The Making of
Modern
Liberalism

The Making of
Modern
Liberalism

Alan Ryan

Princeton University Press

Princeton and Oxford

Library of Congress Cataloging-in-Publication Data

Ryan, Alan, 1940–
   The making of modern liberalism / Alan Ryan.
      p. cm.
   Includes bibliographical references and index.
   ISBN 978-0-691-14840-3 (hardcover : alk. paper)
   1. Liberalism—History.   I. Title.
   JC574.R93 2012
   320.51'309—dc23   2012002052

British Library Cataloging-in-Publication Data is available

This book has been composed in Sabon LTStd text with Bauhaus St. Med display

Printed on acid-free paper. ∞

Printed in the United States of America

10 9 8 7 6 5 4 3 2 1

Contents

Acknowledgments

I HAVE ACQUIRED an immense number of intellectual debts over the years; acknowledging them would amount to writing my intellectual autobiography. Here, I must confine myself to thanking Pratap Mehta for thinking it was a good idea to collect a selection of my work in the first place; Ian Malcolm for gently leaning on me to advance the project; two anonymous readers for their support; Rob Tempio at Princeton University Press for bringing it to completion; and Kip Keller and Leslie Grundfest for deftly editing the text. Particular debts incurred in writing individual essays are acknowledged in the notes; my larger debts to family, friends, colleagues, and students are well known to all of them.

The essays numbered below were previously published in the places listed. Permission to publish them here is gratefully acknowledged.

1. **Liberalism** "Liberalism" in *A Companion to Contemporary Political Philosophy. The Blackwell Companions to Philosophy*, 291-311, eds. Robert E. Goodin, Philip Pettit, and Thomas W. Pogge, Blackwell Publishers, Ltd, Oxford, 1993
2. **Freedom** "Freedom," *Philosophy*, 40 (152), 93-112, Cambridge University Press, 1965
3. **Culture and Anxiety** "Culture and Anxiety" from *Liberal Anxieties and Liberal Education*, by Alan Ryan. Copyright © 1997 by Alan Ryan. Reprinted by permission of Hill & Wang, a division of Farrar, Straus and Giroux, LLC, New York
4. **The Liberal Community** "The Liberal Community" in *Democratic Community*, 91–114, eds. John W. Chapman and Ian Shapiro. *Nomos* XXXV, New York University Press, 1993
5. **Liberal Imperialism** "Liberal Imperialism," in *The Future of Liberal Democracy*, eds. Robert Fatton, Jr. and R. K. Ramazani, Macmillan Publishers Limited, published 2004, reproduced with permission of Palgrave Macmillan
6. **State and Private, Red and White** "State and Private; Red and White," in *Violence, Terrorism, and Justice*, eds. Raymond Gillespie Frey and Christopher W. Morris, Cambridge University Press, 1991
7. **The Right to Kill in Cold Blood** "The Right to Kill in Cold Blood: Does the Death Penalty Violate Human Rights?" *Cleveland Law Review*, Seventy-first Cleveland-Marshall Fund Visiting Scholar Lecture, 2001

8. **Hobbes's Political Philosophy** "Hobbes's Political Philosophy" in *The Cambridge Companion to Hobbes*, 208–245, ed. Tom Sorrell, Cambridge University Press, 1996

9. **Hobbes and Individualism** "Hobbes and Individualism" in *Perspectives on Thomas Hobbes*, 81–105, eds. G.A.J. Rogers and Alan Ryan, Clarendon Press, Oxford, 1988. With permission of Oxford University Press.

10. **Hobbes, Toleration, and the Inner Life** "Hobbes, Toleration, and the Inner Life" in *The Nature of Political Theory*, 197–218, eds. L. Siedentop and D. Miller, Clarendon Press, 1983. With permission of Oxford University Press.

11. **The Nature of Human Nature in Hobbes and Rousseau** "The Nature of Human Nature in Hobbes and Rousseau" in *The Limits of Human Nature*, eds. J. Benthall, Allen Lane, Institute of Contemporary Arts, London, 1973

12. **Locke on Freedom: Some Second Thoughts** "Locke on Freedom: Some Second Thoughts" in *Traditions of Liberalism,* ed. K. Haakonssen, Centre for Independent Studies, Sydney, 1989

13. **Mill's Essay *On Liberty*** "Mill's Essay *On Liberty*" in *Philosophers Ancient and Modern*, 171-195, ed. Godfrey Vesey, Cambridge University Press, 1987

14. **Sense and Sensibility in Mill's Political Thought** "Sense and Sensibility in Mill's Political Thought" in *A Cultivated Mind: Essays on J. S. Mill Presented to J. M. Robson*, ed. Michael Laine, University of Toronto Press, 1991

15. **Mill in a Liberal Landscape** "Mill in a Liberal Landscape," in *The Cambridge Companion to Mill*, 497–541, ed. John Skorupski, Cambridge University Press, 1997

16. **Utilitarianism and Bureaucracy: The Views of J. S. Mill** "Utilitarianism and Bureaucracy: The Views of J. S. Mill" in *Studies in the Growth of Nineteenth Century Government*, 33–62, ed. G. Sutherland, Routledge and Kegan Paul, 1973

17. **Mill and Rousseau: Utility and Rights** "Mill and Rousseau: Utility and Rights" in *Democratic Theory and Practice*, 39–57, ed. Graeme Duncan, Cambridge University Press, 1983

18. **Bureaucracy, Democracy, Liberty: Some Unanswered Questions in Mill's Politics** "Bureaucracy, Democracy, Liberty: Some Unanswered Questions in Mill's Politics" in *J. S. Mill's Political Thought*, eds. Nadia Urbinati and Alex Zakarias, Cambridge University Press, 2007

19. **Bertrand Russell's Politics: 1688 or 1968?** *Bertrand Russell: Whig or Radical?*, University of Texas Humanities Center, 1994

20. **Isaiah Berlin: Political Theory and Liberal Culture** "Isaiah Berlin: Political Theory and Liberal Culture," *Annual Review of Political Science,* 1999

21. **Popper and Liberalism** "Popper and Liberalism" in *Popper and the Human Sciences*, Nijhoff International Philosophy Series, Vol. 19, eds. Currie and Musgrave, Mouton, With kind permission of Springer Science and Business Media, 1985

22. **Alexis de Tocqueville** From Alexis de Tocqueville, *Democracy in America*, Everyman's Library, Alfred A. Knopf, Inc., 1994

23. **Staunchly Modern, Nonbourgeois Liberalism** "Staunchly Modern, Non-Bourgeois Liberalism," in *The New Liberalism*, eds. Avital Simhoni and D. Weinstein, Cambridge University Press, 2001

24. **Pragmatism, Social Identity, Patriotism, and Self-Criticism** "Pragmatism, Social Identity, Patriotism, and Self-Criticism," *Social Research: An International Quarterly*, vol. 63(4): 1041–1064, 1996

25. **Deweyan Pragmatism and American Education** "Deweyan Pragmatism and American Education," in *Philosophers on Education*, 394–410, ed. Amelie Oksenberg Rorty, with permission from Taylor and Francis, 1998

26. **John Rawls** "John Rawls" in *The Return of Grand Theory in the Human Sciences*, ed. Quentin Skinner, Cambridge University Press, 1990

27. **Locke and the Dictatorship of the Bourgeoisie** "Locke and the Dictatorship of the Bourgeoisie" in Locke and Berkeley, *Political Studies*, vol. 13, issue 2: 219–230, 1965, eds. Armstrong and Martin, John Wiley and Sons, 2006

28. **Hegel on Work, Ownership, and Citizenship** "Hegel on Work, Ownership and Citizenship" in *The State and Civil Society: Studies in Hegel's Political Philosophy*, ed. Z. A. Pelczynski, Cambridge University Press, 1984

29. **Utility and Ownership** "Utility and Ownership" in *Utility and Rights*, ed. R. G. Frey, Blackwell/University of Minnesota Press, 1985

30. **Maximizing, Moralizing, and Dramatizing** "Maximising, Moralising and Dramatising" in *Action and Interpretation: Studies in the Philosophy of the Social Sciences*, 65–82, eds. Christopher Hookway and Philip Pettit. Copyright © 1978, Cambridge University Press. Reprinted with permission.

31. **The Romantic Theory of Ownership** Reprinted from *Property and Social Relations*, ed. Hollowell, "The Romantic Theory of Ownership" Heinemann, 1982. With permission from Elsevier.

32. **Justice, Exploitation, and the End of Morality** "Justice, Exploitation and the End of Morality" in *Moral Philosophy and Contemporary Problems*, ed. J.D.G. Evans, Cambridge University Press, 1988

33. **Liberty and Socialism** Reprinted from *Fabian Essays in Socialist Thought*, ed. Ben Pimlott, "Freedom and Socialism" Heinemann, 1984. With permission from Elsevier.

Introduction

PREAMBLE

THE OLDEST OF THESE ESSAYS was published forty-seven years ago, the most recent a year or two ago; they are a small but representative sample of my work over the intervening forty-five years. They possess a consistency beyond that of their authorship, but I would not wish to be tried for my life on behalf of every last sentence in every last one of them. Indeed, I would not have done when they first appeared; the object of intellectual exchange is to have good ideas reinforced and less good ideas corrected. I have also resisted the urge to rewrite them or to write a running commentary on them; everyone knows the mixed sensations provoked by encounters with our former selves and their thoughts. I have silently corrected typographical errors and adjusted some verbal infelicities—I have come to think that the use of "they" and "them" as gender-neutral singular pronouns reads better than "he or she" or "her or him"—otherwise, apart from eliminating some repetitions, I have left the texts untouched. I disavow in passing below some of what now seems incautious or wrong; but this preface is intended for the most part to explain what makes these essays part of a single intellectual project. These essays were written in response to requests from colleagues and have been scattered among different publications and different kinds of publications; the provocation for collecting them here was that former students and colleagues suggested that both the essays and their readers would benefit if some of these essays were collected in one place; I am happy to believe them, especially since it affords an opportunity to bring out their connections to one another.

Like many political theorists, I mix conceptual analysis with criticism of particular writers, and vice versa. If it were not improper to appeal to authority, I would take comfort from the fact that so much of Marx's work was a "critique" of whatever it might be, and that he clearly felt that the best, and perhaps the only, way to articulate what he wished to say about economics and politics, and the methodological difficulties of their study, was to set his own ideas against those of his contemporaries and predecessors. John Stuart Mill, equally obviously, was another writer who thought with and against the writers whose work he discusses in the essays that make up *Dissertations and Discussions* or form the target of book-length works such as *Auguste Comte and Positivism* or the longer and less sprightly

Examination of Sir William Hamilton's Philosophy. If the concept of triangulation had not been discredited by its association with political bad faith, one could say that many of us navigate intellectually by triangulating on our discipline's landmarks. As with navigation in general, that analogy might be the starting point for awkward questions about how and by whom the landmarks were chosen, and whether they lead us into rather than out of danger. I do not ask them here, but plainly, the tradition of political thinking with which I engage is an artifact, not a brute fact.

Intellectual traditions are never made from whole cloth: little of what our more distant forebears wrote was preserved at the time, and little of what was preserved survived thereafter. Generations of political theorists have turned some of what has survived into a canon, but the merits of their selection are far from uncontested, and my own, mildly skeptical view is that what entitles a work to canonical status is only that it turns out to be "good to think with" for a substantial time and a wide audience. But goodness is in the mind of the reader; some readers seek wisdom in a text, others seek the occasion for a rousing argument; some hope to be surprised, and others reassured. There is little more to be said, even though political theorists periodically work themselves into a lather on the subject. Political theory relies very heavily on rethinking the legacy of our predecessors, from Herodotus to Karl Marx, but it is not straightforwardly a historical discipline; it is primarily concerned with the coherence and credibility of the arguments on which it focuses and only secondarily with their causal antecedents and consequences. Historians, even historians of ideas, mostly reverse that emphasis. Political theory relies on conceptual analysis, but is not straightforwardly part of philosophy as taught in the academy; its interest in conceptual analysis is more instrumental than that of philosophy, because political philosophy is, in multiple senses, a "practical" discipline rather than a "pure" one.

Talking to the Dead

There are many questions about the coherence of the project. It is often said that we engage in a "conversation" about "things political" with our departed predecessors; it is as often retorted that there is something odd about talking to the dead, who cannot answer back; and many of us have some difficulty in explaining the difference between "conversations" with silent interlocutors and talking to ourselves. One answer is that unless it is to be an exercise in ventriloquism, we must take seriously the historical identity of the writers we engage with, ensuring that their "otherness" is preserved. We must also exercise a form of self-control whose necessity goes without saying, but whose practice does not come easily. We must not credit past authors with our own favorite—or least favorite—ideas; we care about our forebears and value their insights, but they did not have us in mind when they came to them. Whatever else they were doing, they were not (then) talking to us. Necessary as it is to exercise this self-control, and hard as we should try to remember that our predecessors lived in their world and time and not in ours, it is not always easy; the more engaging a thinker, the harder to preserve the necessary distance. We say "what he must really have meant was . . ." rather than "I wish he had said . . ." usually because we do not notice that sympathetic interpretation has become rewriting.

The historical figures about whom I have written were often fascinating people; but my approach, both here and in the books I have written on Mill, Bertrand Russell, and John Dewey is not biographical as I understand the term. My focus is less on the writers' lives than on their arguments, and the interest of those arguments lies in the way they illuminate the subjects we and their authors are concerned with. The point of getting the biographical context right is that it provides our only assurance that the arguments we explain, criticize, repair, or reject really are those that the author put forward and not figments of our imagination. Four decades ago, it was a common complaint that the "Locke" who featured in discussions of "Locke's theory of private property" was rather distantly related to the historical John Locke; matters were worse with "Locke's doctrine of government by consent." The obvious way to fend off such complaints was to distinguish very sharply between the purposes that the historical John Locke may have had in mind when writing the *Two Treatises* and the literal meaning of what it was he wrote, no matter what purposes animated its writing. In retrospect, I think I was too quick to distinguish as sharply as I then did between "what he meant to say"—which I still take to be essentially a historical question about the author's intentions—and "what what he said meant"—a conceptual question about the implications of the "plain meaning" of the text.

Setting aside the question whether a text ever has a plain meaning, to which the answer is a boring "yes, it is what an uncontroversial paraphrase reveals," any argument over which there has been a good deal of dispute is unlikely to have a truly plain meaning, and a paraphrase is unlikely to be uncontroversial. I would no longer wish to draw as sharp a line as I once did between what an author meant by what he said and what what he said meant. Some sense of how the author intended his words to be taken and some sense of how the audience likely took them are needed before we can settle on the meaning of what he said, at any rate in the extended sense in which the speech act being performed is an aspect of the meaning. This does not mean that an author's intentions are decisive in determining the content of an argument. To explain an argument is to settle, provisionally, on a view of its derivation from often barely visible assumptions, and to grasp its implications, not all of which the author will himself have perceived. Dialectical reasoning would be impossible if we perceived all the implications of what we say; *reductio* is the commonest device employed by critics. It is plausible that an author saw many or even most of the implications of what he wrote, but not that he could have had the foresight to see what his arguments would imply in very different conditions from those in which he lived and wrote. To take an instance in which I certainly misspoke, I would not now say that when Locke writes about property, this reveals a "bourgeois" sensibility; I doubt that the label "bourgeois" suits a British tradition more at home with such expressions as "the middle ranks" of society, and I remain puzzled about the connection in Locke's own mind between "property" in the sense of "lives, liberties and estates" and property in the usual sense of the objects of ownership.

To think we can identify the arguments that writers in the past have put forward, and that it is worth our while to think about them *as arguments*, implies a limited degree of "platonizing." That is, it implies the existence of the intentional object that, in much the same way as an author's wishes, hopes, and fears, we identify as an author's argument. If it we did not do so, we could hardly talk about Pythagoras's theorem and similar entities. Indeed, we could hardly identify what we ourselves have said, are saying, and intend to say in future; *oratio obliqua* (indirect speech) would be impossible, and we would be confined to *oratio recta* (direct speech). There is much to be said about the utility of conversing with the dead, and I shall say only a little of it, and sketchily. The most obvious point is that it stretches the imagination; some people may be able to create out of whole cloth the ideas and insights that Dewey once described as our "funded intellectual capital," but most of us must borrow heavily from the bank of the ages. To take a topic that recurs frequently here, the expressive and communicative aspects of work, it is impossible to use Marx's ideas about *species-being* as a guide to the organization of a complex industrial economy. Working out why it is so is valuable, less because it is a destructive exercise than because the picture Marx paints of the way we can, in some contexts, achieve self-realization and happiness in our work for other people is so attractive. The thought that we see ourselves in our work, in what we make, and in what others make of it chimes with our reaction to gifts that others have created for us, in which we see an embodiment of their affection for us, and in which even the imperfections may be said to speak to us of them.

John Ruskin hated machine-carved statues in the restored churches of Victorian England because they frustrated that possibility: their perfection obliterated the personality of the sculptor, and the object no longer connected the spectator and the creator in the way a work of art, indeed in the way that all good work, should do. That Marx's passion for vastly expanded productivity is at odds with this concern for individual creativity is not hard to see. But if we enter imaginatively into his youthful wish that all productive work should be expressive and communicative, we begin to see not only that it is a utopian aspiration in a modern industrial economy, as he later realized, but also why writers such as Mill, G.D.H. Cole, Dewey, and other enthusiasts for forms of industrial democracy looked for other ways of reconciling the benefits of the improved productivity brought about by modern industrial techniques with ways of giving workers a stake in the productive process beyond the instrumental stake of their wages. Unleashing their creativity elsewhere than in the productive process itself was not a utopian ambition. Nor was it a mistake to emphasize the communicative aspects of production and consumption. Even today, when aspirations to industrial democracy are at a low ebb, consumers are sensitive to the fear that their running shoes or T-shirts embody the forced labor of small children in distant countries, even if they do not much mind whether they rent their cars from a worker-owned or a more conventional enterprise. Selectively at least, consumers feel that the clothes they are wearing speak of their origins and the conditions of their creation. All these phenomena have a history, as does their reflection in the thoughts of the most interesting and imaginative political theorists of the past two centuries.

Beyond this, thinking about politics is essentially historical in a way in which thinking about physical nature, the subject of the physical sciences, is not. The physical sciences have a history, but it is irrelevant to their content. One aspect of this is obvious enough. The laws of physical nature are invariant; either we know them or we do not, but physical nature is not itself engaged in a process of refashioning the laws it obeys. We talk of molecules possessing "memory," but that is strictly by analogy. Similarly, computers do not literally remember as we do: we remember with their assistance. This is not the proposition that all natural phenomena can be deterministically predicted; open systems defy prediction, and any natural phenomenon whose causation depends on human action is no more predictable than that human action itself. Plant biology cannot predict the fate of a tree in a rain forest encroached on by local tribes or industrial loggers. It is of the essence of the laws governing human societies that they are subject to change; the laws of the Medes and Persians may have been a byword for stability, but the empires of the Medes and Persians were overthrown and their laws became of no effect. Crucially, societies run on memory. Not only is their orderliness dependent on their members obeying laws whose validity is a question of pedigree—a matter of their having been accepted forever or having been passed by whatever local process it takes to create valid law; they rely on innumerable commitments above and beyond those encapsulated in law, and anyone intending to honor, or even to evade, those commitments must rely on individual and collective memory to know what they are.

Indeed, the identity of societies and their political institutions is very largely a matter of collective memory. As an organized political entity, a society has internal and external obligations that are binding on it only because it has a persisting identity as that society; even when a society experiences revolution and the postrevolutionary regime engages in wholesale repudiation of the obligations incurred by its prerevolutionary predecessors, the larger social entity persists, and its identity is a matter of language, culture, historical memory, and anticipation. Although a society is not a person writ large, the state that provides its order is, like other institutions, a *persona ficta* (an artificial person) with a life history and a capacity for making agreements and obeying norms. The French legal system regards corporate entities as *personnes morales*, and although they are matters of artifice, they have histories, purposes, and go through birth and death; the U.S. Supreme Court decided more than a hundred and twenty years ago that corporations were legal persons.

Nonetheless, it is only by the continuous, intellectually aware activities of human individuals that states and lesser corporate entities exist at all; without the thoughts and actions of *personae non fictae* there would be no such entities. This imports a degree of indeterminacy into our characterization of these entities, their goals, and their capacities; think of such questions as whether a religious group is a church or a sect. When writing about thinkers remote from ourselves in space, time, or social setting, the indeterminacy is redoubled, since we have to understand both what they wrote about and how they understood it. Was the Athenian polis the Athenian state? Did Aristotle write about "the Greek state" when he wrote about the polis? It is not infrequently said that before the seventeenth century, theorists "had no concept" of the state. What the claim means is hard to tell. One thing it has meant is that when Machiavelli speaks of the prince intending to *mantenere lo stato*, we should not think that he is intending to preserve the state but to hold onto his recently acquired power. It is more of a stretch to go on from that localized and simple point to suggest that when Roman writers wrote about the political system with which they were best acquainted, they were not writing about the Roman state. If that entity was not a state, it is hard to know what it was. Anthropologists who write about stateless societies would not include Rome among their number. By the same token, when we talk of city-states such as Greek *poleis* or the republics of medieval Italy, we appear to regard them as states. Yet we do not wish to say that when Sir John Fortescue writes about the *corpus mysticum* that is the "realm of England" and Hegel writes about the state that is "the march of God upon earth," they are writing about the same thing. The fifteenth-century English state neither did nor could rest its authority on its capacity for the rational management of civil society; nor could the state that Hegel wrote about rest its authority on the thought that Frederick William III was the Lord's anointed. Examples could be multiplied to the point of exhaustion.

Liberalism and Its History

In the context of the essays collected here, the three issues that raise difficult questions about the way other thinkers at other times understood their own societies are whether we can speak of liberalism before the term came into use in the nineteenth century, to what extent writers about freedom have written about the same thing, and what Greece and Rome thought about rights if they did not conceptualize subjective rights as we do—that is, rights amounting to claims that an individual may make or not make at will. These are familiar issues, much discussed elsewhere in the literature, but not much discussed by me except here. The simplest way of answering these questions here is to explain what provides the unity in what follows. I begin with my understanding of the nature of liberalism, continue to an account of the nature of freedom, offer some second thoughts on rights, property, and social justice, and end by explaining very briefly why I have valued the interlocutors on whom I have concentrated. Since these topics are inextricably intertwined with one another, some repetition is inescapable. Since they are also difficult and contentious, what follows is lamentably dogmatic for lack of space to be anything else.

Liberalism as I understand it is essentially a modern creed, but not simply a nineteenth- and twentieth-century one. Its modernity lies in the fact that it is, not in logic but in fact, an offshoot of Protestant Christianity. There is no economic or political reason why liberalism could not have arisen in Athens in the fourth century BCE, but Greek religion and ethics would have had to be very different. In other words, liberalism required a particular intellectual and moral outlook and ways of conceptualizing moral and political issues that existed in no ancient society, but it did not require any particular social, economic, or political structure. The difference is perhaps best seen in the contrast between ancient and modern notions of toleration. Ancient religion was generally less concerned with questions of belief than with ritual practice, and ritual practice was largely concerned with keeping the gods favorably inclined. In the *Iliad*, when Chryses implores Apollo to visit the Greeks with misfortune because the obstinate Agamemnon will not return his daughter for an enormous ransom, he begins by reminding Apollo of all the animal sacrifices he has made. He has done favors for Apollo, and now the god should return them. Greek and Roman cities set a high value on the performance of the appropriate rituals, especially sacrifice, but little on theological orthodoxy. Blasphemy was dangerous because it would lose the good will of the gods; the concept of heresy, as Thomas Hobbes pointed out, was unknown. They were tolerant in the sense of not much minding what anyone thought so long as they behaved like good citizens; Jews and Christians notoriously would not do so, refusing to sacrifice to the pagan gods or to the deified emperor, and so suffered persecution. Many ancient societies found it easy to incorporate other nations' gods into their own pantheons less because they resisted the urge to proselytize on behalf of their own cults than because they seem to have felt no urge in the first place.

This kind of tolerance is collective and unprincipled. There is no suggestion that religious belief deserves a respect that is both grounded in and the ground of respect for the personality of the believer. One should respect priests because ill-treating them makes the gods angry; others must take their chances. "Mere" religious conviction has nothing to do with it. Religious practices should be taken seriously, and we should encourage the young to take them seriously, so that we may keep the gods favorably inclined toward us and preserve social cohesion by instilling respect for our forebears. Mockery should—mostly—be stamped on, and certainly when it amounts to blasphemy rather than Aristophanic byplay. The difference between this attitude and the core of liberalism is that modern toleration is focused on the individual; it rests on a commitment to the sanctity of the individual personality and the inviolability of the individual conscience. This thought lies at the heart of John Rawls's liberalism and explains a great deal both of the apparatus of *A Theory of Justice* and of the concern of *Political Liberalism* to set out a constitutional scheme that can appeal to persons of very different religious or metaphysical convictions without relying on the truth of any of them.

Liberalism Defensive and Principled

This is obvious enough to allow me to emphasize something different. This is that we may take two very different views of what follows from a concentration on the individual; one might say that they yield the liberalism of fear and the liberalism of individual autonomy. Hobbes was not a liberal. Nonetheless, the idea of a Hobbesian liberalism is not pleonastic. Hobbes believed that authority must be absolute. He thought the belief that subjects have rights against their rulers invited anarchy. The right to private judgment in matters of religion, which was advocated by dissenters and which William Godwin later made the centerpiece of *Political Justice*, was anathema. Nonetheless, Hobbes was keenly conscious that individuals who were deeply committed to a particular view of their religious obligations and felt that their salvation hung on their fidelity to those obligations were vulnerable to a particular and deep kind of anxiety. A state that scrutinized their beliefs too narrowly set them to play for their salvation at cross and pile. Where the peace was not threatened, the state would enhance the happiness and diminish the anxiety of its subjects by leaving them as much freedom as possible to practice their faith as they saw fit. It is security rather than sanctity that is doing the argumentative work.

On my reading of both Hobbes and Mill, Mill is a Hobbesian liberal to the extent that he founded the defense of intellectual and social freedom in *Liberty* not on a doctrine of individual rights but on the promotion of utility. But he really was a liberal, as Hobbes was not, because the utility in question was that of individuals eager to exercise their own autonomous judgment in formulating a plan of life; one might say that Mill built a very un-Hobbesian superstructure on Hobbesian foundations. Since I am myself skeptical about rights-based political theories, I have always thought that a Hobbesian foundation for liberalism is as secure as any. Locke, of course, provides a much more obvious starting point, but because Locke's conception of our inviolability as conscientious individuals with a life to live rests so squarely on the idea that we are the workmanship of God, sent here to fulfill his plans for us, it is vulnerable to anyone who thinks that we are not God's handiwork but an interesting biological accident. It is a further consequence of this view of the genealogy of liberalism that just as "Hobbesian liberalism" is not a pleonasm even though Hobbes was no liberal, so "Augustinian liberalism" is not a pleonasm even though St. Augustine was even less a liberal than Hobbes. Hobbes, after all, thought that when men could be relied on to keep the peace, they should be left largely unconstrained. Augustine did not; they had very different views on original sin. The reason for thinking that Augustinian liberalism is not a contradiction in terms is less that Augustine is the patron saint of Protestantism, though there is much to be said for that view, than that Augustine's emphasis on the strictly limited goods we can expect from the political order provides good reasons for states to focus on what they *can* do, which is to provide peace, security, and predictability in managing our earthly affairs, and to refrain from attempting to do what they *cannot* do, which is to guarantee our salvation. Augustine thought it right for the state to protect the church and suppress threats to its survival; but his political reasoning was—if the anachronism is permissible—Hobbesian.

Nonetheless, only when writers think of themselves as liberals does intense argument begin over the nature of liberalism, its compatibility with democratic politics, its vulnerability to mass society, and so on. The acquisition of a new vocabulary makes a great difference to what we think and how we think about it. Nonetheless, it is unduly dogmatic to insist that thinkers cannot hold a political position that they would not have articulated in the same vocabulary as we. This bears on some disputes in political theory to which I am not party: for instance, the claim of Leo Strauss and his followers that there was such a thing as "ancient liberalism." On the view offered here, it is not a conceptual truth that there *could not have been* any such thing, but a factual truth that not enough of the right elements were in place for there in fact to have been any such thing. It is also true, of course, that when it became possible for politicians, commentators, and theorists to apply the term "liberal" to social and political positions, a good deal of linguistic chaos ensued. It is familiar territory that in (vulgar) American political usage, "liberal" means something not far removed from what a European would characterize as socialist or social democratic; it is less familiar territory that in everyday British political terms, it is an open question how far liberalism is committed to free-market economics and to the sanctity of private property, whereas on the European mainland, these commitments are all but definitive of liberalism.

Not only is it intellectually disreputable to try to win political arguments by stipulative definition, but it is also very unlikely to be effective. The most one can aim at is to provide a mixture of *histoire raisonnée* (reasoned history) and helpful definitional scaffolding. As the essay on *Liberalism* reprinted here suggests, I think the core of political liberalism has been defensive, and that as the term suggests, the history of liberalism is the history of a concern to protect individual liberty against a succession of threats. Religious liberty, the security of person and property, and perhaps the ability of those with no resources but their labor to organize to defend themselves against undue exploitation might all be counted among the liberties that the defense of freedom requires. By the same token, one might want to extend the threats to liberty to cases where others substitute their will for mine by means of manipulation rather than simple coercion; indeed, one might be unsure whether the psychological domination of individuals by public opinion that Mill and Alexis de Tocqueville so feared was coercive or manipulative. Mill plainly thought it was the first, but his successors have often thought it was all the more dangerous because it was the second. Indeed, Mill himself seemed to think that just because it did not *feel* coercive, it was all the more dangerous.

Freedom

It is time to revisit the oldest of these essays. Although I do not resile from what I there say about freedom, I should add to it. What I say about the way in which what it is to be free gets its sense from the obstacles to whose absence the appellation "free" is pointing seems to me to be correct, but less bold than it should be, and can be illuminating in a political context only with a lot of fleshing out. It has seemed to me for the past thirty years that there is indeed one concept of freedom, and that it is the positive concept that Isaiah Berlin identified as equating "Am I free?" with "Am I my own master?" It has in itself no tendency to generate a taste for any or all of the horrors that Berlin was concerned to fend off, and half a century after *Two Concepts of Liberty*, it is no unkindness to say that Berlin generated more heat than light about the nature of liberty, and that we may wish he had not talked of two concepts, nor been so slapdash about just who thought just what. The negative concept of liberty that Berlin was defending was not a concept but a very simple theory. It amounted to the thought that for most people most of the time, being our own masters is a matter of there being nobody else who is our master; if what I do flows from what I choose to do rather than from what someone else dictates, I am to that extent free. That fact has the not irrelevant consequence that the dichotomy that the ancient world most cared about—free or slave—is indeed basic. When the Spartans fought the Persians at Thermopylae to defend their freedom, they fought to preserve the distinction between being a citizen and being a slave. The king of Persia's subjects were slaves, not free men. Nobody has ever suggested that the Spartans were enthusiasts for the psychological, moral, and intellectual autonomy that Mill praised in *Liberty*; nonetheless, they fought for their freedom.

Hobbes clouded the issue, not only by objecting to the citizens of Lucca thinking that they were free in ways the subjects of the Ottoman Empire could not be, but by offering several, not obviously consistent, accounts of what freedom was. To say that a man is free when he is not hindered in doing what he has a mind to do was essential to his implausible claim that a man who swears allegiance to a conqueror when the conqueror's sword is at his throat does so freely. It is, of course, true that he is not hindered in swearing allegiance; but it would be odd to suppose that he is not hindered from refusing by the prospect of immediate death. It may be true that if he were to wish to refuse to swear allegiance and so get himself killed, he would refuse; he would not physically be hindered in doing what he had a mind to do. More often, Hobbes seemed to think that freedom is what I am here arguing that it is. A man is free when he is master of his actions; he is master of his actions if nobody else is master of his actions; and another man can become the master of our actions—that is, have the power to dictate them—by two routes: by possessing the ability to make effective threats and, more importantly, by our having yielded ourselves subject or, in more limited spheres, taken on obligations to whomever it is. Hobbes drew some interesting conclusions from this, among them that it followed from the fact that we did not make a pact of submission with the Almighty that "the kingdom of God is got by violence."

What mattered to Hobbes, and is worth emphasizing, is that where we have given someone else the right to determine some portion of our time and activity, we become "not free" with respect to the determination of our conduct in that sphere, but remain as free (or not) in respect of everything else as we were before. Conversely, the prisoner who is freed from jail is free, even if the society into which he is released is a dictatorship with no free speech and no room to organize politically. Again, the ex-prisoner may be married, and until he gets divorced, he is not free to contract another marriage, since he is, in Hobbesian terms, chained by his lips to his existing obligations. The political relevance of this analysis is indirect but worth insisting on. For the past two decades or so, there has been what one might unkindly describe as an outbreak of the politics of nostalgia, with commentators eager to revive an ideal of republican liberty that they contrast with what is taken to be liberal, or "let-alone," liberty. Hobbes is the villain of the piece because of his insistence that the inhabitants of Lucca might or might not have more liberty—which is to say, immunity to the service of the republic—than their contemporaries in Constantinople. If those contemporaries by chance lived under a beneficent sultan, they would have much liberty, and if not, not. The obvious retort is that a slave with an idle master remains a slave; the subjects of the sultan had a master, and the citizens of Lucca did not.

One can admire Hobbes and still wince, since the reply is obviously correct. The crucial point is the answer of the Spartan Demaratus to Xerxes. Xerxes asked whether the Greeks would fight his enormous and invincible army, and was displeased to be told that they would fight to the death to preserve their liberty and to live under their own laws. Greeks were citizens, not subjects, and in their eyes, Xerxes's subjects were not free men but slaves. As to why, Hobbes supplied the explanation: they were chained by the lips to the word of their ruler. Hobbes's dismissive view of the views of the citizens of Lucca rides roughshod over distinctions that we need to preserve, and that he preserves elsewhere. There is, in the universe of *Leviathan*, no room for the distinction between our lawful rulers and the masters or owners of slaves, because there is no room for the idea that our rulers are subject to law; if law is the word of him that by right hath command, and if in earthly matters our rulers have a right to command all things, we are under their absolute command, and not our own masters. We may be slaves who are left to get on with our lives much as we choose almost all the time, and therefore enjoy a great deal of let-alone freedom, but in Spartan terms we are slaves. This, after all, is an implication of Hobbes's insistence that tyranny is monarchy misliked.

The Liberty of the Moderns and Its Connections with Rights

Nonetheless, even if Hobbes was wrong about the incoherence of the republican view of liberty, the politics of nostalgia should be eschewed for the reasons that Benjamin Constant spelled out in *La Liberté des anciens* two centuries ago. The Spartans were collectively their own masters, but individually at the mercy of their fellows. There was no room for private judgment in matters of religion, no room to cultivate private and idiosyncratic tastes. What each individual possessed was his own small share of that collective liberty. Not all Greek city-states were as repressive as Sparta; because it was a commercial state, Athens allowed a great deal more room for individuality than Sparta. Nonetheless, the dichotomy on which Constant insisted was worth insisting on. And it is important to remember that Constant himself was clear that the choice was not between ancient and modern liberty, but between ancient liberty *without* modern liberty—which he thought that the purist republicans had hankered after during the Revolution—and ancient liberty *with* modern liberty. Indeed, in Constant's view, modern liberty could not be preserved unless we took ancient liberty seriously. Unless enough politically active people thought of themselves as citizens with not only a right but also a duty to keep their rulers in check, their liberties of speech, religion, occupation, domicile, and the like would not be secure. Understanding that, modern citizens should understand what representative government can and cannot achieve; hankering after the chance to exercise in person the fraction of sovereign authority that purist republicans would allot us is mistaken, but a readiness to participate in the institutions of representative government—what we now call liberal democracy—is essential. As Mill emphasized forty years later in *Representative Government*, representative institutions cannot achieve self-government in any literal sense; they enable us to take securities for good government, but only if we use them as they should be used.

It is often said that the ancient world did not have our concern for individual liberty because it did not have our conception of individual rights. To dig deeply into this issue is beyond the scope of this introduction, but two things need to be said. The first is that trying to answer the question of what conception of rights the ancient world possessed runs into the difficulty already noted of describing in a non-question-begging fashion the ways in which other peoples at other times and in other places conceptualized their activities and institutions. Today, we plainly have a vocabulary in which we discuss all manner of rights; we distinguish between human rights and property rights, we argue at length about the extent of the obligations imposed by rights, distinguishing at one end of the spectrum a right that may impose no more than a duty of noninterference—as with the right to walk down the sidewalk—and at the other end of the spectrum rights that may impose elaborate duties of specific performance, as when our employer is obliged to pay us an agreed-upon salary. There is almost no simple claim about how we should conceptualize rights that will not be contradicted by someone. It seems tempting to say that nobody now holds the belief in natural rights that Jeremy Bentham savaged in the late eighteenth century; but there are many Catholic thinkers who believe that unborn children have rights under natural law, and it is hard to know what these are if not natural rights, at any rate when natural law is not identified with divine positive law. What is less obvious is what kinds of rights are grounded in that law.

This can be treated as a definitional issue of the kind that Wesley Hohfeld's analysis of rights, powers, and immunities is well designed to handle. Indeed, I think it is best treated in this way. One quick way through the issue is to distinguish between an "objective" conception of rights, in which rights are essentially the immunities conferred by the obligations falling on the person or persons constrained by the duties imposed by law, whether positive, natural, divine, or customary, and a "subjective" conception, in which rights are powers to do or forbear at will, inhering in the possessor of such a right, and the corresponding obligations fall on others in consequence of the rights of the right holder. In the one view, rights are shadows cast by obligations, and in the other, obligations are shadows cast by rights. The rights of the unborn child are immunities to ill treatment or termination, but the unborn child has neither the physical nor the legal capacity to enforce, renounce, or modify those rights. A healthy adult's right to life is more plausibly seen as their normative power to dispose of themselves as they choose. Modern property rights are paradigms of subjective rights. I may do as I please with what I own as a chattel or as real property. One should speak slightly more cautiously than that, of course; the fact that I have all the rights that anyone can have in a piece of property does not mean that I may do just whatever I choose with it. I may own a cow outright, but I have no right to kill it and leave the corpse to decay on the highway; it is infelicitous to think of that restriction on what I may do with the cow as a restriction of my ownership, however, because the things I may not do with *my* cow are things I may not do with *anyone's* cow. There are certainly liabilities, distinct from restrictions on use, that can and do attach to the ownership of a cow, such as the duty to have it vaccinated against tuberculosis. An attractive way of making this point is to say that an owner has in principle all those rights of use and disposal that anyone can have, but that the incidents of property go well beyond rights alone.

Then the claim about the ancient world's lack of our concept of rights becomes the claim that even if many of the incidents of ownership that the modern world recognizes were familiar in the ancient world, as they certainly were, the conception of ownership and the allied conception of rights were closer to an objective conception than a subjective conception. That is, what was absent was not so much property rights narrowly construed as the kind of individual rights enshrined in the American Declaration of Independence; and from that it follows that there was no room for the thought that property in external things was an extension of our rights in and over ourselves. John Locke originated something. The discussion of slavery in ancient authors marks this difference quite neatly. Even Aristotle, who seemed not to object to "man hunting"—that is, forcibly capturing slaves—as an economic activity, thought that slavery was a bad thing in itself; if plows could be set to work on their own and without human intervention, there would be no need of slaves. Since that was a fantasy, slaves were needed, and the only constraint he took seriously was that Greeks should not enslave Greeks.

In the seventeenth century, when Hugo Grotius defended the thought that a man may sell himself into slavery to secure his survival—no more alarming than Hobbes's picture of the way we submit to a sovereign by acquisition—the starting point was self-ownership. It is by an act of my own will that I render myself subject or sell myself into slavery. That idea might seem to be at least latent in the Emperor Justinian's explanation that he possessed absolute authority over the inhabitants of the Roman Empire because the people, who had formerly possessed it, had transferred it to the emperor. The crucial difference, perhaps, is that the authority that had been passed lock, stock, and barrel to the emperor was the property of the people—a collective, and not an individual, possession. What was lacking in the ancient world was the notion of individual sovereignty, or self-ownership, and especially its subsequent liberal, non-Grotian extension: our ownership of ourselves excludes the possibility not only of anyone else owning us, but even of our selling ourselves into servitude.

Property

That perspective explains much of what appears here. Let me now say something about property, work, and social justice, then a very little about the particular authors with whom I have wrestled. Rights of all sorts, but property rights perhaps most intriguingly, demonstrate the human capacity to expand our control over the world and its potential usefulness by organizing ways in which we can guarantee to one another that something we wish to happen in the future will in fact happen. A paradox lies at the heart of the importance of rights of all sorts, particularly property rights: because we are able to generate obligations, we can extend the possibilities of action by giving others the capacity to constrain what we do under determinate conditions. Property rights, of course, go beyond the rights over our future conduct that we can create by promising and the like, since they are rights good against the world and inherent in whoever happens to own whatever it is. As several of these essays suggest, I am not persuaded that the concept of self-ownership illuminates our right to dispose of our own selves and capacities, nor that it provides an explanation of the importance of respecting property rights. A broadly utilitarian perspective is adequate to justify property rights of most sorts, and a proper attention to such matters as the irreplaceability of some sorts of property—a much loved house, for instance—and the ready replaceability of others—insurance contracts, say—illuminates much of what we intuitively feel about the importance of some sorts of ownership and indeed explains why we sometimes do and sometimes do not think that monetary compensation is sufficient for the loss of property.

But a broadly utilitarian justification does not appease two sorts of anxiety. The first is the sense that arrangements that may make very good sense by increasing overall welfare may make much less sense in the way the gains are distributed. There are evidently two ways in which this may be true. One is that the benefit accruing from property rights may simply reflect luck, as they plainly do in the case of holding a winning lottery ticket, and slightly less obviously in the case of being the first person to secure a patent, happening to own a piece of land with oil beneath it, or perhaps "owning" whatever talents and traits of character we happen to have. Whatever doubts I express in passing about the work of John Rawls, I share his doubts about what one might call the "depth" of our ownership of these benefits. The second is the familiar terrain of political philosophy from ancient Greece onward. The benefits of ownership tend to be cumulative; short of abolishing the family, it is extremely difficult to think of ways of preventing the owners of the advantages accrued in one generation from loading the dice in favor of their children in the next.

The problem this presents is in part that loading the dice undermines one of the most important modern conceptions of desert. Broadly speaking, the modern world holds that work, effort, and productivity form the most acceptable basis of a claim to reward, and that harder work merits greater reward—always *ceteris paribus*, of course. The strenuous production of harmful goods, such as attractive narcotics to be sold to schoolchildren, would merit a stretch in jail. Inherited inequality subverts this justification. But I have always been interested in a somewhat different view of the connection between work, reward, and ownership, one less directly tied to the usual concern with social justice and rather more directly tied to a more metaphysical or, more guardedly, more psychological notion of ownership. This is the idea that work provides an outlet for our need for self-expression and that it enables us to "own" the world in the sense of seeing the humanly created and modified world as our product, either individual, for which the obvious paradigm is the work of art, or collective, for which there is no obvious paradigm, though it is not implausible that we may, under favorable conditions, see the world around us as reflecting our talent, ingenuity, and capacity for cooperation. It is this that I call the "romantic" conception of ownership and tie to my view that an important and underexplored— though hardly unacknowledged—aspect of social explanation is this expressive dimension.

Last, then, the thinkers whom it has been good to think with. To a degree that surprises me, I have little sense of having had much control over this. Mill, as I said in the preface to my first book-length account of his importance, was one of the two thinkers who stiffened my teenage resolve to think for myself, and neither to be merely enraged by the prejudices of my teachers nor to give in to them; the other was Bertrand Russell. Because my interests always lay in political theory, Mill provided more sustenance—indeed, enough for a lifetime. Behind Mill as I read him stands Hobbes, the begetter of analytical political theory and an inexhaustible source of puzzlement. They offer opposite attractions. Mill's allegiances are the more congenial, even if he was less liberal in temperament than one might wish. Some of Hobbes's professed allegiances are hard to warm to, but he was liberal by temperament, or easygoing where his amour propre and physical safety were not at stake. Both, of course, repay almost any amount of engrossed poring over the details of what they said; it is almost impossible either to abandon the search for the utilitarian theory of rights that Mill was seeking when he wrote *Liberty* or to believe that we can square the circle as he hoped. By the same token, Hobbes's attempt to give a coherent account of the inner lives of creatures who are fundamentally self-maintaining *automata* remains rivetingly interesting.

Mill relied heavily, perhaps too heavily, on Tocqueville for his view of where an increasingly democratic society and polity were heading. But he did not follow Tocqueville all the way either in his political enthusiasms or in his economic anxieties; nor was Tocqueville particularly attached to Mill's enthusiasm for a liberal ethic of self-fashioning. Nonetheless, Tocqueville is not easily going to be evicted from the liberal pantheon, and certainly not by me. He provides a counterpoise to the "philosophical" mode of argument to which Mill was attached. Tocqueville was sometimes accused of having gone to America knowing already what he was going to see and what he was going to say about it. This is unfair, but there was a French view, articulated perhaps most clearly by François Guizot but widely accepted, that European society had been becoming steadily more egalitarian for many years and that it was a process that might be steered but not stopped. In that view, America was the society that embodied "modernity." In Europe, the increasing "equality of condition" by which Tocqueville was impressed was emerging from societies that had previously been governed aristocratically and whose economies had been feudal; in America, these ancien régime drags on progress were absent. Although Dewey had nothing of the literary charm that Tocqueville possessed in such abundance, I have found him a fascinating interlocutor because he essentially accepted Tocqueville's identification of America with the condition of modernity, though I do not think he ever mentions him.

There are many scarcely visible connections between the thinkers to whom I have been most attracted; some are curious. For instance, Sidney Hook saw Dewey's pragmatism as the philosophy, or post-philosophy, implicit in Marx's more humanistic writings, and even though Dewey himself resisted the thought, Hook was right. In the same vein, Dewey's identification of modernity, democracy, and rationality underlies Rawls's social theory in spite of the world of difference between Rawls's architectural style of argument and Dewey's more meandering prose. Sometimes it is hard to resist the temptation to wish that history had been otherwise, and that connections made that were not. Mill's stepdaughter Helen became friends with Karl Marx's daughter Eleanor; one wishes that stepfather and father could have worked through *Kapital* together. Mill and Tocqueville should have spent time in each other's company; and as long as the better rather than the worse characteristics of each had rubbed off on the other, it would have been a good thing if Russell and Dewey had got on better. Dewey's patience with the intractability of people and politics would have done Russell good, just as Russell's crispness would have done Dewey's literary reputation good. This is to stray self-indulgently, but it allows me to end by saying that I cannot imagine political theory as a discipline that does not encourage the idea of a conversation across the centuries between imaginary friends who might form a revolutionary vanguard or an anxious rearguard, might often find each other exasperating or evasive, but would rarely find each other less than humanly interesting.

PART 1

Conceptual and Practical

1

Liberalism

What Is Liberalism?

ANYONE TRYING TO GIVE a brief account of liberalism is immediately faced with an embarrassing question: are we dealing with liberalism or with liberalisms? It is easy to list famous liberals; it is harder to say what they have in common. John Locke, Adam Smith, Montesquieu, Thomas Jefferson, John Stuart Mill, Lord Acton, T. H. Green, John Dewey, and contemporaries such as Isaiah Berlin and John Rawls are certainly liberals—but they do not agree about the boundaries of toleration, the legitimacy of the welfare state, and the virtues of democracy, to take three rather central political issues. They do not even agree on the nature of the liberty they think liberals ought to seek (Berlin 1969, 122–34).

It is a familiar complaint in writing about politics generally that key terms are undefined or indefinable; the boundaries between "political" and "non-political" behavior and institutions are disputed, the defining characteristics of statehood, along with the necessary and sufficient conditions of legitimacy, are incessantly debated. Liberalism may be no worse off than its ideological competitors, of course. In everyday political practice, all the isms seem to be in the same condition; liberals, conservatives, and socialists can be identified only issue by issue, and their stand on one issue offers little clue to their stand on another. The conservative who opposes railway nationalization supports government subsidies of defense contractors, while the liberal who applauds the establishment of an ethics committee to investigate the financial dealings of politicians will deplore the establishment of a committee to investigate the ethics of schoolteachers.

But even if conservatism and socialism are in the same plight, one is still inclined to ask, is liberalism one thing or many? Is liberalism determinately describable at all (Dworkin 1985, 183–203)? The observation that the terms of political discourse are not easily brought to an agreed definition is not new. More than three hundred years ago, Thomas Hobbes remarked that if anyone had stood to profit from a similar confusion in geometry, mankind would still be waiting for Euclid. While Hobbes's remark suggests that it is the self-interest of priests, intellectuals, and politicians that explains this lack of precise definitions, twentieth-century writers have suggested another reason, that political concepts are "essentially contested" (Gallie 1956, 167–98; Gray 1983, 75–101). A third explanation, and one more relevant to liberalism in particular, is that liberals' political concerns have altered over the past three centuries. All three kinds of explanation suggest, however, that we should be seeking to understand liberalisms rather than liberalism.

One reason for the indefinability of political terms, or the systematic slipperiness of our concepts of the state, the political, or, as here, liberalism, is the use of these terms as terms of praise or obloquy in the political struggle; this is a modern version of Hobbes's view that disputed definitions are the result of competing interests. Since the 1970s, for instance, there has been an intellectual and political movement known as "communitarianism" whose main defining feature is hostility to liberalism (Sandel 1982). Communitarians emphasize the innumerable ways in which individuals are indebted to the societies in which they are reared; liberals, they say, write as if human beings come into the world with no social ties, owing no allegiances, and one way or another entirely detached from the societies they in some fashion inhabit. So described, liberalism is unattractive, built on sociological falsehoods and moral autism. Self-described liberals have naturally said that this is a parody of their views (Rawls 1985, 233; Rorty 1991, 179ff.).

Liberals themselves have sometimes tried to define liberalism in such a way that only the very deluded or the very wicked could fail to be liberals. At the height of the Cold War, it was easy to present the alternatives as liberal democracy on the one hand and assorted forms of one-party totalitarianism on the other. This attempt to narrow the range of political options was itself resisted. *Social* democrats, who opposed both the one-party state and uncontrolled capitalism, believed that their disbelief in the legitimacy of private property in the means of production distinguished them from *liberal* democrats. American conservatives distinguished themselves from liberals by according state and central governments a greater role in preserving national identity and some form of traditional moral consensus than liberals accept, or else by advocating a more laissez-faire economy and a reduced role for government (Rossiter 1982, 235ff.). Their critics retorted that they were nonetheless doomed by American history to remain liberals (Hartz 1955, 145–49).

The attempt to produce a clear-cut definition of a political stance is not always part of a hostile campaign to present the doctrines in question as incoherent or malign. Many political movements have devoted much effort to establishing a creed to which members must swear allegiance. Lenin spent as much time denouncing his Marxist allies for their misunderstanding of scientific socialism as attacking the czarist regime. He thought a revolutionary movement must know exactly what it thought and hoped to achieve. If the fainthearted or intellectually unorganized were driven out, so be it; as the title of one essay proclaimed: "Better Fewer but Better." Of all political creeds, liberalism is the least likely to behave like this. Whatever liberalism involves, it certainly includes toleration and an antipathy to closing ranks around any system of beliefs. All the same, liberals have often asked themselves what they have in common, where the boundaries lie between themselves and, say, socialists on the one side and conservatives on the other.

Another explanation of the difficulty of defining political terms is that they are essentially contested terms, terms whose meaning and reference are perennially open to debate. If we define liberalism as the belief that the freedom of the individual is the highest political value, and that institutions and practices are to be judged by their success in promoting it—perhaps the most plausible brief definition—this only invites further argument. What is liberty? Is it positive or negative? How does the liberty of a whole nation relate to the liberty of its members? Nor is liberty the only concept to invite such scrutiny. Who are the individuals in question? Do they include children? Do they include the senile and the mentally ill? Do they include resident aliens or the inhabitants of colonial dependencies? This might be thought to be unsurprising; any definition opens up discussion of the terms in which the definition is proffered. The sting in the claim that these are essentially contested concepts is the thought that any elaboration will provoke further argument (Gallie 1956, 175ff.).

There is a clear direction in which any elaboration of the definition of a chair, say, must go, and a clear line beyond which discussion is merely captious. This seems not to be true of the discussion of political doctrines. Whether the view that there are essentially contested concepts is entirely coherent is another question. Unless some substantial portion of the meaning of a concept is uncontested, it is hard to see how the concept could be identified in the first place. There must be a central uncontested core of meaning to terms like "liberty" if arguments about the contested penumbra are to make sense. A man in jail is paradigmatically not free; a man threatened with punishment if he writes a book is paradigmatically less free to write it than a man not so threatened (Berlin 1969, 122ff.). Even so, we may agree that political terms are constantly being endowed with new meanings, in much the way the terms of the law are endowed with new meanings in the course of legal argument. Even if liberalism is distinct enough to be identifiable, it still changes over time.

VARIETIES OF LIBERALISM: CLASSICAL VERSUS MODERN

To agree that liberalism may have a variety of institutional manifestations while resting on one moral basis—Locke's claim that men are born "in a state of perfect freedom, to order their actions and dispose of their possessions, and persons, as they see fit . . . a state also of equality" (Locke [1690] 1967, 287), for instance—does not mean that all doubts about the porosity of liberalism have been laid to rest. One argument that has taken on the status of a commonplace is that there have been two kinds of liberalism: one "classical," limited in its aims, cautious about its metaphysical basis, and political in its orientation; the other "modern," unlimited, incautious, global in its aims, and a threat to the achievements of "classical liberalism." Classical liberalism is associated with John Locke ([1690] 1967), Adam Smith ([1775] 1976), Alexis de Tocqueville ([1835] 1964), and Friedrich von Hayek (1973–79). It focuses on the idea of limited government, the maintenance of the rule of law, the avoidance of arbitrary and discretionary power, the sanctity of private property and freely made contracts, and the responsibility of individuals for their own fates.

It is not necessarily a democratic doctrine, for there is nothing in the bare idea of majority rule to show that majorities will always respect the rights of property or maintain the rule of law (Madison, Hamilton, and Jay 1987, *Federalist* 10, 122–25); it is not always a progressive doctrine, for many classical liberals are skeptical about the average human being's ability to make useful advances in morality and culture, for instance. It is hostile to the welfare state; welfare states violate the principle that each individual ought to look to their own welfare, and frequently couch their claims in terms of the achievement of social justice, an ideal to which classical liberals attach little meaning (Hayek 1976). More importantly, perhaps, welfare states confer large discretionary powers upon their politicians and bureaucrats, and thus reduce to dependency their clients and those who depend upon the state for their prosperity.

Modern adherents of classical liberalism often ground their defense of minimal government on what they take to be a minimal moral basis. Minimal government may, for instance, be justified by the prosperity that economies deliver when they are not interfered with by governments; this argument has been current from Adam Smith's *Wealth of Nations* defense of "the simple system of natural liberty" (Smith [1775] 1976, 687) down to Hayek's in our own time. It is not morally contentious to claim that prosperity is better than misery, and it has been given greater credibility than ever by the collapse of the communist regimes of Eastern Europe and the discrediting of military and authoritarian governments elsewhere.

An equally minimalist defense of liberalism as minimal government is provided by pointing to the nastiness of governmental coercion and to the contrast between the negative effects of mere brute force and prohibition compared with the benign effects of uncoerced cooperation. No classical liberal denies the need for law; coercive law represses force and fraud, and the noncoercive civil law allows people to make contracts and engage in any kind of economic activity. Still, every classical liberal holds that all the forces that make for imagination, invention, and growth come from the voluntary sector of the social order.

Classical liberals are not unanimous about the relationship between minimal government and the cultural and moral order, and this is perhaps the most important point about their moral views. Unlike modern liberals, they do not display any particular attachment to the ideal of moral and cultural progress. David Hume was more a political conservative than Adam Smith, but was more inclined than Smith to admire the "brisk march of the spirits" typical of a flourishing commercial society. Tocqueville was doubtful whether liberty could survive in the absence of strong religious sentiment, thinking that the self-reliance and self-restraint that he admired was not natural to modern man (Tocqueville 1964, 310–25), and Hayek was inclined to think that political liberalism rests upon cultural conservatism (Gray 1984, 129–31).

Contemporary defenders of classical liberalism think it threatened by modern liberalism. Modern liberalism, in this view, reverses the ambitions and restraints of classical liberalism, and in the process threatens the gains that classical liberals achieved when they replaced the tyranny of kings and courtiers with constitutional regimes. Modern liberalism is exemplified by John Stuart Mill's *On Liberty*, with its appeal to "man as a progressive being" and its romantic appeal to an individuality that should be allowed to develop itself in all its "manifold diversity" (Mill [1861] 1974, 120–22). Philosophically, it is exemplified equally by the liberalism of the English Idealists and "new liberals" such as L. T. Hobhouse ([1911] 1964).

In practice, it is exemplified by the assault on freedom of contract and on the sanctity of property rights represented by the welfare legislation of the Liberal government in the UK before World War I, by Franklin Roosevelt's New Deal between the wars, and by the explosion of welfare-state activity after World War II. Modern liberalism is usually (but not always) agreed, even by its critics, to be a form of liberalism, for its underlying moral basis is couched in terms of freedom. Negatively, the aim is to emancipate individuals from the fear of hunger, unemployment, ill health, and a miserable old age, and, positively, to attempt to help members of modern industrial societies flourish in the way Mill and Wilhelm von Humboldt wanted them to.

It is liberal, too, because it does not share the antipathies and hopes of a socialist defense of the modern welfare state. Although some defenders of the rights of property claim that almost any restriction on the absolute liberty of owners to dispose of their own as they choose amounts to confiscation (Epstein 1985), modern liberalism has no confiscatory ambitions. Inasmuch as the ideals of the welfare state cannot be achieved without a good deal of governmental control of the economy, modern liberalism cannot treat property as sacrosanct and cannot limit government to the repression of force and fraud; but distinguished modern liberals such as John Rawls argue that personal property is a necessary element of individual self-expression, especially by means of freedom of choice in careers, even if vast shareholdings are not (Rawls 1971, 272–74). Critics of modern liberalism usually insist that it is liberalism, but a dangerous variety.

The fear that modern liberalism is inimical to the spirit of classical liberalism and will, in practice, threaten the latter's gains rests on two things. The first is the thought that modern liberalism is ideologically or metaphysically overcommitted. Mill's vision of man as a progressive being, with its demand that everyone should constantly rethink her opinions on every conceivable subject, is one with at best a minority appeal. To found one's politics on a view of human nature that most people find implausible is to found one's politics on quicksand. There is no need to appeal to such a vision of human nature to support classical liberalism; conversely, it is not clear that the kind of independent and imaginative personalities by which Mill set such store are best produced in a liberal society. History suggests that many of them have flourished by resisting an illiberal and conservative environment (Berlin 1969, 172).

The second is the thought that modern liberalism makes everyone an unrealizable promise of a degree of personal fulfillment that the welfare state cannot deliver, and that its efforts to deliver it will inevitably lead to frustration. For one thing, people resent being forced to part with their hard-earned income to provide the resources that supply jobs, education, and the various social services that modern liberalism employs to create its conception of individual freedom for other people. This creates a hostility between more and less favored groups of citizens that is wholly at odds with what modern liberals desire.

Moreover, the welfare state must employ an extensive bureaucracy whose members are granted discretionary powers and charged by law to use those powers for the welfare of their clients. This means that classical liberals' concern for the rule of law and the curtailing of arbitrary discretion is ignored: bureaucrats are given resources to disburse to their clients, and meanwhile the allegiance of the citizenry is undermined when the state fails to produce the good things it has been asked to provide. The liberation the welfare state promises—liberation from anxiety, poverty, and the cramped circumstances of working-class existence—is easily obtained by the educated middle class and is impossible to achieve for most others. There is thus a grave risk of disillusionment with liberalism in general as a result of its failure when it overextends itself. Some writers suppose that the worldwide popularity of conservative governments during the 1980s is explained by this consideration.

VARIETIES OF LIBERALISM: LIBERTARIANISM AND LIBERALISM

There is a closely related but not identical divide within liberal theory between liberalism and libertarianism. Just as in the conflict between classical and modern forms of liberalism, there is a tendency for the partisans of one side or the other to claim that their version of liberalism is true liberalism and the alternative something else entirely. Contemporary libertarians often claim that they are classical liberals. This is not wholly true. There is at least one strand of libertarian thought, represented by Robert Nozick's *Anarchy, State, and Utopia*, that advocates the decriminalization of "victimless crimes" such as prostitution, drug taking, and unorthodox sexual activities (Nozick 1974, 58–59). There is nothing of that in John Locke or Adam Smith.

The line between liberal and libertarian theories is not easy to draw. Both are committed to the promotion of individual liberty; both rest most happily on a theory of human rights according to which individuals enter the world with a right to the free disposal of themselves and their resources. The line of cleavage lies between the libertarian view that government is not a necessary evil but a largely (and for so-called anarchocapitalists, a wholly) unnecessary evil, and the liberal view that governmental power is to be treated with caution but, like any other instrument, may be used to achieve good ends. Perhaps the most important point of difference is that libertarians see our rights as a form of private property, what Nozick has called "entitlements" (Nozick 1974, 150ff.). The individual is the owner of his or her person and abilities; so viewed, our rights have two sources only—our initial ownership of our own selves and capacities, and the claims on whatever resources and abilities other people have freely agreed to transfer to us. The state, if legitimate at all, may do no more than secure these rights. It has no resources of its own and cannot engage either in the redistributive activities of modern welfare states or in the quasi-charitable activities of such states. Nobody has the right to deprive anyone else of their property by force—if they have committed no crime—and neither does the state.

This is in sharp contrast to the most famous recent account of welfare state liberalism, John Rawls's *Theory of Justice*. In Rawls's account, we arrive at an understanding of what rights we possess, and of how far our liberty extends, by asking ourselves a hypothetical question—"What rights would we all demand for ourselves and acknowledge in others if we were to establish a social and political system de novo, knowing nothing about our particular abilities and tastes, and therefore being forced to strike a fair bargain with everyone else?" (Rawls 1971, 11–17). Rawls's claim is that we should acknowledge two rights: the right to the most extensive liberty consistent with the same liberty for everyone, and a right to just treatment, enshrined in the thought that inequalities are justified only to the extent that they improve the situation of the least advantaged (60–61).

This second principle is often called the maximin theory of justice, since it explains social justice as *max*imizing the size of the *min*imum holding of social resources. This principle is clearly inimical to any account of the state that restricts it to the defense of property rights. The introduction of a conception of social justice into the defense of a liberal political theory rests on the idea that individuals have a right to self-development, and therefore on the kind of theory of individual development that underpins Mill's *On Liberty* and alienates defenders of classical liberalism.

All dualisms ride roughshod over a complicated world. There are forms of liberalism that are nonlibertarian, but also more nearly "classical" than modern liberalism. Locke's *Two Treatises* is, on the face of it, more friendly to private property than the views of Rawls or Mill, and yet Locke shows none of the hostility to the state that libertarians do. The state is obliged to act according to the rule "*salus populi suprema lex*"—"the good of the people is the highest law"—and there is no suggestion that this is only a matter of repressing force and fraud (Locke [1690] 1967, 391). On the other hand, there is also no suggestion that the least advantaged members of society have a right to do as well as possible. Locke suggests that they have to do well enough to make membership in civil society a good bargain—otherwise, they might as well immigrate to some unoccupied part of the world and start again—but he does not suggest that they have any claim beyond that (314–15). Certainly, Locke's individualism treats each person as responsible for his or her own welfare, but Locke's concern with our moral welfare rather than economic well-being means that he was more concerned with religious toleration than with "health and human services."

Liberal Antipathies

Because we are tempted to acknowledge that we are faced with liberalisms rather than liberalism, and are inclined also to say that they are all versions of one liberalism, it is tempting to suggest that liberalism is best understood in terms of what it rejects. Nor would it be surprising to come to such a conclusion. Conservatism is no easier to define than liberalism, and it is not infrequently observed that what conservatives believe is a matter of what they want to conserve and who threatens it. Indeed, Louis Hartz's *The Liberal Tradition in America* argued that conservatives in the United States, as opposed to their counterparts in Britain and Europe, were in a bad way because the society and political system they want to conserve has always been a liberal one; temperamental conservatives are thus forced to be ideological liberals (Hartz 1955, 145–54). However that may be, it is not implausible to argue that liberalism is well defined in negative terms. Its central commitment, liberty, is in general a negative notion—to be free is to be *not* in jail, *not* bound to a particular occupation, *not* excluded from the franchise, and so on—and the history of liberalism is a history of opposition to assorted tyrannies.

ANTIABSOLUTISM

One way of understanding the continuity of liberal history in this light is to see liberalism as a perennial protest against all forms of absolute authority. It is notoriously difficult to suggest a starting date for liberal political theory, or, rather, it is notoriously easy to suggest all sorts of starting dates, running from the pre-Socratics onward, but notoriously difficult to find any kind of consensus on one of them. In British politics, for instance, it was only in the 1860s that the more radical members of the Whigs called themselves the

Liberal Party. Yet it would be odd not to count Locke among early liberals, just as it would be absurd to call Hobbes a liberal even while one might want to acknowledge that he supplied many of the ingredients for a liberal theory of politics in the course of defending absolute and arbitrary authority as the only alternative to the anarchy of the state of nature and the war of all against all.

Whatever liberalism has been concerned with, it has been concerned with avoiding absolute and arbitrary power. It is not alone in this. English constitutional theory had for several centuries an aversion to anything that smacked of confiding absolute power to anyone whatever. Neither Parliament, nor the judiciary, nor the king was entitled to a monopoly of political authority. The imagery of the body politic was called upon to suggest that the elements in the political system had to cooperate with one another for the body to function coherently. What makes liberal hostility to absolute rule liberal rather than merely constitutionalist is the liberal claim that absolute rule violates the personality or the rights of those over whom it is exercised (Locke [1690] 1967, 342–48).

This argument connects Locke's *Second Treatise*, with its claim that absolute and arbitrary authority was so inconsistent with civil society that it could not be considered a form of government at all, with the twentieth-century liberal's contempt for the totalitarian regimes of Nazi Germany and Stalinist Russia. Liberals have disagreed about just which sorts of absolute authority are intolerable. Locke agreed that a general needed absolute authority over his soldiers in battle, and might shoot deserters out of hand. But this was not arbitrary authority—generals might shoot deserters, but not take sixpence from their pockets (Locke [1690] 1967, 379–80).

Mill thought the principles of *On Liberty* did not apply to people who could not benefit from rational discussion (Mill [1861] 1974, 69–70). Elizabeth I and Peter the Great had rightly exercised unaccountable power over sixteenth-century Britain and eighteenth-century Russia, respectively, and the despotic power of the East India Company over its Indian subjects was legitimate. The nineteenth-century British working class, on the other hand, was entitled to full civil and political rights, and women of all classes as much as men. Other liberals have been rather less ready to describe entire populations as "childish," and have thought absolute authority over colonial possessions as indefensible as any other absolute power.

The thought behind liberal opposition to absolute power is not complex, although it has several strands. One is the idea that political authority exists for purely secular ends, toward which we should adopt a rational, scientific attitude, adjusting our political institutions and our policies in an instrumentally efficient way. Negatively, this means that liberals do not see authority as conferred either by the voice of God, as in theories of divine right or charismatic authority, or by the dictates of history, as in Marxist theory, or by racial destiny, as in Nazi theory. Authority exists only to enable a society to achieve those limited goals that a political order enables us to achieve—the security of life, property, and the pursuit of happiness (Locke [1689] 1956, 128–29).

It follows that nobody can claim absolute power, since their title to exercise power rests on their ability to pursue these limited goals efficiently. A second idea that reinforces the first is that the content of these limited goals can be set only by attending to the opinions of all the people under that authority, or at least all those who have not shown themselves to be antisocial or a menace to the political order. To exclude anyone's views is to devalue them; it is also to deny what liberalism relies on for its effect as a moral argument, the claim that we are born free and equal (Dworkin 1985, 191ff.). As free, we must be persuaded to give our allegiance, and as equal, we must be obliged on the same terms as everyone else. This means that government must listen to the people and cannot therefore take to itself any kind of absolute power (Rawls 1971, 221–23).

A third element provides much of the antitotalitarian energy of modern liberalism. Free and equal individuals must be so recognized in the legal system as well as in the political system narrowly conceived. They must be free to form associations for their own purposes and to engage in varied social, commercial, and intellectual activities. Absolute authority is inimical to, and unwilling to share, control over the lives of the citizenry with the leaders of other, secondary groups. The history of twentieth-century totalitarian states indeed shows that such states have always destroyed the independent authority of all other associations they could lay hands on. Liberals believe that the energy and liveliness of a society comes from these secondary allegiances, and therefore that absolute power is both an affront to the moral personality of individuals and destructive of the life of society at large (Dworkin 1985, 193–200).

ANTITHEOCRACY

The opposition to absolutism, which links Locke to Mill and both of them to Rawls, Dworkin, and contemporary liberal thinkers, had its origins in another issue. This was the liberal hostility to the confusion of secular and religious authority, and the liberal obsession with the rights of conscience. It has often been pointed out that the first usage of the term "liberal" in a political context was in the context of European anticlerical politics in the nineteenth century. For many Roman Catholics, the term "liberal" was, except when used to qualify "education," a term of abuse. Voltaire was not a wholehearted liberal, but the cry of "*écrasez l'infame*," with which he attacked the repressive and brutal power of the Catholic Church in eighteenth-century France, became a rallying cry of anticlerical liberals all over Europe.

Liberalism was associated with the nineteenth-century movement of European ideas that was concerned to drive a wedge between church and state and to make the Catholic Church no more influential in the politics of Catholic countries than the various Protestant churches were in the countries where they flourished. In essence, the argument was an argument in favor of religious toleration and against any kind of religious monopoly.

It is sometimes thought that toleration arises when people are convinced that there is no way of knowing what the truth is in matters of religion, and that toleration is the fruit of skepticism. But this is quite wrong. Hobbes was a skeptic, but he was also deeply hostile to supposed *rights* to toleration. It is this that marks him as a nonliberal. The advocacy or denial of toleration as a matter of right divides the liberal and the nonliberal more sharply than anything else. For Hobbes, religious doctrines were too important to be left to private men to pick and choose; even if those doctrines were intellectually quite absurd, they stirred up the passions and so threatened the peace. It was thus the task of the sovereign to regulate what might and might not be said in public on all such matters; if the sovereign failed in this duty, the peace would be broken, exactly the outcome that the sovereign existed to prevent (Hobbes [1651] 1991, 124–25).

Locke put forward the modern doctrine of toleration some thirty years after Hobbes. In Locke's eyes, there were two distinct realms, the sacred and the secular. Locke thought the first much more important than the second, but he also thought that secular authority was quite impotent to achieve anything useful in that realm. The political realm dealt with what Locke termed *bona civilia*, the goods of earthly peace and security, which he otherwise characterized as life, liberty, property, and physical well-being (Locke [1689] 1956, 128). A sovereign who tried to dictate how we practiced our religion was overstepping the proper bounds of his authority. Conversely, a church that tried to dictate the secular law was overstepping the bounds of its authority. The state was essentially a nonvoluntary organization, and one to which we owed obedience willy-nilly; churches were essentially voluntary, and probably plural.

Locke was, as Hobbes was not, a devout Christian, one who thought a great deal about religion as religion rather than from a sociological perspective. It was this that made Locke a passionate defender of toleration. One of the arguments in favor of toleration and against the mingling of church and state was precisely that human beings—especially late seventeenth-century human beings of a Protestant persuasion—were extremely tender about matters of conscience. To force someone to assert a belief he did not really hold was to outrage his deepest nature.

Where Hobbes had suggested that men quarrelled over matters of conscience because there was next to nothing to be known about religion by the light of reason alone, and therefore men ought to be made to assert something in common, simply for the sake of peace, Locke was committed to the view that God required a willing assent and a real faith, so that whatever kind of forced assent the state might induce us to make was an insult to God as well as an outrage upon the individual (Hobbes [1651] 1991, 260ff.; Locke [1689] 1956, 132–33).

Conversely, true religion can make no demands upon the state. This is a view that modern readers find harder to accept. Locke thought it impossible that there might be a valid religious reason for a group to do anything that might come into conflict with the ordinary criminal law. Thus he would have differed with most liberals of today over the case in 1990 in which the U.S. Supreme Court found that the First Amendment guarantees of religious liberty did not entitle Native Americans to use the hallucinogenic drug peyote in their religious rituals once the State of Oregon had banned the consumption of peyote.

Locke would have sided with the Court, but many contemporary liberals thought the demands of any religion should weigh more heavily than that. Locke also confined toleration to opinions that did not threaten the political order; modern readers are often shocked to find that neither Roman Catholics nor atheists would be tolerated in any society that followed Locke's prescriptions. In both cases, the argument was that they were politically dangerous; atheists lacked motives to keep their promises and behave decently, while Catholics professed earthly loyalty to the pope and so could not be relied on by the rulers of whatever state they happened to belong to (Locke [1689] 1956, 157–58).

This reflected Locke's sharp distinction between those matters over which secular authority might be exercised and those over which it must not. Locke argued that earthly governments existed for certain simple tasks and no others, an argument heavily dependent on the idea that it is obvious what the function of earthly government is, and that it does not include saving men's souls. Mill's *On Liberty* took a different route to much the same conclusion, not by arguing that it was obvious what the function of government was, but by showing that a consistent utilitarian who believed in the importance of individuality and moral progress must agree that coercion, especially the organized coercion exerted by governments, was legitimate only to defend certain this-worldly interests—our own liberty and security above all else (Mill [1861] 1974, 119ff.; Gray 1983).

Mill's argument is no more conclusive than Locke's. Enthusiasts for the mixing of church and state may set no value on individuality for its own sake and believe that an enlarged freedom would lead to depravity rather than moral progress. It is on this basis that they demand the union of spiritual and secular authority. In the second half of the twentieth century, liberals have generally taken a less rhetorical, more practical line than Locke and Mill. Totalitarian regimes, the lineal descendants of confessional states, have two great drawbacks. The first is that they employ a distasteful amount of force in securing their goals. Because it is so difficult to tell whether one's subjects are really saved or really loyal to the Nazi Party, or whatever, the temptation is to pile on the penalties for dissent and to engage in acts of exemplary brutal punishment, which does little to secure a real loyalty to the regime and much to make its rulers insecure when they contemplate the hatred of the population they have intimidated (Arendt 1968).

The second is that such regimes are inefficient; they may be effective when fighting a real, all-out war, but they are economically less efficient than liberal societies in which the division of labor between the sacred and the profane is respected in approximately the form Locke laid down. Whether this practical argument captures liberals' deepest beliefs is doubtful. It is hard not to suspect that liberals feel more passionately than that about the wickedness of totalitarian regimes and, for that matter, about the wickedness of authoritarian clerical regimes of the kind typified by the Spain of General Franco. When they feel passionately about such regimes, it is in much the same way as Locke, for modern notions of the violation of personality reflect, in a secularized fashion, Locke's view that the imposition of belief on any individual was an affront to that individual and God their creator (Rawls 1971, 205–11).

ANTICAPITALISM

The history of hatred for despotism, theocracy, and the modern union of the two that is reflected in totalitarianism is a long history. The third of liberalism's antipathies has a shorter history. From the middle of the nineteenth century until today, one strand of liberalism has regarded capitalism as an enemy of liberty (Mill [1848] 1965, 766–69; Dewey [1931] 1984). This marked a great reversal in the history of liberalism. It is not a large oversimplification to say that until the early nineteenth century there was no question of opposing liberalism to capitalism. The movement of ideas and institutions that emancipated individuals from tradition, insisted on their natural rights, and demanded that "careers should be open to talent" rather than birth was a seamless whole.

Just as a man had to think for himself, so he had to work for himself; just as society would progress only if each person took responsibility for their own ideas and moral convictions, so it would flourish economically only if everyone stood on their own two feet. How far this was an articulate defense of capitalism as such is debatable; the term "capitalism" itself did not come into general use until the late nineteenth century, and it is difficult to decide how appropriate it is to characterize as capitalist those societies that possessed nothing one could call a proletariat, whose populations still lived largely in the countryside and worked the land, and that thought of themselves as "commercial societies" rather than "capitalist economies" (Smith [1775] 1976, 399–403).

Moreover, many of the rights to dispose of property just as one wished, to work for anyone willing to employ one, and to contract with anyone for any purpose not obviously damaging to the security and good morals of the commonwealth had been established by successive decisions made by judges appealing to the English common law rather than by legislation of a self-consciously liberal kind. Still, there is an obvious affinity between liberalism on the one hand and the rule of private property and freedom of contract on the other. The liberal view that the individual is, by natural right or by something tantamount to it, sovereign over himself, his talents, and his property is at once the basis of limited government, the rule of law, individual liberty, and a capitalist economy.

But it was apparent from the beginning that property might be employed oppressively as well as harmlessly or beneficially. Apart from the conflict between the rights of property owners and the traditional claims of rural workers—such as customary claims to gather wood or to glean in the fields or to take small game—there was a more general conflict between the liberty of the large property owner to do what he chose with his property and the impossibility of his workers or competitors striking anything like a fair bargain with him. Throughout the nineteenth century, the sentiment grew that if it had once been necessary to liberate the entrepreneur from misguided or oppressive government, it was now necessary to liberate the worker and consumer from the tyranny of the capitalist (Hobhouse [1911] 1964, 22–24, 82–84; Green 1892, 366–70).

Mill observed that the modern wage laborer had as little real choice of occupation as a slave had in antiquity. In that spirit, he defended the right of working people to organize into trade unions to redress the balance of power a little. T. H. Green and L. T. Hobhouse went further, suggesting that capitalism exerted a kind of moral tyranny over the ordinary person, as exemplified by the spread of drinking establishments that destroyed both the health and the self-respect of their victims (Green 1892, 380–85). The "New Liberalism," exemplified in Britain by the social policy of the Asquith government of 1908–16, and in the United States by the demands of the Progressives and the practice of the Democratic Party after the election of Franklin D. Roosevelt in 1932, had many positive ambitions, but one negative assumption was that the workingman needed to be freed from the power of the capitalist. It is this that explains the seeming paradox that late twentieth-century conservatives are often characterized as "neoliberals." The contemporary defense of property rights is not, as it was two centuries ago, the defense of landed property against commercial and industrial capital, but the defense of nineteenth-century laissez-faire and the property rights of commercial and industrial capital against modern reformers.

Liberal Prescriptions

The tidiness of a definition of liberalism couched in terms of its oppositions is only apparent. Certainly, liberalism is antidespotic, anticlerical, and hostile to twentieth-century manifestations of those evils, including the perverted manifestations of totalitarianism. But just as there is a tension between classical and modern liberalisms, the same tension reappears between pro- and anticapitalist liberalisms. And just as most liberals would not wish to pursue the goals of the welfare state to the lengths of threatening the survival of limited, lawful government, so they would not wish to restrain the operations of a capitalist economy to the point at which it turned into a command economy. Whether we start from liberal enthusiasms or liberal antipathies, we find the same controversies.

The wish to find a position that is intellectually attractive and politically responsible exposes liberals to accusations of not knowing their own minds or of being wishy-washy. Liberals have retorted that it is not their fault that the world is a complicated place that requires nuanced handling. One way of underpinning that reply is to provide the positive liberal theory that explains both why liberalism is hostile to the threats to freedom that it encounters and why these threats have varied over time.

A THEORY FOR INDIVIDUALS

In spite of the suggestion that liberalism should confine its attention to political institutions, liberalism is best understood as a theory of the good life for individuals that is linked to a theory of the social, economic, and political arrangements within which they may lead that life. John Rawls's *Theory of Justice* provides some persuasive arguments for the view that we should build a liberal theory for institutional design without committing ourselves to any particular view of "the good life," and those arguments' eventual failure to convince tells us a lot about why a broader theory is needed.

Rawls argues that the search for a consensus in favor of liberal political and economic institutions will go more smoothly if we seek foundations that are neutral with respect to the great, but sharply contested, issues of religion and personal ethics (Rawls 1989, 233–38). Critics have noted, however, that Rawls's minimalist assumptions about "the good life" remain decidedly liberal—he takes it for granted that slavery is an unspeakable evil, that the suppression of conscientious belief is so intolerable that no rational person could trade the chance of being in command of the Inquisition for the risk of being one of its victims, and that freedom of choice in career and lifestyle is essential for life to have any meaning.

The same critics have also pointed out that the principles of justice proposed by Rawls are not suited to absolutely anyone but especially to persons holding a late twentieth-century conception of themselves and the meaning of their lives. The thinness of the premises about human nature and the human good that Rawls builds on do not reflect skepticism or a lack of moral conviction so much as the eminently liberal thought that each person is in command of his or her own moral destiny and that it is not for others to dictate it, as Rawls has subsequently tended to agree (Rawls 1985).

At all events, liberalism viewed as a doctrine for individuals can be understood in terms one might borrow from Immanuel Kant, Humboldt, Mill, Bertrand Russell, or Dewey, since a variety of formulations seize on the same points. The essence is that individuals are self-creating, that no single good defines successful self-creation, and that taking responsibility for one's own life and making of it what one can is itself part of the good life as understood by liberals. Dewey labeled this experimentalism; Kant defined it as the spirit of the Enlightenment; Mill borrowed from von Humboldt to argue that the fundamental aim is to develop human nature in all its diversity (Mill [1861] 1974, 121–22; Dewey [1931] 1984, 114–20; Kant 1991, 53–54).

Its positive attractions become clearer when they are contrasted with pre-liberal or antiliberal views. *Self*-discipline is a great good because nobody can conduct "experiments in living" without the self-control that allows them to stand back and assess their success or failure; submission to discipline, as praised by many Christian writers, and before them by Plato, is not a good in itself (Plato 1941, 127–40). Attachment to one's country and fellow citizens is a great good because few human virtues flourish except against a background of loyalty and strong fellow feeling; "my country right or wrong" is an illiberal sentiment, suggesting an immersion in patriotic sentiment inconsistent with the ideals of individual autonomy.

Plato condemned democratic Athens for its attachment to diversity and variety; liberals condemn Athens for being insufficiently hospitable to diversity and variety as good in themselves. Pericles's famous funeral oration praises the Athenians for their willingness to allow others to live as they pleased, but suggests no positive enthusiasm for variety as a human good, denies that women have any place in public life, and ranks politics higher than any private good. Liberals generally praise public spirit, and most, at any rate, would agree that in time of crisis we are obliged to put aside our private concerns and do what we can for our country, but they would also see this as a sacrifice of one good for another, while Pericles was true to the classical ideal in ranking the goods of private life much lower than the goods of public life (Thucydides 1972, 143–51).

It is true that liberalism has no single positive picture of "the good life for man." It is true because liberals have commonly been empiricists and inclined to believe that only experience can reveal what really conduces to individual flourishing, and also because liberals have often been pluralists and have thought that autonomous individuals might choose a great variety of very different but equally good lives (Berlin 1969, 172–74). It is not, as critics often maintain, that liberals elevate choice to the only absolute good; no liberal would applaud a life of crime merely because the criminal had chosen it. It is, however, true that most liberals have thought that the kind of autonomous individual they have admired can become a fully autonomous being only by exercising their powers of choice. Some people may get lucky and find what suits them without very much exploration of alternatives; others may need to search much longer. But a person incapable of making a choice and sticking to it will have little chance of leading a happy life.

This vision is not uncontroversial, and it is unattractive to many critics. It is unsympathetic to a vision of an orderly universe in which the best lay down the rules of life for the rest of us; it is antiaristocratic, at odds with a belief in Platonic guardians, Aristotelian aristocrats, and the Catholic Christian tradition's claim to know what we must do to be saved. Conversely, it is too strenuous for anyone who thinks most people do well enough by thoughtlessly following the habits and customs of their fellows. It is too optimistic for anyone who believes in the essential depravity of the human race. Liberals look for improvement, not merely to prevent our worse natures from getting out of hand. Writers like Joseph de Maistre and Georges Sorel have not unpersuasively ridiculed this outlook.

Looked at from the other side, it can be criticized as insufficiently serious about its own premises. Friedrich Nietzsche claimed that liberals did not take choice seriously, since they assumed that everyone would share their ideas about what constituted good choices and good reasons for choosing one path rather than another. His successors in the existentialist tradition made essentially the same point. As observed before, liberals are uncomfortably aware that they can seem equivocal at worst or wishy-washy at best in their attempts to steer a tidy course between the critics who complain that they overestimate the value of autonomy and critics who complain that they have not understood that human freedom is a curse and a source of anguish rather than an achievement. It is too late in the day to rely on Aristotle's claim that the truth of these matters is to be found in the mean between extremes, but the liberal can at any rate reply that there is no more reason to suppose that it lies in the extremes than in the ground between them that liberalism occupies.

A THEORY FOR SOCIETY

It is a common complaint against liberalism that it undervalues the role of community. Since the late 1970s, this has been a constant refrain, but it replicates the complaints made by critics of philosophical radicalism in the early 1800s and by philosophical idealists in the late 1800s (Sandel 1982). One response to the complaint might be to list those liberals who took the role of the community entirely seriously—they include Tocqueville, Mill, Green, Hobhouse, Émile Durkheim, William James, and Dewey. This is only the starting point for an answer to the question whether liberalism has or even can have a liberal theory of society. The answer is plainly that it can and indeed that it does. In fact, one might argue that it is only because liberals are so impressed by the ways in which society molds and shapes the lives of its members that liberals are so eager to ensure that society does not also cramp and distort those lives.

Sociologists used to claim that their opponents were attached to a contractual account of society, and by this they meant that their opponents believed that society literally had its origins in some kind of agreement. Although it is plain that no contemporary liberal would think anything of the sort, it is true that liberals find it illuminating to think of society as if it involved a sort of contract. The authority of the group over the individual is not absolute, but extends only to the hypothetical terms of a bargain by which individuals agree to accept that authority (Nagel 1991, 33ff.). The terms of the bargain are what remain in dispute. In his essay *On Liberty*, Mill essentially treated it as a compact for self-protection. Society was, as it were, a device for lending individuals the force of the whole group in fending off attacks on their persons and property (Mill [1861] 1974, 119–22).

This covered only the coercive authority of society. A more elusive topic was what a liberal society would look like, going beyond the question of what rules it might properly enforce on its members. Just as in the case of its account of the values that give point to an individual existence, liberalism is to some extent hampered in giving a very rich account by its attachment to the value of choice. Once we have said that a society full of liberals would be replete with voluntary associations devoted to enhancing the existences of all their members, there is little more to say. We may agree that a liberal would think it desirable that stamp collectors should get together and discuss their enthusiasms, exchange stamps, circulate journals about their hobby, and all the rest, but it defies the imagination to offer a liberal theory of philately.

Liberals would object strongly to any regime that made philately difficult—it would be a pointless interference with liberty—and would divide on the question whether a government might properly assist philatelic societies to get started by a temporary subsidy, as liberals have always been divided in their attitudes to governmental assistance for art, education, and high culture. Beyond that, the liberal answer to the question of what a society attached to liberal principles would actually look like is that the answer is a matter for the society in question. It might have many churches or none, a multitude of different schooling systems or one, an effective public transport system or not; what would matter would be that the individual liberty or human rights of its members were respected in the process of reaching these outcomes. In particular, liberalism is agnostic about what the implementation of the vision of a society of free individuals entails for the economic arrangements it embraces. Certainly, too many state controls threaten liberty, just as a state monopoly of employment threatens liberty (Rawls 1971, 377ff.). So does a capitalism that allows rich men to buy politicians. Where the best feasible regime lies is a matter for experiment.

A THEORY FOR THE STATE

What applies to society does not apply in the same way to the state. Society is the realm of both informal and formal associations, a realm in which public opinion plays some coercive role, but there is much scope for voluntary association; in a manner of speaking, society is a plurality of smaller societies. The state is essentially the realm of coercively sanctioned coordination, and its essence is that it has no competitors or alternatives. That a liberal state must operate according to the rule of law goes without saying; that it must employ as little coercion as possible in its dealings with its citizens also goes without saying. What is more hotly contested is whether liberalism dictates any particular form of government.

Historically, liberals have thought at one time that liberalism was threatened by democracy, and at another that liberalism entailed democracy. What liberalism is always committed to is constitutional government. Except in emergencies, when the preservation of a liberal regime may force governments to take powers that would otherwise be intolerable, the requirements of the rule of law extend to the ways in which governments acquire power and exercise it. How this is best achieved has no fixed answer. It is an ongoing argument whether the British view that governments are kept liberal by public opinion and fear of the voter is more or less plausible than the American view that a written constitution and a formal Bill of Rights are uniquely effective. It is more than plausible that such institutional devices as an independent judiciary, a diverse and free press, and a great variety of watchdog organizations such as the U.S. Council for Civil Liberties are all of them useful, and that one needs both the formal protections of American constitutionalism and a liberal-minded citzenry that makes them more than parchment barriers to oppression (Madison, Hamilton, and Jay 1987, *Federalist* 48, 309).

This leaves the connection between liberalism and democracy for further analysis. If democracy is just a matter of majority rule, it is a contingent matter whether the majority will generally subscribe to liberal views. If it does, there will be a liberal democracy; if not, not. Various devices may be set up to restrain the majority, such as an entrenched Bill of Rights, but all such devices favor liberty by restricting democracy. They are intrinsically undemocratic insofar as they restrict the authority of the majority. On the whole, this view was the view of Jefferson, Tocqueville, and Mill, who were correspondingly anxious to educate the fledgling democracy of their day in order that democracy should not be majority tyranny (Mill [1861] 1974, 62ff.; Tocqueville [1835] 1964, 269ff.).

The alternative view is that liberalism is committed to democracy and that illiberal democracy is not democracy at all. Each individual has a right to take part in the decisions that affect their society. Nobody ought to be governed without their voice being heard, for that is a violation of their human rights or of their right to be treated as a free and equal member of their society (Dworkin 1985, 193ff.). To the objection that majority rule may be inconsistent with liberty, the sophisticated reply is essentially that the authority, as distinct from the power, of the majority is intrinsically self-limiting. We cannot claim the right to vote, for instance, on terms that violate others' rights. In this view, the Bill of Rights does not limit the majority's authority so much as spell out what its authority is. Liberal democracy is not something one may realize if one is lucky; the only legitimate democracy is liberal democracy.

However we decide between these two conceptualizations, liberal government must be limited government. Freedom of conscience, freedom of occupational choice, privacy, and family rights all place limits on what governments may do. Limited government may nonetheless be active government; securing these rights will keep government busy. More to the point, liberal governments will inherit many illiberal arrangements from their predecessors. Abolishing racial and sexual discrimination in the United States has been neither quick nor easy. Reducing the effects of inherited privilege in the United Kingdom has hardly begun. A government that takes liberalism seriously will be a busy government, especially since it will also have to be ingenious in pursuing its goals through lawful channels.

On this point, defenders of classical and modern forms of liberalism can agree. Both deplore the advantages of monopolists; sexual and racial discrimination, and the advantages of inherited position, share in the wickedness of monopolies, for they give undeserved advantages to their beneficiaries and undeserved handicaps to their victims. It may be that classical liberals suppose that once a "level playing field" has been achieved, it will remain level, while modern liberals suppose that it will need constant attention. It is certainly true that modern liberals emphasize the "equal" in equal opportunity, whereas their predecessors perhaps stress "opportunity" and have no particular liking for equality of any other kind. Still, the point remains that limited governments need not be inactive or lazy governments.

Success or Failure?

It is a task of some delicacy to sum up the successes and failures of the liberal project. In the terminology of practicing politicians, it has been avowed conservatives who have prospered in Western democracies since the early 1970s, though they have often been at odds among themselves over whether they were conservatives *tout court* or neoliberals trying to revive the political and economic ideals of the early nineteenth century. "Roosevelt liberals," on the other hand, enthusiasts for an expansive welfare state and for an energetic egalitarianism in social and economic policy, have done rather badly. Here, too, however, it is an open question whether the voting publics in Western democracies have turned against the liberal welfare state or have merely decided that they are grateful for what they have received and are skeptical about the chances of going much further.

One success for the liberal project is the striking collapse of Marxist regimes worldwide. Since Marxist governments drew their legitimacy from the supposed superiority of Marxian socialism over its liberal alternatives, the wholesale failure of Marxist regimes in all possible respects—their failure as economic systems, their inability to secure the political loyalties of their subjects, their failure to secure the human rights of the citizenry, and so on—in effect amounts to a practical demonstration that liberalism of some kind has won.

In this contest, it is liberalism only in the very broadest sense that has triumphed—that is, a liberalism that stresses human rights, economic opportunity, and the values of the open society, rather than one with narrower party-political attachments. This liberalism has triumphed not only over Marxism, but also over the illiberalism of nationalistic military regimes of the kind that once held power all over Latin America. It has, up to a point, triumphed over the apartheid regime of South Africa. Whether a narrower liberalism is particularly popular is another matter entirely, as is the prospect of any kind of liberalism making inroads into military dictatorship in Asia and most of Africa.

That it is only liberalism in the broadest, non-party-political sense that has triumphed is obvious enough. Western conservatives do not support theocratic absolutism, or government by divine right, but would still reject the liberal label as a description of their politics. Liberalism has been equally criticized for the past forty years or so from another direction for its lack of interest in political participation and the development of an active citizenry. Writers who take their cue from classical republicanism think, as do the communitarians, that the liberal view of the individual is of someone essentially cut off from public life, concerned with affairs that are private in the sense of being jealously protected from everyone else. This, they argue, makes for a less healthy politics than the participatory politics described by Aristotle, Niccolò Machiavelli, and other republican writers.

In the republican view, there is certainly a place for the negative liberty—immunity from oppression by the government or any other powerful organization or individual—that liberalism puts at the front of its political demands. But this liberty cannot be preserved unless the citizenry is active in preserving it. In effect, one republican complaint is that liberalism is unable to offer a coherent story about how liberal goals are to be secured, while the other is that liberalism in action tends to turn individuals in on themselves, encourages them to quit the public stage and concentrate only on domestic or economic goals. To this, many liberals reply that the French Revolution of 1789 is a sufficient warning about the dangers of trying to make ancient republicans out of modern Frenchmen and, by the same token, out of modern Americans, Australians, or Englishmen too—as Benjamin Constant's "Essay on the Liberty of the Ancients Compared with That of the Moderns" pointed out in 1818 (Constant 1990, 309–12). Having said so, however, they are as quick as anyone to lament the failure of public spirit and political engagement that seemed to afflict the Western world at the end of the twentieth century.

The liberalism that has triumphed, then, is not an intellectually rigorous system, manifested in its only possible institutional form. It is an awkward and intellectually insecure system, committed to democracy tempered by the rule of law, to a private-enterprise economy supervised and controlled by government, and to equal opportunity so far as it can be maintained without too much interference with the liberty of employers, schools, and families. It by no means embraces laissez-faire with the same fervor that Marxism brought to its attack on property and its passion for rational, central control of economic activity, a point made eloquently by Daniel Bell (1961, 393–407). Moreover, the inhabitants of liberal democracies are deeply, and properly, conscious of the shortcomings of their societies and certainly feel their "success" is an equivocal one.

To know how permanent the success of liberalism is, or how complete it is, one would need a crystal ball rather than the resources of philosophy or political science. In any case, a liberal society can never be more than a partial success by its own standards; its aspirations for the individual, for society, and for the conduct of government guarantee that its ambitions will always exceed its performance. On the other hand, its members may, under most circumstances, feel that their failures are only partial and temporary and that the way in which liberalism institutionalizes self-criticism is itself a guarantee of some progress, even if it is also a guarantee of permanent dissatisfaction.

References

Arendt, H. 1968. *The Origins of Totalitarianism*. New York: Harcourt, Brace and World. First published 1951.

Bell, D. 1961. *The End of Ideology*. New York: Free Press.

Berlin, I. 1969. *Four Essays on Liberty*. Oxford: Oxford University Press.

Constant, B. 1990. *Political Writings*. Edited by B. Fontana. Cambridge: Cambridge University Press.

Dewey, J. (1931) 1984. *Individualism Old and New*. Carbondale: Southern Illinois University Press.

Dworkin, R. 1985. "Liberalism." In *A Matter of Principle*, 181–204. Cambridge, Mass.: Harvard University Press.

Epstein, R. 1985. *Takings: Private Property and the Power of Eminent Domain*. Cambridge, Mass.: Harvard University Press.

Gallie, W. B. 1956. "Essentially Contested Concepts." *Proceedings of the Aristotelian Society* 56:167–98.

Gray, J. 1983. *Mill on Liberty: A Defence*. London: Routledge and Kegan Paul.

———. 1984. *Hayek on Liberty*. Oxford: Blackwell.

———. 1986. *Liberalism*. Milton Keynes, UK: Open University Press.

Green, T. H. 1892. "Liberal Legislation and Freedom of Contract" (1874). In *Collected Works*. London: Macmillan.

Hartz, L. 1955. *The Liberal Tradition in America*. New York: Harcourt, Brace and World.

Hayek, F. von. 1973–79. *Law, Liberty and Legislation*. 3 vols. London: Routledge and Kegan Paul.

———. 1976. *The Mirage of Social Justice*. London: Routledge and Kegan Paul. Vol. 2 of the above.

Hobbes, T. (1651) 1991. *Leviathan*. Cambridge: Cambridge University Press.

Hobhouse, L. T. (1911) 1964. *Liberalism*. New York: Oxford University Press.

Kant, I. 1991. *Political Writings*. Edited by Hans Reiss. Cambridge: Cambridge University Press.

Locke, J. (1689) 1956. *A Letter on Toleration*. In *Second Treatise of Government*. Edited by J. W. Gough. Oxford: Blackwell.

———. (1690) 1967. *Two Treatises of Government*. Edited by Peter Laslett. Cambridge: Cambridge University Press.

Madison, J., Alexander Hamilton, and John Jay. 1987. *The Federalist*. Harmondsworth: Penguin.

Mill, J. S. (1861) 1974. *On Liberty*. Harmondsworth: Penguin.

———. (1848) 1965. *Principles of Political Economy*. Toronto: University of Toronto Press.

Nagel, T. 1991. *Equality and Partiality*. Oxford: Oxford University Press.

Nozick, R. 1974. *Anarchy, State, and Utopia*. New York: Basic Books.

Plato. 1941. *The Republic*. Translated and edited by Francis Cornford. Oxford: Clarendon Press.

Rawls, J. 1971. *A Theory of Justice*. Cambridge, Mass.: Harvard University Press.

———. 1985. "Justice as Fairness: Political not Metaphysical." *Philosophy and Public Affairs* 14, no. 3 (Summer): 221–56.

———. 1989. "The Domain of the Political and Overlapping Consensus." *New York University Law Review* 64:233–55.

Rorty, R. 1991. "The Priority of Democracy to Philosophy." In *Philosophical Papers*, 175–96. Cambridge: Cambridge University Press.

Rossiter, C. 1982. *Conservatism in America*. Cambridge, Mass.: Harvard University Press.

Sandel, M. 1982. *Liberalism and the Limits of Justice*. Cambridge: Cambridge University Press.

Smith, A. (1775) 1976. *The Wealth of Nations*. Oxford: Clarendon Press.

Thucydides. 1972. *The Peloponnesian War*. Harmondsworth: Penguin.

Tocqueville, A. de. (1835) 1964. *Democracy in America*. New York: Random House.

further reading

HISTORICAL

Green, T. H. 1986. *Lectures on Political Obligation*. Cambridge: Cambridge University Press.

Montesquieu, Baron de. 1986. *The Spirit of the Laws*. Cambridge: Cambridge University Press.

Russell, B. 1916. *Principles of Social Reconstruction*. London: Allen & Unwin.

Spencer, H. 1981. *The Man versus the State*. Indianapolis: Liberty Classics.

COMMENTARY

Arblaster, A. 1984. *The Rise and Decline of Western Liberalism*. Oxford: Blackwell.

Rosenblum, N. 1989. *Another Liberalism*. Cambridge, Mass.: Harvard University Press.

Ruggiero, G. de. 1924. *The History of European Liberalism*. Translated by R. G. Collingwood. Oxford: Clarendon Press.

CONTEMPORARY

Ackerman, B. 1980. *Social Justice in the Liberal State*. New Haven, Conn.: Yale University Press.

Flathman, R. 1989. *Toward a Liberalism*. Ithaca, N.Y.: Cornell University Press.

Galston, W. 1991. *Liberal Purposes*. Cambridge: Cambridge University Press.

Macedo, S. 1990. *Liberal Virtues*. Oxford: Clarendon Press.

Raz, J. 1986. *The Morality of Freedom*. Oxford: Clarendon Press.

Rosenblum, N., ed. 1990. *Liberalism and the Moral Life*. New York: Cambridge University Press.

Spitz, D. 1982. *The Real World of Liberalism*. Chicago: Chicago University Press.

Taylor, C. 1990. *Sources of the Self*. Cambridge, Mass.: Harvard University Press.

2

Freedom

Introduction; Explaining and Justifying the Enterprise

IN THIS ESSAY I intend to do two things.[1] The first is to discuss a method of doing philosophy, the method of "ordinary language" philosophy, as it is commonly and misleadingly called. (Its other common title, "Oxford Philosophy," is even more misleading, since the roots of the method lie in Cambridge and many of the most flourishing branches are in the United States rather than England.) If it needs a name, perhaps the best is—adapting Popper to our purpose—"piecemeal philosophical engineering." Such a title would emphasize the attention to detail and the caution about conclusions that characterize the best of such work. The second aim of this essay is to apply the method thus discussed and defended to three questions connected with the concept of freedom. These problems arise out of three recent discussions of freedom—*Thought and Action* and *Spinoza and the Idea of Freedom* by Stuart Hampshire, and *Two Concepts of Liberty* by Isaiah Berlin. The questions I want to ask are the following: What makes the free-will problem so difficult to grasp, and hence so difficult to solve?; What is the moral value of freedom, that is, does it have an "absolute" value rather than a "conditional" value?; In what respects is freedom a "negative" concept? Since I shall not be discussing the three works out of which these questions arise, I ought to say now that this essay is not a critique or criticism of them; their value as contributions to the debate on freedom has been amply proved already.

You may object that the first part of this essay is unnecessary (or should be). If there is something to be said about freedom, why do I not say it at once? If there is not, why do I not admit it at once? By its fruits alone can a technique be judged; if it has some, why not produce them now? I should be inclined to agree, except for two things. The first is that the recent publication of J. L. Austin's papers and lectures has been the occasion for a good deal of argument about the merits of the whole style of philosophy that he represented; and the general estimate of that style has not been favorable. One may think that a certain amount of the criticism has been occasioned by an antipathy to the reputation of Oxford; that a certain amount of hostility is due to an eagerness to be fierce to the memory of a rather fierce thinker; but even if this were true, it is no reason for failing to meet the critics. And, of course, such suspicions are quite out of place where the most acute criticism is concerned. The second thing is very disreputable; it is fear. I am afraid that the method I preach is capable of better things than my practice of it. The sort of detailed, patient inquiry into the way we talk that Austin carried out is peculiarly liable to travesty, however well intentioned, and the evils that would mark that travesty are triviality, pedantry, and obscurity—three of the academic deadly sins. (You may note in passing that to judge by similar disclaimers, most of those who feel closest to Ludwig Wittgenstein's work are afraid of a like danger.) It is thus only fair to admit that what follows is bound to be defective in all dimensions; in length, with the result that the patience and stamina of Austin's work is lost; in breadth, for the completeness of grasp is sadly absent; and worst of all, in depth, with a resulting shortage of that illumination one could suddenly discover beneath the taut, dry, ironic carapace of the severe manner. Austin illuminated issues such as that of free will not by shining a distorting floodlight upon freedom, but by shedding an all-round daylight by way of such papers as "Ifs and Cans" and "A Plea for Excuses." It is the combination of subtlety allied with power that lifts Austin's work out of the ordinary into the inspiring. Hence my fear that what is here defended will be overmuch judged by what is here performed. So far as the performance goes, let me state only that it is an inquiry into the grammar of such expressions as "free to," "free from," "of his own free will," and the like—you may, if you wish, call it an inquiry into the logic of freedom, or even into what freedom is.

Words and Things

People still say that philosophy is not a linguistic matter (and even that it is).[2] Plato, some say, talked about justice, freedom, and happiness with never an inverted comma. Even G. E. Moore, they continue, whom you reverence as a founder of linguistic analysis, was nothing of the sort; why, on one occasion he said that it was the task of philosophy to give a general account of everything there was. But the truth of the matter is surely that to say that philosophy is (or is not) essentially linguistic leads to a variety of errors. One is to suppose that philosophy can be replaced by philology or etymology; this is plainly wrong, and the nearest that anyone has ever come to saying this is Austin remarking that etymology is often a guide to what the words we are bothered by mean. A second error is to suppose that philosophy chronicles usage as its central concern; one of the more absurd jibes of recent years, one that seems to be repeated despite incessant demolition, is that the usage recorded by philosophers is the usage of Oxford senior common rooms. But the issue is (as has been said so often) one of use rather than usage; this is not to say that the meaning of a word is its use, for this is dubious. Rather it is to say that use is very often the best (and sometimes the only) guide to meaning, and also that probably most philosophers are more interested in the use, the point, of words than in anything else about them. And in an important sense, use is nonlinguistic—the point made by Wittgenstein about *Äusserungen*, expressions in which words and nonlinguistic behavior have the same "sense" or point, is a valuable reminder in this context. To talk of usage is to say who says what; to talk about use is to explain why we say what we do. And in the same way that we do not need to look at what other people in the room are doing to know what we are doing, so our asking what we should say when does not require us to record usage, but rather to think what sort of intention we should form.

A third reason why we should avoid saying either that philosophy is or is not linguistic is that this tends to unduly emphasize the differences between what we do now and what philosophers in other times and places have done; this is foolish because it deprives us of the most valuable stimulus we can have, the best thoughts of the wisest of our predecessors. You will recall Austin saying that he came to appreciate just how good was Aristotle's treatment of free will only after hearing someone complain that all Aristotle did was list the sorts of excuses people made. And after all, even in Plato, the arch-philosopher, there is a constant appeal from "when you say . . . you mean . . ." to "therefore we must say . . ." Though there was a good deal of mythology in the account of how what we say means what it does, it cannot be denied that much of Plato's effort went in trying to show people that, for example, if they understood what they were really saying, they could not say that justice was possibly a bad policy for a selfish man. Philosophy is absolutely full of people telling us what we really mean by saying what we do; indeed, the great sign that a philosophical problem is in the offing is that "really," for that appears only when we are quite sure that we do not mean what we are said to mean, but cannot quite see why we do not. More insularly, there has been a very important English (if I may, without prejudice, call David Hume and George Berkeley English) tradition of careful attention to what we actually say, in order to avoid what Thomas Hobbes termed "the insignificant speech of the schoolmen." John Locke likewise you will find complaining, "I think it be not proper to ask if the will be free"; what sort of impropriety is it that is involved? It is not like your mother saying, "Don't thump on the bathroom door to see if it's free; it's not proper." The impropriety of which Locke complains is that there is no such thing as people suppose to be designated by "the will"; the words are senseless; we can ask whether a man is free, because we can see him bound or loosed, in jail or out of it, but since there is no parallel procedure with "the will," there is no genuine question to ask. The impropriety your mother deplores is contravention of the canons of niceness, an offense against "small morals." It is quite clear what a bathroom is, and clear what it is for it to be free—that is, vacant; there is no sort of logical impropriety in thumping on the door; it is just hard on Aunt Ethel, who so enjoys spending hours there. But trivial and trite though the comparison is, it is central to a long tradition from Hobbes through John Stuart Mill to A. J. Ayer, all of whom claim that the grammatical form of "Is the will free?" misleads us into supposing that it is a sensible question like "Is the bathroom free?"

Difference of label is no guarantee of difference of contents, in other words. Terminology changes and interests remain much the same. So philosophers go on doing something recognizably the same, although significantly different too. Plato inquiring into "the Good," Aristotle investigating the "*anthropon agathon*," Moore asking what quality "goodness" denotes, and we investigating how we use words like "good" all understand one another well enough to be able to criticize one another and profit from the exchange. It seems, therefore, that the linguistic versus nonlinguistic battle will generate only heat, not light. A case in point is perception. It has been clear ever since the first sense-data theories were produced that something is amiss with them; it has been clear enough that they derive both their force and their weakness from the questions posed by our reflecting upon the vast range of phenomena involved in seeing, hearing, touching things; that they derive much of their weakness, in particular, from being theories of how we *must* perceive things. Yet people who ought to know better make the strangest statements about the proneness of scientists to accept representative theories of perception, and how this invalidates appeals to ordinary language. Paul Hirst, for instance, reviewing Austin's *Sense and Sensibilia*, declares that a great many neurologists adhere to a representative theory of perception and that we should respect their expertise. But this is misguided. What, as laymen, we respect is the expert's account of what nervous processes take place when we perceive things; but the neurologist has no residual authority about the logic of perceptual language; as a user of perceptual language like the rest of us, in his ordinary life outside the laboratory, he knows when he sees birds and bees, flowers and trees. But when he comes to render this nonexplicit grasp of the logic—as opposed to the neurology—of perception explicit, he starts from scratch with the philosopher. The chief thing, I think, to be said in favor of describing philosophy in linguistic terms is that, at the moment, it is a fairly antiseptic description. It does not convey the impression that there is some special class of problems to be solved by some special techniques. It removes one of the temptations to which philosophy fell prey quite recently—a temptation to eliminate metaphysics and substitute pseudophysics. It may be that this terminology will soon become septic, too. Jerry Fodor and Jerrold Katz may so frighten philosophers into thinking that they are doing some as yet unformed science of linguistics that some other description will become necessary. It does not much matter that at every point in the history of philosophy, many philosophers have discovered that what they want to know can be answered by some substantial science—indeed, this is what progress in philosophy has very largely meant. There will always be something left for people to be worried by.

A final reason why the linguistic-nonlinguistic dichotomy is unhelpful is that the "words-things" dichotomy can, in important cases, be misleading. It is not a new point, but still a crucial one, that Austin makes in "The Meaning of a Word": knowing the meaning of a word is not *just* knowing the meaning of a word. That is, knowing the meaning of the word "cat" and knowing what a cat is are the same thing, not two different things. Similarly, when Ayer's theory of sense-data is put forward as a linguistic theory about the term "sense-datum," it does not look as though this serves to distinguish his doctrine from Moore's apparently empirical theory (the emphasis here being very heavily placed on "apparently," although I am not at all sure it is even apparently empirical). People have suggested that Austin is unfair to Ayer in alleging that Ayer does not really holds his thesis to be a linguistic one at all; but if he is unfair, it is only in complaining that Ayer failed to adhere to a distinction that no one could have reasonably wanted him to try to make in the first place. Words are not things, and confusion is the price of blurring the distinction; but it is worth remembering that things do not appear ready labeled. Alice's cake, saying on its outside "EAT ME," is not paralleled by Hume's external world, arriving in discrete pieces, each with its label: "brown impression," "square impression," and the like. And since things do not appear ready labeled, we necessarily talk about them as labeled by us. Hence, a certain amount of the mystery that has been engendered by the idea that philosophy is a nonempirical inquiry into the way things are can be dispelled by reflecting on the fact that when we can say clearly what we say when . . . , it is not so much that we know more about the world than we knew before as that we now know explicitly what we only knew implicitly before. Perhaps this is a "linguistic" way of saying something of what Kant said—and none the worse for that.

Though the objections to calling philosophy a linguistic pursuit may have been got round, over, or through, a tenacious critic will not be satisfied. It is not just, he may say, that I am committed to language (for that is all right, since we may call it thought), but to ordinary language. And the trouble with ordinary language is that it is the language of plain men, and the trouble with plain men is that they do not think—and are manifestly unworthy of the attention of philosophers. A first distinction that needs to be made is between two sorts of ordinariness in language. The first sort is the contrast between ordinary words and technical terms, jargon, formulae, and so forth; the second sort is the contrast between the ordinary use of a word and its metaphorical use or some other sort of deviant use. The ordinary use of words as opposed to the extraordinary use of them cuts across the "everyday words–esoteric words" line of division. If you took a car, stood it on its roof, and used its rear axle as a winch to fell trees, this would be an extraordinary use to which to put an ordinary machine—anyone with an interest in recondite machinery can go on from there. By and large, philosophers just lately have stuck to the ordinary use of an ordinary vocabulary, but there is no absolutely compelling reason why they should continue to do so. The reason usually adduced is fair enough, in fact; for one thing, ordinary language is our language, the language we all know how to use; it is the language in which most of our dealings are done, and at the very least, it is the language that the scientist uses when he instructs the technician about how he wants the laboratory run. And again, we are always told that philosophical problems are pervasive, common to everyone everywhere. Are we ever free, any of us? Do any of us ever see anything? Do any of us know that anyone else exists or what anyone else is thinking? And the way that such questions are made to worry us is very often by it being said, "When you say . . . , what you mean is . . ." Look at Plato; is it not clear that when we call someone just and when we call someone happy, we do not mean the same thing? Yet Plato almost corners us with the paradox that the just man is necessarily happy, although we have all often enough been tempted to sacrifice justice to our own happiness. You might (I suppose C. L. Stevenson, for example, would) say that Plato was performing the quite legitimate enterprise of getting us to redefine justice. But then an equally interesting question is why does Plato want to coin the two new words "just" and "happy," which bear so striking a surface similarity to the words they are to replace ("just" and "happy"). Everyone who appeals to the propriety of departing from ordinary language is under the necessity of making out a case for this departure, simply because the departure can be understood only if he does so. To merely appeal to a natural right to redefine is to appeal only to a natural right to talk nonsense if one feels like it. To attach significance to a neologism is to attach the neologism to the existing stock of a language's techniques.

This position has been attacked by Bernard Williams as the merest conservatism, and it might be as well to look at some of his objections in concluding this part of the essay.[3] His first objection is that one is committed to the view that all worthwhile distinctions have already been drawn; but this is quite untrue—and is particularly untrue as regards Austin, at whom the objection is chiefly aimed. The point made by Austin was simply that a lot of distinctions have been drawn and that one may be skeptical of the philosopher who proposes to redraw the whole lot after ten minutes thought. The philosopher who wants to divide all perception into cases of veridical perception and cases of illusory perception is rather like a child who sees that sewing involves both cutting and stitching, and thereat proposes to call all his mother's equipment either needles or scissors. Just as mothers are commonly the best judges of what's what in sewing, so most distinctions are best made by those who have experience of unusual phenomena that need sorting out. We have all got a good deal of experience of square towers looking round at a distance, and we just do not need a new language to describe the situation—and particularly we do not need a terminology that assimilates this case to the wiles of a stage magician sawing a woman in half. The second charge is that the position is a Burkean one; by demanding that we should always look at how things work before we make changes, we effectively prevent any changes being made. But this is histrionics, not argument; without a general premise to the effect that every word in a language, every idiom in our vocabulary, is equally important, no such argument would be valid, and the premise needs only to be stated for it to be clear that no one in their right mind would accept it. All one has to hold is that in those areas of everyday life where matters are complicated, for example, perception, moral responsibility, and the like, we should look to see whether proposed large-scale simplifications really are simplifications or whether they are merely impoverishments. Take, for instance, Sir Arthur Eddington's suggestion that tables are not really solid. Susan Stebbing's counter was a simple appeal to a paradigm; tables are solid because being solid is being of the consistency of tables. Williams's response is of the order: "How stuffy you are being. Don't you see that physics has made huge advances, so we are duty-bound to call tables, cast iron, clouds, and water by the same name because they have a common atomic structure, crudely depicted as lumps of matter with gaps between them." But the counter to this is even simpler: "Try eating off clouds. Try swimming in cast iron." The determined disliker of plain men may reply to this by objecting that we may show anything to be of any description we like if we admit appeals to paradigms and ostensive definition. The cry goes up (invariably): "Why cannot the plain man define witches ostensively?" This objection underestimates the plain man. To call a woman a witch is not just to call her a witch; it is to imply that she can do all sorts of things, especially unpleasant things to people. In the case of "solidity," the fact that it may be defined in terms that mean that an object is solid if it is impenetrable by objects impinging on it does not mean that the plain man has a theory about matter in the way that we should be more prepared to say he had a theory about witches. To say that a table is solid is not contradicted by the fact that people can saw it in bits or pass alpha particles through it (just as the statement that there is nothing in the room is not contradicted by saying that there is air in it—save in a very unusual context). Curiously enough, one of the philosophers who took pains to point this out was F. H. Bradley, who held that when the plain man says that the sun rises in the east, he is not mistaken in what he says, although he may have a theory about what the explanation of the facts is that is quite wrong. Williams's last point is that distinctions are put into language by theorists; all distinctions were new once, so why should we be afraid of new ones now? A sufficient rejoinder is no doubt mere skepticism whether it is philosophy rather than necessity that is the mother of invention. But more explicitly, we may revert to our doubt whether those without an expertise of their own, without a field of inquiry in their own right, are the best people to remodel our language. If philosophers do ever have a field of their own, then they will perhaps be able to add useful new terms to the language for making useful new distinctions—after all, Austin, in *How to Do Things with Words*, coined enough jargon to settle once and for all the notion that he was against linguistic innovation as such.

The extent of his opposition to innovation was the extent to which he thought that most philosophical jargon had been confused and confusing, badly defined and probably nonsense. If it is a conservative position to desire to talk sense, then let us eschew more radical attitudes—for as R. M. Hare remarked in this connection, like the highest flights of invention in dancing, the highest flights of linguistic invention are necessarily solo performances.

Finding the Crux

Let us now bring the program to the facts and apply it to freedom. All the symptoms of philosopher's disease are here, and I imagine have always been here. The first of these is the appearance of general and grandiose definitions; the second is their multiplicity; and the third important one is their failure to generate a settlable clash. Thus, some people have defined freedom as being left alone by other people; others as knowing the causes of one's actions; others as pursuing moral goodness for its own sake. Mill, for instance, vacillates between Berlinesque negativism and Coleridgean positivism, beginning with the assertion that a person is free to do an action only if it is true that he will do that action if he chooses, and ending with the statement that only the man of confirmed virtue is truly free; with rough justice, Bradley abuses him for saying the first and proceeds to muddle himself by taking over the second. Even the Book of Common Prayer indulges in paradox mongering about freedom—"whose service is perfect freedom"—*perfect* freedom at that, as if we had not enough theological problems already. But defining freedom in terms of the absence of government or the presence of goodness does not seem to clear the air; indeed, it seems to produce hot air and then beat it vainly. So it will not appear false modesty if I say that I have no answers to the problem of freedom; I fear it will be more than sufficient if we can find some of the problems.

It may be recalled that at the back of our minds we have the three questions: What are the strengths and weaknesses of the thesis that freedom is essentially negative? What is the value of freedom? Why is the free-will problem so baffling?

SUFFIXES

The first set of examples we should look at involves the use of "free" as a suffix and contrasts this with the use of "less."

1. This room is to be kept dust-free.
2. These goods may be exported duty-free.
3. That's a pretty worthless painting.
4. He's a shiftless young rascal.
5. You will have to spend six months on a meatless diet.
5a. You'll be cured only with a totally meat-free diet.
6. "Strained Meatless Broth."
6a. "Strictly vegetarian, meat-free meals served here."

7. That was a careless bit of driving; you'd have missed with a bit more care.
8. Carefree motoring ahead; there's never a care when you drive with Shell.

Taking 1 and 2 as against 3 and 4: rooms to be habitable must be kept without a great quantity of dust on things; similarly a tax, or duty, is something demanded from you in addition to what the goods are really worth. Hence, it is a good thing to keep rooms without dust and a good thing to avoid paying duty if you decently can, that is, if it is legally remitted. But a painting should have worth, either monetary value or aesthetic merit, and a young rascal ought to be able to shift for himself. You may ask then whether "free" is a descriptive term at all; perhaps it is an evaluative term, but the distinction is not useful here. It is a matter of fact whether a room is without dust, for you can look and see (though, of course, standards vary and people look more closely according to whether they are sluts, suburban housewives, or high-powered physicists). And you can find out with the painting too (try to sell it and be disillusioned about the price it will fetch). But clearly the use of "free" rather than "less" implies a good deal about people's wants and purposes, about people's duties, about the uses of objects, and so on. Talking of the so-called fact-value dichotomy here is of little relevance because there is more to be said. If you want to be penniless, then you may enjoy being penniless; you may even, like George Orwell, feel that you ought to be penniless; still, it is a matter of fact that you are penniless, even though it depends on the purpose and point of the use of money in everyday life that "penni*less*" is the right word.

Regarding 5, 5a, 6, and 6a: a fine point, but one we sometimes make. In 5 we envisage the doctor sharing the patient's regret that he will have to abstain from eating meat; while in 5a it is not the abstinence but the benefits of abstinence that are emphasized—perhaps the patient has been eating two-inch steaks for a lot longer than anyone reasonably can who wants to preserve his digestion intact. In either case, it is open to emphasize either the deprivation or the benefit or neither, so that "meatless," "meatfree," or "without meat" would all be equally common; but 6 and 6a show up the difference more clearly. In 6a there is the case implication "No meat and a good thing too; after all, carnivores are a pretty disgusting lot when you think about it." In 6, on the other hand, there seems to be regret at the absence of meat in a broth, perhaps on the grounds that broth with meat in it makes babies both bonny and bouncing. That there can often be at least this much force in a suffix can be seen by reflecting on the oddity of saying that a desert was merely "without water," and the extreme oddity of saying it was "water-free"; the explanation in terms of "free" carrying the connotation of "and a good thing too" is given added force when one thinks of the fact that the house for which no rent is paid is on the one side rent-free and on the other profitless.

In 7 and 8, the suffixes "free" and "less" do not function quite so simply as suffixes. Both "meatless" and "meat-free" are contrasted with "with meat";

but to be careless is to fail to be careful, while to be carefree is to escape being careworn or care-ridden. Once again, it is easy to see the values on which the terms are based. You have to drive carefully; the lives of yourself, your passengers, and other road users depend on your exercising proper care. But when on holiday, although you must still take due *care*, you should not let your *cares* overwhelm you; it is necessarily an evil to the sufferer to be overwhelmed by cares; it means that he cannot enjoy life. Perhaps someone will feel inclined to say that "care" must be ambiguous. Shell cannot be accused of exhorting the motorist to drive without care, so "care" cannot mean the same in "careless" as it does in "carefree," and this spoils our case as so far advanced. But the suggestion seems not to be true. The point rather is that one does not care about the same things in the two cases, for driving a car involves many things, and all must go well for the whole process to be judged an unqualified success. What Shell does is relieve you of the need to care for the mechanical welfare of your car; no one wants to drive while distracted by bangs, thumps, squeaks, groans, and rattles from the works; if your car is in bad shape you have to care about such things. If you feed it on Shell—so we are assured—it will go well and you will be freed of this sort of care. But when you drive your Shellubricated car, however good its condition, you are exercising a skill, the object of which is, among other things, the safe arrival of yourself and your passengers at their destination. Hence, you must exercise your skill carefully in order to secure the object for which it is exercised. Your motoring may be carefree, but your driving had better be careful.

FREE FROM

Let us turn to the use of "free from" as a verbal and adjectival phrase.

1. Oxfam hopes to free Algeria from the threat of starvation.
2. It took Ben Bella ten years to free Algeria from the French.
3. Thanks to penicillin, your wound is free from infection.
4. "May I free you from the weight of that purse?" inquired Dick Turpin of Sir Giles.
5. I've freed the gear lever from the jamming that plagued it all summer.

We can see from the examples dealt with above in "Suffixes" that these cases tie in with the thesis that to free a person or thing from whatever it may be is to remove what is an evil—to them or to most persons or things of that class. So it is not surprising that we may free men from such diverse things as the nagging of wives, debts, promises, prisons, and illusions—cases 1 and 2. Spinoza and Hampshire both seem to hold that since one can free men from illusions about themselves, it follows that a man is free when he knows all about himself. By parity of reasoning, it would appear that if Oxfam is successful, Algeria will be free; yet if Ben Bella has been successful already, is it not true that Algeria is already free? Many critics of Berlin have, in fact, argued along lines like this. The Algerians cannot be free if they are starving, ill, uneducated. But we should take note that while freeing a country from foreign domination does allow the inference that the country is free *tout court*, freeing it from starvation does not. I am not quite clear why this is, but one may suppose it to be due to the fact that a country, considered as a political entity, has specific afflictions, tied in with the criteria of what makes a country one country; these criteria include the existence of a considerable degree of independence from the political control of other countries, and the existence of institutions of its own, so that the imposition of the institutions of foreigners is a specific evil to a *country*, in a way that starvation is not. This is only a supposition, but if true, it has the merit that it tends to explain why the question whether a man is ever free has such ramifications—namely, that an answer depends on elaborating some theory of the goals and purposes and goods specific to man qua man, a task of some difficulty.

Example 3 illustrates the absence of a general inference license from "A is free from *x*" to "A is free" *tout court*. No one will argue from the wound's freedom from infection to its freedom-just-like-that. And even though it is our good, and not the wound's, that is here in question, we do not become freer either, except that we just might want to say someone had become freer of the infection than he had been the week before. And equally with 5: we do not become freer when the gear lever is unjammed, and even the gear lever would be said to be free *tout court* only in the context of just having been unjammed (or perhaps where a contrast was understood with "sticky" gear levers on other cars). These points need greater working out to show convincingly where and when the inference from "is free from *x*" to "is free" is and is not valid; but they do at least show that the inference more often than not is dubious. This somewhat tame conclusion is one of the points behind Berlin's objections to "positive liberty." It may be that I am better off freed from my illusions than freed from your control; it does not follow, however, that you have forced me to be free. And the choice of which evil to escape is not aided by calling the absence of each "freedom."

Example 4 is an ironical case to support the thesis tentatively advanced that to free someone from something is to remove what is an evil to them; for here, of course, the whole point is that Sir Giles is *not* losing what he takes to be an evil; he wants his purse and its contents and has never noticed the weight (which is what would make this a joke if it were slightly funnier). But were the stage not to be set by the suggestion that the weight of the purse is distressing, there could be no joke, only impropriety.

ADVERBIAL FREEDOM

Since we have suggested so far that although "free" is not ambiguous, it is not open to any simple definition, but rather depends for its literal meaning on what the thing is, what the thing is for, or what might go wrong, we should look at the adverb "freely" to see whether the same things hold here too.

1. I can move my leg quite freely now.
2. The engine swung over freely enough.
3. He promised me quite freely that he would come today.
4. Faced with the police evidence, he admitted quite freely that he had committed the crime.
5. He talked surprisingly freely about his wife's illness.

What do these have in common? More or less nothing, except that they all draw attention to the absence of something that might have spoiled whatever it is that we are talking about. It might be thought that I would spoil the case for specificity on the grounds that there is nothing specific that we have to do to move our legs—we just move them. But although it is true enough that we do not have to do anything to move our legs (except move them) in the way that we do have to do something to make a promise, it is still true that specific misfortunes do occur to legs, rendering us unable to move them. So if Jones says that he can move his leg freely again, what we want to know is has it been in plaster or strapped up, or had he ricked a muscle, or whatever? That is, we need a background of absent impediments to make sense of what he says. Example 2, on the other hand, is odd at first sight because we can say such things as "the engine turned over too freely for my peace of mind." Does this spoil the case for saying that we are concerned with the absence of an evil when we talk of freedom? I think not; when we turn an engine over, it is we who turn it, and the engine *should* offer resistance to our effort—so "freely" adheres, as it were, to *our* turning. But you cannot talk of engines being free from compression, only of their lacking it, and it would be strange to talk of an ordinary engine in decent condition as running too freely (it would have to be meant in the sense of "too good to be true").

Examples 3 and 4 are rather similar to each other in that both involve performances that have to reach certain standards to count as valid instances of such performances. Among the things that vitiate both promises and confessions are force or threats of force, or certain sorts of deception; if promises and confessions were always to count, whatever their origin, then they would cease to be useful. So a range of disqualifications is admitted—saving the police and ourselves from temptation. In 5, on the other hand, there is no question of vitiating a performance. Even if the husband had talked hesitantly, he would still have talked. The point is simply that in such cases, persons in his position are often unwilling to say anything, and the force of "freely" here is to point out that he was not.

ADJECTIVAL FREEDOM

Especially in contexts involving the making of promises and related performances, we use the expression "of his own free will." So we ought to have a brief look at it. Hobbes was very cutting about this idiom; just as a free gift is not a free gift but the gift of a free giver, so when we talk of free will, we do not mean that the will is free at all. This is a popular line among English philosophers, and has echoes in Locke, Hume, Mill, and, more recently, Anthony Flew. As an answer to the free-will problem, it has a very grave defect, which is this. The free-will problem is misnamed when it is thought to be a problem about freedom; rather, it is a problem about ability. As we shall see, freedom and ability are not the same thing, although they are related. Thus, however good an account of freedom we got from Hobbes and his successors, we cannot get an answer to the problem of whether it is ever true that a man could have done what he did not do, and it is this latter problem that has been misnamed the free-will problem. To this we shall have to revert in conclusion. Here all we need examine is how good an account of freedom we can give in examining the use of "of his own free will." The paradigm of a free action offered by Flew is pretty crude, reducing almost to "if there are no obvious pressures, such as a gun at his back, or severe social retribution in the offing, then there's an end to worry about the freedom of the will."[4] This, however, is a good deal less wild than Hobbes, who seems to consider any action that we perform at all to be a free one; all actions are voluntary, and all voluntary actions are free. Hence, he does not even allow that a promise made under duress is not binding. But as a matter of fact, it does seem that we are ready to accept more excuses than "I was in jail" or "It was not an action at all." Let's see.

1. Poor old Jones; he's terribly unhappy, and barely a month after his marriage too.

It's his own fault. After all, he married her of his own free will, didn't he?

To which there are quite a number of replies, as, for example:

    1a. No, not really. She was pregnant, and her father would have run him out of town.
    1b. Well, her father was the managing director and Jones was cripplingly poor.
    1c. He would have done absolutely anything to get away from home.
    1d. He did not know it was a wedding; he was drunk at the time and thought it was a joke.
    1e. But he seemed to have every chance of being happy at the time.

If we cannot excuse Jones, we agree it is his own fault that he is married to a woman who makes him unhappy. Do any of these replies tend to show that he did not get married of his own free will? Do any of them excuse him, either wholly or in part? Hobbes, I imagine, would accept 1d, though I am very unsure what account he would give of the relation of knowledge and intention. Flew, I suppose, would have taken 1a and 1d; Aristotle, on the other hand, perhaps Austin and Hart, and, I think, myself would admit all of them as at least shaping up to be good excuses. Example 1a is the case where we should say that he could have done nothing else; the consequences of alternative courses of action were clearly intolerable. In 1b, we are perhaps less ready to accept that the alternatives were intolerable, and 1c may be very suspect from the start. It is true that these initial reactions may have to be overridden. For example, if there was another, nicer girl whose father was almost equally well off, then 1b is immediately written off as an excuse; even 1a could be written off with a good-enough story, but it would need writing off twice over. First, we should have to show that he was not in any real danger from the girl's father (since, for example, there might be a perfectly pleasant town five miles away where he could have been employed and so on). Second, we should have to show that there was no moral obligation on him to stand by the pregnant woman (it was not his child, or she had tricked him by only pretending to be pregnant, and he could have found this out with reasonable common sense). Intolerability, in other words, can be argued about at length, and excuses can be strengthened or weakened in the process. Examples 1d and 1e both rest on a different condition for responsibility, namely, that of the agent's knowing what he was doing. The difference between 1d and 1e shows the difficulties associated with filling out the expression "knowing what one is doing." In 1d, he would have given a different account of the actions he was going through, since, for example, he would have said he was playing at getting married at a party; and this knocks responsibility out completely (other things being equal). In 1e, he would have said he was getting married all right, but he could not perhaps have known that he was getting married to a woman who was going to have an accident and become depressed and depressing. If the consequences of what he was doing *should* have been clear to him, then we do not accept the excuse—an everyday version of the legal test of consequences foreseeable by any reasonable man. But the point of 1e as it stands is to deny that anyone could have foreseen the consequences; it was simply bad luck, not his fault; fate played him a dirty trick.

A further case brings out the point.

2. I darned nearly drowned in that canal.

Well, you went in of your own free will.

No, I didn't; I couldn't let that child drown.

There is no question of compulsion; there is no question but that the man jumped in deliberately, that he did not jump in by accident or that he could help jumping in. The obligation on him was a moral one, however willingly he may have met it, and the existence of the moral obligation is still sufficient rebuttal to the suggestion that he did it of his own free will. It is one of the reasons why it is needlessly paradoxical to adopt the Kantian position that to act of one's own free will is to perform morally obligatory actions; for the whole point of obligations is that they are to be performed whether one likes it or not.

FREE TO

The final examples are cases of the idiom "free to," plus a couple of sentences just involving "free" as a contrast. These examples seem to come close to the heart of the argument between Berlin and his opponents. Berlin's opponents tend to argue that a man with but five shillings in his pocket cannot be said to be free to enter the Ritz; equally, they argue, you cannot say that an Indian peasant is free to do things he has never heard of doing and could not do in any case, because he is illiterate and ill fed. And then they tend to declare that freedom for an Oxford don is different from freedom for an Egyptian peasant, and there is a resounding clash of ideologies. But, let's have a look.

1. Is the doctor free to see me yet?
2. Are you free to come to supper tomorrow evening?
3. You are not free to walk away and leave a drowning man.
4. You are not free to drive as fast as you like on this road.
5. It's marvelous to be free again.
6. India is not free so long as people are starving there.

Now in 1–4, the point is to be clear about what it is that hinders the person from doing whatever it is we have in mind. If the doctor is not occupied with a patient, then his obligations as a doctor allow him to see you, that is, he is free to see you. Here we might just say the doctor is free *tout court*, because a doctor's obligations are specific to his job, that of curing people. He is free (from obligations to other patients, to see to you). If he has broken his arm, then he cannot see you, but it would be misleading to say that he was or was not free to see you. Equally, what makes you not free to go to supper tomorrow evening is a prior engagement, a previous invitation; what makes you not free to leave a drowning man to die is a duty to try to save him; what makes you not free to do ninety on this bit of road might be a speed limit or a promise not to speed. If you feel like doing ninety and you cannot do ninety because the car is flat-out at sixty, then you just cannot do ninety and there's an end to the question. But to say you cannot is not the same as saying you are not free to. Or rather, "cannot" covers both the case of "is not able" and the case of "is not free." (We have earlier suggested that the free-will problem is about the first sort of "cannot" and not the second, in spite of its name.) The point about "free to" is that it invites consideration of whether there is any obligation incompatible with doing whatever it is. But what about the case of a man in example 5 who utters this after twenty years in jail? Was he free to leave jail, or not? Was he merely unable to do so? It is, of course, true of a criminal that he is not free to leave jail even if he can; he not only is obliged to stay there, but is also under an obligation to do so. But we should equally well say a man was not free if he were imprisoned in a house for twenty years by persons who had no authority to keep him there. In his case, it is clear that we think he is free to escape if he can; but it is also clear that, in this case, we should say that being kept where he was, was sufficient for us to say that he was not free.

But does not this precisely push the concepts of inability and unfreedom together? No, because of two things. The first is that here we are not considering the question of what the man is free to do; whereas in the cases to which Berlin objects, it is said that, for example, a man who cannot afford to go into the Ritz is not free to do so. The second is that in the case of a man kept under duress, it is the deliberate restriction of his actions by other human agents that leads us to say that he was not free. But, of course, in the case where a man is not able to do something, there is no point in our saying he is free to do it, or at any rate there is usually no point. In the case of the man kept under duress, we may have a point in saying he is free to escape if he can, even in instances where he cannot, as meaning that any method of getting away is justified. In the case of a man who has not the money to go into the Ritz, this sort of point seems to be lacking. This perhaps explains both the strength and weakness of the sort of statement made in example 5. It brings out the absurdity of talking of freedom if the question of ability cannot be reasonably assumed to have already been settled. We only mock someone who is starving if we tell him that for the first time in centuries his caste is free to buy land and houses anywhere they like. He wants bread, and we offer him the satisfaction of knowing that if he were able to buy a house (which he is not), there would be no legal impediment to his doing so. The weakness of the statement is the suggestion that the starvation is somehow due to the deliberate contrivance of other people; if the peasant cannot vote for a political party because he does not know what party is what, or how to mark his ballot paper or whatever, this is significantly different from his being deliberately impeded in voting by coercion on the part of other men. This is not to take the cheerful view that no country has ever kept its citizens poor deliberately or compelled them to vote in some particular way. It is only to say that not all inabilities can be traced to other people's contriving.

Trouser-Words

At the beginning of this foray into the linguistic undergrowth, we hoped to produce some clues about three problems. The first was the Berlin thesis that liberty is essentially a negative notion. As Berlin argued for this thesis, there was some ground for suspecting that he thought that there is something or other properly called freedom, that this something is entirely concerned with freedom from coercion, especially coercion by government. But this seems to restrict unduly the range of things from which we can sensibly be said to be free, and not to take sufficient account of the implications of saying that someone is free to do something. But behind Berlin's objections there does lie a genuine negativeness about freedom; namely, that it is (to use

Austin's terminology about the other philosophical terrors of "real" and "good") a "trouser-word": it takes its meaning from the absence of something that might have been present but is not. The negativeness involved is that we can always ask the question "What might we have had to free him from?" or "What might have stopped him being free to do it?" The inadequacy of Berlin's position is only that he is too concerned to say that the position he attacks is a mistaken one, whereas he might have done better to explain what its merits are as well as its defects. Of course, it is wrong to say that freedom for an Egyptian peasant is different from freedom for an Oxford don; but it does contain the important truth that it is more vital to free peasants from the threat of starvation than it is to free Oxford dons from their administrative duties, for example. Similarly, it is undoubtedly to our credit that no one coerces the sons and daughters of uneducated manual workers into poorer schools than the sons and daughters of the educated; but it is still true that they go to poorer schools, and we ought perhaps to reflect on that. All the same, the merits of Berlin's position seem unanswerable; it is undoubtedly important to draw attention to the worst evils we see, but it is important too to state clearly what they are, since otherwise it is impossible to choose wisely between courses of action to improve our lot. To offer more government and more bread or not so much government and not so much bread is to offer an intelligible choice; but it is no help to call them both "real" freedom. Equally, it is important because to suggest that freedom is at stake is to invite the question of what social system or what persons are deliberately impeding someone's attempts to lead a happy life. To say that someone is not free because not fed is to imply that someone wants him to starve. And such a covert argument (explicit in much of Marx) leads to fearful resentments and disillusionments. Mankind probably suffers more from incompetence than from deliberate evildoing; and it is no use hoping that radical improvement in the condition of "us" will be made merely by replacing "them."

The second question was that of freedom of the will. You can see how little of a solution we have reached. All we have done is distinguish between the question "Was he free to do x?" and "Was he able to do x?" and suggested that it is the latter that is involved in the problem of the freedom of the will. But it is not clear that it is any easier to see quite how determinism and ability conflict or fail to conflict than it is to see how determinism and freedom conflict or fail to conflict. Hampshire, it is true, attaches a sense both to the notion of getting more free of particular causal laws and to the idea of being more able to do something or other because of having changed our habits. But essentially this is a way of explaining what Hampshire means by freedom, and it is an explanation in terms of ability to change habits because of self-knowledge, as one might expect from his emphasis on the relevance of psychoanalysis. But to the wider problem of getting free of all causal laws, or of acquiring what we may term absolute abilities, we are no nearer an answer. It does indeed look as if Locke is right and that there is (at the moment, at any rate) no more profit in asking whether the will is free than in asking whether virtue is square—indeed, as though there is no more profit in asking whether the man is free (if free means able), which Locke supposed was the right question to ask.

Finally, why is freedom valuable? The question as asked by Hampshire seems to confuse two questions: why do we want to be free? and, is freedom the best of all goods? Hampshire asks for an argument to show that freedom has an absolute rather than a conditional value; but if I am right, this is impossible. We do necessarily want to be free because we want whatever we think good, and to be free to get it is one of the conditions of our attaining this apparent good; it has to be a very nonstandard case for us to want to eat an ice cream and yet not want to be free to eat it. The necessity behind the value of freedom is that to be free of something is to be that much less impeded in the attempt to achieve a good life. But surely, no particular freedom is the best thing there is in life. We might be very much happier if we were, for example, freed from our sexual fantasies, but we must be free from all manner of things first, for example, from the threat of sudden death or starvation, before our fantasies become important at all. To the extent that many people, as life gets easier in some ways, but more complex in many others, enjoy more the sense that they can do things than the doing of most of these things, we can attach some sense to Hampshire's demand; we may say that they are free (to do what and from what, we leave unstated but understood) and that this freedom is what they value most, so that freedom (or rather ability) had acquired a value of its own. But to expect a more satisfactory answer than this seems too much. It is a mistake about the logic of freedom (and one might conclude in parenthesis by saying that this is a horribly grandiose way of saying it is a mistake about the meaning of words like "free").

3

Culture and Anxiety

Some Autobiography

A SOCIETY THAT EMBODIES liberal values—that encourages economic ambition and emphasizes individual choice, that espouses the meritocratic route to social mobility and takes for granted the variability of our tastes and allegiances—may be inimical to the values embodied in traditional liberal education. There is a tension between the self-assertion that a modern liberal society fosters and the humility required of someone who tries to immerse herself in the thoughts and sentiments of another writer or another culture; there is perhaps a greater tension still between the thought that *some* achievements in philosophy, art, or literature will stand for all time and the ambition to use those achievements as stepping-stones to something better. It may be a healthy tension rather than a simple contradiction; renewing the gentlemanly ideal celebrated in Cardinal Newman's *The Idea of a University* in a liberal democracy perhaps requires us to live with such a tension. But this is something to be argued for rather than taken on trust.

I begin with a little autobiography because my own education was itself a training in how to live with this tension. I am what British observers of a certain age call a "scholarship boy": the beneficiary of a meritocratic educational system that plucked boys like myself (girls, too, but less often) from working-class and lower-middle-class backgrounds in order to give us what the clever children of the professional middle classes got automatically—a fiercely academic secondary education, available to London children at schools like St. Paul's, Westminster, Dulwich College, or the City of London School. I was a suitable case for treatment. My grandfathers were a miner and a truck driver; my parents left school at thirteen to work as a boy clerk and a housemaid. My father was a self-improving sort, though without the hard-driving qualities the label suggests. The family dynamo was my mother. Her fearlessness and organizational drive have been inherited by my sister, who runs one of Britain's largest community colleges and is the only woman in such a position. In World War II, my father worked as a clerk in the Royal Artillery, and his commander was impressed enough to urge him to get professional qualifications after the war. He duly did so; my first post-1945 memories are of my father reading endless correspondence units for his accountancy examinations.

I benefited more from his efforts than he did. He became the chief financial officer of a midsized company and prospered, but throughout his career, he preferred the company of a book to that of his fellow executives. I got the liberation he hankered after. My North London "council school"—the local public elementary school—was run by two ambitious head teachers on the lookout for clever and energetic children; they got on well with my parents, and together they set my brain in motion. Tracking—what the British call "streaming"—has become unpopular, but I enjoyed going through school at my own speed, helped by teachers who were tough about making me get things right and imaginative about pushing me forward. The post-1945 London County Council, which ran the schools, was a model of old-fashioned social democratic virtue, but it was a liberal education that we received. We visited museums and grand houses; we sang Handel, Arne, and Purcell; and we had Benjamin Britten's *Young Person's Guide to the Orchestra* played to us by the London Symphony Orchestra under Malcolm Sargent. I was also in debt to the librarians at the local public library, who enjoyed dispensing the riches of their Aladdin's cave.

The London County Council awarded scholarships to various public schools—in the English sense of that expression—and I was awarded one to Christ's Hospital. The school had been founded in 1552 by the saintly boy king Edward VI as part of his plan for putting redundant monastic buildings scattered about London to charitable use. Christ's Hospital was meant to rescue poor but honest children, and on the whole it did. (It was one of a group of institutions of which the best known was the older foundation of Bethlehem Hospital, or Bedlam; visitors to London could watch the lunatics in their asylum and the boys of Christ's Hospital at their meals and prayers.) In 1903, the school moved into the countryside—medieval drainage and the proximity of Newgate Prison bred diphtheria—and set up near Horsham in Sussex. Entry to the school was "means-tested": if your parents could afford to pay for a private education, you couldn't go. My family couldn't afford to pay for my education, so I went. Americans with children at private colleges and universities will be familiar with financial aid given on this basis; in Britain, it still remains an oddity.

During the 1950s, Christ's Hospital was as meritocratic as my elementary school had been in the late 1940s. Most boys left at sixteen to join the sort of City of London firm that had for two centuries employed them in clerical jobs. Charles Lamb was the most famous of them; he spent his working life in the East India Company and his evenings writing the *Essays of Elia* and drinking tea with William Godwin. The small number who could tackle academic disciplines to a level that would get them into Oxford and Cambridge stayed on till eighteen; they included Samuel Taylor Coleridge. The purest example of the self-made academic that the school produced was Sir Henry Maine, the great nineteenth-century jurist and legal historian and a man with a lifelong hunger for academic glory and financial security. I am less driven than he, but I know that I have spent my life trying to meet the standards set for me at Christ's Hospital.

I am vain enough to think the raw material my teachers worked with must have been good enough to inspire such efforts on their part, but my chief sensation is astonishment at my luck at falling in with the people who taught me in Islington, Horsham, and Oxford. For an anxious lower-middle-class child, conscious of the tight budgeting that went on at home and the sacrifice of the present to the future that defines English middle-class life, it was an unspeakable luxury to find this rich and vivid world to which the price of admission was only the desire to join. My brave new world was peopled with writers and my Ellis Island was the school library. There is almost no platitude about the pleasure of having your eyes opened and your mind stretched to which I do not subscribe. At its best, liberal education opens a conversation between ourselves and the immortal dead, gives us voices at our shoulders asking us to think again and try harder—sometimes by asking us *not* to think but just to look and listen, to try *less* hard and to wait for the light to dawn. It is not always at its best, and the contrast between what can happen and what more commonly does is not to be blinked at. Even when liberal education is not at its best, however, it is well worth defending against its wilder critics.

Meritocracy, For and Against

I was not special; innumerable students have had the experience I had; and innumerable students still get the care I got. I mention my education to make a general point about the idea of meritocracy and the pursuit of excellence. Liberalism has a natural affinity with meritocracy; it is attracted to an aristocracy of talent and critical of an aristocracy of birth. Liberal education in the conventional sense also rests on the thought that an acquaintance with intellectual, literary, and artistic excellence is in some (rather debatable and hotly debated) fashion good for us, and that one of the ways it is so is in teaching us to measure ourselves against touchstones of cultural and intellectual excellence. My reflexes are meritocratic. Let me take an embarrassing example. *The Bell Curve*'s claim that measured differences in IQ between black and white Americans reflect different "racial" endowments of native intelligence is entirely ill founded, and the insinuating tone of the book unpleasant.[1] Its insistence that people should be selected for jobs, graduate training, university admission, and the like on the basis of measurable competence is, however, impossible to resist. The cliché defense of meritocracy is that none of us wants to be operated on by an incompetent brain surgeon. That suggests a rather narrow idea of merit; the principle applies more widely. Nobody wants Pushkin translated by someone who knows no Russian, nor do we want the Cleveland Orchestra conducted by a tone-deaf lout with no sense of rhythm. The fact that we can debate the merits of different translations of Pushkin and different performances of *The Rite of Spring* while conceding that all are technically competent makes no difference. Where there is a measurable skill, it should be measured, and the excellent should be preferred to the merely decent. Where standards are debatable, they should be debated. The point is well understood by sports fans, but underappreciated in the arts and humanities.

The case for meritocracy is so obvious that it is tempting to forget that there are respectable arguments against it.[2] Some have been prominent in American life. Let me mention two. First, what we seek in most areas of life is not "the best" but "the good enough." And rightly so. The restless search for the excellent automobile that an automotive perfectionist engages in does not increase his driving pleasure; it merely deprives him of the enjoyment that he would have had if he had settled for a merely decent car. Applied to education, the thought is that most students in high school and college will learn enough math and enough writing and reading skills to get a decent living. They need not be made anxious and dissatisfied by having to face the fact that they will never be very good in either field. Nor is there much of an economic argument for pursuing intellectual excellence. The economy needs very few excellent mathematicians, but a lot of averagely numerate workers. There is an economic case for insisting on a competitive marketplace and the development of excellent products and excellent management, but not for insisting on meritocracy—as distinct from competence—in the educational sphere. Experience suggests that this is a sound view: the United States is the most productive country in the world; its popular culture is as attractive to other countries as its technical expertise in aeronautical engineering and computer software. It is neither an intellectually rigorous nor a culturally ambitious society, however; outside major metropolitan areas, there are few bookshops, the radio plays an unending diet of gospel or country-and-western music, and intellectual pretensions are not encouraged. The nation has prospered without inculcating in its young people the cultural and intellectual ambitions that French lycées and German gymnasia inculcate in their students. Why should it change now?

Most Americans are happy to compete in the marketplace on the basis of the excellence of their products, but few wish to be more discriminating, better read, or whatever else than their neighbors. Most people regard what appears to be intellectual discussion rather as a way of cementing friendly relations among themselves than as a way of changing minds or seeking truth. Many conservatives in the 1990s have looked back nostalgically to the 1950s. But in the 1950s, American high schools taught "life adjustment" classes. Among the topics covered in one New York school system described by Richard Hofstadter in *Anti-intellectualism in American Life* were "Developing School Spirit," "My Duties as a Baby-Sitter," "Clicking with the Crowd," "What Can Be Done about Acne?" "Learning to Care for My Bedroom," "Making My Room More Attractive." Eighth-grade pupils were

given these questions on a true-false test: "Just girls need to use deodor-
ants"; "Cake soap can be used for shampooing." Women friends of mine
were taught how to enter and leave a sports car without allowing their skirts
to ride up and expose their underwear. If the 1950s were wonderful, it is not
because they were years of universal intellectual excellence.[3]

A second persuasive objection to meritocracy rests on a related but rather
different thought: most people prefer stability, authority, and tradition to
uncertainty, freethinking, and openness to the future. Where merit is clearly
defined and relevant, persons should be promoted, and ideas accepted, on
their merits; otherwise, habits of acceptance should be cherished. This is an
old conservative thought, and it is very hard to resist. Karl Popper, the philosopher of science, social theorist, and author of *The Open Society and Its
Enemies*, defended the idea that the policies of governments, like scientific
theories and social practices generally, should be accepted strictly on their
merits, precisely because he thought that the "normal" condition of mankind was conservative and indeed, in his eyes, "tribal." This was why the
"open society"—a liberal, democratic, changeable, and argumentative society—had so many enemies, from the high-minded philosopher Plato at one
extreme to low-minded terrorists such as Hitler and Stalin at the other. Popper's model of the open society was a community of research scientists. Science is a strikingly artificial activity: scientists have to formulate bold hypotheses about how the world works and then submit these hypotheses to
rigorous testing against whatever evidence can be found. Hypotheses may
not be protected from refutation by appealing to our own virtues and our
critics' vices, or indeed by appealing to anything but the best available evidence. If *The Bell Curve*'s hypothesis that IQ is racially determined is to be
tested scientifically, we must not try to discredit it by observing that one of
its authors was a Jew who naturally liked the idea that science showed that
Jews were innately more clever than blacks; and it will not do to defend it
by observing that many of its most savage critics were blacks who naturally
disliked the same idea.

Conservatives are sometimes criticized for advocating laissez-faire in economics but wanting stability in religious, social, and cultural matters. This
seems a mistake; it may not be possible to have what they want, but the
combination of stability in our deepest allegiances and quick-footedness in
our habits of work and consumption would surely make for a happy and
prosperous society. A greater source of anxiety today is that it is not groups
who enjoy the pace of change in American economic and social life who
want stability in their deepest beliefs. Recently, the threat to free speech and
free inquiry on American campuses has come—as it has done for most of the
century—not from the defenders of private property or the defenders of
upper-class respectability but from lower-middle-class groups demanding
"respect" for themselves, their opinions, and their culture. The latter are not
defending privileges that have come under attack, but seeking comfort in a
world they view as hostile and dangerous. Fundamentalist Christians—

almost invariably from rather humble backgrounds—who try to stop colleges and universities from preaching tolerance for the sexual tastes of gays and lesbians genuinely feel as ill-used as the gays and lesbians who want their schools to protect them against the insults of the godly.

The liberal view is hostile to the search for comfort and support, at least partly for meritocratic reasons. All sides are entitled to physical safety, and certainly everyone needs friends, but nobody is entitled to respect—other than the minimal respect that is involved in arguing courteously with one's opponents rather than beating them up. Or, rather, one is entitled to be treated as a rational adult, but one's ideas are entitled only to the respect they earn by being properly thought out, factually well grounded, and the like. It is this distinction that many students, particularly students from families with no previous experience of academic life, find it hard to deal with. The thought that much of what they have hitherto unhesitatingly believed is false, misguided, or simply one among many options produces a lot of anxiety. The wish to assuage this anxiety runs headlong into the view that we must try to believe only those ideas that are good enough to stand up to criticism. None of this licenses rudeness or brutality; it is no doubt true that many professors are socially inept, and others are authoritarian, and still others are so insecure that they cannot bear any criticism of their opinions. All the same, even if we were all as deft and sensitive as could be imagined, the ideal classroom would not be a cozy place. Part of the object of education is to teach us to treat our own ideas objectively rather than subjectively; we ought not to want to believe what will not stand up to criticism, though we all do, and we can hardly hope to discover which of our beliefs are more and which less reliable without a few moments of discomfort. Bullying and insult are intolerable, no matter who is on the receiving end; but shading the truth is the ultimate academic sin.

Liberal Anxieties and Conservative Anger

My first insights into my own education came through reading John Stuart Mill's *Autobiography* and progressing from Matthew Arnold's "Scholar Gypsy" to grappling with Lionel Trilling's *Matthew Arnold*. A predictable result of a liberal education is that its beneficiaries behave like the hero of Saul Bellow's novel *Herzog*—who spent much of his time composing postcards to the immortal dead. Writing about education is particularly likely to involve such a one-way traffic in postcards. Jaroslav Pelikan recently wrote *The Idea of a University: A Reexamination* to defend a conservative and traditionalist vision of higher education in homage to and in dialogue with Cardinal Newman. My antipathy to organized religion, to the Oxford movement, and to the personality of Newman himself means that I admire Newman's prose without much liking the writer. Moreover, Newman wrote *The Idea of a University* to defend the newly founded University College, Dublin, against fellow Catholics who wished it to provide a sectarian education; and this is hardly our situation. We are more likely either to ignore the education of all but an elite or else to be besotted by the needs of the economy. My own touchstone is a book that nobody wrote—*Culture and Anxiety*—but the voices in my head are those of Mill, Arnold, Russell, and Dewey, and, among recent writers, Raymond Williams and Richard Hoggart.[4] Since they were considerable readers, I therefore eavesdrop on their conversations with Marx, Hegel, Freud, Carlyle, and innumerable others.

Liberalism has for two hundred years suffered from three great anxieties. The first is fear of the culturally estranged condition of what has been variously called the "underclass," the "unwashed mob," the lumpen proletariat, or (by Hegel) the *Pöbel*; the second is unease about "disenchantment," the loss of a belief that the world possesses a religious and spiritual meaning; the third is fear that the degeneration of the French Revolution between 1789 and 1794 into a regime of pure terrorism was only the harbinger of revolutions to come. These fears often feed on one another. "We must educate our masters," said the English politician Sir Robert Lowe when he saw that he could no longer resist the Reform Bill of 1867. That legislation gave the vote to most of the adult male inhabitants of Britain's cities. Lowe was frightened by a familiar scenario: unless the working class was educated, farsighted, and prudent, commercial and industrial change would bring in its wake a democratic revolution that would degenerate into mob rule and end with a guillotine in Hyde Park. In the alternative, there would be no revolution, because the mob would follow the first golden-tongued demagogue who cared to woo them. Arnold feared the mob. Mill did not, but he feared Napoléon III. Their contemporary, the social theorist Alexis de Tocqueville, gave Europeans some understanding of how the Americans had escaped both of these disastrous sequences while the French had not.

These political fears are today antiquated in Britain and the United States—but Britain and the United States remain unusual. The recent civil wars in the former communist state of Yugoslavia are but one of many contemporary instances of the way political and economic disruption leads to irrational, violent, and atavistic behavior. They seem to indicate that the first thing a newly emancipated and politically uneducated people will do is follow a dictator. Franjo Tudjman and Slobodan Milošević are nastier and more uncouth than Napoléon III; but everyone who saw Louis-Bonaparte, the nephew of Napoléon and an adventurer of the lowest kind, rise to power after the French Revolution of 1848, on the back of the popular vote, knew how a demagogue could turn the popular vote into a mandate for his dictatorial ambitions.

I want to emphasize the difference between these fears, however. It is clear that we might escape the guillotine but relapse into mindlessness; we might lead culturally vivid lives under the shadow of the guillotine; we might escape both these fates but feel intolerably estranged from the world because a life without strong religious sentiments turns out to be humanly impossible. The three great anxieties are different: the first rests on the idea of a distinctively cultural disaster, what Arnold termed "the *brutalisation* of the masses"; the second rests on the idea that if religious faith and a sense of community together decay, we shall be "unanchored" in the world; the third is more narrowly the fear of political violence. Nineteenth-century Britain and the United States—where modern liberal education was invented—suffered these anxieties to different degrees and in different forms. The French Revolution did not haunt the American political imagination as it haunted British and European writers; indeed, only with the rediscovery of Edmund Burke's attacks on the French Revolution by American conservatives such as Russell Kirk and William F. Buckley during the Cold War did the political excesses of the French Revolution become a theme for American political controversy. Conversely, fear of the solvent effect of immigration affected nineteenth-century Britain only in the narrow and highly specific form of a dislike for Irish migrants in the 1840s and for Jewish and other eastern European migrants in the last two decades of the century; but in the United States, the fear that immigrants from anywhere other than England, Scotland, or Protestant northern Europe would erode the existing common culture was one source of the demand for "common schools" as early as the 1830s, and variations on that theme have been heard in American politics ever since.

I call these anxieties "liberal anxieties," but an obvious objection is that they are everyone's anxieties. My response is that both *anxiety* and *liberal* are to be taken seriously. Liberals have always been on the side of economic, political, and intellectual change; they have hoped that change would culminate in freedom rather than chaos or estrangement, but they have always known that they might unleash forces they could not control. The late eighteenth-century conservative and bitter enemy of the French Revolution, Joseph de Maistre, denounced the liberal philosophers of the eighteenth century for encouraging the aspirations of the common people, and so inciting revolution and bloodshed.

As he observed, it is not the tiger we blame for rending its victim but the man who lets him off the leash. Liberals have wished to raise expectations without being overwhelmed by the consequences, and it is none too clear that it can be done. Tocqueville famously argued that the French Revolution broke out because the population had made enough progress in the years before 1789 to be maddened when progress was not sustained. Americans commenting on the fact that black Americans were more aggressive in demanding their rights *after* Jim Crow legislation had been overturned always refer to what Adlai Stevenson described as "a revolution of rising expectations." It is all too plausible that people who have never been able to raise their eyes to new possibilities will remain docile, while those who have seen new possibilities will rebel if they are then denied the chance to seize them. Liberal anxiety responds to the risk of such a revolution.

Liberals know that it is not irrational to bet against the liberal project from the right or the left, or from both sides at once—that it is quite rational to think that change should be approached much more cautiously, or that it must be embraced much more wholeheartedly. In intellectual and cultural matters, indeed, liberals themselves are often conservative and revolutionary simultaneously in just this way. They see that they are the inheritors of traditions they do not themselves wish to overthrow, but they want everyone to explore those traditions for themselves. When they do so, they may reject them or alter them out of all recognition. The liberal can respond only that this tension lies at the heart of all serious intellectual or aesthetic activity. How could a scientist proceed if not by absorbing the techniques and theories and problems of a tradition of inquiry and then launching out into new work; and are not scientists often disconcerted to find their cherished ideas dismissed as old hat by their radical juniors? Is not the same thing true in art and music?

The concepts of "conservative," "liberal," and "revolutionary" in intellectual matters are used loosely, of course. The context in which they are used more exactly, and where liberals are habitually beset from left and right, is the political. And here is where the difference between anxiety, fear, and anger is most plainly visible. Conservatives have rightly felt fear in the face of the changes the liberals wanted; but since they wanted to preserve an ancien régime society, creedally based political authority, and the habits of a rural economy, they had no reason to be anxious but much reason to be frightened and angry. Socialists and radicals have rightly felt exasperation and anger at the inadequacy of the changes that liberals have welcomed, and at the evils liberals have left untouched as well as at the new forms of exploitation they have brought with them. Conservatives have disliked the liberal, meritocratic ideal of "the career open to talent" because they wished to preserve a society in which hereditary privilege ruled, and not always because it was in their self-interest; socialists have disliked the liberal, meritocratic ideal because it placed unskilled workers at the mercy of financially or intellectually better-endowed people. Conservatives and socialists have often held in common the belief that stable societies in which people know what to expect of life are happier societies than the shifting, insecure societies that liberalism creates.

Nineteenth-century liberals added to their insecurity when they insisted that reform must come through the efforts of its beneficiaries. A chapter entitled "The Probable Futurity of the Labouring Classes" in Mill's *Principles of Political Economy* (1848) set out the argument. Mill took it for granted that benevolent conservatives existed; their flaw was that they wanted to look after the working class. The liberal aim was that the workers should look after themselves; the ultimate aim was a wholly classless society in which individual success depended upon merit. Mill's characteristically sharp way of putting the point was to insist that he wished to live in a society "with none but a working class." Other than children and retired people, nobody was to benefit without contributing to the best of his ability. Self-advancement required intelligence and foresight. It demanded control over fertility. It demanded equality between the sexes. It demanded a transformation of relations at work. Mill was certain—wrongly, as it turned out—that educated people would not accept forever a division between managers and workers, or between capitalists and wage earners. The title of the political scientist Benjamin Barber's recent book, *An Aristocracy of Everyone*, summarizes Mill's aspirations: everyone was to make the best of herself. The revolutionary route to such a result was needlessly painful and unlikely to work; education in a broad sense was the only route. When I say education in a broad sense, I mean that Mill wanted to make society and politics generally more intelligent. He rightly had no thought of throwing open an unreformed Oxford and Cambridge to the English working class of the 1840s.

The Idea of an Educating Society

What Mill, like Arnold, and like Emerson on the other side of the Atlantic for that matter, had in mind was the transformation of the entire society into a community that was reflective and broadly cultivated as well as liberally educated in the usual sense. This is why I said earlier that the ideal of an educa*ting* society, rather than an educa*ted* society, was so important, and why it was the entire society rather than what we nowadays call educational institutions on which discussion focused. What role there was for the ancient English universities in such a vision was not obvious. Until they were reformed by act of Parliament in the 1850s, they could hardly play any role. In the early nineteenth century, they were actually less open to the lower-middle-class or working-class young man than they had been three centuries earlier. What animated reformers was the hope that a more rational society would be governed by a meritocracy; once power was gained by administrative ability and professional expertise rather than by birth, it would both induce the sons of the upper classes to get a decent education and open social and political advancement to their social inferiors. Only when major social institutions gave the stamp of approval to education would ambitious persons seek a decent education. Mill helped govern India from the London offices of the East India Company. The company had set up a school for boys who would go out to govern India—Haileybury College —and there they got a notably modern education, including courses in economics, history, and literature of a kind that Oxford and Cambridge introduced later and reluctantly. The new colleges—such as University College, London, founded in 1828—that were founded in London and the larger provincial cities could more easily than the ancient universities dispense an education both practical and liberal throughout the population.

The wish to be able to boast of the United States or of Britain, as Pericles did of ancient Athens, that our society is a school for all the world is and always has been a utopian ambition. Moreover, it is not an ambition that we can expect everyone to see the point of. The kind of society that sets store by being as self-critical and intellectually ambitious as the society Mill hoped for will not appeal to everyone. Tastes vary. Still, it is easy to imagine that its ideals can readily be realized on a small scale in particular contexts—that liberal arts colleges will form very "Millian" communities, as will many laboratories, some firms, and even some sports teams—and that in many contexts they will not be realized at all. The improvement in working-class well-being in the past hundred and fifty years has moved us both toward and away from that utopian goal. Especially in the United States, the growth of working-class incomes has produced a population that is infinitely less brutal, drunken, ignorant, and alienated than was the urban proletariat of Victorian England, let alone the denizens of New York's Hell's Kitchen seventy-five years ago. It is also a population that is emphatically private in its concerns, and in that way quite different from what Mill and even Arnold would have hoped. Only a bare majority of possible voters now go to the polls in the United States, even in presidential elections. Barely 10 percent of citizens can name their local congressman.

It would be wrong to call the citizens of the present-day United States passive or apathetic; but their concerns are domestic, private, and familial. In 1834, Tocqueville saw this retreat into domesticity as one possible American future, and it was one that he and Mill feared. A prosperous but narrowly self-centered society is better than a poor and narrowly self-centered society; but it is not what they wanted. They hoped that education would produce the wish and the ability dramatically to rebuild social, economic, and political institutions. That economic progress would remove the desire for violent revolution by subverting the ambition for anything other than our own private well-being would have seemed a sad bargain. If liberals have less reason than they once had to wonder whether change would not degenerate into mere chaos, they have every reason to wonder whether they were right to think that a free and prosperous society would also be lively, intelligent, and self-improving.

Brutalization

The fear of brutalization took, and still takes, different forms in Britain and America. Arnold's talk of the brutalization of the masses made perfect sense in a class-divided society; culture was a middle- and upper-class possession. British migrants to colonial America, on the other hand, could more plausibly fear the brutalization of a whole society in a bleak and hostile environment. What led the spiritual leaders of the Massachusetts Bay Colony to establish Harvard College in 1636 had no direct contemporary British counterpart: the feeling of being a small island of Christian culture in a vast wilderness was a physical reality in the New World in a way it could not be in Britain. The feeling was reinforced by the incessant expansion of the country. To establish a college or university—after a church and perhaps a local elementary school—became an outward and visible sign of an intention to cultivate the territory and civilize the citizenry. The process received a great impetus when the American Revolution removed the imperial government's constraints on expansion; but it had already received almost as much from the revivals that were a feature of American religious life from the early eighteenth century onward.

Harvard was two hundred years old in 1836, and the University of Michigan already nineteen. The College of William and Mary was founded in 1693, but when the elderly Jefferson founded the University of Virginia in 1819, he said it was the proudest achievement of his career. Small liberal arts colleges proliferated in the northeastern United States, beginning with Williams College in 1791. The town of Evanston is today a northern suburb of Chicago, but Northwestern University is a reminder that almost the first thing that devout Methodists in the Northwest Territory did was to build a college, just as Oberlin College speaks to the memory of the German educator after whom it was named on its foundation in 1819. After a church and a school, it seemed sometimes that almost the next thing that a respectable town required was its own college; most were evanescent foundations, but some flourished, to our great good fortune.

The cultural environments of Britain and America were less strikingly different than the physical environments. The frontier wilderness was hardly less propitious a setting for high culture than the spiritual wilderness of the British industrial cities in the mid-nineteenth century that so distressed Arnold and many others. Certainly, the British city called out the same response as the American frontier: local worthies and local clergy created civic colleges that eventually turned into the Universities of Manchester, or Bristol, or Leeds. Two differences have always been very marked. The first is the place of established religion, and the second the place of acknowledged class distinctions. The absence of both made the United States the more plausible setting for a democratic intellectual culture; whether they also made the United States a less favorable environment for "high" culture has been argued over for a hundred and fifty years.

The United States was, and Britain was not, committed to the separation of church and state. The U.S. Constitution forbade, while the British continued to accept, hereditary titles of nobility. The fate of England's two ancient universities was tied to the fortunes of the Church of England and to the most conservative forces in national politics. In colonial and independent America alike, a student might well choose a college on the basis of religious affiliation, but there was no question of his being excluded altogether for religious reasons. Nondenominational state universities sprang up immediately after the Revolution. Their presidents had often been admitted to the ministry, and a generalized piety was expected of them; but the contrast with England was striking. There the two great ancient universities were an Anglican monopoly: nobody could even begin an education at Oxford without swearing allegiance to the Church of England, while nobody could graduate from Cambridge without doing so. In both countries, of course, only a tiny percentage of the population attended college at all: Princeton graduated eight or a dozen students a year for many years after its foundation in 1746, for instance, and in Britain, Oxford was a smaller university for the two centuries after the Civil War of 1641–49 than it had been for the century before the war. The role of colleges in defeating brutalization was understood to be a matter of "trickle down," whereby the college-educated would diffuse enlightenment either directly, through the ministry and in teaching, or indirectly, through their support of the arts, libraries, museums, and the like.

The Anglican monopoly of access to the ancient English universities was part of the Anglican monopoly of access to the learned professions, Parliament, and political preferment. Dissenters established very small colleges to train their ministers and to provide a serious liberal education to their children. It was these dissenting colleges that eighteenth-century American colleges resembled in their seriousness, their accessibility to the relatively humble, their liveliness, and therefore their democratic potential. Indeed, when Princeton was founded in 1746, it was to the English dissenting colleges that it looked for curricular inspiration. The established English universities were very far from natural breeding grounds for a democratic culture, and in their eighteenth-century torpor were hardly an educational model of any kind. From the 1820s onward, things changed. With the creation in 1828 of what became University College, London—"the godless college in Gower Street"—England acquired its first secular college. King's College, London, was founded shortly after to ensure that the capital possessed an Anglican college. Outside London, a range of colleges, often founded by Dissenters, started to reach beyond their original, sectarian clientele. The Scots, it has to be said, looked on in some amusement, having enjoyed the benefit of accessible nonsectarian universities in Edinburgh, Glasgow, and Aberdeen for several centuries. It was no wonder that the *Edinburgh Review* took particular pleasure in tweaking the noses of Oxford conservatives.

The early nineteenth century gave the critics of brutalization plenty to fear. The horrors of newly urbanizing Britain were recited by every spectator. Mill was jailed for a day at the age of sixteen for distributing birth-control pamphlets to the working-class houses of the East End; it is said he did so after coming across the corpse of an abandoned baby as he walked to work at East India Company headquarters. The starved and stunted condition of the children who worked in the cotton industry was a commonplace; so was the drunken and brutal behavior of their parents; so was their almost complete alienation from the church; so were their ignorance and illiteracy.

Karl Marx, who relied on Friedrich Engels's *The Condition of the Working Class in England*; Thomas Carlyle, on whose *Past and Present* Engels had himself relied a good deal; and both Mill and his father were in substantial agreement about the horrors of the situation. They were also substantially agreed that the better-off had neglected the spiritual and physical welfare of the worse-off. Revolutionary socialists such as Marx insisted that nothing would change until the expropriators were expropriated; conservative reformers such as the English humanitarian Lord Shaftesbury insisted that it was the proper task of a conservative ruling class to make coal owners and manufacturers treat their workers decently, to protect women and children from exploitation, and to secure the conditions of their spiritual growth. Paradoxically enough, it was the reports of the Factory Inspectorate that Shaftesbury and his allies had shamed the British government into establishing in 1833 on which Marx later relied when he was writing *Das Kapital*.

Disenchantment

In the United States and Britain, the phenomenon of brutalization at its crudest is today a phenomenon only of the decayed inner cities. So far from proletarianization being the lot of the working class, the work and consumption habits of what used to be called the "respectable" working class have become universal. But the end of the twentieth century sees no diminution of anxiety about secularization and disenchantment. The fear has one source, but two distinct aspects. The one source is the increasingly dominant position of the physical sciences among the many ways in which we explain and understand the world. The two distinct aspects are, first, that scientific understanding will drive all the poetry out of the world—that color, beauty, sublimity, will vanish and nothing will be left but matter in motion—and, second, that in the absence of transcendental sanctions, mankind will become as the beasts, without shame, without morality, and without ambitions for perfection. The common thread is the fear that what science reveals is that human existence is accidental; the world has no purpose, humans have no special place in the world, whatever they contrive by way of an existence is wholly up to them, and in the absence of a divine ordering of the world, what they may get up to hardly bears thinking about. "If God is dead, everything is permitted," wrote Friedrich Nietzsche. Many observers of the horrors of the twentieth century have thought that the Nazi death camps were a commentary on that claim.

The Enlightenment was an amorphous movement. Not all skeptical, secular philosophers of the eighteenth century thought they belonged to the movement. Nonetheless, by the end of the eighteenth century, the ideas that mankind was morally and intellectually self-sufficient and that the world was not intrinsically mysterious but would yield to scientific investigation and control were understood as the central ideas of the Enlightenment. The great

German philosopher Immanuel Kant said that the motto of the Enlightenment was *sapere aude,* or "dare to understand." Critics of the Enlightenment complained that their enlightened opponents were bent on driving the poetry from the world, that the world described by science was cold and colorless. William Blake thought that the arrival of Newton had been the death of the human world.

This is not to say that science is irreligious. When the sociologist Max Weber introduced the idea of "disenchantment" in *The Protestant Ethic and the Spirit of Capitalism,* he argued that modern science was a product of the same spiritual impulse as Protestantism. The German word usually translated as "disenchanted" is *entzaubert,* or "unmagicked."[5] The Protestant distaste for magic was a moral and spiritual distaste. To believe in magic was an insult to God. A serious God would not interfere with his creation in a capricious fashion; he could not be cajoled, bribed, or seduced into doing his worshipers a good turn. The Protestant God was *deus absconditus,* the God who had created a universe governed by intelligible natural laws and who had then allowed that universe to operate according to those laws. He himself was absent. This absence left the world to be explained by whatever theories the new natural sciences could validate. This austere picture of the universe sustained, and was sustained by, an ideal of self-discipline that repudiated the use of anything other than our own talents and energy to achieve our ends. It bred a decided moral and intellectual toughness in the process.

The "enchanted" world, in contrast, was a world where we were at home. It was not necessarily a world created by, or ruled by, any of the gods of the great world religions; but it was a world where "natural piety" made sense. William Wordsworth's poetry conveys perhaps more acutely than any philosophical explanation what it was whose loss the critics of the Enlightenment lamented. The Romantic poets had no doubt that what we first encounter is an enchanted world. The child who comes into this world "trailing clouds of glory" needed no teaching or prompting to rejoice in the rainbow or to tremble as the shadow of the mountain stole across the lake. The natural world spoke to him, and he needed only to listen to it. Only when these natural reactions had been suppressed could he think that science could tell him all there is to know about the world. But the suppression of these reactions was a moral and emotional disaster, well captured in the line "shades of the prison house close around the growing boy."

One of Matthew Arnold's more famous essays, "Science and Literature," is devoted to praising poetry and disparaging science as the basis of a concern for culture. It was written as a response to Darwin's ally, Thomas Henry Huxley, who had himself been provoked by Arnold's *Culture and Anarchy* to write in defense of science as the basis for a liberal education. The quarrel of science with poetry is a running theme in the nineteenth century, and one taken up in an interesting way by John Dewey in the twentieth. Its impact on the liberal theory of education is plain enough. Education is notoriously a solvent of traditional forms of religious belief. It is also likely to promote the belief that what cannot be explained by some kind of scientific explanation cannot be explained at all. That, in turn, is likely to promote a view of poetry—and with it, religion—that denies it any cognitive content and sees it as pure self-expression, a matter of sentiment, not intellect. The thought that poetry is "only" expressive is simply the other face of the view that a strictly scientific understanding of the world is all the understanding that there can be. The fear, then, is that neither the individual nor society can sustain an adequate life without an individual or collective conviction that the world itself is in harmony with our desires and affections. It is the fear that we will find life thin, shallow, and unsatisfying if our individual hopes and fears are not supported by rituals, by festivals, and by what, if backed by a supernatural faith, we would call religious belief, and otherwise might call social poetry.

It is no accident that Arnold looked to poetry to supply what the declining credibility of Christian mythology could not, nor that Mill argued that the religion of humanity could satisfy the needs of the heart while it also reinforced the dictates of rational altruism. Once more, it is the liberal who will experience as anxiety the suspicion that these palliatives may not anchor us in our world; the truly devout unfeignedly believe that the visible world reposes upon something deeper; skeptical conservatives hope people will not ask whether it does. Liberals suffer a self-inflicted wound: they want the emancipation that leads to disenchantment, but want the process that emancipates us to relocate us in the world as well. Nietzsche and Weber are only the most eloquent among the voices that say it cannot be done in the way the liberal wants. The anything but eloquent Dewey is the most philosophically astute of those who say that it can.

The Terror

The terror induced by the Terror is an oft-told tale. It is not wholly true that the argument between Edmund Burke's *Reflections on the Revolution in France* and Tom Paine's *Rights of Man* ended in a knockout victory for Burke, but it is certainly true that Burke's forecast—made in 1790—of the subsequent course of the revolution was unnervingly accurate. The revolution did degenerate into terrorism, dictatorship, and ultimately the arrival of a military government. The fear that opening the gate to popular aspirations would lead inexorably to mob rule, violence, and military dictatorship, together with the ruin of the traditional aristocracy, the spoliation of the established church, and an indefinite Continental war thereafter, was enough to make anyone flinch from reform. The liberal reply was naturally that the disaster occurred because reform had come too little and too late and because good sense had been swamped by ideology. This was what Burke himself said in calmer moments; a society without the means of reform is without the means of its own preservation. The argument rattled back and forth for half a century. The young James Mill edited the *Anti-Jacobin Review* when he first came to London in 1803, but twenty years later defended the democratization of British politics in terms that led Thomas Macaulay to prophesy that if James Mill had his way, some future visitor from New Zealand would be left to stare at the ruins of St. Paul's and wonder what had happened to the British.

Macaulay was a Whig, not a Tory. As with the other anxieties of nineteenth-century liberals, the Left and the Right found matters simpler than the liberals did. Macaulay wanted to reform Parliament so that the respectable middle class could play a more active role in British politics; but he feared to go further. The Duke of Wellington and his fellow Tories thought it inconceivable that any change to so perfect a political system could be an improvement, while the Chartists wanted the demands of the People's Charter: annual elections, universal suffrage, and the secret ballot at once. Liberals remained divided among themselves, as they have been ever since. At the time of the fairly mild rioting that preceded the passing of the 1867 Reform Act, John Stuart Mill told the rioters that they should resort to insurrection only if they thought it was absolutely necessary *and* they were likely to succeed, while Matthew Arnold angrily observed: "As for rioting the Roman way was the right one; flog the perpetrators and fling the ringleaders from the Tarpeian rock."

Although Britain and the United States have possessed eminently stable political systems for many years, such arguments persist. In the 1960s, the generally liberal professors of the United States found themselves faced with student insurrection, and reacted with similar ambivalence. As young people who were at risk of being sent off to Vietnam to fight a war they disapproved of made common cause with assorted Maoists, Trotskyites, and even the Deweyan enthusiasts for industrial democracy who had created the Students for a Democratic Society, the old drama repeated itself. Badly needed reforms in teaching and administration threatened to lead to anarchy; and once the Black Panther movement joined the struggle, real violence was never further away than the twitch of a trigger finger. But whatever else was on the agenda, popular insurrection was not. What the state's role in education should be, what degree of abstention from political involvement should be practiced by universities and their faculties, what the place of formal higher education was in the promotion of high culture, and what degree of openness to "low" culture and its fads was proper to a university—these have been perennial questions. That an alliance of students and workers should form a revolutionary vanguard was at most a passing fancy of Herbert Marcuse.

Politics, Culture, Education

If these are the anxieties that beset liberals, and their connection with education is now made out—essentially, that it is not only a little learning that is a dangerous thing for social and individual stability and security—it remains to ask what the role of liberal education is in the liberal view of the world. The answer is that there is no one answer. Once that is acknowledged, it becomes clearer that many of the arguments about the expansion of college and university education over the past century have been arguments about the relative weight to be attached to the provision of a liberal education versus research on the one hand and vocational education on the other, while others have been arguments about the content of what everyone agrees to be a liberal education—what, in an American university, would lead to a bachelor's degree in the college of arts and sciences. A little history may be illuminating as a preface to two famous nineteenth-century arguments, whose echoes rumble on. Before the American Revolution, there were nine colleges: Harvard, founded in 1636, whose doors opened in 1638; William and Mary (1693); Yale (1701); the College of Philadelphia, later the University of Pennsylvania (1740); Princeton (1746); King's College, subsequently Columbia (1754); the College of Rhode Island, later Brown University (1764); Queen's College, later Rutgers (1766); and Dartmouth (1769). All had a common purpose, which was well expressed in the words of Princeton's founders: "Though our great intention was to found a seminary for educating ministers of the gospel, yet we hope it will be a means of raising up men that will be useful in other learned professions—ornaments of the state as well as the church."

The sharp modern distinction between "public" and "private" universities and colleges was unknown until 1819. Most colleges would have been hard-pressed to survive their early years without assistance from their state governments. But when the State of New Hampshire set out to take over the direction of Dartmouth College and turn it into Dartmouth University, it was rebuffed in the U.S. Supreme Court. State courts had held that the college was established for public purposes of a sort that gave the state legitimate authority over it; but the oratory of Daniel Webster persuaded the Supreme Court by a five to one majority that although it was perfectly proper for state governments to establish publicly financed colleges, they could not simply expropriate a private "eleemosynary institution," such as the college clearly was. It is often said that the Dartmouth decision set back the creation of state colleges for some decades and, perhaps more importantly, opened the door to a flood of tiny, and often short-lived, private colleges. Francis Oakley observes that one of its most important results was the feature of American higher education that most astonishes Europeans: the sheer variety of institutions in which it is carried on, and the vast differences in size, prosperity, and, above all, intellectual quality.

Today, some fourteen million full- and part-time students attend all sorts of places, from storefront two-year colleges handing out associate degrees to the graduate schools of Cal Tech and MIT. Rather little of what is on offer is liberal education. In the Ivy League and the liberal arts colleges, 90 percent of students get a traditional liberal arts education; in the entire higher-education sector, loosely characterized "business studies" provide two-thirds of the courses. This is a thoroughly modern state of affairs, dating only from the expansion of the 1960s and thereafter. In the first great expansion after the Revolution, there was no diminution of concern for liberal education. It was only later, with the rise of agricultural colleges and vocationally oriented state colleges, that the primacy of liberal education came under threat. It is worth recalling yet again that even after the expansion of college education in the late eighteenth and early nineteenth centuries, not many more than one American in a thousand went to college. Even in so classless a society as the United States, those who went were markedly upper class.

College education was not in the narrow sense vocational, but it was an education for persons whose vocations were tolerably clear—the ministry, law, medicine—or who would be "gentry." It was not merely decorative, ornamental, or a means of self-expression, but it was not narrowly utilitarian. Learning the craft skills of the preacher, doctor, or lawyer happened elsewhere, commonly on the job. The chance to learn how to comport oneself in no matter what learned profession was something colleges could offer. The students were, as they were at Oxford and Cambridge at this time, very young by the standards of a later day. It was common to graduate at the age of eighteen or nineteen; and although boys entered college young, they frequently took only three years to graduate. The tales of assaults on the faculty, pistols fired at night, and frequent near riots over poor food are reminiscent of what went on at the great English public schools such as Winchester and Westminster in the early years of the nineteenth century, although the religious revivals that swept through American colleges in the early spring were a distinctively American phenomenon. Nothing that we should now recognize as "advanced studies" was possible, nor was it attempted. But this was a society where a man was old at forty-five or fifty, and a boy of fifteen was supposed to comport himself like a man. So it would be wrong to think that colleges like Harvard, Yale, and Princeton were more like modern high schools than they were like modern colleges.

Moreover, in the early and mid-nineteenth century, there began to be the traffic between American (and English) colleges and German universities that opened the eyes of the Anglo-Saxon world to the possibilities of a deeper scholarship than any practiced in England or the United States. And the grip of the English conception of liberal education naturally weakened in a society whose commitments were so self-consciously and explicitly republican. Whether the introduction at an early date of such subjects as "navigation" into the curriculum at Yale and Princeton was also evidence of the familiar utilitarianism of American culture may be doubted, on the other hand. Certainly, Ralph Waldo Emerson's seminal lecture "The American Scholar," in 1837, urged Americans to strike out on their own behalf and pay less attention to "the courtly muses" of European scholarship; but this was not an argument for a utilitarian, practical, or vocational approach to education. It was an argument for an indigenous philosophy and a self-confident, self-consciously American literature. Ten years earlier, Yale had confronted demands for the elimination of dead languages from the compulsory portion of the undergraduate curriculum. The Yale Report, published in 1829, defended traditional classical education; indeed, it was the most famous defense to be proffered in the pre–Civil War period. Yet the Yale president, Jeremiah Day, did not repudiate modern subjects: besides navigation, Yale taught chemistry, mineralogy, geology, and political economy. What was repudiated was not a particular content but a business-oriented scheme of instruction. Geometry and astronomy had always had a place in a liberal education; at Cambridge, indeed, students were required until the mid-nineteenth century to take the final mathematical exam before they proceeded to study classics. (At Oxford, characteristically, the sequence was the other way around.)

Curricular Conflicts; Poetry and Science

The place where liberal education was—largely—to take place was not much contested. It is accurate enough to think of pre–Civil War American higher education as collegiate and to date the rise of the research university from the foundation of Johns Hopkins in 1876. Preparatory schools got young men ready for college, and in college they got a liberal education. Just what constituted liberal education was another matter. Moreover, when one knew what the curriculum contained—if that was what the question of what constituted a liberal education meant—that did not answer the further question of what it was for. The thought I want to offer, which is only half-original, is that the curriculum embodied an ideal of cultivation that had a clearly religious background and that has since retained a dilutedly religious quality. I do not so much mean that many American colleges set out to supply one or another Protestant sect with a supply of educated ministers, though they certainly did. An education intended to inculcate "liberal and comprehensive views" was not narrowly religious. It was, however, intended to give its beneficiaries something one might call ownership of a distinctively Christian culture. With the retreat of sectarianism and the rise of secular education, the object of devotion was not the truths of biblical Christianity so much as the cultural values embodied in great literature.

Arguments over "the canon" in the last dozen years mimic amusingly the arguments that occurred in the late nineteenth century when modern literature in English was fighting its way into a curriculum in which literary studies had always been dominated by the classics. The question whether to substitute *Paradise Lost* for the *Iliad* is not obviously one that must provoke fury, any more than the question whether to save unused bread after the celebration of communion must provoke fury. But churches have remained separated from one another over the reservation of the host, and professors have thought that liberal education stood or fell with the standing of non-vernacular literature. Meanwhile, another argument, elegantly chronicled in W. B. Carnochan's *The Battleground of the Curriculum*, was going on, which was essentially an argument over the merits of specialization versus the virtues of a general education.[6] This could be, and often was, presented as a choice between a general and literary education on the one hand and a deeper, more specialized, and scientific education on the other. This did not raise only the familiar issue of the place of science versus the place of literature in liberal education. It also raised—as early as the 1840s—a question that still puzzles universities and colleges today. A general, literary education is better given by a scholar than by an ignoramus. A literary scholar is—it has optimistically been thought—naturally and happily a teacher; was it so obvious that a scientist, eager to conduct research, would wish also to teach his subject to unskilled neophytes?

To add more confusion to the confused scene, even before the Civil War there were many voices raised in defense of avowedly nonliberal education; and a more narrowly vocational training was indeed provided by the first state colleges devoted to "agricultural and mechanical science." Or, rather, they set out to provide such a training, but until the last quarter of the nineteenth century had an extremely checkered career. For one thing, state legislatures were unwilling to finance them at a reasonable level; even the least luxurious provision for the basic chemistry and biology that a serious interest in scientific farming implied was beyond the imagination of legislators and taxpayers. For another, the enterprise suffered from divided aims. Was it to educate scientifically minded farmers and mechanics, or was it to provide a general education to men who would not enter the learned professions but would earn their living on the land or in business? The first goal did not appeal to practically minded critics who thought that the skills of any occupation were best acquired on the job; the second goal did not appeal to critics of liberal education, since it seemed to be the extension of liberal education to people to whom it would do no good at all. Both versions of the enterprise also suffered from the fact that there were so few high schools available for the potential students at such colleges. Preparatory schools existed to prepare young men to go to college, but precious few public high schools did. There were exceptions—Jefferson's beloved University of Virginia was a state university; it was secular; and it provided a variety of courses of study from which students might choose. But even the University of Virginia had terrible difficulty attracting students who could benefit from higher education, and its intellectual standards were for many years lamentably low.

The state colleges as a class of institution were rescued by a combination of circumstances. One was the availability of money after the Morrill Acts of 1862 and 1890 provided a sufficient amount of federal lands to support state colleges, and especially after the second act provided for their receiving predictable annual appropriations. More importantly, perhaps, they benefited from the general growth of the American economy after the Civil War.

It may appear paradoxical, although it is hardly so in fact, that colleges whose origins lay in the need to train scientific farmers and mechanics flourished at just the moment that urban colleges began to flourish, too. In both cases, however, the possibility arose because money became available just at the time that a new clientele arose, one that challenged the traditional belief that college education was only for the elite.

Three other developments are worth noticing before we return to the high theoretical issue of the virtues of science and the virtues of poetry as foundations of a liberal education. The first is the rise of graduate education. Unlike Britain, the United States took to the German model of university education with gusto. What excited American visitors to Germany was the graduate seminar. In the United States, there was nowhere to touch Berlin, Jena, Tübingen, or Heidelberg; nor was there anywhere where advanced research in medicine could be pursued. To Germany, therefore, went a stream of young men who came back to launch American graduate education, including G. S. Hall, who became the first president of Clark University; Charles W. Eliot, who revitalized Harvard from his appointment in 1869; Andrew White, who created Cornell; and Daniel Gilman, who had the greatest impact of anyone because he made such a success of Johns Hopkins from the moment it opened in 1876. Because so much of modern university education takes place in graduate school, the rise of graduate education is not wholly irrelevant to the question of what a modern liberal education is for and where it can be had. But in its origins, it was part of the revolt against the liberally educating liberal arts college. The first nonhonorary PhD was given by Yale in 1860; by 1918, some five hundred a year were being awarded nationally. Late twentieth-century students will probably not wish to know that John Dewey received a PhD from Johns Hopkins after two years of study—the standard timescale—and that his dissertation took only five weeks of his final semester to write. The modern semipermanent graduate career is a very recent development, and one that we may hope is already on the way out.

The second is the rise of education for women. In spite of the fact that Oberlin College was coeducational as early as 1833, there was, in the first half of the nineteenth century, almost no opportunity for women to pursue genuinely postsecondary studies. Most "female seminaries" were essentially high schools, and their intellectual standards unrigorous. Only after the Civil War did matters change, and then quite swiftly. Wellesley, Smith, and Vassar colleges date from the 1860s and 1870s; older establishments such as Mount Holyoke and Bryn Mawr began to raise their standards. Radcliffe and Barnard were established adjacent to Harvard and Columbia, while midwestern and western institutions either became coeducational or began as coeducational institutions from their foundation. Some of the commentary on female education was—appropriately—perfectly hysterical. Men who ought to have known better announced that the effect of excessive study would be neurosis and sterility; racial degeneration would be inevitable if upper-class women undertook studies that would result in their having fewer children than they ought to have for the well-being of the nation.[7] Once again, the relevance of women's education to liberal education is much like that of the movement for state colleges. The public thought that it was pointless to educate either workingmen or women beyond what the needs of their future careers as workers and wives dictated.

The third is the opening of higher education to black Americans. The usual objection to educating black Americans was, of course, that a man whose role in the world was to hoe and plow had no need of an education at all, let alone higher education. Like most American colleges in their early years, only more so, black colleges were chronically underfunded and usually short-lived. Interestingly enough, two black Americans—Edward Jones and John Russwurm—graduated from Amherst and Bowdoin in 1826, some fifteen years before Oberlin awarded the first three bachelor's degrees to women. Few pre–Civil War black colleges survived into the twentieth century; the best known is Lincoln University in Philadelphia. After the Civil War, the Freedmen's Bureau and a number of northern missionary societies set out to establish colleges for the emancipated Negro population—including Fisk, Morehouse, and Howard. As with those who wanted to found colleges for women, the founders of black colleges wanted to provide for blacks an education indistinguishable from the education that whites found acceptable. The reality, however, was that the inadequacy of the secondary education available to black students was so marked that only Fisk and Howard University were able to teach anything resembling the traditional liberal arts syllabus.

As they did over other aspects of black emancipation, Booker T. Washington and W.E.B. Du Bois quarreled over the conclusions to be drawn from this state of affairs. Washington thought it would be easier to gain white support for black education if the education of black Americans was confined to practical subjects. Du Bois thought that this was a cowardly concession to white prejudice. Again, the relevance of this piece of history to our topic is only that it shows a familiar argument in yet another setting. The one final point to be made is that in the last third of the nineteenth century, the demand for higher education gathered strength. By the time the United States had entered World War I, there were 350,000 students in some form of higher education. This was only some 4 percent of the age group, but it was three times as high a percentage as in Britain, and it was a period when only 7 percent of the population went to school after the age of fourteen.

I conclude this account of the origins of our contemporary hopes and uncertainties with a last look at the claimed preeminence of literary studies in a liberal education. To do this, I draw on Mill and Arnold, the two preeminent liberals who made "culture" their subject. Mill never had the impact in the United States that he had in Britain and France, but even in an American context, he epitomized reforming, public-spirited, secular, and democratic values. Arnold, the purveyor of "sweetness and light," was in both countries contrasted with the man whom Charles Eliot Norton described as an "intellectual iceberg." Those who thought Mill represented "science" and that science stood for progress preferred the iceberg. In the early 1880s, the students of G. S. Morris at the University of Michigan complained of their diet of German idealism and Christian moral uplift, and expressed the suspicion that their teacher did not tackle Mill and Herbert Spencer because he dared not. Arnold reinforced American anxiety about the uncultured quality of American life, about the hostility of self-made men to "college men," and about the hold of old-fashioned Calvinism on colleges and universities. Both Mill and Arnold had the United States very much in mind while writing about the prospects of late nineteenth-century Britain, and both saw the United States as the place where the compatibility of liberalism and high culture would be put to the crucial test. Only Arnold ever visited, several times.

To my earlier question whether the term "liberal" means the same when it qualifies "education" as it does when it qualifies "anxieties," Mill and Arnold return different answers. Mill's conception of an adequate liberal education was tailored to his politics. The self-aware, self-creating hero or heroine of *On Liberty* sets the standard by which liberal education is to be judged. Mill took pains to say that such a creature will appreciate many of the things that reflective conservatives have valued, whether this is an appreciation of the natural world, an affection for traditional forms of behavior, or an acceptance of the importance of authority in cultural and intellectual matters. (These attempts to proffer an olive branch to conservatives fell flat; Mill's observation in *Considerations on Representative Government* that the Conservative Party was "by the law of its being, the stupidest party" gave too much offense.)[8] Still, just as Mill insisted in *Representative Government* that democracy had no need of "a party of Order" and "a party of Progress," because order was no more than a precondition of progress, so the "conservative" elements of character are all ingredients in a life built around the ideal of autonomy.

Arnold is harder to pin down. At times he seems to be opposing the values of culture to the values of liberalism; this is certainly true when culture is understood as a subordination of our own judgments to "the best that is thought and written in the world," and liberalism is understood as one of the laissez-faire enthusiasms of mid-Victorian British governments. This is the Arnold to whom late twentieth-century defenders of high culture so frequently appeal. They are quieter than Arnold was about the fact that "sweetness and light" are in opposition to commerce and to Protestant self-abnegation; but they approve of his emphasis on the disciplinary effects of high culture. More importantly, Arnold suggests that it is an inadequate, thin, and ultimately self-destructive liberalism that confines government to matters of economic management—a matter on which he and Mill were as one, though they had different ideas about how governments might express their concern with culture. A concern for the culture of all its people is a proper concern for a liberal political order. In that view, a cultivated liberal is not only a cultivated person but also a better liberal. It still remains true, however, that the connection between education and liberalism is, so to speak, an external one. The cultivation that a liberal education provides corrects and restrains the bleaker and more utilitarian tendencies of the politically liberal mind.

Mill wrote about culture in terms of his famous opposition between Bentham and Coleridge. He painted what he saw as the two main conflicting tendencies of the age as a conflict between two representative figures: the utilitarian philosopher, political theorist, and legal reformer Jeremy Bentham and the poet, philosopher of religion, and cultural critic Samuel Taylor Coleridge. Bentham was, in Mill's eyes, the man who epitomized the eighteenth-century Enlightenment: analytical, reform minded, critical of existing institutions, contemptuous of what he called "unexamined generalities." Coleridge epitomized the nineteenth-century Romantic reaction against this excessive rationalism: discursive, historic minded, reform minded too, but in a conservative fashion that involved recalling the English to their own traditions. In what Bentham had dismissed as unexamined generalities, Coleridge found the deep wisdom of the human race waiting to be elicited. It was true, said Mill, that Coleridge's views on economics were those of an "arrant driveller," but Coleridge's understanding of how a society held together, what its people needed to know, and where it might draw its spiritual sustenance was infinitely superior to Bentham's—indeed, Coleridge understood the subject, and to Bentham it was a blank. What Coleridge offered, as Mill well understood, was a theory of culture. It sustained a theory of education and announced the need for a learned class—what Coleridge coined the term "clerisy" to describe—who could serve the functions of a learned clergy but on a secular, or at least a nonsectarian, basis.

What Mill drew from Coleridge's work was the thought that there might exist a form of cultural authority that would transcend political authority in the narrowest sense and yet would sustain it, and that would be simultaneously intellectual and emotional. In part, this was to draw on Shelley's well-known claim that poets were the "unacknowledged legislators of mankind"; in part it was to take up Coleridge's insistence that the state could not secure a willing and intelligent obedience unless it embodied a national spirit, a sentiment of unity, and attachment to a particular national culture. This was, though Mill never developed the idea, potentially an elegant way around the problems posed by what was later baptized "multiculturalism." For it allowed a liberal nationalist to acknowledge with pleasure the multiplicity of different cultures in the world and to encourage their expression in a national setting, while also suggesting that a plurality of more local cultures in a society would need some form of appropriate political expression, too. Looking forward from Mill in the 1830s and 1840s to ourselves a century and a half later, it appears that Mill reverses the implications that John Rawls or Ronald Dworkin draw from the fact of cultural plurality. They claim that the state must be "neutral" with respect to all those cultural allegiances that do not themselves amount to attacks on a liberal state. Their reasons are good ones—primarily that state incursions into religious or cultural allegiances cause misery, alienate the victims, and do little good to anyone else. Mill would not have doubted it. He was, however, more ambitious than they, and hoped that an intelligently governed society could weave together what one might term "subnational" cultural attachments into something that sustained a sense of national identity.

Mill's essays on Bentham and Coleridge were, during the 1950s, part of the canon of exemplary works on the idea of a national culture that F. R. Leavis and, after him, Richard Hoggart and Raymond Williams taught to a generation of mildly left-wing students of English literature. But they never seized the educated imagination in the way that Matthew Arnold's *Culture and Anarchy* did. Written in 1869, it was both blessed and cursed by Arnold's facility with elegant aphorisms. The very title ensures that conservative readers will think the book was written for them rather than for liberals. But Arnold's intention was essentially liberal and democratic; he wished the blessings of a literary high culture to be extended to the working class. For this to happen, the ruling elite had to become cognizant of what cultivation was, and the middle class had to raise its eyes from its account books. Arnold hoped to convert the barbarians and the philistines for the benefit of the populace. "Barbarian" was his happy label for the English governing classes, who might profess a muscular Christianity but might equally profess nothing more than muscularity. They might collect an empire in a fit of absence of mind and impose a rough-and-ready order on the world, but they could not civilize the estranged proletariat of a modern industrial society, because they had no idea what civilization was. They had no sense of those touchstones of human existence—"the best that is thought and said." The "philistines" were the middle-class dissenters whose lives rotated around a narrow sense of duty; respectable and legalistic, they distrusted pleasure, beauty, and the inspiration of the senses. John Dewey described the Congregational Protestantism of his Vermont childhood in very much these terms, and Arnold himself complained of the impact of dissent on American life in his mean-spirited essay "American Civilization." Political authority in Britain was slowly slipping from the hands of the barbarians and into those of the philistines—which is to say that an aristocratic politics was being transformed into a middle-class politics. The leading lights in this movement, thought Arnold, were John Bright and William Cobden. They were pacifist, free-trading, and insular Little Englanders, who, he thought, had no sense of what it might be to be a citizen of the world, to reckon success by noncommercial measures.

Thus far, Mill and Arnold are natural allies. Both, evidently, think the ideals of liberal education to be even more important for an industrial and commercially minded society than for its simpler predecessors. Against the critics of liberal education in nineteenth-century America, who thought a

more utilitarian, practical, and vocational education should replace traditional liberal education, their reply is that just because society offers so
many incentives to acquire the vocational and practical skills we require, it
is all the more important to balance these pressures by disinterested, noninstrumental, and, in that sense, impractical instruction. This is an ideal of
"cultural literacy" in a stronger sense than that of E. D. Hirsch. As for a
modern university education, and for a modern high school education, it
implies, at the very least, the ability to "read" a poem in a fashion that goes
beyond merely stringing the words together and to read a novel in a way
that goes beyond merely following the story—and by extension, the ability
to understand how other societies and traditions of interpretation have
thought of such things. And in implying this, it suggests the need for more
ambitious programs in history, literature, and languages than most high
schools and colleges dare to contemplate.

I want to end by opening up the question of the place of science in a liberal education and by making some last observations on the kind of liberalism a liberal education might sustain. Surprisingly enough, the two topics
are related, and Mill and Arnold show why. Mill's ideal of a liberal education was firmly rooted in an attachment to the classics, as his rectorial address to St. Andrews University insisted. What the classics were to teach was
another matter. Mill admired the Athenians for their politics, for the vitality
of their citizens' lives, and for their democratic aspirations. Athenians did
not confine their interests to a literary education, and they were not superstitious about the wisdom of their ancestors. In short, a concern for the classics
was to feed a concern for a lively democratic politics and for a kind of political and intellectual ambition that Mill thought Victorian Englishmen lacked.
It followed that when Mill asked the question whether we should seek an
education for citizenship or an education in the classical tradition, he inevitably answered "both," and when he asked whether such an education
ought to be a scientific or a literary education, he unhesitatingly answered
"both" once more. These were not Arnold's politics, nor Arnold's educational ideals.

In politics, it suffices to remind ourselves that Mill was unbothered by the
protests that terrified Arnold at the time of the Second Reform Act. Mill
embraced self-assertion in politics in a way that Arnold could not. Mill was
a democrat of a kind Arnold could not be. Arnold's reluctance to embrace
the modern world colored their educational differences. Arnold insisted that
science could not provide the basis of a liberal education. The capacity for
"criticism" to which he thought education should train us up was essentially
poetic and literary. It was also, one might complain, very passive. Learning
physics or chemistry could hardly be expected to inculcate the kind of sensibility Arnold had in mind. It is all too easy to see why radical professors of
literature take Arnold as representative of everything they dislike. If the
study of literature amounts to the establishment of a canon of indispensable
work to which we are to pay homage, any red-blooded young person will

want to dynamite the study of literature so conceived. Arnold, of course, had a much more complicated view of what the study of literature in a university might involve; he had an almost boundless respect for German scholarship and for the historical and philological studies for which German universities were famous. The views for which he is best known applied not to higher—or deeper—scholarship, but to the impact of literature on the nonscholarly. In that sense, it is not unfair to juxtapose Arnold's conception of education against a more aggressive modern conception of a radicalizing education.

More interestingly, and more paradoxically, however, Arnold begat the twentieth-century thought that culture is for us what religion was for our forebears by analyzing religion as essentially poetry. The effect was first to alienate readers who saw that Arnold was announcing the death of literal Christianity and the futility of sectarian differences, and second to persuade his later admirers that culture was religion. Every commentator has observed that the recent culture wars have been fought in the heresy-hunting spirit of the religious wars of the sixteenth and seventeenth centuries. If the point of culture is to save our souls, whether in a transcendental sense or a more secular one, culture wars are just religious wars. In *The Culture of Complaint*, Robert Hughes mocked Americans for subscribing to the view that art is either religion or therapy, and there is something mad about recent arguments. But it is not willful silliness. We are trapped by ideas put into circulation by the Romantic poets, by Matthew Arnold, and later by T. S. Eliot. The residual effect persists; F. R. Leavis's belief in the potentially redemptive properties of the Cambridge English Tripos (honors examination) is mirrored in every literature department in the United States, where "theory" is nowadays thought to yield insights into the human condition that orthodox philosophy, sociology, or political science cannot.

What can we learn from this quick foray into the past? Perhaps the *half-*comforting thought that our anxieties and uncertainties are not new. We have been wrestling for a century and a half with the question of what culture a liberal education is to transmit, what the place of science, classical literature, modern literature, history, and linguistic competence in such an education must be. We have for as long been wrestling with the question of how far to sacrifice the pleasures of individual scholarship or deep research to the demands of teaching, just as we have been arguing about what education can achieve, and for whom—whether it is to put a polish on an elite, to open the eyes of the excluded, to permeate society with a secular substitute for the faiths of our ancestors, or to link a new society with an old tradition. The fact that we have been arguing about the same problems for a very long time is only half-comforting, since it suggests that we may not come to anything like a consensus for many years yet. On the other hand, it offers the mild comfort that our condition today is not an especially fallen one, and that even in the absence of general agreement about what we are doing and why, we can do a great deal of good.

4

The Liberal Community

WHAT FOLLOWS IS NOT MEANT to be the last word on the "liberal-communitarian debate."[1] It is, however, an attempt to change the terms of that debate.[2] My strategy is simple. Part I argues that the conflict between liberalism and communitarianism that the "debate" supposes is a figment of the imagination; many paradigmatic liberals have been communitarians, and many paradigmatic communitarians have been liberals.[3] A sample is offered, biased to my purposes. Though the sample is biased, I emphasize some illiberal-sounding remarks of T. H. Green and L. T. Hobhouse in order not to cheat. Part II argues that epistemological, methodological, psychological, and moral issues have been muddled together, and when they are unmuddled, it emerges that there is no one general issue at stake. Nonetheless, the various issues I uncover are connected, and I say something about how they are connected. Part III offers a sketch of a liberal community and its social, economic, and political attachments, and finds several tensions that could properly be called tensions between liberty and community. In this part, I also say a little about community and democracy, though hardly enough to satisfy even myself.

I

An undernoticed feature of the so-called liberal-communitarian debate is its resemblance to two late nineteenth-century debates.[4] The first debate was over the empiricist conception of the self; the second over the idea of the social contract. One episode in the first debate was the assault launched by the English Idealists on their utilitarian predecessors; one episode in the second was Émile Durkheim's assault on anyone who denied the autonomy of sociology. The implications of these arguments concern us in Part II. Here we need notice only that Durkheim and most of the Idealists were unequivocal political liberals, whereas one of their main targets, J. S. Mill, was not backward in recognizing the claims of community.[5] It is, of course, commonplace that turn-of-the-century British "New Liberalism," which coincided with Durkheim's heyday and with the last years of the Hegelian revival, was communitarian in both its politics and its epistemology.[6]

In the second half of the nineteenth century, Idealist critics of Mill and Bentham attacked what they called "one-sided" or extreme individualism, a term sometimes replaced by "atomism." This was not primarily a political criticism; in economics, Bernard Bosanquet was more an individualist than Mill, and it is a fine call whether Green was not also.[7] The crux was epistemological, or metaphysical, though it carried moral consequences. The battlefield was conceptions of the self. The best brief statement of the Idealist case came in one of F. H. Bradley's footnotes: "Mr Bain collects that the mind is a collection. Has he ever thought who collects Mr Bain?"[8] To put it more lengthily, the Idealist target was what has come to be known as the "punctual" or "serial" view of the self. If a person was merely a succession of instants of consciousness, together with some cumulative memory of those instants, there could be no genuine personal identity.

Mill was a tempting target, directly or through his follower Alexander Bain. Mill's analysis of the external world in terms of "permanent possibilities of sensation" invited the question, if a sensing self creates the identity of external objects, what provides the sensing self with *its* unity?[9] Idealists thought these questions unanswerable in an empiricist and associationist framework.

Their criticisms mirrored Kant's criticisms of Hume, and when they edited Hume, Green and T. H. Grose made much of Hume's avowed incapacity to find his self within, but distinct from, the flow of sensory experience.[10] The connection with political issues was indirect. The Idealist view was *not* that Mill's political and social views were simply wrong, but that even their merits showed up the defects of their metaphysical (or psychological) supports. Bradley was unusual among the English Idealists in thinking Mill's liberalism was mischievous, but Bradley's arguments against it were independent of his arguments against Mill's conception of personal identity. *Ethical Studies* was unkind to all of Mill's opinions, but even Bradley did not suggest that the wickedness of Mill's politics followed deductively from the incoherence of his view of the self. The case was more broad-brush. Mill's system was incoherent in its foundations and its superstructure. Green, D. G. Ritchie, Edward Caird, and liberal Idealists were no kinder about Mill's metaphysics, but shared most of his political ideals.[11] Green was even ready to agree that utilitarianism had done much for moral progress, at any rate when it was detached from a hedonistic theory of motivation.

No liberal Idealist deplored the ideals of *On Liberty*. Liberal Idealists, too, thought a morally serious agent must keep his or her life permanently under review, assessing it by the ideals of autonomy, rationality, and openness to the claims of novel experience. When Mill insisted that his defense of individual liberty was not a defense of "mere selfishness," they believed him. They knew that when Mill based the doctrines of *On Liberty* on "the utility of man as a progressive being," he espoused a wholly congenial vision of the unity of a well-lived life. They complained that such ideas were impossible to ground in Mill's atomistic psychology—not that Mill did not believe in them, nor that they were worthless. Where they differed with him, it was because they were more nearly orthodox Christians than Mill and did not see religion as a threat to liveliness and variety. This, and their belief—perhaps the same belief—in the ultimate rationality of the universe certainly gave their views a different coloring from Mill's. Bradley's demand that we must live life as a whole, and make of ourselves a more perfect whole, displayed an optimism about the attainability of harmony that Mill did not share, as did Green's account of the way individual good shared in the goodness of the world as a whole.

Otherwise, the Idealists' *idée maîtresse* owed as much to Aristotle as to Hegel: to describe someone as happy or unhappy, vicious or virtuous, involves the appraisal of long-run dispositions and experiences. Something, as already suggested, carries over from the metaphysical disagreement; Mill was quicker to look for disagreement between one individual and another, and slower to look for conciliation, than T. H. Green, say. There are ways in which Green did and Mill did not think that the highest good was a common good. Further than that it is impossible to go. They were at one in their view that moral analysis looks at life holistically and in the long term. Take Mill's emphasis on character: in the *System of Logic*, Mill tackles the Owenite argument that because our characters are the product of education and our actions the product of our characters, our actions are not under our own control.[12] Mill replies that we can make our actions our own by making our character our own. It is not the plausibility of Mill's answer that is at issue, but the readiness with which Mill invokes the idea of character.

Utilitarianism offers another striking instance. When Mill considers the objection that persons whose decisions are based on self-interest cannot act morally, he replies that we create a moral character that tides us over the temptations of self-interest. The plausibility of this reply is again not at issue, merely the way Mill appeals to the work of a fixed moral character in explaining how distinctively moral motivation squares with his hedonic theory.[13] A last example is provided by Mill's account of punishment and guilt in his *Examination of Hamilton*. There he writes of the criminal momentarily succumbing to temptation and being reproached for the rest of his life by the better self that deplores his bad behavior: "After the temptation has been yielded to, the desiring 'I' will come to an end, but the conscience-stricken 'I' may endure to the end of life." Again, the issue is not whether such a self can emerge from Mill's raw materials, but what his conception of moral agency, responsibility, and character is.[14]

This does not settle the question of how "communitarian" Mill was. It shows that his conception of moral agency was not dictated by the "punctual" or "abstract" conception of the self that recent writers have deplored, but that is only the first step.[15] The second step is to recognize that he insisted that we develop our fixed and persistent characters because we are embedded in our social relations; indeed we can hardly think of ourselves apart from them. This deep social connection develops the conscience, since we internalize the known or assumed disapproval of others for actions that damage their interests. Mill was also anticommunitarian, but in such a way that only someone who was so impressed by the capacity of society to make itself felt within its members' souls could be.[16] Far from ignoring the reality of community, Mill was so impressed with the community's power over its members that he devoted *On Liberty* to ways of holding that power in check: not by destroying it or denying its existence, but by teaching his readers when they ought and when they ought not to deploy that power.

The third step is to notice that later liberal writers, such as L. T. Hobhouse in Britain and John Dewey in the United States, had no doubt they were defending liberalism even if it was a communitarian liberalism. They were liberals because they justified political and social action by reference to liberty rather than simple welfare. T. H. Green claimed that the wage laborer was to all intents and purposes a slave, and in need of liberation, whereas Hobhouse defended the nascent modern welfare state as an essential support to freedom.[17] The romantic prose aside, Bertrand Russell's *Principles of Social Reconstruction*, although overtly committed to guild socialism, is in the same vein.[18] Neither Green, nor Mill, nor Hobhouse, nor Russell thought a simple opposition between individualist and communitarian social theories reflected a conflict between liberalism and communitarianism.

Several things explain the appearance, and often the reality, of conflict in this field. First, T. H. Green (and Hobhouse and Dewey) said things that seem illiberal to the last degree. Green famously insisted that we could not have rights against the state because the state was the precondition of our moral identity and existence.[19] He analyzed an individual right as representing "a capacity for contributing to the common good," and Hobhouse followed him. John Dewey explained rights in almost identical terms. According to Bradley, "Have I a right?" means "Am I in this the expression of law?" No present-day American reader can help flinching at the thought that we have no rights against the state, and no one who thinks of rights as "trumps" can help flinching at the claim that rights are to be explained as features of our duty to promote the common good. To some extent, these anxieties can be palliated: the state against which one can have no rights is not an actual government, but the ideal embodied in the community's social and legal arrangements. The claim that we have no rights against this entity is less illiberal than tautological. Nor is such a theory of rights indefensible. If one supposes, as John Rawls does, that rights can be claimed only by rational agents who interact with similar agents in a network of rights and duties, one is halfway to the Green-Hobhouse view. I think the view is wrong to leave out the way rights protect interests regardless of a capacity to contribute to anything. Still, it is not indefensible.

The other contributor to these deceptive appearances is the rise of sociology during the last half of the nineteenth century. Durkheim sometimes seemed to think sociology had shown that there was simply no such thing as an individual. If there were no individual, it would be hard to make sense of liberalism's concern for individual liberty. Durkheim's unrelenting emphasis on the priority of society over its members, on the coerciveness of social facts, and his hostility to using psychological and biological considerations in explaining social behavior can easily make one think that Durkheim must have been a political collectivist and authoritarian. The truth is quite otherwise.

Durkheim's conception of the imperative power of morality relied on his view of the connection between the *conscience collective* (common consciousness) and the individual conscience. Unless so linked, an individual's moral views would not be moral views, but personal whims or tastes, which is echoed in the arguments employed by Charles Taylor in his recent work.[20] But, Durkheim never suggested that the *conscience collective* is or must be or ought to be employed on behalf of authoritarian or conservative moral sentiments. Modern morality regards the individual as sacred and treats his or her projects as demanding moral respect. The difference between Durkheim and other moral theorists lies in his understanding of how morality is dictated, not in his view of its content. The principle of respect for persons that Kant enunciated and on which Dworkin bases his liberalism is the dictate not of the noumenal self but of the *conscience collective*.

Mill and Durkheim did not see eye to eye on everything, but they agreed on more issues in social theory than one might expect. Mill agreed wholeheartedly that society had to be a felt unity if society was to exercise moral authority and governments were to be able to draw on that authority.[21] He quoted Coleridge to this effect when he wrote his famous essay on him, lifted the passage bodily for the *System of Logic*, and treated it as the intuitive statement of a fundamental truth of political sociology.[22] In his treatment of representative government, Mill anticipates Durkheim's enthusiasm for secondary associations as schools of public spirit, drops his father's suspicion of "sinister interests," and treats local government and local forms of organization as training grounds where individuals develop public spirit by performing public tasks.[23]

Even on the methodological front, Mill and Durkheim shared antipathies. Durkheim was fiercely hostile to any appeals to social contract. It was absurd to think society could be constructed by a contract between individuals. The very idea of a binding contract presupposed a social setting where *pacta servanda sunt* ("agreements must be kept") was already accepted. But utilitarians had always thought contract theory absurd. Mill agreed it might be useful to think of our duties to society in a quasi-contractual way; we receive the protection of society and owe a return for that help. But before conceding even as little as this, he insisted that no good purpose is served by explaining rights as arising from a social contract.[24]

Durkheim and Hobhouse wrote very different sociology, and had very different moral styles, but it would be hard to separate them on the issues that defined the "new liberal" position. Both agreed that the modern world's conviction of the importance of the individual was essentially a moral conviction. Both agreed that it involved individual liberty understood both positively and negatively. *La carrière ouverte aux talents* (careers open to the talented) meant that individuals ought not to be shoehorned into traditional occupations and statuses *and* that a positive effort was required to find them occupations in which their abilities would be employed to the advantage of society at large, and in which the combined economic and psychological rewards for conscientiously doing their job would be and would be *felt* to be a just return for their contribution.[25] Unrestricted laissez-faire capitalism was a poor background for this ambition; the anomic distribution of success and failure unrelated to merit and contribution that characterized a regime of boom and slump was morally intolerable, and state intervention was required to bring some order to it. On the other hand, the individualism of their moral positions meant that neither thought the state should literally own and run any substantial portion of industry or commerce. Like many others of their kind, Hobhouse and Durkheim were welfare-state liberals, hard to separate from moderate socialists, not wholly at odds with Christian democracy, but entirely opposed to traditional conservatism or Marxian socialism.

II

Liberal views have always had a communitarian component, and many liberals have launched their liberalism from a basis in communitarian sociological theory. The so-called liberal-communitarian debate cannot be what its name implies, a debate between liberals and communitarians. I suggest there are at least four different debates, of which two are not liberal-communitarian debates at all, although two might be so described, but not entirely perspicuously. Nothing hangs on the labels offered here, but for present purposes, we can distinguish, first, an argument about accounts of the self that could be called "atomist-holist"; second, an argument about sociological and moral inquiry that could be called "holist-individualist"; third, an argument about substantial moral commitments that might be called "collectivist-individualist"; and last, an argument about social, moral, and political change that might be called "traditionalist-innovative." The last two will be glossed as a conflict between communitarianism and liberalism by those who think liberalism must be both individualist and innovative and that any invocation of communal values is necessarily collectivist and traditionalist. In any account, only the first two issues are genuinely dichotomous. The last two cry out for resolution by "more or less." None of the four is so conceptually intertwined with any other that there are relations of implication between a stand on one issue and another; but there are affinities stronger than merely accidental connection between them.[26]

As pointed out in the first section of this essay, the relation between conceptions of the self and society on the one hand and substantial moral and political positions on the other is indeterminate. Most of us have views, however inchoate, about human nature and social structure, and we use them to justify our moral and political views. But it is an open question how far our views about social nature and human nature demand philosophical justification or imply a definite social theory. Certainly, we have to believe that people possess whatever characteristics it takes if they are to be suited by the social values we are defending, socialist, conservative, or liberal as they may be. But we may hold views about what features people have and about what suits them without being able to say much about why they are in fact like that, let alone being able to say why they must be like that.

Thus, it is not an objection to Rawls's account of justice that we cannot imagine what it would be like to be one of the individuals placed behind the "veil of ignorance." An individual who knew neither where he or she was, nor what sex he or she was, nor what abilities or tastes he or she possessed would find it hard to give sense to being anyone in particular. The "rational actor" who features in theories of rational choice, and his cousin, "rational economic man," are in the same boat. Orthodox economic theory has prospered by adopting this austere notion of the rational actor, even though it is as hard to imagine what it would be like to be one as to imagine life behind Rawls's veil of ignorance. Empirical remoteness is not an objection to a theory. We make sense of economically rational man by treating his behavior as a limit case, and we can make sense of the abstraction from our present identities required by Rawls's theory by treating that as a limit case of what we do when we set aside self-interest and consider what is fair. To attack Rawls's procedure, we must show not that it embodies a counterintuitive conception of personal identity, but that a procedure successful in economic analysis is unsuccessful in moral and political argument.

The claim that abstraction is misguided leads us to the second of our four kinds of argument, the defense of holistic approaches to social and moral theory. Here Michael Sandel's objections to Rawls's approach in *A Theory of Justice* bite as they do not when the subject is personal identity, though the fact is obscured by the way Sandel moves from criticisms of what he calls "deontological liberalism" to criticisms of liberalism *sans phrase*. The arguments for holistic and "unabstract" moral theory are many and varied, but the possibilities are readily illustrated. Bernard Williams's *Ethics and the Limits of Philosophy* criticizes Kant's search for a demonstratively true moral theory that is rationally rather than morally compelling, and binding on agents who share few of our human characteristics. Kant's error was not that he believed in a "noumenal self," but that he failed to see that ethics has a history; that moral considerations apply to embodied creatures with particular hopes, beliefs, and aspirations; and that ethical demands cannot provide reasons for action for creatures too radically different from ourselves. The message is that we must start in medias res. We must recall the ways in which we differ from the members of other, earlier cultures; we must, in a manner of speaking, employ Aristotle's understanding of ethical argument without Aristotle's finite and local conception of human nature.[27]

One could call this "antiabstractionism" rather than "holism," except that what underlies the attack on abstraction is the claim that individuals do not invent morality by legislation ex nihilo but by striking out from the commitments they find in the language and life of their own social setting. This idea reappears in the recent work of Charles Taylor, whose *Sources of the Self* is an ornament of communitarian liberalism.[28] Taylor recognizes the difference between holism as a methodological commitment and collectivism as an ideological commitment, and argues for the sanctity of the individual via a historical phenomenology whose form is Hegelian, though its exposition is blessedly less portentous than the master's own. Taylor claims that we must accept some form of liberalism; social and conceptual change, mutually interwoven, have made it true that our best reasoning yields a liberal account of the tasks of the individual and the social setting in which to pursue them.

Taylor's political allegiances are not implied in his methodology. The conservative or socialist may share Taylor's tastes in moral reasoning even though reading the same record teaches a different lesson. Political agreement can, by the same token, coexist with methodological disagreement. Durkheim's account of the division of labor in modern society and its moral implications is methodologically and politically close to Taylor's, for both believe that what is revealed by the appropriate moral inquiry is what it is that forms the moral ideals of the modern individual. Both eschew the state of nature inhabited by the heroes of *A Theory of Justice* and the passengers on Bruce Ackerman's spaceship.[29] That is how holistic liberals differ from contractarians.

One last point. The criticism to which *A Theory of Justice* was subjected inspired its author to further explanations and reformulations. Those reformulations move the discussion of the positive doctrines of *A Theory of Justice* onto the terrain occupied by Williams and Taylor. Rawls now says that the conception of the self implicit in the book is "political not metaphysical"; he did not commit himself to any theory of personal identity, but only to whatever would best illustrate the conception of justice to which "we" subscribe.[30] The idea that a theory of justice should seek an "overlapping consensus," again, is a recommendation especially apt to anyone working in the unabstract, holistic, contextual way Rawls's critics commend. To build liberalism on a presumption of ignorance about the good is, in the abstract, very odd advice. Decoded, it turns out to be a reminder not to think a liberal regime will be sustained in the contemporary United States by a mass commitment to the ideal character portrayed in Mill's essay *On Liberty*.

A certain briskness in pressing on may be excused by the need to leave methodology for substantial moral and political issues.[31] These are even slipperier than those already encountered, because the number of ways of being a moral and political collectivist is certainly large but probably indeterminate. I split off an analytical issue that preoccupies some theorists, most notably Charles Taylor, then take up two collectivist claims, one for the importance of certain sorts of collective entities, the other for the superiority of goods provided and enjoyed in common to goods provided and enjoyed privately. I wish to inspect the claim that some goods are misunderstood if they are not understood as essentially collective. Taylor suggests as an example the experience of an audience listening to an orchestra giving a live performance, in which the orchestra's consciousness of the audience and its response to the audience enter into the quality of what we experience. It is not the experience of an aggregate of individual goods.

What is at stake is obscure. Taylor contrasts the provision to a large number of people of some good that each values self-interestedly, such as garbage collection by the municipality of Montreal, and common goods like concertgoing. His invocation of self-interest clouds the issue. There is nothing unself-interested about listening to a concert. The distinction seems to lie between an instrumental and noninstrumental view of the presence of one's companions; six of us may pool resources to share the cost of a taxi while each wishing to be able to hire it for himself or herself alone, and this is different from wishing to be part of an appreciative audience, in which everyone else's presence and pleasure is an element in one's own. But if that is all that is at stake, a moral and political individualist may set as high a value as you like on such goods.[32]

We can now turn to positive collectivism. Its first element is the view that some collective entities, such as the state, or the local community or the family or the church, are the proper objects of one's ultimate loyalty, and certain virtues, such as submission to their authority or a deep understanding of their purposes and natures, are the greatest virtues. Hegel understood the Greek polis to embody a claim of this sort. The individual was submerged in the political and social life of his own city, his virtue a matter of his contribution to the city's life. There was an immediate identity of individual and community.[33] The deeds of great individuals were the stuff of Greek poetry and history, but they were not following what we think of as individual moral projects; they were fulfilling roles already laid down by and implicit in the nature of the social or political whole to which they belonged.

The second element is the view that collectively provided and enjoyed benefits are to be esteemed more highly than individually enjoyed benefits. Public health care may be held to be intrinsically superior to private health care because one thing that unites the human race is the common hazard of ill health and eventual death. Because society exists to unite our resources in the face of the hazards of nature, common provision by a national health service is an apt expression of a determination to tackle a common fate. The individual receives medical attention, but also an assurance that he or she is valued by the community, that he or she will continue to be cared for regardless of his or her ability to pay, and so on. Those who provide help make just such morally reassuring gestures as well as providing treatment.

It is easy to see how the argument must proceed. The individualist who repudiates the argument from the value of a collective entity may insist that the state in particular should not be an object of loyalty, because it is violent and thrives on the human disposition to find enemies. Or the individualist may agree that we owe it some noninstrumental loyalty, but argue that it is more often worth only an instrumental loyalty, to be rationally valued for its aid to non-state-related individual virtues, such as kindliness, imagination, and intellectual curiosity, and thus to other collective entities such as churches, universities, and clubs. The individualist who repudiates collective goods may, in the extreme, regard collective activities with a sort of fastidious loathing, as Nietzsche sometimes seems to have done, or not see their point, as Edward Bellamy did not when he preferred piped music to concert-going.[34] He may more moderately argue only that there is no general reason to prefer collective goods to private, individual goods. Its collective qualities may make concertgoing attractive in just the way it is, say, but the only question about health care is whether people get decent treatment at a nonexorbitant cost. Private insurance and national health services are to be compared strictly instrumentally.

Now we can broach the fourth of my dichotomies. Rarely will this be an all-or-nothing struggle between those who insist on the absolute subjection of the individual's moral judgment and imagination to the traditions embedded in his or her community's existing understanding of their moral and political condition, and those who insist on every individual's absolute obligation to think out afresh every item of their moral system. Nor is it necessary that an insistence on the role of tradition be tied to a community that bears that tradition. Still, most writers who insist on the role of tradition insist also on submission to the community's understanding of that tradition or to community practices in which the tradition is embedded.

Enthusiasts for tradition change their minds, too. Alasdair MacIntyre now makes more of tradition's role as tradition than he does of its relation to any particular community that embodies it or to that it gives substance to. The "Thomist tradition" in Catholic thought is more strongly recommended by its intellectual power and its ability to absorb the merits and correct the demerits of other systems of thought than by its embodiment in the community of the Catholic faithful.[35] This is a more intellectualist and less communitarian defense than one found in *After Virtue*, where it was their qualities as communities that commended Benedictine monasteries or the Icelandic settlements of the Norse sagas.[36]

Ideals of moral and political innovation on the one hand and ideals of faithful submission to tradition on the other do not divide the terrain neatly and do not align at all with positions on either the nature of personal identity or the sociological analysis of ethical systems. What is involved in moral innovation and inventiveness may be as cautiously spelled out as it was by Mill or as recklessly demanded as it was by Nietzsche; equally, submission may be demanded with all the blandishments of Edmund Burke or at the point of the sword by Hobbes. For Burke, submission flows gently from an acknowledgment of our sociability; for Hobbes, the demand comes most urgently from our need to escape from a war of all against all.

The most dramatic demands for moral innovation, Nietzschean or Sartrean, are beset by paradox. They need as a background a general belief in the fixity and permanence of our identities that Taylor makes so much play with, but have to claim that it is an illusion we subscribe to out of cowardice. Anyone with a more moderate taste for change, a respect for innovation, and a taste for an expanded moral imagination can agree that our selves are, at any given moment, more or less fixed. They need observe only that our present selves can always be the starting place for the process of becoming something else. If the method and prescription are not confused with each other, the most that ontological or methodological considerations can tell us is how hard it will be to behave in one way rather than another, or how to find out how hard it may be. Only if the prescriptions are smuggled back into the ontological or methodological considerations—as they often are—can ontological or methodological theses foreclose our moral and political options.[37]

The "communitarian liberals" on whose existence I have been insisting think that it is possible to draw on tradition but to innovate too. They are not radical innovators in the way Sartre and Nietzsche are, but they insist that human nature is open-ended, that moral and political discoveries are yet to be made, and that the existence of some fixed points on the moral compass does not preclude the existence of open options. Liberal innovators will generally be interested in innovations in novel individual aspirations. They may not be interested only in these. Among the options not foreclosed are varieties of the common good and kinds of association not yet widespread. Individual innovation is not limited to experiments in solitary or self-centered activities. The string quartet was an invention; so was the democratization of concertgoing; and both are "collective" activities. Nor are all calls for innovation calls for liberal innovation. *After Virtue* ends with an appeal to its readers to create a community not yet born but latent in the insights of Leon Trotsky and St. Benedict.[38] When we distinguish between the upholders of tradition and enthusiasts for invention, we must remember that this dichotomy, too, will not lie neatly on top of the others we have been looking at.

III

My last task is to ask what one can sensibly say about the liberal community. I cannot deal with the view that the term "liberal" has become so degraded by political controversy, and so indeterminate in its application to Britain, Europe, and the United States, that nothing at all can be said about liberalism, nor with the view that we must distinguish between a (good) narrowly circumscribed political theory and a (bad) larger theory of life. It is not that nothing can be said for and against these views, merely that it cannot be said here. My object is only to show how distinctively liberal aspirations may be defended by someone who has absorbed everything the Idealists usefully said against their predecessors, and everything Durkheim usefully said against earlier social theorists.

The theorist who has absorbed these things but believes, like Mill, that mankind is so much a social animal that he needs to be given some breathing space—or who believes, like Russell, that unbridled laissez-faire will not do but that *Brave New World* is worse—will want to argue for a nonstifling communitarianism. This is not the "dialogical" openness of Bruce Ackerman's liberal society, nor the rationalism of Jürgen Habermas's system.[39] It is a looser, less philosophically ambitious ideal, content to look for no more precision than the subject allows. For all that, it is more eager to proselytize than Richard Rorty's aphilosophical defense of "late capitalist bourgeois liberalism"—or whatever tongue-in-cheek characterization he at present prefers—and hopeful that it is possible to lurch less violently between the extremes of abstractness and localism than John Rawls's successive characterizations of his view of justice have done.

According to the communitarian claim, we each need *some* complicated emotional, moral, and intellectual support from those we live among. The liberal claim holds that this support should be support for an individuality that goes beyond the fulfillment of a social role. It has many aspects. One is what Charles Taylor labeled "expressivism," the German romantics' ideal of a distinctive character whose expression is akin to the expression of the artist's capacities and vision in his art. A second, more austere thought makes each of us responsible for our own existence and indicates that we must be scrupulous about the burdens we impose on others. This is not just the desire to stay off the welfare rolls that animates so many neoconservatives. It is a fastidiousness about demanding from others more than a fair share of their time, attention, and resources, and a positive ambition to make one's own way in the world.

A third, more relaxed aspect says we are entitled to pursue the harmless pleasures and interests that the variety of human nature has handed out to us. Mill's essay *On Liberty* is a hymn to expressivism, combined with a casual defense of the third view and a strong dose of the second. Mill's critics have complained of his elitism, arguing that this first ideal demands too much from those who have nothing very individual to express. Yet, the third view bulks as large as any and is emphatically unelitist. Mill says that a man needs a warehouse full of clothes if he is to find a jacket that fits him, and how much more so a whole life. The image is not an elevated one, and is not supposed to be. Still, the point is not to defend or criticize *On Liberty*. It is to ask what the connection is between these ideas about the individual's moral and social fate and an appeal to community. The answer is self-evident. Unlike Rawls and Dworkin, the communitarian liberal insists that liberalism needs a community of liberals to flourish.

Writers who merely demand toleration for harmless activities do not demand as much as this. They will be content if they can secure the majority's indifference. But liberalism has historically demanded much more, for it is clear that reliance on indifference is dangerous. Toleration for the odd pleasures and weird pursuits of others must rest on something more secure than indifference or it will not last the first outbreak of ill temper and dislike. Without a public opinion committed to the belief in a right to toleration, toleration is insecure. Dworkin's attempt to provide what is needed by invoking the state's duty of neutrality is not as unhelpful as it may seem, because he distinguishes so sharply between the state's duty to remain neutral between ideals of the good life, on the one hand, and the liberty we all have as private persons to defend such ideals as and when we can, on the other. Still, something has to motivate the demand for neutrality, and it is hard to see what it can be other than a full-blown defense of the liberal vision of what members of the same society owe one another by way both of assistance and forbearance.

Such a community would be united in defending the negative liberties of its members. The most ambitious vision of a liberal community would go further and hope for a community where we each tried to sustain the positive individuality of our fellow citizens. We might turn Charles Taylor's image of the orchestral concert to a different purpose. We shall not divide the audience from the performers, but will think of a community as simultaneously audience and orchestra. Each member contributes to the *Gesamtkunstwerk* that we hope we can make of our social interactions. For some purposes, deciding on the town drainage system, for example, this will be a hopelessly overblown and highfalutin image, but for many it will not. Such an image is not the property of liberals alone. The liberal character of any such vision comes in its taste for innovation (the orchestra does not stick to the standards but improvises, divides into chamber groups, experiments with mixtures of old and new, and so on). This terrain is one on which familiar political divisions are visible. The grimly Hobbesian variety of conservative thinks we have too little time left over from keeping *homo homini lupus* ("man, a wolf to man") under control to engage in social play; the disciples of Maistre try to beat us into a submissive recognition of our irreparable sinfulness; the Marxian does not repudiate the aspiration but insists that between us and its realization lies the long haul of proletarian revolution.

This is the aestheticist version of a communitarian liberalism, attractive to Schillerians and enthusiasts for the more romantic facets of Mill's work, and perhaps catching something of what Rorty defends by celebration rather than cerebration.[40] This essay is less concerned to argue for it than to place it in the intellectual landscape, along with the practicalities of the maintenance of a society in which persons are as far as possible self-maintaining, career-pursuing, self-respecting citizens, and the maintenance of whatever combination of barriers and positive support it takes to preserve toleration and the rule of law.

I return to three dry, familiar, central issues. The first is the relation of community to liberty in the economic realm. The role of private property is a central issue. Too rigid an insistence on the sanctity of property takes us back to the kind of contractarianism that Durkheim denounced as morally and explanatorily inadequate; too casual an acceptance of the need to curtail property rights for the sake of public benefits threatens security, innovation, and the motivation to be a self-maintaining member of society. To Durkheim, it seemed obvious that property was both sacred and in need of collective supervision. An argument in favor of the style of argument offered here represents this as an argument within liberalism as well as one between liberals and others. The economic equality that Charles Taylor defends in *Sources of the Self* may or may not be as important to modern liberalism as he thinks, but it is clear why it may be and clear how this view recapitulates the old view that the emancipation of property from traditional and familial constraints was a needed spur to progress and individuality while the later manifestations of a regime of unfettered ownership and absolute freedom of contract threatened to produce new forms of slavery.

Because the liberal conception of community sees common provision as an aid to individual freedom, the defense of economic equality is not based on considerations of solidarity, whether proletarian or other. Rather, a degree of economic equality and some collective control of the economy are nowadays required to ensure general access to education and employment and to ensure that average wages will keep body and soul together and provide for a decent family life, especially if the family is to produce the kind of individual the liberal wants society to foster. Conversely, the importance of *la carrière ouverte aux talents* is enough to make the liberal prefer a market to a command economy, to prefer a private-property-based economy to a collectivized economy, and to demand no more equality than is consistent with giving people an incentive to seek employment and to better their condition. It would be foolish to pretend that this yields a determinate result. But if we cast the argument in this way, tensions within the liberal vision are clearly distinct from tensions between liberalism and alternatives. Different facets of individual freedom may come into conflict, may be accorded different degrees of priority on different occasions, but those "intraliberal" arguments are different from arguments between defenders of individual liberty on the one hand and enthusiasts for unthinking integration on the other, and different again from arguments between defenders of individual liberty and enthusiasts for revolutionary solidarity, the historical mission of the proletariat, or whatever.

Second, the politics of communitarian liberalism unsurprisingly turn out to be the politics of a pluralistic representative democracy. The reasoning behind this has two facets. One lies in the considerations eloquently brought out by John Rawls. To exclude anyone from the process of decision making in his or her society is inconsistent with the self-respect we seek for each individual. Nobody has a natural title to rule, and nobody can expect to rule except by way of the consent of his fellows. This is the principled argument for representative democracy. According to the pragmatic argument, the diversity and changeability of our ambitions, as well as our ordinary self-interested desires, can hardly be accommodated in any other system for legitimating our rulers. Both reasons depart quite drastically from some obvious alternatives, such as the thought that in economic class conflict, the superior resources of time, money, and organizational skill enjoyed by the possessing classes will infallibly reduce the laboring classes to poverty unless they can devise a political system to counterbalance those advantages.

Third, consider the question of constitutional restraints upon government and society. Within our framework, there will have to be, de jure or de facto, some analogue to what Rawls secures by talking of the priority of the right over the good. This is not the place for a long discussion of the comparative merits of written constitutions and unwritten conventions. The considerations that lead to a stress on both individuality and community are enshrined in famous essays in advocacy such as Locke's *Letter on Toleration* and in famous documents such as the U.S. Constitution. The communitarian liberal is unlike John Rawls in setting more store by social and political action than Rawls does. Whereas Rawls sees politics in essentially coercive terms, and wishes to keep government at bay in all sensitive areas, the communitarian can see government as more creative yet still think that in many areas—religious allegiance and sexual preference being two obvious ones—the community may properly foster a respect for taking such matters seriously, but must not require any particular choice from the individual.[41] It is otiose to repeat the demonstration that this will still allow a good deal of dissension internal to liberal theory while drawing a clear line between liberals and their opponents and critics.

In conclusion, two things need to be said. First, this has been an arm's-length account of its subject matter. No one could take an interest in the topic without some sympathy toward the intellectual and political leanings involved. Still, it has been the intention of this essay to lay out a view in such a way that it can readily be assaulted. My own understanding of democracy, for instance, is closer to the "domesticated class warfare" conception of democracy than to the liberal view. Second, it is time to make good on my opening paragraph. Having denied the existence of any general "liberal-communitarian" conflict, I agreed that within communitarian forms of liberalism, tensions arose that could be seen in that light. This section ought to have revealed how such a conflict arises. A viable community is cherished for the sake of the liberty and self-development of the individuals composing that community; yet occasions must arise when the community must be preserved by measures that frustrate the freedom and self-development for which we value it. A nation at war curtails its subjects' civil liberties. A nation at peace may preserve the peace by means that violate an ideal right to free expression. Not all liberal societies would allow a Nazi procession to march through a Jewish neighborhood.[42] Affirmative action is an issue that reveals an inescapable tension between trying to establish a community outlook that is genuinely favorable to *la carrière ouverte aux talents* and a regard for the liberty of employers and employees to strike whatever bargains they can. These tensions are part of the messiness and incompleteness of political and social life, not to be deplored nor swept out of the way by conceptual cleverness. I claim that a good liberal can be a good communitarian, not that he will find life simple.

5

Liberal Imperialism

IN THIS ESSAY, I argue that liberalism *is* intrinsically imperialist and that we should understand the attractions of liberal imperialism and not flinch. But I argue against succumbing to that attraction. This is for low reasons of practicality rather than on high moral principle, though "practicality" has considerable moral force when people's lives are at stake. The essay sustains an argument for a nonmilitary but morally uninhibited global liberalism, *if it were pursued intelligently and consistently*, and for that I offer no apology. I regret the topicality of the subject—I have been bothered by it in the terms set by this essay since the Suez and Hungarian invasions of the fall of 1956.

I also regret that I have not been able more elegantly to integrate my few thoughts about Thomas Jefferson into the broader argument and have therefore inserted them as a sort of intermezzo.[1] Jefferson is, for my purposes, altogether too good an illustration of the temptations to which liberals can succumb, as well as an illustration of the very unusual conditions that have to obtain if the liberal imperialist is to be successful. But he has been so variously assaulted for his views on slavery, his treatment of Native Americans, and a great deal else that a short essay on the pros and cons of liberal imperialism—or idealist interventionism—cannot hope to do justice to Jefferson in passing. My last preambulatory point is this: philosophers argue extreme cases, which is good practice in the company of other philosophers but rhetorically unhelpful in other circumstances. The extreme cases in this essay serve a heuristic purpose: to make one think about what would have to be true for the case the essay makes to be compelling as a guide to practice. Anyone who dislikes the argument can think of it as a form of reductio ad absurdum.

I

Liberal imperialism, or liberal interventionism, is the doctrine that a state with the capacity to force liberal political institutions and social aspirations upon nonliberal states and societies is justified in so doing. Let us begin by noticing that contrary to the orthodoxy in political theory, there is nothing odd about the suggestion that we can force an individual or a society to be free. It is impossible to force either of them to "do freely" what we force them to do; doing it freely and doing it under compulsion rule each other out. That, however, does not settle the matter. Imagine a small colony, as it might be Malta under British rule; imagine the imperial power having tired of its responsibilities toward the inhabitants of this small colony, but the inhabitants not having tired of being a colony. If Britain were to walk away from its imperial role, it would have forced freedom on Malta; in fact, something not unlike this happened to Malta and to some of Britain's Caribbean colonies that found more self-government thrust upon them than they at that time desired. Were it not for the certainty that a savage civil war would have followed, the British government might have forced freedom on Ulster. You may be tempted to object that this is a stretch in the notion of forcing anyone to do anything: Britain did not "use force" in the ordinary sense, but rather refused to go on operating as the ruling authority. What one might describe as a "refusal to govern" may seem to have too few of the features associated with the employment of force in international affairs to provide much illumination.

It is not intended to provide a lot of illumination, only to show that forcing communities and individuals to be free is not an incoherent notion. The refusal to govern forced its former beneficiaries to do without the previous assistance, and so forced freedom upon them. Take an individual case. A man may become habituated to life in prison and be unwilling to leave. The time comes when his sentence is completed and the prison wishes to be rid of him. He refuses to go; a struggle ensues, and he is pushed out the door. Under those conditions, he has had his liberty forced upon him. Cases may be multiplied. A married man is not free to marry; as the unwilling victim of a divorce thrust upon him by his wife, he becomes free to marry. He, too, has been forced to be free. In general, once one has identified what condition it is that constitutes being free in the appropriate respect, the question whether someone else can force that condition upon us is something to be answered empirically. You may say that the prisoner expelled from jail and forced into freedom need only break a window to have himself rearrested and reincarcerated, and that is true enough. We can force freedom upon him, but we shall have a hard time keeping him in the condition into which we have forced him, a consideration that applies with equal force at the societal level. The victim of an unwilling divorce, on the other hand, may remain unhappily free to contract another marriage but without any inclination to do it, and find that his newfound freedom is just about inescapable.

Such examples push out of the way any suggestion that there is a conceptual barrier to liberal imperialism. There may be any number of objections of practicality and morality, but it cannot be said that the very suggestion of forcing societies and their members "into freedom" is sheerly incoherent. This is not an argument that Americans ought to resist. During the American Revolution, there was no settled majority in favor of breaking ties to Britain; it is more than likely that until late in the war, most colonists were dubious about a total breach, unsure whether they could sustain a government of their own if they were to succeed, and none too certain that their immediate neighbors would be less inclined to tyranny than the distant George III and Lord North.

The methods employed by the patriots were not those that twenty-first-century American governments approve when employed by liberation movements in foreign countries—the doubters were driven from their homes and farms and threatened with death or injury if they returned. To these disadvantages of refusing to join in the revolution, there was added the positive incentive that adherence to the revolution was a quick way to acquire the farms and property of loyalist neighbors. By comparison, the African National Congress has all along behaved astonishingly well. No American will say that those who were forced *out* of dependence on the colonial rule of the British and subsequently *into* the republican arrangements concocted by Madison and his friends were less free—politically speaking—at the end of the day than at the beginning. They might be poorer, injured in the war, unsure what the future would hold; but they were free. The change was less dramatic than advertised by those who instigated it, but there was and remains a well-understood sense in which republican institutions are paradigmatically the institutions of free government, and monarchical institutions of the British sort are not. Free institutions had been brought into the world not just by dissenters from the old regime severing their ties to it, but also by forcing a sufficient number of grudging American colonists to join in too. Out of mutual coercion comes freedom.

The cases that we nowadays have to think about, and the ones that raise problems in their most acute form, are those that rest on the thought that liberal Western nations ought to at least protect and, where possible, to spread liberal values, and to do it by brute force when necessary. I want to take two actual cases and one nineteenth-century text, and then draw some inferences from them. As always, my stalking horse is John Stuart Mill, a thinker who was not only the author of the essay *On Liberty*, but also the senior London-based civil servant in charge of the government of British India. Before he became examiner of India correspondence not long before he retired in 1858, Mill occupied the wonderfully ambiguous role of attending to the political arrangements of the "Princely States," the Indian entities that were governed by their own maharajahs under the tutelage of a political officer of the East India Company (EIC). Since Mill was always admirably frank in acknowledging that the EIC exercised a "despotic" government over the subcontinent, he could have made some interesting observations on the nature of the indirect despotism that he himself had operated.[2] He did not.

Indeed, one of his more striking, though not wholly admirable, rhetorical gestures was to dismiss colonial issues from the opening pages of *On Liberty* with the observation that despotism is a legitimate method of governing barbarians so long as their improvement is the aim of government and the result of its activities in fact. Queen Elizabeth—the First—along with Charlemagne and Akhbar, is among the beneficiaries of this somewhat broad-brush theory of government. We ought not to be too hard on Mill, because he in fact gave a very elegant justification of the despotic rule of the EIC when he appeared before the House of Lords committee that was considering the last renewal of the company's charter in 1852. Their lordships were less shocked by Mill's assurances that the company provided good government in spite of lacking the usual apparatus of checks and balances that secured good government in Britain, than by his insistence that as soon as the company had taught Indians the arts of self-government and had provided a proper infrastructure of law on the one hand and docks and railroads on the other, it would be time for the company to pack up and leave. The self-eliminating imperial project was a cleverer political concept than their lordships were accustomed to dealing with. As Mill feared, once the EIC was abolished in 1858, the British decided that the Raj was not a training ground for the arts of liberal self-government but the greatest jewel in the imperial crown and not to be given up lightly.

It is important, though Mill was not absolutely clear about it in front of the committee, that Mill did not suggest that the British government or the EIC should patrol the world looking for countries that might be dragged willy-nilly into liberalism and representative government. In this, he was much more cautious than Bertrand Russell, who several times suggested that instead of fighting one another, European nations should gang up and divide the world between themselves in order to civilize it. Mill thought that no nation has a right to civilize another against its will; what he says in *On Liberty* about the U.S. view that a "civilisade" should be launched against the polygamist Mormons of Utah embodied that thought.[3] Three things are worth noticing. First, Mill thought that *whatever the origins* of the EIC's control of the Indian subcontinent, there was a liberal account to be given of the way the EIC should now behave, given that it was in a position to act—and, indeed, given that once it was the only plausible power in the subcontinent, a failure to act would plunge its Indian subjects into chaos, disorder, and exploitation that would be far worse for them than the rule of the EIC. The EIC may have had no right to be in India in the first place, but once there, it had to act. What is interesting about Mill's House of Lords evidence is that Mill held that *given* the EIC's situation, its proper course of action should not be dictated by the self-interest of Britain, the imperial power, but by the requirements of the political development of India, construed in a liberal fashion.

Second, Mill's view was that even if we had a right to go around civilizing people against their will, there would be a very strong case for not doing it. I shall elaborate on that in due course, but the obvious basis for Mill's assertion that we have no right to civilize anyone against their will is the same as the basis for the argument that even if we had such a right, we ought not to exercise it. If one person can take civilizing measures at his own discretion, so may any other person, and there will be chaos. This is a consequence of

Mill's consequentialist and utilitarian view of rights, and fits in with what he says elsewhere about why each of us has the right not to be murdered even if the world would, on balance, be better off for our death. If one person can make that decision, then so may anyone, and the safety and predictability that is the object of any system of rights to promote will have gone down the drain.

Third, Mill is delicacy itself compared with Marx. Inheriting Hegel's view that history is a "slaughter-bench" or, in the alternative, a court of justice where the only available sentence is death, Marx thought that the EIC was certainly wicked, but no more so than any other capitalist enterprise. It went without saying that men were motivated by greed and the desire to accumulate wealth and that the EIC was organized so as to bring home to Britain whatever could be extracted from India. Just as Hegel held that we were doing the work of God—or, more properly, *Geist*—when our wicked behavior propelled history toward the rational freedom of the modern world, so Marx held that the EIC was justified because it dragged its Asian victims into modernity. By the same token, he thought Bismarck justified in taking Schleswig-Holstein by force and thereby dealing reactionary, old Norse nationalism its deathblow. He was not inclined to flinch at the brutality with which Asian stagnation was overcome. The Left is not immune from the temptations to which Mill might be thought to have succumbed.

A second historical example is provided by World War II. There is no denying that the Axis powers were bombed into liberal democracy. There are ways of softening this thought. We may say that the German people had been enslaved by Hitler and that bombing Germany into acceptance of the Allies' view of the world was less a matter of bombing the nonliberal German people into a relatively liberal frame of mind than a matter of bombing Hitler and his friends out of their capacity to enslave the rest of their countrymen. Nobody thinks there is anything wrong with using force to free someone *other* than the target of that force. If you are held captive by a hostage taker and I contrive to hit him over the head and liberate you, I have employed force to free you, and I have freed you by force, but nobody would say that I have forced you to be free. Only if you had become so beguiled by your captor that when I immobilized him, you tried to remain where you were would there be a question of my having to force you to be free. Only if you tried to stay in the bank cellar where he had imprisoned you, and I had to drag you out by main force would it be plausible to say that I was forcing you to be free.[4]

In fact, neither Germany nor Japan in 1945 was unequivocally—or in Japan's case, even halfheartedly—a free society fallen into the hands of oppressors. Both were substantially committed to following their authoritarian leaders into the disastrous courses to which that obedience led. Certainly, eliminating the bad leaders was a crucial step toward liberation; that is, it was a large part of the movement toward freedom to disable those who could have prevented the citizenry from creating a free regime. It might well have been a crucial negative step in another sense, which is that by disabling rulers whose legitimacy rested on their ability to deploy force successfully, and on little else, the Allies did more than literally disable the erstwhile rulers; they delegitimated militaristic regimes.

Since I am offering these thoughts in a somewhat arm's-length fashion, I ought to stress that I am unequivocally committed to the implications of that last sentence. To survive, a rights-respecting regime must show itself to be as capable of maintaining order and enforcing the rule of law as any of its illiberal competitors. This is not difficult as a general rule; in times of peace, liberal regimes have lower crime rates and better compliance with commercial and tax laws than their rivals. What is less obvious is that liberal regimes are in general as militarily effective as their illiberal competitors. Soldier for soldier, the German armies in World War I and World War II were perhaps 50 percent more effective than their American and British opponents, not because of individual courage, so far as I know, but because of the quality of the military staff. What the Axis powers could not do, and their enemies could, was to mobilize the entire nation to throw everything into the war; nor could they sustain cooperation with allies who were dubious about the relationship or hostile to it. (Nor, for that matter, could the Soviet Union sustain effective alliances.) So I do not want to suggest that it was a small matter that the Allies could put together the resources to smash the German war machine. If there were a choice between liberalism and effective government, life would be even more difficult than it already is.

It is central to the question that I raise—how far can nations with the capacity to impose liberal institutions and allegiances go in doing so?—that the positive impact was more than the elimination of dictatorship: it was the compulsory installation of liberal democracy. Importantly, what was installed was at any rate modestly well adapted to the local cultures—Japan became a parliamentary constitutional monarchy rather than a rip-roaring republic, for instance. Indeed, one of the most obvious reasons for being extremely wary of spreading liberalism at the point of a bayonet is just that it is extraordinarily difficult to insert new ideals into cultures that are very foreign to one's own. At least one element in the postwar success of the Allies must have been the fact that six years and four years of total war had created something closer than usual to a tabula rasa for their nation-building efforts. Still, the locals were not asked what sort of arrangements they would like after the bombing had stopped; they were presented with a new constitution and told to endorse it. More than that, they were occupied by the troops of the victorious powers until it was apparent that the liberal virus had sufficiently infected its host. The subsequent fifty-seven years have thus far been a good advertisement for the Allies' actions in the immediate postwar years. Italy, Germany, and Japan are not models of Jeffersonian virtue, nor can one imagine their populations (or anyone else's) staying up late to read Mill's *On Liberty*. Nonetheless, they are solidly liberal democratic societies, and they got that way by being bombed into that condition. That is the thought on which I want to insist. Many people dislike this sort of argument so much that they deny that any such events as these occurred. They would do better to agree that they occurred, but to argue that they are such special cases that they cannot bear the construction I put on them. So I shall now show why they might be special cases, then why they may not be very special.

So, what reasons might lead us to think my two cases are so special that no general principles can be drawn from them? First, India. The danger, we agree, is to believe that any nation that thinks itself civilized may go around liberating whatever other nations it can bend to its purpose. Kant thought that no state had the right to civilize another state by force, and Mill sounded the same note in condemning the U.S. treatment of the Mormons. The concept of a "civilisade" was one he repudiated. How might we distinguish the Indian case and the Mormon case? Mill's argument was that the EIC had simply found itself in control of India. Nobody had decided to add the political responsibilities of government to the commercial undertakings of the EIC; but having been led step-by-step into a situation where the government had fallen into its hands, the EIC had only two choices—to govern well or to allow anarchy to prevail. Nobody had found themselves in control of the territory occupied by the Mormons, and what was being proposed was an invasion on the basis of pure moral principle.

Second, Germany and Japan. Leaving aside the technicality that Britain declared war on Germany rather than vice versa, World War II was a defensive war. Just as nobody could accuse me of forcing good behavior on the burglar whom I disarm, nobody can accuse the Allies of forcing liberalism on the aggressor nations they disarmed. Between teaching the burglar the error of his ways and leaving him to go on and burgle other people, one should surely do the former. It would be absurd and counterproductive to arrest everyone within sight who struck us as vulnerable to temptation and then lecture her or him on the evils of burglary. Having begun the war in self-defense, we may legitimately end it by imposing liberal institutions, but its origins in self-defense are what legitimate our doing anything whatever. In short, if accident puts us in the way of *having* to act, or self-defense does the same, we may act; otherwise, we have no right to act. The consequentialist liberal is half-impressed; he will want an argument that underpins talk of when we have a right to intervene, and will think that such an argument must be consequentialist and that if it is sound, it supplies all we need without a diversion through a discussion of the rights of states. Consequentialists are inclined to think that appeals to "rights" are abbreviations of more complicated discussions of consequences, a necessary shorthand but no more; and it is from that standpoint that this essay is written.

Consequentialism has no room for the idea that situations are special. Once we have accepted that we are not going to patrol the globe looking for folk to turn into good liberals, we are little further forward with the question of how we are to conduct our interactions with the rest of the world.

The consequentialist takes seriously the state of the world as it now is. Two centuries ago, one could have decided that the best the liberal could do was to mind his own business and leave everyone else to mind theirs, but in an increasingly intermeshed world that is implausible. "Mind your own business" must now express an old-fashioned realism. Realism in this context is the injunction to ask only what we have to gain from any given interaction in the foreseeable future, ignoring everything that goes on within the borders of another state as none of our business. A government animated by realism will take its own citizens' moral commitments—liberal, conservative, pacifist, or militarist—into account to the degree that they influence its ability to pursue the national self-interest; but it will not take them seriously *as* moral commitments.

The liberal who is not quite an imperialist cannot be a realist in this sense. The liberal must say something like the following. Realism is a perfectly possible policy; a state can operate in international affairs by asking only, "What is in it for us?" Clean-hands abstentionism is not a possible policy for liberals. We may try to avoid violating the rights of other nations by avoiding interaction, but we shall fail; if we do not molest others, they will molest us, either by accident or design, or by way of third-party interactions, and we shall then have to form a policy toward them. In any case, abstentionism is not obviously clean handed. Should we let Ethiopia starve when we could help it with grain? Is this not too like ignoring the starving baby left on our doorstep? If grain, why not medical supplies? If medical supplies, why not a few peacekeepers so that the supplies can get to those who are injured in the latest civil war? If . . . Either we pursue a policy of clear-eyed selfishness, or we open up the argument to the question of how much good we should aim to do more generally. To this, the only answer is that we should try to do as much good as possible, remembering all the while that we may need a great deal of self-restraint on those occasions when doing nothing is the best we can do. But if a liberal wants to do as much good as possible, then the good he or she wants to do must be colored by liberal ideas regarding what that good is.

II

This is the moment to contemplate Jefferson. On the face of it, Jefferson stands at the opposite end of the intellectual and political spectrum from anyone who is moved by the argument of this essay. His hostility to overseas entanglements was often and vigorously expressed; his desire that the United States should have no standing army and no navy was notorious; however it was that liberty might spread through the world, it was, on its face, not by means of American aggression against the illiberal and the reactionary. Yet Jefferson not only imagined that the United States might within fifty years be a nation of fifty million inhabitants, but also did his best to provide it with the necessary space by the Louisiana Purchase. Nor was he prepared to acquire territory only by purchase. He threatened the Native American peoples who stood in the way of endless expansion with "extermination" and envisaged seizing Canada in order to chase them into their last refuge and exterminating them there. From the point of view of the original inhabitants of the continental United States, he committed the United States to a war of conquest. The purpose for which he did it was to spread freedom and enlightenment. One critic who dislikes Jefferson's conception of enlightenment has compared him to Pol Pot.[5]

Curiously enough, at the same time that the nascent United States pushed westward into the interior of the continent, the czarist government of Russia began its nineteenth-century expansion eastward, to the Caucusus and beyond into Siberia. For the prudential considerations that this essay is intended to keep in the forefront of our minds, both the Americans and the Russians were favored by one crucial fact—the territories into which they expanded most readily were sparsely populated by nomadic and seminomadic peoples at a much lower level of technological and political development than themselves. That fact, however, renders their expansion uninteresting for our present purposes. From the perspective of the liberal consequentialist, it goes without saying that it was better to bring the American continent under the control of a generally liberal, democratic, and rights-respecting regime than it would have been to subject it to an inefficient bureaucratic despotism. But that leaves out of consideration the prior question whether the accumulation of territory is a legitimate goal, let alone the situation of the dispossessed aboriginal inhabitants. The peculiarity of Jefferson's behavior from the perspective of this essay is that much of his early reflection on politics suggests a commitment to what I previously called clean-hands abstentionism, as though it were enough for American to set about preserving freedom and self-government within the new United States and to leave the rest of the world alone. Reinforced by his prejudice that self-sufficient farmers were the salt of the earth and all other occupations corrupting to a greater or lesser degree, this view dismissed most trade as an "entanglement," and was hardly a basis for an aggressive liberalism that might take political salvation to other peoples, sword in hand. Conversely, when Jefferson imagined a vastly expanded America, he dismissed many of the inhabitants of other countries as simply inapt for freedom. Indians who show no sign of turning into quiet farmers are not to be persuaded but "exterminated." This is infinitely far from Mill's idea of tutelary despotism, and by the same token, infinitely far from the temptation that this essay is trying to make real, the temptation to use military and other resources of a highly developed country to—and the issue we have not yet confronted is that of how far the process is to go—at least eliminate brutal and inhumane regimes where possible and replace them with something closer to liberal democracy, and perhaps engage in wholesale cultural reconstruction to provide the newly built regimes with adequate support.

The one element of Jefferson's lifelong views that we may want to recall at this point relates less to the liberalism of the liberal imperialist project than to its imperialism. Jefferson, like his educated contemporaries, thought about eighteenth-century America in the light of English history and a tradition of republican theorizing that went back to Cicero. In this tradition, there are always two things to remember about empire; the first is that it rarely does for those who are subjected to imperial rule quite what the imperialists have in mind, and the second is that imperialism corrupts republican politics. Taking the first for granted—that is, taking it as read that the history of the past several centuries gives us few grounds for confidence that even well-intentioned imperial powers in fact know how to make things happen as they hope—the second is worth focusing on for a moment. Eighteenth-century Englishmen fearful of the effects of Indian wealth on English politics were no doubt partly anxious only about the rising cost of a seat in Parliament, but behind that anxiety was an unease that went all the way back to the last century of the Roman Republic. Rich men accustomed to lord it over the semislave inhabitants of whatever the latest conquered territory might be were not to be trusted in domestic politics when they came home. In the twentieth century, one might have added to these anxieties the suspicion that the brutality of European rule in Africa had come home to roost in the savagery and racism of European politics between 1914 and 1945. The prudent liberal imperialist will be almost as fearful as Jefferson of the dangers of turning democracy into plutocracy by imperial accident.

III

Leaving Jefferson aside, then, the remainder of the essay first of all defends the attractions of what is often taken for wickedness before conceding much of the case of the critics. We may start with a "maximalist" argument: the duty to maximize the number of decent liberals in the world; and then move to a more minimalist argument from the universal duty to defend anyone's fundamental rights when they are threatened. The liberal's answer to the question of what is the most good we can do in international affairs is that we should do our best to promote liberal values and liberal institutions. One (and only one) interpretation of this is that we should try to maximize the number of committed liberals in the world, since they will create and sustain the liberal institutions that are good in themselves and will in turn shelter committed liberals who . . . and so on.

This means that we should do what we can to transform all states into liberal states (starting at home); and since they will not remain liberal states without a liberal political culture to support them, we should also do what we can to ensure that there exist no political cultures except liberal ones. This sets limits to enthusiasm for political-cultural pluralism. There may be arguments such as Mill sketched in *On Liberty* for preserving enough individual conservatives, fundamentalists, bigots, flat-earthers, and whatever else to provide liberals with the opposition they need to keep their argumentative muscles in training, but it is implausible to think that we need bigoted regimes to keep liberal regimes in good heart. An *advocatus diaboli* is one thing, but a diabolical state another. Cultures in the broader sense occupy a middle ground, and it is obvious enough that liberalism is not best promoted by Kulturkampf; not only is cultural imperialism likely to produce backlashes of a degree sufficient to undermine the entire project of dispersing liberalism more widely, but in only a very few cases is the connection between cultural allegiances and political arrangements so inflexible that it would be literally inconceivable that a person would have to renounce all her or his cultural attachments in order to operate political institutions that a liberal would find perfectly acceptable.

Even the most aggressive kind of consequentialist liberal—indeed, especially the most aggressive kind of consequentialist liberal—must be permitted the use of ordinary political intelligence. It is as obvious to him as it is to anyone else that nations should not in fact go around launching "civilisades" at their own whim and discretion. It does not follow that they ought not to—for instance—use their commercial muscle for the purpose, that they ought not to beam in propaganda, and that they ought not to find other means of influencing people and governments that do not threaten chaotic consequences. There will doubtless be states where propaganda in favor of free speech, a free press, the rule of law, frequent and uncorrupt elections, and universal suffrage will be received with the indifference that greets the double-page advertisements for the thoughts of the Dear Leader that the North Korean government places in British broadsheet newspapers; but this will not always be true, and not everyone will ignore it. The effort that the Soviet bloc used to put into jamming broadcasts from the West suggests that propaganda unnerves the ruling elite at least. Where regimes are simply intolerably brutal, the argument that states should not embark on military action for liberal purposes ad hoc is an argument against vigilante justice; but the proper replacement for vigilante justice is not to sit on our hands, but to establish a police force. Liberals who take themselves seriously should therefore try to form alliances up to and including something like a world government so as to have an orderly process for coercing the illiberal into decent behavior.[6]

This kind of consequentialist argument is familiar to everyone; welfare consequentialism is the operating theory of most democratic governments in domestic matters, and this is a more ideologically driven version of consequentialist reasoning in international relations. Of course, liberalism is also a theory of individual rights, and the explanation of what rights are and which rights we possess is not wholly easy in a consequentialist moral theory. Happily, that is not much to the point in this context; consequentialist liberalism is not a complete moral theory, and it does not have to commit itself on the ontological status of rights, even though it will mention few of them and will be insouciant about the rights of states, though not those of individuals. The consequences to which consequentialist liberalism attends here may be regarded as already embedding liberal rights within them: that is, we are thinking of maximizing the number of people and regimes that take the rights of individuals with sufficient seriousness and that hold the values that encourage this. What is to the point in this context is that consequentialist arguments are open ended in what they require; they may require action or inaction, coercive measures or fastidiously uncoercive measures. Since they require us to promote a goal, the two chief constraints are not to do what damages that goal and not to do what threatens other sorts of damage worse than a failure to achieve that goal. A strong sense of practicality will focus on the danger that an action or string of actions will damage the value that it sets out to promote. Consequentialist liberalism is always vulnerable to the fear that an unduly aggressive liberalism will provoke such a backlash that the end will be worse than the beginning. Head-on assaults on religious orthodoxy, for instance, may provoke worse sectarianism; a softer and gentler approach may diminish it.

On the other hand, consequentialism is flexible. What no sane person would try to achieve by violence, we may achieve by education, not to mention by nagging or seduction. There is no limit to the considerations that consequentialist arguments can properly take into account. And because there is a lot more to life than those parts of it that are best discussed in a liberal framework, it is unlikely that we shall think very often of doing anything that violates the ordinary taken-for-granted rights to life and security of persons that governments exist to protect, unless the governments whose lives we mean to make difficult have themselves done something sufficiently dreadful—in particular, have begun to murder their own citizens on a scale that suggests that the casualties of war will be much lower than the victims of inaction, or have singled out some particular section of the population for genocide. The aspirations of the maximalist will be different from those of the minimalist, but the policies promoted by both are likely to be very similar; the difference between them is that the minimalist will think he has no right to contemplate doing what the maximalist thinks we have every right to contemplate, but usually every reason not to do.

Thus, on my analysis, Saudi Arabia is a society whose religious, social, and political structure ought to be pressured in a liberal direction by any liberal government that has relations with it. Elementary realism about oil supplies and military alliances urges on us greater caution than we might feel in many other cases, as does the anxiety that political instability might open the door to a still more reactionary government. Still, it is impossible to be a liberal and not think that the world is a worse place for the existence of the government of Saudi Arabia as presently constituted. There is undermining and undermining, however. One modest bit of undermining would be to make it clear on all occasions that its legal system, the repression of women, theocratic politics, and the rest of it are not charming local options but deeply offensive in the modern world. Another would be to make more fuss than we habitually do about the asymmetry of Saudi appeals for toleration in its favor while the regime practices wholesale religious intolerance itself. In the same way, the United States should be much sharper than it is about the Israeli government's readiness to act in brutal and unconsidered ways, and should not be deterred by the rhetoric of anti-anti-Semitism. Sometimes countries live up to their duty to nag their neighbors into good behavior; it was a good thing that the other countries in the European Union put pressure on the British government over the methods it used to police Northern Ireland and on more culturally touchy issues such as the right of homosexuals to serve in the armed services. Nagging is the obvious tactic when drastic measures would be foolish.

One familiar objection to this way of thinking rests on the claim that no state has a right to interfere in the internal workings of another except in self-defense, and that every state has a right to the exercise of whatever rights inhere in its status as a sovereign state. That is exactly what this essay is arguing against. This essay rests on the assumption that sovereignty is not a fundamental right and that states are not fundamental rights holders. When we talk about rights, we should stick to the view that individuals have a good many negative human rights—particularly against ill-treatment by states—and one positive human right: the right to free action consistent with protecting the same right in others. States, in this view, have many moral obligations to their citizens, but none of their rights over their own citizens or against other states are human rights, and all their rights are conventional; they are also vastly important, but they are important because well-observed conventions are important in international relations. That is not in contention. The point is that states are, in the crucial respects at issue here, quite unlike individuals. An individual may damage himself without violating the rights of others and is to be condemned for nothing more than imprudence, and not generally to be coerced out of his foolish behavior. A state cannot in the same way damage only itself; there is no "itself" to damage, only its citizens severally. The reality is thus that the wielders of coercive power are either neglecting their subjects' welfare or violating their subjects' rights, and probably both. The question then arises of what violations of individual rights legitimate intervention; I take it for granted that a bad enough neglect of citizens' welfare will constitute a violation of their rights, since it will amount to starving them to death.

Common sense suggests that intervention—which will always be denounced as imperialism by some of those on the receiving end and elsewhere—is most justified and will secure the greatest support within the interventionist society when it is politically and culturally uncontroversial. This implies that minimalism will always triumph in practice. It also implies the priority of humanitarian intervention to prevent gross violations of a limited set of rights—to secure rights against torture, massacre, and assault; intervention on these grounds is humanitarian rather than distinctively liberal, and overlaps with, but does not depend on a liberal view of, the grounds for intervention. Arguments against intervening even on these grounds must be arguments of pure practicality unless they are to hang on the thought that the answer to the question whether I am my brother's keeper is a firm no, that is, unless they are to rest on a very fierce realism. John Rawls and Michael Walzer have always argued that a philosophically defensible law of peoples will rule in humanitarian intervention but rule out intervention to establish a liberal state, and they have lately been joined by Michael Ignatieff. Their arguments have a good deal of force, but one caveat is that if we find that only more or less liberal states will reliably protect human rights in this minimalist sense, there may be little room to intervene on humanitarian grounds alone without embarking on regime creation too.

To see how far a consequentialist-liberalism defense of intervention overlaps with arguments for intervention based on human rights, we can push this argument further. If the rights we think we should intervene to protect include minimal political, social, and religious rights, we get the beginnings of a liberal basis for intervention. By the same token, we get a decreasingly strong case for thinking that the violation of rights *as such* justifies outside intervention. The question whether we should intervene thus falls into a question of the consequences of so doing or not so doing. There are two neatly opposed consequentialist arguments here. The first has just been mentioned: if we intervene on humanitarian grounds and against the will of the incumbent regime, as in Kosovo, we could wreck the local government by intervention and would have to rebuild it. We had better rebuild it along liberal lines, at least in a minimalist sense. *How* minimalist is a good question that is simply evaded here. Minimalism must at least mean that we hardly look further than to the rule of law and fair elections; that is, we do not consider such matters as whether local religious practices are scrupulously egalitarian as between the sexes, what the state of the law on abortion is, how egalitarian education is, and so on.

Conversely, anyone who doubted that a *liberal*, as distinct from just any sort of law-abiding and efficient, government was required to avoid humanitarian disaster would argue that we ought to try to create a government that is in tune with the local culture to the greatest extent possible without risking the basic humanitarian goal. A government may be law-abiding but otherwise nonliberal; imagine a conservative Catholic government in nineteenth-century Europe, for instance. A political system built on a culture in which there is intense social pressures for sexual and ethnic apartheid but a fastidious attention to the rule of law and nonbrutality in its enforcement is not a completely incoherent notion, and if that turned out to be the most stable regime to institute, the minimalist who is a humanitarian rather than a liberal must follow that logic. The prudent liberal who accords priority to humanitarian considerations but does not give up on the wider aim of creating a more liberal world will then think that the task is only half accomplished and settle down to "nagging."

Finally, then, we come to the person whose views about the rights whose violation licenses intervention—*if it works*—incorporate liberal maximalism, and who thinks a state violates our human rights in failing to provide us with adequate opportunities for self-expression, moral growth, and the development of an autonomous personality. That view of human rights takes over the consequentialist's aim of maximizing the number of liberals in the world but dresses it up in the language of rights. It thereby dilutes the notion of a right by making it aspirational rather than peremptory. There is much to be said against doing any such thing; first, because talk of rights is most appropriate when we can show that what we are claiming is something that we can *demand* and that the appropriate persons have a real duty and capacity to provide it. *Non*abuse—abstaining from torture, murder, robbery, and the like—is something we can demand from everyone, and governments in particular, and nobody has any excuse for not meeting their duty. Benefiting from other people's positive contributions is always more difficult to think of as a right, and from positive contributions to the sustaining of a liberal culture impossibly difficult. The Lubavitcher Rebbe violates my civil rights if he clubs me about the head and utters racial insults while doing so; there is no argument to the effect that he violates my rights simply by holding illiberal views on many issues. If he violates anyone's rights, it is by the roundabout route of limiting the intellectual liberty of children who are brought up in narrowly Orthodox households; and the analysis of parental rights on liberal principles is a subject this essay steers well clear of. Second, liberal goals are typically such as to be best promoted by argument, information, and noncoercive means, not only because that is the best way to make them stick, but because liberalism sets an intrinsic value on argument and information as routes to change. The maximalist will always be asking whether he or she is threatening the achievement of a liberal goal by adopting illiberal means. Arguments about rights are less adapted to such balancing; at best, they announce the conclusion of a balancing argument. Third, and however, even when the maximalist has agreed, first, that there is no human right to have our government create and sustain a liberal culture of the John Stuart Mill variety, and second, that even if there were, it is absolutely unthinkable that it would be a right enforceable by outside intervention, and third and most important, that there is such a variety of liberalisms, culturally speaking, that one could not possibly have a right to the existence of any particular one, the maximalist will still want to say something like the following.[7]

Humanitarian considerations come first, both in the sense that they trump others in extreme cases and that without a humane political environment, liberalism is an impossible project. Non-self-defense-based arguments for liberal imperialism will more often be broadly humanitarian than distinctively liberal. But it is a plausible hypothesis that what we ordinarily think of as liberal-democratic regimes are more reliable sustainers of humanitarian decency *for their own citizens* than any other; even if we think it sensible to adopt the usual international-relations norms about coercive intervention—self-defense, first; humanitarianism, second; and nothing else to count in justification, whatever guidance it may provide once you have won—we should do what we can to spread political liberal democracy by all means short of war. And third, it is a plausible conjecture that liberal democracies will last better if they are sustained by liberal sentiments in the political culture; what these are is matter for a different argument, but it seems plausible that they can come in many varieties and be grounded in many religious and cultural traditions. This is a thought on which it is hard to disagree with the Rawls of *Political Liberalism*. One can be a better Catholic siding with John XXIII than with Pius IX; one can be a liberal rather than an illiberal Catholic, just as one can be a liberal rather than an illiberal atheist. It implies that one should encourage liberal trends within whatever cultures we interact with, not that we should imagine ways to reduce them all to secular uniformity.

The minimalism that this essay takes seriously therefore is this: in general, we should in practice err on the side of caution; that is, we should contemplate *neither* the employment of the U.S. marines to maximize the number of good liberals in the world, nor even their employment to maximize the number of decent liberal regimes; however, the reason is not that we have no right to do it, but that it just does not work. It does not work for too many reasons to spell out, but they begin with the difficulty of securing a consensus on policy in the intervening country, continue through the difficulty of knowing how to secure the goal we have in mind, and end with the justified resentment of the intervened-upon, who are treated like children in the interests of their own self-government. Even if it were more likely to work than it is, we still ought not to do it in other than very rare cases, since the liberal values of autonomy and self-reliance imply that it matters that people attend to their own liberation and that we respect their autonomy by allowing them to do so. The good liberal will adopt a liberalism that is consequentialist and unbounded in principle, but at anything beyond the level of agitprop, she or he will be as cautious as anyone else. One further thing the good liberal will be conscious of is that the humanitarian motives that pull us into intervention—a distaste for bloodshed and cruelty—are exactly those that make war so disgusting in the eyes of liberals. It is all too easy to do more harm (defined in physical and emotional terms) than good, and that harm may very easily outweigh the value of the freedom brought into existence. One can irreparably damage liberal values by trying to implement them by force; and a creed that insists on the value of choice is the last creed that should be rammed down anyone's throat. Consequentialist liberals ought therefore to be tempted by imperialism—but under most conditions, they should resist.

6

State and Private, Red and White

Philosophy and Violence: Some Anxieties

THIS ESSAY ASKS some quintessentially philosophical questions about violence and terrorism: Is violence "special," demanding a particular kind of moral treatment? Can a state properly be called "terrorist"? Is there anything worthwhile in the old radical distinction between "red" and "white" terror? It begins with a prior question, whether philosophy has anything to contribute to the discussion of violence in the first place. The philosophical treatment of violence, and particularly of terrorist violence, suffers more than most political philosophy from a disproportion between the inevitable and proper impracticality of philosophical inquiry and the all too urgent practicality of the problems addressed. Every time the Irish Republican Army blows an innocent family to pieces, and each time an Israeli reprisal raid on a Palestinian camp reduces a child to bloody rags, the life of reason is mocked and the hope recedes of a politics based on debate and conciliation, a politics based, if you like, on "reflective equilibrium" rather than partisan passion. It is all too easy to see why an ordinary citizen, not otherwise ill disposed to intellectual activity, might question the point of a *philosophical* account of violence and terrorism. He or she would surely think a political sociology of terrorism was worth having; if it was soundly based, we might understand what drove the warring factions into violent conflict, and that might enable us to see the terms of a peace treaty and how we might deflate their readiness to act violently. By the same token, the ordinary citizen would think a psychopathology of violence worth having as offering some hope of identifying, and then isolating and controlling, those who are too readily attracted to political violence. What comparable promise can philosophy make?

In one view, gallantly defended over many years by Richard Hare, philosophical clarification can contribute something useful, though nothing very exciting. By attending carefully to the logic of moral discourse, we can separate factual disputes from differences of moral outlook. Sometimes people will see that their disputes are merely factual disputes, and *moral* passion will evaporate. Sometimes they will see that their views are not moral views at all, and they will see them as mere expressions of taste or of simple self-interest. If they really want to be governed by morality rather than self-interest or the passions of the moment, they will rethink the morally proper path of action. Whether rethinking will lead to agreement—or enough agreement to reduce the amount of violence in the world—does not depend on the logic of moral discourse. The character whom Hare nicknames the "fanatic" will pursue his moral goals even if the result is destruction for himself, and with him there is no arguing. The only hope must be that there are few, or no, reflective fanatics. If the old empiricist view is warranted, and human nature is sufficiently uniform for few ultimate moral differences to survive genuine factual agreement, then we may hope that if we become clear about what separates us, we shall find that little does.[1]

Hare's critics have observed that the real difficulty lies in getting even the unfanatical to engage in such reflection in the first place, and have doubted whether this is a task for philosophers at all. Most writers gloomily accept that a readiness to engage in such reflection postdates the attainment of peace and cannot be expected ahead of that event. Hobbes can speak for many. Whether or not he meant to say that even coherent speech depends upon the existence of a sovereign power sufficient to "overawe them all," he was sure that the theorems of his philosophy had authoritatively to be dinned into people's skulls before they would do any good.[2] Once there was peace, people would see the point of peace and would listen to the arguments; until there was peace, they would be carried away by self-love, pride, and religious frenzy. Securing the peace could not be left to philosophers.

The example of Hobbes, indeed, shows how few philosophers have said anything both useful and interesting about violence. Hobbes himself aimed to be useful, but not to say anything philosophically interesting about violence. Although he explores the philosophical complexities of basing political obligation on natural insecurity and the fear of sudden and violent death, he does not offer a "philosophy of violence." He was an original theorist of the problems of deterrence; he was theologically unconventional in his insistence that God had obtained his kingdom "by violence." Still, it was not a *philosophically* interesting fact that men feared violent death above all else. It was important, for it provided the essential motivation for peace, but the treatment of the fear of violent death is rhetorically rather than intellectually central to the plot of *Leviathan*. Hobbes's rhetoric performed the task that Richard Hare brackets away—it got people to think morally. Hobbes rubbed people's faces in their fear of violent death because the philosophical demonstration of the laws of nature would have an impact only on people who had been put in the right frame of mind by that earlier psychological move.[3] One might say the discussion of violence was intended to be useful rather than philosophically illuminating.

Conversely, philosophers who have thought that violence was a central part of politics and a subject for philosophy have not intended to be useful. Hegel's "Owl of Minerva" flying at dusk reminds us what politics and law are, not what they ought to be,[4] and it is no part of Hegel's philosophy of history to deny that history has been a slaughter-bench or to encourage us to lament the fact.[5] Nietzsche's political reflections have been domesticated by writers who think that he *should* have had the aim of teaching us how to be less violent because less repressed, but it is hard to see such humanitarian concerns in the text.[6] He was no friend to political violence in its modern form because he was no friend to the modern state or to modern political concerns in general. Nonetheless, even if the modern hero is an artist, a poet, or a philosopher, he must also be a *hero*, and the impulse behind the demand that he stake his life on his quest for a meaning to his life comes directly from archaic heroes whose lives were literally staked on the outcome of violent personal encounters. The last thing Nietzsche hoped to be in appealing to this image was useful. Georges Sorel has often been softened in the same fashion because he emphasized that frustrated liberal rationalists were bloodthirstier in their disappointment with their fellows than "pessimists," who never expected to create utopia in the first place.[7] There, too, it is hard to accept that Sorel's hard-boiled insistence that he preached no messages disguised a humanitarian soul. His pessimists accept violence as natural and proper; their ethic is the ethic of a good fight, not of the avoidance of a fight. It is proper to observe that Sorel is no friend to terror, murder, or torture; but he is not interested in "violence minimization."

Recent Arguments: More Anxieties

The list could be prolonged, but it is long enough. In the past two or three decades, there have been three kinds of "philosophies of violence," two of which have operated in the same metaphysical mode and have therefore taken in each other's washing, while the third has defended a toughly utilitarian stance and provides much of the substance of this essay. On the one side, there have been the existentialist or Sartrean reflections of Frantz Fanon, emphasizing the purgative and creative role of violence.[8] In this view, violence is indeed at the heart of politics, and the fact is to be understood, and embraced when understood. This line of thought is indebted to Nietzsche, but even more to the idea that social subordination, especially the racial subordination of colonized blacks, exists because the oppressed sees himself through the eyes of his oppressor. Kill the oppressor, and you not only reduce the enemies' ranks, you add a brand-new individual to the ranks of the revolted. This positive enthusiasm for violence need not rest on a Nietzschean or Sartrean foundation, of course. Sartre's own reflections on violence occur in a work that claimed that twentieth-century philosophy is essentially Marxist, and the New Left was quick to embrace Marx's suggestion that the proletariat discovers itself only in the process of insurrection and that the need for revolution is apparent only to those who engage in it.[9] Whether or not power flows from the barrel of a gun, self-understanding does. The supports for such a view are many; sometimes, as with Fanon, the emphasis lies on the psychological transfiguration of the actor; sometimes, as with Baader-Meinhof, the thought is that a social order that relies on a disguised (but real) terrorism to secure itself against its victims will be forced to unmask itself and provoke the retaliation from below that Marxists have awaited since 1848; sometimes, as with Marx himself, the thought is that combat welds us into a fighting force and makes clearer what the conflict is about.[10] What holds these disparate ideas together is the thought that the hierarchical order of all political systems, and the unequal distribution of the costs and benefits of all economic systems, are, in the last resort, sustained by violence; whether countersystem violence clarifies our minds, strengthens our resolve, or replaces repressive violence by creative and progressive violence, everything rests on a sociological assumption about the way order is sustained.

It would be tiresome to dwell on what often accompanies such thoughts—the attempt to reconceptualize "violence" and "terrorism" in such a way that inequality just is a form of violence, or in such a way that the gaudy consumer society of the middle 1960s appears as a society of psychological terrorism by its very nature. It is worth noting such brazen reconceptualizations, however, since one way in which the costs of violence and the evils of terrorism may be played down is by insisting that violence and terrorism "are always with us," and so suggesting that revolt, murder, assassination, and hijacking are pretty much on a level with the continued prosperity of Macy's and Bloomingdale's.[11] Skepticism about such claims is no obstacle to agreeing that prosperous societies may harbor a lot of violence in their bosoms, as the United States plainly does, or may impose a great deal of it outside their own boundaries, either through the deliberate actions of their rulers or by unwittingly causing upheavals elsewhere that lead to indigenous violence. Nineteenth-century Britain was domestically tranquil, but frequently engaged in violent, though usually small-scale, conflicts abroad; and all developed countries have inadvertently brought the sort of social and economic disruption to simpler societies that has led to domestic violence there.[12]

The antithesis to this thesis, so to speak, is represented in Hannah Arendt's *On Violence*. It addresses the Sorelian or Fanonesque enthusiasm for violence, but its primary purpose is to contradict the New Left thought that power flows from the barrel of a gun. Power is quite another phenomenon from violence, and entirely at odds with violence: "Politically speaking, it is insufficient to say that power and violence are not the same. Power and violence are opposites; where the one rules absolutely, the other is absent. Violence appears where power is in jeopardy, but left to its own course it ends in power's disappearance. . . . Violence can destroy power; it is utterly incapable of creating it."[13] Her account of what power is and how it relates to the characteristic means employed by governments and their opponents is enigmatic, but it suffices to pick on two thoughts. The first is that violence represents "one against all"; the solitary man with the rifle tries to overawe numbers of other people. Power represents "all against one"; the community opposes its will to the will of the single individual. It is thus a failure of social will that creates a shortage of power and leaves people only the recourse to the *techniques* of violence.[14] The second, which follows, is that power rests on agreement; it is because the many constitute themselves a political body that they have a single will that they can oppose to that of any single individual. Although Arendt's formulation of these points reflects concerns familiar in *The Human Condition* and elsewhere, such as her distaste for the human sciences and her insistence that politics is profoundly non-"natural," the contrast between the deliberative and willed nature of politics and the suddenness and reactiveness of violence is not unfamiliar in other writers. The enigmatic formulation of her views sets her at a greater distance from everyday sociological views than does their substance.

Talcott Parsons's view of power as essentially residing in the hands of an organized community and consisting in a capacity to set and achieve societal goals may not be terribly persuasive as a general definition of power, but it picks up one concern of those who want to distinguish private violence from public power, and it does it in much the same way as does Arendt's view.[15] In this Parsonian view, power is creative, whereas violence is essentially destructive; and although he makes nothing of it, it is also important that power is public. Nobody need be ashamed of exercising power; violence belongs with the surreptitious and the antisocial. Ceteris paribus, employing violent means is a source of shame.[16] Once again, violence is special, but this time deplorably so.

The third strain of thought is tough-mindedly utilitarian and strives for matter-of-factness. It has many exemplars. If Romantic Marxists hanker after Götterdämmerung, the ranks of the toughly utilitarian are swelled by unromantic Marxists ready to calculate the costs and benefits of insurrectionary politics and the revolutionary overthrow of whatever social and political order is under their gaze. To avoid clogging this account with excursions into the distinctively Marxian aspects of the case, however, we may here concentrate our attention on Ted Honderich's *Violence for Equality*— an expanded version of his earlier *Three Essays on Political Violence*.[17] Honderich does not need to insist that much of the inequality he is concerned with is instituted and maintained by force. It plainly is, particularly in dependent colonized or neocolonial societies, or in nominally independent states that in fact are dictatorships sustained at arm's length by American or Soviet pressure. There is no need here to balance Honderich's emphases by pointing to the conjunction of economic *equality* and political subordination that was characteristic of the satellite states of Eastern Europe, where it was *equality* rather than *inequality* that was forcibly instituted and sustained.[18] All this can be put to one side to isolate the one argument at stake, which is that liberal political theorists are prone to suggest that violence is never a legitimate means to secure egalitarian social goals, whereas from a utilitarian standpoint, it is clear that *some* equalizing of economic outcomes would increase general well-being, and that the question whether egalitarian violence is justified reduces essentially to a calculation of the costs of that improvement. In this view, either it is presumed that violence is not peculiarly evil, or it is presumed that even if it is, the ills to which it is addressed are themselves so awful that the evil of violence is not different in kind from the evils it may put a stop to—one must presume this to see the issue as amenable to utilitarian decision making at all.[19] Violence, in this view, is the use of a lot of force; terrorism is the use of particularly frightening kinds of force and threatened force. That both states and individuals can resort to violence and terror is obvious. The utilitarian radical's preference for "red" terror is simple enough. Red terror is simply terror employed in the interests of justice and equality, white terror simply terror employed in the interests of an inegalitarian status quo. Since there is nothing morally peculiar about violence, all interesting questions can be translated into issues of the high social and psychological costs of achieving or resisting social change. Again, the one thing to notice is that anyone trying to lessen our discomfort at the thought of violent measures will, even if he or she is of an unromantic and utilitarian turn of mind, want to remind us of "the violence of normal times," the quantity of unacknowledged, removable, but systematically applied damage done to individuals without overt or visible violence, but possible only because real violence lurks in the background.[20]

This position is unexceptionable in its own terms, although insofar as it is a classically utilitarian argument, it must suffer from the difficulties that beset all utilitarian arguments. But the remainder of this essay comes back to this point a long way round, by first tackling two issues that obstruct our adopting so simple a position. The first issue is whether it is right to treat all violence as essentially alike, or whether we must distinguish between state violence and individual violence; and in asking that question, terrorism is a paradigm case. If states employ violence to get their own way, and if states can be terrorist states in just the same way as individuals can be individual terrorists, then terrorism is discussable in simple utilitarian terms, for violent means are simply violent means, and their drawbacks can be set against the ends they serve.[21] It is clear why we can expect this result; utilitarianism has no special place for such notions as legitimacy, and is intrinsically hostile to trying to give a special moral status to the distinction between de jure—that is, official and licensed—exercises of legitimate *force* and de facto—that is, unofficial and unlicensed—*violence*. The question we face is how far we can go in carving out room for such notions in a generally utilitarian framework. The second issue, tackled very briefly, is whether there is any distinction between red and white terror. On the face of it, anyone of a utilitarian disposition will think the distinction farfetched or an awkward way of making a tautological point: whether terror is employed for supposedly "progressive" purposes—red terror—or for supposedly "reactionary" purposes—white terror—is neither here nor there, since the only question worth asking is whether the costs of either promoting or resisting change are outweighed by the gains of so doing. Again, our problem is whether we can find some room for the distinction, either to discredit or, more guardedly, simply to complicate a utilitarian perspective.

Can There Be a Terrorist State?

Arendt claims that violence is an individual or antipolitical use of force, whereas what a state employs is, strictly speaking, power.[22] The first reaction of many of her readers is to throw up their hands and insist that violence is a matter of the kind of force employed, and the amount of force employed, and the degree of resistance that has to be overcome rather than a matter of who employs it or whether they are licensed to employ it or whether they have the majority of the people with them. The British army in Northern Ireland meets IRA violence with official violence; certainly, it relies on its own legitimacy to secure the uncoerced support of the bulk of the population in its fight against IRA terrorists, but what it employs against the terrorists when it has to is violence. Yet there is a certain awkwardness about saying simply that the IRA's campaign of unofficial violence is being met with a campaign of official violence. Or, better, anyone who said that would mean it as a criticism rather than as a neutral description of the facts. So the reader who throws up his or her hands at Arendt's sharp distinction between power and violence may need a more elaborate response.

A fortiori, if we flinch at the idea that what is leveled against the IRA is just "official violence," then the thought that the state meets IRA terror with legitimate, or official, terror will seem even more awkward. The neatest route to good sense is not wholly clear, however. It is not enough merely to stare at such terms as "force," "violence," and "terror" as if we might divine their essences; we have to come to terms with the reasons why we are pulled in two directions, recognizing on the one hand that states secure obedience by coercing the recalcitrant and threatening violently inflicted harm to anyone tempted to rebellion, and on the other that states regard such sanctions as something to be relied on only when appeals to authority have failed. In spite of Max Weber and Jeremy Bentham both, we are not tempted to *define* a state's authority in terms of its ability to command a monopoly of legitimate violence, though we may well be willing to concede that a state cannot be expected to exercise the authority it claims unless it can also command a (near) monopoly on violence.[23] It appears, on inspection, that there are some quite strong reasons behind our sense of the awkwardness of certain ways of talking, even if they do not license categorical claims of the kind that Arendt makes.

In thinking about the state's use of terror, one writer takes a position extreme enough to anchor one end of our argument. This is Joseph de Maistre, whose *St. Petersburg Dialogues* contain a long and rather revolting description of a man being broken on the wheel for blasphemy or parricide. The point of the passage is the ambiguous status of the hangman. The hangman cannot be thought of as a member of society, though he prays in God's church and is evidently one of our species. For he lacks crucial human qualities, and what he does cannot be made sense of in ordinary human terms. Nonetheless, he is the key to social order: "And yet all grandeur, all power and all subordination rests on the executioner: he is the horror and the bond of human association. Remove this incomprehensible agent from the world, and at that very moment, order gives way to chaos, thrones topple, and society disappears."[24] That is, in Maistre's scheme of things, states secure themselves by terrorist methods. To call them terrorist methods needs a little explanation, and in giving it, we can see what is peculiar about terrorism in the usual sense and why it is worth distinguishing it from legitimate force.

The point is this: the activities of terrorists are marked by two characteristics. The first is a willingness to employ methods that deprive their victims or targets of the power of a graduated, rational response. This is what Maistre thought authority required. It is certainly what most people think is intolerable about terrorism. There is a disproportion between the goals aimed at and the sanctions threatened that takes terrorist "bargaining" out of the realms of bargaining as usually understood and turns it into the simple imposition of the will of one party. Consider the IRA. The goal of a united Ireland is not a simple goal—it is exceedingly hard to say what arrangements would be needed to stabilize a united Irish state, because so much would depend on the frame of mind of the citizenry at the point where a united state was instituted. Even if there is less "pure" mutual detestation between the two communities, North and South, than there appears to be, there is a great deal of mutual apprehension; a combination of high apprehension and a belief that it might be possible to unscramble any union would surely be likely to replace IRA terrorism with Ulster Volunteer Force terrorism in an attempt to take the Six Counties out of a united Ireland. The resolution of the difficulties facing union, or rather reunion, would be a complicated matter to bargain one's way through, assuming we had two governments and a good many community representatives at the bargaining table. If IRA terrorism is seen as a way of getting a united Ireland that anyone wants to live in, it must look absurd. Its only purpose must be to so intimidate and alienate the army, Ulster Protestants, and the ordinary civil authorities that they acquiesce in some *simple* demand—such as "Brits Out." Similar tactics got the British out of Palestine, even if the subsequent forty years are a bad advertisement for securing nationhood in such a way. As Arendt remarks, though apropos of nowhere in particular, the main thing that violence is good at bringing about is more violence.[25] Governments that refuse to negotiate with terrorists almost perpetrate a pleonasm inasmuch as it is not the terrorists' intention to negotiate over anything except the question "What will you give me to stop?" This question, the blackmailer's or the terrorist's question, suggests that the terrorist's demands are, as they commonly say, "nonnegotiable" and that the terrorist is interested only in applying whatever pressure is necessary to get his or her own way in something simple and immediate.[26]

In so doing, the terrorist reveals the other aspect of terrorism that sets it apart from ordinary politics. The terrorist operates essentially by being willing to do what others would not knowingly and in full consciousness do. To be a terrorist is to notify everyone else that there are literally no limits to one's willingness to behave badly. The terrorist in effect declares that in his or her moral universe, the categories of innocence and guilt have been abandoned; children may be taken hostage, old women thrown out of airplanes—anything goes so long as it terrifies one's opponents. The two things go hand in hand; the element of shock involved in declaring one's willingness to behave atrociously is both a natural and a predictable social response to the atrocious behavior itself, and the felt atrociousness of the behavior is partly a consequence of our sense that the terrorist really will stick at nothing. The degree of shock may also reflect baffled outrage at something that is a consequence of these two things, and that is the sense that the terrorist is inviting us and defying us to break all our own rules; the Irish Free State put down the IRA in the 1920s by executing hostages, and part of the horror of terrorism is just that it incites such wickedness in those whom it threatens. The glee of ordinarily decent Americans at the bombing of Tripoli in the spring of 1986 is perhaps a commentary on such tensions.

This may be the key to the urge to draw a categorical or conceptual distinction between—however one puts it—legitimate force and mere violence, between the state's threat of punishment and the terrorist's threat of "punishment," the urge to say that power is one thing and violence another, the urge to deny that power can flow from the barrel of a gun, to deny that authority is accepted and effective threatening. For a state to trade in the currency of authority, and to claim the *right* to have its demands taken seriously, the state must work within a rough moral consensus; not only must its demands on the citizenry be demands that citizens think it reasonable to make of one another—the repression of violence, the security of contract, and so on—but their sanctions must also fall within that consensus.

This is not a precise claim. Little of the empirical literature on political ideology and citizen loyalty is precise even where it is considerably bolstered by statistical data, and I know of no empirical literature on just this point. Still, it explains two things that are obvious enough but readily overlooked. The first is the extent to which governments secure obedience without drawing attention to the sanctions that underlie their demands for it; individuals do what they are asked because they think they ought to do it whether asked or not, and their interest in their government's capacity to wield sanctions is confined to the question whether the government can prevent others' taking advantage of their own compliance.[27] Taxpayers pay their *fair* share willingly enough so long as they believe that others who are tempted to cheat can be prevented from doing so; rational people put away their guns so long as they believe that the government can disarm others who might be tempted to take advantage of their unarmed state. We do not ask whether the state can terrify *us* into obedience. The other is the informal convention about the limits of punishment under which most societies appear to operate. Capital punishment for parking offenses would make vastly more difference to the number of parking offenders than it would to the murder rate. It would, however, be quite mad to hang someone for meter feeding or overstaying the allotted time, or for being ten feet nearer a hydrant than allowed. Herbert Hart refers to the idea of a "tariff" that guides judges and legislators in their view of what punishments to impose and how far to go in making use of the penalties provided for. Only serious outrages justify severe penalties. What seems at first glance to be the utilitarian view—that a very, very few judicial executions would have a disutility overwhelmingly offset by the increased utility of all those millions of occasions on which it became easier to park somewhere—is at odds with this "tariff" conception, according to which each crime can draw down only a penalty that is a good match on the same scale.[28]

This is confessedly an imprecise claim. It makes tolerably good sense nonetheless. In the first place, there are penalties and judicial practices that we—twentieth-century, liberal-democratic we—regard as dreadful, and yet understand as not all that dreadful in context. Treason, for instance, was punished in classical Roman law and in medieval English law not only by hideous physical ill-treatment of the actual traitor but by what amounted to perpetual disinheritance of the traitor's family. It, so to speak, "tainted the blood" of the perpetrator. This strikes us as unjust and superstitious, and it was ruled out by the U.S. Bill of Rights, by the revolutionary constitutions of France, and by modern practice; but we do not feel inclined to hold that against the Romans and the medieval English. They held curious views about the divinity of authority, they were more inclined to merge individual and collective responsibility, and they lived in shakier societies than ours, ones where unusual deterrents seemed more reasonable.

A second thing that is illuminated by the thought that governments must generally stick within the accepted moral boundaries in making and enforcing law is the Bill of Rights prohibition of "cruel and unusual" punishment. One might think it sufficient to prohibit punishment of "excessive" cruelty or some such thing; but the idea that we want to prohibit unusualness has a certain logic to it. Terrorists ply a trade to which ingenuity and surprise are all too relevant; a terrorist organization whose tactics and methods were predictable would be out of business in a week. Equally, they have to beware of inducing a resigned acceptance of their activities among the population they attack. The IRA suffers to a degree from the fact that it tries to behave somewhat like an army and therefore murders a predictable group of people; since it kills fewer people than do everyday murderers in an average American city of the same population as the province, its activities can be put up with, even if not exactly shrugged off.[29] Yet a campaign to create "pure" terror would put it at odds with its claims to be the army of a future republican government. The Baader-Meinhof gang caused more alarm in Germany than the IRA causes in Britain not just because German society is more readily alarmed than British—though it may be—but because its activities and targets were so much less predictable. Since its aim was to force the state to reveal its own terroristic aspect, its tactics were to unsettle and panic the government by opportunistic violence against targets it selected as peculiarly representative of capitalist oppression—judges and businessmen prominent among them—but without much apparent logic about who out of a large group was likely to be attacked.[30] There lies another crucial difference from the behavior of governments: predictability and regularity are of the essence of government. Governments do not wish to leave their citizens in the dark about what is going to happen next. Indeed, there is something like a conceptual connection between purporting to be a *government* and attaching fixed sanctions to known demands. Hence, the thought that a government might resort to unusual penalties is not just disturbing as a matter of inducing anxiety among the citizenry; it is also disturbing as a blow to the idea that the government really means to govern.

Two Obvious Counterexamples

To any claim about such a conceptual or near-conceptual connection between being a government and eschewing terror or violence, there are obvious counterexamples—certainly Nazi Germany, and probably both Nazi Germany and Stalin's Russia. The government's reliance on terror as a standard tool of government features prominently in most definitions of a totalitarian state.[31] Such states display no sense that cruel and unusual punishment is somehow at odds with being a government at all. Anyone who finds this obvious will certainly think that I have absurdly underestimated the number of counterexamples. All too many governments have gone down the same track; Pinochet's government in Chile and the military regime in Argentina connived at, sponsored, and perhaps deliberately organized the abduction, torture, and murder of women and children as well as of suspected terrorists; the Indonesian government behaves quite as badly in East Timor. Indeed, governments that engage in such activities may well outnumber those that do not.

There is no point in trying to maintain that the governments of Nazi Germany and Stalinist Russia were not governments—Aristotle might well have thought that whatever they were, they were not political regimes, and Augustine would have had no qualms about describing them as mere "armed bands of robbers," but that is not much help here.[32] General Pinochet's government was, for better or worse, the government of Chile; the Argentinian junta was manifestly the government of Argentina. If we think that there is, all the same, a large distinction between these and nonterrorist regimes, and thus wish to illuminate their relations with their subjects, and the odd combination of terrorist and legalistic behavior these involved, there is more mileage in the thought that such regimes have declared war on some segment of the population. That means that the government stands in a slightly odd relationship to its victims, treating them both as subjects and as enemies. Often such governments have themselves faced domestic terrorism, and claim that their behavior is a reaction to it. This is consilient with one liberal argument against terrorism, namely, that the great defect of terrorism is that it cannot undermine a determined government but does lead to the destruction of civil liberties. A government that behaves atrociously in the Argentine fashion accepts the declaration of war from below and fights with as few legal restraints as there would be on the field of battle. Since its opponents are not, in fact, enemy soldiers but all too often unprotected and innocent civilians, we have the horrors of civil war compounded.[33]

Of course, cases vary. In Chile, there was no justification for Pinochet's savagery; but in Argentina there had been enough urban terrorism to give some color to the government's claim that it was already fighting a virtual civil war, though the revolting behavior of its agents exceeded anything done by Pinochet's forces. No such argument applies to Nazi Germany or Stalin's Russia. One of the many madnesses of Hitler's Germany and the Russia of the purges lay in the way they fought a crusade against their own subjects, none of whom had taken up arms against the regime, and few of whom had much idea wherein their offense lay. At the other end of the spectrum, British civil and political liberties have perhaps not been much more eroded by the campaign against the IRA than they would anyway have been under a prime minister of Margaret Thatcher's temperament. Still, the campaign has seen some nasty innovations in reducing the defendants' rights in criminal trials and has involved a good deal of passing brutality, some cases of what amounts to murder by the police, and the erosion of the rights of free travel and free speech.[34]

The rather feeble conclusion toward which this points is thus that the bold conceptual claims of writers such as Arendt pick up something important even if they misstate what it is. There is every reason in morality to wish governments to observe a distinction between force and (mere) violence, between legitimate punishment and attempts to terrorize their subjects, and there are plenty of empirical grounds for supposing that a stable and productive society is possible only if such distinctions are built into the legal practice of the society. But no conceptual argument could show that a government cannot maintain itself by terror or that it would cease to be a government if it did; certainly it sacrifices consent to brute force, but plenty of regimes have been happy enough to do that. One can see why so many writers have wanted to say that what exists in such conditions is not law, or is not government, or is not politics; but it seems better to admit that it is politics of a particularly disgusting kind than to get embroiled in conceptual squabbles. The point, after all, is less to find a label for it than to try to stop it.

Red and White: A Redundant Distinction

This discussion has been tied almost entirely to the question whether a government can be accused of behaving like a terrorist toward its own subjects. It has taken for granted that no useful distinction is to be drawn between red and white terror, since it has taken for granted that terrorism is no way to secure either justice—which is characteristically the goal of red terror—or order—which is the goal of white terror. To subvert that conclusion, one would have to demonstrate that there was some essential connection between the aspirations of the progressive and conservative forces and the brutalities they resort to. It is not impossible to make a start on such an argument. Jeane Kirkpatrick's much-mocked defense of the United States' authoritarian allies in Central America relies on the thought that totalitarian regimes have no logical stopping place in the infliction of violence; they wish to remodel human nature, and this is an endless task. The less horrible kind of authoritarian regime merely wishes to frighten a finite number of enemies so that the status quo can be maintained.[35] Still, one might wonder what this implies about Hitler's Germany, which was, by most lights, conservative or reactionary and showed no signs of such self-restraint; and in any scale of horror, General Galtieri's Argentina does as badly as any regime of the left. The truth seems to be rather that regimes that live by brute force have every reason to go on using it, since they must create enemies as fast as they kill them and may well create imagined enemies a great deal faster than that. To find the distinction between red and white terror useful, we have to swallow a great deal of contentious sociological theory, which is, at the least, outside the scope of this essay.

Terrorist States

It is time to conclude by listing fairly briefly some ways in which governments can straightforwardly be accused of engaging in terrorism and a few ways in which they may contentiously be said to be so engaging. The first two cases are simply those in which a government hires or employs or sponsors terrorists to attack either its own citizens or those of other countries. The status of the death squads of Central American countries such as Guatemala and El Salvador is, for for obvious reasons, veiled in obscurity; but in each case, they were probably hired, and certainly protected, by the regime of the day, and that, by anyone's reckoning, made it a terrorist regime. If Syria paid for, protected, equipped, and assisted hijackers and would-be bombers of El Al aircraft, that makes the Syrian regime a terrorist regime. In neither case does it make the regime merely a terrorist regime, any more than the fact that governments of liberal democracies rely on armed force and possess large standing armies makes them merely military governments.

But just as relations between government and the military in many democracies suggest that the continuum between military and nonmilitary regimes really is a continuum (even though the distinction between *gaining* power by military force and gaining it by other means remains a difference in kind), so the distinction between terrorist and nonterrorist regimes lies on a continuum where some hands are dirtier than others (though the distinction between states where the rulers *acquired* power by murder and violence and those where the rulers acquired power through the ballot box also remains a difference in kind).

There is, however, a rhetorical force to "terrorist regime" that goes beyond observing that regimes exist that hire assassins, hijackers, kidnappers, and bombers. There is at least a suggestion that these are regimes that are happy to do so and would rather get their way in this fashion than in any other; they are regimes that have been seduced by the allure of the gunman. Now, when one comes to decide which countries belong in this category, contentiousness is the order of the day; visiting Martians might well think that several Middle Eastern countries are in that condition—not *official* Iran, perhaps (if such an entity exists), and certainly not Egypt, but unofficial Iran, Libya, and Iraq quite plausibly. It is not a description these countries would themselves accept; and it is one that has been overused in American and Israeli rhetoric. On the other hand, visiting Martians might think that the Israeli government showed some of the symptoms, and that the actions of the Mossad were not far enough removed from those of Hezbollah to sustain the moral weight the Israeli government would like to place on the difference.

Martians might be persuaded either way by further argument; they might think that the Mossad was fastidiously controlled as a result of its official status, that it was careful in its choice of targets and sufficiently accurate in its operations to sustain the moral difference between a covert war against noninnocent enemies and a mere campaign of terror designed to shut up political dissent. They might, however, find themselves thinking that what was going on in the Middle East was a total war in which there were no innocent parties, and that Hezbollah was fighting as legitimate a war as anybody else. This essay is not committed to siding with one claim or the other, but to making some sense of the rhetoric in which arguments in this area are dressed.

If one accepts the suggestion that succumbing to the allure of the gunman is part of what makes a government a terrorist government, the moral mess into which governments can get themselves is not always far from home; the British government's readiness to hero-worship the Special Air Service is unlovely enough, and a taste for, and a belief in the possibilities of, covert violence has marked the behavior of the United States ever since the end of World War II. It is a vice that is likely to infect any regime that gained its nationhood by force of arms in the not too distant past; one of Israel's difficulties in sustaining its own moral principles is just that Irgun and the Stern

Gang were successful. It is doubtful whether the visiting Martians would think any government absolutely immune from at least the temptation.[36]

War and "Official Terrorism"

Finally, there is "ordinary" warfare. This is commonly taken to be a paradigm of what terrorism is not; it is violent, but it is overt, legitimate, directed against combatants, started and finished by legally recognizable acts, and so on. But this all supposes that governments do in fact manage to sustain all these crucial differences, and in the twentieth century there is no evidence that they do or that they have seriously intended to. "Total war" is, on the face of it, terrorism under the aspect of war; the British firebombings of Hamburg and Dresden were deliberate attempts to break civilian morale by killing as many noncombatants as possible. It was not a matter of arguing that munitions workers in Hamburg were as important to the war effort as soldiers on the Russian front and therefore legitimate targets, though it is sometimes passed off in that way. It was a deliberate attempt to erase a whole city, and that is to say that it was a deliberate attempt to massacre a large civilian population. President Truman's justification of the destruction of Hiroshima and Nagasaki, like the British defenses of the firebombing of Hamburg and Dresden, relied on the consequentialist argument that fewer people got killed that way than would have got killed if the war had been allowed to go on. Nonetheless, this was a defense of a massacre of the innocent, and thus a defense of essentially terrorist methods. It does not follow—except in some interpretations of just-war theory—that the defense is unacceptable.[37]

Couching things in those terms is, of course, rhetorically impossible to square with the repeated insistence of current Western governments that it is illicit to meet terrorism with terrorism and that the resort to terrorist methods is absolutely wrong. So used are we to the picture of the terrorist as *essentially* private and engaged in some revolutionary cause on the red end of the spectrum that we find it a wrench to contemplate the idea that terrorism can also be massive in scale, officially organized, delivered by people in uniform, subject to legally certified orders, and so on. But all the usual features of terrorism apply to total war; it is waged without distinction between the innocent and the guilty, and although we have got used to the idea that nuclear war is the ultimate horror of our time, we ought not to forget that its horrors are only those of Hamburg and Dresden magnified a good deal. Burning women and children to death as an instrument of policy is the same act whether the means chosen include incendiaries and high explosives or nuclear weapons.

Total war resembles terrorism in its contempt for negotiation, too. The demand for unconditional surrender may once, on the battlefield, have simply been a way of making the point that the opposing, losing army was in no condition to carry on.[38] In the two world wars of this century, it became the decision that the Allies would stop at nothing to win and that winning was a matter not of inducing the other side to return to the negotiating table from the battlefield, but of annihilating its capacity to sustain the war. Aside from the tactics—it may well be that a better postwar settlement could have been achieved if the Allies had, from the very beginning and certainly after 1943, offered a negotiated peace to anyone who could remove Hitler and open negotiations—the morality of "unconditional surrender" is open to question. In its absolutism, it too much resembles the "nonnegotiability" of the terrorist's demands.

We must now end by coming back to our utilitarian starting point. Does this bring us all the way back to the highly plausible view that violence is violence, whoever perpetrates it, and that whether it is public or private, we can ask only the question we began with—is it morally justified by its results? Not quite. If it is true that twentieth-century warfare has turned into officially practiced terrorism, not as a definitional or conceptual matter but morally speaking, we may still want to hang onto some of the moral and conceptual claims made in the just-war tradition, not, so to speak, seeing them as deliverances of pure reason or natural law, nor seeing them as somehow built into the fabric of the world, but seeing them rather as distinctions and calls to self-restraint that we may be able to enshrine in international law and international organization if we work at it.

One powerful domestic argument for maintaining regular, legal government is that it replaces the feud, private vengeance, and other forms of self-help that not only are frequently ineffective, but also readily degenerate into uncontrolled brutality and cruelty. Once one sees that the international system of self-help that is what war amounts to can operate in a controlled way but generally does not, one can begin to see how states can use force to get their own way without behaving too hideously, but also how perilous this process is and how likely it is that they will be faced with the choice between behaving as terrorists and making a humiliating retreat—or, as in the case of the United States in Vietnam—stumbling into doing both. If there is anything to be said for the philosophical investigation of such issues, it is that it can help us make our way more steadily through this moral minefield.

The Right to Kill in Cold Blood
DOES THE DEATH PENALTY VIOLATE HUMAN RIGHTS?

THIS ESSAY BEGAN life as a public lecture, and I have not tried to remove the informality of style appropriate to such an occasion. The essence of the argument is this: all punishment must be inflicted in cold blood; whatever damage we do to others not in cold blood is not punishment but self-defense or revenge; what we have a right to inflict in cold blood is a question of the rules of just social cooperation and especially the justice of the sanctions required to sustain those rules; it is here argued that the fundamental principle is that we may inflict whatever punishment is necessary to deter wrongdoing and is not disproportionate to the offense; I do not dismiss "pure" retribution as a goal of punishment, but I do not discuss it here. I invoke only a diluted concept of retribution in the form of the concept of a "proportionate" response to crime. The central issue of fairness is, then, that of the process by which alleged criminals are pursued and caught, questioned, tried, and sentenced; in the view taken here, the death penalty raises no questions of justice that are different in *kind* from those raised by other forms of punishment, but that death as contrasted with incarceration may be thought to raise questions about irreversibility that are different in degree. One reason for insisting that a failure of fairness in the criminal justice system makes *all* punishment suspect is that an undue attention to the death penalty (by both defenders and opponents) diverts attention from too many of the other injustices perpetrated in our name. Finally, the essay turns to the question of how we should discuss the penalty of death in particular, and I invoke the shade of Joseph de Maistre for the purpose.

I hope that you will be unable to detect whether I am an enthusiast for the death penalty, an opponent of capital punishment, or deeply ambivalent. You may have your suspicions about where my allegiances lie, but I shall do my best to leave you uncertain whether your suspicions are well founded. I ought perhaps to mention that one of my philosophical heroes, John Stuart Mill, not only believed in the indispensability of the death penalty as a deterrent, but also personally launched a private prosecution for murder against a brutal British governor of Jamaica, with every intention of having Governor Eyre hanged.[1] What you should have no doubt about is my answer to the question I pose in my subtitle. My answer is that whatever objections one might have to the death penalty, they should not be objections to its compatibility *in principle* with any plausible account of human rights. If anyone wants to know only my answer to the question whether the death penalty *must* always and in principle violate human rights, they have it—it is *no*. But I doubt whether anyone does want to know only that. The 65 percent (today) to 85 percent (in the 1980s) of the American people who say in response to questionnaires that they believe in the death penalty already believe that it does not violate human rights, and do not need me to reassure them. Nor will the 20 percent or so who think that it is intrinsically barbarous and morally disgusting, and that it will inevitably be administered in a racially and economically biased fashion, much care whether *some* version of the death penalty might be operated without violating anyone's rights. The very small percentage of the American people who share my professional interest in the history of arguments about human rights know without my telling them that lawyers, philosophers, and legislators over the centuries have argued not only that our rights do *not* include the right not to be subjected to the death penalty under appropriate conditions, but also—as did Immanuel Kant, G.W.F. Hegel, and some of their late nineteenth-century disciples in Britain and the United States—that criminals have a positive right to be executed.

So why do I chase this particular hare again? Partly because of the contrast between the light-heartedness of Governor George Bush over the likelihood that the death penalty has been carried out on Texans who were not guilty of the crime for which they were executed, and the anxieties of Governor Ryan of Illinois, who declared a moratorium on executions as soon as he became unsure that everyone on death row was properly there.[2] Partly because it is a very striking fact that the United States is a country that takes rights seriously and yet refuses to subscribe to various international declarations of human rights because they state that the death penalty violates those rights. Partly because of something I do not myself fully understand. The European Convention on Human Rights (ECHR), which was first ratified in 1950 by a number of European states, including Great Britain, was modified in 1983 to include a protocol (the Sixth Protocol) prohibiting the use of the death penalty except in time of war by any of the states that were signatories to the convention. This would have been impossible at the date of its first creation. Not only Britain, but France, the Benelux countries, and most others as well not only had capital punishment on the statute books but actually carried out executions. The French, indeed, abolished executions by means of the guillotine only in 1981, having carried out the last execution in 1977. The British slowly relinquished the use of hanging, but after a near miss at abolition in 1947, further attempts to abolish the death penalty in the 1950s came to nothing, and a royal commission reporting in 1953 declared itself uncertain on the facts, but inclined to think that death was a "unique deterrent." The discussion in those years never suggested that even if it was a unique deterrent, it violated the human rights of the executed prisoner. Lawyers assumed an existing consensus on the limits of lawful punishment; lawful punishment, inflicted only after a fair trial and a sound verdict, might be ineffective, might have bad consequences of one sort and another, but was not itself a violation of the rights of the condemned. It was assumed that the processes of the law were sufficiently respectful of the rights of the accused and of the condemned.

I do not know why sentiment against the death penalty moved so swiftly and completely in Europe, moved rather reluctantly and incompletely in Britain, and swung dramatically back and forth in the United States. In the United States, opinion was firmly in favor of the death penalty in the 1950s, swung against it to the extent that supporters were in a minority in the 1960s, then swung back again until at present it is supported by 64 percent of those polled, after attaining a high point of support at 84 percent.[3] One needs to begin with a well-known but underappreciated paradox. In no country where capital punishment has been abolished has it been abolished with the support of the electorate. To put it the other way round, in no country has the electorate demanded the abolition of capital punishment and then seen legislators follow public opinion by abolishing it. There are many countries where capital punishment no longer enjoys the support of the majority of the population; in all countries, the number who support it varies quite dramatically according to whether the most recent event in the public mind is the murder of a small child by a sexually deranged adult or the execution of a probably innocent person. But in no Western society has the death penalty been abolished because the public at large demanded its abolition.[4] The common pattern is that it is abolished because legislators decide that it is either not a deterrent or that too many doubtful convictions have occurred, or that it is for whatever reason distasteful, and the electorate then gets used to it not existing; as that happens, so legislators get used to not trying to restore it, and the public eventually goes off the whole idea. But principled opposition to capital punishment is not a common trait in democratic electorates. Nor is principled support for it important in Europe. That punishment *ought* to reflect some version of "an eye for an eye" is felt by many people, but it is not argued for by pressure groups or politicians. This contrasts with other issues that attract similar degrees of passion when they flare up in the public mind. In Britain, there is a persistent though low-key campaign by right-to-life groups to have the rules on abortion tightened up and to have the 1967 act regulating abortion either repealed or made much more restrictive. Similarly, pro-gay groups persistently campaigned for many years to have the age of consent made the same for homosexual and heterosexual relations—it is now sixteen in all cases—and MPs introduced legislation to this effect from time to time. Nothing of the sort happens with respect to the death penalty. Two rather halfhearted attempts at reinstatement shortly after repeal are all there have been. Large numbers of the public insist, when sufficiently excited and goaded on by interviewers from the tabloid press, that sex offenders should be hanged—preferably after prolonged torture culminating in castration; but there is no steady, persistent pressure on the legislature to reintroduce even the sanitized executions by lethal injection that American states have instituted.[5]

This returns me to the oddity of the European Convention on Human Rights. Although Canada and some other not very European countries have observer status at the Council of Europe, the United States cannot do so, because the retention of the death penalty is inconsistent with membership. (Actually, that is not strictly true; as always with treaties that commit states to acknowledging the provisions of a convention, there is room for derogation and reservation. Britain for some years preserved as a matter of law, though not of practice, the death penalty for those rare persons who committed piracy with violence on the high seas or committed treason, a crime that included the seduction of the sovereign's daughter as well as betraying one's country to an enemy in time of war. Even in its present, apparently absolute form, the convention allows states to use the death penalty in time of war, a concession not allowed for the use of torture, which is banned absolutely.) The Sixth Protocol, proposed in 1983, does not go into details about the change of heart on the death penalty, but simply notes that in the thirty years since the convention was initially promulgated, European opinion had turned against the death penalty and most European countries had given up its use.[6] This does not amount to saying that at some time during that thirty years they had noticed, discovered, or decided that the death penalty was a violation of human rights. Nor, in fact, is the chronology of the death penalty's falling into desuetude quite as neat as that suggests. There was a considerable gap in many countries between their ceasing to execute anyone in practice and their abandoning the penalty in theory; the Swedes last executed anyone in 1910, but abolished the penalty only in the 1950s, while Eire took from 1954 to 1990 to bring abstentionist theory into line with abstentionist practice. Britain last executed anyone in 1964—the victim on that occasion, a man called Joseph Hanratty, may well have been innocent, but even if not, there had always been enough anxiety about the matter to make it an appropriate case to pause on—and the penalty was abolished for everything except piracy and treason in 1973; only in 1998, when Britain prepared to incorporate the convention into British law, did Parliament take the last step and abolish it entirely. Nobody noticed, and there was no evidence that either the royal family or our mariners slept less easily in their beds and hammocks. Part of what lay behind the movement in Europe was a change of heart within the Catholic Church; traditionally, the church had no qualms over the death penalty, but for the past thirty years or so, whether the pope was a liberal like John XXIII or a conservative like the present pope, the church has been opposed to execution and has exposed itself to numerous rebuffs from American states by appealing, and usually in vain, for reprieves for convicted criminals on the verge of execution.

Now, it is, of course, true that if we define human rights in positivist terms—that is to say, as those rights that are protected by some applicable convention or other and accepted by the government within whose jurisdiction the question arises—then it is true of all citizens of those states that are signatories to the ECHR and members of the Council of Europe that the imposition of the death penalty on *them* and *there* would violate their human rights. And conversely, for citizens of the United States in the United States, it would not. The situation of European nationals in American courts would be conceptually problematic in this view, though in law, their position is covered by the Vienna Convention. Failures of individual states to take any notice of the convention have recently placed the U.S. government in some difficulty on the matter. But a positive account of human rights is highly implausible. The thought that the human rights of Europeans are different from the human rights of Americans empties the concept of human rights of all meaning. The point of talking about human rights is to claim that what lies behind the positive rights set out in a convention are deep rights, rights that ground the convention rights rather than simply flowing from them or reflecting them. Human rights are what we used to call "natural rights" or "moral rights" or just "rights."

What I claim is that the infliction of death is *not* a violation of the human right of a convicted felon under appropriate conditions and, in the converse, that individuals and society as a whole have the right to inflict such a sentence, but I am also going to argue that this has moral force as a defense of the death penalty only if many other rights are in place. There are many rights of the accused and convicted that have to be respected, and many conditions that must be in place before we may justly exercise our right to kill in cold blood. I go this long way round for something other than the pleasure of performing philosophical arabesques. In the summer of 2000, an essayist in the *New Republic*, engaging in the journal's favorite pastime of irritating such liberals as still read it, argued that the rise of DNA testing in capital cases might backfire on the liberals who had demanded it. *They*, he observed, had demanded DNA testing on the assumption that it would show condemned felons to be innocent; but what if it showed that they were guilty? Would that not open the way to their execution?[7] To which the answer, of course, is that *pro tanto* (to that extent) it must. To remove one obstacle to execution is to remove one obstacle to execution. Why liberalism should be thought to be inconsistent with elementary logical inference is not clear to me, nor why the *New Republic* thinks itself so clever in pointing out a tautology. But the *New Republic* and I are at one on the logic. The right not to be executed—nor to suffer any other penalty—for a crime one has not committed is the most basic right that must be respected if we are to have the right to take a life in cold blood. If guilt is established without doubt and by just and transparent means, the most important obstacle to execution has been cleared away.

Let us approach this conclusion from the opposite direction: the right to punish anyone for anything, a right that Robert Owen and most anarchists have denied that we possess, but that I shall defend. The first step is to distinguish punishment and self-defense; the right to self-defense is the right to retaliate against immediate attack and, by extension, to do whatever is needed to prevent an assailant from immediately attacking us.[8] The (potential) victim of an attack may do whatever is necessary under the circumstances and must use his or her best judgment as to what that is. That best judgment is subject to scrutiny. If you are kicked in the leg by a five-year-old child, you cannot shoot her dead and pass that off as your best judgment; you have committed murder. If you are attacked by a madman with a knife, on the other hand, you will be excused the death of your would-be assassin on the grounds that there was no way of knowing quite what he might have done, and there is no upper bound to what you may need to do to protect yourself. There is no settled doctrine about these limits, as attested by that lamentable case in Louisiana five or six years ago in which a householder shot dead a Japanese schoolchild who knocked at the door to ask for directions, and was acquitted of all wrongdoing by a local jury. John Locke, the theorist of mild and constitutional government, insisted that defending our property in the absence of government assistance licenses the use of deadly force. Someone who set out to rob us might do us worse harm still, and any degree of self-defense is licit.

But the right to inflict punishment is not identical with the right to self-defense. Punishment is what we threaten ahead of time and inflict after the event, but it is not whatever damage we may happen to do to someone from whom we are defending ourselves. We may properly describe the institution of punishment as part of society's battery of means of defending itself, but that is a different matter. The right of self-defense is not the same as the right to inflict punishment. Punishing people is not merely something that we do in cold blood, but something that we morally—and almost logically—*must* do in cold blood. First, the inflicter of the penalty must be authorized to impose the penalty and see to its carrying out; courts are so authorized, lynch mobs are not. Locke thought individuals were so authorized in the state of nature; Hume thought Locke's view made no sense. But both saw the same difference between doing something that could qualify as punishing and doing what amounted simply to harming someone else. Locke was eager to insist that governments could acquire only rights that individuals gave them. If governments had a right to punish, they must have got it from individuals who transferred it to them. Hume thought the institution of punishment just grew in the same way as property rights and government generally. Second, the recipient of the penalty must be guilty of an offense and must have been found guilty by a reputable procedure. The *point* of a system of punishment is not primarily to respect the rights of the criminal;

but none of us can pursue our purposes while violating the rights of others, not even the rights of criminals, so when we purport to punish someone, we must not violate their rights in the process. Third, the purpose of punishment is to secure the rights of the noncriminal and to requite a proper measure of justice on the wicked. Reliable systems of punishment based on proper adjudication and sentencing are as good a way as anyone knows to reduce the insecurity and uncertainty of a world where we are vulnerable to theft, assault, sexual assault, and fraud on the part of others, without creating new forms of insecurity as bad as or worse than those we prevent. This is what Herbert Hart many years ago called the general justifying aim of punishment.[9] If you follow Locke and say that individuals have a right to punish by the light of nature, what does this mean? It means that they may threaten others with harm that they will inflict on them if they damage other people's legitimate interests; *but* it must be noticed—what Locke agreed his readers might think very strange—that the persons threatening punishment are behaving as if they were, so to speak, little governments before any real government existed. This is because of the fourth point: punishment must be aimed at any breach of the law, no matter who is harmed. We say not that if someone hurts *us*, we shall *retaliate*, but that if they hurt *anyone*, we shall *punish* them. The implausibility of imagining that persons bereft of government will in fact consult John Locke before they act is obvious enough. We do not think that individuals will act on behalf of others as energetically as on behalf of themselves; indeed, we think they will act too energetically on behalf of themselves and not at all on behalf of others—that what we call "punishment" will in fact be revenge when our own interests are at stake, and nonexistent otherwise.

Nonetheless, this objection itself shows what punishment really is and therefore what we have a right to impose on others, and it shows what accused and convicted people have a right to. To dogmatize, all of us have both a right and a duty to make a system of punishment, but not a system of simple revenge, work as it should. We owe this to other people, and we owe it to them as part of a cooperative and fair system of mutual help for the sake of security and prosperity. Everyone has a right to benefit from this system *unless* they forfeit that right in whole or in part by some violation; and among their rights are some they cannot forfeit because other human beings can never have the right to treat them unjustly, cruelly, or wickedly. What we have the right to inflict by way of punishment is now the crucial topic. On the face of it, we can inflict whatever meets two requirements; the first that it is effective in deterring and adequate in retributing misconduct; the second that it does not violate rights that a criminal cannot forfeit or imply rights on the part of the punisher that nobody can have. Innumerable governments have violated this second condition. The Spanish government of the seventeenth century made it a capital offense to import books from foreign publishers; nobody had a right to impose such a sentence, and being so sentenced violated the criminal's rights. However fastidious the legal process by which one's guilt was ascertained, the offense was not (morally speaking) an offense, and the penalty not proportionate.

If we take these thoughts in sequence, we reach the following position. Because the infliction of punishment is itself a bad thing to the extent that it is the causing of misery, the amount of punishment to be inflicted must be the minimum necessary to achieve the goals of deterrence and retribution.[10] To retribute to someone more than is proper is itself a violation of justice and therefore of their rights; it is also to cause more misery than strictly necessary, though that is a utilitarian argument rather than an argument from rights, and sustains an argument from rights only once you add that it is unjust that anyone should suffer more than is absolutely necessary to achieve a defensible goal. To threaten by way of punishment more than is necessary to secure compliance (or effect just retribution) is to declare yourself ready to violate the rights of anyone whom we punish in fact. The question whether it is right to threaten to do what it would be wrong to do in fact was much debated during the 1950s by Catholic critics of nuclear deterrence; many theorists of deterrence claimed that in order to keep the peace, it was necessary to threaten to launch a nuclear war if the Soviet Union launched the first strike, even if we knew that no good purpose would be served by retaliation and doubted whether we would actually do it. Much elegant deterrence theory rests on the thought that it is good to lead your opponent to believe that you are stark raving mad and might retaliate from atop a radioactive ash heap. Many Catholics held that if it would be wicked to launch a retaliatory strike, we had no right to threaten to do it.

There is an analogous situation vis-à-vis the death penalty in the following sense. If the death penalty is not much of a deterrent in the case of murder and armed robbery, it surely would be in the case of parking offenses; and yet everyone is clear that to *threaten* death for overstaying one's time on a meter would be wicked—even if we were perfectly sure, on the one hand, that the deterrent would be so effective that nobody would ever overstay and, on the other, that if they were to do so by some mischance, we would find some way of remitting the sentence. It follows that if the death penalty is out of proportion to the crimes for which it is inflicted, or if some much lesser threat would secure everything that a system of deterrence needs to secure, the death penalty would be illicit as a punishment for those crimes too. In short, punishment is not just something threatened for the sake of deterrence, but must also be an *apt* response to the crime for which it is threatened. The overstayed parker is guilty only of mildly inconveniencing the rest of the public, if that, and a small pecuniary penalty is adequate. We have, you might say, a right to threaten that much, and nobody can have a right not to be threatened with that much, but we all have a right not to face the threat of more than that.

My own view is that some argument of this sort is cogent; perhaps more to the point in this context, it is felt by most people to be cogent. It can be given some unusual philosophical tweakings, however. Immanuel Kant, for instance, held that the right to punish was implicit in a hypothetical social contract—one that nobody had in fact signed, but that we could imagine everyone signing and could imagine embodying the conditions of mutual obligation that lie at the basis of social cooperation. This contract allows each of us to invoke the assistance of everyone else in preventing others from violating our rights so long as we do our part to secure their rights as well; the contract guarantees our freedom from assaults on our lives, persons, and property as long as we cooperate in securing the same freedom for others. Since this vision of the role of the state implies an essentially defensive role for it, there is no suggestion that the state's task is to make us better, more amenable, more morally virtuous, or adherents of the true faith; all those things are tasks for individuals working under the protection of the state, but not under its instructions. The role of punishment in this scheme is striking. We commit ourselves to the contract on terms that in effect *instruct* others to inflict on us for breaches of the law the penalties we stand ready to inflict on others. *Not* to punish criminals would be a dereliction of moral duty, and Kant observes in a footnote that a society that knew it would perish from the earth in the middle of the night should ensure that the murderers in its jails were hanged before the society was destroyed.[11] Even in Texas, this might be thought a bit fierce, but the grounds for Kant's views are not as odd as the conclusions they ground. To be part of a law-abiding society is to be part of a scheme of rights observance; in effect, we are estopped from complaining that others hold us to standards of rights observance that we have advertised ourselves as accepting. We do not become *outlaws* by violating the rights of others, tempting though it is to say that we forfeit our immunity to the assaults of others if we break the rules that protect them against the assault of ourselves. What we forfeit is only our immunity to whatever punishment is properly imposed by the agents of the criminal justice system. We become criminals, not outlaws, which is to say that we are still within the ambit of law, and are treated as beings with rights, not beings without them.

This is plainly correct, and it makes sense of some of the things that distress critics of capital punishment, such as the suicide watch that is kept on condemned criminals. If the only thing we were interested in was that condemned criminals should be dead, we would presumably not mind how they became dead—and quite a lot of hard-boiled commentators have suggested that leaving a bottle of something lethal readily to hand would be a cheap way of disposing of the condemned who chose to go of their own volition. It would, however, be a lawless way of proceeding, and for those who care that punishment should be a lawful undertaking, this is intolerable, however perverse the results appear. But this is running ahead of things, because the more crucial question is how people actually get onto death row in the first place. Here, issues of rights violation really rear their heads.

The first thought is that if capital punishment is felt to be special, as it plainly is in Western societies nowadays, then all the usual rules have to be observed with extreme scrupulousness. What are they? Begin at the beginning; we all have a right not to be condemned for any crime that we have not committed, even if this is barely overstaying at a parking meter. How fastidiously this right has to be observed before there is a serious injustice is another matter, however; to complain that my rights were seriously violated by a parking authority that did not maintain its parking meters in tip-top condition would be going a bit far. To complain that my rights were seriously violated by a state that hired known drunks to defend me in a capital case would be putting the matter quite lightly. This point runs right through the whole of criminal justice, and I want to say two things that may seem surprising. The first is that capital cases are not, to my mind, as special as the public inclines to think, and the second is that the issues raised by capital cases run disquietingly through the whole criminal justice system. Let us start with the banal thought that we have a right to be tried on one issue only, namely, whether we committed the crime of which we stand accused. There is no law against being black, against having a low IQ, or against being poor. It is, however, inconceivable that any well-off white person of reasonable intelligence would run much risk (not, that is to say, no risk at all, but very much less than a poor, not very bright black person of comparable wickedness) of suffering the death penalty in the United States. Nor is this primarily a racial matter; as the case of O. J. Simpson sufficiently illustrates, anyone with really substantial means need not worry unduly that they will suffer execution if they put their minds to escaping it. I ought to say that this is not a uniquely American phenomenon, nor one relevant only to the death penalty. The prisons of Britain contain disproportionately many young black men, and the criminal classes are overwhelmingly drawn from the ranks of the poor and the educationally subnormal. But these are banal observations, so why are they worth noticing?

If the justice of punishment depends on its being part of a general scheme of social control under which we all observe the law in order to share in the benefits of general law-abidingness, there must be some rough equity in how we are requited for our forbearance. Contrary to some radical views, the poor, the intellectually unadvantaged, and members of low-status groups certainly get something from the legal system, and in some ways they get more than is apparent. If the law is scrupulously observed, they are protected from exploitation and especially from being bamboozled by the quick and the clever, as well as from being subject to arbitrary ill-treatment at the hands of the majority. They may have little property to protect, few contracts to enforce, and meager estates to bequeath, but they have their lives, limbs, and security to protect, as much as anyone else. Nonetheless, they are, as Bentham observed, required to keep their hands off the property of the rich, they are obliged not to take shortcuts to obtain the property of others, and they ought to be adequately recompensed for this abstention. One form that that recompense might properly take is being guaranteed the real, as distinct from the nominal, protection of the law. So far as the law of property goes, individuals who have little property must have what they do possess fastidiously protected, and the widow's cottage must be as safe from harm as the plutocrat's mansion. The life and times of John D. Rockefeller, John Jacob Astor, and Henry Clay Frick suggest that we do not always live up to that. When it comes to the criminal law, the thought is even starker. Your life and liberty must not be at stake because your means are slender. So one right we must have in place before the death penalty can be imposed without a violation of rights is a genuine right to free and equal justice, and that must mean that the quality of legal assistance available to the badly off must be no worse than that available to the well off.

But aside from the utopian quality of that aspiration, does it pick out the needs of defendants in capital cases only? This is where things get more complicated. It is generally assumed that capital cases are special, but I want to raise some doubts about that. You may think that this is British callousness, and that only in a country where they used to execute fourteen-year-olds for sheep stealing and where the theft of five shillings was capital—and indeed, where the families of those condemned to hang used to pay the hangman a few pence to be allowed to pull on the feet of their relatives to ensure a quicker and more merciful death—could anyone doubt that capital cases are special. Now I do not deny that the death penalty has *become* special, inasmuch as those who are eager to see it imposed have gone to enormous and expensive lengths to ensure that it can be—it being, on average, three times dearer to kill a criminal than to keep him in jail for thirty-odd years—and the intricacies of what the Supreme Court does and does not permit have become pretty extraordinary. But this is what you might call factitious specialness; it results from people thinking that the death penalty is special, and it provides no independent reason to think that it is. The most obvious difference between death and all other penalties is that the death penalty has a finality that no other punishment has. Even this, however, ought not to be exaggerated. When inmates of Angola, the Louisiana State Penitentiary, go in on a life sentence without parole, they stay in Angola until they die, as much as if they were going in only until they are executed; like those who are executed, they will leave only in a coffin. Nor is the death penalty final in the sense of being passed and implemented speedily so that the whole thing is over and done with at once. We cannot today draw the same sharp distinction as we can between the finality of the old English system, in which there was no appeal and if the judge did not exercise mercy, you were hanged at the conclusion of the assizes, and "Angola finality" extending over forty years. The average stay on death row is almost two decades, so what those who are executed in fact receive is a life sentence followed by a lethal injection. Perhaps the finality we care about most is symbolic: the sentence expresses our conviction that you cannot be rehabilitated, that we have finally given up on you. Or perhaps it is merely precautionary: the only thing we are interested in is making sure you do not do whatever it was again, and this is an effective way of achieving that.

The thought that this is the sort of finality that many people want is supported by the fact that supporters of the death penalty moderate their support if offered the alternative of life without parole. There surely are some people whom we just want out of the way; and death, on the one hand, and throwing away the key, on the other, are not very different ways of achieving that. The sort of finality that disturbs critics, on the other hand, reflects the fact that death is irreparable and that it is too late to change our minds about guilt or about the justice of a sentence once we have killed the person sentenced to die. That is both irrefutable and important, but it also suggests some of the reasons that lead me to say that *all* punishment can raise similar issues. Consider Ian Gordon, acquitted in October at the age of seventy of a murder he almost certainly did not commit fifty-two years ago. He has an IQ in the eighties, and when he was eighteen, he was shy, hesitant, eager to please, and just the sort of person who would confess to a crime he did not commit in order to be helpful. You cannot exactly give him back his life. Nor can we do very much for another not very bright middle-aged man who has been in jail for twenty-seven years because he will not admit to having committed the murder for which he was sentenced at the age of seventeen. Since he seems not to have committed it, one can hardly blame him for saying so, but no parole board will release him until he "comes to terms" with his crime. It is not clear that these men's plight is very much less than that of the person who has been executed, and it is not clear that the finality with which their ordinary lives were terminated was very much less than the finality of death. We think, intuitively, that killing people is very much more dramatic than locking them up, and I do not want to deny that it is. But I do want to say that we now think so for reasons that have more to do with our attitudes toward the death penalty and less to do with what we actually inflict on the criminal who is punished.

Let us leave finality and rest on this: although there is nothing about the death penalty that means, intrinsically, that we may not inflict it, and that the victim of it has a right not to have it imposed on him or her under any circumstances, there are a set of rights to just treatment under a system of criminal law that constrain what can justly be done to anyone. We all have a right to be subject only to a *fair* system of investigation, arrest, interrogation, and prosecution. This *might* perhaps cover a limited amount of so-called racial profiling, in the sense that it is not unfair—if it is done scrupulously and sensitively—to keep a particular eye on people who are more likely than the rest of the population to have committed some crime or other. Known homophobes cannot complain, in this view, if an obviously homophobically motivated crime is followed by some scrutiny of their actions, just as the discovery of a road-death victim with a great smear of white paint on their clothes rightly sends the police looking for white cars and panel vans. It does not license a priori assumptions about the likelihood that any given murder was committed by a member of some racial or income group. A person who can reasonably claim that the police set out to stitch him up or that they did not question their own assumptions about who was guilty of the crime can reasonably claim that their rights have been violated. (Of course, they may be guilty nonetheless.) This applies to all crimes and all penalties and, only to the extent that the death penalty is special, applies with special force to capital cases.

The process of chasing, catching, interrogating, and processing for prosecution is one part of the story. Since some people are unusually vulnerable to ill-treatment and unusually inept in self-defense at this stage, the foregoing arguments apply more sharply to them, which is why I made some tart remarks about the educationally subnormal. As for the trial itself, I have already said that the same considerations apply with even more force. If we are to jail people, let along hang them, we must be sure that *all* that can be said on their side has been said. This entails defense lawyers no less competent and no less well provided for than the lawyers for the prosecution. I perhaps ought to say that I do not think of a good lawyer in quite the way that many Americans do in this context. I do not think that the adversarial theory of justice means that the task of a defense lawyer is to get his client acquitted no matter his guilt or innocence. Lawyers are agents of the system of justice as much as or more than they are agents of their clients. They are officers of the court as well as hired help for the dubiously well behaved. It is easy to confuse two distinct thoughts: the first that the best way of ensuring justice is to operate an adversarial system of justice so that each side can properly scrutinize the other side's case, and the other that justice is whatever results from having two sides fight it out as best they can. The second is not true; a criminal trial is not a boxing match—in the latter, the object is to batter your opponent into a condition where he cannot continue to fight, but in the former, the object is to discover an objectively true answer to a part-factual, part-legal question: did the accused commit the crime of which he is accused? Just as the finding of this answer is frustrated if the defense lawyers see it as their job to trip up the prosecution by any means possible and to get the jury on their side by any degree of grandstanding, misrepresentation, and whatever lies or near lies that the judge will let them get away with, so it is frustrated—and much more frequently—if the accused has poor representation. It is in this sense that my own answer to the question whether the hundred and forty people executed in Texas under the auspices of Governor Bush had their rights violated would be yes. They may or may not for the most part have been guilty, and perhaps even have been guilty as charged of the crimes for which they were sentenced, but they did not have an adequate defense, and they were not pursued, arrested, interrogated, and prosecuted under a squeakily clean system. It was not their being put to death but their being put to death *as part of that process* that was the violation of rights, and the rights that were violated would have equally been violated if they had been jailed for twenty years instead.

Now, one response to this sort of argument—and one that I am more sympathetic to than you might suppose—is that no system of criminal justice can be squeaky clean in the sense I am demanding. Hard-bitten cops and criminal lawyers sometimes observe that it is warfare out on the mean streets and that a fastidious concern for justice on the battlefield is likely to get you killed. Let us take the analogy seriously. Those who make war on civilized society cannot complain of injustice if society makes war on them. But that thought is covered by the right of self-defense and immediate retaliation. Persons who adopt a posture of incipient aggression cannot complain if they are taken seriously, and a cokehead with a toy gun who has the bad luck to wave it at an armed shopkeeper suffers bad luck but no injustice if he is shot. But even in warfare there are rights in plenty to be considered. The first is that noncombatants have the right to be immune from aggression; too casual an attitude to victims caught in the cross fire and too casual a view of what evidence we need before we decide that someone is an incipient enemy remove the case from lawful self-defense and turn it into wanton aggression. And there are further arguments behind that one. One is that we should not accept the hard-bitten view too swiftly. Far from turning ordinary criminal justice into domestic warfare, the task of civilized states has always been that of trying to make real warfare more like domestic criminal justice. We try—and we do not wholly fail—to conduct war as a measured exercise in deterrence and retribution rather than an all-out exercise in slaughter and incapacitation; the notion lying behind the attempt to do so is in part that we want enemy societies to rejoin the society of nations in due course. If that is an ideal, then too much dwelling on the idea of the control of crime as a sort of domestic warfare is unhelpful.

In short, I end where I started. There are no grounds for saying that the death penalty is always and everywhere a violation of rights. Few people think, to take a concrete instance, that Adolf Eichmann's rights were violated when Israel hanged him, even if they think that Israel might have done better to hold the trial and then let him go, or at any rate to have found him guilty and not hanged him. A death penalty imposed for those crimes, if any, for which it is uniquely effective as a deterrent and to which it is not disproportionate as a penalty does not violate a criminal's rights so long as the criminal was arrested, tried, and convicted according to the strictest rules of justice, and so long as the criminal was of sound mind and fully responsible for their actions. This, in effect, is to say that I agree with the Supreme Court's decision in *Furman v. Georgia* in 1972, but that I would take rather more persuading than the Supreme Court has lately taken that the appropriate degree of fastidiousness has been maintained.[12] My guess is that no society that persistently thought as the majority in *Furman* thought would in fact impose the death penalty, but it might, and especially in time of war. If it did not, I suspect it would be because any society that thought in that way would mind about things in addition to rights—such as compassion and forgiveness and reconciliation and rehabilitation—and would simply not wish to employ capital punishment. But there are many things we have the right to do that we do not do, and that we think ourselves right not to do.

Which brings me to a last, entirely informal coda on the question of the death penalty in its own right. I have said that all punishment works by depriving people of things they value, whether money, liberty, or life itself; that we employ the threat of such deprivation as a deterrent to lawbreaking; and that *what* we may threaten is restricted by a constraint of retributive appropriateness such that the harm we inflict on the wrongdoer must not be disproportionate to the harm he or she inflicts. These principles allow the defender of the death penalty to claim that death is a proper harm to threaten for crimes of a sufficient degree of gravity—murder in our society, but blasphemy in others, corruption in others, and drug dealing in many. My purpose has been to argue that it is all the things that may go wrong between the commission of a crime and the execution of the offender that should concern us. But I now turn briefly to some speculation on why the death penalty is felt by so many people in the United States to be peculiarly appropriate. Notice the limitation of time and place; in societies where incarceration is difficult and expensive, physical penalties such as beating, mutilation, and execution have an obvious utilitarian justification they do not have for us.

In the American context, a trawl of pro-death-penalty Internet sites, some of which are of considerable sophistication and display an impressive grasp of the empirical literature, suggests that above all they are animated by the conviction that it is a divine commandment to kill murderers. The role of religion in the debate is thus interestingly confused. Thirty-nine Christian denominations have made formal and official declarations against the death penalty, including those not otherwise noted for their cultural liberalism, such as the Southern Baptists; but there seems to exist among the population at large a fundamentalist and literalist determination to take the words of the Old Testament at face value and to repudiate the attempts of church leaders to invoke Christ's gospel of forgiveness in condemning the death penalty.

This is not to deny any of the obvious empirical evidence that opinion alters when the death penalty is compared to other punishments such as life imprisonment without parole, that enthusiasm for the death penalty drops when it is explained that it is not cheap, or that it is not particularly effective as a deterrent. One may be motivated by a religiously based morality but still pull back from its implications if they are at odds with other values or with common sense. Still, we need some explanation of the fact that some Americans, and particularly Americans in some parts of the United States, are attached to the death penalty for reasons that evidently do not move their fellow countrymen in Michigan or New Jersey. Supporters of the death penalty who concede that it is too expensive a form of punishment *concede* the point; they do not welcome it. This is different from the 20 percent of the sampled population who shift from supporting the death penalty to opposing it when they are asked to compare it with life imprisonment without the possibility of parole. They plainly hold a "throw away the key" view of the matter, and if assured that the key can be thrown away more cheaply without killing people, they take the alternative. The rest think death is what counts.

Together with the anecdotal evidence of the websites, this suggests that the familiar finding that the United States is the outlier among developed countries in being more or less immune to secularization has implications in penology too. It may also be related to a feature that the United States shares with Britain. In both countries, criminals are more inclined toward a strongly retributive and generally rather violent view of punishment. Felons support the death penalty more strongly than the population at large; this leads some advocates of the death penalty to suggest that this is "horse's mouth" support for the deterrent effect of the penalty, and leads opponents to suggest that it confirms that human beings are poor judges of their own motivation. At all events, what we might conclude is that simple, firmly structured worldviews facilitate the thought that death is the apt and appropriate penalty for murder in particular. One might observe in passing that the Old Testament catalogue of death-penalty offenses, though shorter than the list of 222 that the British penal code ran to in the eighteenth century, is a great deal longer than that of the modern supporters. Bestiality and adultery are not offered up as candidates for stoning and incineration.[13] Nor is blasphemy.

But this raises the question of what it is about the culture that sustains this selective but energetic espousal of a religiously based approach to punishment. One possibility is that it reflects a form of cultural pessimism. This is not to say that it is pessimistic about economic growth or about the possibility of making large fortunes or about a good deal else. What, then, might it be pessimistic about? Perhaps about the innate sinfulness of mankind, about the immovability of the stain of evil that wicked actions place upon us. It is hard to give a clear account because the cultural view itself so colors the things we are describing; but the thought I have in mind is this. A wholly secular view tends to be forward looking and not entirely judgmental: given that a criminal committed crime x, what are the odds that they will do it again, what is the risk that letting this one out will weaken the deterrent effect of the penalty, and so endlessly on. The nonsecular view is that the person had stained their soul, and might seek divine mercy but could not look forward to divine justice with any optimism. When I say the cultural view colors the phenomenon, I mean that the secular mind tends to see the past as in some sense eradicable and forgettable, whereas the religious mind tends not to. If people have incurred the stain that merits death—not that death erases it—then death it is. You might agree that people have become changed characters since their crimes, and much else besides, but you would harden your heart in the interests of preserving the rigid connection between the crime and the penalty.

As to why we must *kill* criminals, the best account was given by a two-thirds mad aristocrat and emigré some years after the French Revolution. In his *St. Petersburg Dialogues*, Joseph de Maistre gives a particularly disgusting account of a public execution in which he imagines a man being broken on the wheel—that is to say, being stretched out across a cartwheel and being killed by having all his limbs systematically smashed by the executioner. The scene ends with the executioner walking through the crowd, which draws aside at his passing; "Justice drops a few coins into his hand, from a distance," says Maistre. Then he goes on to argue that honor, glory, and civilization itself rest on "this incomprehensible agent." It is precisely the fact that killing people is so strictly forbidden that makes it the thing to do when we wish to make a point; the man who does the killing would be a murderer or a butcher if he were not an agent of the state. It is this that means we cannot quite approve of the executioner, no matter how skilled he may be. It also means that we—collectively, that is to say—cannot quite make up our minds about the way we want death inflicted. If it is to be an exemplary spectacle, it should be public, and the degree of brutality involved is not especially important. There is a degree of cruelty beyond which the motives of the state might be impugned, so limits must be observed; but making it easy for the criminal is not the object of the exercise—if it were, he might be given poison unawares. (Nevada did try in the 1920s to asphyxiate the condemned by pumping gas into their cells while they slept; it did not work.) If it is not to be an exemplary spectacle, the temptation is to medicalize the whole business as if it were a form of euthanasia—as when people executed by lethal injection have their arm swabbed with antiseptic before the fatal needle is inserted. That defeats several of the objects of the exercise, but I would not suggest that the choice before us is to embrace public and exemplary hanging on the one side or to give up on the death penalty entirely on the other. The social costs associated with public execution are just one further topic that has been left unexplored in this already overextended essay.

PART 2

Liberty and Security

8

Hobbes's Political Philosophy

THIS ESSAY DISCUSSES some large questions in Hobbes's political philosophy. My aim is to identify what, if anything, Hobbes thought to be *the* central problem, or problems, of politics and to link the answer to an account of why the state of nature is so intolerable, of how we may leave it, and whether the manner of our leaving is well explained by Hobbes. I then turn to the implications for Hobbes's account of the rights and duties of the sovereign, and then to the contentious issue of the subject's right, in extremis, to reject his sovereign and rebel. In the course of that discussion, I also consider Hobbes's account of the nature of punishment and the question whether his two rather different accounts are not one too many. In answering these questions, I shall say something about Hobbes's conception of the law of nature, his theory of political obligation, and the role (or lack of a role) of religious belief in his political system.[1] I say a little about Hobbes's account of liberty and link its oddities to the politics of his own day.

Hobbes's Career

It would be otiose to say much about Hobbes's career here; that has been done elsewhere. I will emphasize some features of his life only to frame the discussion of the central arguments of his political philosophy and the interpretative problems they present. Hobbes observed that fear and he were born twins into the world because his mother had gone into labor upon hearing the (false) rumor of the approach of the Spanish Armada in the spring of 1588. "His extraordinary Timorousness Mr Hobs doth very ingenuously confess and attributes it to the influence of his Mother's Dread of the Spanish Invasion in 88, she being then with child of him," says Aubrey.[2] Hobbes made much of this, treating caution as one of the primary political virtues, arguing that anxiety was the main stimulus of religious belief, and thinking that religious belief gave fear a useful focus.[3] We shall see below how important fear is in explaining the causes and character of the "war of all against all" in the state of nature, in motivating persons in the state of nature to contract with one another to set up an authority to "overawe them all" and make peace possible, and in persuading them to obey that authority once it has been established.

Hobbes's education at his grammar school in Westport and at Oxford was a literary one; in Oxford it was literary and "philosophical" in a traditional and non-Hobbesian sense. His first employment as a tutor and confidential secretary in the Devonshire household made use of the skills of a man of a literary and historical education; those are what he taught his charge, the young earl of Devonshire, and Hobbes's first published work was a translation of Thucydides's *History of the Peloponnesian War*. The publication was, in part, a compliment to Hobbes's employer. It was not the only possible choice for a man who translated Homer into passable English verse in his extreme old age and wrote his autobiography in Latin verse (and much of his philosophy in Latin prose), as he did when he celebrated the marvels of the Peak District.[4] He might have chosen many other ways to compliment his employer; the choice of Thucydides was a meaningful one, and its meaning was plain enough: "Thucydides is one, who, though he never digress to read a lecture, moral or political, upon his own text, nor enter into men's hearts further than the acts themselves evidently guide him; is yet accounted the most politic historiographer that ever writ."[5] As to the implications of Thucydides's work, Hobbes stressed that as far as Thucydides's opinions of forms of government were concerned, "it is manifest that he least of all liked the democracy."[6]

Twentieth-century readers admire Athens more than seventeenth-century readers did, and today we admire Pericles's famous Funeral Oration without reflecting on the fact that Alcibiades (who urged the Athenians into the disastrous Sicilian expedition, the overwhelming defeat of which cost Athens the war) exerted more influence over Athens than Pericles ever did. We try not to notice when Thucydides observes that, under Pericles, Athens was a democracy in name only and a monarchy in fact because of the authority that Pericles could exercise. Hobbes emphasizes what we flinch from.

> And upon diverse occasions he noteth the emulation and contention of the demagogues for reputation and glory of wit; with their crossing of each other's counsels, to the damage of the public; the inconsistency of resolutions caused by the diversity of ends and power of rhetoric in the orators; and the desperate actions undertaken upon the flattering advice of such as desired to attain, or to hold what they had attained, of authority and sway among the people.

Not that Thucydides was a friend to aristocracy either.

> He praiseth the government of Athens when it was mixed of *the few* and *the many*; but more he commendeth it, both when Peisistratus reigned (saving that it was an usurped power), and when in the beginning of this war it was democratical in name, but in effect monarchical under Pericles.[7]

Hobbes took to heart Thucydides's message that democracies collapse into factionalism and chaos as their search for freedom and glory ends in civil war and self-destruction. Hobbes's first work was historical and so was the work of his last years. *Behemoth* is perhaps a strange example of its genre, inasmuch as it takes the form of a dialogue in which the two parties exchange hypotheses about the causes of the English Civil War. Nonetheless, it was historical in form and in purpose; it was intended to unravel the course of particular events and to draw a moral from them: "the principal and proper work of history being to instruct and enable men, by the knowledge of actions past, to bear themselves prudently in the present and providently towards the future."[8] Since this essay considers Hobbes's science of politics, and Hobbes explicitly contrasted that science with a historically based prudence, it is worth keeping in mind the fact that Hobbes also wrote history.

One last aspect of Hobbes's career worth mention is his connection with the law during his brief career as amanuensis to Francis Bacon, inductivist and lord chancellor, and in his later excursion into jurisprudence in the *Dialogue between a Philosopher and a Student of the Common Law*. I shall argue that Hobbes's political philosophy is "absolutist" in a slightly curious sense, namely, that perhaps his greatest wish was to show that a political system had to settle the question "What is the law?" with a clear, unambiguous, and indisputable answer; that the way to achieve that was to secure universal agreement that only one source of law existed; and that whatever that source declared as law *was* law. The so-called Hobbesian problem of order was cast by Hobbes in a particular light: how to escape from a situation in which there were no clearly enunciated and scrupulously enforced rules of conduct into a situation in which a determinate, ultimate, omnicompetent authority laid down the law and enforced it. Any authority with that standing and intended to perform that task must be legally absolute, that is, unchallengeable in the name of any other legal authority.[9]

There were many problems in the way of establishing such an authority; one was the arrogance of the common lawyers who held that "the law is such a one as will have no sovereign beside him." The greatest of the common lawyers of Hobbes's day, Sir Edward Coke, held that the "High Court of Parliament" was the only authority able to change the common law by statute, but he fell under the same Hobbesian anathema. The High Court of Parliament, in Hobbes's account of the matter, could change the law only to the extent that the sovereign empowered it to do so. Qua court, its authority was derivative. Other obstacles included the foolishness of those who believed that only a republican, or "free," government could be legitimate, and who therefore complained that the laws of a monarchy limited their freedom and had no binding force. They had simply failed to understand that all law limited freedom. The liberty at which republics aimed "is not the Libertie of Particular men; but the Libertie of the Commonwealth," that is, its independence as a sovereign state, and "whether a Common-wealth be Monarchicall, or Popular, the Freedome is still the same."[10] A greater obstacle still was the arrogance or madness of religious fanatics who believed that God had spoken to them in their dreams, licensing them to legislate for others according to their inspiration or absolving them from the decrees of the unrighteous. Hobbes's view of unauthorized inspiration is well known: "To say that he hath spoken to him in a Dream, is no more than to say that he hath dreamt that God spake to him;"[11] his skeptical criticism of dissenters and enthusiasts reflected his view that religion must be subordinate to law so that law would not be subordinated to the ambition of priests. For Hobbes, the dividing line between religion and private fantasy was to be drawn by the sovereign authority as a matter of "law not truth." It was to establish one unequivocal source of law, not to demonstrate the truth of some particular religious creed, that Hobbes waged his campaign to undermine the credibility of the unofficial prophets.

Political Science versus Political Prudence

The final feature of Hobbes's life to be borne in mind was his acquaintance with the greatest scientific minds of the day. He quarreled with several of them and was on the losing side on several occasions.[12] Nonetheless, he was as deeply conscious of living in the middle of an intellectual revolution as he was of living in a period of political and religious revolution. The bearing of this fact on this essay's concerns is simple: Hobbes's political philosophy was distinctive in its ambition to be a science of politics. Hobbes's positive understanding of what this involved is a matter of controversy. Hobbes explained what a science of politics was by contrasting it with political prudence; the latter was practical wisdom, practiced in the light of the best advice that we can draw from a storehouse of historical examples. Thucydides was a model of political prudence as well as the source of instructive examples, but Hobbes proposed to improve on him. The Romans, Hobbes remarks, rightly distinguished between *prudentia* and *sapientia*; we call both wisdom, but we ought to follow the Romans and distinguish them: "As much Experience, is *Prudence*; so, is much Science, *Sapience*. For though we usually have but one word of Wisedome for them both; yet the Latines did always distinguish between *Prudentia* and *Sapientia*; ascribing the former to Experience, the later to Science."[13] Prudence is the knowledge of events and affairs that comes from wide experience and reflection and from recapitulating the experience and reflection of others as recorded in history. Prudence is *essentially* experiential; its method is historical—whether it is a matter of retrospective reflection upon our own experience or upon that of mankind in general—and its object is sound judgment in particular cases. The best evidence of prudence is continual good judgment. Prudence is a genuine form of knowledge, yet it is always knowledge of particulars; it is a knowledge of how things have worked out in the past and what *has* happened, not of how they *must* work out nor of what *must* happen. Generalizations based on such experience are always in danger of being falsified by a novel, unexpected event.[14]

Sapientia is based on science. Science is hypothetical, general, and infallible. Most commentators have found nothing very surprising about the thought that science deals in hypothetical generalizations. Modern analyses of causal laws (water boils at 100°C, say) as universal propositions of the form (x) Ax → Bx ("If anything is water, it boils at 100°C") treat them as just that. Yet nobody has offered an entirely persuasive account of Hobbes's view that science is infallible; modern accounts of causal laws emphasize their fallibility, finding their empirical content in their capacity for falsification.[15] Hobbes's account becomes no clearer with his insistence that the only science we possess is geometry. For our purposes, we may decently avoid controversy and suggest that Hobbes's assimilation of geometry and politics is best understood by analogy with economic argument. Economic theory explains the conduct of a rational economic agent by laying out the optimal strategy for such an agent to pursue. It is normative as much as descriptive because its explanations of what actors *do* do are parasitic on its accounts of what for them is the thing *to* do.[16] I shall use an analogy I have used before and try to place no more weight on it than I must. Hobbes's science of politics is a form of blueprint making; it sets out a rational strategy for individuals placed in the dangerous and anxiety-ridden state of nature, individuals whose goal is assumed to be self-preservation and whose means of survival are minimal. Politics so understood is a normative discipline, and in this resembles modern economics.[17] The blueprint sets out what rational individuals must do if they are to form a political society; it does not predict that they will do. Far from offering a disconfirmable prediction of what they will in fact do, Hobbes's politics relies for its rhetorical power on the fact that men have so often failed to do what the blueprint dictates and have thus caused themselves appalling misery.

Political science sets out what men rationally must do. Its relationship to empirical accounts of human psychology, anthropological investigations of nonpolitical societies, political socialization, and a great deal else that the twentieth century embraces under the general heading of "political science" is thus complex. It plainly has some vulnerability to factual considerations. If mankind were empirically so constituted as inevitably to fail to follow Hobbes's prescriptions, we should at least lose interest in them—as we should lose interest in a theory of pedestrian safety that enjoined us to rise vertically ten feet above onrushing traffic. Short of that, it is hard to set out general rules for adjusting Hobbes's science to the facts or the facts to Hobbes's science. To the extent that actual agents pursue the recommended strategy, whether knowingly or unknowingly, their behavior will be both explained and justified by the theory; and to the degree that the world matches the world posited in the theory, their actions will "infallibly" produce the results predicted. The practice of modern economics suggests that Hobbes was right to link geometry and politics. Hobbes's account of the horrors of the state of nature has, in recent years, often been interpreted as a prisoner's dilemma problem, and contemporary economics places the analysis of strategic interactions at the very heart of its concerns.[18]

Hobbes's contemporary Sir James Harrington, the author of *Oceana*, began the tradition of accusing Hobbes of slighting the historical understanding of politics in favor of his own scientific understanding.[19] It is surely true that Hobbes thought that the scientific understanding of politics was superior to a historical one, and in that sense, he preferred "modern" prudence to "ancient" prudence.[20] But this is far from implying that he despised historical analysis. What he despised was the habit he saw in many of his contemporaries of flaunting their historical erudition not to advance their understanding of their own age's dilemmas, but to show off their learning. This was particularly foolish because it amounted to retailing secondhand experience in preference to their own.

> And even of those men themselves, that in the Councells of the Commonwealth, love to shew their reading of politiques and History, very few do it in their domestique affaires, where their particular interest is concerned; having Prudence enough for their private affaires; but in publique they study more the reputation of their owne wit, than the successes of anothers businesse.[21]

He also despised the habit of taking past political actors, beliefs, or systems as authoritative models in current conditions. That the Athenians had practiced democracy was their misfortune; that the citizens of ancient republics had thought their governments free and all others servile was their mistake. To follow them blindly was to repeat their errors and to refuse to learn from experience. Learning from experience was not to be despised, particularly since it reinforced the lessons Hobbes's political science taught. If Hobbes had not thought so, he would hardly have wasted his time writing *Behemoth*. Nor, for that matter, could he have published *De Cive* ahead of the rest of his projected system, on the grounds that it was "grounded on its owne principles sufficiently knowne by experience."[22]

There was much that science could not prove. It could tell us that no society without an ultimate and absolute legal authority possessed a sovereign and that it was to that degree not a state at all; but it could not demonstrate that a monarch would make a better sovereign than an assembly. Experience tells us it is highly probable that monarchy is the best form of government, but Hobbes did not think he had demonstrated this conclusion, and he may well have doubted that it could be demonstrated.[23] Demonstration handles large structural features of political life and leaves experience to deal with particularities. The science of politics tells us that anything we can properly regard as a state must have a certain constitution; to learn what a prudent empirical implementation of that constitution is, we must turn to experience. It could tell us what laws are, but not what the laws of any particular country are.[24] Hobbes cannot have thought that a feckless monarch would be better than an assembly of thoughtful and prudent senators, any more than he could have thought that science could tell us whether a given judge would take bribes or listen to a case carefully. Science tells us what law *is*. In the light of that, we can appreciate the qualities to look for in a judge, such as a willingness to subordinate his private judgment to the commands of the sovereign. It cannot tell us whether Francis Bacon, Lord Verulam and a noted bribe taker, was a wise choice for lord chancellor.

This leaves much of the methodological detail of *Leviathan* unresolved. In particular, it leaves unclear why Hobbes should have devoted so much of the first two books of *Leviathan* to an elaborate account of human beings considered as elaborate automata. The emphasis on a speculative physiological reduction of the most important emotional and intellectual qualities of human beings does not, on the face of it, add much to what Hobbes might have achieved by starting with persons in the state of nature and elucidating the dangerousness of their condition as a preliminary to offering the only secure way out of it.[25] To the extent that this physiological and psychological speculation provides a foundation for later arguments, it is by leading us to think, in a broadly constructivist way, that were we in the position of God, first creating the world, then man, and then exploring the consequences of putting man in such a world, there would be only one rational route to self-preservation available to man. This captures Hobbes's talk of the way we create the state by analogy with God's creation of the entire natural world; it is, after all, the very first thing he tells us: "Nature (the Art by which God hath made and governed the World) is by the *Art* of Man, as in many other things, so in this also imitated, that it can make an Artificial Animal."[26] It also leaves a great deal untouched. In particular, it leaves untouched Hobbes's own skepticism about our knowledge of just how God rules the world. Hobbes elsewhere stresses that we can never know what God's perspective on his creation is. We might draw up a system that seems rationally compelling to us, but God's free choice cannot be limited by what seems rationally compelling to us.

The Natural Condition and Its Horrors

Perhaps the most famous single phrase in Hobbes's entire oeuvre is his observation that life in the state of nature is "solitary, poore, nasty, brutish, and short."[27] The interest of Hobbes's view emerges by contrast with the views of his predecessors and successors. Aristotle, whom Hobbes savaged throughout *Leviathan*, sometimes by misrepresenting him for the purpose, had claimed that "the polis is one of those things that exist by nature, and man is an animal made to live in a polis."[28] Hobbes's break with the teleological perspective of Aristotle's *Politics* made this claim not only false but also absurd. States exist by convention, and conventions are manifestly man-made, so states are self-evidently artificial and thus nonnatural. But Hobbes dissented from Aristotle on the substance of human nature, too, even though he cheated in his statement of the difference. Men, said Hobbes, were not political by nature as bees and cattle were; their association depended on an agreement to observe justice among men who disagreed about who ought to receive what, and thus they needed common standards of right and wrong to regulate their affairs.[29] This was hardly a hit against Aristotle. He had claimed that bees and cattle were sociable or gregarious, but not political—for just the reason Hobbes cited against him.[30] Bees and cattle simply congregated together, but men could live together only on the basis of agreed principles.

Still, the difference persists; Aristotle thought that there was some kind of natural attraction toward the good and toward life in society. Hobbes thinks that at best there is a common aversion to the *summum malum* (supreme evil), or death, and that we become "apt" for society only by being socialized into decent conduct. Almost equally important is Hobbes's insistence on the natural equality of mankind. For Aristotle, the social order can—and when things go well, does—mirror a natural hierarchy in which the better sort of person is plainly distinguished from the less good: aristocrats from their inferiors, men from women, adults from children, free men from slaves, and Greeks from barbarians. Hobbes rejected this view of the world. Not only was it false, but it also violated two conditions of political peace: one, that we should reckon everyone our equal and demand no more from them than we allow them to demand from us; the other, that everyone should acknowledge the sovereign as uniquely the fount of honor.[31] An aristocrat was anyone the sovereign declared to be an aristocrat, no more and no less.[32] The pride of descent that aristocrats displayed was a threat to peace; it made them think they were entitled to demand political preferment, it made them touchy about their honor, and it provoked needless fights. Thinking of humanity as morally, politically, and intellectually on a level reinforced the view that the state rested on universal consent rather than on a tendency toward a natural hierarchy.

Hobbes's successors held a variety of views about the state of nature, ranging from the view that there had never been a state of nature, so that considering what it was like and how we might have emerged from it was a waste of time, to Rousseau's view in *Discourse on the Origins of Inequality* that it was a peaceful condition, prehuman in important respects, and perhaps a model for a kind of innocence that we might hope to recover in a social setting at the end of some very long process of change.[33] I shall contrast Hobbes's account of the state of nature with Locke's and Rousseau's accounts, and will, in passing, mention Robert Filmer's patriarchalist theory of government as a contemporary, but diametrically opposite, view.

Hobbes writes of the "condition of mankind by nature" without anxiety about its historical accuracy. He is quite right. As he says, the heads of all governments live in a state of nature with respect to one another. The state of nature is simply the condition in which we are forced into contact with one another in the absence of a superior authority that can lay down and enforce rules to govern our behavior toward each other.[34] Like many of his contemporaries, Hobbes thought that the Indians of North America were still living in the state of nature. More importantly, the inhabitants of Britain had been in that condition during the Civil War; so not only was the state of nature a historical fact, but relapse into it was also a standing danger. Indeed, the state of nature with which Hobbes is concerned is more nearly the condition of civilized people deprived of stable government than anything else. This can be seen by a simple thought experiment.

There are many societies that anthropologists call acephalous. They have no stable leadership; there is nothing resembling law or politics in their daily life. Such societies persist for long periods. They have no apparent tendency to self-destruction, although they are easily wrecked by contact with more advanced societies. Hobbes seems to suggest that their existence is impossible to explain. In the state of nature, he says, we are governed by no rules, recognize no authority, are therefore a threat to one another, and must fall into the state he describes as a war of all against all. But, we counter, if that were so, acephalous societies would self-destruct. It is easy to think of reasons why they might not. Hobbes plays down such possibilities by saying only that the concord of the American Indians "dependeth on naturall lust" and by going on to observe that they live in a "brutish manner."[35] The brutishness of their existence is, however, not the decisive point. The decisive question is whether they can—at least on a small scale—get by with the laws of nature alone. On the face of it, they can. Hobbes never suggests that we cannot know what rules we ought, both as a matter of prudence and as a matter of morality, to follow. The members of acephalous societies can understand the laws of nature.

For enforcement, the institutionalized practice of the blood feud may serve well enough. If you murder me, I cannot revenge myself, but my brother can do so on my behalf. In a small society, it is likely that the murderer would be immediately obvious; if he has killed me only because he is murderously inclined, he will not find allies to help him resist vengeance. The knowledge that he faces the vengeance of my family will, one may hope, act as a powerful deterrent when he contemplates murder, so the whole process of taking revenge need never start. For this to work, several things have to be true that will not be true in large and complicated societies. It is crucial that my death must be known at once to my family, on whom the burden of revenge falls, and the probable killer must be easily discovered and brought to justice. This is not true in larger societies: if I am traveling on business and am robbed three hundred miles away from home, I must depend on institutionalized police power for help or on my own unaided force. Many people have suggested that Hobbes's state of nature is peopled with the men of the seventeenth century; properly understood, this may not be a defect in the theory. That is, the theory may be designed around the problem of sustaining and policing a large, prosperous society, in which most people are known well only to a few friends but want to transact business and hold intellectual converse with distant strangers.

What is Hobbes's theory? We are to consider men in an ungoverned condition. They are rational, that is, able to calculate consequences; they are self-interested, at any rate in the sense that they ask what good to themselves will be produced by any given outcome; they are vulnerable to one another—you may be stronger than I, but when you are asleep, I can kill you as easily as you can kill me; they are essentially anxious.[36] They are anxious because they have some grasp of cause and effect, understand the passage of time, and have a sense of their own mortality. It is these capacities that Rousseau, for instance, denies that we possess merely qua human animals, and in their absence, he claims, we would be like other animals, heedless of any but present danger. Hobbesian man is heedful of the future. This means that no present success in obtaining what he needs for survival can reassure him. I pick apples from the tree now, but know I shall be hungry in six hours; my obvious resource is to store the surplus apples somewhere safe. But the logic of anxiety is remorseless. Will the apples remain safe if I do not find some way of guarding them? I find myself in a terrible bind. To secure the future, I have to secure the resources for my future; but to secure them, I have to secure whatever I need to make them safe. And to secure it. . . . This is why Hobbes puts "for a generall inclination of all mankind, a perpetual and restless desire of Power after power, that ceaseth only in Death."[37]

Such creatures encounter one another singularly ill equipped in the natural condition. Each appears to the other as a threat, and because each appears as a threat, each is a threat. This is not because of any moral defect in us. Hobbes wavers somewhat on the subject of original sin, but the miseries of the state of nature would afflict people who do not suffer from original sin but who do have the anxieties that Hobbes ascribes to us. Nor does our knowledge of the moral law, that is, of the laws of nature, make any difference. Each of us has the natural right and the natural duty to preserve himself. This right is an equal right. You have no greater right over anything than I have, and I have no greater right over anything than you have. In the absence of a secure system of law to protect us from each other, we all have a right to all things; that is, we have no obligation to defer to anyone else or yield to them. This equality of right is matched by a rough equality of capacity and, therefore, an equality of hope. It is this combination that brings us to grief.

Each of us is a potential threat to everyone else because each of us faces a world in which other people may cause us harm. The reasons for this are threefold. First, the state of nature is a state of scarcity. You and I may both want the same apple, and even if we do not, we both want to be sure of having enough to eat. This sets us at odds. This is the condition described by Hobbes as competition. However modest we may be in our wants, we face the fact that other people's use of the world may deprive us of what we need. I may be happy to drink water rather than champagne, but if your anxiety about future water supplies has led you to sequester all the local water supply, I shall have to do something to extract from you enough water for my needs.

The second cause of trouble is fear or diffidence. The logic of fear is something with which humanity has become extremely familiar during the past fifty years. It is the logic of interaction between two persons or two societies that can each annihilate the other, and neither of which possesses second-strike capacity, that is, the ability to revenge itself on the other post mortem. Two nuclear powers that can each wipe out the other side's nuclear forces if they strike first, and therefore cannot revenge themselves on the other side if they do not strike first, would be the post–World War II illustration of Hobbes's theory. The point to notice is that the horrors of the situation do not hinge on either party's wishing to attack the other. People in this situation are driven to attack one another by the logic of the situation, no matter what their motives. Thus, I look at you and know that you can kill me if you have to; I know that you must have asked the question whether you have to. Do you have to? The answer is not entirely clear, but a plausible reason is that you will have looked at me and have understood that I have every reason to be afraid of you because you might need to attack me. But if that is true, you do need to attack me, and if I know that about you, I can see that I must attack you. If I let you strike first, my loss is complete. So however little I incline to attack you, I have a strong incentive to do so. Or, as Hobbes puts it: "From this diffidence of one another, there is no way for any man to secure himselfe, so reasonable, as Anticipation.[38]

Both these first two reasons for conflict can be dealt with fairly easily. Competition can be dealt with by the achievement of prosperity; if I can be sure that my efforts to achieve subsistence will indeed secure my continued existence, I have no further reason to fight. It is sometimes suggested that Hobbes failed to understand that markets help overcome scarcity, but this is surely as false as the equally common view that Hobbes's politics are only about maintaining markets. The obvious reading of Hobbes is that once mine and thine are defined and enforced, we shall successfully look after our own welfare: "Plenty dependeth (next to Gods favour) meerly on the labour and industry of men."[39] Similarly, once there is a system of police, fear makes for peace rather than conflict. I see that you have every reason not to attack me, so think you will not; you see that I have every reason not to attack you (because we are both threatened with the same sanctions by the sovereign) and think I will not; now we both know that neither of us has any incentive to attack, so we both have even less an incentive, and peace is established.

The third cause of conflict is not so easily dealt with. This is pride, or vainglory. Hobbes insists that a peculiarity of human desire is its indeterminacy. Not only do we constantly change our ideas about what we want; we are chronically unsure whether what we want is worth having. There is no tendency to gravitate toward the truly good, for our desires are the psychological outcrop of a physiological mechanism that is in constant flux. But one crude test of value is the envy of other men.[40] This presents a worse problem than the other causes of conflict. "Vain Glory" is satiable only when we reach the top of the heap, and the criterion of success is universal envy; vainglory cannot be slaked by prosperity, and it creates a competition that security cannot defuse. There logically cannot be more than one top position; if that is what we seek, the conflict between ourselves and others is absolute. It is not surprising that Hobbes treats pride as the worst threat to peace and assails it both in aristocrats who take pride in their descent and in their social inferiors who strive for riches and social position. It is the one attitude that has to be suppressed rather than merely assuaged or diverted, and it is apt that *Leviathan* is the story of the genesis of the creature who was king over the children of pride.[41]

The combined pressure of competition, diffidence, and glory leads to the war of all against all and to a life that is poor, solitary, nasty, brutish, and short. To escape this condition, men must devise institutions that will enforce rules of conduct that ensure peace. To discover what those rules are is to discover the law of nature. We are so familiar with such an argument that we may fail to see how different its assumptions were from the political assumptions on which most of Hobbes's contemporaries relied. Filmer, for instance, argued in his *Patriarcha* that men had never lived outside government; the Bible and secular history concurred in tracing political history to life in small, clanlike groups governed by the absolute authority of the father. The Roman *patria potestas* (the power of the head of the Roman family) was much like the authority of Old Testament fathers; it was a power of life and death, a power to sell one's children into slavery. It was the proper model of political authority. Although few modern readers think much of Filmer's history, there is something deeply engaging about his response to the assertion in state-of-nature theory that men are born free and equal: they are not. Many others of Hobbes's contemporaries would have thought it simply needless to stray outside English history in looking for the foundations of government. The realm of England had a traditional structure: it was an organic community to be governed according to familiar principles by the king, the Lords Spiritual and Secular, and the Commons. Hobbes thought that it was essential to go behind these debates. The polity had to be founded on the laws of nature, not on habit or on local myth.

Hobbes's account of the laws of nature is distinctive. "A LAW OF NATURE (*lex naturalis,*) is a Precept, or generall Rule, found out by Reason, by which a man is forbidden to do, that, which is destructive of his life, or taketh away the means of preserving the same; and to omit, that, by which he thinketh it may be best preserved."[42] Hobbes sees that their standing as laws is problematic; in both *Leviathan* and *De cive*, Hobbes insists that a law is the word of someone who by right bears command. The laws of nature, conceived as deliverances of reason, are thus not, in the usual sense, laws. Hobbes sees this; he calls them "theorems," which they surely are. Laws, properly, are commands rather than theorems, and thus exist only when someone issues them as commands.

> These dictates of Reason, men use to call by the name of Lawes, but improperly: for they are but Conclusions, or Theoremes concerning what conduceth to the conservation and defence of themselves; whereas Law, properly, is the word of him, that by right hath command over others. But yet if we consider the same Theoremes, as delivered in the word of God, that by right commandeth all things; then are they properly called Lawes.[43]

This approach contrasts in an interesting way with that of Locke. For Locke, the argument runs through the inferred wishes of God and could not be sustained otherwise. That is, in the Lockean state of nature, a man first comes to the view that he is sent into the world about God's business as the creation of an omnipotent maker, and then concludes that such a maker requires him to preserve himself, and others as far as that is consistent with his own preservation.[44] This is a process of ratiocination and is, to that extent, like the process Hobbes invokes; but it is not the same process.

Hobbes, then, claims that we can see that the rules we ought to follow lay down that we must preserve our lives, and that we have an absolute right to do whatever conduces to that end. What most conduces to it is to seek peace, and that is accordingly the first law, just as the statement that we have the right to do anything necessary for self-preservation is the fundamental right of nature. We can then infer that the way to achieve peace is to give up as much of our natural right as others will. It appears that we must renounce all our rights, except only the right to defend ourselves in extremis. It is to be noticed that Hobbes does not suggest that we shall generally have any psychological difficulty in seeking peace. Some people have bolder characters and perhaps a taste for violence; they will present a problem, since they will not be moved by the fear of death that moves most of us to desire peace.[45] Most of us are not like them, but, in fact, wish to be protected against them. Hobbes's account of the way we are forced into conflict explains the conflict not as the result of our wish to engage in aggression, but as the result of our wish to lead a quiet life.

Moreover, we can see why it is a mistake to assimilate too closely Hobbes's account of our situation to the prisoner's dilemma of recent game-theoretical discussions. The prisoner's dilemma is superficially very like the Hobbesian state of nature. The dilemma is that each of the two parties to the dilemma faces a situation in which, should he do the cooperative thing and the other person not, he suffers a great loss, whereas if they both do the noncooperative thing, they both do badly. A Hobbesian who, say, disarms himself without being sure others do so also may now be killed more easily by others; so he had better keep his weapons, even though everyone will be worse off if all are armed than they would be if all were disarmed. This looks very like the problem of a noncooperative, aggregatively inferior outcome dominating a cooperative, aggregatively superior one.

		B	
		adheres	violates
A	adheres	2,2	4,1
	violates	1,4	3,3

The matrix above does not put values on the outcomes, only on their ranking in the eyes of self-interested participants. Each participant ranks as his favored outcome the one in which the other party (party B) keeps his agreement and he (party A) benefits from that agreement while violating it. This occurs, for example, if the other person disarms himself and I take advantage of his unarmed condition to take what I want from him. Hobbesian man is supposed to repress this desire. This is why the state of nature is not a true prisoner's dilemma. The essence of a prisoner's dilemma is that because the parties to it are utility maximizers, opponents in the game will always try to exploit each other, and they know it. Hobbesian man will not. He is not a utility maximizer, but a disaster avoider. Your proper response to my disarming myself is to disarm yourself, not to kill me: to seek peace, not to maximize advantage. I do wish not to be vulnerable, not because I know you will exploit me if you can, but because I am not certain that you will not exploit me. In modern discussions, utility-maximizing assumptions ensure that none of the obvious ways of getting out of the dilemma will work. The most obvious is to agree to follow the cooperative route and to set up an enforcement system to enforce the agreement. But if we are utility maximizers, it will both be overstretched (because everyone will renege on their agreements when they can profit from doing so) and underoperated (because its personnel will not do their job as enforcers if they think they can do better by slacking off). In a manner of speaking, utility maximizers are rational fools, for they *cannot but* ignore agreements if it profits them to do so. Hobbesian man is obliged to keep his agreements unless it is intolerably dangerous to do so, and Hobbes does not suggest we will be tempted to stray, as long as we keep our eyes on the need to avoid the state of nature. Once Hobbesian men have agreed on the cooperative path, they will follow it not only until they can see some advantage in not doing so, but unless and until it threatens their lives.[46] Hobbes relies heavily on his subjects' fear of the return of the state of nature to motivate them to keep their covenant of obedience; as he says, fear is the motive to rely on, and he spent much of *Leviathan* trying to persuade them to keep their eyes on the object of that fear.

The Contractual Escape Route

The explanation of this demands an account of the Hobbesian contract and its place in his political theory. Hobbes's first two laws of nature tell us to seek peace and to be ready to give up as much of our right to all things as others are for the sake of peace. The third law of nature is "that men perform their covenants made." This law is central to the entire edifice. It is also a slightly odd law. All the other laws, whether the basic injunction to seek peace or elaborate corollaries such as the requirement to give heralds safe conduct, are injunctions of a clearly moral kind. The requirement that we keep promises is peculiar because it seems to be both moral and logical. A covenant specifies now what we shall do in some future time; if it did not bind us (ceteris paribus), it would not be a covenant. Consider how often we try to evade a regretted obligation by saying something along the lines of "It wasn't really a promise, only an expression of hope." To know what a covenant is is to know that it is a way of incurring an obligation. This thought is what lies behind Hobbes's claim that breach of covenant is like what logicians call absurdity, in effect saying that we shall and shall not do whatever it may be.[47]

The reason for Hobbes's concern with covenants is obvious enough. If we are to escape from the state of nature, it can be only by laying aside our right to all things. That is, we can do that only by covenanting not to do in future what we had a right to do in the past—mainly by agreeing not to use and act on our private judgment of what conduces to our safety in contradiction of the sovereign's public judgment, except in dire emergency. Hobbes sees that there are difficulties in the way of contracting out of war and into peace. Since we are obliged not to endanger our lives, we shall not keep covenants that threaten our safety, and a covenant to disarm would do that unless we could rely on everyone else keeping their covenant to disarm too. But how can we do that if there is as yet no power to make them keep their covenants? One of Hobbes's more famous pronouncements was that "covenants, without the Sword, are but Words, and of no Strength to secure a man at all."[48] It seems that in order to establish a power that can make us all keep our covenants, we must covenant to set it up, but that the covenant to do so is impossible to make in the absence of the power it is supposed to establish. Hobbes, in fact, understood the problem he had posed himself.

He did not think that all covenants in the state of nature are rendered void by the absence of an enforcing power. The laws of nature bind us *in foro interno* (literally, "in the inner court"); they oblige us to intend to do what they require; a person who makes a contract is committed to carrying out his side of the agreement if the other party does and if it is safe to do so. If, upon making a contract, he finds that the other party has indeed performed and that it is safe to perform himself, then he is obliged *in foro externo* (publicly), too, that is, as to the carrying out of the act. It is no use pretending to recognize an obligation *in foro interno* but then failing to act when it is safe to do so. The only conclusive evidence of a sincere recognition of an obligation *in foro interno* is acting when it is safe. If I shout across the ravine that keeps us from injuring each other that I will place ten apples at some agreed-on spot if you agree to place five pears there when you pick up the apples, and I then place the apples there and retire to a safe distance while you collect them, you are *obliged* to leave the pears. If I can spare the apples and do not endanger my life by leaving them there, a Hobbesian, though not a twentieth-century game theorist, would think I did well to risk disappointment if you take my apples and leave no pears. Experimentally, of course, people behave as Hobbes suggests and try to create cooperative arrangements by engaging in tit for tat: if you take my apples and leave no pears, I "punish" you by not cooperating the next time; if you leave the agreed-on pears, I leave apples again.[49]

Can this explain the obligation to obey the sovereign and get out of the state of nature? Perhaps it can, even though most commentators have been sure it could not. Remember that not all of us are watching for an opportunity to take advantage of other people's compliance with the laws of nature; we are watching only lest they take advantage of our compliance. It is, of course, absurd to imagine that we could literally make the sort of covenant that Hobbes describes as a "covenant of every man with every man, in such manner, as if every man should say to every man. . . ."[50] It is far from absurd to imagine that we could, in effect, indicate to others that we proposed to accept such and such a person or body of persons as an authority until it was proved to be more dangerous to do so than to continue in the state of nature. In a manner of speaking, we do it the entire time inside existing political societies.

Hobbes was not apparently very anxious about such puzzles. Two reasons may be guessed at, although guessing is all it is. The first is that the usual situation in which we find ourselves is not that of setting up a state ab initio, but of deciding whether to swear allegiance to an existing government. That is, modern commentators are fascinated by the puzzle of how to create a sovereign by institution, but Hobbes paid more attention to the rights of and duties owed to a sovereign by acquisition. Hobbes published *Leviathan* when he came back to England and made his peace with the Commonwealth established by Cromwell after the deposition and execution of Charles I. He said that he thought the book had framed the minds of many gentlemen to a conscientious obedience, by which he meant that they had been moved by his arguments to understand that they could give allegiance to Cromwell without dishonoring their previous allegiance to Charles. So Hobbes's topic was the "sovereign by acquisition" rather than the "sovereign by institution." The second reason is that Hobbes's most strikingly counterintuitive claim about the contract that binds us to the sovereign is that it is valid even if extorted by force.

> Covenants entred into by fear, in the condition of meer Nature, are valid. For example, if I Covenant to pay a ransome, or service for my life, to an enemy; I am bound by it. For it is a Contract, wherein one receiveth the benefit of life; the other is to receive mony, or service for it; and consequently where no other Law (as in the condition, of meer Nature) forbiddeth the performance, the Covenant is valid.[51]

What Hobbes imagined was the situation in which we find ourselves, after the end of a war or the end of a decisive battle, at the absolute mercy of the victor. He is entitled to kill us if he wishes; we are in a state of nature with respect to him; we are, to use Hobbes's terminology, an enemy. This does not mean someone actually engaged in fighting him, but someone who is not pledged not to fight him. The victor has the right of nature to do whatever seems good to him to secure himself, and killing us to be on the safe side is no injustice to us. In Hobbes's unusual terminology, it cannot be unjust, since all injustice involves breach of contract and there is no contract to be breached. He may offer us our lives on the condition that we submit to his authority. Now we have a choice: to refuse to submit and so draw our death upon us, or to submit. What Hobbes insists is that if we submit, we are bound. To cite the fact that we submitted out of fear is useless because we always submit to authority out of fear: "In both cases they do it for fear: which is to be noted by them, that hold all such Covenants, as proceed from fear of death, or violence, voyd; which, if it were true, no man, in any kind of Commonwealth, could be obliged to Obedience."[52] The only thing that can void a contract is an event subsequent to the contract that makes it too dangerous to fulfill it. Nothing that we could take into account when we made the contract counts against its validity. Most readers find Hobbes's view quite shocking, but it is, after all, true enough that when we go and buy food at a grocery, we regard ourselves as obliged to pay for what we purchase even though we are ultimately driven to eat by fear of starvation. Hobbes's point was that both contracts—the contract of all with all, and the contract of the individual with the person who has his life within his power—are based on fear; and both are valid.

Contractualism and Obligation

In some ways, the greater oddity of Hobbes's work is the insistence that each of us is obliged only because each of us has, implicitly or explicitly, contracted to obey the sovereign. Of all the routes to obligation, contract is at once the most and the least attractive. It is the most attractive because the most conclusive argument for claiming that someone has an obligation of some kind is to show them that they imposed it on themselves by some sort of contract-like procedure. That route is uniquely attractive because promising is a paradigm of the way we voluntarily acquire obligations. It is unattractive for the same reason; few of us can recall having promised to obey our rulers for the very good reason that few of us have done so. American schoolchildren, who are obliged to pledge allegiance to the Stars and Stripes and "the republic for which it stands" most mornings of the school year, are an exception to this. It is odd that schools tend to drop this ceremony when children reach the age of reason and might be held to account for their promises.

The example of the pledge made by American schoolchildren shows one or two other problems. The most obvious is just what Hobbes tried to defuse with his claim that fear does not invalidate covenants. If we had approached a flag-burning dissident at the time of the Vietnam War and reminded him that he had once pledged allegiance, he would not have been much moved. For one thing, he might have said, he had had no option; if he had wanted to attend school, he had to say the pledge or face expulsion. How could a pledge extorted by such methods have any binding force? For another, students might plausibly complain that they had had no idea what was involved in pledging allegiance. How were they to know that the Republic for which the flag stood would subsequently turn out to be intent on sending them to get killed in Vietnam? Here, too, Hobbes's response is that what we pledge is obedience to a person or body of persons, and in doing so we renounce any right to discuss the terms of that obedience thereafter. It is just because we renounce *all* our rights that Hobbes's theory has the character it does. It is also what made it vulnerable to the complaints of Locke, who observed that it would be folly to defend ourselves from polecats by seeking the protection of lions; leaving the state of nature by exposing ourselves to the absolute, arbitrary power of the sovereign appears less than rational.

It seems odd that Hobbes should insist that obedience rests on a covenant, and that he should have so argued himself into a corner that he had to give a very counterintuitive account of the way in which coercion does and does not affect the validity of contract. One wonders what drove him to do so. Some aspects of his argument seem easily explicable; they were driven by the political needs of the day. It is part of his argument that when the person whom we acknowledge as sovereign can no longer protect us, we may look for a new ruler. The bearing of this on the situation of anyone who was formerly a loyal royalist and now had to consider whether to acknowledge Cromwell's Commonwealth is obvious enough. To do this, though, he had to defuse the objection that a person who joined the service of a sovereign out of fear would feel himself permitted to leave it whenever things got hot. Hobbes denies this twice over. In the "Review and Conclusion" of *Leviathan*, he states:

> To the Laws of Nature, declared in the 15. Chapter, I would have this added, That every man is bound by Nature, as much as in him lieth, to protect in Warre, the Authority, by which he is himself protected in time of Peace. For he that pretendeth a Right of Nature to preserve his owne body, cannot pretend a Right of Nature, to destroy him, by whose strength he is preserved: It is a manifest contradiction of himselfe.[53]

But he had earlier said clearly enough that what we do when we promise to recognize a given person or body of persons as sovereign is to sustain that authority in all necessary ways, particularly by paying our taxes willingly and by not quibbling over ideological issues.[54]

Less explicable is Hobbes's insistence that obligation is self-incurred. Sometimes this insistence is diluted, as when Hobbes claims that by accepting our lives, property, and liberties from a sovereign who can lawfully kill us, we have in effect contracted to obey him. More commonly, it appears to have reflected a deep conviction that in the last resort, everything hinges on the thoughts and actions of individuals. Hobbes, we might say, saw himself as addressing his readers one by one, trying to persuade each of them to accept his case for obedience to an absolute sovereign. It is a vision that seems on its face not wholly consistent with his view that persons possessed of sufficient power can simply force others to subscribe to their authority. "The Kingdome of God is gotten by violence," he observes; what that seems to mean is that because God's power is irresistible, only he has unique authority not based on our contracting to obey him.[55] But even then one wonders whether God's dissimilarity to any human authority may not be the true point of Hobbes's observation. At all events, Hobbes's individualism is in the spirit both of the methodological tactics of the opening chapters of *Leviathan* and of the concentration on each individual's fears for himself and his own concerns that underpins Hobbes's account of the state of nature. And Hobbes's individualism is important in his insistence that the limits of our obligation to obey the sovereign are set by our inability to give away our lives. We may say to him or them, "Kill me if I do not perform," but not "If you try to kill me, I shall not resist." It is one of the many peculiarities of Hobbes's cast of mind that he insists that the rights of despotic sovereigns are just the same as those of sovereigns by institution, and yet still claims, "It is not therefore the Victory, that giveth the right of Dominion over the Vanquished, but his own Covenant. Nor is he obliged because he is Conquered; that is to say, beaten, and taken, or put to flight; but because he cometh in and submitteth to the Victor."[56]

Rights and Duties of the Sovereign

When the sovereign is instituted, or acquires his power by succession or conquest or some other conventional route, a strikingly lopsided situation arises. We the subjects have nothing but duties toward the sovereign, but he is not, in the strict sense, under any obligation to us. Hobbes's argument for these alarming conclusions is a tour de force, but it has always struck critics as more bold than convincing. In the case of the sovereign by institution, Hobbes points out that we covenant with one another, not with the sovereign. Strictly, we are contractually obliged to one another to give up our natural rights in the sovereign's favor. The sense in which we are obliged to the sovereign is somewhat tricky to elucidate. In one sense, he is the beneficiary of our contracts but not a party to them, as would be the case if you and I promised each other to look after a neighbor's child. Are we obliged *to* the child as well as in respect of the child? Opinions vary. In Hobbes's theory, it is a moot point, for the sovereign is the beneficiary of our promised intention to do whatever he tells us, which is just the position he would be in if our obligation was to him as well as to one another in respect of him. In any case, the central issue is Hobbes's determination to show that the sovereign has no obligations to us.

Almost every commentator is so intrigued by this argument that it usually passes unnoticed that in the case of the sovereign by acquisition, the contract is made with the sovereign, who does therefore have—momentarily—

an obligation to us. The step to be attended to is that the sovereign's obligation can be instantly fulfilled. The sovereign in effect says to us, "If you submit, I will not kill you." When he spares us, he has fulfilled his obligation. Our obligation, on the other hand, endures indefinitely. So the same situation comes about as comes about in the more complex case of sovereignty by institution: "In summe, the Rights and Consequences of both *Paternall* and *Despoticall* Dominion, are the very same with those of a Sovereign by Institution; and for the same reasons."[57]

Nonetheless, the sovereign has duties. Indeed, he has obligations to God, although not to any earthly authority. For the natural law binds the sovereign, and as long as his or their subjects are more or less well behaved, this law binds the sovereign not only in conscience but also in action.

> The Office of the Sovereign, (be it a Monarch, or an Assembly,) consiseth in the end, for which he was trusted with the Soveraign Power, namely the procuration of *the safety of the people*; to which he is obliged by the Law of Nature, and to render an account thereof to God, the Author of that Law, and to none but him. But by Safety here, is not meant a bare Preservation, but also all other Contentments of life, which every man by lawfull Industry, without danger, or hurt to the Common-wealth, shall acquire to himselfe.[58]

The inference is hard to shake: we are obliged to obey the laws of nature except when it is too dangerous to do so, and if the sovereign is moderately effective, it will not be dangerous for him to do so. No doubt a conversation might be imagined between Machiavelli and Hobbes on the question of what the sovereign should count as danger and how scrupulous he should be in following natural law.

For all that, Hobbes insists quite energetically both that there is no question of our holding the sovereign to account for anything he might do, and that he should be guided by the moral law. It is not too much to claim that Hobbes's ideal sovereign would be absolute in principle, but indistinguishable from a constitutional sovereign in practice. Or, to put it otherwise, we cannot demand constitutional government as a matter of right, which is why Hobbes is never going to turn into a Lockean; but a ruler, when it is safe to do so, ought to govern in a constitutional fashion. This is, to belabor a point, a place where the coincidence of utilitarian and deontological considerations is very apparent. What other writers might demand as a matter of right, Hobbes derives from such obvious considerations as the fact that threats of punishment, say, will enhance the well-being of society only if people know what will happen to them under what conditions, and know how to avoid them. Retroactive punishment is thus contrary to the purpose of civil society, and so is to be deplored regardless of whether we have a right not to suffer it. Hobbes, in fact, comes close to letting a right not to be so punished back into his lexicon by a sort of conceptual sleight of hand.

> Harme inflicted for a Fact done before there was a Law that forbad it, is not Punishment, but an act of Hostility: for before the Law, there is no transgression of

the Law: But Punishment supposeth a fact judged to have been a transgression of the Law; therefore Harme inflicted before the Law made, is not Punishment, but an act of Hostility.[59]

The sovereign's duties under the law of nature fall into three roughly distinct categories. On the one hand, there are restraints on his actions that stem from the nature of sovereignty, of which the most important are those that forbid the sovereign to divide or limit his sovereign authority. He can transfer it whole and undivided, set out rules for its transfer to his successor, and do whatever does not destroy it, but any action that seems to part with a vital element of sovereignty is void.[60] The second class of actions embraces those things that the law of nature forbids or enjoins. A Hobbesian sovereign who observes these requirements will go a surprisingly long way toward recognizing everything that human-rights advocates demand of governments, except for one thing—conceding subjects a share in government as a matter of right. I shall return to that point almost at once, since it bears on Hobbes's understanding of freedom. It is perhaps not surprising that the requirements of the law of nature coincide with the requirements of most human-rights theories; but it is worth noticing that those requirements forbid disproportionate punishments, forbid the ex post facto criminalization of conduct, forbid anyone to be a judge in his own case, and much else besides.

The final class of actions occupies most of Hobbes's attention in the second book of *Leviathan*, in which he discusses what one might call the standard political tasks that a prudent and effective sovereign will have to perform. For the most part, they contain no surprises. We might wonder at the vanity that leads Hobbes to suggest that the sovereign would be well advised to have the doctrines of *Leviathan* taught to the entire population in order to keep their minds on the horrors of war and the blessings of order, but these chapters are in general not unpredictable in their concentration on the need for adequate taxation, security of property, and so on. They do contain two possible surprises for the modern reader. One is the prominent place Hobbes gives to the sovereign's role in judging what doctrines may be publicly taught and defended. It is, says Hobbes, against the sovereign's duty to give up the right of "appointing Teachers, and examining what doctrines are conformable, or contrary to the Defence, Peace, and Good of the people."[61] Hobbes's views on religion were very complex, but two simple things can be said of them. The first is that Hobbes was so appalled by the way religion led men into civil strife that it was obvious to him that the secular powers had to control religious institutions and decide what might and might not be preached in the pulpit. Hobbes was in general an antipluralist, in the sense that his insistence on the sovereign's unique standing as the source of all law meant that no subordinate body such as a church or university could claim any independent authority over its members, other than what the state might grant it. But what they could not claim as a right, they might well be given as a license to engage in harmless and possibly useful inquiry. As far as the church went, Hobbes was entirely opposed to ecclesiastical claims to the right to impose secular penalties. Hobbes anticipated Locke's *Letter on Toleration* by arguing in his essay on heresy that a church should have no power over its members beyond that of separation from the common worship and, more contentiously, that the first secular laws against heresy were intended to apply only to pastors, not to the laity.[62]

The other thing one can say of Hobbes's view was that he saw that the degree of religious uniformity the state needed to impose would vary with the temper of the people. If there was much doctrinal dispute, the state must settle at least the externals of behavior, such as whether altars were or were not to be used and whether we must pray bareheaded. These were conventional signs of honor, and it was a proper task of the state to set those conventions. Beyond that, Hobbes hoped that with the return of common sense, men might return to the condition of the early church and to "independency."[63] Too much intervention would be destructive of felicity.

The second surprise comes not at what Hobbes proposes to regulate in a way we might think excessive, but at what he proposes not to regulate. Hobbes was not a "capitalist" thinker, nor a theorist of commercial society; in many ways, he was hostile to the life of moneymaking and had a thoroughly uncapitalist preference for leisure over labor. Nonetheless, he advised the sovereign to concentrate on defining property rights, cheapening legal transactions by such devices as establishing registered titles to land— something not achieved for another two and three-quarter centuries—and encouraging prosperity by leaving his subjects to look after their own well-being. This was not a pure laissez-faire regime. Hobbes's proposal was much nearer what we would call a welfare state, with provision for the sick, the elderly, the infirm, and the unemployed.[64] Yet it shows once more how insistent Hobbes was that the central task of politics was to settle who had the ultimate legal authority and to make sure that the possessor of authority could get the law enforced. It did not follow that busybody legislation was prudent or useful. Indeed, once the matter was framed in such terms, it clearly was not.

All this is set out with no suggestion that the sovereign's political self-control reflects the subject's rights. Indeed, Hobbes is at pains to deny it. As we have seen, the subject, having given up his rights, cannot now appeal to them. Moreover, the one area in which Hobbes breaks entirely with later writers on human rights is his insistence that we have no right to have a share in the sovereign authority and that any system in which we try to set up a collective sovereign embracing many people will almost surely be a disaster. His grounds for so thinking are partly historical; that is, he believed that democracies characteristically collapsed into chaos and factionalism, and doubtless thought himself vindicated by the behavior of Parliament in his own day. Even more interesting, he broke with the tradition that held that one form of government, and one form only, pursued freedom. His view was summed up in a sentence from a passage we have quoted already:

"There is written on the Turrets of the city of *Luca* in great characters at this day, the word *LIBERTAS*; yet no man can thence inferre, that a particular man has more Libertie, or Immunitie from the service of the Commonwealth there, than in *Constantinople*. Whether a Common-wealth be Monarchicall, or Popular, the Freedome is still the same."[65]

Hobbes defines liberty in two not entirely consistent ways. First, in the state of nature, "by Liberty, is understood, according to the proper significance of the word, the absence of externall impediments."[66] Second, civil liberty, under government, is the *absence* of law or other sovereign commandment: "The Greatest Liberty of Subjects, dependeth on the Silence of the Law."[67] Both accounts make it entirely possible to act voluntarily only from fear, and neither suggests that freedom has anything to do with the freedom of the will. Hobbes disbelieved in free will and conducted a running battle with Bishop Bramhall on the contentious issue of freedom, necessity, and foreknowledge. His two chief purposes are clear enough. As we have seen already, he wanted to argue that a contract made out of fear for our lives is made freely enough to be a valid contract; the common view that coerced contracts are invalid ab initio he explained as a reflection of the fact that we are normally forbidden to force people into making contracts by the positive law of the sovereign. That civilized societies will forbid coerced contracts makes perfect sense. It is clear that there are sound reasons of policy for keeping force out of economic transactions.

The second great aim was to enforce the claim that freedom was not a matter of the form of government. In one sense, freedom and government are antithetical because we give up all our rights when we enter political society, except, as Hobbes observes in his discussion of the liberty of subjects, the right to defend ourselves against the immediate threat of death and injury. Had we reserved any rights upon submitting to a sovereign, we should have left open endless occasions for arguments over the question whether a given law does or does not violate one of those reserved rights. This would have frustrated the object of entering political society in the first place and so would have been absurd. Once we are members of political society, there is a further issue, which is the extent of the control our sovereign wishes to exercise over us. A despot who largely leaves us alone leaves us more liberty than a democracy in which the majority is constantly passing new legislation. This is the point of Hobbes's reference to Constantinople. Being part of the sovereign does not add to one's liberty; Hobbes is not Machiavelli, nor is he Rousseau. He felt strongly that the classical education of his day and religious enthusiasm could, in this area, combine to delude people into thinking that they could be free only in a republic: "And as to Rebellion in particular against Monarchy; one of the most frequent causes of it, is the Reading of the books of Policy, and Histories of the ancient Greeks, and Romans."[68]

The thought that killing one's king is not murder but tyrannicide is, says Hobbes, an encouragement to anarchy. To the degree that classical republicans talk sense at all, the freedom they have in mind must be the freedom of the republic as a whole from domination by outsiders. This plainly was a large part of what Machiavelli admired in the Romans, but hardly all of it. Here as elsewhere, Hobbes is not entirely scrupulous about painting his opponents in the colors that most flatter them.

Resistance

Hobbes was not a liberal, and this statement goes beyond the observation that "liberal" is a term not employed in English politics until around 1812; Hobbes was strenuously opposed to many of the things that define liberalism as a political theory. Nonetheless, many things about his political theory would sustain a form of liberalism, and he held many of the attitudes typical of later defenders of liberalism. It is easy to feel that as long as nobody talked about their "rights," a Hobbesian state would be indistinguishable from a liberal constitutional regime. The sovereign has excellent prudential reasons for listening to advisers, allowing much discussion, regulating the affairs of society by general rules rather than particular decrees, and so on indefinitely. Allied to the natural-law requirement to respect what we might call the subjects' moral rights, something close to a liberal regime emerges.

Still, the antipathy to claims of right is a real breach with liberal political ideas. Whereas Locke insists that we enter political society only under the shadow of a natural law whose bonds are drawn tighter by the creation of government, Hobbes relegates that law to the realm of aspiration. If the sovereign breaches it, we are not to resist but to reflect that it is the sovereign whom God will call to account, not ourselves. It is an unlovely view, for it suggests all too unpleasantly that if Hobbesian subjects are told to kill the innocent or torture prisoners for information, they will do so without much hesitation. They may think it very nasty, but they cannot engage in conscientious resistance, or if they do, they must not incite others to resist with them. They may embrace martyrdom, but not engage in rebellion.

This is the aspect of Hobbes that many readers find repugnant. It cannot entirely be got round either. Still, we may in conclusion see whether even in this area there is something to be said for Hobbes's views. We may approach an answer by way of Hobbes's account of punishment. Hobbes has two accounts of punishment; they serve much the same purpose, but they are very different. The purpose they serve is to insist both that there is a real difference between legal punishment and the treatment of "enemies," and that we are not obliged to submit to punishment without a struggle. The difference lies in whether the right to punish is a right the sovereign has gained upon the creation of the state or a right we all had in the state of nature that everyone but the sovereign has relinquished on submission. The first view would be an ancestor of Rousseau's and Kant's; the second view would be very like Locke's were it not for the fact that Hobbes does not anticipate

Locke in distinguishing the state-of-nature right to punish from the state-of-nature right to do whatever we need to defend ourselves from our enemies.

The first view follows from Hobbes's discussion in chapter 30 of the nature of the obligation to obey the sovereign. He says unequivocally that the obligation imposed by civil law rests on the prior natural duty to keep covenants:

> Which naturall obligation if men know not, they cannot know the Right of any Law the Sovereign maketh. And for the Punishment, they take it but for an act of Hostility.[69]

The second is offered in chapter 28, where Hobbes insists that

> to covenant to assist the Soveraign, in doing hurt to another, unlesse he that so covenanteth have a right to doe it himselfe, is not to give him a Right to Punish. It is manifest, therefore, that the Right which the Common-wealth (that is, he, or they that represent it) hath to Punish, is not grounded on any concession or Gift of the Subjects.[70]

In the state of nature, we all have the right to subdue, hurt, or kill anyone we think we need to in order to secure our own preservation; what the covenant does is commit us to helping the sovereign to employ that right. What then distinguishes punishment from hostility is the regular, predictable, lawful, and public nature of the harm so inflicted.

The reason why any of this matters is straightforward. On the one hand, Hobbes must mark a difference between our vulnerability to punishment if we enter political society and then violate the rules, and our vulnerability to being treated as an enemy if we remain in a state of nature with those who have entered political society. Unlike Rousseau, who suggested that we might remain in something like state-of-nature relations and still be treated decently, Hobbes insists that if we were to remain in this situation, we could be treated in any way the sovereign thought fit, ignoring his own insistence that the law of nature at least urged the recognition, *in foro interno*, of acting with no more than the barely necessary force. By signing up for political membership, we sign up to suffer no more than the penalties prescribed by law if we break the law at some future point. This supposes that punishment is something other than the ill-treatment properly applied to enemies for our own protection.

The view that punishment rests on the sovereign's state-of-nature right of self-defense has some awkward consequences. One is that we appear to remain in the state of nature vis-à-vis the sovereign, and that legal relations are always, as one might say, horizontal, holding between subject and subject, but not between subject and sovereign. It is a complex operation to analyze the ways in which we do and do not leave the state of nature in our relations with the sovereign. At one level, it is harmless enough to suppose that we do not. The sovereign and ourselves can transact most of our business on the basis of the law of nature, especially since the law of nature would enjoin us to respect the sovereign's laws whether or not we had ever contracted to do so. It is perhaps in the general spirit of Hobbes's account that legal relations in the usual, conventional sense hold between subjects only. Thus, we must abstain from taking one another's property, but the sovereign is not bound by the same rules. All the same, there is an awkwardness to it; it fails to distinguish, except in a shadowy fashion, between the regular, law-governed treatment of the citizens' property by way of such things as properly legislated taxation, on the one hand, and peremptory expropriation, on the other. This case is much like the case of Hobbesian constitutionalism. The sovereign ought to behave as a constitutional sovereign would behave, but there is no suggestion that the sovereign must do so for constitutional reasons. Ex hypothesi, the sovereign is the fount of law and is "absolute" in the sense of not being bound by his own rules in the same way as his subjects are bound by those he promulgates; nonetheless, he ought to consider himself bound *in foro interno* and by the law of nature.

Many later writers, perhaps overimpressed by the difference between punishment and mere ill-treatment for a purpose, have suggested that the fact that the subject willed the punishment was a morally significant aspect of the institution.[71] Hobbes was very much not of that camp. It was clear enough that the rational person had to commit himself to the existence of a system of sanctions: other people would not sign a contract of submission to sovereign authority unless he signed up as well, and they would not believe he was bound unless they saw he was vulnerable to sanctions. He must, therefore, say something equivalent to "if I do thus and such, you may try to kill, imprison or fine me." What he could not say was "I will endorse your doing so as you do it." He could not refuse to resist.

And here Hobbes's system encounters its moment of truth. Hobbes is eager to say three things, and they may not be entirely compatible. The first is that as long as the sovereign preserves my life and possessions, I must assist him to retain his power. If he calls an army together, I must fight or pay for a soldier to serve in my place.[72] If the enemy is at the gate, I must fight regardless. Useless sacrifice is certainly useless, but readiness to take risks on behalf of the power that protects us is indispensable. The second is that I am, in the last resort, entitled to do whatever seems best to me to save my life. I need not, and probably cannot, give myself up to prison and death. I have a right to self-preservation that overrides everything I may have formerly said. But, third, we cannot encourage others to resist the sovereign with us.

The conjunction of these last two claims presents problems. The absence of the first claim would amount to the dissolution of the whole political system upon the first crime committed against it. The absence of the second would not only, as we have seen, make it impossible to see why the formerly loyal subjects of Charles I might later swear allegiance to Cromwell with a whole heart and a clear conscience. The absence of the third would come close to admitting that people might foment revolution when it seemed to them that revolution was to be preferred to submission. But the third is inconsistent with the obvious possibility that the best way to secure myself against the sovereign's ill will is to ally myself with others who can resist him. If we are, for whatever reason, enemies of the sovereign, we must seek the best way we can find to our own safety.

At that point, Hobbes requires some much less formal way of explaining which forms of resistance are morally acceptable and which are mere criminal conspiracies. It is not hard to see the ingredients of such an explanation in his own writings, but it would be wholly at odds with the spirit of his political philosophy to seek them out and elaborate anything we might call a "Hobbesian theory of resistance." The point of his system was to discredit any such theory. The genius of Hobbes was to produce a theory that, because it was built on individualist and rationalist foundations, must, in spite of its author's intentions, leave room not only for individual resistance but also, in extremis, for full-fledged revolution. *Leviathan* may well have framed the minds of many gentlemen to a conscientious obedience, but it also framed in many other minds a disposition to ask whether the sovereign had failed to secure our peace and safety or was visibly about to do so. In so doing, it was inadvertently a prop to the revolutionaries of the next fifty years.

9

Hobbes and Individualism

THAT HOBBES WAS one of the begetters of modern individualism is widely asserted. Quite what it was that he thus begat is equally widely disputed. Here I try to show that Hobbes espoused a consistent (though not in all respects persuasive) form of individualism in intellectual, moral, and political matters. I draw on two earlier essays of mine, though I do so in order to advance beyond them, not to rest on them.[1] One problem is gestured at by my title: What kind of an individualist was Hobbes? Was he the "economic" individualist and booster for capitalism that C. B. Macpherson described?[2] Was he perhaps less a "market-oriented" individualist than the advocate of the self-centered but self-abnegating bourgeois moral style depicted in Leo Strauss's famous account, or of the "privatized" individualism described in Sheldon Wolin's *Politics and Vision*?[3] I suggest at the end of this essay that Hobbes's individualism was moral and intellectual, not economic, a doctrine of moral and intellectual autonomy—in essence, the individualism of the "modern" character described in Michael Oakeshott's essay *On Human Conduct*.[4]

Hobbes was a systematic thinker, and his conviction that he had created a science of man and society raises intriguing questions about the connections between his epistemological and his moral commitments. How does Hobbesian individualism relate to the atomism of Hobbes's mechanical materialism? Is there a logical tie, a conceptual affinity, or no relationship at all?[5] I shall argue that there is a conceptual affinity between his atomism and his intellectual individualism, but something closer to a logical tie between his intellectual individualism and his political individualism.

That Hobbes was in several senses an epistemological individualist is hardly disputable. One of those senses is given by his contempt for intellectual authority. "Goliath defied the host of Israel, and Mr Hobbs defyeth the whole host of learned men," complained Alexander Ross, and he was echoed by most other critics.[6] Yet Hobbes defended the absolute and arbitrary authority of the sovereign, and one might suppose that in a system as tightly constructed as his, all forms of authority must stand or fall together; Hobbes plainly thought not. Were his views at odds with one another or as consistent as he supposed? I try to show their consistency.

In part, my case is that Hobbes was impressed by the self-sufficiency of most individuals in everything other than mere self-preservation. Self-indulgent pride, intellectual or political, was deplorable; self-confidence was not. But this picture is methodologically individualist in implying that all modern, politically governed communities are sustained by individual commitment to the terms of cooperation, and it gives rise to an awkwardness (to put it no more strongly) that I have to defuse in the second section of what follows. Within Hobbes's political theory, in the narrow sense, there is a tension between his insistence that a man is obligated to obey the sovereign only by some positive act of his own and the utilitarian flavor of his account of the sovereign's powers and duties. The first is individualistic in asking the question "Why am *I* obliged to obey?" the second less so in asking, "What overall good is achieved when there exists a sovereign whom everyone obeys?" Within the more individualistic construction, there is also a tension between his insistence that we renounce all our rights in favor of the sovereign and his insistence that it is up to the individual to decide when he would do better to flee or resist rather than obey and submit.

I cannot promise a conclusive resolution of these anxieties, but I hope to provide the apparatus needed for the purpose. It comes in three parts. First, a treatment of Hobbes's epistemological antiauthoritarianism and individualism; second, a discussion of Hobbes's theory of obligation and its moral basis; last, a defense of the view that Hobbesian individualism is neither quietist, nor capitalist, nor "bourgeois."

Epistemological Individualism

"He was wont to say that if he had read as much as other men, he should have knowne no more then other men."[7] Aubrey's tribute to Hobbes's confidence in the resources of his own mind and his conviction of the absurdity of claims to intellectual authority is echoed by hostile critics: "Mr Hobbes consulted too few Authors and made use of too few Books."[8] They found it hard to believe in Hobbes's wholesale contempt for Aristotle, for tradition, or for the pretensions of any body of men to lay down the truth about the world; they set it down to brazen pride and a taste for novelties. Yet Hobbes's position was plain. We could be obliged to *say* what the sovereign wished, where the point was to express allegiance and not to assert a matter of fact. The sovereign might require us to utter phrases expressing allegiance to God and to worship him in sentences that were literally meaningless but expressively valuable: even if *"Spirit Incorporeall"* is an unintelligible epithet, it is excusable when they that so call God do so "not *Dogmatically*, with intention to make the Divine Nature understood; but *Piously*, to honour him with attributes, of significations, as remote as they can from the grossenesse of Bodies Visible."[9] What no sovereign can do is require us to *believe* propositions that might not in fact be true. Authority can lay down only what experience cannot decide. It is because the question whether the world has a beginning or not, to take an example from Hobbes himself, is unanswerable by human reason that authority may properly decide it.[10]

Hobbes's argument was in part political and defensive: belief is not under the control of the will and cannot be commanded. As subjects, we feel safer if we do not fear that sovereigns may command us to do what is not in our power to do. Political prudence prompts the sovereign too to self-restraint; belief can be dissimulated because the mind of man is not visible to anyone but its owner, and authority would be rash to provoke opposition by trying to discover whether people really believe what they will not avow or disbelieve what they will.

More importantly for our purposes, authority stands in the way of the growth of knowledge. Hobbes insists that each man must make up his mind for himself and believe only what he has good reason to believe; otherwise, superstition prevails and science is throttled. We do not *know* that which we merely take on trust: "He that takes up conclusions on the trust of Authors, and doth not fetch them from the first Items in every Reckoning (which are the significations of names settled by definitions), loses his labour; and does not know any thing; but only beleeveth it."[11] Hobbes was not alone in taking this stand. The admired Bacon, whose amanuensis he had briefly been, had said the same; the disliked Descartes did so too. Hobbes's opponents recognized the similarity. Condemning Hobbes as a monster of intellectual arrogance, they relied on Descartes's theological ill repute to discredit Hobbes when they pointed to the similarities between his views and those of the *Discourse on Method*.[12]

The difficulty is to give a convincing account of how the various elements in Hobbes's antiauthoritarian theory of knowledge hang together. The problem is that his most salient view, and the one most loathed by his contemporary critics, is his insistence that the subject's duty is to take the sentence of the sovereign for his guide to good and evil.[13] How, in the light of that, he still insisted on the importance of judging for ourselves in everything else it is not easy to see. It is quite clear that it cannot rest on an individual right to free speech or free thought. Hobbes had no time for what the Dissenters claimed as the "right of private judgment." The explanation must lie in his epistemology, but it is hard to find. It is not persuasive to assimilate Hobbes's philosophy of science to Baconian inductivism and empiricism; Hobbes was contemptuous of much empirical experimentation—though not of all experiment—and seems to have had no conception of inductive inference at all.[14] It looks equally implausible to suppose that Hobbes was a defender of Popper's methodology of conjecture and refutation *avant la lettre*; in Hobbes's account, true science renders refutation inconceivable. Moreover, one cannot suppose Hobbes a friend to Popper's program of showing that science and liberal democracy make good bedfellows.[15] It is more persuasive to assimilate Hobbes and Galileo. Galileo thought that geometry was the key to celestial mechanics and that experiment illuminated the operation of mechanisms whose modus operandi, once it was spelled out, was a matter of necessity. Hobbes's view of the relationship between the axiomatic method of geometry and our knowledge of geometry's applicability to the empirical world remains obscure; but he may well have shared this view, even though he was prone to insist on the arbitrariness of God's decision to construct his universe at all, and on the variety of means by which he might have produced his effects. But the analogy drawn in *Leviathan* between the art whereby God created the world and the art whereby man creates both geometry and the state suggests a less dramatic arbitrariness behind the universe.

It is a view that surfaces again in Locke's *Essay*.[16] Geometry sets out the rules for constructing figures and, therefore, bodies; it is hypothetically certain in the sense that geometry shows that if there are cubes, spheres, or whatever, then such and such are the properties they must have. It is an applied as well as a pure science, because empirical evidence and a priori construction converge to show that we live in a Euclidean space. Locke is as emphatic as Hobbes in stressing the difference between our a priori grasp of geometry and our a posteriori grasp of the laws of empirical science, but they are at one in suggesting that in the eye of God at any rate, all is a priori. We see a posteriori what he constructs a priori.[17] Hobbes insisted, famously, that reason cannot tell us the nature of anything other than what we ourselves create and thus that physics could not, strictly speaking, be a science. Yet it is not hard to see how a slightly more relaxed view would close the gap between the rational and the merely empirical while preserving the distinction between geometry and physics. Indeed, Hobbes's own discussion of the relationship between science and prudence is far from suggesting that science is wholly a priori, and far from ruling out any role for experience in science. It is not their concern for empirical evidence but their lack of concern that Hobbes complains of when he says that those who "love to shew their reading of Politiques and History" generally "study more the reputation of their owne wit, than the successe of anothers businesse."[18]

The connection between this view of science and epistemological individualism is indirect, in the sense that Hobbes strongly suggests, but does not try to prove, that each of us is capable of reaching the truths both of geometry and of statecraft if we will only cleave to a good method and avoid obscure speech and obfuscating symbols.[19] Here, too, his critics objected, insisting that doctors, lawyers, philosophers, and theologians needed the specialized terminologies of their disciplines and that Hobbes was encouraging the vulgar to set up their limited judgments as a standard to their betters, a charge anticipated and repudiated in his comments on *nosce te ipsum* ("know thyself"), "which was not meant, as it is now used to countenance, either the barbarous state of men in power towards their inferiors; or to encourage men of low degree, to a sawcie behaviour towards their betters."[20] The rules of good method are indeed simple enough—the avoidance of insignificant speech, the scrupulous distinguishing of words that refer to things from words that refer to words, the analytical disentangling of conceptions into their simplest elements, and extreme care in their recombination. Hobbes's encounter with Euclid, and with Plato's demonstration that

Meno was capable of proving Pythagoras's theorem from his own internal resources, would have pressed in the same direction.[21]

Knowledge, then, is an individual possession, which each of us can secure for himself or herself. Yet Hobbes acknowledges that we need the intellectual services of others to be wholly successful in the quest for it. Each individual is, to a degree, at the mercy of his own idiosyncratic physiology and psychology. What we have hold of is not the world itself, but its impact on our sensory and recording apparatus; our bodies change in the same way as everything else, and with them, the quality of our present grasp on the world and even on our own past thoughts and experiences. The difference between private fantasy and something we might dignify by the name of knowledge lies not only in the quality of our definitions and inferences, but also in the degree to which these are conformable to the definitions and inferences of others. Our thoughts are dictated by what we attend to, and our attention is driven by our passions; out of the company of others, all men are fantasists: "The most sober men, when they walk alone without care and employment of the mind, would be unwilling the vanity and Extravagance of their thoughts at that time should be publicly seen: which is a confession, that Passions unguided, are for the most part meere Madneses."[22] Hobbes remains an epistemological individualist, but recognizes the place of social discipline in epistemic reliability. Unless we are controlled by common standards, we may fly off in all directions. Moreover, just as the passions are implicated in the unreliability of isolated individuals, so the sin of pride appears as a social and an epistemological threat wherever men are excessively self-confident and mistake their own reasoning for the dictates of right reason: "And when men that think themselves wiser than all others, clamor and demand right Reason for judge; yet seek no more, but that things should be determined by no mans reason but their own, it is as intolerable in the society of men, as it is in play after trump is turned, to use for trump on every occasion, that suite whereof they have most in their hand."[23]

This mixture of individual achievement and social control means that the establishment of agreement can be a means to achieving a grasp of the truth, but consensus is not the test of truth. Hobbes was disinclined to trust group sentiment in this or any other area; many intellectual communities have a vested interest in teaching their members to talk various sorts of nonsense. Hobbes's view of the Roman Catholic Church's vested interest in obscurity is too well known to bear discussion. It seems that a community that can assist its members to search for the truth must have no vested interests, or an interest only in peace, security, and the advancement of humanity through the conquest of nature. Is this not, in spite of everything, leading us back toward an almost Popperian picture of science?

We need to belong to a community with an interest in truth; it must exercise a certain restraint on its members' fantasies, but it must not exercise a dogmatic authority over them. It is this last antiauthoritarian requirement that makes this an individualist philosophy of science, whether in Hobbesian or Popperian form. Progress demands individual boldness tempered by respect for the opinions of others. What of my earlier claim that it was implausible to assimilate Hobbes's philosophy of science to Popper's? We must distinguish the tactics of scientific progress from our view of what science achieves when it is successful. We may reject Popper's description of the findings of science as no more than "conjectures" that have thus far escaped refutation, yet see some role for his conception of the ideal scientific community in which every individual is encouraged in intellectual boldness.

If science is defined in the rationalist terms of Hobbes's account, it is still plausible to suggest that the inner resources on which the individual draws in constructing a theory are decisive, but can adequately be exploited only with the help of others. The detection of contradiction and ambiguity can be managed single-handed, but is best managed by like-minded groups. A proper appreciation of the "social" character of the creation of scientific knowledge still leaves Hobbes free to adopt the arrogant and violently anti-traditionalist approach that so distressed his contemporaries—though he is surely condemned out of his own mouth as a man who could not accurately distinguish between confidence and pride and who thus failed to live up to his own standards.

This antitraditionalist view of knowledge is, in strictly logical terms, independent of the mechanical materialism to which he also subscribed. Once again, the mere mention of Popper suffices to show that epistemological individualism (in the sense of an imperative to think for ourselves) is consistent with an antireductive willingness to believe in minds as well as matter and even with a belief in a Hegelian third world of objective mind.[24] Nonetheless, there is an affinity between the two things in Hobbes's work. The bridge between mechanical materialism and epistemological individualism is provided by the view that men are a species of self-regulating automata. If the natural order contains self-maintaining bodies that preserve a complicated internal organization and that manage complex interactions with the outside world for the sake of self-preservation, we best explain knowledge of the outside world as a component of this self-maintenance. Hobbes is innocent of evolutionary speculations about just why such entities must have reliable information about the outside world, let alone of any speculations about the value of seeing such creatures as mapmakers interested in continuously sophisticating their maps. Hobbes is not Karl Popper, nor even Jean-Jacques Rousseau.[25] All the same, Hobbes espoused a naturalistic and therefore an individualistic epistemology; it is individuals, in sensory interaction with the world, who are the bearers of knowledge of the world. This is the vision Hobbes shared with orthodox empiricism.[26]

Critics may by now feel that I have diluted Hobbes by first making him a precursor of Popper on the sociological front and now making him a quasi empiricist on the epistemological, and that the bare "affinity" suggested is too slender a basis for any very satisfying analysis. But one can certainly say that Hobbes's vision is individualistic enough to be distinctively anti-

Hegelian and anti-Wittgensteinian; it is naturalistic enough to be decidedly anti-Kantian in spite of Kant's professedly individualist Copernican revolution. Hobbes supposes that the interactive process between the individual and the material world provokes the conceptualizations by way of which we make sense of that world; but he is a naturalist in supposing that there are no privileged categories, whether built into the individual mind or given by "forms of life," that we impose upon the world. The affinity with mechanism gives a distinctive content to Hobbesian epistemological individualism of a kind that sustains the earlier suggestion that Hobbes believed that membership of an intellectual community was causally important in keeping our thinking on the rails, but not in providing the conceptual possibility of all thinking whatever.

Political Obligation Revisited

Hobbes's account of political obligation has been so thoroughly analyzed in recent years that one might reasonably despair of adding anything new to the discussion. This section sticks pretty narrowly to the "individualist" aspect of Hobbes's theory. There are two ways in which Hobbes's account of obligation is contentious; both involve a seeming conflict between Hobbes's insistence that nobody can be under an obligation to obey another except by virtue of some previous agreement to do so, which is a piece of moral individualism par excellence, and his claims, on the one hand, that we are under an obligation to obey the law of nature with no suggestion of our having consented to do so, and, on the other, that "a sure and irresistible power confers the right of Dominion, and ruling over those who cannot resist."[27] In pursuing this issue, I take it for granted that Hobbes's understanding of obligation is that obligation is a moral, and not simply a prudential, matter.[28] That is to say, the proposition "I am obliged to do x" is not reducible to "I am forced to do x," and "I ought" does not reduce to "I had better." The question is whether we have obligations only after imposing them upon ourselves, not whether Hobbes has a peculiar view of what obligations are. What I shall do is first show that our relations with God are so different from our relations with any earthly creature that a proper attention to that difference may resolve both of the problems just stated, though I have some anxieties about the resolution. Then I revert to the question that underlies this entire section: whether Hobbes's insistence that each of us alone is responsible for his or her own allegiance and obedience represents a distinctive moral individualism.

Leviathan explains how we come to have an obligation to obey the sovereign because of the terms of our having promised to obey. In the unusual event of our jointly instituting a sovereign, we promise one another to obey the person or body of persons so nominated; in the more usual case of the sovereign by acquisition, we submit to the person or body of persons who could, without injustice, take our life, receiving our lives in return for submission. Hobbes insists that it is submission that creates the obligation, not merely the threat of death, nor merely defeat in battle: "Nor is he obliged because he is Conquered; that is to say, beaten, and taken, or put to flight; but because he commeth in, and submitteth to the Victor."[29] This is the point of his claim that nobody is obliged but by some act of his or her own. The promises involved are odd in the sense that when a sovereign is instituted, the sovereign is not a party to the covenant and therefore does not stand in any reciprocal relation of obligation to the subject; conversely, although we do covenant with the sovereign in the case of sovereignty by acquisition, the sovereign immediately performs his side of the bargain by refraining from killing us, and thereafter is under no further obligation to us. So curious is this doctrine that one can suppose only that Hobbes was drawn to it by a thought he very much did not wish to give up, namely, that we really have put ourselves under an obligation that we ought to keep except where our lives would be endangered by the attempt—or more weakly, except where we fear that they would be so endangered. The polemical thrust of *Leviathan* in the interregnum context is presumably that since the gentlemen whose minds Hobbes wishes to frame to a conscientious obedience have already as good as promised to obey the Protectorate government, they would be foolish not to make that promise articulate when asked to do so—whence Clarendon's assertion that *Leviathan* was backed by thirty legions.[30]

There is no analogous process in the case of our obligation to obey the law of nature. There are some interesting difficulties posed by Hobbes himself. The laws of nature are precepts or general rules "found out by Reason, by which a man is forbidden to do, that, which is destructive of his life, or taketh away the means of preserving the same";[31] but he also describes them as being more properly theorems, an understanding of which is, so to speak, programmed into the self-maintaining entities that Hobbes considers us to be.[32] Under some conditions, the attempt to preserve ourselves leads to the war of all against all, and reflection on the causes and miseries of that state leads to our seeing the need for some power able to overawe us all. It leads to the injunction that we should seek peace whenever possible, and to the permission to use all helps and advantages of war if we cannot safely seek peace. The obligatoriness of the law of nature has not bothered most critics of Hobbes, the one serious exception being Brian Barry.[33] Critics interested in the problem of obligation have since the late 1960s worried away instead at the question of how individuals who are trying to maximize their own utilities can subscribe either to Hobbes's laws of nature or to the dictates of the sovereign. Their problem is this. Hobbes requires us to keep the laws of nature unless it is too dangerous to do so; it is this law-of-nature obligation that underlies our duty to obey the sovereign. But the maximizer of his or her own returns will surely obey only when it is maximally advantageous to do so, and will disobey if it is not.[34] I do not think this was the problem that faced Hobbes. Though Hobbes indeed describes the mechanisms of desire and motivation in terms that suggest that each person is indeed bent on maximizing his or her own enjoyment, it emerges on closer inspection that Hobbes readily envisaged us "satisficing." The twentieth-century obsession with the prisoner's dilemma and with the temptation to be a "free rider" presupposes a theory of motivation that Hobbes did not believe in. What Hobbes's individuals maximize in the state of nature is power. They do not do so because they like power, nor because they want to maximize the enjoyment of anything positive. They are forced to maximize their power even though they would be content with a moderate living.[35] This is because isolated individuals have no other means of security; they are not utility-maximizing but danger-of-death-minimizing creatures. Risk aversion is built into their physical constitution and, if they understand themselves, into their psychical constitution too. The prisoner's dilemma is thus a red herring.

Our question is not whether egoists can meet their obligations, but how "theorems found out by reason" can impose obligations. Hobbes was always careful to distinguish counsel or advice that we may take or leave at our peril from law or command.[36] Hobbes's answer to the puzzle is well known: if the laws of nature are considered as the commands of God, who by right commandeth all things, they are laws and they oblige.[37] This shuffles off the problem to a different area of Hobbes's philosophy, namely, the sense in which we are obliged to obey God even though we have not given our consents. Brian Barry has suggested that Hobbes ought not to have said that we have an obligation to obey the law of nature. We ought to obey, but the duty to obey the law of nature derives from its content, not from our obligation to obey its promulgator. This seems to me to be wrong, though accurate enough as an account of how we should view the duty to take notice of the laws of nature considered as theorems, which are counsel, not commands. Hobbes offers two possibilities; they are, I think, alternative and mutually inconsistent. Both rest on a further consideration of some interest, even if it hardly removes the inconsistency.

The first possibility Hobbes opens is one that denies the assumption we have thus far been working on, namely, that we do not consent to the government of God. In *Leviathan*, Hobbes seems to say that those and those only who consent to the government of God are properly under an obligation to obey him.

> Subjects therefore in the Kingdome of God are not Bodies Inanimate, nor creatures Irrationall; because they understand no Precepts as his; Nor Atheists; nor they that believe not that God has any care for the actions of mankind; because they acknowledge no Word for his, nor have hope of his rewards, or fear of his threatenings. They, therefore, that believe there is a God that governeth the world, and hath given Praecepts, and propounded Rewards, and Punishments to mankind are God's subjects; all the rest are to be understood as Enemies.[38]

Believers alone *sin* when they violate the law of nature, though atheists are also accused of treason to the Almighty because they deny his authority when they deny his existence.[39] There is another awkward question, however. In what sense do those who believe in God consent to his government? It seems that it must be, but cannot be, in the same sense as the subject consents to the government of his earthly sovereign. The motivation for submission is the same as ever—fear of death—and the believer has the added incentive that God grants and withholds eternal life, so there is a better argument for submission to God than to any earthly sovereign. On the other hand, God does not make us an offer of life upon terms that we may accept or reject, so submission does not amount to contract.

As to the atheist who is shut out by this argument, Hobbes insists that an atheist is rightly described by the Old Testament as a "fool" rather than a sinner or, more exactly, as one guilty of a sin of imprudence, not of injustice.[40] It is rash not to believe that there probably exists a God who brought the world into existence and who can exercise alarming sanctions. To be on the safe side, we should believe and obey. How far we can believe in this prudential fashion is a moot point, as is its consistency with Hobbes's insistence on thinking for ourselves, and I should hesitate to go much further than suggesting that Hobbes recommended what one might call hypothetical belief—we should conform ourselves in the way belief and submission would dictate. But this account, which derives obedience from submission, is not the only one Hobbes offers. The other account derives God's legislative authority from his power: in the first place by a route that has earthly analogies, and in the background by a route that has none.

Each of us comes into the world with a right to all things. This is a useless right because we lack the power to do anything with it; we therefore renounce it and leave the sovereign alone in possession of this initial right and, through our submission, with the power to make use of it. If any of us had sufficient power to rely on his own resources and thus to have no incentive to renounce his natural right to all things, he could become sovereign. God is uniquely in the position of requiring no earthly assistance to exercise his rights. He has no reason to renounce any of his rights; therefore, he retains the right to all things, including the right to rule us as our sovereign: "They therefore whose power cannot be resisted, and by consequence God *Almighty*, derives his Right of Soveraignty from the *power* it selfe."[41]

But as soon as we articulate this account, we can see two alternative criteria for the existence of obligation running into head-on conflict. On the one criterion, we infer the existence of an obligation from the existence of law, and the existence of law from the existence of a lawmaker. It is God's right to rule that explains our obligation, and our submission appears not to play much role in the story. We are all born with the right to rule, that is, with authority; for human beings, it is a perfectly useless right, since everyone else has the right to take no notice and we have no power to make them take notice. But God is differently situated, and can and does exercise that right. On the other criterion, the authority of any lawmaker is to be traced back to the submission of those subject to the law. What makes law law is certainly the fact that it is the word of him that, by right, has command, but what gives him that right is our submission; he has authority only because each of us authorizes him. The two criteria have very different implications for the concerns of this essay. When Hobbes begins with the thought that everyone has a right to all things, the notions of submission, consent, and authorization are only weakly present, and the account only weakly individualist; acts of submission do not so much transfer to another rights over our conduct that he could not otherwise possess as offer him reassurance that we shall not resist the exercise of rights he already has. When Hobbes plays down this (exceedingly counterintuitive) account of what a "transfer" of right really means, his theory of obligation remains strikingly individualistic. We have those obligations that we impose on ourselves, and no others. Sovereigns have authority because they are given it. Each man is by nature the author of his own actions only; for the sovereign to be able to be the author of the acts of all his subjects, his subjects must authorize him.

Which reading of Hobbes ought we to prefer? It is hard to tell, but a case for supposing that Hobbes is anxious to take the second route can be drawn from considering how different the earthly sovereign and God really are. Hobbes was always impressed with the story of Job. Job finally turned and reproached God, pointing out, and not before time either, that he had done all that God commanded, and what he had got out of it was bankruptcy, skin diseases, and the death of most of his household. God did not reply that Job was being sacrificed in a good cause or that he had really behaved badly by being so proud of his own righteousness. Those utilitarian or Kantian responses are strikingly absent, especially in Hobbes's interpretation of the story. What God replied was "Where wast thou when I laid the foundations of the earth?" which, as Hobbes justly observed, was not an argument drawn from his goodness or from Job's sin, but from his power.[42]

How should we understand it? What kind of argument is it? Merely to point out to Job that if God chose to behave atrociously there was little Job could do about it would have been both otiose and intellectually and morally feeble. The only answer that makes adequate sense is that God pointed out to Job that since he had created Job, ex nihilo, Job was wholly and entirely his to do as he chose with. Hobbes says that the right of nature whereby God reigns over men and punishes those that break his laws is not derived from the fact of his having created them. This, however, is not in conflict with my account, for what Hobbes is concerned to deny is any thought that "he required obedience, as of Gratitude for his benefits," and my account is at one with Hobbes's in relying on God's power, not his subjects' gratitude.[43] So far as earthly sovereigns go, we have to authorize them because we are, by nature, the authors of our own actions and responsible for them, and sovereigns can claim authorship of our actions only when we have granted them that right over us. God, on the other hand, made us; he is the author of our being and therefore, without further ado, the author of our actions. He cannot commit an injustice against us any more than I can commit an injustice against the clay pot that I throw on the wheel and then break up because it is ill made. As Hobbes's critics pointed out, this makes God the author of our sins and is theologically exceedingly unorthodox—but it is a point in favor of my interpretation that they should have so latched on to one of its implications.[44]

If this is right, a familiar tension in Hobbes's account of the sovereign's duties appears in a new light. When an earthly sovereign is instituted, it is entirely on the consent of his subjects that his authority depends. Each subject has a choice between staying in the state of nature and thereby risking the enmity of the sovereign and, on the other hand, submitting to the authority of the sovereign. One might suppose that Hobbes thought that only a madman would risk staying outside the covenant and risk death by refusing to acknowledge an existing sovereign's authority or by refusing to submit on the battlefield. Hobbes did not quite say that. If someone refuses to submit because he is sincerely convinced that God will avenge the slight done to him by earthly submission to an illicit sovereign, he may be rash in drawing down death on himself—he could, after all, submit with mental reservation—but Hobbes does not suggest that the Christian martyrs were simply silly, though he does suggest that anyone so intent on attracting death without an explicit commission from God must be more or less deranged. Again, a man might scruple to break an oath freely made in the past. So far from describing him as mad, Hobbes is quite clear that a sense of honor is an estimable character trait and useful for society. Fear may be the motive to rely on, but it is not as admirable a motive as a sense of honor or disinterested love of others.[45]

If the ordinary view of human motivation is not much damaged by Hobbes's materialism, and his insistence that each person is bound only by his own decisions is taken seriously, there remains a tension between Hobbes's insistence that subjects have no rights against their sovereigns and his insistence that subjects retain the right to decide whether the covenant is off. It is not simply that there is a tension between the utilitarian, public-interest-oriented prescriptions for the sovereign's conduct of government and the individualism of the story of the covenant. Certainly, recent philosophers would insist on that tension, and John Rawls's *Theory of Justice* is founded on the need to prevent individuals from being sacrificed in the public interest. But just as Hobbes does not, when scrutinized, turn out to believe that individuals seek to maximize their own utilities, so, when scrutinized, he turns out not to believe that sovereigns ought to maximize the sum of the utilities of their subjects, even if this entails sacrificing some of them. It is individual safety that plays the most important role, then the promotion of opportunities for individual advancement, or "commodious living."[46] The sovereign must above all else maintain the rule of law; what has aptly been called Hobbes's "moral constitutionalism" is a very obvious feature of the theory.[47] But although this means that there is no tension between a utilitarian perspective and an individualist one, there is a tension between the individualism that underpins Hobbes's prescriptions about fair trials, scrupulousness about retrospective legislation, and so on, on the one hand, and the insistence that the subject has no rights against the sovereign on the other.

It is a tension that Hobbes does his best to defuse. The sovereign has a duty to observe the laws of nature, a duty that falls on him as a private person rather than a public one; he can do more good than anyone else by so doing because he has more power than anyone else. It may therefore be that his duty is more exacting because he has less excuse for nonobservance than anyone else, being generally less at risk than anyone else. This account allows Hobbes to insist that none of his subjects can call the sovereign to account for a breach of the law of nature; the sovereign is answerable to God and his conscience alone. Conversely, this means that we have no right to have the sovereign behave in this way; it is simply that he ought to do so. If he has an obligation to do so, it is an obligation of natural law, not positive law.

Nonetheless, what remains firmly in the hands of the individual subject is the right to decide whether obedience is worth it. There is no right of revolution in Hobbes; but private individuals do not promise to stop thinking about their own preservation and that of their families and friends. They are obliged to obey because they have promised, but if things turn out too dangerously, they have the right to break their promises too. This has some faintly comic effects; one familiar one is the way in which Hobbes insists that the unusually timid should be allowed to pay for someone else to go and fight in their place and ought not to be expected to fight themselves. The noncomic effect is that creatures as forward-looking and anxious as Hobbesian men cannot be supposed to wait until the knife is at their throat until they raise the question whether obedience is too unsafe. They must surely spend much of their time watching the performance of the government in crucial respects. Certainly, "*every man is bound by Nature, as much as in him lieth, to protect in Warre, the Authority, by which he is himself protected in time of Peace,*" but once they have discharged that duty, it is their right to consider their own safety.[48] To us, this seems perhaps only a small concession in a generally authoritarian scheme; to some of Hobbes's contemporaries, it was tantamount to denying the sovereign's authority altogether. For anyone deriving sovereignty from divine right, Hobbes's account is trebly obnoxious: the story of Job marks an absolute breach between divine power and earthly power; the sovereign is created only by the voices of the people; the sovereign's power has strict and easily recognized limits. Those who thought of the sovereign as a simulacrum of God must have thought Hobbes's "mortall God" much too mortal and quite insufficiently godlike.[49]

"Privatization"

This essay has been thus far engaged in arguing two cases not exactly at odds with each other, but not usually found in company. The first is that

Hobbes's view of human motivation is, at an empirical level, not particularly surprising, though it is novel at the analytical level because of its entrenchment in a mechanistic psychology. In the same vein, I have tried to show that Hobbes's "epistemological individualism," as I have called it, is not at odds with many of the commonplaces of the sociology of science, though again it has distinctive features because of the underlying mechanical psychology and Hobbes's obsession with geometry. But in the second place, I have been trying to suggest that Hobbes's contemporaries often found him alarming, not because of the authoritarianism and defense of despotism that his twentieth-century readers notice, but because of an individualism that was both like and unlike other individualisms of the time, but in being a form of individualism at all, was hostile to an emphasis on community, tradition, ecclesiastical authority, and the derivation of political authority from a Christian view of the world.

In conclusion, I should, without exaggerating the novelty of my position, distinguish it from some others that could also make these two claims. In particular, I should briefly suggest why the individualism outlined is usefully described as moral and epistemological and not as capitalist, bourgeois, or privatized. The notion that Hobbes was writing to defend or even merely to express the worldview of capitalism is implausible. The most famous argument to this effect, offered by C. B. Macpherson, is essentially circular. It starts from the assumption that Hobbes was living in a market society, either nascent or full-fledged, and from the companion assumption that political theories reflect the economic conditions associated with their production. So Hobbes's picture of human nature is not a picture of human nature, only that of market-oriented man; the undoubted contrast between Hobbes's methodology and Aristotle's has to be reinterpreted as a contrast between the outlook of a market society and the outlook of a classical, nonmarket society. Once these assumptions are firmly in place, everything in Hobbes's theory that is friendly to capitalism becomes an argument in their favor. The circularity involved is evidently that the interpretation of Hobbes's text that supports the premises is reached only by scrutinizing the text on the assumption that those premises are correct.[50]

Still, there is something to be said for the interpretation. Hobbes does argue for something close to laissez-faire in some economic areas; the sovereign ought to define property rights as clearly as possible, remove uncertainty about title—for example by establishing a land register so that it would be clear who owned what—refrain from unpredictable or sudden alterations in the rules, and avoid sudden and unpredictable taxes; given that, the sovereign could leave the population to get on with their economic life more or less unimpeded. Is this a positive argument for capitalism, however? There seems no reason to think that it is; Hobbes does not admire merchants and does not admire most employers, who, he thinks, are interested in driving people to work at the lowest possible wages. Moreover, he is explicit about the need to create some sort of welfare arrangements for those who are too old or ill to work. Equally, and entirely at odds with the ethos of capitalism, he advocates sumptuary legislation to diminish class antagonisms. The belief in the virtues of unlimited accumulation that Macpherson puts at the heart of a defense of capitalism is very far from being a belief shared by Hobbes. Hobbes sees the accumulation of wealth as a threat to social harmony. People who accumulate do so to get power, to drive down wages, or to flaunt their wealth in ways that merely irritate their inferiors, an argument that Strauss struggles vainly to defuse.[51] It is this last misuse of wealth that he particularly deplores and that he relies on sumptuary laws to stop. Of course, a last-ditch defense of an interpretation of Hobbes as an apologist for capitalism could perhaps claim that this assault on the flaunting of wealth is capitalist inasmuch as it implies that investment or some other virtuous wealth-increasing employment of funds is harmless and useful. This will not do, however. In the first place, Hobbes does not say anything of the sort. Moreover, it is essential to the picture of Hobbes as a capitalist apologist that he should assume that "human nature" is suited to the operation of a capitalist economy. That is just what he does not seem to do; harmless, moderate persons may need no more than security and opportunity to make themselves prosperous and happy, which is an argument for a relatively laissez-faire policy, but they need protecting also against the arrogance, greed, and acquisitiveness of the rich.

Now that the whole idea of a "bourgeois revolution" in seventeenth-century England has been so thoroughly discredited, it is no argument against Hobbes as capitalist apologist to show that Hobbes was both the friend and devoted employee of an aristocratic household, and that when his enemies assailed him, it was for corrupting the brisk wits at Charles II's court rather than for the espousing of bourgeois and antiaristocratic attitudes.[52] For it is equally true that the Devonshire family was an investing and improving family as well as a landed family of great house builders, and true, too, that those whose aristocratic pretensions amounted to pride in their descent rather than their abilities did not care for Hobbes's reminder that the sovereign was the fount of honor and that honor was a sort of price.

Still, Hobbes's defense of industry, prosperity, and science-propelled social advance was not distinctively or interestingly capitalist. It was modernizing, no doubt, and revealed a distinctively modern belief that history might be an indefinite upward path rather than a cyclical and repetitive course. It was individualistic, certainly, in its acceptance of the fact that individual intelligence and energy might take a man away from his social and geographical roots. But to have been an articulate defender of capitalism, Hobbes would have had to have a much more calculating, accounting outlook than he actually possessed.

The same point disposes of the "bourgeois" Hobbes and equally of the "privatized" Hobbes. Hobbes's bourgeois image is drawn by Leo Strauss from Hobbes's assault both on pride, or "vainglory," as the great threat to civil order, and, as Strauss thinks, on the aristocratic sense of honor in consequence. Hobbes's theory of human nature gave him every reason to be insistent on this point; in his account of the condition of nature, the three great causes of war are competition, diffidence, and vainglory. Now, competition for the resources for survival or for a commodious living can be deflated by prosperity. If there is plenty for each of us, the only reason to struggle for a monopoly is fear that the current abundance will be cut off by physical attack. This, though, is just what the cure for diffidence also cures; once the sovereign is able to impose his will on us all, we need neither fear immediate theft nor accumulate power in order to insure ourselves against future predations. Thus, curing diffidence provides for prosperity, which provides the cure for competition.

Pride is unamenable to such treatment. To be proud is to wish to emerge on top of whatever competition is at issue, to wish to have more of any good thing than anyone else; it is essentially incurable because abundance cannot choke it. There cannot be more than one summit. Hobbes's insistence on the subjective nature of value puts a distinctive extra gloss on the reasons for fearing pride; the only test of success is the envy of others. Pride demands the simultaneous abasement of others. It is therefore intrinsically antisocial and must be stamped out.

Is this a "bourgeois" view? There seems no particular reason to think so. The truth seems rather that in Hobbes's view, anyone might display pride and anyone might be decently sociable and amenable to the discipline demanded by social coexistence. The lowborn fanatic insisting on the truth of his idiosyncratic illumination displayed an antisocial pride in wishing the world to bow to *his* truth and being unwilling to learn from its views. Hobbes's opponents certainly did not think of pride as a peculiarly aristocratic vice from which the bourgeois were naturally free; all rounded on Hobbes and denounced him as a monster of intellectual pride. Thomas Tenison taunted him with doing everything "in a way peculiar to himself" and "with such a confidence as becometh only a Prophet or Apostle."[53] Of course, aristocrats are prone to one form of pride that nobody else is so prone to, namely, pride of ancestry. The general point, however, is wholly classless; it is that we should try to purge ourselves of all those passions that are essentially antisocial, and antisocial passions are understood as those that not only set us at odds but also have a zero-sum quality about them. Nor did Hobbes's opponents associate the pride he denounced with any particular social class. They thought he was absurdly hypocritical in denouncing a vice to which he was himself so prone. What they attacked was his inordinate vanity over his own originality and cleverness. As for social allegiance, they took it for granted that the people he tried to impress were "gentlemen" and that among the disagreeable sorts of pride that Hobbes himself displayed in the course of attacking that vice, boasting of his connections with the court and the aristocracy was pretty salient.

We can finally turn to "privatization." As will be evident, if Hobbes were the defender of the worldview of the capitalist bourgeoisie, he would also be a defender of a privatized worldview. That is, he would hold that our interest in government is instrumental and that the purpose of government is to enable us to pursue private economic goals in peace; the goals would be understood in terms familiar to twentieth-century social theorists, that is, they would be inwardly directed, concerned with the welfare of the nuclear family, and it would be taken for granted that the way to achieve that welfare is by work as an employee or by profitably employing others. In Hannah Arendt's *The Human Condition* and Sheldon Wolin's *Politics and Vision*, Hobbes is seen as one of the founders of the liberal worldview, and the liberal worldview as essentially self-centered and apolitical.[54] Without challenging Wolin's association of liberalism with anxiety, which certainly seems plausible enough in Hobbes's case, I should like to enter a note of caution about the too-quick move from the thought that Hobbes espoused a self-centered politics to the thought that he espoused an apolitical politics.

The caution is a double one. In the first place, Arendt's vision of the politics-centered world of classical antiquity may be challenged; it is not true that Aristotle offers a particularly exuberant picture of life in the agora, and the undeniable zest with which Machiavelli writes of ruses, wiles, stratagems, and battles won and lost is neither based on, nor the basis of, a political theory of public man. So the contrast between a classical, publicly oriented vision of politics and a modern, privatized vision has to be treated cautiously. In the second place, Hobbes resembles Machiavelli in writing with great zest of a grim business. Hobbes's opponents never forgave him his mastery of a prose style that relied on innuendo, analogy, and metaphor to achieve what bald argument could not, but whose felicities were simply too obvious to be denied. His stylistic enthusiasms certainly encourage the "privatized" interpretation, too. By the time Hobbes has finished suggesting that men are wolves, lions, tigers, wild cats, and whatever, we might be forgiven for thinking that Hobbes supposes we should all become *bons petits bourgeois* and leave public life alone.

In fact, there is nothing to be said for such a view. Certainly, Hobbes is hostile to "ancient prudence" and to the view that only under democracy or some form of popular republic is there freedom; but a belief in negative liberty is no argument for or against active participation in public life. Hobbes is no liberal, but his argument is a pluralist one. Generous spirits will participate in public affairs; nobody should force the timid to join in if they do not wish to. Again, participation is subordinate to order. Sovereigns will, if they are wise, take the best advice than can get; if they do not, we have no right to insist that they should. But then again, they should recall that whatever their rights and our obligations, they cannot expect an ill-governed state to survive as long as a well-governed one. Politics in the twentieth-century sense is an optional activity in the good life, but a well-run Hobbesian state may have quite a lot of it so long as politicians remember that they are only the sovereign's advisers.

Hobbes's individualism is "private" only in the sense that Michael Oakeshott's account of the modern individual implies.[55] Mankind does not need to be told what ends to pursue, what the good life is, or how private life is to be conducted; certainly, we need the company of others to get anywhere with pursuing our own intimations of the good life, but we do not need to be forced, to be legislated at, or to have others legislated at in order to get on with it. Private life is not, however, "privatized" life—it is eminently sociable, outward looking, friendly, and spontaneously cooperative. What it demands from the res publica, however, is not aid or instruction in how to live it, but only a shelter within which we can pursue it. It may be that a society that understands its politics in that way will organize its economic life in a "capitalist" fashion; it may create a social grouping properly termed "bourgeois"; by ill luck, it may go through periods of narrowly self-centered and "privatized" existence—but all this is contingent. What is not contingent is that distanced, self-reliant, self-conscious stance that is so distinctively Hobbesian.

10

Hobbes, Toleration, and the Inner Life

IT ALWAYS SURPRISED ME that John Plamenatz wrote so perceptively, so incisively, and so well about Thomas Hobbes.[1] On the face of it, he ought to have found Hobbes as little to his liking as he found Bentham and James Mill.[2] Hobbes's famous injunction to consider men in the state of nature as if they were sprung out of the ground like mushrooms, without engagements to one another, seems to be what Plamenatz deplored as the root of bad practice in social thought. The *idée maîtresse* of *Man and Society* is just that: social and political arrangements are not matters of artifice, not constructed for the presocial and prepolitical purposes of self-contained individuals. The Hegelian emphasis on the organic unity of society may reflect an unintelligible metaphysics, but it rests on a sound methodological instinct. Individuals are *essentially* social, and their aspirations are such as only members of a social and political community could conceive. What we count as individual achievements, individual hopes, and even individual miseries, could not come into existence except in a social setting. It is not only Hegel who is praised for seeing this, of course; Rousseau is sometimes chided for incoherence, but he is always praised for his understanding of the degree to which our relations with our society are internal relations. Even Pascal, of whom it is certainly true that the anarchy he fears is a spiritual anarchy whose cure lies in submission to God, must be credited with a subtler sense than Hobbes of the genesis of our restlessness and our vanity, and a subtler sense of how society may do something to control them.[3]

Plamenatz certainly enjoyed the vigor and the crispness of Hobbes's thinking and writing. Whether reading Plamenatz or arguing with him in tutorial, there was no mistaking the pleasure that Hobbes's "brisk witt" gave him. Hobbes's own aggressiveness and self-confidence evidently encouraged a like response; no one need have qualms about arguing against Hobbes with every weapon he possessed. Hobbes's description of the man armed with science as an utterly invulnerable fencer almost reads like an invitation to a duel, and everything we know of Hobbes's own behavior as a controversialist suggests that the cut and thrust of argument did much to give him pleasure; better, perhaps, a strenuously and confidently wrongheaded thinker like Hobbes than a muddled and slackly right-minded one like J. S. Mill.[4]

What follows is intended to explore what I imagine Plamenatz himself would have thought a nonexistent subject. Is it not verging on the frivolous to suggest that Hobbes has anything to say about the inner life? No doubt, he has a good deal to say about the infinitesimal interior motions, or endeavors, that are the beginnings of voluntary action. He has a good deal to say about how perception as well as emotion is to be explained by internal pressures; but these are not part of our inner lives in anything except a flatly physiological sense. Can it be said that such matters as our religious convictions, our moral aspirations, our views on the meaning of life, and so on get anything but the roughest and most peremptory treatment? Whether the materialism that leads Hobbes to explain our thoughts and beliefs in terms of "phantasms" with physiological causes is intrinsically inimical to a serious concern for the private moral and intellectual aspirations we generally reckon as our "inner life" is arguable; what seems less so is that Hobbes was a materialist who gave the inner life short shrift.

Even those who would allow that there is more to be said about it than that would still generally deny that what Hobbes speaks to is the inner life. When Sheldon Wolin explains Hobbes as something like an illiberal proto-liberal, it is because Hobbes thinks that a man's rational concerns are essentially with his private interests, and that politics matters only insofar as it impinges upon those interests. The end result, in Wolin's account, "was to destroy the distinctive identity of the 'political' by merging it with interest," but for our purposes, two points alone are worth noticing.[5] Hobbes certainly attacks classical and republican conceptions of politics; in the process, he invents a new meaning for the term "liberty," which he uses to deny that republics possess liberty while monarchies do not and, indeed, uses positively to insist that a man may live with more security against intervention in a monarchy than under a popular government. Liberty as unimpededness is the only sort of liberty there is, and what men rationally desire is to be as little impeded as possible in the pursuit of their own interests. The first point is that among the sorts of liberty to which Hobbes displays any tenderness, liberty of conscience is not one; the second is that this "privatization" of our aspirations is tender to private economic aims, not to an interest in our inner lives. For it to be anything of the latter sort, Hobbes should surely have shown a sympathy toward religious sects and small communities of believers that he was very far from showing.

It is commonplace and true that throughout *Leviathan*, Hobbes is hostile to religious dissent and claims for freedom of speech; he is eager to keep universities firmly under control, and shows no scruples about what is and what is not under governmental control. Nor is Hobbes casual in his illiberalism; he does not suggest that sometimes and in dire emergency we can resort to censorship, nor does he say that because men's opinions on religion and morality are of little importance, it is all one whether governments choose to control them or not. He argues exactly the opposite: states that take no care to secure doctrinal and liturgical uniformity are storing up trouble for themselves; precisely because opinion does matter, the sovereign must ensure a good deal of uniformity in opinion. Hobbes insisted: "It belongeth therefore to him that hath the Soveraign Power, to be Judge, or constitute all Judges of Opinions and Doctrines, as a thing necessary to Peace; thereby to prevent Discord and Civill Warre." This requires that he must decide "on what occasions, how farre, and what, men are to be trusted with-all, in speaking to Multitudes of people; and who shall examine the Doctrines of all bookes before they be published." And this is because "the Actions of men proceed from their Opinions, and in the wel governing of Opinions, consisteth the well governing of mens Actions, in order to their Peace, and Concord."[6]

The questions this raises are how far that control of opinion can go and how far Hobbes thought it should go. That Hobbes did not think complete uniformity of opinion or desire would ever be achieved is evident enough from the way he contrasts the sociability of those nonhuman creatures that simply coincide in their aims and behavior with the contrived sociability of human beings.[7] Even so, it might be said that once an artificial society had been constructed and a sovereign instituted, there was room for the remaking of human nature by educating men into a new uniformity of opinion and desire. That *something* of the sort is proposed by Hobbes is a reasonable inference from the famous footnote to *De Cive* in which he insists that "all men, because they are born in infancy, are born unapt for society . . . man is made fit for society not by nature, but by education."[8] This, however, leaves us with three possible interpretations of Hobbes's position. The first would suggest that somehow or other the sovereign could and should exercise complete control over our opinions and render dissidence literally unthinkable. This imputes a very totalitarian ambition to Hobbes, and I shall later suggest that something of the same ambition can be found even in paradigmatically liberal writers like Mill and Russell. The second view is the most usual one, and essentially amounts to saying that he was extremely anxious to secure uniformity of profession in matters of religion and jurisprudence (the latter category embracing the former, in his view) but minded about little else.[9] Public profession could be divorced from private conviction, and the control of opinion therefore amounted to no more than the control of opinion's public expression.[10] The third view is that Hobbes had more positive concern for freedom of speech and for the exercise of individual conscientiousness than is generally thought. I shall end by coming back to the usual view, but I hope to show that there is a good deal in Hobbes to which it does not do justice.

It is a commonplace that Hobbes saw two great causes of civil strife in England. The first was a lack of agreement on the legal supremacy of the Crown; the other was the eagerness of private persons to set up their religious intuitions as a guide to themselves and everyone else—one consequence of which was the extreme quarrelsomeness that men must feel if they think their eternal salvation depends on their political disputes.[11] These disagreements opened the way for interested parties to claim an overriding authority—judges, members of Parliament, Presbyterians, and papists among them. It is worth noting that Hobbes's intellectualism is not so extreme as to suggest that the Civil War sprang solely from intellectual errors about the nature of authority. Men will believe whatever fosters their power, so that although it is true that some men's power springs from the acceptance of error, it is also true that the disposition to accept these errors rests on the search for power. Hobbes was very attached to the view that peace might be preserved indefinitely if sound doctrines were widely diffused—if *Leviathan* was prescribed as a textbook in the universities; but he was quick to say that interested error could not be eliminated by argument alone.

The importance of securing doctrinal agreement is obvious from the way in which half of *Leviathan* and *De Cive* are devoted to the subject. The twentieth-century reader of *Leviathan* pays little attention to books 3 and 4, and even for those who do pay attention to them, it is rather puzzling that Hobbes should have been so alarmed by the papacy's contribution to the "Kingdome of Darknesse" as late as 1651, unless this reflects his experiences in Paris.[12] Nonetheless, the last two books crucially complement the first two. Once Hobbes has explained the matter and generation of the commonwealth in secular, naturalistic, and this-worldly terms as a contrivance of men's hands for their this-worldly welfare, he needs to show that a Christian commonwealth is not qua commonwealth affected by being a *Christian* commonwealth. It is worth noting that Hobbes has to approach this topic from a particular direction; he has to ask whether and in what way the obligations of a subject are affected by the subject's being a Christian and, again, whether and in what way the rights of sovereigns are affected by their being Christian sovereigns. The target, always, is the suggestion that ecclesiastical authority can be different from, or even superior to, lay authority, with its implication that some religious authority can release the subject from his obedience to the sovereign. Hobbes's main concern, in both *De Cive* and *Leviathan*, is to argue that the city and the church are one—that there is one and only one test of the lawfulness of doctrines and practices, and that is whether it has pleased the magistrate to permit or forbid them. What we ordinarily call the authority of the church in spiritual matters is the power vested in "pastors lawfully ordained, and who have to that end authority given them by the city."[13]

The implied premise here comes from Hobbes's views about the motive for obedience. Since we cannot be obliged to do anything that threatens our lives, and since the earthly sovereign can only threaten our earthly lives, while God can threaten our lives in eternity, any suggestion of a clash between the commands of God and the commands of earthly rulers has to be avoided. To this end, Hobbes argues over and over again that the only thing we are commanded by Christ is to believe in him; since we cannot believe in him unless we believe in God the Father, we must profess our belief in him too. It follows that no minimally Christian sovereign ever gives us ground for disobedience; the criterion for his being a minimally Christian sovereign is that he cannot command his subjects "to deny Christ, or to offer him any contumely," since to do that would just be to profess himself not a Christian.[14] Everything else is a matter of doctrinal speculation; crucially, everything else, in Hobbes's account of it, is a matter on which God has not *commanded* us to say or think something in particular. Evidently, this leaves open the question of how the Christian must treat the commands of a non-Christian sovereign. In matters temporal, insists Hobbes, obedience must be absolute, and if, in matters spiritual, we cannot obey, Hobbes's only advice is "go to Christ by martyrdom."[15] What is not clear is when this moment might arrive; given that Hobbes seems to be convinced that we could safely worship graven images or even deny Christ if commanded and escape the consequences by mental reservation, we might wonder whether anyone of Hobbes's views would ever go to Christ by martyrdom.

The purpose of Hobbes's arguments seems to be to drive scriptural considerations out of politics in order to deprive the church of any independent political power. At a time when those who thought about political morality at all generally did so by reference to the Bible, this was a bold move, but essential if Hobbes was to demolish the aspirations of those who thought that the goal of polities was to establish God's kingdom in England. Hobbes says, in *Leviathan* and many other places, that there is no useful sense in which any earthly kingdom can be identified with God's kingdom. The divines speak of God's kingdom metaphorically, as meaning the life hereafter, but he wishes to confine the name of God's kingdom to the one case in which God did indeed rule over his chosen people by covenant. God's government of the Jews was "constituted by the Votes of the People of Israel in peculiar manner; wherein they chose God for their King by Covenant made with him, upon Gods promising them the possession of the land of Canaan."[16] The kingdom of God by nature, on the other hand, is not and cannot be instituted; God rules all those who have the wit to recognize his existence and follow his laws, that is to say, all those who can work out that there must be a God and that the laws of nature must be his laws. He also, in a manner of speaking, rules those who acknowledge no such thing, since his irresistible power can rightly be unleashed against anything and anyone. But, viewed from the side of God's subjects, it is only those who believe and who acknowledge his laws who can properly be termed subjects. The rest are, in Hobbes's technical sense of the term, enemies. There is one obvious implication of this, which is that atheism is no injustice and no sin, though loss of faith might well be held to be such. It is the fool, not the sinner, who says in his heart, "there is no God." The important conclusion, though, is that since God no longer licenses prophets, there is no question of re-creating the special relationship he enjoyed with the Jews; no band of religious enthusiasts can be taken seriously in their desires for re-creating God's kingdom on earth, since their aims are either unrealizable or realized already.

Part of the object here is, evidently, to defuse the thought that the Bible might itself be an independent source of authority. Over and over, Hobbes insisted that the only way an interpretation of scripture could become uniquely lawful or be made unlawful is by command of the sovereign. All the same, Hobbes did not wholly oppose the translation of the Bible into the vernacular, and was not fearful of the results of independent judgment, so long as proper distinctions were drawn between what we might call speculative questions about the origin and nature of the universe and its government, on the one hand, and practical questions about liturgical conventions, on the other. Hobbes's arguments in favor of uniformity in the latter area—always drawn from the consideration that what one man thinks a way of honoring God another might think ridiculous—are entirely consistent with the defense of a large measure of speculative freedom, though they suggest a circumspect view about publication. The energy with which *Leviathan* berates scholastic philosophy might suggest that Hobbes was simply hostile to philosophical speculation; but that is belied by his defense of true philosophy, and Hobbes is more usually at odds with the power-hungry clerics who seek political influence by heresy hunting. Hobbes's undistinguished little history of heresy shows a decided hankering after the original sense of the word—"which signified no more than a private opinion, without reference to truth or falsehood"—or, failing that, a return to the legislative restraint of Constantine, when heresy had "by virtue of a law of the Emperor, made only for the peace of the church, become a crime in a pastor."[17] The implication is obvious: doctrinal uniformity may be a necessity in the officers of a church, since otherwise the organization will suffer, but that does not suggest that laymen need be chased after by zealots for orthodoxy.

It is for all that certainly true that Hobbes laid it down as an important task for the sovereign to tell teachers and subjects how to interpret the scriptures. He does so as part of a general doctrine about the sovereign's role in intellectual matters, a doctrine that he himself applied to *Leviathan*. In his "review and conclusion," Hobbes reports that on looking through his work, he thinks that it is true and demonstrable, and he hopes that it may occur to someone to have it printed and taught in the universities. (In fact, his own university had it burned in the Bodleian quadrangle.) The reason is that "the Universities are the Fountains of Civill and Morall Doctrine, from whence the Preachers and the Gentry, drawing such water as they find, use to sprinkle the same (both from the Pulpit and in their Conversation) upon the people."[18]

Hobbes was also anxious to insist that he had looked to see whether anything he had said was unlawful, and that he thought nothing was. Moreover, in such unsettled times, a novel doctrine could not be accused of upsetting the (nonexistent) peace, and precisely because times were unsettled, there was all the more reason to explore this avenue to peace. Hobbes seems to be asserting both that what he writes is true and that it would be usefully imposed as an orthodoxy—that is, given a unique place as the only doctrine publishable. Hobbes also distinguishes the question of the truth of his doctrine from his right to publish it, for he readily admits that if the sovereign had forbidden its publication, he would have had no right to publish. This raises the obvious questions of how truth, utility, and publishability are connected; of how far the sovereign can go in imposing doctrines; of what frame of mind the search for uniformity is supposed to achieve in subjects; and of what limits, if any, governmental activity in this area is subject to.

An extreme view might be culled from what Hobbes says in *De Cive* about the way in which an agreement on terms creates truth. The proposition that 2 + 3 = 5 is said to depend on our will, for we have decided that "the number // is called two, /// is called three, and ///// is called five," and by the will of those who have thus called them, "it comes to pass that this proposition is true, *two and three taken together make five*."[19] Since agreement on meanings depends on the existence of a linguistic community, and the existence of a community depends on the existence of a sovereign, we might infer either that *all* truth depends on the sovereign or, more minimally, that some truths will depend on the meanings he imposes. This would imply that there was no room for disbelief in what the sovereign lays down as truth, and that subjects would simply have to believe it. There could be no room for objection so long as the meanings thus imposed did indeed lead to peace. The picture is not wholly intelligible, once it is scrutinized in detail, however; even in the example Hobbes offers, it is only the linguistic expression of the mathematical truth that is conventional. The only sense in which 2 + 8 = 5 could be made true is if "8" were to be employed as "3" is now; nothing else is amenable to linguistic fiat.

This does not entail that there is no useful role to be played by laying down a vocabulary; if coherence is not the whole of the truth, ambiguity is certainly inimical to the pursuit of truth. It is not too fanciful to see Hobbes groping after the analogy of the draftsman's blueprint; here, in a manner of speaking, it is the will of the draftsman that determines whether an actual object "truly" conforms to what he has laid down. Statecraft, for Hobbes, is very obviously a matter of laying down blueprints, and of course, just as there is no preexisting object for the blueprint of a new model of car, say, to copy, so there is no such natural thing as a "natural" state for Hobbes's blueprint to copy. But whether a motorcar made according to the blueprint will actually work is not a question of anyone's will, but one of fact. Evidently, it is a precondition of it working that there are no incoherent instructions in the blueprint, but another condition is that it should not demand impossibilities of the material out of which the vehicle is to be built. Moreover, it is a matter of what people want from the vehicle that determines how good a car it is at last. Analogously, we may lay down a geometry or a number system; whether it is coherent, accurate, and useful is something we do not lay down but discover. If this is so, we may credit Hobbes with a milder doctrine: truth and utility cannot for long diverge, and where there is no question of truth (or truth is impossible to ascertain), the sovereign must simply lay down conventions. The subject who understands Hobbes's philosophy will not demur at this, even if his private opinion is different from the sovereign's; and the sovereign who understands Hobbes's philosophy will remember the injunction of *De Corpore Politico* to leave his subjects as much natural liberty as he can. He will not stretch their willingness to obey him in things necessary to peace by inquiring minutely into their private opinions.[20] This suggests that the view we offered as commonplace—that Hobbes is the illiberal forebear of liberalism—is not quite right; Hobbes's reticence about securing intellectual uniformity is liberal enough in its own right.

What allows Hobbes to occupy this position is partly the inclination toward nominalism that we have seen above, and partly a kind of nonnaturalism in his ethics. By nonnaturalism here, I do not mean that Hobbes lays the foundations of his ethics anywhere other than in human nature, but that Hobbes insists that evaluations are not descriptions.[21] The goodness or badness, as much as the justice or injustice, of actions and states of affairs implies a human agent (and in the case of notions like sin, a divine agent) by reference to whose desires these attributions make sense. For

> whatsoever is the object of any mans Appetite or Desire; that it is, which for his part calleth *Good*: And the object of his Hate, and Aversion, *Evill*: And of his Contempt, *Vile* and *Inconsiderable*. For these words of Good, Evill, and Contemptible, are ever used with relation to the person that useth them: There being nothing simply and absolutely so; nor any common Rule of Good and Evill to be taken from the nature of the objects themselves.[22]

There is therefore no question of the truth or falsity of such judgments, though what *is* true is that peace depends upon our being got to utter harmonious appraisals on the same occasions. That is, only if I can be got to regard it as "good" that, say, you walk quietly down the road as you desire and already think good will I easily live in peace with you.

Even more important than Hobbes's appreciation of the role of convention here is the effect of his skepticism about the amount of information to be derived from natural theology about the nature and wishes of God, for it is this skepticism that allows him to detach the essentially political question of who ought to interpret the scriptures authoritatively from the metaphysical question of who made the world and decided how it worked. The effect is to make uniform public worship a political good and not a religious issue in the usual sense while strongly suggesting that private opinion can be left unfettered—a view we have already come to by one route and will come to again. How valuable the liberty is is another question; so often we find Hobbes seeming to suggest that freedom of thought is necessarily secure—because one man cannot pry into another's mind—that it is easy to think him uninterested in it. It can, however, at least be said that one objection to minute inquiry into our private thoughts is not just that we can dissimulate them, but that we have little control over them and cannot justly be held to account for them. Thoughts and desires break in upon the mind, and we cannot be compelled to keep them out when this is impossible; what we may be compelled to observe is some discretion in divulging them: "The secret thoughts of a man run over all things, holy, prophane, clean, obscene, grave, and light, without shame or blame; which verball discourse cannot do, farther than the Judgement shall approve of the Time, Place, and Persons."[23] Security would be threatened by much prying, so much prying is condemned. Of course, this is light years away from Mill's insistence in *Liberty* that freedom of thought means nothing without freedom of speech; Hobbes's point is precisely that we can conjoin private liberty and public regulation.[24]

Hobbes's briskly skeptical account of religion is familiar enough: anxiety about relations of cause and effect makes us work backward from effects to causes until we "come to this thought at last, that there is some cause, whereof there is no former cause, but is eternall; which is it men call God."[25] All the same, we hardly understand the conclusion we draw, since we "cannot have any Idea of him in the mind, answerable to his nature."[26] We are like blind men warming themselves at the fire; we know that something warms us, but we know not what. Many commentators have said that Hobbes was an atheist, even the father of atheism, but we need not draw any such conclusion. He is always eager to insist that we know that God is omnipotent; and he seems sincere enough in holding that the Gospels provide men with a clear and adequate moral code, their allegiance to which ought not to be shaken by sectarian wrangling.

Still, it is true that Hobbesian natural theology is extremely agnostic. Since we can form no clear idea of God, we can infer nothing about Him. Most of what we say about God is grammatically misleading, for it is really affirmed of our *in*capacities rather than his capacities. To call God omnipotent is not to say how much power God has, but to admit our incapacity to say how powerful he is.

> Hee that will attribute to God, nothing but what is warranted by naturall Reason, must either use such Negative Attributes, as *Infinite, Eternall, Incomprehensible;* or Superlatives, as *Most High, most Great*, and the like; or Indefinite, as *Good, Just, Holy, Creator*; and in such sense, as if he meant not to declare what he is, (for that were to circumscribe him within the limits of our Fancy,) but how much wee admire him, and how ready we would be to obey him.[27]

Although Hobbes mocks those who call God a "body incorporeal," which is a mere contradiction, he agrees that the description may not be absurd in use. The expression may be used not "*Dogmatically*, with intention to make the Divine Nature understood; but *Piously*, to honour him with attributes, of significations, as remote as they can be from the grossenesse of Bodies Visible."[28] The view is obviously attractive; when we shout, "May the King live forever" at his coronation, we know that he can do no such thing, but the wish is neither insincere nor absurd.

This suggests that one thing likely to be lost from our private concerns is an anxious attention to exactly what God requires from us for our salvation. By reason, we know that he requires us to keep his laws, but those we can work out by rational reflection—they are "theorems" first and divine commands second.[29] Faith in Christ, in the sense of secure conviction, is a gift of God, but we are obliged—by revelation rather than reason—to try to have that faith. Given the extent to which absolutely everything else may lawfully be determined by the sovereign, it is hard to see why anyone should worry very much about meeting God's requirements. Hobbes's insistence that God demands only a minimal amount of faith, plus obedience to the civil laws, seems to render the anxious inner life of Puritanism more than somewhat pointless.

This does presuppose that once we have cleared the decks for an extreme conventionalism in regard to religious practice, there will be no difficulty in carrying out the program. On the face of it, the distinction between private views about the nature of the world and public conventions about what counts as worship in this state rather than some other is an easy one to maintain. Yet this seems to understate the extent to which beliefs about the Deity infect attitudes to conventions. If God delights not in burnt offerings, will he not delight even less in five-part masses? A man who has read the first in scripture will find it hard to confine himself to saying that he does not know whether God likes music, and that he is prepared to leave the question for God and the sovereign to settle in due course. Most of the doctrines Hobbes is eager to control are ones that claim secular power for ecclesiastical bodies, but if conviction and convention are implicated more than he suggests, the sovereign must go either further toward securing uniform belief than Hobbes seems to want, or less far toward securing any sort of uniformity.

Perhaps the difficulty we face here is the result of taking Hobbes less radically than we should. That is, Hobbes's claim throughout is that religion is a matter of law not of truth, and his aim always is to show that there is no way in which our duty to obey God can conflict with our duty to obey (at any rate Christian) sovereigns. If we keep this point steadily in mind, we end up accepting that Hobbes thought that his own skeptical account of the bearing of scripture on politics was simply the truth, and that it ought to be taught as orthodoxy in order to calm the passions that led to civil strife. Whether or not it was true, it would certainly be a useful doctrine to have believed, since it would prevent strife; but given an audience that genuinely minded about its prospects for eternal life, it would make no sense to say that. Hobbes had to claim that his view was true and useful.

This, however, throws the issue of private judgment and its lawful expression back from religion in particular to law in general. That is, we still have the question of how far the sovereign may or must go to secure convinced or committed allegiance to his laws. The thought that we may think what we like, and want what we like, so long as we obey the law is an obvious first thought here; the question, of course, is once again whether we can so completely detach private judgment from outward allegiance. Now, it is clear that Hobbes's central claim is always that any society needs a single sovereign of legally unlimited authority, but this does not at all imply that the wielders of authority only impose laws. They can, and are morally obliged to, ask perfectly straightforward questions about what laws would best achieve the ends of civil society. The question of what would be the best way to legislate on a given issue is a perfectly straightforward question, and it can be answered on a commonsensical basis, by the sovereign or anyone else with the appropriate knowledge. Hobbes thinks the sovereign ought to get the best advice he can about the answer—this being part of what F. C. Hood calls the "moral constitutionalism" of the theory.[30] Hobbes himself suggests in his *Dialogue of the Common Law* that excessive litigation is the result of the lack of a proper system for registering land titles.[31] So there is no doubt that questions about the desirability of law are issues for individual judgment. The main burden of the *Dialogue*, however, is the familiar one: what the law is is a different question from that of what it ought to be. There is no direct connection between the reason of anyone and the validity of the law—not even when it is the reason of the very rational Sir Edward Coke. Origin, not content, determines the validity of law; bad laws laid down by "him that by right hath command" are still laws. The subject may say to himself that the law is a bad law; nonetheless, he must obey it and must do nothing to discourage others from obeying it.

Need the sovereign go further than this demand for outward obedience? Or, to put it differently, does the Hobbesian state require a deeper consensus than this? One suggestion that it does might be thought to be implicit in Hobbes's account of the natural dissensus of desire. After arguing, as quoted earlier, that terms like "good" and "evil" apply to objects not in virtue of properties of the objects but in virtue of the desires of agents in respect of those objects, he goes on to say that the goodness and badness of anything is, in a commonwealth, to be taken from "the Person that representeth it; or from an Arbitrator or Judge, whom men disagreeing shall by consent set up, and make his sentence the Rule thereof."[32] Now, given Hobbes's redefining of "justice" and "injustice" to mean legal and illegal, it is not difficult to see how we have to admit that what the sovereign *declares* for justice and injustice *are* justice and injustice. What is less obvious is how we are to take the claim that we are to take for good and evil what the sovereign declares for such.

It seems that we might take two different views, one of which would not really involve any new evaluations, the other of which would; it would then be a separate but related question whether either of these tied the goodness and badness of things directly to the sovereign's say-so. The first view is that the sovereign's ability to punish us for transgressing his rules makes situations good and bad in ways that they were not before, but not in any sense in which they were not before. Thus, in the state of nature, I regard your having the apple you now have as bad and the state of affairs that would obtain if I had it instead as good. (That is, I want it, and I therefore dislike your having it.) In the commonwealth, your possession is ownership, and I should be punished for interfering with it; anticipating the punishment, I now think that your having the apple is (relatively) good. But this does not seem to have introduced rules for judging goodness and badness; it seems only to have introduced new consequences. I do not think your having the apple is in itself good, or my having an apple that is not mine as bad; it is only my-having-the-apple-and-being-punished that I regard as bad. There are common rules all right, but they seem not to be rules for evaluation, and one might claim that unless they were rules for evaluation, they would not lend legal observance the moral support it actually needs.

The other view is that we do have a shift in evaluation. Anticipating the kind of account of the growth of conscience that is a commonplace of Mill's utilitarianism, Hobbes may be suggesting that what we come to think is that my-having-an-apple-owned-by-you is bad in itself, and that coming to think in this way is just what it is to develop a conscience.[33] Punishment may be necessary to instill such a conscience in us; but once instilled, its judgments are not consequentialist. Now, it is certainly true that Hobbes shares with later utilitarians a tendency to vacillate between a view of society that sees fully formed adults setting it up de novo and a view that rightly recognizes this as a methodological fiction and that then tends to take society for granted and inquire about how to socialize children into apt members of it.[34] It is an odd aspect of the English liberal tradition—or its utilitarian wing—that it places a great deal of the burden of preserving social order on the educational system in this way, but one can see how there would be two rather different images of what difference the sovereign makes. Self-interested adults contracting into a new political society would presumably apply their old evaluative habits to new situations—would value stolen fruit as highly as ever, but not want it for consequential reasons; their children would simply not want stolen fruit because they had been taught to disvalue it. In this second case, it does seem plausible to say that the sovereign has laid down rules for judging as opposed to simply attaching consequences of a novel kind.

As to the directness of the connection between the sovereign's say-so and new evaluations, we may distinguish three possibilities. The first picks up the first line of thought suggested above: we see the point of the sovereign's rules, and we see them creating instrumental goods. Without those rules there would be no property, and without property, no secure enjoyment; therefore, we think enforceable rules about property are good. We and the sovereign share evaluations, but this rests simply on the facts of the situation. The second possibility is rather different; it is that once there is security, things appeal to us intrinsically that did not do so before, and that perhaps hardly could do so before. There is a pleasure to be had from keeping promises, showing ourselves faithful to our friends, and so on; but this is a pleasure that can emerge only once we are safe enough to engage in morally satisfactory dealings with one another, and that is, in a sense, a second-order or emergent good. It therefore marks a rather larger break with the condition of mere nature. All the same, this is the sort of good that, as it were, grows naturally in fertile soil, and our thinking these things good seems to owe nothing to the sovereign's calling them good. Third, then, there is the possibility that the sovereign simply conditions us into calling good those things that he calls good, presumably by conditioning us into desiring what it is that he desires that we should desire.

It is the possibility of his doing this that forms what one might call the soft underbelly of liberalism. Liberalism insists, against the gloomier forms of Christianity, that human nature is not irretrievably wicked and that the right environment can mold beliefs and desires in the right direction. Critics of J. S. Mill have often argued that Mill's liberalism is essentially a better-than-nothing solution to the problem of achieving a society in which happiness is scientifically pursued and secured.[35] Huxley's *Brave New World* may be to some extent a parody of the aspiration toward the scientific manipulation of human nature for the sake of happiness, but it struck the normally liberal Russell as one recipe for peace, and perhaps a recipe that we ought to swallow.[36] What is characteristic of the brave new world is that its inhabitants are so conditioned that they cannot think their way round the possibilities it offers; gammas are glad to be gammas and think green is the nicest of colors, while betas are equally pleased with their lot and much admire blue. They do not want the same things in the sense that they can agree whether blue or green is the prettier; but they want what it is good for harmony in society that they should want.

One difference between this sort of conditioning and anything apparently envisaged by Hobbes is that Hobbes seems to want to circumscribe our choices by way of the imposition of names and agreement on definitions. It is a seemingly more intellectualist and less associationist theory altogether, although readers of Orwell's *1984* will wonder whether Hobbes has not anticipated Newspeak. Much like Wittgenstein, Hobbes seems to think that the limits of language are the limits of our world, so that if the sovereign can secure the necessary grip on our language, he can secure that our whole world, inner and outer, is under his control. Why should Hobbes be so eager to insist on his account of terms like "injustice" if not because he hopes that once we think it is a definitional truth that the sovereign can commit no injustice, we shall not rebel against "iniquity" but will think ourselves unable to rebel with a good conscience at all?

I hope that what has been said already is sufficient to cast doubt on the idea that Hobbes was hoping to define us into through-and-through conformity, and that the fact that Hobbes places so much weight on definitions and not on the association of ideas casts sufficient doubt on the idea that he was eager to condition us into parroting the sovereign's judgments of good and evil. In spite of the marvelous frontispiece to *Leviathan*, in which subjects are depicted as literally making up the body of the state, and in spite of Hobbes's assurances that when a state is founded, "it is a reall Unitie of them all, in one and the same Person," there is no submergence of individual substances in some superior whole.[37] Hobbes is neither Rousseau nor Hegel, and we ought not to try to turn him into either. There is still one obvious question that we ought to answer, however: if Hobbes is not bent on abolishing the individual, and yet certainly shows no great enthusiasm for moral and spiritual individualism, and if he is not particularly delicate about the inner life, but is tolerably clear that the interest of states is the interest of their members, then what interests do we have, and do any of them amount to an interest in our own inner lives?

The temptation is to make Hobbes into the spokesman of the bourgeois—or even of the suburban middle classes of today.[38] When Hobbes lists the horrors of the state of nature, the worst is the fear of violent death; but the state exists for more than mere survival. It exists for commodious living. This can readily attract a commercial gloss: luxury goods cannot be imported in the absence of maps and navigators, ships and sailors, merchants and bankers; we cannot live in decent stone houses with glass windows and nonsmoking fires unless we have roads and quarries and literate architects. It would be silly to underestimate Hobbes's attachment to useful knowledge; he may be less millenarian than Bacon, but he is as ready to assume that reason lights the way to peace and prosperity. But we ought not to go too far down the path of making him a spokesman for the nascent capitalist and the rising bourgeoisie.[39] His utilitarianism makes him accept as much freedom of trade as is for the general good and no more; nor does he think that property rights are sacred. We own what the sovereign says we own, and on the terms the sovereign lays down.[40] If the sovereign takes your property and gives it to a favorite, you have no grounds for complaint—though the sovereign ought not to do it in the first place, your rights are good only against fellow subjects. Again, Hobbes's views on the virtues have been described as bourgeois.[41] He was extremely hostile to the excesses of the aristocratic concern for honor; men who seize on the slightest excuse to pick a quarrel are menaces to the peace. Yet Hobbes was not exactly a bourgeois apologist; his patron, the Earl of Devonshire, may have been interested in iron smelting, but he was no bourgeois, and the virtues of fidelity and a willingness to forget old grudges are, if not classless, particularly the virtues of a gentleman.

To put it somewhat differently, there is certainly something about Hobbes's account of human psychology that irresistibly suggests the behavior of an indefinitely expanding enterprise in a "*race* we must suppose to have no other *goal*, nor other *garland*, but being foremost";[42] but this picture of men without any natural standards of success and failure other than the envy or contempt of others is not a picture of commercially minded man. The pleasures of civilized men are not themselves commercial or mercenary enjoyments; the affection of our friends, the disinterested search for knowledge, and the pursuit of literary excellence are all private goods in their own right. It may be true that when we enjoy an intellectual discovery, we experience the enhanced vital motions resulting from a sense of our talent for discovery, but we must be careful not to deflate Hobbes too far. Self-congratulation is an inescapable property of the physical organism, not the discovery of a cynical Hobbes. Hobbes has no quarrel with the claim that we enjoy one another's company quite disinterestedly, nor with the usual distinction between self-interested and disinterested intellectual activity.

I incline, therefore, to think that most of what we ordinarily think is valuable in the inner life was thought valuable by Hobbes. The worth of peace and security is that they enable us to enjoy civilized pleasures. These include the pleasures of having a quiet conscience and an easy mind; knowing that we have been generous, kindly, and charitable to the needy is the sort of pleasure Hobbes approved of.[43] It is one of the rewards of decent behavior that is unavailable in the state of nature; it is, for all that, not imposed upon us by the sovereign, even though it intrinsically inclines us to peace and will further incline us to obedience when we think of its dependence on the existence of good order. This being so, we can see again that the sovereign need not do anything very extraordinary to induce us to behave peacefully; he does not need to engage in thought control or in the invention of Newspeak, because our private occupations will in any case engross us. These occupations are, as we agreed earlier, the occupations of apolitical men, of subjects rather than citizens. For all that, Hobbes commends those that yield pleasure to the mind, not the satisfaction of sensual appetite.

It ought to be stressed, however, that the furthest this can take us in finding a case for intellectual liberty and mutual toleration is no farther than a utilitarian argument can go. The degree to which it is worth the sovereign's while to intervene for the sake of peace seems to be an issue of technique, not principle—that it is only for the sake of peace that he ought to intervene is the only principle in the case. Hobbes's sovereign cannot condition children as the Director in *Brave New World* can, and therefore should not try. There is no evident reason of principle to stop him from applying the techniques when they are discovered. Just as Hobbes shares with avowed liberals like Mill and Russell a tendency to vacillate between adapting society to adults and conditioning children into society, so he shares with them the difficulty of providing a principled stopping-place for governmental control of the mind. That the sovereign need not control most intellectual activities is one thing; that he may not even if he wishes to and knows how to is another. Mill and Russell evade the issue somewhat by appealing to a principle of "growth," which requires a liberal environment.[44] Hobbes is tougher and more consistent in simply employing the rule that the search for conformity is self-defeating if it only maddens the unorthodox.

Taking this together with what we saw earlier about the limits to the power of "imposing names," we can now end by suggesting that the sense in which Hobbes has principled reasons for toleration must always and only be that he has epistemologically principled reasons, never morally principled reasons. There are things we cannot get people to think, and where we cannot, we ought not to try. All else is a matter of expediency in that large sense in which the laws of nature bind sovereigns to act expediently rather than selfishly or arbitrarily. That Hobbes is inclined to let men alone but not to offer a principled defense of toleration is unsurprising. He paints a vivid picture of some parts of our inner lives—of anxiety, fear of ghosts, practical and impractical curiosity. But a man whose enthusiasm for music seems to have been limited to an appreciation of the good effects of singing upon his lungs is unlikely to get much further than that. He would no doubt have understood the fears of Soviet poets and writers in the face of Stalin's arbitrary cultural diktats; but it seems unlikely that he would have appreciated how far they minded about their art rather than their skins.

The Nature of Human Nature
in Hobbes and Rousseau

OUR IMAGES of human nature are centrally important ideological phenomena, for the evident reason that what distinguishes an ideology from a merely random string of moral and political imperatives is the way it incorporates the validating assumptions of those imperatives. The assumption that these imperatives—whether taken for granted, defended desperately, or pressed for the first time—have their roots in "human nature" is one main condition of their very intelligibility. Philosophical theories of ethics that have analyzed their subject matter in formal, nonnaturalistic terms—Kant's *Groundwork* or Hare's *The Language of Morals*, for instance—are unsatisfactory just because they cut themselves off from recognizable answers to the question "What is the point of acting in such and such a way?"[1] But if any viable ideological position implies the possession of an image of human nature, this is far from suggesting that most cultures have felt any great need to articulate that image. Indeed, it is arguable that this possession, like many others, is noticed only when it is lost. A society in which the going rules are universally accepted, in which conflicts of interest do not appear to be intense or deep, may well get along in the belief that how men ought to behave there is how men ought to *behave*, because how men are there is how they *are*. Whether there are many, or any, such societies is unclear; the old sociological image of "primitive society" may simply be a myth that tells us less about the moral orderliness of savages than it does about the anxieties of our own social theorists. At any rate, what is clear is that an account of human nature is intrinsic to moral and political argument, and the need for an explicit account is the more urgent when moral and political argument becomes fiercer and gets more swiftly down to basics. Thus, the discovery by the Greeks that their way of life was so different from that of many of their neighbors provoked at once the question of how convention was, or was not, rooted in nature. Was there one justice, since fire burned in Athens and Persia alike; or was there nothing coherent to be said about the relative merits of different social arrangements?

The question to which students of human nature inevitably address themselves is, what are men *really* like? And it is important to stress that "really," since it is at the heart of all sorts of problems. If we were to ask what men are like, we might invite a mere catalogue—men here have such and such beliefs, men there have such and such other beliefs. The tricky word "really" tells us that this will not do. When we add "really," we always mean to rule out some possible deceptive factor—is she really blonde, or does she dye her hair? Is that really a Great Dane, or will it turn out to be a rug when I put my spectacles on? Now, we have to ask what "really" rules out when it appears in this context. What kind of tampering or deception are we ruling out? Plainly, the tampering is that stemming from social conventions, moral, religious or political brainwashing. The point of asking what human nature is like is to see through—or behind—what men locally believe, want, approve, and abhor, to uncover the substratum beneath man as he locally appears. But this presents us with a problem to which no wholly compelling answer has been given, certainly a problem that Hobbes and Rousseau set for us rather than solved. Men always live in society; so far as we can see, all the more complex forms of behavior that we regard as characteristically human are ones we learn slowly through social interaction. But if our evidence of human capacities comes from socialized man, what can we infer about nonsocialized man's resources for good and evil? Even to ask the question shows up more problems. It is, in the first place, not clear that anyone does want to know what men would, as a matter of fact, be like without socialization. Rousseau explicitly denied that this was his concern, and neither he nor Hobbes would have gained much moral purchase from the occasional feral child. In the second place, if we hope to get at human nature by "stripping away" the effects of socialization, it looks as if we must already know what the effects of social life are. To then explain the effects of social life by reference to an underlying human nature looks very like arguing in a circle. No wonder, then, that practically the first remark that Rousseau makes is "*écartons tous les faits*" (let us lay aside all the facts); the concept of human nature is confessedly a theoretical construction.[2]

All the same, it is worth making one methodological point here; up to this point, nothing said about the difficulties of getting at human nature implies that these are different in kind from those involved in getting at the nature of nonhuman objects. To the seventeenth-century scientist—and to John Locke—a knowledge of the nature of lead was beyond us; for all we know of lead is what happens to samples of lead in various experimental situations—just as all we know of men is what happens to samples of humanity in those experiments that we call society. But a sufficiently dashing scientist would not stop there; he could reply that he had such a good deal of elaborate chemical and physical theory about the internal structure and organization of lead that he was justified in believing that he knew the nature of lead and knew why samples behaved as they did in experiments. No doubt the internal organization of men is imperfectly understood, and no doubt the variety of effects that the environment exerts on that structure is far beyond our present knowledge. But there is, in principle, no more reason to despair of knowing the nature of man than there is to despair of knowing the nature of lead.

Such, anyway, would have had to be the reply of Thomas Hobbes (1588–1679), and there have been no more dashing or ambitious figures in English

philosophy. The very blandness with which he announces that all the conclusions of *Leviathan* except the preexcellence of monarchy are demonstra-
tive truths is immensely appealing in view of the shock and outrage that
those conclusions created. For a man who prided himself on his caution,
even cowardice, in political matters, he was extraordinarily brave in intellectual fields. The ideological collapse that provoked Hobbes's response
was, of course, an overt and very far-reaching one, and Hobbes was an acute
observer of its near and remote causes. The disorder Hobbes most minded
was literal civil war, the collapse of law and order. The source of disorder
was men's inability to agree about the status and grounds of the rules that
ought to maintain the legal and political system. Two particular causes of
these disagreements were, in the first place, the conflict between the defenders of the traditional common law, who held, with Edward Coke, that the
fundamental rules were traditional, built in, not open to change by royal
say-so, and the defenders of royal prerogative, who held that law was what
the sovereign said it was; and, in the second place, the multitude of religious
prophets who preached doctrines of individual illumination that were, in
implication, anarchic in the extreme. Now, it is easy to make two related
errors about Hobbes's work. The first is to detach it too completely from its
time—for Quentin Skinner has certainly shown that *Leviathan* had immediate political implications that were perceived by Hobbes's contemporaries.[3]
They knew that his equation of de facto and de jure authority implied a duty
to swear allegiance to the new Commonwealth. But the second error is to
underestimate the oddity and originality of Hobbes's arguments in this context. He saw more plainly than his contemporaries that an entire picture of
the natural order had been dealt a mortal blow. The old Christian-cum-
Aristotelian metaphysics was simply played out; the usual inquiries about
man's place in the natural hierarchy were therefore nonsensical. Attempts at
a rational inquest into the good life for man as laid down by Nature or God
were old-fashioned scholastic junk. To understand nature, human nature,
and the imperatives of social life, it was essential to throw out this meaningless rubbish and begin on scientific foundations. No account that sees Hobbes
as other than a secular, materialistic utilitarian is an account of Hobbes at
all, which is why Leo Strauss's attempt to present Hobbes's science as a mere
tarting-up of old-fashioned conceptions of the state as a remedy for sin just
misses the point.[4] So equally do more recent attempts to present Hobbes's
political system as a derivation from Christian theology.[5] Hobbes's own
contemporaries knew better than more recent commentators: orthodox supporters of royal prerogative knew that this secular, calculating politics was
a creed quite unlike a belief in the divinity of kings.

Hobbes's science of human nature is part of his science of nature in general—a fact that instantly puts Hobbes on the "hard" side of today's debates
about the status of the human sciences. Hobbes's science of nature is the
science of bodies in motion; what he is committed to is a universe in which
there is nothing in the world except matter in motion. Hobbes's psychology

is in principle reducible to physiology, and ultimately to physics. Again, this puts Hobbes into some thriving contemporary company—that of those philosophers who call themselves "identity theorists" or "central state materialists" on the strength of identifying psychological and physiological processes as the same processes. A good deal of (not very successful) ingenuity is devoted by Hobbes to trying to account for, for example, memory in terms of "interior motions": if present perception involves "phantasms" caused by the physical interaction of the internal motions of our brains and the corpuscular emanations of bodies external to us, then memory is a weakened "phantasm." This ignores all sorts of difficulties, the most obvious of which is that my now remembering having read a book last week is nothing like my now reading a book—either a neat or a dilute version of that event. Hobbes's physical analysis of human activity would no doubt have been more persuasive had his experience of "machines" extended beyond the clocks and watches that were the common basis of seventeenth-century corpuscularian analogies and on to that twentieth-century source of analogy, the computer. Certainly, what Hobbes wanted to tell the world was that human beings are self-regulating and self-maintaining mechanisms. That he was faced with the intractable difficulties we, too, face in explaining the "emergent" properties of self-maintaining physical systems is only one more of the things he shares with us.

It is a consequence of Hobbes's mechanistic approach that he presents men as having two crucial properties. First, their actions are wholly determined. There is no such thing as free will; men are free in just the same sense that anything else in the world is free, and no more so. A stream runs downhill freely when nothing impedes its progress—though that progress is certainly caused. A man acts freely when there is no external impediment to his actions, but those actions have determinate causes. What men call the will is simply the last appetite in deliberation; willing is in no sense a voluntary act, as the nonsense of saying, "I will to will . . ." shows. As we shall see, there are a good many hidden problems here. The second crucial quality is human selfishness. Not only are our actions determined, but they are determined by our desire to maximize our own pleasure. The successful maintenance of the human organism is accompanied by pleasure—pleasure is, so to speak, the way that the maximization of vital motions appears to us, just as "phantasms" are the way our sensory interactions with the external world appear to us. Thus, the self-maintaining mechanism pursues the maximum of pleasure for itself. Hobbes was quite aware that the assertion that we always try to pursue our own pleasure is fraught with danger. A friend saw him giving alms to a beggar and raised the obvious question of how a believer in selfishness could act in this seemingly altruistic way. Hobbes's reply—absolutely correct according to his theory—was that the beggar's distress caused him distress, and by relieving the beggar, he relieved himself.[6] But the reply itself creates another puzzle, for it reveals an ambiguity in the concept of pleasure. If it is a necessary truth that every action is done to maximize the apparent pleasure of the actor, then it is certainly not necessarily true that men are selfish or pleasure seeking in the usual sense of the terms. It is not true that the benevolent man is "really selfish"; rather, the reason why we call him benevolent is that his gaining pleasure depends upon the pleasure of others. The difficulty for Hobbes is that if it is only in this rather formal sense that men are pleasure seeking or selfish, this in itself offers no reason for thinking that they will be selfish in the usual sense. But only if they are selfish in the usual sense will they get themselves into the kind of trouble that Hobbes's state of nature describes and that the Leviathan is supposed to rescue them from.

Self-maintenance is clearly the major imperative facing the Hobbesian man. The organism is, so to speak, programmed to keep itself in existence. So clear is this to Hobbes that he regards suicide as proof of madness; and this imperative underlines his claim that the one thing we cannot promise to do is destroy ourselves even if our absolute ruler requires us to, for nothing would count as a genuine promise to do so, so contrary is it to our basic nature. Equally importantly, it explains Hobbes's claim, made in opposition to the Aristotelian tradition, that there is no natural *summum bonum* (supreme good) for men, although there is a *summum malum* (supreme evil). The open-ended imperative to survive means that we must do what looks like the survival-enhancing thing on each occasion. Felicity in this life is not attained in a condition of happy and tranquil rest, for all life is incessant motion and incessant change of desire; felicity can consist only in achieving the objects of our different desires one after another. But the absence of vital motion is an absolute evil; death, the cessation of all desire and activity, is the *summum malum*. Hence, Hobbes's assumption that the great evil of ineffective government is the way it exposes us all to the danger of violent death; hence, too, his belief that it is our common interest in avoiding such risks that provides the securest foundation for the power of Leviathan.

Before leaving Hobbes's premises about human nature for his conclusions about the plight it gets us into, it is worth summarizing the legacy he has left us. His belief that explanation in terms of matter in motion—mechanical, causal explanation—is the only satisfactory kind of explanation has been triumphant since his day. During this century, the goal of tough-minded scientists has been to reduce the psychological vocabulary of desire, purpose, and intention to something more akin to the austere vocabulary of mechanics. The efforts of psychologists of the persuasion of Clark Hull or John Watson has, to a large extent, been directed to the Hobbesian program, though in a more empirical and inductive way, and one that is more cautious in hypothesizing interior mechanisms.[7] Crucially for our comparison, it is the suspicion of talk about mental entities that carries across the centuries, the fear that talk about the contents of consciousness verges on mysticism. Conversely, the problems that Hobbes found intractable remain intractable today for the same reason. Hobbes, for example, tries to graft an account of the conventional meaning of words onto a causal foundation by showing words provoking ideas—a sort of stimulus-response backing. But he cannot manage it with any ease; to raise merely one problem, logical constructions such as "if . . . then . . ." are utterly recalcitrant to a name-object analysis. And attempts to resolve the problem invariably wind up in circularity, since the only way of identifying the appropriate response to the word stimulus depends on already knowing the meaning of the word that the response is meant to explain. Who, after reading Noam Chomsky's devastating attacks on B. F. Skinner's view of language, would not agree that Hobbes's difficulties are alive and unsolved and living in Harvard?[8] Again, all the phenomena of self-consciousness—except, perhaps, anxiety about the open future— receive a rough analysis from Hobbes. Is the process of trying to make up our minds only a matter of overhearing the decision-making machinery hunting through its routines—the conflict of one good reason with another a matter of the ebb and flow of motions until a decisive shift is made? Do we stand as such spectators in our own bodies that what seems phenomenologically to be a choice is no more than a spasm when the machinery settles down? Like his successors in this tradition, Hobbes found it hard to explain consciousness without thereby explaining it away.

The condition of hypothesized selfish, rational man is familiar today from another contemporary hypothetical science—strategic studies. Our natural condition is one of merciless competition. For rational, selfish creatures, competition has three sources—scarcity, fear, and pride (or vainglory). Scarcity hardly needs elaboration, but the other two causes do. The effects of fear are, again, the commonplaces of deterrence theory. In a condition in which there is no power sufficient to overawe us all—which is, by definition, the condition we are in without government—we know that another man can, by brute force or by guile, do us any injury up to and including death. The ability to kill one another is the one basic equality that Hobbes assumes, and it gives us all an approximate equality of vulnerability. It also gives us all a powerful motive to strike first rather than be struck against. I know that any of my fellows sees me as a threat; he knows that my only certain defense against him is to eliminate him before he can eliminate me; he knows, too, that I know this—that I have, therefore, every reason to strike at once—and that knowledge gives him every reason to beat me to it. When each of us has a lethal first-strike capacity, and none of us has any second-strike capacity at all, the strategic logic necessarily leads to a war of all against all—individually, it is irrational to forgo the preemptive strike, but individual rationality leads to destruction for all. This is not to say that men have any intrinsic lust for conquest, desire to dominate their fellows, or the like. That men seek restlessly for power after power throughout their lives is a result of their insecurity. Men, unlike animals, can fear tomorrow as much as today. We cannot enjoy the goods we have at the present moment unless we have some certainty that we can enjoy them in future, and this means we must have some way of protecting them. But the demands of power are inexorable, for we must always protect the position from which we protect our goods: to eat the apple, we grab the tree; to defend the tree, we build a fence; to protect the fence, we dig a ditch; and so endlessly on. But as if this were not enough, Hobbes endows man with an urge to emulate, to outrun his fellows. Not that Hobbes moralizes about pride; he merely asserts that since men can recognize other men as essentially like themselves, they begin to compare their own success with that of other men and, having done so, become dissatisfied with any position other than the best. We do not merely wish to survive; we wish to survive better than anyone else. And this introduces a kind of scarcity that nothing can cure and a kind of competition to which there can be no end. When we are all intent on occupying first place, and the evidence that it *is* the first place is the envy of the defeated, there is no possible way to create enough goods to go round. The state of nature is thus overdetermined.

Recent writers on deterrence have argued that the war of all against all can be averted by the creation of second-strike capacity. The urge to launch a preemptive strike disappears when it is obvious that it will bring only lethal retaliation in its train. In the nuclear field, doomsday machines or a belief in the human urge for revenge is enough to create the plausible threat. For Hobbes's system, it is the Leviathan who provides second-strike capacity; if you murder me, I certainly cannot kill you in reply, but the state can, and this knowledge ought to powerfully reduce your enthusiasm for making the first move. In short, Hobbes applies the logic of the game theorist to human nature, and much like Anatol Rapaport arguing that rational egoists will get into an irrational mess, Hobbes shows us that the state of nature is a state of universal war.[9] And like his successors, Hobbes argues that some enforceable system must be found whereby it is made the interest of every party to pursue the common interest in peace.

But what does the Leviathan do when he creates order in this chaos? I have argued all along that the point of inquiring into human nature is to inquire into the underlying reasons why social order is both necessary and possible; it must also be to show what kind of order is required. And here Hobbes seems to offer two responses, which are worth distinguishing rather sharply. In one view, the sovereign creates a minimal order of peace and security. Men may do whatever they wish within the limits of keeping the peace. The sovereign certainly judges, for example, what religious views may be put forward—but he does not judge their truth; all he does is ensure that ceremonies of praise and honor to a deity are agreed on and cause no dissension. Religion, as Hobbes insists, is law, not philosophy—conventions, not truth. What men choose to believe in the privacy of their hearts concerning such contentious matters as the origin of the world is their own business. In other words, there is no legal limit on the sovereign's authority and no theoretical limit on what he may find it necessary to regulate. But men being what they are, an effective government can be a very laissez-faire one. Much of what Hobbes says supports this view. It accords well with his jokes against original sin and his dislike of interfering clerical authority. And this side of Hobbes suggests that the association between liberalism and secular utilitarianism is more than a historical accident.

Yet there is another side to the story, less obvious, but well brought out in John Watkins's *Hobbes's System of Ideas*.[10] In this view, the Leviathan is more than a mere contractual arrangement. It is, as Hobbes says, a real and perfect unity of them all. We become literally one body—though an artificial body, nonetheless a real one. The famous frontispiece to the first edition of *Leviathan* is to be taken quite literally. Now what this suggests is a much more radical jump from prepolitical man to political man. The state is to take each of us and so mold us that we become elements of it. Yet the way in which this is to occur is not through coercion, but through teaching us the language of civility, a vocabulary in which treason becomes unsayable, hence unthinkable. Since the Leviathan is, although a body, a body whose sinews are conventions, its parts—the citizens—must have as little choice about keeping these conventions as have things in the natural world about obeying the laws governing them. Hence, Hobbes makes it a primary task of the sovereign to lay down rules by which acts are to be named and judged. Common rules of right and wrong are to be established, and Hobbes appears to envisage these as being so established that it will appear self-contradictory to question them. The simplest example is Hobbes's claim that what the sovereign does is, by definition, just—"just" means here "in accordance with the sovereign's commands"—so nobody can think himself unjustly treated by the sovereign. This is a profoundly totalitarian image, and one that speaks to our contemporary terrors. Orwell's Newspeak and Jean-Luc Godard's dictionary-eating computer in *Alphaville* are powerful images of the ways in which vocabulary may shape political possibilities. But Hobbes's state is still light-years away from the horrors of the twentieth-century totalitarian state. His successors in our century are fictional ones—the rulers of *Brave New World* and the planners of *Walden Two*. But the only moral that I want to draw is that—as the preceding account of a more liberal Hobbes shows—utilitarian, manipulative accounts of human nature are not bound to lead in this direction. The revolt against recent applications of a certain kind of Benthamite rationalism, which several writers have documented—none more soberly or clearly than Stuart Hampshire—is a revolt against possible rather than inevitable applications.[11] But what is true is that once we have, with Hobbes, taken up this secular, mechanical, naturalistic approach to human nature, we are left with no absolutely forbidden actions, no intrinsically wicked behavior. The limits of politics, even when pursued by the undeniably benevolent, are set by psychological technology rather than by independent standards of human dignity or the like.

But if human nature is so manipulable, one of the functions of the notion of human nature is much impaired, for it plays a much-reduced role in setting a limit to political possibility. Unless something substantial, basic, and important survives the process of socialization and remains intact behind social appearances, we are unable to say anything very profound about how well or how ill social arrangements satisfy human needs and aspirations. Hobbes begins by setting up social arrangements to cater for human needs, but ends by teaching us how to remake human beings to fit social arrangements. Certainly, the friendly relativism of a lot of sociology owes what respectability it possesses to a similar emancipation of the social sciences from their psychological basis. Societies create their own raw material; they can, therefore, be coherent or incoherent in the way that they do it; if they are too incoherent, then they will grind to a standstill, but between two equally coherent societies there seems nothing to choose—neither would satisfy the "human nature" created in the other, but each satisfies the "nature" it creates. But there is no question of a society coherently violating human nature. The suspicion that appeals to human nature were politically ineffectual in just this way was one of the many doubts that tormented Rousseau. I do not want to embroil us in a blow-by-blow account of the similarities and divergences between Hobbes and Rousseau, but I do want to show how this suspicion fits into a use of the concept of nature that is different from Hobbes's in important ways. If Hobbes's descendants are the "tough-minded" behaviorists, then Rousseau's are a ragged collection ranging from revisionist Marxists through to the existentialists and beyond.

The disorder to which Rousseau responded most keenly was psychological disorder. It was the chaotic condition of the individual self that distressed him, and although he insisted that this condition had social causes and social consequences, it was the fusion of the personal and the political that unified his essays, his novel, his autobiography. He described the disorder he saw as alienation: "*l'homme est devenu hors de lui-même.*" Men cannot live within themselves; they are not self-sufficient, either singly or together. This was both the cause and the effect of inequality and injustice. But whereas Hobbes is willing to accept the world's account of who wins and who loses in the social race, Rousseau says that everyone loses. One man thinks himself the master of many and yet remains a greater slave than they. Competition breeds greed, envy, servility, false conceit, and false humility. It forces men to perform for the sake of public approval, and where they cannot or will not, it forces them to retire into themselves, to dream of revenge and preeminence founded on fear. Rousseau was a great admirer of his own talents as a painter of the human heart, and he excels himself at the end of the *Discourse on Inequality* with a description of the lonely crowd that encapsulates an entire tradition, pre-echoing Hegel and Freud and looking back to Plato's account of the self-enslaving tyrant in book 9 of the *Republic*.

But how had men got into this condition, where had they taken a wrong turning, and could they have done better? Rousseau provides no one answer, and his hopes for improving the human condition are minimal. But there are some illuminating suggestions. In the *Discourse*, Rousseau claims that men without society must be mere isolated animals. For him, natural man is not the noble savage, nor is he Hobbes's rational egoist. Both these conditions are social conditions and, in an important sense, nonnatural. As an animal, man is neither moral nor immoral, but amoral; his conduct cannot sensibly be judged by moral standards, any more than that of animals can be. Such "natural goodness" as man does possess, he possesses only in potentiality—and this potentiality is by no means certain to be realized. As an animal, natural man shares with animals an advantage denied to social, truly human man. He is lacking in any sort of self-consciousness, and therefore he is lacking in any kind of anxiety. Animals are afraid in the presence of a terrifying thing that provokes their fear, but the haunting fear of extinction that pervades human life, the factitious anxieties about how we look in the eyes of others—these are fears the animal knows nothing of. That these anxieties are a central element in the human condition and are importantly nonnatural is, of course, one respect in which Rousseau anticipates the central commonplaces of existentialism. But human nature contains seeds of a total transformation that animals cannot undergo—we alone are so educable that we change individually over an entire lifetime, and so adept at transmitting what we have learned that as a species we change as drastically. An animal is the same after a few months as during its whole life; the species is the same at the end of a thousand years as at the beginning. Only human beings can properly be said to have a history; but once we enter history, our former nature is irretrievably lost, and knowledge of it merely hypothetical. This capacity for indefinite transformation Rousseau terms *perfectibilité*, but it is by no means a capacity to make ourselves perfect—indeed, its chief effect is to put us quite at odds with ourselves. Our "natural" condition, in the sense of our existence as mere isolated animals, is not an elevated condition—we eat, sleep, copulate at random, and fight at necessity—but it is one in which desires and their satisfaction are matched to each other. Dissatisfaction has not yet entered the world. And this matching of desire and attainment gives the state of nature a moral quality for Rousseau, though not that of prescribing how we should behave in society.[12] It is rather as an image of harmony, the opposite of the restless, striving competitiveness of civilization, that it finds its moral role; but the critic with an ear attuned to Rousseau's pessimism catches the implication that such harmony is possible only where everything that is distinctively human—speech, self-consciousness, individual and social aspiration—is absent.

The arrival of language and society drastically transform the situation; they make morality possible—but they also make men depraved: "*L'homme qui pense est un animal méchant*" (The thinking man is a depraved animal). The raw animal material of morality was the twin sentiments of self-love and sympathy; we shun, by an instinctive reaction, both pain to ourselves and pain to our fellows. The arrival of reason transforms these into principled benevolence and a proper, conscientious self-respect. We recognize other men as entitled to correct treatment, and we claim it from them in return. We also, more alarmingly, become able to grade men for their qualities, to rank them as more and less estimable. And we can therefore desire to be esteemed ourselves. At this point, someone emerges who closely resembles Hobbes's natural man—proud, selfish, competitive. Rousseau draws attention to the fact, and goes on to draw Hobbes's conclusion that this will be the prelude to the war of all against all. But he is at pains to point out that the state of war exists only within society and as a consequence of social dealings. This claim is not, of course, a straightforwardly historical or sociological one. Rather, it is a way of denying Hobbes's comparatively cheerful assumption that if this is how men are, then we had better construct a social order that will accommodate them without bloodshed. The perpetual motion of Hobbesian man is not a neutral phenomenon, but a disease to be cured. And Rousseau's concern for the damage done by universal competition is not limited to fearing that we shall make war on one another, that the fist, the knife, or the gun will replace the market. It is not the danger that we shall damage one another that agitates Rousseau; it is the certainty that we are damaging ourselves.

Civilization is a condition in which we lose touch with ourselves. We put on masks; we play particular social roles as if we were actors in the theater, or even puppets on a string. Rousseau was fascinated and repelled by the theater—it was both an allegory of the falseness of social life and a celebration of that falseness. The more society develops, the more elaborate its games become, and then the greater become the temptations that beset the man who tries to be himself and to live within himself. Social distinctions are, of course, merely conventional—but nonetheless real. It was quite impossible for Rousseau to address his aristocratic patrons as if they were his equals, just as it was impossible for him to pretend that he thought their disparity in rank was based on a like disparity in merit. Once the conventions are set, they are as much an objective part of the world as anything else is. And if they give us no chance to build up a liveable-with character, that, too, is a fact about the nature of civilization. What haunted Rousseau was the fear that there might be no real self behind the several masks we wear; this emerges even in his *Confessions*, in which he both promises to reveal everything about himself and yet produces such a variety of disparate revelations that we can suppose only that even he was unable to find one single coherent story about a single coherent self.

But where, we might ask, does Rousseau go from here? What escape is there, and how does the knowledge of human nature help? One thing only is certain: that he found the status quo quite intolerable. Moreover, he had enough of a sense of history to feel that our situation had to be explained genetically, that the present is unintelligible until related to its origins in the past. Unlike his historicist successors Hegel and Marx, he had no faith that the process would ultimately reveal itself as benign. The obvious similarities between his ideas and theirs make it the more necessary to insist on this difference—as Marshall Berman's otherwise excellent book fails to do.[13] But if there is no optimism about the benefits of history, there is no assumption that we can simply go back on our tracks. If the present is intolerable, the condition of natural man no longer charms us; and even Rousseau agrees that a refusal to embark on human history at all is no answer to the question of how to be both human and happy. Not that natural man is unimportant as a critic of civilized society—the mindless paradise of Adam and Eve testifies to the vitality of the image. But the presocial state is not offered as a utopia to which we might aspire. And the simple lives that Rousseau does praise are, at most, nearer nature, and they are not exactly paradise either. The Caribs of the *Discourse* are already corrupted by vanity, and they are cruel too; the shepherds of the Haut-Valais are more attractive, but even they are clumsy and ignorant by the standards of civilization.

The question remains whether the things that are lacking in the simple life really are losses—are they goods that we have bought at too high a price, or are they not really goods anyway? It seems to me that Rousseau's answer is the former. Certainly, it is more than mere rhetoric when Rousseau claims that the simple life is better than the life of Paris; but the situation is not simple. Maybe we are the better for suppressing our literary talents, but we are also the poorer; these are genuinely human talents we have suppressed. Harmony would involve the blending of our many and diverse skills; all we ever seem to achieve is discord; therefore we would do better to settle for unison. Still, all this is, in a sense, beside the point; for Rousseau's major claim is that even if we saw that the simple life was the better life, *we* could not choose it. Rousseau's propagandist motives are infinitely less direct than were Hobbes's. We would die of boredom in the Haut-Valais and of disgust among the Caribs. And Judith Shklar is more than persuasive when she claims that Rousseau's utopias set no positive goals—that they serve to point out the irremediably rotten condition of this society, not a perfection to be found in some other.[14]

That the simple life of this kind is not intended by Rousseau to be a picture of the good life is suggested too by the most famous of all Rousseau's works, the *Social Contract*. For there Rousseau contrasts the condition of natural man with the condition of the man who is both free and virtuous—indeed, free only because he is virtuous. The life of impulse is a form of slavery, but obeying laws that we prescribe for ourselves is freedom. All this shows one further important aspect of Rousseau's concern with human nature. Presocial man's desires and satisfactions coincide; civilized man's desires and satisfactions are drastically at odds with each other. The depravity of society and the arbitrariness of social convention create an obsession with personal prestige that is utterly self-destructive. One of the insights that Durkheim extracted from Rousseau was the idea that nature could be re-created inside society; for this to happen, social rules must possess the same degree of impersonality, nonarbitrariness, and externality to our desires that the descriptive laws of nature possess. This links up with some very characteristic ideas in both the *Social Contract* and in *Julie*. The legislator of the *Contract* has to know how to abolish human nature and create something new and socially adaptable. And Wolmar's talent is precisely that he can do this for his own charges—his wife, children, and servants—by so arranging the environment of Clarens that the obvious (or natural) path is the path of virtue. But all this remains as ambiguous as everything else in Rousseau's work—the legislator of the *Social Contract* seems to end up with nothing more attractive than Sparta to his credit, which hardly suggests that Rousseau was the originator of totalitarian democracy. And Wolmar's Clarens is not the greatest success we can imagine—Julie remains in love with Saint-Preux, and the artificiality of the life at Clarens is eventually reflected in her unwillingness to go on living it. Something in her nature must surely have been mortally abused, and Wolmar is as much her murderer as her benefactor.[15]

The Rousseau whose views of human nature I have sketched so briefly and crudely is not, of course, the only Rousseau to be found in the writings of that ambivalent and alarming man. There is a good deal of straightforward Hobbes-like utilitarianism in the *Social Contract*—where Rousseau acknowledges with perfect calm that conflicting interests makes society necessary and shared interests make it possible. But what there is in Rousseau that possesses a curiously current interest is the fear that not enough of our nature is visible or recoverable to provide us with a clear guide to what viable self we can create. The anguish at having so many masks to wear, so many roles to act, so many choices with so few guides on how to make them—this is something that really does seem to have begun with Rousseau. It is all too easy to read Sartre, Hegel, or Marx back into Rousseau and thereby blur the contributions of all of them. But even the most austere and historically cautious writer can hardly ignore that new tone of voice. To become as familiar as it has, it had to start a long tradition, one that has recently reemerged in sociological theory, literary criticism, and philosophy. But if Rousseau's successors have added their own, original contributions, he ought, I think, to get the credit for starting the argument in these distinctively modern terms.

12

Locke on Freedom
SOME SECOND THOUGHTS

ALTHOUGH THE THEME of Knud Haakonssen's collection of essays is "traditions of liberalism," it is a moot point whether Locke is best understood as "a founding father of liberalism."[1] I do not mean by this that judged by some timeless test of liberal virtue, Locke is disqualified from joining the liberal club. Rather, I mean that Locke was notoriously secretive in life and remains elusive in death. Exactly what his own intentions were, it is hard to say; exactly what lessons secular, pluralist, twentieth-century liberals might draw from the devoutly Christian Locke, it is even harder to say. Certainly, one way in which historians of ideas have been having second thoughts about Locke for the past thirty years is that the old picture of Locke as a slightly muddled liberal who tried to balance consent, property ownership, and the public good as alternative bases for political authority has been discredited. He has been seen as a covert Hobbist, defending absolute government; as the defender of the rising bourgeoisie; as the defender of capitalist landowners; as a Calvinist emphasizing the arbitrary and contingent quality of all earthly hierarchy; and as a revolutionary and a regicide (Cox 1960; Macpherson 1962; Wood 1984; Dunn 1969; Ashcraft 1986). None of these views is wholly without merit; none is wholly satisfactory. The elusiveness that did much to save his skin (see Ashcraft 1986, 426ff.), posthumously does much to save him from the interpreter's oversimplifications. Of the innumerable topics this essay might tackle, I address only a handful. The main topic is the familiar question of how Locke's account of government in his *Two Treatises* can be a solution to the problem of reconciling freedom and authority, which I take to be *a*, even if not *the*, central problem of liberal politics.[2] In the course of providing a fairly simple answer to that question, I say something about the connections between freedom and property, a little about the connections between freedom and republicanism, and lastly something about the dismissal of liberalism as an essentially "privatized" view of the world by Hannah Arendt and Sheldon Wolin (Wolin 1961, 309ff.; Arendt 1961). It will be apparent that on all of these, I am offering second (third, fourth, and later) thoughts, but very few conclusions.

Preliminaries

If men are born naturally free and equal, there is a problem about how they come to live under political authority. There are problems familiar from game theory: if everyone is willing to obey an authority but everyone fears that other people are not, how is mutual assurance to be achieved? If matters are worse than that, if we should all like to exercise authority but would also like to avoid obeying it if we could, how then can we set up any sort of political and legal authority? If, *per impossibile*, we can achieve that, how can we decide *who* is to exercise authority? Ordinarily, persons who exercise authority are authorized to do so; but to make an authoritative appointment demands that someone already possesses or has acquired authority. Readers of Hobbes will have asked themselves and him such questions. It is Hobbes who insists that we cannot infer from the Bible what authority to obey until we are told by some authority how to understand the Bible, just as it is Hobbes who seems to turn the establishment of any authority into a prisoner's dilemma game. There is, however, a sharp difference between Hobbes and Locke. Locke did not ask himself such questions, and this was not out of carelessness or inattention but because he did not think he needed to. If men were born free and equal, they were not born outside all forms of authority. They did not face the problem that Hobbesian men face, that of pulling themselves up by their moral or legal bootstraps.

Their freedom and equality consisted of the absence of earthly hierarchy; but they were in all conditions governed by a law of nature that was intelligible to anyone who consulted his reason. Men were the handwork of God. Moreover, they were his handwork in a way that no object of human manufacture could be; God created the world ex nihilo, whereas men merely reassemble the ingredients they find around them; God inspires us with a soul in a way that defies rational explanation. We are therefore God's property in a very special way, quite different from the way our earthly property is ours. God may dispose of us as he sees fit. No human being has this sort of authority, neither over himself nor over anyone else, nor even over anything else. Since our lives are God's and not our own, our property in our own persons amounts to the freedom to choose how to employ our talents and time in order to realize the purposes intended by God.

Freedom is therefore not the arbitrary domination of our will, but the uncoerced following of the law of nature: "Freedom is not, as we are told, *A Liberty for every Man to do what he lists*: (For who could be free, when every other Man's Humour might domineer over him?) But a *Liberty* to dispose, and order, as he lists, his Person, Actions, Possessions, and his whole Property, within the Allowance of those Laws under which he is; and therein not to be subject to the arbitrary Will of another, but freely follow his own" (2:57). Although Locke insists, as Hobbes had, that law supposes the will of a superior, his view of law is, for all that, Aristotelian, and less Hobbesian or

"Benthamite" than most modern commentators find congenial. God's law is "not so much the Limitation as *the direction of a free and intelligent Agent* to his proper Interest" (2:57). It is more than a set of coercive rules founded on general utility. Although God's goodness means that he wills the happiness of his creatures and the flourishing of all things as far as possible, the law of nature is not merely, as I once suggested (Ryan 1984, chap. 1), a utilitarian moral scheme. A utilitarian account of natural law and natural right would see the primary role of law as the defense of each of us against the ill usage of other men, rather as Mill's essay *On Liberty* does, and it is true that the content of the utilitarian schema and the law of nature as described by Locke overlap. Reason "teaches all Mankind, who will but consult it, that being all equal and independent, no one ought to harm another in his Life, Health, Liberty or Possessions" (2:6). Nonetheless, the rationale of this injunction is not that its acceptance forms the basis of a social peace treaty — as it is with both Hobbes and the utilitarians — but that it directly points out to each individual what God requires of him.

Men are the servants of one sovereign master, "sent into the World by his order and about his business"; they are "his Property, whose Workmanship they are, made to last during his, not one anothers Pleasure" (2:6). The individual acting in the light of this Lockean law will not harm another, but whereas the Hobbesian or utilitarian perspective makes mutual forbearance central to the justification of the rule of law, the Lockean perspective does not.[3] Locke's is a Christian perspective in which the fact that we have been sent here about the Almighty's business yields both the content and the authority of natural law. In my view, therefore, the prior authority of God is one of the supports of an insistence on the rule of law in earthly politics; Shirley Robin Letwin and I agree that Lockean individualism allows the individual no ultimate freedom to decide his or her own ends—these being set by God—but I dissent from her suggestion that this sort of freedom is necessary to a defense of the rule of law.[4] Even piously motivated preemptions of the rights of others are ruled out by Locke as a violation of the sanctity of the individual's own judgment and the individual's own relationship with the Almighty.

Property and Liberty

If we focus on the connections between freedom so conceived and Locke's account of property, we get two strands of argument. The first is that human beings sent into the world on God's business are required to make good use of the world's resources. They cannot do this except by appropriating them; food for eating and water for drinking must be taken into our bodies before they are any use to nourish life. We must therefore have the right to make things "ours": "There must of necessity be a means *to appropriate* them some way or other" (2:26). The property rights thus acquired are chronically misrepresented in the literature; Macpherson, for instance, assumes that Lockean property rights are unencumbered freeholds and that what we get by initial acquisition is the *ius utendi et abutendi* ("right to use and destroy") of the Roman lawyers. He further muddies the waters by contrasting Locke's conception of property with that of Aquinas and other medieval writers and misappropriates the labels of "exclusive" (or "exclusionary") and "absolute" to define this conception. This makes a fearful tangle in the following several ways.

Lawyers have a use for the distinction between "absolute" and "nonabsolute," which is technical and unlike Macpherson's distinction. Whereas he means "under the unfettered discretion of an owner unencumbered by customary or communal claims upon the property," the lawyers distinguish between forms of property law that start from the presumption of a single owner who possesses all the powers (be they few or many) over his property that the law recognizes, and systems that do not. English land law was archetypically an example of the second and remained so until 1925. Yet it is in the context of landed property in seventeenth-century England that Macpherson is writing.

Certainly, to say of someone that he had an "absolute" property right is often a way to conjure up the thought that he "can do what he likes" with his property and that nobody may say him nay; but even here, there is a misleading suggestion in the air. Roman law, which is the paradigm case of a system founded on an absolute-in-the-lawyers'-sense conception of ownership, actually gave the owner less power to create dependent interests in his property than did the common law. Parting with the *ius fruendi* (right of enjoying another's property without destroying it), for instance, because it was a personal contract, was a less satisfactory way of creating a lease than the English leasehold; it was the system that lacked the absolute conception of ownership that, perhaps paradoxically, gave the owner most scope for the imaginative control of his property. If the powers of owners over their property were greatly expanded during the seventeenth century (and it is not at all clear that they were), this did not introduce the "absolute" conception of ownership into English law (Macpherson 1962, 220–21; Lawson 1958, 8–9; Reeve 1986, 13–23, 45–51).

Similarly, Macpherson's emphasis on the "exclusive" conception of property thoroughly confuses conceptions of property with ideas about who is to do what with whatever property is in question. Macpherson contrasts the power of the capitalist to exclude others from access to the means of production with an "inclusive" conception of property that guarantees access to the means of production. Precapitalist societies had collective ownership of one sort and another, which allowed villagers to graze their cattle on common land or run their pigs in the woods, or gave them access to strip fields to grow wheat, and so on. Under socialism, the forms of ownership will be very different, but the same thought holds: property will be property for access. This, however, muddles two different issues. In the first place, *all* property is exclusive; when a village owns a common, it has the right to exclude nonmembers from access to the common. If it has de facto control over a hunting run, what it has is the power to exclude members of other tribes or villages from access to the hunting run. The power is held by all the group and not by individual members; but the power is just as much (or as little) a power to exclude as the power of the capitalist. Moreover, the emphasis on the capitalist's powers of exclusion is misconceived in another way; the capitalist needs to employ his capital in setting workers to work. If he had no power to exclude some, he could not employ others, but unless he does employ some, he will not long be in business. In that sense, one might well say that his property forces him to offer access to those he employs. It is impossible to see how there would be any conception of property under socialism that was not also an exclusive conception, even if property was employed to include as many people as possible in the workforce.

Whether property conceptually includes a right to exclude is a wholly distinct issue from the question of the extent to which people either may or habitually do use their ownership for private gain. It may be that those who own the commons are unconcerned to do anything more than live as they always have; and it is certainly true of socialist economies in practice that they have been eager to avoid unemployment and have therefore tended to guarantee employment to all who are halfway willing to work. All the same, the rights of the Soviet state over Soviet industry are very like the rights the British state has over nationalized industries. The idea that a society dedicated to securing full employment either has or needs to have a different *conception* of property is a confused way of making points that could readily be made without entering into such territory (Reeve 1986, 32ff.).

We must, therefore, try to decide what Locke's views on these issues were, without unduly encumbering the issue with extraneous matter. To get to this point we must begin with Locke's conception of rights. Locke evidently begins with duties rather than rights. God's design for the world gives us duties and sets us tasks; we must therefore have the rights that are necessary if we are to fulfill those duties. This vision is very different from the one that Nozick ascribes to Locke (Nozick 1974, 174ff.; but on 58 at least acknowledges some of the distance between them). We are obliged to preserve life, and therefore must have the right to what is necessary to preserve it; this is how the duty to preserve life lies behind the right to appropriate property. It is not a self-centered conception of rights at all: "Every one as he is *bound to preserve himself*, and not to quit his Station wilfully; so by the like reason when his own Preservation comes not in competition, ought he, as much as he can, *to preserve the rest of Mankind*, and may not unless it be to do Justice on an Offender, take away, or impair the life, or what tends to the Preservation of the Life, the Liberty, Health, Limb or Goods of another" (2:6).

Because the law of nature is God-given and imposes duties before it confers rights, Locke took seriously the record of what Adam's rights and duties were. Against Robert Filmer, who started from the thought that Adam had an arbitrary and unlimited dominion that was at once magistracy and own-ership, and ended with the conclusion that Charles I had the same, Locke claimed that Adam had not even the right to destroy the inferior creatures for his own use: "who, as absolute a monarch as he was, could not make bold with a Lark or a Rabbet to satisfy his hunger" (1:39). Adam had do-minion over but not, in the usual sense, ownership of the animal kingdom. Adam's property extended only to the vegetable kingdom (contrast Genesis 1:31–32 with Genesis 9:31). It is noticeable that Locke does not suggest that Adam would have been even freer than he was in the Garden of Eden if he had been allowed to slaughter animals too. Freedom remains firmly *within* the bounds of God's law.

The "duty-based" conception of rights is important in making proper sense of Locke's "strange doctrine" that we all begin with the right to exe-cute the law of nature against offenders. If this were a liberty right, it would imply that we might execute the law of nature if we felt like it and not if we did not. This reading of the matter would be alarming in the sense that it would provide an incentive to anyone violating the law of nature to go to the length of murdering his victim, since if the right to punish violators was simply the liberty to do so if we chose, there would be a good chance that nobody other than the victim would choose to do it, and therefore that the violator's best hope would be to eliminate his victim entirely. This was the logic of Hobbes's war of all against all. Locke's view was that we had a duty and *therefore* a right to enforce the law of nature; we might not be able to enforce it, but wherever we could do so, we ought to do so. By the same token, it was only if the duty lay behind the right that the social contract setting up government could create what we wanted—not a government that had the right to enforce the law of nature if it felt like it, but a govern-ment whose duty was to enforce the law and that had, as individuals did not always have, the power to do its duty. Here as elsewhere, Locke has the advantage of Nozick, who simply omits any explanation of how "protective associations" are to be made to do their duty (compare Nozick 1974, 137–40, and Locke 2:9).

Unsurprisingly in the light of this duty-backed view of rights, the acquisi-tion of property is the fulfillment of a duty, and only for that reason the exercise of a right. The literature on Locke's theory of property is extensive, but chronically underattentive to this feature of Locke's theory. James Tul-ly's long and careful account, for instance, tries to make sense of Locke in terms of what one might call the "embodiment" of personality in property (Tully 1980, 110). This is not wholly wrong, but it is subtly misleading in that it starts from a concern that is distinctively more modern than Locke's; to the extent that Locke thought of property as connected with personality at all, it was only via the thought that person is a "forensic notion," that what made persons persons was their capacity to obey the law, take respon-sibility for their actions, and generally live up to the standards of natural, moral, and divine law.

Tully, to be sure, maintains that "Locke's use of the term 'person' is also traditional." He cites Thomas Aquinas, Francisco Suárez, and Samuel Pufendorf; but in so doing he emphasizes the thought that to have a personality is to be a free agent and that the free man is defined as proprietor of his own will. It is this that strikes a false note. Although Rousseau, Kant, and Hegel picked up old traditions of thought when they emphasized the role of the will, their vision of the embodied will is distinctively modern and very un-Lockean. A modern reader cannot stress the embodiment of the will as Tully does without picking up such Kantian and Hegelian themes. What we have to stress instead is that Locke was light years away from accepting the Romantic (or even the English Idealist) doctrine that personality as such demanded expression in the external world, except in the limited sense that the world had to allow a man scope to do his duty. Self-expression was something about which Locke was at best ambivalent; it came close to the pure willfulness that he was always eager to repress. The "self" that was to be allowed expression was so circumscribed by the duties laid upon it by God that there was no scope for Hegelian or Romantic notions of *Bildung* in the Lockean universe, not even when Locke was writing about education.[5]

Macpherson's emphasis on the theory of differential rationality, which he—uniquely—discovers in Locke's works, suggests, rightly, that there is a rational imperative to acquire a property in external things, but Macpherson goes on to infer, wrongly, that "unlimited appropriation" is the mark of rationality. If John Dunn exaggerates a little when he says that Locke "must be supposed to have had about as much sympathy for unlimited capitalist appropriation as Mao Tse-tung," he does not exaggerate much (Macpherson 1962, 232–38; Dunn 1969, 209). Nonetheless, it remains true that rationality requires us to acquire property. In the first place, it is only by taking and using what nature offers that we can survive at all. Reason enters the equation in the following way: what human beings ought to do is a matter of what their essence or nature dictates. Our natures, like the real essences of anything else, are a matter of God's construction. *An Essay Concerning Human Understanding* denies, of course, that we possess genuine "knowledge" of the real essences of things other than those we have ourselves created—though Locke seems at times to have wondered whether Newton might not have penetrated the veil of appearance and somehow read the mind of God after all. In the case of geometry, which is a human construction, we do possess an a priori, and in that sense godlike, knowledge of the objects thus constructed. Indeed, we have the same knowledge wherever an action or object is made what it is by meeting a standard we have laid down. We do not know the essence of gold, because "gold" refers to whatever it is that gold turns out to be like, but we do know the essence of adultery, because "adultery" refers to an activity that satisfies criteria we ourselves have set (Locke 1964, 2:66–70; Ashcraft, 1987, 44–46).

What of the knowledge of ourselves? There seems no certain or simple answer to be had to this question. Locke does place the knowledge of our own selves in the same category as mathematics and morals, but how much we know about our own selves and what it is that we know is not spelled out very satisfactorily. Locke needs simultaneously to insist that we do not know how God has wrought us in order to insist on God's authority over us and its difference from earthly authority, and yet that we know enough about our own construction to reveal the dictates of natural law. It is not clear that there is any way of reconciling these demands. What there is is a loose analogy with the *Essay*'s strategy of showing that we have knowledge sufficient to our needs. The Gospel, Aristotle, common sense, and a view of what is needed for happiness all converge on the same point. It is contrary to reason to suppose that God would create us with desires that he chronically intended to frustrate. Our search for happiness and our attempts to avoid misery were implanted for good reason; and success in them—both here and in the hereafter—is not impossible. Obedience to the law of nature makes for happiness, both because God's injunction to live modestly and at peace with our neighbors, to practice charity, and to place our happiness in what is eternal rather than transitory makes for earthly happiness anyway, and because God's capacity to inflict eternal punishments on those who violate his laws and give eternal rewards to those who keep them ensures that over the infinitely long run, virtue and happiness coincide.

The dependence of all this on a Christian framework is complicated; indeed, it is multiply complicated. One dimension of the complexity, to which we must return, is that Locke intends to drive religion out of politics and politics out of religion; but he proposes to do so for what one might call "religious" reasons. Another, of immediate concern, is that Locke evidently thinks that Christian and non-Christian reflection will coincide in an agreement on what the law of nature requires. The Aristotelian, teleological framework of classical natural law picks up the natural presumption that things that serve human needs so exactly are there to do just that. Apples, so to speak, are there to be eaten for our benefit; the rational man will eat them, not use them as missiles, nor will he gorge on them. The needs of any sort of social interaction similarly dictate what sort of moral code we must follow. The Swiss and the Indian bartering for trade in the woods of inland America know perfectly well that *pacta servanda sunt* ("agreements must be kept"), though they share no common religion. Perhaps the Christian, equipped with the Gospel and the unique enlightenment it offers, is better off than anyone else, but the law of nature is not unavailable to anyone who is both rational and of moderate goodwill.

This is not a complete answer to our question; Locke seems also to doubt whether men are so much at one in their moral views as he himself suggests in his more optimistic moments. His *Essays on the Law of Nature* admit that "there is almost no vice, no infringement of natural law, no moral wrong, which anyone who consults the history of the world and observes the affairs of men will not readily perceive to have been not only privately committed somewhere on earth, but also approved by public authority and custom. Nor has there been anything so shameful in its nature that it has not been sanctified somewhere by religion, or put in the place of virtue and abundantly rewarded with praise." Nor does he go far along the path of trying to distinguish between the more or less utilitarian considerations on which one might expect mankind to agree—the need to keep faith, tell the truth, abstain from violence within at any rate a certain social circle—and ideas about the good life, the sexual virtues and vices, family life, and the like, which one might expect to vary much more dramatically (Hampshire 1983, 164–7; Locke 1954, 167). It is perhaps surprising that he does not do so, since the general pattern of his politics is to insist on the need to provide a framework of enforceable law within which individuals may pursue their own intimations of the good life. But it is easy to see that Locke's concern in his *Essays on the Law of Nature* is to fend off Hobbes; contra Hobbes, it is crucial to insist that morals are not validated by convention and do not rest on individual self-interest. It would only weaken the case to stand back and contemplate cases that are more nearly conventional.

Still, even if we cannot press Locke very hard on this, we can now return from the law of nature to property and see what this implies for his views on freedom. Without unduly rehearsing an old story, the gist of the Lockean account is to insist on *use* as the moral basis of proprietorship. The definition of ownership, as distinct from its moral basis, is, however, firmly linked to consent: "For I have truly no *Property* in that, which another can by right take from me, when he pleases, against my consent" (2:139). It is the concept of use that allows him to say that the grounds of legitimate appropriation are set by the law of nature, as are the limits of such appropriation: "The same Law of Nature that does by this means give us Property, does also *bound* that *Property* too. *God has given us all things richly*, 1 Tim. vi. 17 is the Voice of reason confirmed by Inspiration. But how far has he given it us? To *enjoy*. As much as any one can make use of to any advantage of life before it spoils, so much he may by his labour fix a Property in" (2:31).

For familiar reasons, Locke needs to show that although God gave the earth to mankind in common, each individual may establish property in what he acquires, without the consent of everyone else. Filmer had argued, as a reductio ad absurdum against those who began from the claim that men were born free and equal, that the institution of property could never have got off the ground; each joint owner would have had to give his consent to the appropriations of any individual. As Locke later said, men would have starved in the midst of plenty if they had had to get such consent before they could pick acorns or drink from the brooks. Filmer's answer had been to trace title from the right of Adam or else, and more interestingly, from the rights of any paterfamilias who had no earthly superior. If men were simultaneously the fathers, owners, and governors of their offspring, individual property could be explained as the legitimate grant made by former owners.

If Adam had owned everything and everybody and had had an absolute arbitrary power over all of it and all of them, subsequent rights had a pedigree
(Filmer 1949, 10–14). Locke needed to fight off that account.

He did it by mixing several elements familiar from Roman and natural
law, but in a curiously English-common-law fashion. That is, Locke did not
need to, and did not in practice try to, turn anyone into an "absolute" owner.
The English law's familiarity with the idea of an "estate in" whatever it is
allowed Locke to see proprietorship as necessarily including the right to
exclude others from enjoyment of whatever it is, in the respect in which we
have a property in it, without having to suggest that this follows from our
having an absolute and arbitrary power over it. "Property" in is the crucial
notion. Locke mixes English and Roman conceptions by tying together first
appropriation and labor as ways of gaining ownership. Roman Law recognized both these; Locke, in effect, needed to be able to answer the question
to which first appropriation was an answer—namely, how does it come to
be his in particular? But he wanted to do so in a framework that built in the
view that we could acquire only what we could make use of, and the view
that God sent us into the world to make something of his creation. So labor
sometimes collapses both into using and into first appropriating—as when
we lean over the brook and drink—but at other times stands out as part of
an argument from justice—when we make fields fertile and therefore work
hard to improve God's donation to us, we deserve the benefits we reap.

This matters a good deal, because it raises the question of how free we are
to deal with the world so appropriated. It is not clear that Locke offers one
and only one account of this, but I incline to agree with Richard Ashcraft
that there is a strong suggestion that the Lockean state of nature is a two-
stage state of nature, in the second stage of which many of the simplicities
of the first stage are lost. If that is right, then the first stage is one of Golden
Age innocence; it needs only simple moral rules about when we must regard
things as taken under the control of particular others. We shall have rules
about when the fish in the lake become yours rather than mine; where we go
in for cooperative hunting and gathering, we shall have rules about how the
spoils are divided. None of these establish freeholds in the earth as opposed
to its fruits; and since the objects owned are so perishable, the rules leave it
wide open how far powers such as the power of bequest go along with ownership. The capacity to give what is ours to our friends and children plainly
is part of ownership even in this simple state, but bequest is very different
from *inter vivos* gifts (gifts between the living).

What we are entitled to when we own something is innocent use. This
rules out letting things spoil in our possession; Locke suggests that spoliation is a form of theft from others, but this seems implausible in the state of
affairs where we can so easily leave "enough and as good for others." The
more plausible thought is that God gave nothing to man to destroy; anyone
who destroys what lies in his possession is therefore acting beyond the limits
of his proprietorship. Ownership is derivative from God's gift; spoliation

violates the terms of God's donation. If we apply the same thought to the acquisition of land as well as the fruits of the earth, what we get is the thought that in order to make the land more fertile and fruitful, we must be able to rely on exercising *some* control over it. At least there must be a presumption that once we have enclosed and cleared it, we are entitled to reap the fruits of our labor and entitled also to say who shall and shall not have access to it.

This does not mean that we shall get bequeathable freehold ownership. Locke's mode of argument reverses Kant's—Kant sees ownership as a claim to sovereignty over the substance of external things and therefore sees land-ownership as prior to ownership of crops, which are "accidents"; this is a thoroughly Romanized conception. Locke builds up toward ownership in the full, liberal sense defined by A. M. Honoré by extending the functional requirements of "use" (Honoré 1961, 108ff.; cf. Ashcraft 1987, 142ff.). If landed property demands a good deal more than the simple rights over perishables, which we have in the Golden Age, it does not immediately demand outright freehold ownership. Quasi leasehold such as simple agricultural societies have would do the trick—the rights of Fijians over their gardens and plantations are far short of English freeholds, but establish the conditions Locke had in mind. Locke's own example of the way Spanish villages allowed short-term ownership of wastelands brought into cultivation is equally removed from freehold ownership but a perfectly plausible solution to the use-based requirements of Locke's theory.

The difficulty lies less in grounding increasingly elaborate rights in increasingly long-term uses than in securing that the crucial limitation on the freedom to appropriate—leaving "as much and as good for others"—is satisfied. It is a limitation that in the early stages can hardly help being satisfied; men are few, the world is empty, and it is hard to deprive others except by deliberately wrecking the environment—by polluting a stream, say. However many acorns or however much fruit we consume, we shall leave as much and as good for others: "And thus considering the plenty of natural Provisions there was a long time in the World, and the few spenders, to how small a part of that provision the industry of one Man could extend it self, and ingross it to the prejudice of others . . . there could be then little room for Quarrels or Contentions about Property so established" (2:31). In that state, even land presents no problems; the fact that it is finite in quantity is not a problem, because the numbers who want it are so small. Even in Locke's time, there would be enough land to give some to everyone who wanted it, if it had not been for the invention of money.

So we must distinguish two states of nature: the one innocent of money, the other equipped with it. In the former, the only uses to which anything can be put are near-immediate consumption and simple barter. In these conditions, there is no incentive for elaborate accumulation of property, and therefore presumably no accumulation. Once money comes in, everything changes dramatically. Money has two vital properties. In the first place, though useless for any immediate purpose, it is exchangeable for what is useful. In the second, however much of it anyone has, they are in no danger of it spoiling and therefore in no danger of violating the prohibition on letting things perish uselessly in our grasp. Locke does not raise the question whether one man's accumulation of money means that there is "as much and as good" left. And for this there is a very good reason.

Locke's account of property is oddly unconcerned with the actual stuff over which people claim ownership. The reason for this is that Locke thinks that God gave us the world so that we might have a good living; to fix our hearts on any particular things would be a violation of God's purposes and would display the sort of willfulness he was anxious to remove in the course of education, for instance: "As to the having and possessing of Things, teach them to part with what they have easily and freely to their Friends; and let them find by Experience, that the most *Liberal* has always most plenty, with Esteem and Commendation to boot, and they will quickly learn to practise it" (Locke 1968, 213). Now, if the use to which one man puts the world increases rather than diminishes the chances of another man having a good living, the first has not taken anything from the common stock but has added to it. So the account we get of the role of money and trade and its impact on equality and on landed property is intriguingly two-edged. The love of money is the root of all evil; once money appears, the *amor sceleratus habendi* ("accursed love of possessing") can get a grip on us. Locke is one of the philosophers Rousseau described as explaining human depravity by the introduction of gold and silver. On the other hand, money allows trade, the division of labor, and economic progress. Without it, we should not be eating white bread and living in houses with glazed windows. Locke follows Hobbes in thinking of these as innocent improvements in our conditions of life—not, as Rousseau was to do, as signs of how far we had fallen from Carib innocence or Spartan toughness.

How this bears on landownership is a familiar point. A man who has money may pay another to bring wasteland under cultivation, paying the other a wage and reserving to himself ownership of the land. In this way, ownership and actual labor are detached from each other, though not ownership and use. A man may own more land than he himself can cultivate or consume the produce of because there are other uses to which the produce can be put—it can be sold to people who themselves can acquire more of the useful things of life by working at something other than growing their own food. Unlike Plato and Aristotle, who thought trade dangerous and the handling of money a sure route to corruption, Locke is ready to acknowledge the utility of trade and therefore to see it as fulfilling God's purposes. If one effect of this is to put all the land into private ownership, this occurs without violating anyone's freedom.

How it occurs without violating anyone's freedom, on the other hand, is less easy to spell out convincingly. The crucial point is that Locke is, contrary to the view of him taken by Robert Nozick and James Grunebaum, not a "first appropriation" theorist; that is, it is not true that Locke derives ownership titles from an inquiry into pedigree that terminates in the appropriative act of whomever first set out to exert his will over whatever it is that is in question. There is, therefore, no temptation for Locke to think that we all come into the world entitled successfully to appropriate something in particular—land, for instance. If we were to enter the world with such a right, those who happened to arrive before us would not have been entitled to appropriate all the land for themselves, or at any rate, not in such a way as to claim outright freeholds. The only just system would be one in which some sort of rearrangement of titles occurred on the death of existing owners and on the birth of new arrivals—or on their reaching the age of majority perhaps (Steiner 1982, 513–33; Spencer 1851, 1145; Reeve 1986, 82–86; Tuck 1979, 77ff.) If, conversely, the entitlement to appropriate was an entitlement to appropriate only what was not already appropriated, we could reach the other extreme conclusion, namely, that those already in lawful possession of the earth could treat all newcomers as trespassers and refuse to allow them to live except on such terms as the owners thought good. Locke plainly regards any such idea as preposterous, though Grotius did not.

So what we have instead is the idea that those who among them own the landed property of a country such as England have a duty to see that the nonowners can live by working (Nozick 1974, 177). That is the conclusion to which Nozick comes, too—one of the rare occasions when his account is genuinely Lockean. Ownership on such terms violates none of the rights of the nonowners, who may secure their share of the good things of life by labor; and it does not impose unreasonable demands on the owners, whose property is at all times to be considered entrusted to them, subject only to the maxim *salus populi suprema lex est* ("the welfare of the people is the highest law"). Locke clouds the issue by arguing also that whereas appropriation in the simple, nonmonetarized state of nature occurs without the need to secure the consent of the rest of mankind, money exists only by consent; we consent to it, and thus to its consequences also. This, however, seems a pretty feeble argument. Money exists by consent only in the weak sense that conventional monetary instruments are indeed conventional. There is no suggestion that in using money I have consented to the existence of a monetarized economy—or if there is, everything Hume says against the social contract can be said against this suggestion too. Locke's strongest argument is instrumental, and it is as strong as it is because it is not just an instrumental argument but is backed by a vision of natural law that settles issues of justice and individual right that a secular instrumental theory would not.

Liberty and Republicanism

Locke spends a great deal of time on the nature of property, as he ought in view of its role in his theory. I have therefore spent most of my time on the same topic. However, it would not do to evade some further questions that

Locke provokes without himself raising them. Locke's view of political legitimacy relies on the theory of property in our persons to distinguish parental, despotic, and political authority in a way reminiscent of Aristotle's treatment of the subject. Just as Plato lumped together the authority of husbands over wives, owners over slaves, and rulers over subjects, failing to acknowledge that political rule was distinctively the rule of a statesman over freemen, so Filmer lumped together ownership, despotic authority, parental authority, and political authority. Aristotle took it for granted that free government existed only in a constitutional republic—though a lawful monarch appears to be perfectly consistent with his insistence on a government of laws, not of men. Locke seems, in his discussions of the constitutional framework of a legitimate state, to take it for granted that it would have many of the features of the England of his day—that it would be a constitutional monarchy. It is of course true that much of the point of his saying so was to lead on to the argument that a king who refused to summon Parliament was in a state of war with his people and might properly be resisted and deposed. This raises the question whether Locke was in any sense a "republican" theorist, and invites the reply that in the sense made familiar by Machiavelli and his successors, and objected to by Hobbes, Locke does not seem to be concerned with republican liberty.

This is a complicated topic to straighten out; I want to suggest that Locke is more nearly a republican than he might appear at first glance, and in the process to cast some doubt on the distinction between ancient and modern prudence, first made by James Harrington (1977, 161) and recently echoed by J.G.A. Pocock (1983, 235ff.). This is a two-stage process: this section tries to establish one way in which Locke connects republicanism and freedom, and the final section tries to clear Locke and liberalism more generally of an antirepublican hostility to political involvement.

The recent enthusiasm for the history of civic-humanist theories of government and the taste for seeing the Machiavellian moment recurring from sixteenth-century Florence to nineteenth-century America make it harder than ever to get Locke straight. Locke, to be sure, reads like neither Machiavelli nor Harrington; however, he would have agreed with Rousseau in distinguishing between states that were predictably in search of the common good and were thus republican, and states that were predictably dominated by the will of some person or class and were therefore tyrannies, whether of the one or the few or the many—though I say no more than Locke "would have" done so, since he never raised the question in quite this form. Republican government in this sense—that is, constitutional, public-spirited government whose authority stems from its commitment to the public good—is calculated to reconcile freedom and authority in the sense that individuals are never required to obey the arbitrary will of another (which is Locke's own polar contrast to freedom under law) and never required by the law to do what they morally ought not to.

This "republicanism" is a long way from the sense in which Harrington might be said to have defended a Machiavellian conception of republican liberty (Pocock 1974, 384ff.). The Baconian and Harringtonian vision of republican liberty relates to landed proprietorship in what is by now a familiar way: the yeoman is the backbone of the country, far different from the French peasant, who is a mere ground-down laborer, or "base swain." The yeoman is a fighting man whose like exists nowhere in Europe: he is attached to his own land, he has a stake in the country, he is fit to vote and play a part in politics. The enthusiasm for colonialism and expansion that we find in both Bacon and Harrington is part of their vision of freedom—the nation is master of its fate and its fortunes, just as its citizens are master of theirs. Freedom consists of following one's own will, not that of tyrants, nor that of external necessity. Locke equally wished men to follow their own wills, not those of tyrants, but he was a "negative" libertarian in focusing on the citizen's treatment by his rulers, not a "positive" libertarian in focusing on an expansive state. But this latter distinction may not be as solid as it looks. Machiavelli, to whom Bacon and Harrington are deeply indebted, did not insist that only expansive states were free. A state invulnerable to domestic tyranny and foreign conquest was a free state. Locke surely went that far. As we shall see, there is an obvious difference between Locke and the classical republicans in their conception of the ultimate goods of life; but we ought not to conclude too quickly that Locke was unable or unwilling to connect political liberty and constitutional forms. He was not Hobbes.

An area in which Locke agreed with the Machiavellians was in their antipathy to standing armies as opposed to citizen militias; but again, this was not because he saw the armed farmer as peculiarly the defender of liberty. Locke was hostile to standing armies, and to that extent a Harringtonian de facto, because he thought the monarchy of his day was determined to reduce the English people to servitude. Charles II's desire to establish a standing army was part and parcel of his intention to govern without Parliament and to force his people to convert to Catholicism as he had promised Louis XIV he would. Locke's belief in the supremacy of the legislature over the executive reveals a more nearly de jure commitment to republicanism, evidenced by the decision to *publish*—as opposed to the decision to *write*—the *Two Treatises* when he did. For Locke's view of the Glorious Revolution was drastic and republican in just the way Edmund Burke later objected to. Where the soberer Whigs were ready to go along with the fiction that James II had abdicated, leaving the throne to his nearest Protestant relative, otherwise his son-in-law William of Orange, Locke was insistent that what had happened was a dissolution of the old constitution and therefore that Parliament had become a real constitutional convention that had authority to start all over again. This was doubly a trope out of ancient prudence, both in its emphasis on the possibility of a fresh start and in its emphasis on the powers of the legislature.

Locke's whole theory of government, in fact, leads in a republican direction because of its emphasis on law and consent. Traditionalists would have derived the authority of the sovereign from his occupancy of a throne inherited from his father and grandfather before him. Locke, by contrast, made legislative authority the central feature of the state. If there is a hereditary monarch, the right to inherit is itself given to the monarch by the legislature; supremacy belongs to the legislature because it represents the whole people considered as a legislating body. Thus, the nature of authority is swung away from any picture in which monarchy can sustain itself in its own terms; hence my earlier claim that Locke and Rousseau were at one in their view of the republican quality of a constitutional monarchy.

As to the freedom that republics preserve, that is a matter of some banalities and some very seventeenth-century matters. Crucially, Locke identified absolute monarchy with the Catholic despotism of Louis XIV. This trampled on individual conscience, violated the individual's security of person and property, and damaged the liberty of trade and occupation on which prosperity depended. This is one way in which Locke's claim that government is instituted for the preservation of property latches onto the pressing concerns of the improving classes, who were most hostile to Charles II and willing to go to all lengths to stop his brother, the Duke of York, from ascending the throne as James II. But the antipathy to monarchy was a seamless web. The republicans still alive and in opposition after the Civil War were as fiercely hostile to an established church as they were to the despotic pretensions of Charles II. Their republicanism was not merely a matter of insisting on legislative supremacy and a dislike of the person of Charles II; it neatly combined a belief in the traditional liberties of the Englishman with an insistence on his right to representation and a new doctrine of toleration, which picked up the ancient belief that the state's interest in religion was confined to the preservation of good public morals.

If Ashcraft is even halfway right in his account of Locke's political activities—though he, too, is forced by Locke's efficient covering of his tracks to resort to surmise more often than is comfortable—there is no doubt that from the 1670s onward, that is, from the time he joined Shaftesbury's household, Locke was allied to the radicals who kept alive the alliance between dissent and republicanism. His religious convictions marched in step with his political convictions. Locke became steadily less convinced that Christianity required of us anything more than the faith that Christ is the Lord. Curiously, he began and remained wholly hostile to Hobbes, who seemed to his contemporaries to be a principled opponent of toleration; yet Hobbes had himself argued exactly as Locke had, that Christianity required only commitment to the truth that Christ is the Son of God and our Savior.

Hobbes may have been a greater friend to toleration than has usually been thought, but the crucial point on which he and Locke agreed was that there was no doctrinal basis for a church establishment (cf. Ryan 1988; Ashcraft 1986, 48–52). Freedom, for Locke, was evidently tied, all but conceptually, to the right to worship God as we chose, according to our own convictions. Hobbes, of course, admitted no such right, but thought sensible people would allow one another so much liberty, and in the meantime, thought them foolish to mind what worship men performed in private;

Locke thought the law of nature included the injunction to give *public* praise to the Almighty, and had to admit an individual right to worship publicly in the way that seemed best to us. Locke was almost bound to be tempted by the Romans' uninterest in a religious establishment and to think that republics generally offered a safer home to religious liberty.

"Privatization" and Liberalism

There has been a tradition of distinguishing between classical, participatory political liberty and liberal, apolitical private liberty. It was started by Benjamin Constant's famous *Essai sur la liberté des anciens comparée à celle des modernes*, though one might without exaggeration see the same story in Hegel's *Philosophy of History* and *Philosophy of Right*. But Constant's account differs strikingly from what we have had over the past thirty years from Arendt and Wolin; he wrote to praise a liberalism that he understood as a possible importation from Britain into France, whereas they wrote to criticize a liberalism that is essentially that of postwar America. Though it is an agreeable exercise to wade into these arguments and start throwing punches in all directions, I confine myself to two small issues. The first is whether it is true that Locke's vision of liberty is privatized; the second is whether, to the extent that it is, it is indefensibly so.

The republican critics of liberalism, if so we may call them, start from a somewhat unfair advantage in being able to call on Arendt's vivid but misleading account of politics as "virtuosity" (Arendt 1958, 77–78, 305ff.). Once one has put together Heidegger's contrast between mere happening and genuine acting, on the one hand, and Machiavelli's injunctions to boldness, on the other, we have something bound to make most other political theory look slightly pallid (Arendt 1958, 42–46). But there is reason to think that the effect is achieved at the cost of historical accuracy (Skinner 1984, 203–12). Machiavelli was not the theorist of virtuosity that he is made out to be, and the emphasis on acting in front of others, and on performing on the public stage, is a foreign, Heideggerian importation. Machiavelli was a soberer, more cautious defender of private goods and negative liberty than Miss Arendt suggests.

There is a second, less metaphysical aspect of the contrast between public actors and private behavers, which equally tells to the discredit of liberalism. This is the suggestion that republican theory concentrates on the search for the common good, while liberalism aims only at individual, essentially private satisfactions. Now, I do not wish to say that there is nothing in any of this, though I do wish to begin by recalling that Locke's account of political power stresses that authority exists only in order to promote the common good. Power is not given to anyone for their own exclusive benefit; governments possess the public power and must therefore be guided in all things by the maxim *salus populi suprema lex est*. The retort of the republican is evidently that the *commonness* of the common good is intrinsic to its goodness in the republican theory, but is only a matter of instrumental efficacy in liberalism. That is, in liberal thought, individuals have an essentially private interest in the maintenance of public goods such as defense and law and order; republican thought makes freedom the highest good, and sees it as a matter of participating in a shared enterprise—the glory of Athens or whatever. Put differently, the liberal reduces the common good to the product of compromises between bargaining interests, in the way recent political science has done. The republican seeks to infuse a desire for the common good in every citizen, and thus relies on citizen virtue rather than bargaining to produce the common good.

This seems implausible as an attack on Locke. It may have some force as an attack on Hobbes, whose famous definition of freedom as "immunity to the service of the commonwealth" (Hobbes 1914, 113) certainly betokens a concern to detach the concept of liberty from a defense of classical republicanism. Against Locke it is very much less powerful; Locke insists that the state has those rights and duties that individuals concede to it. One of those is to enforce the law of nature against malefactors, as we saw earlier. This means that Locke's individuals do not enter the world with no interest in anything but their own welfare. On the contrary, they enter the world with duties to the public. The state is a device for assisting them in doing their duty to others as much as a device for protecting them against the ill will or irrationality of others.

Is this the pursuit of a genuinely common good? As I have agreed when mentioning Locke's republicanism, if we have in mind the patriotic conception of a common good that identifies the common good of the Spartans with their being Spartans, Locke does not have any room for that. Indeed, it is very hard to see quite how anyone really belongs to some given country in the Lockean scheme of things—and one might well imagine that Locke himself had no great sense of belonging to a country that he twice had to leave in haste (Ashcraft 1986, 122–23, 406ff.). But doing one's duty by God and natural law is certainly not a private good in the disapproved sense.

We need to look a little more closely at the ultimate goods of the Lockean universe before we can conclude the case. There is no doubt that the ultimate goods are private in the sense that they are a matter for God and the individual. The Puritan concern to be able to account for ourselves at the Day of Judgment animates Locke as well. It is, however, not a distinctively private concern in the same way that private economic interests are private. Private interests compete with public interests; my salvation does not compete with anyone else's. It is certainly true, as Machiavelli observed, that in rough times, a man who minds about the safety of his soul may be unable to do what the safety of the republic demands; it is not true that a man who minds about the safety of his soul will always or even often have to choose between his duty to God and his duty to his fellows. Locke, after all, served Shaftesbury and his fellow Whigs without hesitation; in quieter times, he served William and Mary on the Board of Trade. One can do one's individual duty to the Almighty by public service. It remains true that Locke's concern to give a good account of himself to his creator is distinctively Christian and unclassical. It gives a dimension to life in which we are not merely private but alone. It is a dimension of moral thinking distinctive and peculiar to western Europe, and there is no bucking the difference it makes to comparisons between us and, say, the classical Greeks.

All the same, if it makes for a sort of moral loneliness, it does not make for privatization. Quakers are famously public spirited and rich in good works; New England town meetings may rarely have been quite as impressive as we would like to believe, but they do not come a poor second to the agora in Thebes or Corinth. Nor should we underestimate a Puritan society's capacity for friendship and for a common intellectual life. Locke himself combined a well-founded and self-centered fear of what the agents of Charles II would do to him if they laid hands on him, with a great capacity for friendship and for loyalty to his friends. So we must not jump from a proper emphasis on the individualized and internalized vision of the good to which Locke undoubtedly subscribed to saddling him with a purely instrumental, self-centered political vision to which he did not subscribe (Cranston 1957, esp. 342ff.).

Last, however, one ought to admit that Locke's vision of freedom is not a particularly political one. In Constant's terms, he was an enthusiast for modern rather than ancient liberty. He was almost certainly much more a democrat than we have hitherto thought, but he was not inclined to set political activity at the center of the moral universe—differing twice over from Aristotle in this (Aristotle 1947, 5–6; Ashcraft 1986, 128ff.). But we ought not to raise our eyebrows at this and treat it as a knockout blow for the "privatization" thesis. As Constant observed, one reason why the Greeks took so much interest in politics was that they were constantly in a state of war with one another; another was that when they were not, there was rather little to do. Life in antiquity had longueurs that could be coped with only by fights, games, and debates, to coin a phrase. Lockean freedom is negative freedom, though it is also moralized freedom—liberty is not license. It is negative freedom for good reason, namely, Charles II's assaults on the constitutional, religious, commercial, and private liberties of his subjects. Politics is not itself a realm of free action, a concept Locke would have found odd in any case. But political involvement may, for all that, be a duty for anyone who cares about freedom and the common good as much as Locke evidently did.

References

Arendt, Hannah. 1958. *The Human Condition.* Chicago: University of Chicago Press.

———. 1961. "What Is Freedom?" In *Between Past and Future*. London: Faber.

Aristotle. 1947. *Politics*. Translated and edited by Ernest Barker. Oxford: Clarendon Press.

Ashcraft, Richard. 1986. *Revolutionary Politics and Locke's Two Treatises of Government*. Princeton, N.J.: Princeton University Press.

———. 1987. *Locke's Two Treatises of Government*. London: Allen and Unwin.

Constant, Benjamin. 1964. *Sur la liberté des anciens compareé à celle des modernes*. Paris: Pléiade.

Cox, Richard. 1960. *Locke on War and Peace*. Oxford: Clarendon Press.

Cranston, Maurice. 1957. *John Locke*. London: Longman, Green.

Dunn, John. 1969. *The Political Thought of John Locke*. Cambridge: Cambridge University Press.

Filmer, Robert. 1949. *Patriarcha and Other Writings*. Edited by Peter Laslett. Oxford: Blackwell.

Hampshire, Stuart. 1983. *Morality and Conflict*. Oxford: Blackwell.

Harrington, James. 1977. *Political Writings*. Edited by J.G.A. Pocock. Cambridge: Cambridge University Press.

Hegel, G.W.F. 1941. *The Philosophy of Right*. Translated and edited by T. M. Knox. Oxford: Clarendon Press.

———. 1954. *The Philosophy of History*. Translated by W. Sibree. New York: Dover.

Hobbes, Thomas. 1914. *Leviathan*. London: Dent.

Honoré, A. M. 1961. "Ownership." In *Oxford Essays in Jurisprudence*, series 1, edited by A. G. Guest. Oxford: Clarendon Press.

Lawson, F. H. 1958. *The Law of Property*. Oxford: Clarendon Press.

Locke, John. 1954. *Essays on the Law of Nature*. Edited by W. von Leyden. Oxford: Clarendon Press.

———. 1964. *An Essay Concerning Human Understanding*. London: Dent.

———. 1967. *Two Treatises of Government*. Edited by Peter Laslett. Cambridge: Cambridge University Press.

———. 1968. *Educational Writings*. Edited by James Axtell. Cambridge: Cambridge University Press.

Macpherson, C. B. 1962. *The Political Theory of Possessive Individualism*. Oxford: Clarendon Press.

Mill, John Stuart. 1912. *Utilitarianism, Liberty, and Representative Government*. London: Dent.

Nozick, Robert. 1974. *Anarchy, State, and Utopia*. Oxford: Blackwell.

Pocock, J.G.A. 1974. *The Machiavellian Moment*. Princeton, N.J.: Princeton University Press.

———. 1983. "Cambridge Paradigms and Scotch Philosophers." In *Wealth and Virtue*, edited by Istvan Hont and Michael Ignatieff, 235–52. Cambridge: Cambridge University Press.

Reeve, Andrew. 1986. *Property*. London: Macmillan.

Ryan, Alan. 1965. "Locke and the Dictatorship of the Bourgeoisie." *Political Studies* 13:205–11.

———. 1984. *Property and Political Theory*. Oxford: Blackwell.

———. 1988. "A More Tolerant Hobbes." In *Essays on Toleration*, edited by Susan Mendus. Cambridge: Cambridge University Press.

Skinner, Quentin. 1984. "The Idea of 'Negative' Liberty." In *Philosophy in History*, edited by Richard Rorty, J. B. Schneewind, and Quentin Skinner, 193–221. Cambridge: Cambridge University Press.

Spencer, Herbert. 1851. *Social Statics*. London, Chapman.

Steiner, Hillel. 1982. "Land, Liberty, and the Early Herbert Spencer." *History of Political Thought* 3:513–33.

Tuck, Richard. 1979. *Natural Rights Theories*. Cambridge: Cambridge University Press.

Tully, James. 1980. *A Discourse on Property*. Cambridge: Cambridge University Press.

Wolin, Sheldon. 1961. *Politics and Vision*. Boston: Little, Brown.

Wood, Neal. 1984. *John Locke and Agrarian Capitalism*. Berkeley and Los Angeles: University of California Press.

PART 3

Liberty and Progress, Mill to Popper

Mill's Essay *On Liberty*

JOHN STUART MILL is—surprisingly—a difficult writer. He writes clearly, nontechnically, and in a very plain prose that Bertrand Russell once described as a model for philosophers. It is never hard to see what the general drift of an argument is, and never hard to see which side he is on. He is, nonetheless, a difficult writer because his clarity hides complicated arguments and assumptions that often take a good deal of unpicking. And when we have done that unpicking, the task of analyzing the merits and deficiencies of the arguments is still only half completed. This is true of all his work and particularly true of *On Liberty* (hereafter referred to simply as *Liberty*). It is an essay whose clarity and energy have made it the most popular of all Mill's works. Yet it conceals philosophical, sociological, and historical assumptions of a very debatable kind. In his introduction, Mill says:

> The object of this essay is to defend one very simple principle, as entitled to govern absolutely the dealings of society with the individual in the way of compulsion and control, whether the means used be legal penalties, or the moral coercion of public opinion. (*Liberty*, 68)[1]

More than a century and a half after the essay first appeared, Mill's commentators still do not agree about just what that principle was, nor about just how it governs the dealings of society with its members.

It is easier to see what Mill was trying to argue if we have some sense of the context in which Mill was writing—both the biographical and intellectual context so far as Mill himself was concerned, and the social and political context for which *Liberty* was intended. It is worth remembering that Mill himself thought of his essay as aimed almost wholly at an English audience; it was the intellectual and social oppressiveness of Victorian England that was his target, and the lesson he preached was, he thought, one that most of Europe did not need to be taught. Mill thought that Britain was *politically* much freer than most of Europe—where, indeed, parliamentary government and a free press were in 1858 almost unknown. Conversely, he thought that *socially* most of Europe was freer than Britain—the British were intellectually timid and conformist, whereas Europeans were much more willing to question traditional moral and religious beliefs. Although *Liberty* is, by a long way, the best remembered, most admired (and most criticized) of all his works, it was, and is best understood as, a product of its own time and place.

Mill painted his own picture of his times and gave his own account of what he thought his intellectual duty to his contemporaries amounted to in the most immediately readable of all his work—his *Autobiography*. It is, as Mill intended it to be, interesting as the record of an extraordinary education. He was brought up by his father, with the advice and assistance of Jeremy Bentham and Francis Place, to be something like a one-man Open University, a storehouse of advanced thinking on all matters who would enlighten the politically influential middle-class audience that read the political quarterlies. Readers of his *Autobiography* will not need reminding of the strenuous educational program this required. He was taught Greek at three (with the aid of flash cards of the kind still used by educational psychologists); read enormous amounts of Roman history, Greek drama, and European poetry before he was in his teens; and rounded off the diet with logic, utilitarian moral philosophy, and the latest ideas in economic theory. Most of us feel exhausted merely reading the titles of the books that Mill got through before he was sixteen; and few of us are surprised that Mill had a nervous breakdown in his early twenties.

A strange feature of this nervous collapse is that although none of Mill's friends or contemporaries appear to have noticed that anything was amiss, it mattered so much to Mill that he made his account of it the centerpiece of the *Autobiography*. It seemed to him that the collapse was brought on when he asked himself a fatal question—"If everything he had campaigned for was suddenly achieved, would that make him happy?" The answer seemed to him to be an unequivocal no. And the sense that the social and political good works to which he was devoted really had a feeble hold on his heart and his imagination plunged him into profound depression. He had assumed, as a convinced utilitarian, that the projects to which Bentham and James Mill and the other Philosophical Radicals had devoted themselves would make people happy and would make their benevolent promoters happy too. The experience of disillusionment and his struggle out of it had a profound impact on Mill's thinking. He came to believe that the event was a symbol of the tensions of the age and that his recovery from it was an exemplary case—to put it dramatically, he thought that the lesson he had learned for himself was one that the age at large needed to learn. But what was that lesson?

For himself in particular, Mill thought that he had been trained too hard in the use of his analytical abilities and too little in the development of his emotions; his imagination had not been sufficiently stretched, and he had never been taught to understand the variety and flexibility of human nature. And this failure to appreciate imagination and variety was a failure of old-fashioned utilitarian radicalism itself. This implied that his main task was to reeducate the radicals and reformers. He did not think that his teachers had been wrong to try to make him a social scientist and a utilitarian; all his life he was absolutely clear that if there was to be any hope of social reform, or of introducing an acceptable socialism into economic life, or acceptable democracy into political life, or equality between the sexes, this would require the best knowledge of social cause and effect that we could achieve. Such knowledge was not to be left to "intuition" or tradition; it had to be a matter of social science. The difficulty was that all previous accounts of that science had been far too narrow. The economic theories of his father and David Ricardo had rightly been complained of as contributions to the "dismal science"; they were dismal because they made it look as if workingmen were everywhere and always doomed by necessity to live and work as they did in early Victorian England. His father's politics, as spelled out in his *Essay on Government*, were founded on the view that people were inevitably self-interested. But this was plausible neither as description nor prescription. So Mill was left to argue that before we offered recipes for social reconstruction based on the new social sciences, we had to widen our understanding of human nature—social science was useless otherwise.

Similarly, Mill never renounced his early allegiance to utilitarianism. He always defended what he believed to be the fundamental idea of utilitarian ethics—its commitment to rationality. He never wavered in the belief that rationality meant that we must have some ultimate standard by which to justify all the rules of conduct society requires, and that that standard can only be the general happiness. But, once again, he thought that his teachers had had a terribly narrow idea of what people were like and what human happiness consisted of. From Goethe he borrowed the slogan "many-sidedness," and argued whenever he had the chance that what made man different from the beasts was a spirit of divine discontent, which made individuals strive after their own self-perfection. In *Utilitarianism*, he argues "better Socrates dissatisfied than the fool satisfied"; and there, too, he argues that "self-perfection," the search for one's own better self, is not only a means to the general happiness, but is, properly speaking, also part of happiness itself. This allowed him to clear utilitarianism of the charge leveled against it by Thomas Carlyle, that it was "pig philosophy," passing off the contentment of the swinish multitude as the highest goal of ethics. Mill's utilitarianism had—he claimed—plenty of room for the highest aspirations of mankind.

Last, we have to bear in mind Mill's reaction to the rise of democracy. Mill was a democrat; or to be more accurate, he was a committed defender of representative government. But he was a frightened democrat. He read Alexis de Tocqueville's *Democracy in America*, and was alarmed at the picture the book painted of a society in which equality led to conformism and uniformity. Equality was an admirable ideal; Mill always defended equality of opportunity, always attacked snobbery, always condemned aristocracies that insisted on their privileges but refused to accept their obligations. Nonetheless, he thought that the point of equality was as an aid to justice and merit. Only if everyone started equal would success fall to the most meritorious; only if success were proportioned to merit would justice be achieved. Mill was what one might call a "moral aristocrat"; he thought that some men were simply the moral superiors of others, just as some men were the intellectual superiors of others. Moreover, he believed that all social progress depended on the efforts of those few superior characters and intellects. So equality of opportunity is, paradoxically, defended by Mill as a means of finding and liberating the intellectual and moral vanguard on whom progress depends. And what Mill feared was that a general social equality would result in a gray uniformity of opinion and attitude that would stifle vitality and progress.

We should pause for a moment to see what sort of oppression Mill learned from Tocqueville to fear above all else, and how that was related to his fears about democracy. The oppression Mill expected was what Tocqueville described as the coming of a society of "industrious sheep." Neither Mill nor Tocqueville anticipated the police terror of modern totalitarian states such as Nazi Germany and Stalinist Russia. What they expected was a "soft despotism." They thought that a society in which uniformity and conformism had got the upper hand would be one in which everyone would try to think like his or her neighbor, would regard public opinion as the final court of appeal on all subjects, and would be frightened to strike out on an independent tack in anything. This would not be a conformism enforced by brute force or the terrors of the Inquisition. It would be enforced by a silent ganging up of the majority against the minority. The pressure of public opinion would be felt in the form of judgments that nonconformists were "odd," "not normal," not quite nice. It would be the sort of pressure that sustains clubs, school common rooms, suburban housing estates—those declared "odd" would be shunned, their views would not be taken seriously, they would find themselves unobtrusively shut out from friendship and success. Because Mill and Tocqueville thought that an egalitarian society would be anxious for a *comfortable* life above all else, they did not think that such a society would become passionately attached to political or religious causes that would lead to persecution by an Inquisition or a Cheka or the ayatollahs. They thought it would be the uniformity of a flock of sheep that they had to fear, not the ferocity of a pack of wolves.

But it was, for all that, a form of social oppression that was almost more dangerous than that of the persecutor with a sword in his hand. For it was a pressure that worked continuously, silently, unobtrusively. Violent persecution arouses its own opposition; its victims may not be able to protect themselves, but they are likely to want to resist. The pressure of public opinion is not like that. It is much less likely to arouse opposition except in the hearts of those who have strongly independent characters already. Certainly, Mill was anxious about the political consequences of such a social conformism. In the nineteenth century, government was increasingly under the sway of public opinion, even if it was not formally a parliamentary democracy. Public opinion could therefore dictate the shape of legislation, and a conformist public opinion that did not recognize the right of individuals to do as they pleased wherever the vital interests of others were not at stake would not hesitate to pass oppressive laws. Temperance legislation, to take an obvious example from *Liberty* itself (156–58), could be expected from a society that insisted on minding everyone else's business. Censorship of books, state regulation of school syllabuses, an insistence on subscription to some formal religious organization or other—all these might well be enshrined in law as the result of the pressure of opinion. But law not backed up by public opinion provokes resistance. What does not provoke resistance in anything like the same way is public opinion. It is opinion, therefore, that is the underlying danger. Most of us are likely to succumb to the pressure to conform; worse yet, many of us are likely to avoid any disagreeable conflict between our own views and those of the public at large by adjusting our own views in advance, even before argument breaks out. When society

> issues wrong mandates instead of right, or any mandates at all in things with which it ought not to meddle, it practises a social tyranny more formidable than many kinds of political oppression, since, though not usually upheld by such extreme penalties, it leaves fewer means of escape, penetrating much more deeply into the details of life, and enslaving the soul itself. (*Liberty*, 63)

By no means *all* social pressure is a disaster. Society only exists because we are amenable to social pressure; children begin, even if not by being simply selfish, at any rate by being pretty unbothered about the welfare of everyone else. They are, as Hobbes had remarked two centuries earlier, "born inapt for society" and have to be trained for it. That training consists in part of being forced into good habits, and in part of being got to believe things that we *could* certainly argue about, but simply do not. But it is important that society should confine this sort of coercive and nonrational pressure to children and the incapable; people "in the maturity of their faculties" have to be dealt with in other ways.

Like Tocqueville, Mill thought that the great need of democracy was to preserve "the antagonism of opinions," so much of *Liberty* is about the social requirements of that antagonism. What makes *Liberty* something quite other than a commentary on Tocqueville is that Mill had complicated philosophical views that went beyond Tocqueville's sociological and political insights. Mill defended his insistence that society should coerce individuals only in order "to prevent harm to others" with an account of the nature and scope of morality and more particularly of the area of morality covered by the idea of "rights" that was a philosophical tour de force. Since our interest lies primarily in Mill the philosopher, it is time we turned to these details.

Mill begins *Liberty* by sketching the rise of democracy; as a defense against mismanagement and ill will by monarchs and aristocrats, the people at large had to build up their own power. But this process has now gone so far that what men are discovering is that "self-government" turns out not to be the government of each man or woman by himself or herself, but the government of each of us by all the rest (60–62). Moreover, says Mill, matters are made much worse by the lack of any agreed-upon principle by which to decide when government ought or ought not to act. It is, he says, only the "likings and mislikings" of mankind that have determined the issue—a phrase to which we shall have to pay careful attention in due course. Some people have thought that wherever anything was amiss society, government should act and correct it; other people have so feared government that they would tolerate any amount of mischief rather than give more powers to government. What has been lacking is any coherent theory of what does and what does not justify coercive measures against individuals. It is important to understand that Mill's aim was not simply to diminish the role of government; indeed, he advanced a much enlarged role for government and public opinion alike in making parents meet their obligation to educate their children and in making couples meet their obligation to avoid bringing into the world children who would be a burden to the rest of society. These "private" matters, which many people even now consider too sensitive and too private for outside pressure, were not so described by Mill. Mill intended to produce a principle that, though it would certainly reduce many of the present pressures of government and public opinion, would equally certainly add to those pressures in other areas.

So we must recur to the crucial question Mill asks himself: on what general principle is the coercive interference of society toward its members to be organized? Mill is careful to confine his question to the coercive interferences of society toward its members; many people—including Gertrude Himmelfarb throughout her introduction to the Penguin edition of *Liberty* and her longer book *Liberty and Liberalism*—ignore this vital point. They think that Mill's view is that society should be "neutral" about the private or "self-regarding" behavior of its members. But Mill expressly disavows this interpretation of *Liberty*. He is, on the contrary, eager to assert just the opposite: our usual notions of good manners make most of us reluctant to tell other people just what we think of them. We are reluctant to tell them that we think they have low tastes or that they lead lives fundamentally lacking in the concern for self-perfection that alone makes our lives better than those of beasts. But this is a great mistake, says Mill. We owe it to one another to try to keep one another up to the mark; what we do not have is the right to force other people to live according to our standards. It is coercion that Mill is concerned to circumscribe.

"Exhortation and entreaty" are not coercive, says Mill, and whereas we may not coerce others, we certainly ought to exhort and entreat them to make the best of themselves. Not to do that is not to practice a virtuous neutrality about their conduct, but to display a selfish unconcern for their higher welfare. Mill's critics' failure to take this point is not entirely blameworthy; many of us would feel that being exhorted and entreated to live up to our better natures would, if it went on for long or went on very often, be just as bad as the coercion of public opinion, and we might wonder about the point of Mill's distinction between the coercion of opinion, on the one hand, and "entreaty" on the other. But it is to such doubts that Mill thought he had an answer.

Mill commits himself to the view that we may force others to act in ways they do not wish only for the sake of "self-protection." This causes Mill a problem. He was a utilitarian, and on the face of it, a utilitarian is committed to one principle only—that we should do whatever maximizes happiness. Suppose that paternalism made people happier—the paternalistic legislator, moved by the sufferings of his ignorant and incompetent fellows, is happy when they have been protected from themselves; his ignorant and incompetent fellows do not much mind the laws and other pressures that restrict their freedom, and they are manifestly better off when not doing themselves a mischief through their own folly. In *Liberty*, Mill denies that this gives anyone the right to act paternalistically. Having enunciated his "one very simple principle," he glosses it by saying,

> His own good, either physical or moral, is not a sufficient warrant. He cannot rightfully be compelled to do or forbear because it will be better for him to do so, because it will make him happier, because in the opinions of others, to do so would be wise or even right. These are good reasons for remonstrating with him, or reasoning with him, or persuading him, or entreating him, but not for compelling him or visiting him with any evil in case he do otherwise. To justify that, the conduct from which it is desired to deter him must be calculated to produce evil to someone else. (68)

Many people have thought that in asserting this, Mill was simply renouncing utilitarianism. Writers such as Immanuel Kant did denounce paternalism as an outrageous despotism; but they did so as part of an attack on utilitarian arguments. For Kant, the sovereignty of the individual was the starting point of moral argument; it was a metaphysical presupposition of ethics that each individual was an end in himself, a member of a kingdom of ends, someone whose highest achievement as a human being was to lay down the moral law to himself. But this is not the language of utilitarianism. The utilitarian considers individuals sentient creatures, experiencing pains and pleasures, with an interest in having as few pains and as many pleasures as possible, so from where is Mill to derive the prohibition on paternalism, and the insistence that coercion is appropriate only in order to defend others from harm? Before we answer that question, we must notice that Mill himself sharpens the problem for himself. He says, almost at once,

> It is proper to state that I forgo any advantage which could be derived to my argument from the idea of abstract right as a thing independent of utility. I regard utility as the ultimate appeal on all ethical questions; but it must be utility in the largest sense, grounded on the permanent interests of a man as a progressive being. Those interests, I contend, authorize the subjection of individual spontaneity to external control only in respect of those actions of each which concern the interest of other people. (*Liberty*, 69–70)

So we have to answer the question of how Mill comes to think that utility implies the principle that the only basis of a right to dictate how others behave is self-defense. Some part of the answer will have to be spelled out shortly, when we follow Mill's defense of freedom of thought and discussion, and when we follow his argument about individuality and the need for experiments in living—for it is in the course of these arguments that Mill relies on his picture of "man as a progressive being" to whom freedom is a prerequisite of happiness. But the interesting semitechnical question we must answer at once is that of how Mill derives concepts like that of a *right* from utility.

There is no agreed-upon answer to this; indeed, disagreements on the issue are the staple of discussions of both *Utilitarianism* and *Liberty*. But the elements of an answer are as follows. The principle of utility is not itself a principle that anyone does or should follow; it is a principle for assessing the goodness or badness of *anything* whose goodness or badness we might wish to assess. It is not itself and straightforwardly a moral principle. It cannot be that, because absurdities would result. Suppose I go to the cinema and see a film I enjoy much less than I had expected. This is a bad outcome, and I made a mistake. I did not, however, commit a wrong in going to it; even if I did not bother to check up on the film, made no effort to make sure I would enjoy it, and even after the event did not care much that I had not enjoyed it, I should not have acted wrongly. A person who does not take care to choose sensibly will no doubt waste his or her money and be imprudent; but folly and imprudence are not the same thing as wickedness or wrongdoing. Mill's aim is to draw the line between folly, on the one hand, and the violation of other people's rights, on the other, in the place where reflective common sense and utilitarianism would coincide in placing it. It is this principled drawing of the line between legitimate and illegitimate intervention and nonintervention that is meant to replace the "likings and mislikings of society" as the guide to coercive interference.

How does utilitarianism draw the line? Mill thinks of morality as essentially concerned with enforcement and punishment; to call an action wrong is, by definition, to say that it is the sort of thing that other people are, in principle, entitled to stop. This is not to say that everyone ought, in fact, to try to stop every wrong action; there are innumerable actions that are indeed wrong, but that we must simply let pass on the grounds that their prevention would be a greater evil than they. This also is a matter of degree. Every promise creates a right in the beneficiary; if I promise to provide you with a house, deliver a signed contract, and then go back on it, the law is right to intervene and give you damages in the first place, and if I have committed a fraud, to punish me too; but if I promise to make you a cup of coffee and then decide I cannot be bothered, you will be justified in reproaching me, but not in trying to haul me into court. Mill's view, in outline, is that society is to be understood as a device whereby we are protected against the ill will and aggression of others, and are enabled to rely on them in cooperative activities by means of social pressure on individuals. Society is not based on a contract, but our relationships with one another can usefully be visualized as if it were. Mill explains what he means in chapter IV, "Of the Limits to the Authority of Society over the Individual":

> Though society is not founded on a contract, and though no good purpose is answered by inventing a contract in order to deduce social obligations from it, everyone who receives the protection of society owes a return for the benefit, and the fact of living in society renders it indispensable that each should be bound to observe a certain line of conduct towards the rest. This conduct consists, first, in not injuring the interests of one another; or rather certain interests, which, either by express legal provision or by tacit understanding, ought to be considered as rights; and secondly, in each person's bearing his share (to be fixed on some equitable principle) of the labours and sacrifices incurred for defending the society or its members from injury and molestation. (*Liberty*, 141)

One difficulty in Mill's account is that it is not entirely clear how to draw the line between the area of morality concerned with rights and the wider area of morality generally. Mill seems to draw it along two lines. The first is by asking whether it would be good to protect the "interest" in question by coercive measures—which is why Mill refers to "certain interests . . . which ought to be considered as rights"; the other is to ask whether it is essential to security to protect an interest. So, for instance, the right to life plainly succeeds on both counts—it is for the greatest good to protect our interest in continued existence, and but for such protection, we should feel exceedingly insecure. My right to the fulfillment of small promises succeeds rather better on the first count than the second; I might not be much harmed by many nonfulfillments, but the whole business of promising and cooperating on the strength of promises to one another would be frustrated if we did not enforce promises.

Except where the obligation rests on agreements and promises, most "rights" will impose duties of a negative kind. Your right to life primarily imposes on me the duty not to kill you. Your right not to be assaulted primarily imposes on me the duty not to attack you. But this is only the general rule; there are, says Mill,

> many positive acts which he may rightfully be compelled to perform, such as to give evidence in a court of justice . . . and to perform certain acts of individual beneficence, such as saving a fellow creature's life or interposing to protect the defenceless against ill-usage. (*Liberty*, 70)

So Mill's crucial test for a "right" is not attached by definition to the idea that other people's rights can impose only duties of abstention on us. That would be the doctrine of "abstract" right, which he rejects.

One further point that is worth noticing is that when Mill discusses rights in the body of *Liberty*, he explains them in terms of interests. In essence, he holds that there are some interests that utilitarianism requires us to treat as rights. If we set great store by this explanation, as I think we should, we can then see that Mill asks himself the question "What interests would it promote the long-run happiness of humanity to treat as rights?" If society is, as he often says, impossible except on the understanding that it exists in the first place to afford security to its members, it is evident that rights as immunities must be the most basic and the best-protected rights we possess. It is also evident, however, that such rights as the right to a fair trial, which impose on others duties of giving evidence in a court of law, are readily defensible as protecting the sort of interests whose protection utility would demand. This position reflects the flexibility of a utilitarian, interest-based theory of rights. This flexibility is equally apparent when Mill qualifies the opening statement of his case by pointing out that he intends it to apply only to "human beings in the maturity of their faculties" (*Liberty*, 69). He has two exceptions in mind: children and young people on the one hand, and "those backward states of society in which the race itself may be considered as in its nonage" (69). Until they are of an age to be improved by argument and discussion, both require paternalistic government. Mill's twentieth-century readers tend to flinch at the cheerfulness with which Mill (as befitted a senior permanent official of the East India Company) accepted the virtues of colonialism and despotism. There are also twentieth-century critics who think Mill entirely underestimated the capacity of young people. Two other points are perhaps more likely to be overlooked. The first is that Mill's argument is in no way a criticism of the growth of democracy in Britain; the British working class—he thought—had long since passed beyond the stage at which arguments directed at children or the population of India applied to it. The other is that this is one of the places where Mill's utilitarian account of rights diverges sharply from an account such as Kant's. For Kant, despotic government was simply wrong. It was no use for the East India Company, Akbar, or Charlemagne to point to their benevolence and superior wisdom, for the point was that they simply had no right to govern without consent. Mill was entirely serious in saying that he appealed to utility.

All the same, the utility in question was that of a progressive being, and the interests at stake were the interests of progressive beings. We now need to follow Mill through the central chapters of *Liberty* to see how this makes a difference. In these chapters, Mill first defends an absolute freedom of thought and discussion, and then gives an account of the virtues of individuality before recurring to a general discussion of the line between the individual's sphere and society's, and some awkward examples. Mill's claim for the absolute inviolability of thought and discussion is one of the most famous parts of the entire essay. It is dragged into all sorts of twentieth-century discussions where it is rather dubiously at home, but even if we are fastidious about avoiding that, we are in controversial terrain enough.

The first thing to notice in the argument is that Mill does not employ his principle about not coercing others except in self-defense. He does not try to do anything very elaborate to show, for instance, that we are not "harmed" by hearing opinions we very much dislike. In this area, Mill seems ready to admit that we may be shocked by, or very much dislike, a professed opinion, but he insists that this does not give us grounds for repressing it. What he rests on is an argument about fallibility and an argument about the worthlessness of merely conventional belief. To put it simply, the argument is, first, that suppressing opinions deprives humanity of the opportunity of discovering whatever truth they may contain and, second, that it is important that our ideas should genuinely be *our own*, a condition that can be fulfilled only if we have some experience of hearing arguments against them and learning how to fend off those arguments. It is plain that a utilitarian argument for this case is going to have to rely quite heavily on the idea that mankind is in some sense progressive. A utilitarian who thought that mankind was, and should be, content to stagnate would happily argue that utility demanded that conventional opinion should always be upheld as far as possible. If people were happy only when they were undisturbed, the utilitarian argument against intellectual, moral, artistic, and any other sort of innovation would be conclusive. So we must dig into Mill's view of progress a little.

Mill was unlike his father and Bentham in being obsessed with history. They knew perfectly well that "time and place" made a difference regarding whether laws would work and what sort of government it would be wise to install. Mill, however, held that the central discovery of the social sciences was that history progressed in a certain direction and did so under the impact of changes in ideas. As I have said, it is this conviction that justifies Mill's entire lifework. Mill's abiding hostility was to forms of philosophy that suggested the ultimate test of truth was "intuition." In his *System of Logic*, he attacked the philosophy of science put forward by William Whewell, because Whewell claimed that the truths of mathematics and geometry were known intuitively and that the fundamental laws of nature were also known by intuition, even though it might take a lot of experiment and observation to make those laws as intuitively obvious as they ought to be. Mill detested this way of thinking: he saw that what made intuitionism in mathematics and the philosophy of science attractive to its defenders was ultimately that it provided support for intuitionism in ethics.

Intuitionism in ethics seemed to him to sanctify custom and tradition and to encourage people in what they are anyway all too ready to do, that is, in believing that their own strong feelings on ethical matters are argument enough and render further debate superfluous.

Mill was an empiricist. He thought that knowledge grew only by observation and experiment and reflection upon their results; increased knowledge in ethics could come only through deepening our understanding of human nature and its needs, and for this, absolute freedom of inquiry was essential. Intuitionists cut short this process by claiming that we already know all the most important moral truths and cannot need further argument for them. Mill claimed two things in reply: first, this amounted to an unwarranted boast of infallibility, and second, even in cases where truths were, in the end, unchallengeable, they lost their life and their power over the imagination if men were not allowed to challenge them. Indeed, says Mill at one point,

> so essential is this discipline to a real understanding of moral and human subjects that, if opponents of all-important truths do not exist, it is indispensable to imagine them and supply them with the strongest arguments which the most skilful devil's advocate can conjure up. (*Liberty*, 99)

Mill's argument is intended to be extreme and absolute. He explicitly repudiates any suggestion that his arguments for free speech must not be taken to extremes. It is, he thinks, necessary that they should be taken to extremes. So we have to ask what sorts of doctrines are included in the scope of Mill's case. In the United States, for instance, the sellers of pornography have, with varying degrees of success, argued that the constitutional prohibition on abridging free speech implies that they can sell their magazines and show their films, subject only to the usual restrictions on how anyone carries on any commercial activity. Needless to say, Mill does not address exactly this case—he does address the sale of narcotics and the carrying on of prostitution, but not as a question of free speech, of course. Mill's position is, however, clear enough. As to speech, narrowly construed, it must be lawful for anyone to express any opinion whatever. So, for instance, if the Pedophile Information Exchange confined itself to ventilating the question whether sexual relations between adults and children did either party any harm, it could not, in Mill's world, be touched by law, and even more importantly, it ought not to be touched by any unofficial "ganging up" of polite society against its members. Even if it advocated the abolition of most of the present laws against sexual relations between adults and children, it should not be touched. But between this absolute license and *incitement*, a sharp line had to be drawn. The same argument runs right the way through Mill's case. It would be impossible in a society run as Mill intended to forbid anyone from publishing the view that white Anglo-Saxon Protestants were chronically stupider and idler than Jews, Indians, or whoever, and impossible to forbid anyone from publishing the reverse view. But the line would always be held between that and incitement to attacks of one sort and another. Unlike most of us, who tend to attach a high value to free speech and to public order, and then to worry about how to square the National Front's desire to march through Brixton with the local inhabitants' desire not to be insulted by their enemies, Mill thought his utilitarian account of rights could be relied on to yield an answer—not necessarily a simple answer, but an answer.

This answer is, in effect, that we should have no protection against the discomfort of knowing that other people have a low opinion of us—they might be right to have such an opinion, it would not be for the long-term good of humanity to protect us against such discomfort, and the desire for emotional security carries no weight against long-run utilitarian factors. But society would be intolerable unless everyone had complete protection against the sudden and uncontrolled worsening of his or her position, and against actual attack by others. Applied to a case such as that of pornography, Mill's arguments fall awkwardly. One reason for this is that Mill himself expressly ruled out questions of decency and indecency from his discussion; there are many innocent actions that it would be indecent to perform in public—urination and defecation are in themselves innocent, but it is indecent to engage in them in a crowded street; sexual relations between married people are paradigmatically innocent, but if performed in the middle of Oxford Street are every bit as indecent as sexual intercourse between unmarried persons. Mill simply pushes such questions to one side, and it is impossible to guess how he thought utilitarianism could handle them. The shock of merely knowing that others have strange sexual tastes is not one that Mill would wish to protect us from, any more than from the shock of any other form of knowledge. (Equally, Mill would not wish to prevent Jews and Muslims from knowing that their neighbors eat pork.)

What there is no discussion of in Mill's account is the principles on which social space is to be shared by people with very different sexual or religious taboos. This is a genuine loss to the theory, for Mill envisages a plural society, and therefore ought to offer some solution to the question of how we are to cohabit peacefully while pursuing different intimations of the good life. The obvious answer would seem to involve an extrapolation of the principle of nonaggression—I may eat pork, but I may not, so to speak, eat it *at* my Jewish neighbors'; I may pursue my tastes as a rubber fetishist, but I may not *obtrude* them on the old lady next door. Mill thought that utilitarianism dictated our ordinary intuitions of what constituted "fair shares," and he may have thought it obvious that the only solution in cases like this is fair shares too, allowing everyone space to pursue their own way of life, but preventing them from encroaching on the deep-seated feelings of others. On the other hand, he may have taken a more directly utilitarian line and thought that the only rights and immunities that people really had were those they would have asked for if they had been fully informed utilitarians themselves. What division of social space we have to have now is, then, not a matter of principle in the allocation of fair shares, but a matter of the tactics that will bring about an enlightened utilitarian society in which these prejudiced, instinctive reactions do not occur. But what the inconclusiveness of any such attempt to extrapolate from Mill's discussion of opinion to twentieth-century concerns with sexual issues shows most plainly is how different Mill's own concerns were.

What they were, in addition to his concern to defend his account of progress and strike another blow against intuitionism, included an anxiety to stop respectability and Christianity from ganging up against eccentricity and agnosticism. He was outraged by the way in which people had been denied justice in English courts because they would not swear on the Bible, but wished to affirm instead. He was outraged by the way workingmen were boycotted by employers for holding unorthodox religious views or none. He insisted that such unofficial pressure was as bad as outright persecution, seeing that a man might just as well be put in jail as denied the chance of earning a living. His hostility to Christianity in particular—not as a creed, but as manifested in the oppressive habits of his contemporaries—was increased by his sense that Christians had better reason than most to beware of persecution. He observed that there was nothing that a Victorian Christian could say in favor of suppressing dissent that had not been said before and better by Marcus Aurelius in favor of suppressing Christianity. He rejected the cant view that persecution never really destroys a doctrine; on the contrary, says Mill, wherever persecution is persisted in, it succeeds in its objects. Catholicism survived wherever sixteenth-century governments persecuted their Protestant subjects with any determination; Lollards, Hussites, and Anabaptists were all wiped out without any hope of revival. The only thing to be said on the other side is that where a suppressed belief is literally true, there is the prospect that it will be rediscovered over and over again until eventually its discovery coincides with a period of toleration. Although it is not true that *Liberty* is primarily concerned with Christian intolerance, it must be said that it bulks large in Mill's concerns—much larger than sexual intolerance.

Chapters III and IV of *Liberty* belong together; they belong together because in chapter III, Mill unveils his account of individuality, and in chapter IV draws the implications for where the line is to be drawn between individual freedom and social control. Mill begins the discussion of individuality by agreeing that actions are not as free as opinions. It is here that he employs his famous example of the opinion that corn dealers are robbers of the poor, which "ought to be unmolested when simply circulated through the press, but may justly incur punishment when delivered orally to an excited mob assembled before the house of a corn dealer, or when handed about among the same mob in the form of a placard" (*Liberty*, 119). But, says Mill, this restriction is comprehended under the requirement that a man must not make himself a nuisance to others. The purpose of the chapter is to defend the proposition that where others are not primarily concerned, individuals must be allowed, at their own risk and expense, to live according to their own opinions.

The elaboration of this case, considered as a philosophical defense of Mill's proposed line between the coercible and the noncoercible, comes in chapter IV and has, to some extent, been anticipated in our discussion of Mill's utilitarianism. What precedes it is Mill's defense of individuality as a good in itself. This is not philosophically very elaborate; it contains, rather, what one might call an extended picture of what individuality consists in, why Mill thinks it matters, and what about the present age threatens it. Mill's argument is two edged. One edge amounts to a claim about what the individual gets out of individuality; the other, a claim about what the rest of mankind gets out of it. And, again, part of the argument is negative—showing what we lose by taking any other view—and part positive, celebrating the pleasures of active individuality.

Mill's hero is Wilhelm von Humboldt, whose book *The Sphere and Duties of Government* provided Mill with the epigraph to *Liberty*:

> The grand, leading principle, towards which every argument unfolded in these pages directly converges, is the absolute and essential importance of human development in its richest diversity. (*Liberty*, 57)

Where this concern for diversity, originality, and individuality is lacking, "there is wanting one of the principal ingredients of human happiness, and quite the chief ingredient of individual and social progress" (*Liberty*, 120). Individuality consists in our having a strong sense that whatever views we hold and whatever way of life we adopt should be truly ours. In effect, it amounts to holding the view that justifies Mill's argument in favor of freedom of opinion—the view that it is not just a matter of what we believe and do, but a matter of the liveliness with which we believe and act.

Negatively, Mill observes that a person who is prepared to take the opinions of others as a complete guide to life needs no other talents than "the ape-like one of imitation" (*Liberty*, 123). Positively, Mill claims that using all our faculties is itself a contribution to happiness. The man who feels himself to be fully stretched feels a happiness not available to anyone less vigorous. This is Mill's argument in *Liberty* that corresponds to his claim in *Utilitarianism* that Socrates's discontent is better than the fool's contentment, that Socrates would be unhappier if he were less moved by his discontent. It is an argument with which many philosophers have quarreled, but which others have frequently tried to resurrect. For there is an obvious difficulty in asserting that a man who is, say, clinging with his fingernails to a cliff is at that very moment "happy"—he may not be enjoying the experience in the least and may be longing to get down or get up. But we are also moved by the thought that he would not himself want to have avoided his predicament; he has chosen to be there. His being there is, we must admit, in some sense *a good for him*; and it is this that Mill relies on. The psychological fact that makes Mill's case impressive is, of course, that it is such "stretching" activities that those who practice them are most reluctant to give up. If the natural test of whether somebody finds happiness in an activity is the enthusiasm with which he pursues it, Mill's case is a plausible one. In essence, Mill is relying on an asymmetry in the attitudes of his fully active characters and their more custom-minded fellows. Once fully awoken, people do not wish to go back to sleep; when the sleepers wake, they are glad. It is not an elaborate argument, but it strikes many people, on reflection, as about the best that this sort of discussion admits of.

Mill's attack on other conceptions of life proceeds along a path that is, by this stage in the essay, a familiar one. That is, he assails the Calvinist view that the proper attitude to ourselves is one of self-abnegation. Certainly, the ability to subordinate our own interests to those of others is essential to social life; extreme self-abnegation may sometimes be essential too. There are good utilitarian reasons for agreeing to these claims: some ability to act unselfishly is needed if society is not to dissolve into civil war, and occasional emergencies demand heroic self-sacrifice. Nonetheless repression is a false ideal. What we want is strong characters capable of standing up for themselves. Even if they sometimes act wrongly, it is better to take that risk than to have a society of enfeebled creatures such as the repressed ideal aims at. At this point, Mill begins to sound a little like Friedrich Nietzsche, and his attack on the Christian ethic begins to sound a little like Nietzsche's attack on "slave morality." But as many people have pointed out, it is more than a little unfair of Mill to saddle Calvinism with such a self-destructive view of the world. Calvinism is notorious for producing decidedly strong-minded, self-reliant, and independent-minded individuals—they may be rigid, one-track, intolerant, and tough, but they are not exactly given to slavish imitation of their fellows. Mill might have done better to go down the same track as Matthew Arnold and say outright that he wanted somehow to combine the Protestant conscience and the Greek ideal of the good life.

As for why the rest of mankind should allow us to pursue our individual excellence in this fashion, the answer is simple enough. Just as we ought to be glad to see others think differently from ourselves, since their doing so is an exploration of ideas from which we may possibly benefit, so we ought to be happy to see others explore the possibilities of other ways of life, even if we have no inclination to pursue them. We are the gainers by their experiments—if they discover new sources of happiness and new ways of life, we benefit, and if they discover dead ends, we benefit by learning which roads not to travel. Something that is less visible is an assumption that may underlie a lot of Mill's argument. This is that if people become more convinced of the truth of a generally utilitarian picture of morality, they will cease to feel threatened by their differences from their fellows. Mill's arguments are, so to speak, better arguments for utilitarians than for anyone else. Since Mill supposes that rational people will become utilitarians, he must suppose that he can argue with them on two fronts—persuading them to see the world in utilitarian terms, and persuading them to interpret utilitarianism in the way he does.

That this process of argument is more necessary now than ever before follows from Mill's perspective on history generally. Once, it was essential that society should try to get the upper hand over individuals; violence and self-assertion were the order of the day, heroic individuals were two a penny and a menace to their neighbors. Progress demanded order. It was important, too, that this order be more than skin deep. It would not have been enough for law and order to be established without an underlying moral commitment to the idea that the well-being of society at large was a legitimate reason for restricting the freedom of individuals. But, Mill thought, as he so often said, in the contest between sociability and antisocial individuality, sociability had got the upper hand to such a degree that further progress demanded a redressing of the balance. Mill was reading a lesson to his friends in saying this, as well as fighting a holy war against social conformity. For it was reformers like Auguste Comte and administrators like Mill's friend Edwin Chadwick who risked sacrificing individual liberty for the sake of the general welfare. Comte was a "liberticide" by temperament as well as by theory; Chadwick had none of the wildly dictatorial ambitions of Comte (who saw himself as the creator of a new religion and a new church as well as a new society), but his benevolence made him unperceptive about the threats to freedom that his tidying up involved. The explicit, centralized desire for order that came from politicians and administrators worked with the other pressures of the age. The development of the economy meant that organization, communications, education, marketing—all were on the side of uniformity and the predominance of the large-scale over the individual. Mill did not quite anticipate the twentieth-century idea that the manager and the bureaucrat were the central figures of our age, but he came very close.

> What, then, is the rightful limit to the sovereignty of the individual over himself? Where does the authority of society begin? How much of human life should be assigned to individuality, and how much to society? (*Liberty*, 141)

With these large questions, Mill begins chapter IV of *Liberty*, and in the pages that follow he spells out the implications of the answer he gave at the beginning of the essay. That is, he spells out the implications of his claim that individuals may be coerced out of attacking others and coerced into bearing their fair share of "common defence"—and otherwise may only be exhorted, entreated, and persuaded. As we saw, Mill is sometimes thought to be arguing for a "let-alone" policy, but he denies it.

> It would be a great misunderstanding of this doctrine to suppose that it is one of selfish indifference which pretends that human beings have no business with each other's conduct in life, and that they should not concern themselves about the well-doing or well-being of one another, unless their interest is involved. (*Liberty*, 142)

Moreover, Mill is also eager to point out that he does not suppose that how people act in "self-regarding" matters can be a matter of indifference to others. If we ourselves have any sorts of standards, we are bound to have strong views about the behavior of others. We cannot think that our own tastes and interests are ones that serious people would share and not think the worse of people who do not share them. The man who spends all his time watching video nasties or drinking too much does not harm us, violates no positive duty towards us; but we are unlikely to think he is the sort of man we want as a friend, and we shall hardly be able to help thinking that he is a pretty poor specimen of humanity. Mill does not wish us to think anything else. What he wishes is that we should not think we might punish him for his self-regarding vices. This requires us to draw a careful line between what we may and may not do. Mill's thought is that punishment is essentially social; if we think someone is punishable, we think that we ought to gang up with others in inflicting punishment. But if we think only that in the exercise of our own freedom of action we may avoid the company of another, this is not a matter of encouraging everyone to gang up against him, only a matter of claiming for ourselves the freedom we do not deny him. Certainly, it is true that if someone is such a low specimen of the human race that none of us can bring himself or herself to make friends with him, the effect is the same as if we were to organize a boycott. Nonetheless, it makes all the difference which way we think of it.

To enforce this line of argument, Mill insists on some familiar distinctions and fights off some obvious objections. The familiar distinction between wickedness and imprudence is one that Mill has to rely on in the same way as the rest of us. If we ask what the logic is of describing behavior as "imprudent," it is plain that it is all to do with the agent's own welfare; if, when we point out that an action is imprudent, he says either that he does not care or that he can avoid the ill consequences, our objections on the score of imprudence must be much reduced. A wicked action, on the other hand, is much more plausibly one that does damage to others. Were the agent whose actions are complained of to reply that he does not much mind, or that he can bear the results, our response would be to try to *make* him mind, whereas it seems rather odd to try to back up claims about imprudent behavior by making a man mind.

Similarly, Mill relies on a commonsense view of the distinction between direct and remote consequences. It may well be that a man does self-regarding actions that eventually and remotely make him behave in a way that is genuinely culpable; Mill's view is that this gives us no license to repress the self-regarding behavior, but only the other-regarding behavior that directly violates rights. It may, say, be the case that I rarely read anything carefully; unpredictably, I fail to read the manual of the coach I am driving, and so crash and injure my passengers. Mill insists that we cannot force people to read carefully just in case; what we do is hold people responsible if they cause accidents, and punish them particularly severely if they cause accidents by carelessness. Analogously, merely getting drunk is no offense; but a man who loses his temper because he is drunk and then assaults another is punishable for the assault. If he does it again, he is then punishable more severely. The same doctrine applies to the effects of circumstances. It is obviously a matter of my free choice when I go to bed—but not if I am on sentry duty or driving a train. Mill's consequentialism resists any suggestion that we somehow try to see whether an action is *essentially* self-regarding or other-regarding. Many actions that would be self-regarding under some conditions become other-regarding under others. But since society is not always under the same conditions as an armed camp, no good purpose is served by abolishing the distinction in usual conditions.

We then have to step back once more and ask why Mill resists the suggestion that since he is a utilitarian, he ought to accept that *any* methods are legitimate if they achieve the appropriate goal. But the answer is simple enough. Mill maintains the nature of the goal is such that coercive measures simply are not in place. That is, once we have decided, because of the arguments in chapter III, that a major part of the utilitarian goal is itself the creation of a certain sort of character—fearless, tolerant, many sided, and so on—the means we can use to promote that goal are also fixed. We cannot create heroes by compulsion, we cannot make people spontaneous by fiat, we cannot really even make people prudent by compulsion—we can, at best, prevent the worst consequences of their imprudence.

What Mill has to attack is the thought that we are entitled to have others either live up to our standard of personal excellence or to do for the public at large everything they are capable of doing. This, of course, he has done throughout the essay. Here he argues it again in the context of laws against drink. Temperance campaigners claim that their "social rights" are invaded if they have to live in a society in which people drink too much; Mill, in effect, asks what degree of tyranny such a principle would *not* license. None of us would be safe from the moral preconceptions of other people, and there would be an end to all forms of liberty.

> So monstrous a principle is far more dangerous than any single interference with liberty; there is no violation of liberty which it would not justify . . . The doctrine ascribes to all mankind a vested interest in each other's moral, intellectual, and even physical perfection, to be defined by each claimant according to his own standard. (*Liberty*, 158)

It is obvious to Mill that nobody can seriously propose a theory of rights that has such a result. Once again, we see the strength of Mill's belief that his brand of utilitarianism supports an account of rights that favors libertarianism.

Mill's "applications" of the argument in his final chapter are interesting less for what they rule in and out than for the subtlety with which the argument develops. Mill, that is, is eager to argue not only that various legal restraints should no longer exist, and that various social pressures should no longer be applied, but also that social and even legal pressure should be imposed at points where it is not at present applied. Basically, Mill's approach is simply to take particular issues and show the consequences of his case. Thus, he insists that the sale of poisons is an area where governments may not stop people buying poisons, but may insist on their signing a register so that if there is misuse, it is simple to trace whether suspects have purchased the means of crime. Recurring to the question of laws against drink, he concedes that a man who cannot get drunk without becoming violent may properly be penalized for getting drunk—because *in his case* the connection is direct enough to warrant it. More interestingly, he argues for the prohibition of people selling themselves into slavery on the peculiar ground that "it is not freedom to be allowed to alienate [their] freedom" (*Liberty*, 173). It was not slavery that he had in mind, but marriage, for the principle he wants to defend is the principle that people should not be allowed to bind themselves to personal ties that are legally irrevocable. Slavery is an acute example, but marriage was a more pressing one.

Mill's claim that selling oneself into slavery is not freedom is awkwardly made. On the face of it, if we have the right to dispose of ourselves as we please, and we please to be a slave, then it is in the exercise of our freedom that we renounce it. No doubt it is the last free choice we make, but so too is the free choice of suicide as a better alternative to a painful and lingering death by some fatal illness. Mill might have done better to employ an argument that surfaces in his *Principles of Political Economy*. That is, he might have pointed out that buying and selling—entering into marriage too, for that matter—all require social conventions that back up the arrangements we make. Property is essentially conventional, as is marriage; the grounds for creating and sustaining such conventions must be utilitarian and libertarian, namely, that they extend people's choices. Slavery and irrevocable marriage both frustrate that goal; they ought, therefore, not to be recognized. If someone wishes to behave in a slavish fashion, that is his business; but that is infinitely far from suggesting that the rest of us ought to support institutions that force him to go on behaving in a slavish fashion when he has changed his mind.

In general, Mill does rest on the thought that trade is a conventionally assisted activity. The regulation of trade may often be an error—which is why laissez-faire is a sound principle—but it is not in principle illicit. But there is a difficulty in this, which is that some sorts of trade look as if they are no more than an application of Mill's principle that whatever a man is free to do he ought to be free to do in common with others (subject to the usual restriction that the effects of their so doing ought not to be damaging to others). If applied to prostitution and gambling, this seems to imply that brothels and gaming houses ought not to be prohibited. Gambling itself cannot be—except when, as in the case of the drunk who gets aggressive, the gambler is out of control—and fornication cannot be—though it may provide grounds for divorce. What of those who provide the service? Mill says that these are cases that are exactly on the border of two distinct principles, and evades giving a decisive answer. The general principle is not too hard to work out, however; the dangers of gaming houses and brothels are what Mill himself had earlier called "contingent"—that is, there is always a risk that the owners and managers will cheat, rob, defraud, or blackmail their clientele, or will themselves be preyed upon by other criminals. So some sort of regulation is needed, whereas prohibition is not.

Mill, however, was most interested in cases where dependent individuals needed to be protected from those to whom they are closest. This interest comes out clearly when he discusses the state's role in education. Parents owe their children a duty of education; indeed, they owe that duty not just to their children but also to society at large. Not merely are their children dependent on them for the intellectual and psychological resources they will need in later life, but the whole society is dependent on their not sending out into the world young people who are a drain on everyone else's resources. Society is entirely within its rights in insisting that parents see to the education of their children. Mill was, of course, eager that the state should not monopolize the provision of education; the whole of *Liberty* implies that educational provision should be as diverse as possible. But it would obviously be intolerable if parents were compelled to provide education in spite of their poverty, so the general principle has to be that they should be compelled to see that their children get an education, the education itself provided by a diversity of bodies that can be supervised for their factual efficiency, but not for any sort of doctrinal orthodoxy, and the parents given grants if they need them, or some schools provided free as an alternative. Mill's general stance is to shy away from the state providing either all education or a free backup service.

> An education established and controlled by the state should only exist, if it exist at all, as one among many competing experiments, carried on for the purpose of example and stimulus to keep the others up to a certain standard or excellence . . . If the country contains a sufficient number of persons qualified to provide education under government auspices, the same persons would be able and willing to give an equally good education on the voluntary principle, under the assurance of remuneration afforded by a law rendering education compulsory, combined with State aid to those unable to defray the expense. (*Liberty*, 177)

The hope is rather that the state will provide experimental education to balance any lack of variety in the marketplace. Only in underdeveloped societies must the state take the lead.

Mill's insistence on intervention in this area goes along with an insistence that it is within the state's proper sphere to regulate marriage. People who marry without the resources to provide for the children they will certainly have are in effect imposing burdens on others—they are violating the rule that they must not make themselves nuisances. So Mill was perfectly happy that there should be "laws which, in many countries on the Continent, forbid marriage unless the parties can show that they have the means of supporting a family" (*Liberty*, 179). These did not exceed the legitimate province of government; those who objected to such laws showed the odd state of thinking on the subject in Britain.

> When we compare the strange respect of mankind for liberty with their strange want of respect for it we might imagine that a man had an indispensable right to harm others, and no right at all to please himself without giving pain to others. (*Liberty*, 180)

Mill ends *Liberty* with what is strictly a digression from its main theme, namely, the consideration of those cases where government action is legitimate in terms of his "very simple principle," but where there are other objections to it. Though it is a digression, it is a topic that reappears in his *Considerations on Representative Government* and in the famous fifth book of his *Principles of Political Economy*, and it is the centerpiece of his theory of government. Moreover, it might be said that it fits in perfectly with the rest of *Liberty* simply because it is a restatement of the creed of "self-dependence," to which the essay is devoted. Mill claims first that, generally speaking, people manage their own affairs better than a government manages them for them—this is not true of colonial dependencies, but they are, as we have seen, precisely the sort of exception he is concerned with. Second, and more to the point, when individuals look after their own affairs, it does them good. They learn new skills, acquire more energy, take a wider interest in the world. So whenever there is a choice between government activity and voluntary organization, we should always choose the latter. Finally, the growth of bureaucratic government is itself a bad thing. It deadens the energies; it drains talent out of the rest of society and sends it to sleep in the government service. A good bureaucracy must be a small bureaucracy. Russia, China, and, to a large extent, France among European nations show the evils of allowing the governmental machine to absorb too large a share of the life of society. And this is a lesson that reformers ought to bear in mind. Better to cure evils slowly than to create a state that dwarfs its members. For that is the self-defeating conclusion of such reform—such a state

> will find that with small men no great thing can really be accomplished; and that the perfection of machinery to which it has sacrificed everything will avail it nothing, for want of the vital power which, in order that the machine might work more smoothly, it has preferred to banish. (*Liberty*, 187)

It is a proposition that every reformer appalled by the slowness and disorder of the process of improvement ought to have engraved on his heart.

14

Sense and Sensibility in Mill's Political Thought

THE ESSAY THAT FOLLOWS is the antithesis of what Jack Robson, the great editor of John Stuart Mill's *Collected Works* and author of *The Improvement of Mankind*, does so well. Loosely tethered to the solid ground of the text and weakly controlled by the details of Mill's biography, it ventilates some thoughts on the relationship between the biography and an intellectual assessment of Mill's work that I have long repressed. It is a kite flown in celebration of Robson's life and career.

This essay asks in a general way what we can learn about Mill's intellectual project from attention to his biography, and particularly from attention to his *Autobiography*. Much of the essay is about just that; I then go on to say something about the case of *On Liberty*, arguing that the complexities of the *Autobiography* reveal something about the complexities of *On Liberty*, and end with a bare paragraph or two of suggestions about how the *Autobiography* illuminates some of the silences of *The Subjection of Women*. I shall not trace again the territory I have traced before, in stressing the anticonservative purposes of Mill's *System of Logic* and his *Examination of Sir William Hamilton's Philosophy*.[1] On this occasion, I want to discuss the way Mill's depiction of his own life and personality illuminates his social, political, and intellectual allegiances.

This is a task I embark on with a certain trepidation. The vulgarity and silliness that has characterized many contributions to psychohistory puts many people off any attempt to mix biography and intellectual analysis. The one full-length attempt at a psychobiography of James and John Stuart Mill produced so far was so inept that it was an embarrassment to read or review.[2] Nor is it only the introduction of psychoanalytic theory that is likely to distort the attempt to provide intellectual illumination by biographical means. Too urgent an introduction of present anxieties and allegiances does almost as much damage. An excessively present-centered history of ideas gives the reader the uncomfortable sensation that truth is being sacrificed to propaganda, and even if not literal truth, then certainly understanding. To take one example only, *On Liberty* has many virtues and many vices, but it is unlikely that it has much to do with the excesses of the American Left in the late 1960s, nor with the wilder varieties of American feminism.[3] Gertrude Himmelfarb was a wonderfully acute and stringent critic of Bruce Mazlish's excesses, but herself proved quite unable to resist the urge to write a propagandist history of ideas.[4] Yet it is impossible to write a history of ideas that is not in some sense present-centered. What we find interesting in the past is, truistically but not unimportantly, what we find interesting. When we make an effort to set aside our own interests and preoccupations, to get into the skins of the protagonists of an earlier and different time, the results will display the shadow or afterimage of what it is we have set aside. Generosity and flexibility can be aimed at and with luck achieved; a godlike perspective in which all times and places are equally transparent cannot. We may think of the history of ideas as an ideal conversation across the centuries in which we aim to be good listeners as well as good questioners. Nonetheless, it is a conversation between two parties, in which both voices will be audible. This would all be utterly trite were it not that every generation seems doomed to fight over the various ways in which any text, event, or life has "a meaning," and our generation seems doomed to fight worse and more inconclusive battles than did our predecessors.[5]

All these warnings taken to heart, Mill offers an irresistible temptation, and I propose to take Oscar Wilde's way out—and yield to it. Mill's *Autobiography* is a work written in massive (though tremendously sympathetic) bad faith, in which Mill's efforts to give his life a particular public shape and meaning are constantly subverted. His attempts are doubly subverted: by the internal incoherence of the meaning he tries to give his life, and by the way his memory of events releases emotions that cannot be contained by the smooth didactic prose of the book. Compare Mill's *Autobiography* with the *Autobiography* of his godson Bertrand Russell or the *Confessions* of Jean-Jacques Rousseau. Mill's essay is the work of a man who turns his emotions into pieces of evidence for a social theory. To take the most obvious example, Mill denies that there was anything very special about his famous mental crisis. Yet he devotes a whole chapter of the book to that unspecial event. The justification that Mill offers to his reader for paying attention to this portion of his life is founded in social theory rather than in experience. (It will be remembered that Mill opens his *Autobiography* with the forbidding observation, "I do not for a moment imagine that any part of what I have to relate, can be interesting to the public as a narrative, or as being connected with myself." Readers who want anything more than an account of the "successive phases of a mind which was always pressing forward" must look elsewhere.)[6] The crisis is explored at length because of its status as a typical event in the lives of those who lived in the emotionally and ideologically incoherent early nineteenth century, a time Mill always described as "an age of transition in opinions."[7]

Indeed, as commentators have observed, Mill's description of the crisis mimics his historical theory, and particularly his view of the French Revolution. His inner life first displayed the aridity of the eighteenth century; it was revealed as a "sham" (to use the expression Mill so liked in Thomas Carlyle's *French Revolution*), with the inevitable result that once he knew the truth about himself, he could no longer sustain the proper management of his existence. Finally, but only after a period of uncertainty and emotional disorder, an appropriate mix of romantic and rationalist attachments restored good order.[8] Though this is a dramatic and indeed a highly dramatized account, the reader is asked to believe that Mill did not much mind that it was *his* mental crisis, only that it was *a* mental crisis. The strained coolness with which Mill tries to treat this most dramatic episode is undercut by the dramatic account he gives of it. He simultaneously implies and denies that his mental crisis interested him primarily as an example of the problems likely to be faced by educational reformers insufficiently attentive to the emotional needs of children, and beyond that as typical of the intellectual and moral rebuilding that intelligent people had to engage in during a transitional age.

To the extent that he remains in command of his account, Mill remains resolutely detached from his own experience. In the face of similar episodes, Russell and Rousseau preserved no such distance. They had no doubt that their feelings mattered, both because they mattered to themselves, and because they were special—deeper, more intense, richer in metaphysical resonance than other people's. Mill strenuously denies that such a thought has ever crossed his mind. Yet the attention he gives the mental crisis, the enormous care with which he describes it, the way he picks out the events that start it and end it—the whole dramatic structure, in short—presupposes that either the events themselves or his understanding of the events go beyond the commonplace. It is this that defeats attempts to question the accuracy of his account of his mental crisis, even though we know that none of his friends suspected he was in such a state. Honesty compels Mill to admit he had been in a "low state of spirits" when he first asked himself the fatal question whether the realization of all his political, reformist hopes would make him happy, just as he admits that he sometimes felt gloomy even after the reading of Jean-François Marmontel's *Memoirs* had liberated him from the awful dry state of feeling that constituted the crisis. But his didactic and typifying purposes mean that no niggling questions about the literal accuracy of his recollections can subvert his account as a whole. Its honesty lies in the honesty of those public-spirited purposes. Mill need not ask himself whether he honestly believes that his feelings are not special, because he is offering himself only as an instance. Self-revelation is not the game he is trying to play. Even as author, he is more object than subject of the *Autobiography*.

Yet the *Autobiography* is a bildungsroman as moving as anything in the genre, and the determinedly public manner in which it is written excites one's curiosity in a way a more blatant text cannot; Russell's *Autobiography* frequently leaves the reader wondering whether what Russell says is true, but not terribly eager to know more of what Russell felt about any particular topic, person, or event. Much the same goes for Rousseau. Mill, on the other hand, begins with what must be the chastest description of an author's origins in the whole history of autobiography: "I was born in London, on the 20th of May 1806, and was the eldest son of James Mill, the author of *The History of British India.*"[9] The *Autobiography* is not to be a "narrative" of his life, let alone of his *vie intérieure*, but an account of an education. That education was, in its beginnings, firmly in the hands of his father, James Mill, a philosopher, civil servant, and polemicist. As we have known since the discovery and publication of the Early Draft, Mill by no means ignored his mother's existence when he first sat down to write his autobiography, but from the published text, one would suppose that Mill had come into the world as "the product of a writer and a book," as the historian Frank Manuel remarked in conversation some years ago.

The *Autobiography* paints an exceedingly artful picture of its supposedly artless author. The liberal Mill is a dictatorial author who insists that the reader must read Mill's story only as the record of an unusual education. Moreover, the sense in which we are allowed to think it unusual is strictly circumscribed. Mill certainly presents himself as a learner, a receiver of factual information and moral instruction from older, wiser, more imaginative, or merely stronger spirits than himself; but he draws the eye simultaneously toward and away from one absolutely crucial way in which his education was unusual. This is the fact that so much of it was supplied by Mrs. Taylor, and so much of it took place when Mill had for some years earned his own living in the offices of the East India Company and had already begun on his prolific career as a practitioner of the higher journalism.

Mill's view of Harriet Taylor has been the subject of continual, mostly hostile, comment ever since the first publication of the *Autobiography*. I want not to raise the usual questions about the extent of her influence on him, about her responsibility for the central doctrines of *On Liberty*, or even about the radicalness of her feminism.[10] It is a different question that I want to raise: what is her literary or dramatic role in the *Autobiography*, and does our answer to that question have any intellectual consequence for the understanding and assessment of Mill's major work? Is Taylor to be seen as the mother who supplies what Mrs. Mill, the ground-down hausfrau, could not, or as an essentially sexless being who happens to combine Carlyle's sensibility with James Mill's practical-mindedness and is therefore fitted to "finish" the student whose father had taught him only half of what he needed to know? We know that Mill addressed Sarah Austin as *Mütterlein*, which suggests the first reading; the second is overtly in the text, and we also know that John Sterling briefly occupied almost the same place in Mill's life in the 1820s and 1830s, which suggests that Harriet Taylor ought to be seen as John Sterling's heir rather than Mrs. Mill's or Sarah Austin's.[11]

What is the intellectual interest of such a question? Setting aside a perfectly proper and nonprurient curiosity that anyone might feel about anyone else's *vie intérieure*, there is an underexplored disjunction between the doctrines put forward in Mill's best-known essays in social and political theory and the emotional style the *Autobiography* seems to display. To put it starkly, the *Autobiography* is a curiously passive work to have come from the pen of the author of *On Liberty*, let alone from the pursuer of Governor Eyre and the admirer of Marx's address on the Paris Commune.[12] That the *Autobiography* is an unbalanced work is a commonplace. The first twenty years of Mill's life occupy almost two-thirds of the book, and the first thirty almost three-quarters of it. That would be explicable, and would not make the *Autobiography* appear in the least unbalanced, if it had been the work of a different temperament or of a man whose career had been strikingly different. Someone unfeignedly obsessed with his own processes of maturation might easily write such a work.[13] But Mill's account of his education is, in crucial ways, not an account of his growing up. It is not an exercise in emotional parricide, and in a crucial way, Mill did not grow up.

The story of an education—conceived in the romantic style, with a romantic male hero—ought properly to stop at the point where the young man strides out into the world, alone or with the mate of his choice, unafraid, complete, master of his own fate at last. An *Autobiography* that had concluded with the end of the "mental crisis" would have been less dramatically awkward than the completed text; and again, if Harriet Taylor had been a different sort of person and their relationship a different sort of relationship, the story might well have ended with Mill's account of their meeting. "Reader, I married her" is not exactly Mill's style, but had he fallen in love with an unmarried Harriet Taylor, he could properly have stopped there, leaving his public life a matter of public record and his private life a matter for himself and his wife. The fact that she was already married, and their relationship thus as awkward as possible, meant that he had to say nothing about it or say a great deal. All the same, an *Autobiography* that relegates to a near appendix the thirty years in which he published *A System of Logic, Political Economy, On Liberty, Utilitarianism, Representative Government, An Examination of Hamilton, The Subjection of Women,* and a host of essays in the periodicals of the day is odd. A bildungsroman must either describe the grown-up fate of the author or leave it entirely to the reader's imagination; it cannot suggest that once the author had left one tutor, his life consisted in finding another and becoming the inadequate mouthpiece of his or (as it happens) her ideas.

In Mill's case, the oddity is heightened by the fact that the works for which he remains best known to all except professional philosophers or historians of economics are hymns to individuality, to intellectual boldness and fearlessness, to an intellectual life in which we care intensely that our thoughts and feelings should be ours.[14] It might be said that it is not so surprising that Mill was less committed to individuality than I suggest, and that *On Liberty*, like many other works, contains much that is consistent with the *Autobiography*. Romantic individualism is not the fundamental doctrine of Mill's mature years; he was the utilitarian he said he was. I and a good many others have expended a lot of energy endeavoring to show that *On*

Liberty is the utilitarian treatise that Mill says it is, and that an adequate utilitarianism is a plausible foundation for Mill's kind of social and political liberalism.[15] Still, even then such interpretations essentially proceed by demonstrating that there are good (second-order) utilitarian grounds for approving something very like the (first-order) dictates of romantic individualism.[16] We may agree that Mill approves of authority as well as individuality, but there is no escaping his insistence on individuality—it is, after all, the title of a chapter of *On Liberty* and "authority" is not. *The Subjection of Women*, moreover, ends with an entirely unutilitarian appeal to precisely that urge to be one's own master or mistress that is almost (but importantly, only almost) wholly missing in the *Autobiography*. Mill, it will be recalled, considers the benevolent opponent of feminism who is genuinely concerned for the welfare of women and asks why women should want an uncomfortable freedom rather than a comfortable dependence on fathers and husbands. The reply runs thus:

> What citizen of a free country would listen to any offers of good and skilful administration, in return for the abdication of freedom? Even if he could believe that good and skilful administration can exist among a people ruled by a will not their own, would not the consciousness of working out their own destiny under their own moral responsibility be a compensation to his feelings for great rudeness and imperfection in the details of public affairs? . . . Let any man call to mind what he himself felt on emerging from boyhood—from the tutelage and control of even loved and affectionate elders—and entering upon the responsibilities of manhood. Was it not like the physical effect of taking off a heavy weight, or releasing him from obstructive, even if not otherwise painful, bonds? Did he not feel twice as alive, twice as much a human being, as before? And does he imagine that women have none of these feelings?[17]

It is an important fact about the *Autobiography* that this urge for independence is not entirely suppressed. The passage in which Mill describes the first lifting of the gloom after his winter of depression is justly famous. The completest amateur in psychoanalytic theory would be inclined to read this passage as the expression of a powerful wish to see his father dead and himself in his father's place. Long before psychoanalysis came into the world, writers knew perfectly well that images such as Marmontel conjures up have a powerful charge of ambiguity, that we cannot but be appalled at the thought of a parent's death yet also be eager to see how we shall cope on our own. But we do not need to chase down that road. We need only note that whether or not Mill's sense of being dependent, passive, and a perpetual child led him to harbor unconscious wishes for the death of his father, he certainly felt dependent and passive and helpless, and that it was a passage of literature about a young man boldly assuming responsibility for himself and his family that so effectively cheered him up.[18]

Yet what followed was not the assumption of responsibility but the search for further teachers; the search was successful inasmuch as Sterling and Carlyle offered new insights, unsuccessful inasmuch as Carlyle demanded an unthinking loyalty to whatever he came up with, and Sterling fell ill and died. In this perspective, Mill's correspondence with Comte is an important exhibit: Mill hesitates to reveal his dissent even from Comte's dottier views, and disagrees with Comte only in the most deferential way, even when he knows full well that Comte's views are not just mad but obnoxious.[19] Comte's regime of *hygiène cérébrale*, the policy of reading nothing that might unsettle his existing convictions—a regime that constituted the absolute antithesis of the pursuit of contradictory ideas advocated in *On Liberty*—is passed over as a policy permissible in a man as well read as Comte but dangerous in a lesser thinker.[20] Can Mill really have thought so? One doubts it. Only when Harriet Taylor denounced the feebleness of Mill's criticisms of Comte's views on the intellectual inferiority of women did Mill speak his mind.[21]

Mill was perhaps someone who, by temperament, disliked personal conflict and tried to avoid it—though he was comparatively fearless in public. What seems clear is that his search for teachers was both cause and effect of a certain emotional passivity. Taylor was all he could want, but she did not exactly allow him to grow up. Their correspondence during the short years of their married life can hardly be read without pain. The "rejected leaves" from the Early Draft remark on Mill's inability to dress himself as a child.[22] His letters to his wife show him unable to buy his own underwear, puzzled by the fact that the house consumes more coal in winter than in summer (and this from the creator of the canons of the experimental method), and unable to confront either the rats in the coal shed or the next-door neighbor's anger about them.[23]

The point of assembling these familiar facts is to found the following argument. Mill's emotional dependency is in many areas not a handicap but a source of intellectual strength. In particular, it makes *On Liberty* a more interesting essay on individuality than it might otherwise be, because *On Liberty* recognizes numerous arguments in favor of various kinds of authority as well as the central case for individual liberty. *On Liberty* is not an essay about doing your own thing; it is an essay about finding the best thing and making it your own. But there is one area in which Mill's dependency on Taylor damages his thinking, and this is in the realm of sexual relationships, and thus of marriage. Mill's ideal of marriage is in many ways admirable and in some ways all the more admirable given Taylor's strong-willed insistence on a woman's right to work and her unsentimental demolition of Mill's occasional expression of the view that a woman's role is to "beautify" life. Nonetheless, it is a curiously bleak picture of married life that emerges from Mill's reflections. This is the topic of the last page or two of this essay. First, I want to turn to the way that *On Liberty*'s case for the freedom of speech and thought is illuminated by attending to the psychology revealed in the *Autobiography*.

That *On Liberty* is not much deformed by Mill's own ambivalences is something some readers will refuse to believe at any price and others will think it quite otiose to demonstrate. The latter will argue that the essay offers so compelling a case for individual freedom that no biographical information can alter our view of it one way or the other. There may or may not eventually be a scientifically validated account of the psychological conditions of the production of philosophical arguments, but the quality of Mill's arguments would be untouched by any account of the causal route by which he came to put them forward. By the same token, his critics think the essay so misguided that nothing can count in its favor. The point these responses miss is that biographical information and psychological conjecture may be enlightening in identifying the arguments of the essay even before we turn to assessing their merits.[24]

To take a simple example: there is a familiar crux in *On Liberty* in which Mill is concerned to defend a near absolute right to free speech as a means of securing the truth. We may not forbid another to speak his mind, however sure we are that he is talking nonsense; he may be right, or if wrong, partly right, or if wholly wrong, a valuable irritant impelling us to views more nearly true than our existing views. The truth can advance only if it is open to anyone to challenge any and every received opinion; moreover, it can be felt to be a living and vivid truth only if it is one we are accustomed to defend against its critics. It looks as if Mill's case is an instrumental one, a version of Sir Karl Popper's falsificationist account of scientific progress. The detection of error and the discovery of truth demand an unflinchingly critical approach to received doctrine. It is an impressive case but a vulnerable one. Critics have always pointed out that because it is an instrumental defense of free speech, it is vulnerable to empirical disconfirmation.

Critics who have read T. S. Kuhn on the nature of normal science can plausibly argue that it is not free speech that advances knowledge but a combination of limited freedom of speech and considerable authoritarianism.[25] Researchers are to speak their minds about the solutions to "puzzles"; they may be individualistic and independent minded about the way to fill in previously identified gaps in our understanding of the world. But woe betide them if they should challenge the consensus about what constitutes a puzzle and its solution, or about what gaps exist to be filled. Even loyal disciples of Popper, on record as regarding Kuhn's views as a threat to civilization, acknowledge that Popper's own demand for "tenacity" in giving a hypothesis a proper run for its money may, in practice, be hard to distinguish from acceptance of the role of the paradigm in disciplining the intellectual efforts of a profession.

But a careful look at Mill's text suggests another and different difficulty. When we look at what Mill is concerned with, it seems not to be a matter of scientific truth so much as the "truths" of religion and morals. He is not concerned with truth in the narrow sense of correspondence to fact. Rather, he is concerned with something quite different—namely, the state of mind in which we entertain whatever beliefs we do entertain about the meaning of existence and the ends of life. What he is concerned with is the contrast between views taken unthinkingly on trust and views we have really made "our own." The former need nothing more than the apelike faculty of imitation—that is, the ability to repeat what we have been told; the latter need to be thought through independently. It is in these latter views that we should value criticism and opposition.[26]

It is sometimes suggested that Mill's conception of the route to intellectual progress vacillates between an inductive and a more Popperian falsificationist conception of good method. In the former conception, scientific progress is made by observation and experiment, and by extrapolation and generalization from the data of such information-gathering exercises; in the latter, progress is made by treating generalizations as hypotheses to be exposed to falsifying tests. It is certainly true that Mill elsewhere writes as if induction is the method of science, though I do not think he is to be taken as espousing what it is that Popper and other falsificationists denounce. In *On Liberty*, he equally certainly defends a falsificationist position, asserting that no belief is really known except by someone who knows what can be said against it. Still, that does not quite line him up with subsequent philosophers of science. Mill seems rather to be laying down a prescriptive test for what is to count as knowing something, and not a methodological precept for scientists.

If truth were only a matter of correspondence to fact, the frame of mind in which one believed a proposition p would be irrelevant; so long as it was true that p and one believed that p, one would hold a true belief. Mill is evidently concerned that belief should be living, lively, vibrant, and fruitful. We ought not to exaggerate the extent to which an unemotional acceptance of the factually accurate would suffice in science. It is plausible to suppose that science, too, would make no progress unless at least some of its practitioners were passionately committed to the theories they came up with. If they treated the most basic doctrines of their discipline as flatly factual, on a par with propositions about the cleanliness or otherwise of the lab floor, they would have little motivation for further exploration. All the same, it is only of propositions of a more distinctively ethical or quasi-religious cast that we feel inclined to say that their point, or even their meaning, lies in the fact that they attract belief of a wholehearted kind.

Why should we exercise ourselves about this? For the simple reason that Mill's case for freedom of speech and thought plainly has three distinct levels. In the first place, there is an appeal to the "harm principle"; we cannot suppress someone else's utterances unless those utterances are likely to do us harm. Even then, how they harm us must be taken into account; that we dislike what is said is neither here nor there; that if people are persuaded of what is said, we shall lose some existing privilege or benefit is neither here nor there. If the effect of what they say is that we lose out in economic competition, that is neither here nor there. It is only cases analogous to that of the placard waved at an angry mob that count. Recently, Robert Nozick has seemed to suggest that "harm" occurs only when the persons causing the injury have no right to do so; if I am driven out of business by a competitor using his property more efficiently than I use mine, he has not, in the appropriate sense, harmed me.[27]

Mill held a better view. In this view, if corn dealers rob the poor, corn dealers have no right to go on doing so and ought to be stopped. They ought not to be stopped by a violent and angry mob, but by due process of political persuasion and legal provision. They have no right to rob the poor, but they have a right to a fair trial. There is no suggestion they would suffer no harm by losing their illicit advantages, only that they plainly cannot call on the harm-preventing institutions of society, such as the law and the police, to protect them in harm-inflicting activities. They will be worse off if they lose their ability to exploit the poor, just as thieves will be worse off if they go to jail—but thieves ought to be sent there nonetheless. In the light of this reading of Mill's case, one might say that the first level of argument for free speech allows people to speak their mind when they do not harm anyone else, or harm them only by way of legitimate procedures for doing justice to those who themselves cause harm, or harm them only in the course of competitive activities whose overall utility is enough to justify the harm done to losing competitors.

The second level of argument is the argument from truth. This, we have seen, may be persuasive at the level of a *ceteris paribus* claim that generally it is a condition of successful scientific inquiry that people can put forward any hypothesis they like, offer it for test, and not be deterred by threats of disapproval, ostracism, or worse. It is an imperfect argument, in the sense that what it sustains is not a right of free speech but a social convention of argumentativeness and a right of free speech only in the sense that within that convention, people must live by that convention. It is imperfect also in the sense that it may mislead readers about the extent of variety, argumentativeness, and imagination in run-of-the-mill, puzzle-solving science. Nonetheless, it is a powerful argument; even when we discount for the observations of Kuhn, it remains true that unless there is a free-speech ideology in science, progress is unlikely. The example of Trofim Lysenko's baleful impact on Soviet science is overused but decisive.

At the third level, there is an argument of a very different kind. Here we are in the realm of pure ideal-regarding arguments. The defense of free speech is part of the defense of the search for the kind of life-enhancing truth discussed above. Views we dislike are far from harming us; we are all the better for being able to contemplate, discuss, and accept or reject the views that others hold. Our own views are less our own in the absence of a clear sense of how they differ from those of other people. It is in this context that Mill insists that the eccentric does the rest of the world a service by reminding them they must have grounds for their beliefs and cannot rely on their universality to prove them true.[28]

This, then, is a pure defense of individual moral and intellectual sovereignty. It is a defense of nonpassivity, and has its psychological origins in Mill's education. He bitterly resented the suggestion, made by Carlyle in particular, that he was a "made man," the product of his father's and Bentham's schemes. The same insistence that we could all be our own creations appears in his discussion of free will in *A System of Logic*; it is there that he discusses the Owenite attack on punishment as the unjust ill treatment of people who cannot help acting as they did. To the Owenite insistence that our actions are the result of our characters and our characters the result of our education, made *for* us and not *by* us, Mill replies that we can help create our own characters. Certainly, the materials must be present for us to have any chance of constructing the character we desire, but if they are present, the person who so desires *will* act, and the one who does not will *not*.[29] We see a tension in Mill's view of the world and of himself. He understood he had been shaped by his father; he had to believe he could reshape himself. It is tempting to guess that he often felt he could not, and that it was something of a relief to settle for reshaping by Taylor or Carlyle. He felt himself to have been bullied by his father, indoctrinated, turned into a calculating machine, and deprived of a soul. He might have argued, but did not, that in his own analysis of the poet's sensibility, this meant that his father had made him passive but had failed to develop his passive sensibilities. In effect, his father had imposed on him a vision of the successful man as a self-controlled, strong, and effective character, and had created in him a conviction that he had failed to live up to this ideal. He had damaged his will, but he had not taught him to understand the passive virtues.

The cure for his mental crisis was a belief that it was possible, after all, to create a character of his own and to establish his own system of ideas, as well as the belief that what was needed for him was needed for society at large. It would take Wordsworth, Coleridge, and Shelley to complete the Benthamite view of social and political progress. But the conviction was not solidly founded; the curious tetchiness with which he often responded to criticism, as well as the cruel and inhumane way he treated his family at the time of his marriage, suggests that he was very much less secure in his new view of himself than he doubtless hoped to be. No doubt another part of the story was that he had little sense of how far he could go without betraying his father. Oddly enough, he had fewer grounds than he thought for the sense that he was drastically at odds with his father's social intuitions and political allegiances. James Mill was worried about his son's connection with Harriet Taylor, but he was quick to approve the essay "Civilization," which at face value seems to be an all-out attack on what his son took to be the utilitarianism of his father and Bentham.[30]

* * * * *

What Mill lacked was a sense of how one might combine the passive sensibility he admired in the poet with the strong sense of self that would allow him to call his ideas his own. What makes Mill engaging is the way this internal conflict appears, transformed, in his formal writing. It makes an essay such as *On Liberty* something more complex than a hymn to self-assertion, for it makes it a hymn to a self that has been properly educated, and that is still susceptible to the authority of the more enlightened or more cultured. *The Subjection of Women* is a less interesting work because it is less complex. That is not to say it is anything but a lively and spirited defense of its simple case: that women are not destined by nature to occupy dependent and inferior positions, to be always under the tutelage of husbands, brothers, or fathers.

What, however, it—or Mill himself—seems to be short of is a positive image of an egalitarian sexual, or indeed any other form of intimate, relationship. It is in that sense (and deliberately in many other ways) a very negative piece of work. It is tempting to speculate that Taylor may have exacerbated what was obviously a general difficulty. Mill may initially have been ready to throw away his career and reputation for the sake of love, and he may have envisaged the two of them taking the unrespectable route of a new life in Paris or Florence. No such thing crossed her mind. It is hard these days not to say that censoriously, as if she ought to have subscribed to our standards of sexual liberation and emotional warmth rather than to her own. This is plainly no way to write intellectual history. Still, there is some connection between Mill's ambivalence about passivity and self-assertion and the arguments of *The Subjection of Women*.

There are two views one might take of this matter. One would be to argue that liberalism is ideologically committed to an unsatisfactory view of marriage and perhaps of all close personal relationships; the other would be to argue that there is no particular reason why a satisfactory liberal view of these matters cannot be developed, but that Mill himself fell a long way short. My own sense is that the second is the right view, but there is something to be said for the first.

If contractual relationships are the paradigm of voluntary association for the liberal, it is plausible to see marriage as essentially a contract. It may be a peculiar contract, but a contract it must be. The question then arises of what it is a contract for. The difficulty that any answer faces is nicely illustrated by Kant's extraordinary suggestion that the marriage contract must in law be a mutual and exclusive contract for the use of the sexual organs. If this is preposterous, it shows by its very absurdity that the contractualist faces the difficulty that everything one might adduce as the point of the contract can be satisfactorily taken care of in some other way—except, depressingly, for legalized sexual relations.[31]

This is hardly decisive as an argument against the thought that marriage is, inter alia, a contract, nor against the thought that the liberal conception of marriage ought to acknowledge the libertarian and egalitarian aspects of the contractual relationship while still insisting that within the contractual framework established by the law there will be goods of an intimate, personal kind that may in themselves have little or nothing to do with liberalism, but that will certainly be valued in a liberal culture subscribing to ideals of self-exploration and self-creation. Again, a modern view presupposes a background of an impersonal public life—at work, in politics, in all sorts of instrumental relationships—against which an environment where intimate, relaxed relationships and highly specific emotional attachments flourish will have an even greater value. Mill, it seems to me, could not bring himself to see that sexual intimacy might be an important ingredient of such relationships and an important aspect of such attachments. For all his emphasis on the value of diversity and variety, and for all his instructions to himself about the need for many-sidedness, he rarely saw anything in sexual relations other than "animal functions," and saw those as a matter of men imposing their unconsidered and inconsiderate lusts upon whatever woman the law had placed in their power. Without belaboring the point, it is surely inadequate to discuss marriage on so limited a basis.[32]

If this is right, generally or in part, it may provide an answer to our question of the intellectual bearing of Mill's biography. Indeed, it may provide a more interesting answer than one might expect. For it suggests there are many areas of Mill's work in which we learn a lot about the motivation of the argument—about, say, the political motivation behind his attack on intuitionist and a priori accounts of mathematics and logic—but almost nothing of interest about the content of the argument. There are other areas where we learn something about the content in learning something about the motivation, and this, I have suggested, is particularly true of *On Liberty*'s arguments about freedom of speech and the search for truth. Finally, there are still other areas where we acquire what one might call negative insights, insights into why Mill did not or could not employ certain sorts of arguments, insights into what it was that he characteristically overlooked or even had to overlook. In accepting this, we may come to think that an adequate intellectual biography of Mill may, at one and the same time, be adequate to both the intelligence and the biography, and indeed be adequate to each only in being adequate to both. If Mill's own *Autobiography* is not the last word in intellectual biographies of this sort, it is surely a good enough example of the genre to make one hunger for more.

Mill in a Liberal Landscape

MILL'S ESSAY *On Liberty* had both the good and the ill fortune to become a "classic" on first publication. The immediate success of the book, dedicated as it was to preserving the memory of Harriet Taylor, could only gratify its author. Yet its friends and foes alike fell upon it with such enthusiasm that the essay itself has ever since been hard to see for the smoke of battle.[1] *That* it is a liberal manifesto is clear beyond doubt; *what* the liberalism is that it defends and *how* it defends it remain matters of controversy. Given the lucidity of Mill's prose and the seeming simplicity and transparency of his arguments, this is astonishing. Ought we not to know by now whether the essay's main target is the hold of Christianity on the Victorian mind[2] or rather the hold of a monolithic public opinion of whatever kind; whether its intellectual basis lies in utility, as Mill claimed, or in a covert appeal to natural right; whether the ideal of individual moral and intellectual autonomy is supposed to animate everyone or only an elite; and so indefinitely on?

The account of Mill's essay I offer here does not settle these issues. My account is neither conclusive nor comprehensive, nor will it resolve very many of the problems that Mill's readers have had with the essay. My argumentative aim is to emphasize the difficulties a late twentieth-century reader will have with Mill's liberalism and to mark quite sharply its differences from many contemporary—that is, late twentieth-century—liberalisms. I therefore begin with a sketch of Mill's argument, then say something about the context of Mill's discussion, that is, about whom the essay was aimed at, negatively and positively; I conclude by contrasting Mill's liberalism with the liberalisms of John Rawls and Isaiah Berlin in order to bring out some of the ways in which Mill was and was not a pluralist, did and did not attend to "the separateness of persons" (Rawls 1971, 27), did and did not espouse a full-fledged teleological and ideal conception of the autonomous individual.[3] I make no secret of my preference for Mill's ambitious and comprehensive theory over Rawls's more limited and defensive (the latter a narrowly "political") liberalism, nor of my uncertainty about quite what to say about Mill's seeming blindness to the attractions of colorful but illiberal cultural alternatives—such as that presented by the Indian subcontinent, whose political affairs he directed.[4] There is much in Mill's essay that I do not discuss here, but I have tried to avoid repeating what I have written elsewhere and what others have (to my mind, at any rate) dealt with adequately.[5] It is in the nature of classics that their students are exhausted before they are.

Mental Pemmican

Mill's essay was conceived in 1854 when he discovered that he and Harriet were suffering from consumption and might well die in the near future. It was to be part of the "mental pemican" that they would leave to thinkers "if there should be any" after themselves (J. S. Mill, *Later Letters*, in *Collected Works* [hereafter cited as *CW*] 14:141). The absurdity of their fears for the wholesale collapse of British intellectual life has often been commented on, and the kindest gloss on it is that no two people who had waited to be married as long as they had should be chided for excessive gloom when they so soon afterward discovered that their long-deferred happiness was to be snatched away.[6] *On Liberty* was conceived at a time when Mill was, for the first time, contemplating a long essay on Comte, his intention in part being to counter the excessively favorable impression that his use of Comte's work in *A System of Logic* had created. Mill abandoned the Comte essay for the rest of the 1850s (it eventually appeared in 1865), but *On Liberty* has the marks of Mill's ambivalence about Comte all over it.[7] On the one hand, Mill thought highly of Comte's appreciation of the need for a scientific reorganization of social and economic life; on the other, Mill condemned Comte's version of that project as "liberticide." On the one hand, Comte saw deeply into the need for some kind of moral system to play the role in individual lives that Christianity had formerly played; on the other, Comte's version of the religion of humanity "could have been written by no man who had ever laughed" (J. S. Mill, *Comte and Positivism*, *CW* 10:343). On the one hand, Comte understood that as society became increasingly complex, the bonds of duty must tie us ever more tightly to one another; on the other, he wholly failed to see that unless we lived for ourselves as well as for others, nothing would be worth living for, nothing would exist for which it was worth doing our duty. Of course, Mill had many other writers in mind. *On Liberty*'s famous epigraph invokes Wilhelm von Humboldt and the German concern for *Bildung*;[8] the historical sociology of democratic culture on which Mill relied to explain the nature of the threat to liberty posed by that culture was lifted bodily from Tocqueville's *Democracy in America*. But the intellectual and political vision that Mill was anxious to check is one that his friends and colleagues found tempting—not just the "soft" despotism in the form that Tocqueville feared, but that of a benevolent bureaucracy also.

Like that of *Utilitarianism*, the argument of Mill's essay is not so much familiar as notorious: "The object of this Essay is to assert one very simple principle, as entitled to govern absolutely the dealings of society with the individual in the way of compulsion and control" (*On Liberty*, *CW* 18:215). Commentators have complained about Mill's appeal to one very *simple* principle; they have said that little in human life is simple, and the question of when to interfere with one another's liberty is not part of that little. This complaint may be mistaken; simple principles are often complicated to apply—a planning minister or his civil servants may be required not to withhold consent "unreasonably" when a citizen applies for permission to build a house or a garage, but that simple requirement leads to complicated lawsuits. Mill's simple principle is that we may coerce others into doing what they do not choose to do only for the sake of self-defense and, by extension, to make them perform a small number of good offices (such as giving evidence in a court of law) that are required if others are not to be harmed by their inaction. It *is* a simple principle, however complicated it may be to apply.

Mill was less interested in employing the principle to restrain coercion by single individuals than to restrain the coercive actions of groups. It is not the fear that we shall individually assault or incarcerate others when we ought not that motivated him, but the fear that we shall collectively gang up on eccentric individuals when we ought not. The fear is based on two things. The first and more obvious is Tocqueville's observation that Americans had less freedom of thought and speech than one might suppose from their constitutional arrangements; Americans were notably bad at thinking for themselves, and were vulnerable to the desire to think like everyone else and to the desire that everyone else should think like them (Tocqueville 1994). The second and less obvious is an idea that Mill picked up from the Saint-Simonians during the late 1820s and early 1830s. This is the view that the progress of modern civilization is a movement away from individual genius and toward action en masse (J. S. Mill, "Civilization," *CW* 18:121). Mill largely relied on the first thought. It was a corollary to the view of the history of democracy that he had come to, partly under Tocqueville's tutelage, but quite largely independently of that influence. The ordinary people of a country like Britain had successfully altered the balance of power between themselves and their rulers until the country was in practice, though not in constitutional principle, democratic; but they had not noticed that in fending off the tyranny of monarchs and aristocrats, they had rendered themselves vulnerable to a different and more insidious tyranny, the tyranny of all collectively over each individually.

The insidiousness of this tyranny was not only that "self-government" often meant in practice the government of each by all the rest, but also that this was a soft, constant social pressure for conformity rather than a visible political tyranny. The consequence was that they tyrannized over themselves as well as over one another:

> Reflecting persons perceived that when society is itself the tyrant—society collectively, over the separate individuals who compose it—its means of tyrannizing are not restricted to the acts which it may do by the hands of its political functionaries. Society can and does execute its own mandates: and if it issues wrong man-

dates instead of right, or any mandates at all in things with which it ought not to meddle, it practises a social tyranny more formidable than many kinds of political oppression, since, though not usually upheld by such extreme penalties, it leaves fewer means of escape, penetrating much more deeply into the details of life, and enslaving the soul itself. (*On Liberty*, CW 18:219)

There was nothing to be done about the movement toward political democracy. It was a movement that Mill thought inevitable, and like Tocqueville, Mill thought it was, on balance, morally desirable on the grounds of justice and liberty alike. All the same, a new view of liberty was needed to counter the threat posed by the tendency of the public to suppose that once its mind was made up, dissentients should defer to public opinion. Mill's "very simple principle" was intended to provide part of that counter. Individuals must acknowledge the right of society to coerce them out of behavior that harmed other people, that violated their rights, that damaged their legitimate interests; over all else, each individual remained sovereign.

Critics have complained not only that Mill's principle was too simple, but also that he had no business offering it as an "absolute" principle. Mill himself was aware that it was dangerous for a utilitarian to offer any other principle than utility as one "entitled to govern absolutely" the dealings of society with its members. Utilitarians prided themselves on having reduced morality to principle: ethics had been rationalized when the principle of utility justified the everyday morality that utilitarians accepted and the noneveryday morality with which they wished to improve everyday morality. The status of any other principle was thus a delicate matter. Mill was ready with his answer. The individual's sovereignty over him- or herself was not based on natural right; it was derived from utility. It was absolute not in the sense that the liberty principle is "ultimate," but in the sense that it is exceptionless. This claim, however, raised another difficulty. The impetus to the writing of *On Liberty* was to protect freedom from the assaults of illiberal dogooders—as it were, an advance warning against the "bourgeois, benevolent and bureaucratic" Sidney and Beatrice Webb when they should arrive on the scene, and perhaps a warning against his own good friend Edwin Chadwick, with his enthusiasm for Prussian efficiency. This supposed a conflict between the pursuit of freedom and the pursuit of the general welfare; but Mill proposed to defend freedom for its contribution to the general welfare.

In essence, the rest of *On Liberty* spelled out how the principle of *no coercion except to prevent harm to others* promoted utility. The first step was to point out that the utility involved had to be taken "in its largest sense": it was the utility of "man as a progressive being" that was at stake, not only the bread-and-butter utility of man as a consumer, with fixed tastes and desires.[9] Giving a persuasive account of what the utility of such a person was based on, as most critics have seen, forms the substance of the work.[10] It is worth noting that Mill's expansive conception of the utility of a progressive being rested on a sober basis. To use a term from recent discussions,

Mill's liberalism is "perfectionist" in the sense that it proposes an ideal way of life; in the sense in which his contemporaries would have understood such a term, it was more nearly "antiperfectionist," inasmuch as it repudiated the idea that the state or society generally had a right to *make* individuals conform to some existing ideal of good character. In any case, Mill's concern for individual liberty rested both on a doctrine of self-protection and on a doctrine of self-development. We have two great needs that rights protect: the first and most basic is for security, and the second is for room to expand and flourish according to our own conception of what that entails.[11] In *Utilitarianism*, Mill went on to explain the achievement of security as the province of *justice*, and to tie the notion of justice to the notion of rights. Our interest in security has the character of a right that must be protected against threats from other persons.

Although Mill was not a functionalist, he plainly thought that organized human society and its legal and political arrangements existed to provide each individual with a collective defense against such threats. One of the ways in which the principle of "no coercion except to prevent harm to others" is glossed by Mill, therefore, is to include the right of society to make each of us bear our share of the burden of sustaining the institutions that provide collective security. The refusal to give evidence at a trial is not a matter of our making a legitimate decision to withhold a kindness to the person whom that evidence would help, but a threat to the arrangements on which everyone's security depends, and so is a case of harm to others; we may therefore be coerced into giving evidence:

> There are also many positive acts for the benefit of others which he may rightfully be compelled to perform; such as, to give evidence in a court of justice; to bear his fair share in the common defence, or in any other joint work necessary to the interest of the society of which he enjoys the protection; and to perform certain acts of individual beneficence, such as saving a fellow-creature's life, or interposing to protect the defenceless against ill-usage, things which whenever it is obviously a man's duty to do, he may rightfully be made responsible to society for not doing. A person may cause evil to others not only by his actions but by his inaction, and in either case he is justly accountable to them for the injury. The latter case, it is true, requires a much more cautious exercise of compulsion than the former. To make any one answerable for doing evil to others, is the rule; to make him answerable for not preventing evil, is, comparatively speaking, the exception. Yet there are many cases clear enough and grave enough to justify that exception. (CW 18:224; cf. 276)

Mill's argument that rights are to be elucidated in this way remains contentious; it was, and is, a bold move to defend the right to liberty as something other than a *natural* right. Consider, for example, the relationship between Mill's views and those of such recent writers as H.L.A. Hart and Robert Nozick. Mill's view that the limits of our liberty are to be understood by reference to the purpose of our living in society is squarely at odds with

Nozick's natural-rights-based view. And while Mill's view that we may be made to bear our fair share of the burdens of maintaining society is on all fours with the natural-rights-based views of H.L.A. Hart (1955), Mill's argument reaches that conclusion more directly than does Hart's. Hart explained our obligation to obey the law by arguing that a society may coerce its members into doing their fair share to sustain institutions from which they derive the same benefits as those they help. This was intended to explain how someone who enjoyed a natural right to "maximum equal liberty" may still be under an obligation to obey the laws of his or her community, including laws that impose obligations of the sort discussed by Mill.

Nozick's (1974, 92–93) response to Hart's argument was to argue that if we have a right to equal liberty, it is only our own consent that can give others the right to demand such positive assistance as our giving evidence in a law court. Merely being part of a community in which we benefit from the assistance of others is not enough to generate obligations of "fair play." It might be true that it would be *good* of us to return something for the benefits we received, but it would violate nobody's rights if we did not. Mill would surely have concluded that this and similar disputes among rights theorists showed the superiority of his utilitarianism. He relied on a simpler thought: that society is a mutual-aid system designed to protect our fundamental interests; we are born into society, not into a state of nature, and within that society we are obliged to sustain the protective system from which we benefit. Everything then hinges on explaining our fundamental interests as persuasively as possible.

Mill appears in much of *On Liberty* to take it for granted that his readers will understand the principle of "no coercion except to prevent harm to others" in much the same way as himself. That is, there is no very elaborate discussion of what constitutes harm; and as Jeremy Waldron (1987) has argued, there seems every reason to believe that at least some sorts of distress—such as being startled to discover that our neighbor is not a Trinitarian Christian, or that she is not heterosexual, say—would have been counted by Mill as positively good for us and not in the least "harmful." Mill's confidence in the transparency of the concept of harm on which his argument relied meant that he argued in a way that bypasses much of the argument of recent years. Two common arguments against his position he hardly bothered to rebut except in passing. One, made popular thirty-five years ago by Lord Devlin (1965), is that if society is to defend each of us against assault, robbery, breach of contract, and so on, it will also be necessary for society to defend a common morality covering all aspects of social and individual, or all aspects of public and private, life. James Fitzjames Stephen had produced during Mill's own lifetime a related but by no means identical argument; Stephen's crude utilitarianism implied that we should beat good behavior into people whenever the policy offers sufficient prospect of success. Utilitarianism is therefore not a basis for, but at odds with, Mill's self-abnegating doctrine. Stephen prided himself on his roughness, as his nickname "the Gruffian" suggests, but the argument is far from easy to defeat.[12] Stephen in particular was opposed to the idea that freedom was as important to the utility of "man as a progressive being" as Mill supposed; but the problem posed by a no-holds-barred consequentialism of the sort he represented is quite general. One of its implications, for instance, is that if Mill thought that a taste for liberty was an element in a good character, he ought to have been ready to beat a taste for liberty into the recalcitrant, too.

Devlin's view was not so much a dismissal of Mill's concern with freedom as the claim that a plausible account of Mill's harm principle would license the defense of a collective morality. Devlin thought, at a time when most of public opinion was against him, that the Victorian laws against homosexual acts between consenting adults ought to be abolished. This, however, was not because they infringed liberty in the abstract, but because they violated a concern for privacy and for intimate relationships that was inherent in existing British moral attitudes. To set up an abstract test of the kind Mill proposed was to invite the unraveling of social cohesion. The reply implicit in Mill's essay would, however, answer both Devlin and Stephen. In essence, it is that the facts are against his critics. *Some* common morality must be generally enforced, and its features are just those that Mill suggests; but there is no reason to believe that a failure to secure uniformity of belief on disputed conceptions of the good life will bring about any harm other than whatever discomfort is attendant on being required to think for ourselves. Conversely, there is good reason to suppose that trying to enforce more than the basic morality Mill had in mind would result in the damage that *On Liberty* laments.

It is sometimes suggested that a utilitarian defense of liberty is a nonstarter; utilitarianism would license any degree of interference that gave enough pleasure to the majority. If people *want* to believe in a shared morality, the majority has a right to have a common morality enforced, on the utilitarian basis that the enforcement will provide pleasure to the majority. Mill's response to this vulgar but not implausible argument was offered glancingly, in several places, and in three installments. One was an appeal to the intuitive idea that any claim that others should behave as I wish *just because* I wish them to do so has no merit. Mill knew that nobody *avowed* such a view. The buried premise of Mill's argument against it therefore was that where enough moral discord existed to excite the desire for uniformity, the demand that others should do anything in particular for the sake of a "shared morality" is tantamount to the claim that they should think like me and act like me because I want them to. This is what Mill denounced as his contemporaries' belief that their "likings and dislikings" should be a universal guide (*On Liberty*, CW 18:222). The second was sketched in the previous paragraph: the content of the "common morality" that any society must enforce was essentially limited to the defense of each of its members against a limited range of harms, and to the enforcement of the common rules of interaction that made life more prosperous and more rationally controllable—the morality that underlies the making and keeping of contracts, the doing of jury duty, recognizing the obligation to go to work and earn a living, and so on. Any greater uniformity would do more harm than good. The third was essentially an elaboration of the conception of "more harm" that was involved in such a response; that elaboration supplied the bulk of the positive argument of *On Liberty*. Mill denied that enforcing uniformity would be a good bargain in utilitarian terms; the entire essay was an argument to that effect, since it was an argument against yielding to the desire for uniformity of sentiment, whether for its own sake or for the sake of the general welfare.

Mill's concluding admonition to beware of creating a society whose animating spirit has been sacrificed to the perfection of a bureaucratic machine summed up Mill's underlying theme: a society of what Tocqueville had called "industrious sheep" was the only alternative to the lively and flexible (and emotionally uncomfortable) society that Mill was arguing for. It is a famous peroration:

> The worth of a State, in the long run, is the worth of the individuals composing it; and a State which postpones the interests of their mental expansion and elevation, to a little more of administrative skill, or of that semblance of it which practice gives, in the details of business; a State which dwarfs its men, in order that they may be more docile instruments in its hands even for beneficial purposes—will find that with small men no great thing can really be accomplished; and that the perfection of machinery to which it has sacrificed everything, will in the end avail it nothing, for want of the vital power which, in order that the machine might work more smoothly, it has preferred to banish. (*On Liberty*, CW 18:308)

Some of Mill's elaborations of what follows from his very simple principle have become justly famous. Others have languished in an unwarranted obscurity, among them his insistence that it was no illicit interference with liberty for the state to demand that young people who proposed to marry should demonstrate that they had the means and the intention to look after the probable children of their union (*On Liberty*, CW 18:302–4); others, such as his insistence that the state should on no account take a large part in the provision of education (302), have been much less attended to than one might have expected, perhaps because modern liberals both British and American take public education for granted, while enthusiasts for the privatization of education have not generally been Millian liberals in other respects. In the contemporary United States, enthusiasts for home schooling are overwhelmingly concerned to keep their children at home in order to indoctrinate them in creationism or some other quirk of fundamentalist Protestantism; they are not natural allies of Mill. It is a matter for regret that commentators have been so eager to assimilate Mill's ideas to those of mainstream twentieth-century liberalism that they have not seen what a very awkward ally of twentieth-century liberals he is.

The same cross-purposes have been visible in much subsequent commentary on Mill's defense of an almost absolute freedom of speech. Characteristically, attention has been divided between two different modern concerns.

On the one hand, Mill's insistence that such a freedom is the best route to the discovery of the truth has been subjected to some anxious scrutiny in light of a more skeptical view of the lessons of the history of science, while on the other, his view that speech is intrinsically not a source of harm to others has been scrutinized equally anxiously in the light of American First Amendment jurisprudence and both British and American obscenity law. What emerges most clearly, however, is that Mill's concern with truth has more to do with religious "truth" than scientific truth, and that he had almost nothing to say about indecency and nothing at all to say about pornography. Mill's arguments are interesting just because his concerns were so unlike the concerns of recent theorists.

It is perhaps more surprising that Mill has not only little or nothing to say about sexual freedom, but also nothing to say about the concept of privacy, the basis of most modern arguments. This is, I think, a real defect in his treatment of the subject. For one thing, it is because we mind so much about privacy and about the near sanctity of intimate relationships that we flinch from Mill's insistence that society should impose financial requirements on people intending to marry and have children. Again, many of us would think that the same considerations were a powerful argument for abolishing penal laws against homosexuality—and that even if some harm were to be done by their abolition, the argument that their enforcement was an outrage against privacy would be a powerful argument in the other direction. For Mill's own purposes, a simpler case sufficed. He drew a distinction that good sense requires, between arguments from decency and arguments from harm, and left it at that. The distinction is simple enough and best illustrated by an imaginary example. A married couple having sexual intercourse in Piccadilly Circus in broad daylight engage in an indecent act, but not one that violates any obligation they owe to each other. Conversely, an adulterous liaison may be objectionable because it violates the trust that the injured spouses had placed in their errant partners, but if conducted discreetly, it could not be condemned as indecent. Decency is essentially a matter of not obtruding offensive displays upon others. A moment's thought about our insistence on the privacy of defecation shows plainly how often decency is concerned not with the *moral* content of acts that nobody has ever suggested are immoral in themselves, but with the fact that they would be indecent if done obtrusively in public:

> Again, there are many acts which, being directly injurious only to the agents themselves, ought not to be legally interdicted, but which, if done publicly, are a violation of good manners, and coming thus within the category of offences against others, may rightfully be prohibited. Of this kind are offences against decency; on which it is unnecessary to dwell, the rather as they are only connected indirectly with our subject, the objection to publicity being equally strong in the case of many actions not in themselves condemnable, nor supposed to be so. (*On Liberty*, CW 18:296)

One might regret that Mill so cavalierly waves away arguments about decency, but he had other fish to fry. Most of Mill's argument about freedom of thought and speech had two aims. The first was to establish that freedom was an essential condition for discovering truth; the second was to elaborate an account of what sort of truth he had in mind. Much of the argument was negative, in the sense that it was devoted to repudiating familiar arguments against freedom. Thus, Mill denied that the defense of free speech amounted to the acceptance of the war of all against all; he thought himself entitled to the conventional distinction between mere speech and incitement, as in his famous claim that we must be free to publish the opinion that corn dealers are thieves but not to put it on a placard and wave it at an angry mob outside a corn dealer's house: "An opinion that corn-dealers are starvers of the poor, or that private property is robbery, ought to be unmolested when simply circulated through the press, but may justly incur punishment when delivered orally to an excited mob assembled before the house of a corn-dealer, or when handed about among the same mob in the form of a placard" (*On Liberty*, CW 18:260). Some critics have affected not to see the point, but a brief consideration of the abolition of slavery enforces it well enough. Slave owners ought not to own slaves: their property is simply illicit. Nonetheless, private citizens ought to try to abolish slavery by peaceful means if at all possible. John Brown was rightly hanged for murder, even though slavery was an atrocity and he was an abolitionist.

More interestingly, at least in the sense that his seeming espousal of a "proto-Popperian" position was in some tension with his usual inductivist views, Mill argued that truth was internally related to controvertibility. The only ground we have for believing in the truth of what we believe is that it has been or can be exposed to attempted refutation and that it has survived or will survive it. To believe something, properly speaking, is to understand what would controvert one's belief in it and to have confidence in that belief's ability to withstand test. This appears to be Mill in proto-Popperian mode rather than Mill the inductivist. Yet even here, Mill's interest did not lie where Popper's lay. Mill did not offer an empirical claim to the effect that scientific progress depends on an intellectual regime of "conjecture and refutation."[13] What he put forward was a strongly normative conception of belief that entailed, among other things, that most of what we describe as our "beliefs" are not so much "believed" as acquiesced in. Much the greater part of Mill's chapter on freedom of thought was concerned with religion; as this might suggest, Mill's concern was with strong conviction and lively belief, and much of his argument was an argument for trying to maximize the liveliness of our beliefs. A mere recording machine could pick up and reiterate the ideas of others, and might by coincidence reiterate the truth; a human mind might do much more (*On Liberty*, CW 18:245). The question how far Mill's conception of the self allowed him to appeal as unselfconsciously as he did to the importance of making our beliefs "our own" is a difficult and underexplored one, but that is what animates his argument. It is one of many arguments in the essay that rests upon a "positive" conception of liberty.[14] Mental freedom is a form of positive possession of our ideas.

The argument is plainly more persuasive when applied to moral and religious beliefs than when applied to scientific ideas. This is yet another field in which Mill's argument was directed not toward our anxieties but toward his own. We have become used to the arguments of T. S. Kuhn (1962) and Paul Feyerabend (1975), who have claimed that scientific truth is established in a more coercive and nonconsensual fashion than previous philosophers of science supposed. So far from making bold conjectures and accepting painful refutations, scientists habitually preserve orthodoxies and run dissenters out of the lab.[15] But Mill was not interested in what made science "special," nor in discussing the difference between establishing low-level facts and high-level theories. He was interested in the degree of conviction with which people held their beliefs about the ends of life. Unless they were in the habit of arguing for their views, they were not in full command of them: "However unwillingly a person who has a strong opinion may admit the possibility that his opinion may be false, he ought to be moved by the consideration that however true it may be, if it is not fully, frequently, and fearlessly discussed, it will be held as a dead dogma, not a living truth" (On Liberty, CW 18:245).

When we turn to the argument for freedom of action in the forming of our own plans of life, the considerations Mill adduces remain within the same framework. In part, Mill was concerned to deny that society was in the condition of an armed camp where everyone must devote all their efforts to the well-being of their fellow creatures. There were emergency situations in which individual claims to freedom had to be more or less denied, but everyday life was not such a situation. A man on sentry duty might be shot for falling asleep; in everyday life, we may choose our own bedtimes. A sentry might be shot for drunkenness on watch; in everyday life, we may generally drink as we like. The rationale for the distinction is the familiar one; we are answerable for the predictable harm we cause others: "No person ought to be punished simply for being drunk; but a soldier or a policeman should be punished for being drunk on duty. Whenever, in short, there is definite damage, or a definite risk of damage, either to an individual or to the public, the case is taken out of the province of liberty, and placed in that of morality or law" (On Liberty, CW 18:281).

Mill was particularly concerned to deny that a proper concern for the moral welfare of our fellows must take the form of censoring their thoughts and inclinations. This is a feature of his argument that has received less attention than it deserves. He drew a very careful distinction between coercive and uncoercive means of altering other people's behavior, and was anxious to insist that where coercion was illicit, noncoercive measures might well be appropriate. Mill knew that he was vulnerable to the objection that On Liberty put forward a doctrine of ethical laissez-faire that encouraged pure self-centeredness and an unconcern with the well-being of others—and he duly denied in several places that he was doing anything of the sort.

> It would be a great misunderstanding of this doctrine to suppose that it is one of selfish indifference, which pretends that human beings have no business with each other's conduct in life, and that they should not concern themselves about the well-doing or well-being of one another, unless their own interest is involved. Instead of any diminution, there is need of a great increase of disinterested exertion to promote the good of others. (*On Liberty*, CW 18:276).

He was eager to point out that it was absurd to suppose that the choice lay between indifference on the one hand and force on the other: "But disinterested benevolence can find other instruments to persuade people to their good, than whips and scourges, either of the literal or the metaphorical sort" (276). This is an echo of Locke's sardonic observation in his *Letter on Toleration* that we can concern ourselves with other people's spiritual welfare without throwing them in jail or burning them at the stake.

Mill argued that we must think of ways of noncoercively encouraging other people's highest aspirations, carefully distinguishing between even the most strenuous exhortation on the one hand and punishment on the other; we may, and we should, tell other people exactly what we think of their behavior in matters that reflect on their character. If we deplore their drinking, we should say so. If we think their literary tastes are vulgar, we should say so. Ordinary standards of politeness militate against this, but so much the worse for ordinary notions of politeness.

> Though doing no wrong to any one, a person may so act as to compel us to judge him, and feel to him, as a fool, or as a being of an inferior order: and since this judgment and feeling are a fact which he would prefer to avoid, it is doing him a service to warn him of it beforehand, as of any other disagreeable consequence to which he exposes himself. It would be well, indeed, if this good office were much more freely rendered than the common notions of politeness at present permit, and if one person could honestly point out to another that he thinks him in fault, without being considered unmannerly or presuming. (*On Liberty*, CW 18:277).

Himmelfarb (1974, 49–51) quite rightly notices that Mill himself was quicker to object to other people taking a nonpunitive interest in his conduct than this passage supposes he ought to have been. But this does not in itself impugn the distinction. Punishment involved penalties that were organized either overtly and institutionally by the legal system, or covertly and unconsciously by the operations of a censorious and collective public opinion. Penalties were intended as threats before the event and as retribution after; they involved visiting their target with evil.

Mill's contemporaries were puzzled by his insistence on the difference between penalties strictly speaking and the accidental misfortunes that might befall us as a result of differences in taste. To Mill, it was of the greatest importance because he saw moral coercion as the opinion-based shadow or background of legal coercion. In a democratic society, even in the absence of a democratic political system, public opinion was an organized force. Mill absorbed Tocqueville's conviction that what made the force so impressive was its silent and unobtrusive quality (Mill, *On Liberty*, CW 18:219; Tocqueville 1994, 1:264)); whereas physical penalties aroused resistance in the person punished, the penalties of opinion worked in his soul. He might, indeed, become his own mental jailer.

Mill's argument in *On Liberty* was deliberately repetitive. He was laying siege to a frame of mind that he thought permeated English society, and he set about driving it from one position after another. He also believed that few people had thought about the problems he identified, and thus that it was particularly difficult to make the argument he wished to make (Mill, *On Liberty*, CW 18:226). This was not always in the interest of extending freedom. It was sometimes, and quite startlingly, in the interest of restricting it. Too few critics attend to the fact that Mill was not attacking only the habit of interfering with harmless conduct. He was equally concerned to attack the absence of rational and publicly understood principle that allowed harmful conduct to flourish unchecked while harmless conduct was repressed. "I have already observed that, owing to the absence of any recognised general principles, liberty is often granted where it should be withheld, as well as withheld where it should be granted," wrote Mill (*On Liberty*, CW 18:302–4) in the context of his claim that society took too little interest in the improvidence and fecklessness with which young people contracted marriage and brought children into the world without having any idea how they were to be reared and educated. His argument was squarely in line with the basic principles underlying *On Liberty*; to produce children who could not be brought up properly was a double offense, once against the wretched children, and second against society at large:

> It still remains unrecognised, that to bring a child into existence without a fair prospect of being able, not only to provide food for its body, but instruction and training for its mind, is a moral crime, both against the unfortunate offspring and against society; and that if the parent does not fulfil this obligation, the State ought to see it fulfilled, at the charge, as far as possible, of the parent. (302)

To throw unproductive extra bodies onto the labor market was an antisocial act.

Mill's unconcern with twentieth-century anxieties about privacy and intimacy is a striking feature of his bleakly high-principled acceptance of restrictions on marriage as well as on parents' rights over their children.

> To undertake this responsibility—to bestow a life which may be either a curse or a blessing—unless the being on whom it is to be bestowed will have at least the ordinary chances of a desirable existence, is a crime against that being. And in a country either over-peopled or threatened with being so, to produce children, be-

yond a very small number, with the effect of reducing the reward of labour by their competition, is a serious offence against all who live by the remuneration of their labour. The laws which, in many countries on the Continent, forbid marriage unless the parties can show that they have the means of supporting a family, do not exceed the legitimate powers of the State: and whether such laws be expedient or not (a question mainly dependent on local circumstances and feelings), they are not objectionable as violations of liberty. (*On Liberty*, CW 18:304)

Mill was perhaps unwise to make so few concessions to the popular feeling that even where there are good prudential reasons not to marry, the impulsiveness of youth must be given some leeway. It appears to be an emotional blind spot that led him to pay so little attention to the more elaborate sentiment that intimate relationships are so valuable that we should make more room for them than narrowly prudential arguments can provide. At all events, it may have been such austere moments that gave him his reputation as an "intellectual iceberg."

The concluding chapter of "applications" added little to the argument of *On Liberty* in the narrow sense, but much to one's sense of what Mill was after. He faced difficulties familiar to later generations. One awkward question was whether it was right to prevent people getting together to do collectively what they had an individual right to do. Running a brothel would be an example: fornication is not illegal or to be repressed by the collective censoriousness that he described as the "penalties of opinion," but one might wish to prevent people living off immoral earnings or trading in sexual services. The same thought applies to gambling houses; one might not object to individuals getting together in an informal fashion to gamble, but still fear the effects of gambling dens (*On Liberty*, CW 18:296). Mill's approach generally concentrated on detaching genuine offenses from their nonpunishable causes. A man who gambled away his family's housekeeping money was to be blamed and, if necessary, forced to look after his family; but he ought not to be treated worse than if he had spent the housekeeping money on failed attempts to invent electric lighting. Still, Mill also understood the problem of attractive nuisances, and he hesitated to put his name to the principle that what a person is allowed to do another person must be allowed to advise him to do (296).

Mill also reminded his readers of a view that he made rather more of in his *Principles of Political Economy* and *Representative Government*. There he argued that just as private individuals may exhort and encourage where they may not coerce, so governments may take a position on matters where they may neither forbid nor require any particular line of conduct. Moreover, governments may act on such views when they consider how to distribute the burden of taxation. Mill was ferociously opposed to temperance agitation, partly because temperance reformers claimed that drinkers violated their "social rights," and Mill thought the appeal to social rights tyrannical. Yet he was ready to agree that while governments were not entitled to tax alcoholic drink at a level designed to stop its consumption, they were entitled to put a tax on alcoholic drink rather than on tea or bread; supposing the tax to be necessary at all, its incidence would be less damaging if it fell on drink than if it fell on tea or bread (*On Liberty*, CW 18:297).

The Tyranny of the Majority

The question at whom and at what Mill aimed the weapons of *On Liberty* has partially been answered by this sketch of the argument. There were several distinct targets of his attack, and a brief list may fix our thoughts. At its vaguest but most encompassing, the target was the mid-Victorian middle-class conception of respectability and the stifling effect it had on individuals whose lives were circumscribed by its demands. Mill and Harriet Taylor were, in their own eyes, victims of its effects. Mill sometimes suggested that England was uniquely blighted by this, as it were, mass fear of and mass imposition of public disapproval of the unusual. To Pasquale Villari, he wrote that his essay "n'a guère de valoir que pour l'Angleterre" ("has little value except for England"; *Later Letters*, CW 10:550).[16] This was hardly his considered view, but he was convinced that Italy and France were less socially repressive even when they were more politically repressive than Britain.

The largest target was the democratic disposition of mind deplored by Tocqueville in *Democracy in America*. To the extent that Tocqueville had been an accurate observer of opinion in the United States and a not absurdly overanxious spectator of the march of democracy in France, Mill's essay must have had some purchase both in France and in the United States as well as in England. The democratic frame of mind was an elusive prey, but exceedingly important to Mill. The distinction between true and false democracy was one that he continually recast; by the time of *On Liberty*, the most salient distinction lay between genuine self-government and the tyranny of the majority. Self-government certainly embraced most of the goals that professed democrats sought, including a chance for the ordinary person to exercise an influence on government by way of the ballot box and other devices; but for Mill, it also had to embrace such character-improving devices as the requirement that everyone must play some part in actively managing the affairs of his or her own community, whether in jury service or serving on parish councils or in some novel way (*Representative Government*, CW 19:411–12).

The more urgent point, however, was to escape the tyranny of the majority. Following Tocqueville, Mill thought that the everyday understanding of democracy was insufficiently attentive to the difference between ruling oneself and being dominated by everyone else. It had been one of Mill's complaints against Bentham years before that Bentham had failed to make this necessary distinction; Mill agreed that it was progress to curtail the unbridled power of the former ruling classes, but it was not much progress if all it did was give unchecked power to "the majority" ("Bentham," *CW* 10:106–8). What one might call the democratic frame of mind was the belief that there was something special about the opinion of the majority once the majority had settled on it, something over and above the mere fact that it happened to be the opinion of more than half the people in question. This majoritarian superstition was a peculiarly American vice, but it had more than a little in common with the passion for respectability that drove the English middle classes. That is, both were examples of the habit of thinking that if "everyone" believed something or other, it was faintly improper for an individual to doubt it.

Although there is little solid evidence to rest such a case on, it is not implausible to think that the passion with which Mill wrote *On Liberty* owed much to his antipathy to this deadly conjunction of the forces of respectability and the inevitable march of democracy. Paradoxically, the antiliberal pressure of public opinion was increased by a factor that one might have thought would work in the opposite direction. Mill was almost as depressed by his contemporaries' inability to recognize intellectual authority where it was appropriate as by their readiness to defer to mere feelings that were not entitled to authority at all. It was the honor of the ordinary man that he could be led to embrace great things with his eyes open (*On Liberty*, *CW* 18:268). Nonetheless, he had to be led. He could not do all the work of self-development himself. Mill distinguished as sharply as he knew how between the pressure of the "likings and dislikings" of mass opinion and the persuasive force of insights and arguments that could sustain a rational scrutiny and a dispassionate assessment. One must not exaggerate the role of *rational* assessment in the acceptance of the insights generated by the outstanding individuals on whom Mill relied; to the extent that Mill had poets and social critics such as Goethe or Wordsworth in mind, some of their authority had to be ascribed to the *affective* force of their insights. The point remains that Mill passionately wished his countrymen to acknowledge *some* form of intellectual, moral, and spiritual authority, one they could acknowledge freely and intelligently; if they were to do so, they had to also understand how different such an acknowledgment was from mere subservience to social pressure (267–68).

Behind this thought lay Mill's lifelong complaint against the influence of intuitionist philosophy. Intuitionism in any form was committed to the claim that indubitability was the mark of truth and that there were many truths about the world, both scientific and ethical, that we knew because when we scrutinized them, we were convinced that they *could not be* false. Mill was never particularly careful to make the intuitionist case as plausible as it might be made, but he understood well enough that intuitionism did not set out to guarantee large numbers of particular truths by appealing to their indubitability. The object of intuitionism was to guarantee principles and generalizations, such as the principle that every event has a cause, or the law of the conservation of matter, or the priority of the right over the good. Mill thought the doctrine was superstitious in whatever form it was presented. It was, he said, the great support of conservative doctrines and attitudes, and encouraged people to believe that any conviction that they held sufficiently strongly was warranted (*Autobiography*, CW 1:270). Since people were all too inclined to swallow whatever local orthodoxy they encountered and to regard it as revealed truth, the object of philosophy ought to be to unsettle this passion for certainty rather than to pander to it.

The difficulty that faced the would-be unsettler was not only that people find challenges to their ideas more or less painful, but also that many people had been taught not to obtrude their own ideas upon others. This was where Mill's antipathy to Christian ethics became significant. It was not that he wished to destroy the existing clergy and replace them with a Coleridgean "clerisy." He did hope for the growth of a Coleridgean clerisy, but he had little anticlerical animus. Nor was Mill eager to see Christianity as a social force in British life destroyed before it had been improved; in France, he thought, it was too late to rescue Christianity from the damage done to it by both the church and the anticlerical, but in Britain, it was possible to revive it. Nonetheless, *On Liberty* was more committed than were Mill's more conciliatory discussions of Christianity to reducing the influence of the Calvinist view of the self.

The target of Mill's assault was self-abnegation (*On Liberty*, CW 18:254). He contrasted Christian self-abnegation with pagan self-assertion, the latter being a force capable of working great evil but also of doing great good. "Pagan" was perhaps two sweeping a category; neither Plato nor Aristotle were theorists of the will to power, and the Stoic doctrine of *apatheia* taught something very like self-abnegation as the route to freedom. Mill, of course, was mostly concerned to attack the effects of Calvinism; it, he thought, had rendered its adherents timid, fearful of their own desires, and unambitious. Critics have, quite rightly, complained that Mill's association of Calvinism with weakness of will does an injustice to the many striking conjunctions of Calvinist allegiance and stiff-necked intransigence that we find both in fact and in fiction. Mill is not wholly without resources in his own defense, for it is certainly true that Calvinism denounced "self-will," and its characteristic view of education was that the first step was to break the child's willful ways. Even John Locke's relatively benign and "child-centered" views on education insist that the beginnings of instruction lie in breaking the child's will. In any event, one can forgive Mill for following Machiavelli in praising "pagan self-assertion" to the detriment of the Christian ideal of self-abnegation. In gross, at any rate, that contrast holds up perfectly well.

We can now begin to see why *On Liberty* seemed to so many readers to be a root-and-branch assault on the English society of its day. For the truth is that it was such. Protestant self-abnegation was a poor foundation for Humboldtian *Bildung*; questioning received opinion was not something that came naturally to people brought up on middle-class Protestantism. The peculiarly English conviction that skepticism was both wicked and unrespectable was likely to deaden such flickerings of independence as might occur. If they were then further stifled by the prevalence of intuitionist ideas about the irrefutability of commonplace moral and political convictions, the prospects for intellectual and cultural independence were slender indeed. As if this were not enough, Mill knew that there were many reasons of a wholly unsuperstitious kind why individuality would be hard to preserve in an industrial society. Such a society required more complicated forms of cooperation and collaboration than its agrarian predecessors; people would live closer and closer together, and therefore would have to be more careful of one another's interests. In sewerage, lighting, transport, and much else, they would need to make collective provision for their needs. Society would thus have to become more *organized*, more of a consciously organic whole. If this were not to bring on the tyranny of the majority—or the tyranny of the benevolent, bourgeois, and bureaucratic Fabians or Comtists—a different social psychology would have to prevail. This could be built only on a positive enthusiasm for variety, eccentricity, novelty, strenuousness, and self-overcoming. These were virtues more obviously at home in the writings of Goethe, whose work he knew well, and Nietzsche, whose work he never encountered, than in those of Bentham and James Mill.

Perfectionism

The view I ascribe to Mill is, evidently, a view of liberty that is teleological, consequentialist, and genuinely, though awkwardly, utilitarian. It falls, because of its attention to the ideal perfection of individual character, within the class of what are today called perfectionist theories, even though Mill's contemporaries would have noticed that Mill had stolen the clothes of the antiutilitarian moral theorists of his day in arguing so emphatically that a concern for individual perfection was a utilitarian concern. Being comprehensive, teleological, and even ambiguously perfectionist, it stands in sharp contrast to later contractualist theories, such as that offered by both of John Rawls's accounts of the basis of a liberal society. Less obviously, it is also at odds, though less simply as well as less obviously, with the pluralist liberalism of Isaiah Berlin's *Two Concepts of Liberty* (1958), and, for that matter, with the Idealist liberalism of T. H. Green (1886) and the pragmatist liberalism of John Dewey (1935). Now that we are tolerably clear about what Mill believed, it is easier to understand why *On Liberty* relates so awkwardly to its successors. What follows is not a comprehensive account of Mill's later admirers, critics, and rivals, but an attempt to extract particular points of contrast for our more local purposes. I begin with the contrast between Mill and Rawls, since this is so striking, then say something about the role of pluralism in Mill's work, then say a little more about the communitarian and anticommunitarian aspects of his liberalism in order to sharpen our sense of how Mill's ideas were and were not assimilable within the Idealist-pragmatist tradition.

The contrast between Mill's defense of liberalism and John Rawls's rests on what is now a commonplace, though the implications of that commonplace for discussions of liberalism are perhaps less well understood. Rawls has insisted, particularly in his recent *Political Liberalism*, that liberals must not try to impose a "comprehensive moral doctrine" on their society, but only to establish terms on which persons who hold a plurality of different comprehensive views can live with one another (1993, xvi–xvii, 154–57). The reasoning behind this fastidiousness is complicated but persuasive. In part, it rests on the plausible thought that social stability is easier to achieve if we do not thrust contentious moral and religious ideals upon people unwilling to receive them. It is a central element in Rawls's liberalism that the "strains of commitment" should not threaten the social order, and it seems obvious enough that we would feel less committed to a social order that espouses moral values we disapprove of (xviii–xix, 134–44). In part, however, it rests on a moral value that goes to the heart of Rawls's view of the basis of liberal politics. This is the idea of the inviolability of the individual.[17] An important element of that inviolability is the inviolability of the individual conscience. Such considerations give each person a right not to live under institutional arrangements that violate his or her conscience. A constraint on anyone claiming such a right is that their conscience must not be so "unreasonable" that they impose unfair burdens on others; the difficulty—perhaps greater in theory than in practice—is to give an account of what it is to have "reasonable" conscientious scruples on which secular liberals, secular conservatives, religious conservatives, and religious liberals can agree.[18] This, however, is one of the things that a constant attention to fairness may cope with, although my own belief is that it will not, and that the ground of consensus must be sought for in a prior agreement on the facts of social life and the consequences of change, rather than in a principled abstention from taking them into account.

The details of Rawls's developed theory are not our concern. The contrast with Mill is. Rawls begins with a conception of society as *essentially* a contractual arrangement between individuals; the considerations on which we have just focused reflect the view that society is, for purposes of moral discussion, best understood as an agreement on terms by individuals concerned to preserve the central core of their interests. Almost all of Rawls's differences from Mill follow from Rawls's contractualist beginnings. So, for example, the "strains of commitment" interpreted as strains upon our consciences are not a simple sociological fact; people feel them only when they have a particular conception of themselves, one in which their conscientious scruples play an important part. It is arguable that late twentieth-century Americans have retained much of their seventeenth-century Puritan prickliness, and that this is therefore a proper starting point for an account of liberalism in the United States. Mill, on the contrary, thought that the problem in Victorian England was to rouse people to understand that their convictions were something that they could revise in the light of the evidence and their other convictions. Individuals were under too little strain of commitment rather than too much. They either stood pat on the deliverances of conscience or took the majority opinion as they encountered it as definitive of what any rational person could believe.

Someone who resisted armchair sociological speculation of this sort might say that it is an obvious moral truth that we should start from some such principle as the inviolability of the individual conscience, no matter what the degree of local fastidiousness. But Mill would have resisted the claim that we should *start* with such a principle. This is not to deny that we should take the principle seriously; Mill took it very seriously. Yet we may still believe that it is not a foundational principle, but a derivative one. It is certainly a central element in liberal morality; but we should think of it as a principle that becomes increasingly important in the collective life of "man as a progressive being." Just as freedom becomes an essential element in the welfare of an individual with a strong sense of his or her own individuality and a commitment to self-development, so the passionate attachment to following our own consciences that is expressed in the claim of inviolability would spring up in a liberal society—though it might well spring up in others as well.[19]

Whether we begin from Mill's position or Rawls's makes a great difference to what one supposes the liberal project is, even though it makes less difference to how that project should be pursued. Rawls writes as though the liberal project is to create a society of individuals whose primary commitments are to their own private well-being, on the one hand, and to their own consciences on the other. Given that view of the opening situation, what liberalism must be "about" is the task of finding fair terms of social cooperation among individuals who are willing to respect others' rights on the condition that their own are equally respected (Rawls 1971, 3–7). It is not surprising that this results in the thought that justice is the first of all social virtues; nor is it surprising that the liberal commitment to freedom emerges as a branch of the liberal commitment to justice. This is why Ronald Dworkin (1981), explicitly explicating liberalism as understood by Rawls, explains liberalism in terms of the right to equal concern and respect. To Mill and his disciples, that must seem wrong. Certainly *some* freedoms will be protected by the attempt to secure justice; the utilitarian account of justice as concerned above all with security implies that freedom of movement, personal safety, and, no doubt, many freedoms of speech and association should be secured to individuals. But Mill's liberalism is centered on Mill's account of what freedom is and why it matters; and part of that argument is an argument against an excessive concern with security.

Rawls's subsequent account of the implications for international law of his theory of justice as fairness is worth glancing at for its implications for domestic politics. Rawls raises a question that Mill's notorious essay "A Few

Thoughts on Non-Intervention" (CW 21:109–24) had raised a hundred and thirty years before: when and on what grounds may an outside power violate the sovereignty of other nations? Rawls has recently argued that any society that does not violate the fundamental rights of its population should be immune to intervention from other societies for the sake of whatever economic, social, religious, or moral principles those other societies may have in mind. This is the natural counterpart to his insistence in *Political Liberalism* that social groups that do not violate the fundamental rights of their members are entitled to immunity within a single society. This provides the basis of what Rawls calls a "reasonable" pluralism. We are now faced with two possibilities. The first is that we can give a nonliberal account of fundamental rights: a just society is one in which no group attempts to impose its view of the world on any other, though everyone stands ready to aid persons whose fundamental rights are violated, either by members of their own or any other social group. The assumption would be that protection from assault, deliberate starvation, acute emotional deprivation, and so on are fundamental rights, but that nobody has a "right to be free." If they did, then it would, in principle, be possible for outsiders to police the groups to which they belong in order to make sure that that right had not been violated. The second possibility is that we explain fundamental rights in terms of liberal values and so give society at large the right to police constituent groups within our own society, and to police other societies where we can do it, in order to impose a liberal worldview. Rawls plainly wants to avoid the second position, but he may, in the process, have abandoned too much of what traditional liberalism seeks to achieve, for it looks as though the pluralism he accepts could embrace a society in which every cultural allegiance was to illiberal values so long as no group's members acted aggressively toward any other's and so long as members who wished to leave a particular group (or country) could do so. Whether such a situation would be stable over the long run is debatable; one might think that any group ready to allow its members to exit would adopt more liberal values over time or, conversely, that any group countenancing a thoroughgoing illiberalism would soon refuse to allow its members to exit freely. Whether it is a form of liberalism at all is also debatable.

Still, our concern is rather with what Mill's liberalism amounts to in contrast. It is an awkward consequence of Mill's consequentialism that *in principle* it licenses liberals to promote the growth of freedom by all means whatever. Mill himself denied that any society had a right to civilize another by brute force (*On Liberty*, CW 18:290), but it is not obvious why he thought so, nor that he was consistent in so thinking. What liberals want is the greatest possible expansion of the values of individuality, open-mindedness, and self-criticism; as a good consequentialist, Mill cannot escape the thought that we may contemplate coercive means to such an end. We may suppose that there are all sorts of good reasons for not trying to force liberation on unwilling adults. The case of India was offered as an explicit exception to the general rule against paternalism, in much the same spirit as Elizabethan England and the Russia of Peter the Great. Still, conservative religious groups such as the Hasidic Jews who follow the Lubavitcher Rebbe or the Amish farmers of Pennsylvania, who surely do no harm to anyone except (arguably) themselves and their children, may think that relying on Mill's judgment about when the rest of the human race has reached "the maturity of their faculties" (On Liberty, CW 18:224) is a dangerous business. Moreover, Mill's emphasis on protecting children from the neglect or ill treatment of their parents, together with his feminism, would give them reason to fear that they would be prevented from doing what they very much wish to do—that is, from isolating their children from the secular currents of the wider society. More interestingly, perhaps, they might find their marital relations held up to unkind scrutiny, too, since the considerations that suggest we should liberate children from their parents also suggest that we should curtail the authority of husbands over wives.

Mill expressly repudiated this view of the consequences of his doctrines. Writing of the Mormon practice of polygamy, he observed:

No one has a deeper disapprobation than I have of this Mormon institution; both for other reasons, and because, far from being in any way countenanced by the principle of liberty, it is a direct infraction of that principle, being a mere rivetting of the chains of one half of the community, and an emancipation of the other from reciprocity of obligation towards them. Still, it must be remembered that this relation is as much voluntary on the part of the women concerned in it, and who may be deemed the sufferers by it, as is the case with any other form of the marriage institution; and however surprising this fact may appear, it has its explanation in the common ideas and customs of the world, which teaching women to think marriage the one thing needful, make it intelligible that many a woman should prefer being one of several wives, to not being a wife at all. Other countries are not asked to recognise such unions, or release any portion of their inhabitants from their own laws on the score of Mormonite opinions. But when the dissentients have conceded to the hostile sentiments of others, far more than could justly be demanded; when they have left the countries to which their doctrines were unacceptable, and established themselves in a remote corner of the earth, which they have been the first to render habitable to human beings; it is difficult to see on what principles but those of tyranny they can be prevented from living there under what laws they please, provided they commit no aggression on other nations, and allow perfect freedom of departure to those who are dissatisfied with their ways. (On Liberty, CW 18:290)

That is about as unequivocal a statement of the noninterventionist view as one could wish. It is one that puts Mill squarely on the same side as the Rawls of Political Liberalism.

But Mill was not exactly of one mind. He opened the floodgates himself by remarking in so casual a fashion that until people are capable of improvement by rational discussion, they had better be dragged down the path of progress by Akhbar, Charlemagne, Elizabeth I, or Peter the Great—and doubtless by the East India Company (*On Liberty*, CW 18:224). He was eager to insist that in countries such as Britain and the United States, the time had long since arrived when everyone was to be presumed amenable to rational persuasion. Nonetheless, he was quite right to raise the possibility of what I have elsewhere called "compulsory liberation." The thought behind compulsory liberation is not that we ought to tour the world looking for people to emancipate, by brute force if necessary. Mill did not hold liberal-Kiplingesque views about the white man's burden being to rescue his fellow man from immemorial torpor. It was, rather, the thought that if we found ourselves for whatever reason in a position where we had to act, we should not flinch from forcing liberal values on those we could affect.

The positive argument for compulsory liberation is thus no more elaborate than the suggestion that if we *can* force people into the liberal fold, we may. For Rawls, and for liberals who think like him, the rights of individuals and peoples rule out such a suggestion from the beginning. In a utilitarian perspective, the question turns on the grounds, which were provided by Mill but not much addressed by him, for not engaging in intra- or international wars of cultural liberation. There are four that can be extracted from *On Liberty* without violence to the text and its spirit. The first is essentially prudential; the second is recognition of the importance of family and social loyalties; the third hinges on the good of *self*-development; the last on the (possibly) intrinsic value of variety and plurality. The first and second close the gap between Mill and Rawls on matters of practice while leaving them at odds over principle; the third closes both the principled and the practical gap between Mill and Idealists such as Green and pragmatists such as Dewey; the last raises some awkward questions about both Mill's liberalism and that of Isaiah Berlin.

Mill's position is that a government may espouse but not enforce what Rawls calls a comprehensive theory of the good life. The liberal view that I have so far ascribed to Mill amounts to the thought that it is a legitimate object of social policy to bring into existence as many autonomous, self-critical, public-spirited men and women as possible. There are two things to be noticed about this view. The first is that Mill treats governments as if they are individuals writ large; individuals can advocate moral visions without imposing them on others, and in Mill's eyes, governments can do so too. This view animates his distinction between the coercive and the educative roles of government in the discussion of governmental action in his *Principles of Political Economy* (CW 3:799–804). For all its merits, it may embody a mistake. One might say that governments are essentially the bearers of authority, so their advocacy cannot be on all fours with that of individuals. Their resources, too, are greater than those of any individual; they must be tempted, as individuals are not, to employ increased resources to bear down opposition or disbelief. (In some contexts, such as that of the contemporary United States, of course, the argument would run in the other direction—that government is so unpopular, and its agents have so little moral authority, that they would do better not to espouse any particular good cause lest they give it the kiss of death.)

It might be said, in the spirit of Robert Nozick's *Anarchy, State, and Utopia*, that governments do not own the resources they employ in the way individuals do; if I choose to spend my money on publishing views that others do not share, that is my business, but because a government's resources are really the taxpayers' resources, governmental action is more like my spending your money to advocate views that I hold and you detest. This last point Mill would have had little difficulty with. That governments drew upon the labor of their subjects he acknowledged; that their subjects had a natural proprietorship over their incomes and resources of the kind this argument presupposes, he denied. The previous objections he seemed not to consider with the seriousness they deserved.

If Mill regarded governments as endowed with the same right to press a moral case as anyone else, he also saw that there were many reasons for them to tread very gently. For one thing, Mill was well aware that governments are intrinsically clumsy. Where individuals might cajole, charm, seduce, and woo others into an acceptance of a new worldview, governments were all too likely to arouse their resentment and antagonism. As Mill tartly observed, one argument against the public enforcement of *any* moral view was that when governments interfered in private life, they were overwhelmingly likely to do so in the wrong place (*On Liberty*, CW 18:283). This would be one prudential argument against unrestricted interference. All the same, Mill's view was not Rawls's. Rawls's *Political Liberalism* proposes that liberals should reassure the devout that they will not be put under pressure, but Mill merely proposes that liberal governments should act delicately.

Consider an example where the difference between them might make a difference. The famous U.S. Supreme Court decision in *Wisconsin v. Yoder* (1972) established that the Amish were exempt from the requirement to send their children to school beyond the eighth grade. One view of this decision might be that it was rightly decided as the result of a "balancing act" between different policy considerations. A society that values religious commitment *and* an educated work force may have to trade one against the other; in this case, however, the Supreme Court rightly held that the Amish were unlikely to let their children become unemployed, whatever their acquaintance with formal education, and that the balance thus tilted toward allowing the Amish to withdraw their children from school at fourteen. One can imagine Mill agreeing: truth aside, passionate religious conviction is valuable and deserves protection. Family ties deserve some consideration, too, and governments ought not to interfere where all members of a family appear to be in agreement. Once again, this is not Rawls's view. Rawls's grounds for agreeing with the Court rest on the idea that an insistence on children being educated to the age of sixteen imposes a comprehensive secular liberal view of the good life on a group that does not share it.

But one might think—and Mill might have thought—that the case was wrongly decided. On one liberal understanding of the interests of the child in this case, it was a violation of the interests of the child to allow the parents to withdraw him from school. The child's interests "as a progressive being" lay in preserving an open mind until the end of adolescence. If the Amish cannot preserve their hold over their young people without preventing them from learning whatever an American high school might teach them after the age of fourteen, they have no business trying to preserve their way of life at all. The crucial question is not the rights of the parents, but the interests of the child. Quite what follows then is obscure. On one view, a Millian ought to be moved by the changes between nineteenth- and twentieth-century society to extend Mill's insistence on the duty of parents to fit their offspring for the society in which they will later live—and thus insist that young Yoder remain at school. On another, young Yoder's chief obligation in later life is to be self-supporting and not a drain on other people's resources, and his parents have done enough to ensure that he can do that. Had the boy wanted to go to school, his parents might have been made to let him do so. If not, not.

One might suppose that Mill's position ought to have been something like this: liberal consequentialism does not license attempts to bully Amish parents into changing their minds about their own lives. Any such attempt would surely be counterproductive, ineffective, and therefore pointless.[20] The adult Amish's beliefs harm only the adult Amish (if they are restrained from hobbling their children's acquaintance with the outside world), and this puts them squarely into the class of self-regarding actions that are protected from coercive interference. Children are another matter. They are, ex hypothesi, susceptible to something other than rational persuasion. They are, from the liberal perspective, to be protected against youthful indoctrination that makes them incapable of freedom as adults.

It is thus good liberal policy to insist that they go to school until sixteen, painful though that is for their parents. The principle that parents may not inhibit the development of freedom in their offspring has far-reaching consequences. Many of them are quite at odds with the practice of American governments and perhaps at odds with a principled adherence to the separation of church and state. A liberal government might insist that parochial and religious schools teach comparative religion alongside whatever particular faith animated their founders and the parents of the children they teach, in order that the children should at least know what the world has to offer. Since liberalism is distinguished from other comprehensive views by its attachment to criticism, there can be no question of protecting *it* from criticism in such classes, but the classes themselves would be justified as a means of allowing children to decide for themselves when they reach the age of reason what view of the world to adopt.

Given the resistance such policies would surely arouse, it is easy to see how Mill and Rawls might end by advocating similar but not identical policies in practice. Mill's sensitivity to the imprudence of more than modestly aggressive policies to favor a liberal perspective would yield the same results as Rawls's principled forbearance. But there may be unaggressive possibilities that a Millian liberal would seize and a Rawlsian liberal would have to forgo. Consider the potentialities of a national broadcasting service, or the educational possibilities latent within a national health service. Mill's liberalism would encourage us to make the most of them; Rawls's view that the state ought to be neutral toward competing conceptions of the good life would apparently require us to forgo such opportunities.

A more principled argument against an energetic state frequently employed by Mill will lead us from Mill's differences with John Rawls to his differences with his Idealist and pragmatist successors. Mill suggests, in support of his "no coercion except in self-defense" rule, that it matters very much that we come to our mature view of ourselves by self-chosen paths. This means, among other things, that if, *per impossibile*, there were a pill that we could swallow in order to make ourselves good Millian liberals, we probably ought not to swallow it, and if we concluded that we ought to swallow it, we should do so with regret. This provides another reason for noncoercion when dealing with adults. We might go to the length of nagging couch potatoes—perhaps by airing public-service announcements during breaks in televised football games to suggest that they should engage in strenuous rethinking about their lives—but that is about it. The reason is not that individuals possess an inviolability that entitles them not to be badgered and harassed, but that one of the goods of the pursuit of individual autonomy is precisely that it is *our own* pursuit.

The fact that this yields a requirement of liberal self-restraint similar to that produced by the principle of individual inviolability may tempt some critics to think that this shows what others have said, that Mill relies much more heavily on a natural-rights view of liberty than he is willing to admit. The better gloss is that talk of rights is a shorthand; the deeper considerations are those of social prudence and individual self-development. "No coercion except in self-defense" summarizes the liberal's calculation of where the arguments for and against coercive liberation come down. To talk of rights, said Mill, was to talk of important interests, and an important individual interest that reinforces the prudential arguments for a restrained policy is an interest in self-development.

This suggests how Mill's liberalism relates to that of an Idealist like Green or a pragmatist like Dewey. Mill, Green, and Dewey held surprisingly similar views on individual development in spite of their very different metaphysical—or in Dewey's case antimetaphysical—convictions. I do not deny that Green thought of the self with which we ultimately identify as godlike or even God, nor that Dewey turned away from Green's moral philosophy in the early 1890s because Green separated the empirical selves of individuals too sharply from the Self that was the reality behind the universe as a whole.[21] I want only to emphasize the importance to all three of the idea that we become who we are by creating a self that we regard as "ours." It is because we want people to identify strongly with the views and aspirations that they think of as constituting their own identity that we mind that they arrive at their allegiances by an autonomous route. Unlike the prudential argument that coercion causes pain and resentment, or the "balancing" argument that asks us to set family and local loyalties in the scale against the value of liberty, this is a genuinely liberal argument for restraint in the pursuit of liberal goals.

Where Mill and later liberals of a Greenian or Deweyan stripe differ more sharply is in their understanding of the relations of individuals and their communities. Mill was, in several senses of the term, a "communitarian liberal." He thought social philosophy should begin by contemplating human beings not in a state of nature or behind a veil of ignorance, but immersed in their social setting. He shared neither the ontology of Hobbes and Locke nor the methodological convictions of Rawls. Mill had no doubt that it was an important truth that we grow up in communities of different kinds and form our ideas and ideals in the course of learning to live with others. He thought that most of us find it difficult to imagine ourselves outside the social settings in which we move; and he wanted to create a *society* of liberals, not a collection of liberal monads (*Utilitarianism*, CW 10:230; *On Liberty*, CW 18:220).[22] All this he shared with Green and Dewey, and with most people who have not acquired some strong theoretical reason for thinking differently.

Nonetheless, Mill was not a communitarian in at least two further ways, and these set him sharply apart from Green and Dewey. Because Mill was an empiricist and a naturalist, he thought of individuals as only partially socialized creatures. Idealists and pragmatists were disinclined to stress the way in which embodied beings like ourselves were to some degree at the mercy of psychophysiological forces over which we have limited, and quite slowly developed, authority. One might say that this was Mill's nontheological acknowledgment of the concept of original sin. In Green, the idea of original sin was replaced by his emphasis on the distance that remains between empirical selves and the universal self that is God; Dewey deplored any talk of original sin whatever. While Mill did not believe in the theology of original sin, he believed in a good deal of the psychology and sociology it implied. But not all our unsocial and unsocialized promptings were to be treated with caution. Many were beneficial. We might light on new visions of the world and new ideals of human happiness. Once these visions were understood, they could be imparted to our fellows with some hope of acceptance by them. Until then, however, we might have to stand by them at the price of social isolation. Mill thus wanted to encourage a degree of separation from our social attachments to which Dewey and Green would have been hostile. I have always thought Mill was right and they were wrong.

When assessing the merits of one or another interpretation of liberalism, we inevitably balance different liberal aspirations against each other. Which liberalism we find most congenial is a matter of emphasizing one aspiration rather than another. It is time to take account of one last aspiration. Mill dedicates *On Liberty* to "the absolute and essential importance of human development in its richest diversity" (CW 18:215; see note 8 to this chapter). It is thus a treatise on a form of pluralism. Yet Mill was quite clear that ways of life had no right to exist unmolested simply because they added variety to the human landscape. The British were not invited into India, but the East India Company's government of India had transformed Indian life very drastically, and Mill justified this intervention as a means of development (*Memorandum of the Improvements in the Administration of India during the Last Thirty Years*, CW 30:91–160). Mill was not in the usual sense an imperialist. He had no particular enthusiasm for imperial projects and thought that once the British had given the Indian subcontinent the tools of self-government, their next task was to go home and leave the Indians to work out their own destiny. Still, Mill had no doubt that until that time arrived, the East India Company was acting in the best interests of the Indian people and ought to continue doing so. There was little room in Mill's mind for the thought that what he saw as the superstitious, indolent, and intermittently violent life of the Indian subcontinent was to be enjoyed as one more variant on the theme of a diverse and contradictory human nature. Comparison with one distinguished twentieth-century pluralist, Isaiah Berlin, may sharpen the point. Berlin is a moral pluralist, and one of the grounds he offers for placing a high value on negative liberty is that there are many different acceptable ways of life, and negative liberty allows them to coexist. Mill, in contrast, was committed to the view that there is, in principle, a "right answer" to every moral question; since the British knew what the Indians did not, and were in a position to make the right answer stick, they had better do so.

This is a very different outlook from that which holds that one community has no right to civilize another against its will, which was set out by Kant (1970). But it is also at odds with the principle of no coercion except in self-defense, a principle that has sometimes been taken as coextensive with Mill's "very simple principle." But "no coercion except in self-defense" is not identical with "no coercion except to prevent harm to others"; the first places a constraint on *who* may engage in coercion that the second does not. The first implies that a fitting reply to the suggestion that the British might properly try to teach nineteenth-century Indians how to become good Victorian liberals would be that it was none of their business, since the Indians were doing the *British* no harm. The second is less restrictive; if we thought that the Indians were doing "harm" to their children, their neighbors, or whomever else, we might decide it was our business—that is, that it was the business of anyone who could act to prevent the harm in question. A direct appeal to the utilitarian backing of the entire essay is even less restrictive; Mill was clear enough that paternalism was justified *if* the facts warranted it. The anxiety that the moral hyperactivism implicit in utilitarianism induces in many critics is only exacerbated by the suggestion that "we"—whoever "we" are—occupy a morally privileged position from whose height we can decide the fate of the less privileged. Obviously, one form of pluralism is sustained by the counterclaim that there are no right answers in ethics and that nobody can occupy that privileged position by virtue of having that answer.

To a degree, Mill weakened the force of the claim that there were right answers to moral problems by suggesting that even though the "right answer" was right for utilitarian reasons, it was delivered by the judgment of a suitably sensitive critic, and not by any very simple utilitarian algorithm (*Utilitarianism*, CW 10:211). This might imply that there could be several incompatible "right answers" to a given question, an idea not as odd as it sounds: the paintings of Monet and Cézanne provide right but different answers to the question of how to render a landscape for late nineteenth-century sensibilities. If one thinks of ultimate moral questions as having much in common with, and perhaps even as being identical with, aesthetic questions about the shape of a life, it is not foolish to think that discussion of the ends of life will result in plural answers.

Pluralism and liberalism—at any rate, some liberalisms—are thus awkward allies. One form of pluralism, indeed, is consistent with thoroughgoing illiberalism, namely, the form in which an overarching, unconstitutional, undemocratic, and anything-but-liberal political authority allows specified social groups to handle the affairs of their own members. The Ottoman Empire was not a liberal enterprise, but operated after such a fashion. Another form is liberal in the sense that it amounts to the creation of a peace treaty between groups in order to give each group the freedom to conduct its life as it chooses; but the establishment of a peace treaty does not secure the prevalence of liberal values outside anything other than the political realm, nor does it secure to group members more freedom than their group cares to grant. A pluralism of this kind might be consistent with the Roman Catholic Church being able to visit heretics with sanctions, perhaps to deprive them of their livelihoods, so long as the church does not attempt to control the lives of non-Catholics and does not prevent members from leaving the church. The Dutch state is more liberal than most, yet it financially aids Catholic universities that can dismiss theologians whose doctrines they dislike.

Such a peace treaty presupposes a liberal state in the background, since that allows members of the church to leave without suffering civil disabilities. A theocratic state, as opposed to a liberal state, might tolerate more diversity than we would suppose likely, but would not offer legal guarantees of this kind. One view of the transformation of the Catholic Church in the

United States is that it has been forced to become more liberal, and to be more liberal than it is elsewhere, precisely because its members are guaranteed an unsanctioned exit. The theory put forward in John Rawls's *Political Liberalism* is liberal in this fashion; the requirement that groups do not violate the human rights of their members constrains the authority any group can exercise over its members. But the theory is not comprehensively liberal; there is no suggestion that the group should be urged or encouraged to adopt liberal conceptions of authority or liberal arrangements for its internal government. Catholics may not chase after their departed members to do them ill, but they may violate equal opportunity in recruiting for the priesthood and impose burdens that liberals would disapprove of: they are not obliged to accept women as candidates for the priesthood, and they can impose the requirement of celibacy.

The moment of truth for a pluralist comes when he is asked whether he is happy to see a great variety of nonliberal ways of life flourish for the sake of variety, or whether he really wishes to see only a variety of liberal ways of life, even if the result is less variety than there would be by admitting nonliberal ways of life. Mill ducked that question by insisting that as things stood, we had too much to lose by curtailing anything but grossly illiberal ways of life; we knew too little about what would, in the end, suit human beings to be justified in curbing all but the most approved liberal ways of life. Isaiah Berlin's liberalism causes his critics some difficulty because his pluralism is straightforward and his liberalism is therefore not; Berlin would rather see vivid, nonliberal ways of life flourish than see them suppressed for the sake of the spread of liberal principles. The question, then, is not whether there are nonliberal forms of moral and political pluralism, but whether liberalism entails pluralism at all and whether Mill believed that it did.

Mill thought it entailed one kind of pluralism, about which he and Berlin agree. We have no definitive, unchallengeable answer to the question of what the good life consists in, and we must allow experiment to winnow out the mistakes and refine the better answers. There is one kind of pluralism over which Mill and Berlin disagree. Mill thought that in the last resort a rational morality reduced to a single principle, and Berlin dissents. Berlin is, and Mill was not, an ethical pluralist. Berlin holds the commonsense view that freedom is one thing and happiness another; Mill argued that the search for freedom was a search for happiness.[23] What is left standing is two puzzles. The first is whether Mill thought that answers to the question "How shall we live?" would eventually converge and so eliminate diversity; the second is whether Mill thought that irrespective of the answer to that question, sheer variety was something to be valued for its own sake. We know that Berlin's answers to the two questions are no and yes—that answers to "How shall we live?" do not converge, and that variety is intrinsically worth preserving.

I do not know the answer to my question. It is possible that Mill was not of one mind about the answer; it is possible that he never put the questions to himself in quite the form I have given them, and so never confronted ambiguities in his own views; it is possible that he had a clear but complicated view and never found an occasion to spell it out. The difficulty it makes for his liberalism is simple enough to describe. Mill argues, against liberticide theorists like Comte, that we do not know enough about human well-being to warrant us in trumping individual choices except to prevent harm to others. This suggests that Mill may have thought that *if* we knew enough about human welfare, we might trump misguided choices on paternalist grounds, so that, in the end, science trumps liberty. But he might equally have thought that *if* we were ever to reach the point where that was a live possibility in principle, it would not be a live possibility in practice, because nobody would simultaneously be sufficiently in their right mind to be a claimant to the usual liberties and yet so perverse as manifestly—that is to say, *really* manifestly—to act against their own interests.

Mill's arguments always revealed traces of his attraction to and skepticism of the Saint-Simonian and Comtist view of the transition from the present critical phase of history to the organic phase that will end it. By the time he wrote *On Liberty*, he had lost the enthusiasm visible in early essays such as *The Spirit of the Age*. Even in the 1860s, however, Mill seems to have thought that something like the Saint-Simonian view of history might be true, but that the Saint-Simonians generally, and Comte particularly, were much better at explaining why the critical phase had been going strong for eight centuries than why we should expect it to end within the next thirty-five years (*Comte and Positivism*, CW 10:325–26). In other words, the arguments for freedom and experiment in *On Liberty* might be superseded by the discovery of the ultimate truth about how we should live, but that discovery and its universal, uncoerced acceptance would be several centuries off, and therefore not an option worth discussing now. A further difficulty, however, is that Mill relied on the analogies between scientific and moral progress and at the same time resisted them. Thus, Comte scorned the idea of free speech on the grounds that there was no free speech in science. Mill acknowledged that the authority of the properly trained was, in science, very great; but he also noted that a scientific consensus was not maintained by coercion, and then suggested that moral debate was anyway not on all fours with debate about findings in chemistry. So it appears that the response to Comte was first to deny that there was no place for free speech in science, and second to deny that moral progress was sufficiently like scientific progress to sustain any argument like Comte's.

I am inclined to believe that Mill held the following view. There *is* an answer to the question what ways of life best suit human beings; it is not a unitary answer, because human nature varies a good deal from one person to another and therefore yields diverse answers—though these are answers that have a common form, since they will be answers about what conduces to the long-term well-being of the people in question. To reach those answers, we need experiments in living, because human nature is exceedingly ill understood. What we see is the manifestations of human nature as it has been socialized in a variety of ways, of which many are inimical to human flourishing. Mill argued more continually in *The Subjection of Women* than in *On Liberty* that we have little idea of what we might achieve if we adjusted the ways we socialize the young so as to enable them to live more flourishing and self-actualized existences thereafter, but the thought plainly sustains *On Liberty* too (*The Subjection of Women*, CW 21:259–340; *On Liberty*, CW 18:260). Women might be the most immediate beneficiaries of a deeper understanding of how far the interaction of socialization and human nature distorts or hides the possibility of new forms of happiness, but humankind generally would be the ultimate beneficiary of such an understanding. Hence, Mill's never-realized hopes for the science of ethology.

Human nature is malleable, and as we work on our own characters, so we open up some indeterminacy in the answer to the question of how best to live. We not only come to be better at pursuing happiness, but also change our view of what happiness is. We can also change our own characters so as to be better able to live by the views we come to. Mill, as I have argued elsewhere, suggested that the answer to ultimate questions about what sort of happiness to pursue lay in the realm of aesthetic judgment.[24] Aesthetic judgment has a tendency not to converge in any very straightforward way; it is, in that sense, the antithesis of scientific judgment. Mill is hard to interpret because he wanted both to emphasize the place of scientific rationality and to leave space for aesthetic judgment in determining the ends of life. The experimental life would, if this is a proper interpretation of Mill, have a tendency to settle some questions while opening up others. It would thus promote and destroy pluralism at the same time.

How much pluralism does this yield? It yields as many distinctive and therefore different lives as there are different people; it does not yield as many different political systems as there are human communities. There are many common tasks that governments must perform, and any society concerned with efficiency will have them performed in the same way. It does not yield an infinity of cultural options (in the anthropological sense of "cultural"): many cultures now visible will vanish because they rest on superstitious beliefs that cannot withstand inspection. In other senses of "cultural," it yields room for infinite variety; there is no sign that the number of available musical, sculptural, literary, and other aesthetic formulae will soon diminish, and no sign that we shall soon settle down to repetitively re-creating works of art to a single pattern. Since Mill's borrowings from Humboldt and Goethe imply that aesthetic invention is the model of experiments in living, we should have no fear that Mill's liberalism is likely to reduce the number of available cultural options to one. Mill's pluralism remains less hospitable to nonliberal and illiberal ways of life than Berlin's pluralism, though perhaps not very much less hospitable. The reason why the gap may not be as great as one would imagine at first sight is that vivid, fully realized lives, for the sake of which Mill, like Berlin, defends freedom, may also be realized in nonliberal settings. Where they are, the liberal will face a familiar transition problem: how much of the vividness and commitment can be kept when beliefs and attitudes change in a liberal direction? It is every modernizer's question. That Mill was more inclined than Berlin to sacrifice vivid traditional societies to less vivid modern ones goes without saying. That he was wrong to make that choice is a more contentious claim. It is also one that there is no space to discuss any further.

References

Berlin, Isaiah. 1958. *Two Concepts of Liberty*. Oxford: Clarendon Press.
———. 1969. *Four Essays on Liberty*. London: Oxford University Press.
Devlin, Patrick. 1965. *The Enforcement of Morals*. Maccabean Lecture in Jurisprudence. 1958. Reprint, London: Oxford University Press.
Dewey, John. 1935. *Liberalism and Social Action*. New York: Putnam's Sons.
Dworkin, Ronald. 1981. "Liberalism." In *Public and Private Morality*, edited by Stuart Hampshire. Cambridge: Cambridge University Press.
Feinberg, Joel. 1984. *Harm to Others: Moral Limits of Criminal Law*. Vol. 1. New York: Oxford University Press.
Feyerabend, Paul. 1975. *Against Method*. London: New Left Books.
Gray, John. 1983. *Mill on Liberty: A Defence*. London: Routledge and Kegan Paul. Rev. ed., 1996.
———. 1993. *Post-Liberalism: Studies in Political Thought*. London: Routledge.
Green, T. H. 1886. *Lectures on the Principles of Political Obligation*. London: Longmans, Green.
Hamburger, J. 1991. "Religion and 'On Liberty.'" In *A Cultivated Mind: Essays on J. S. Mill Presented to John M. Robson*, edited by Michael Laine, 139–81. Toronto: University of Toronto Press.
Hart, H.L.A. 1955. "Are There Any Natural Rights?" *Philosophical Review* 64:175–91.
Himmelfarb, Gertrude. 1974. *On Liberty and Liberalism: The Case of John Stuart Mill*. New York: Knopf.
Kant, Immanuel. 1970. "Perpetual Peace." In *Kant's Political Writings*, edited by H. B. Reiss, 93–130. Cambridge: Cambridge University Press.
Kuhn. T. S. 1962. *The Structure of Scientific Revolutions*. Chicago: University of Chicago Press.
Mill, John Stuart. 1963–91. *The Collected Works of John Stuart Mill* [cited as CW]. Edited by John M. Robson. 33 vols. Toronto: University of Toronto Press.
Moir, Martin. 1990. Introduction to *Writings on India*, by J. S. Mill. In *CW* 30.
Musgrave, Alan, et al., eds. 1970. *Criticism and the Growth of Knowledge: Proceedings of the International Colloquium in the Philosophy of Science*. Vol. 4. London: Cambridge University Press.
Nozick, Robert. 1975. *Anarchy, State, and Utopia*. New York: Basic Books.
Popper, Karl. 1959. *The Logic of Scientific Discovery*. London: Hutchinson. Originally published as *Logik der Forschung*, 1934.
———. 1974. *Conjectures and Refutations*. London: Routledge and Kegan Paul.
Pyle, Andrew, ed. 1994. *Liberty: Contemporary Responses to John Stuart Mill*. Bristol: Thoemmes.

Rawls, John. 1971. *A Theory of Justice*. Cambridge, Mass.: Harvard University Press.

———. 1993. *Political Liberalism*. New York: Columbia University Press.

Raz, Joseph. 1983. *The Morality of Freedom*. Oxford: Clarendon Press.

Rockefeller, Steven. 1991. *Religious Faith and Democratic Humanism*. New York: Columbia University Press.

Ryan, Alan. 1970. *The Philosophy of John Stuart Mill*. London: Macmillan. 2nd ed., New York: Macmillan, 1988.

———. 1995. *John Dewey and the High Tide of American Liberalism*. New York: Norton.

Taylor, Charles. 1989. *Sources of the Self*. Cambridge: Cambridge University Press.

Tocqueville, Alexis de. 1994. *Democracy in America*. London: Dent.

Waldron, J. 1987. "Mill and the Value of Moral Distress." *Political Studies* 35:410–23.

Wollheim, Richard. 1979. "John Stuart Mill and Isaiah Berlin." In *The Idea of Freedom*, edited by Alan Ryan, 253–70. Oxford: Oxford University Press.

Zastoupil, Lynn. 1988. "J. S. Mill and India." *Victorian Studies* 32:31–54.

16

Utilitarianism and Bureaucracy
THE VIEWS OF J. S. MILL

I BEGIN, reluctantly, by begging some interesting—and for my purposes, rather important—questions that have recently agitated both historians of ideas and historians of administrative reform. I say "reluctantly" because these are questions on which I have formed some opinions and would by no means hesitate to expound on them in the right circumstances. But in the light of this essay's immediate purpose, I shall dogmatize briefly and hope to carry only enough conviction to get on with the exploration of those dilemmas about administration that we can see in the writings of J. S. Mill. The first large doubt raised by historians of ideas is—to put it crudely—whether the ideas of professional thinkers and the ideas of the great and nearly great social and political theorists have *any* definite influence at all.[1] Do we have any justification for calling political changes—be they reformist or revolutionary—Lockean, Benthamite, Rousseauist, or even, to take the fiercest line, Marxist? Mostly, there is no reason to think that politicians and administrators are at all well versed in what the "great men" said. We can take over Keynes's remark about the hold exercised on practical men by obsolete theorists and add to it the observation that even where the theorists in question are not obsolete, they are likely to be secondhand and second rate. We can all think of good reasons why the minds of practical men will be open to the secondhand rather than to the new, the original, the highly developed, and the finely articulated. Even when we consider men like Lenin or Trotsky, who had read widely and were well versed in a social and political theory by which they professed to direct their activities, is it not clear that what they actually took up and developed was more closely rooted in the needs of their own situation than in the words of their mentors? We can hardly begin to conceive of the views formed by theorists surviving the transition from thought to action unimpaired; we praise the work of the theorist for its subtlety, elegance, sophistication, but the political actor requires above all to make an impact on a rough and unpredictable world of brute fact. It is no wonder, therefore, if we find the theory bending to meet the facts; it is usually a great deal easier to match the idea to the reality than to bend reality to match the idea.

Plainly, we can pile up considerations of this sort so as to carry a good deal of weight, and some of the points made are simply unanswerable. But the case is not conclusive; we might, for instance, retort that ideas circulate by other means than the reading of books and the explicit adoption of creeds.[2] The popular notion of the "climate of opinion" at any rate points toward a recognizable phenomenon in intellectual life, even if it leaves a lot of interesting questions unasked and unanswered.[3] Again, it can be said that it is an oversimplification to look at the political theorist as if what he provided was an exact timetable, a fully drawn blueprint for social and political amelioration. Not only is there a historical puzzle about what practical conclusions, if any, men have drawn from the social and political thinkers of their day, there is a prior intellectual puzzle, that of determining whether logic compels us to draw one conclusion rather than another. The great diversity of interpretations current in the academic discipline of "traditional political theory" suggests that it rarely does so. Thus, the denial of a direct prescriptive influence is too easy an intellectual victory; the kind of influence that is shown not to exist is not the kind of influence anyone expected to find in the first place. The notion of "influence" must be elaborated in some subtler way than this.

Without undertaking to settle the issue, I should say that I am sure we shall have to refine our ideas about the spread of intellectual influence as our knowledge of how ideas are diffused becomes more adequate in the light of historical research and sociological theory alike. But for my present purpose, this hardly matters. Nothing in what follows commits us to the view that political philosophies operate as direct and immediate causes of social change, nor to the view that political philosophers who originate them stand behind the scenes with their hands on ghostly but nonetheless effective levers. All I take for granted is the banality that men in general act for reasons—usually declared, but often only to be extracted with difficulty from their actions—and hence that a large part of historical explanation is devoted to showing what kind of reasons people had for doing what they did, whether they were frustrated by events or not.[4] The relevance of social and political theorists for the historian lies in the fact that to a large extent, the reasons that men offer for their actions make sense only within some particular weltanschauung, some conceptualization of the world within which the agent is situated.[5] This is not to deny that people with a great variety of practical views may share the same conceptual scheme, and it is not to deny that people with radically different conceptual schemes may well agree about what to do in practice. Nonetheless, our descriptions of the facts, and our assessments of what these imply for our actions, rest on our acceptance of what, in other contexts, has been called a "paradigm";[6] to elucidate what kinds of problems a given paradigm will make visible and what it will tend to hide is thus a contribution to the historical understanding of what men have and have not achieved.

To descend from the theory to the instance, I must say a few words about the case of nineteenth-century administrative reform in particular. At this level of specificity, the obvious question is, to what extent can we explain the changes in the organization, recruitment, and functions of the English bureaucracy as a result of deliberate planning by ideologically sophisticated reformers? One recently popular answer is, to no extent at all.[7] There are two distinct strands in what, following MacDonagh, we may call the "anti-ideational" case. The first is a plainly empirical argument to the effect that changes in the range of tasks performed by government and in the machinery by which these tasks were performed took place according to no plan whatever. The process was one of incoherently responding to the felt pressure of events—abuses were discovered, were felt to be "intolerable," were remedied ineffectively, then tackled more effectively; the social and political effects of all this were cumulative, and none too clearly perceived, although they were such as to move English society in the "collectivist" direction that Dicey described.[8] But this was essentially a process that no one foresaw and that no one involved in would have supported had he understood it to be in train. On this argument, I have only two comments. The first is that it is essentially a factual matter how the various areas of bureaucratic regulation came to grow and thus that it is a matter that awaits resolution by empirical investigation. The second is that it follows from this that we cannot a priori show MacDonagh's account, when it is generalized to provide a "model," to be any more plausible than what would be my own guess—that different departments probably had very different histories.[9] The tone, rather than the content, of MacDonagh's 1958 article leads me to suspect that he subscribes to some more general philosophy of history that plays down the role of ideas in the causation of events. But in the absence of any explicit and argued statement of this philosophy and the grounds on which it rests, I cannot judge whether it would rule out influences of the kind I hope to elucidate below.

The second aspect of the anti-ideational case presents no problem, for it is the claim that no matter what the actual processes, they were not inspired by utilitarian aims and ideals, and that these latter had no great part in bringing about administrative reform. To regard the series of nineteenth-century reforms as Benthamite is to ignore the facts—they were neither inspired by Bentham and his followers, nor did they proceed in accordance with their hopes.[10] On this issue, my conclusions hereafter will be mostly negative. I am inclined to think that there was no such thing as *the* utilitarian view on administrative reform, no such thing as *the* utilitarian view of the proper role of government and the best mode of its fulfilling that role—any more, I suspect, than there was any such thing as *the* nonconformist view or *the* evangelical view. Rather, what was involved in accepting a utilitarian view of social and political life was the acceptance of a theoretical framework within which certain ways of describing and explaining social and political matters got to the heart of them; it did not involve the possession of answers to problems of social and political practice so much as the assurance that certain ways of posing these problems was the right way of posing them. Where there were answers to be had, it involved the belief that certain reasons for thinking them to be answers were, in principle, good reasons.[11] But it is plain enough that many of the assumptions of utilitarianism were, up to a point, at home in other ways of perceiving the world—for example, in unitarianism after Priestley—a fact that must then have rendered communication as much easier as it now renders the ascription of influence more difficult.[12] And, a final caveat, at the level of biographical adequacy, we must remember that all of us are subject to the influence of more ways than one of looking at the world, so that among the ideas to be found in the minds of secular utilitarians there will be ideas that come from other, quite foreign sources—foreign, that is, to the calculus of pleasure and pain. In this respect, as in others, John Stuart Mill has an obvious claim on our attention.

The goal of this essay then is the examination of Mill's views on the civil service—its role, its mode of recruitment, and so on—in order to assemble a tolerably clear picture of the kinds of difficulty that confront the utilitarian theorist of politics. Mill's writings are readily accessible, both those that stem from his work as a senior civil servant in the East India Company and those that are represented by more theoretical works such as *Representative Government*. In addition, when Sir Charles Trevelyan was canvassing support for his proposals, Mill wrote him a letter that Trevelyan described as "the best we have received."[13] It is, in fact, a document in which the twin personae of administrator and theorist are strikingly united. For our present purposes, Mill's views have several aspects of some interest. As all the world knows, he was a man whose mind had supposedly been made for him by a utilitarian education amounting to indoctrination, but who spent his life deliberately exposing himself to influences of which his mentors would often have disapproved.[14] Mill's views thus show us how utilitarian doctrines could be strengthened and weakened by influences from such unlikely sources as Coleridge's romantic conservatism, Saint-Simon's managerial positivism, and the continental liberalism of Humboldt and Tocqueville. Again, Mill was a man both of the study and the office, and while this in no way lessens the primacy of his intellectual achievements, it does mean that when he talks about government, he speaks from thirty years' experience of earning his living as an administrator. In *A System of Logic*, Mill defended his father against the charge of being an impractical doctrinaire by pointing out how extremely practical his father had been when involved in the world of everyday business.[15] And the same claim could be made on behalf of the son. Indeed, anyone who thinks that a concern for the theoretical foundations of politics is necessarily a disqualification for practical life would do well to think hard about the more than adequate services rendered to the East India Company by James and J. S. Mill.

In drawing on the evidence of Mill's work at East India House, we ought to bear in mind the importance of India in the context of the nineteenth-century administrative reformation. Merely at the level of personalities, several notable reformers served the government of India, among them Trevelyan himself. More importantly, the need to govern India brought to light some characteristic dilemmas facing nineteenth-century thinking about politics. It raised the question of democratic versus paternalistic government, the merits of a noisy public opinion as opposed to those of a silent expertise; it raised the problem whether governments should aim at conserving the existing social fabric or whether they should try to innovate and bend their efforts toward the rationalization of institutions.[16] And a variation on the theme permanently to be heard in nineteenth-century English arguments about education occurs in the debate over Indian education too—how much ought the lower orders (or natives) to be educated, and in what kinds of subjects? When Mill gave evidence to Trevelyan, he was emphatic that civil-service reform should provide a stimulus to national education—an aim shared with Benjamin Jowett, Henry Halford Vaughan, and others.[17] Edward Hughes long ago dismissed this as "a quite irrelevant educational emphasis," but nothing could be further from the truth.[18] For it was about issues of this sort that there clustered many of the most basic political differences separating utilitarians from nonutilitarians. Utilitarian arguments of a rationalizing kind concerning the need for accurate information when making decisions confronted nonutilitarian, often antirationalistic arguments about the benefits to be had from a wider, more emotionally supportive "culture." And such arguments both at home and in India mingled with arguments about whether to stamp Western "scientific" learning on an alien culture, or whether to try to fuse it with the rich, but superstition-riddled native product.[19]

The East India Company's government of India originated not only the term "civil servant"—distinguishing those of the company's servants in its civilian employment from those who served in its armed forces—but also many of the practices of efficient bureaucratic government. Thus, to take a minor aspect of the matter, when Mill came to describe the working of the company he drew attention to its control over its records.[20] The government of India was necessarily and essentially a "government of record" in the sense that it was clearly impossible to exercise detailed control over the decisions made in India, but that much of the effect of doing so could be achieved if every decision was recorded, its grounds noted, and comments on it sent back.[21] Thus, the company obliged every one of its servants to record his decisions and to send a copy of the record to London, where it was duly filed. Naturally, this raised questions about the vast army of clerks and the huge mountains of paper that such a system would seem to require. But Mill's reply was that the material was indexed with great accuracy, so that all files were immediately at hand; present-day enthusiasts for systems of instantaneous data retrieval will understand Mill's pride in his system, though no doubt we all regret the other factor that Mill cited on behalf of it—the cheapness of copying done by native labor.[22] Still, a concern for filing systems, though certainly utilitarian enough, could hardly warrant our interest in the East India Company's dealings with utilitarianism.

The more substantial question that the careers of both father and son raise is that of how essential it is to good government that it should also be self-government—obviously a central issue in colonial administration. On the matter whether good government could be provided other than by the people themselves, the two Mills stood in rather different positions. Indeed, there is a tension in utilitarian thought generally whether government *for* the people entails government *by* the people. One of the ways in which Bentham and James Mill stood outside the mainstream of liberalism is that they both believed that so long as government operates for the benefit of the governed, their actual participation in their own government is immaterial. In the case of Britain, they both came to believe that only a government controlled by the people would govern in the general interest and not in some "sinister interest." And in Bentham's case, the conversion to democracy was slow and incomplete.[23]

But so far as India was concerned, there was no place for the arguments relevant to Britain. The ordinary objection to foreign rule over a native population was that the foreigners would exploit and plunder the natives and quite fail to attend to their interests. But the case was vastly different with the East India Company's dealings with the native population of India. Even before James Mill joined the Company, he had written of it in his famous *History*:

> In the highly important point of the servants or subordinate agents of government, there is nothing in the world to be compared with the East India Company, whose servants as a body, have not only exhibited a portion of talent which forms a contrast with that of the ill-chosen instruments of other governments, but have . . . maintained a virtue which, under the temptations of their situation is worthy of the highest applause.[24]

The virtues of the Company were placed in high relief by contrast with the corruption, ignorance, inefficiency, and superstition that permeated native rule in India; and as between efficient government by foreigners and inefficient government by natives, utility could decide only one way. Self-rule—and hence the valuing of democracy or some form of home rule above no matter how efficient an administration—was alien to the temperament of the theorist and the logic of the theory alike. For James Mill, who saw in government few questions other than those of cheapness, orderliness, and effectiveness, the despotism of Britain over Asia was no temporary staging post on the way to some other form of association.[25]

But for J. S. Mill, the stage of despotic government could be justified only if it really were a stage on the way to self-rule and independence.[26] The relationship between despotic rulers and their despotically governed subjects is morally tolerable only on what amounts to an educational basis—that the despot is the teacher and the subjects are genuinely instructed; and for examples of such relationships, Mill cites Peter the Great and Queen Elizabeth.[27] In the well-known passage of *On Liberty* that discusses this issue, he says: "Despotism is a legitimate mode of government in dealing with barbarians, provided the end be their improvement, and the means justified by actually effecting that end."[28] We may recoil from the readiness with which nineteenth-century Englishmen equated the richness of Indian culture with barbarism as much as from the readiness with which they believed that what England had to offer was unequivocally progress; but the argument is not illiberal. Even though any particular claimant was often in danger of seeing the argument used as a reductio ad absurdum against him, it was a commonplace among writers from Aristotle to Locke that despotism was warranted where there was a sufficiently clear superiority of ruler over ruled.[29] And Mill certainly improved on the racialist assumptions of intrinsic superiority, which became common after his death, in emphasizing that what the English possessed, they could pass on to the natives of India. In India, he observed a more acute version of what was to some extent visible in England as well—a population that, while perfectly capable of improvement, did not know its own interests, because of ignorance, and therefore needed advice, information, and leadership.

What was significant about India was that the tension inherent in utilitarian thought, when it came to analyze the relative importance of the politics of self-government versus the honesty of administration, was there resolvable in only one way. In India there was no room for the kind of problem that besets the politician under parliamentary arrangements—no need to gain popular support, no maneuvering for votes, no conciliating public opinion. The only problems were those that faced benevolent and enlightened administrators. This is important for a central but not very much discussed reason. Because utilitarian ethics aim at maximizing the sum total of happiness, there is a strong current in the theory that exalts good management as the greatest of skills. Maximizing happiness is a task that calls for organization and methodical administration; hence there is a tendency to look forward to a time when interests need not be conciliated and the political virtues will be summed up by beneficent legislation and the correct administration of the law. Yet, of course, utilitarianism is equally an ethical system predicated upon a view of human nature that assumes conflicts of aims and a continual competition for benefits, so the problems of ethics are problems of conciliating and adjudicating these conflicting claims.[30] In this view, the best kind of politics must surely be the politics of free competition, in which all interests can express themselves, strike bargains and rally support. But in India, this dilemma could make no impact, since there were none of what would now be called the "functional prerequisites" of this kind of politics; thus, the government of India could become, both in utilitarian theory and to a large extent in East India Company practice, a question of good management. It is thus no wonder that Mill was so concerned to stress the company's managerial efficiency, both to the Select Committee in 1852 and in the *Memorandum* of 1858.[31] Such efficiency was to a large extent the company's raison d'être. But this efficiency and the probity claimed for the behavior of the company's servants are at odds with what utilitarian theory leads us to expect from unchecked governments; the whole point of the utilitarian advocacy of representative democracy was the underlying assumption that unless some check could be exercised by the ruled upon those who ruled them, there would be no hope of curbing the standing inclination of all governors to rule in their own rather than their subjects' interests.[32] Short of taking the standard way out—ascribing the puzzle to Mill's notorious inconsistency—we should expect a man of Mill's intelligence to have given the matter some thought. And indeed, Mill provides a rather coherent explanation of the unlikely state of affairs—an explanation directly relevant to the efforts made by Trevelyan and others to remove patronage from the English civil service.

Although Mill's most interesting explanation of the merits of company government relates to his concern for the antagonism of opinion, and is therefore discussed below, he certainly attached great importance to how the company's methods of recruitment and training avoided the characteristic evils of patronage. Although appointments in the company were matters of patronage, Mill claimed that the evils of such a system were, so far as possible, absent.[33] One can hardly do better than quote his own summary of the causes of this happy state:

> Among the first of these seems to me to be, that those who are sent to administer the affairs of India are not sent to any particular appointment; they go out merely as candidates; they go out when young, and go through the necessary course of preparation in subordinate functions before they can arrive at the higher ones.[34]

Mill explained that candidates spent an initial period in India simply learning the routines of the office before they were called on by senior officials to fill some particular vacancy. It is a practice still recommended. The other great merit that Mill saw in the system was that those who made the appointments in India had no interest in considerations other than having the duties performed efficiently by those who were appointed to them; from a variety of causes, among them the rotation of directors of the company, there was little need for them to consider how to satisfy some young man's patron.

> A second great advantage of the present system is, that those who are sent out as candidates to rise by degrees are generally unconnected with the influential classes in the country, and out of the range of Parliamentary influence. The consequence is, that those who have the disposal of offices in India have little or no motive to put unfit persons into important situations, or to permit unjustifiable acts to be done by them.[35]

The Select Committee's questioning suggests that Mill may have been exaggerating the absence of patronage, but his replies to their other questions certainly show his hostility to patronage and to the social assumptions surrounding it. It was, of course, impossible to claim that entry to the company's service was open, so long as aspirants had to go through Haileybury and had to obtain the recommendation of a director to attend the college. But Mill was more than ready to agree that attendance at the college ought not to be a precondition of service.[36] And when asked how he would dispose of the patronage of the company if it were to be removed from the hands of the directors, he replied:

> I think in that case the only proper system, and one which I should myself consider as intrinsically the best would be to bestow it by public competition, by *concours*, as some offices are given in France; to give it to the best qualified among all persons of requisite age and education who might compete for it.[37]

That this entailed opening the service to persons from any social background, Mill freely admitted. The committee asked:

> When you speak of competition, do you mean a bona fide public competition, open to all the world, or would you require any particular qualifications or previous course of education on the part of the candidates?

Mill's reply was: "I would admit persons to compete in whatever manner they had been educated, and at whatever place." And to the question "And in whatever condition of life they might be?" he answered, "And in whatever condition of life."[38]

That Mill meant exactly what he said emerged during two further exchanges with the committee, in one of which he put forward his view that the elevation of the native population to self-rule was part of the object of the company's government: "In proportion as the natives become trustworthy and qualified for high office, it seems to me not only allowable, but a duty to appoint them to it." The committee asked, "Do you think that in those circumstances, the dependence of India on this country could be maintained?" To which Mill replied: "I think it might, by judicious management, be made to continue till the time arises when the natives shall be qualified to carry on the same system of Government without our assistance."[39] The other occasion was less significant perhaps, but it casts an amusing light on the social implications of Mill's radicalism, and in the light of recent debates about the extent to which middle-class pressure for reform was a movement designed to secure employment for middle-class children, it at any rate shows up some less utilitarian motives on the part of the defenders of the status quo. Two successive exchanges went like this:

> [Committee:] Is it not a curious circumstance that the son of a horse-dealer should be sent to India as a cadet?

> [Mill:] The son of a horse-dealer is as likely to qualify himself in the subordinate positions for succeeding to the higher as the son of anyone else."

[Committee:] But that is not exactly the class from which you would select persons to be the companions of gentlemen who are to fill honourable positions?

[Mill:] It is not the class from which writers or cadets are generally selected; but I see no reason why such persons should be excluded.[40]

Throughout his life Mill was unwilling to make any concession at all either to snobbery or to silly fears about the "tone of society." As we shall see below, his letter to Trevelyan defends precisely the attitude that his replies to the Select Committee evidenced in 1852.

Before we turn to the final flurry of Mill's career, when he defended the company against the government's plans for its dissolution in 1858, there is one further matter on which the company's activities shed some light. This is the problem of why utilitarians were so ready to defend its administrative activities if they were, as Dicey believed, enthusiasts for an individualist and laissez-faire creed. The problem has been more or less effectively dissolved by Dr. Parris's reexamination of Dicey's views; but it is worth stressing the difference between a doctrine that is, as a matter of logic, both atomistic and mechanistic and one that supports either a romantic or a rugged individualism.[41] So far as the *logic* of utilitarianism goes, the only questions we can ask about private versus public initiative are questions of relative cost and efficiency. There is no reason to suppose that the earlier utilitarians recoiled from the public provision of any particular good for any reason other than their belief that it would be wasteful; and certainly there is in Bentham none of that enthusiasm for individual liberty that is so characteristic a feature of the writings of J. S. Mill.[42] Much the strongest objection to public enterprise seems to have stemmed from hostility to the aristocratic incumbents of governmental positions, who could be calculated to turn the public service into a series of jobs for their friends. The creation of an honest and patronage-free bureaucracy would, in principle, have gone a long way toward meeting the objection.

And even this leaves out one characteristically nineteenth-century note, the concern for improvement; although governments might in general be less efficient than private enterprise in providing goods and services, they could still play a valuable role in initiating improvement by supplying goods and services of the right kind to a society whose state of civilization was too low for them to be provided unaided. Schools and communications are two very obvious examples—especially obvious in the context of India. Moreover, the example of India illustrates two of this essay's contentions quite neatly. James Mill was a firm believer in improvement, and what he wanted to see was improvement on a broad front, for it extended to the intelligence, probity, and diligence of the Indian population, which he had characterized so unkindly.[43] And, unsurprisingly in view of what we said earlier, much of this improvement coincided with the spiritual regeneration planned by the evangelicals for the superstitious Hindus.[44] But we can also see the areas of similarity and dissimilarity in earlier and later utilitarianism here. For J. S. Mill also shared the belief that among the benefits to be sought were the moral and mental improvement of the subject population; he also called that population by some pretty unflattering names; and sometimes his conception of improvement seems no wider than his father's—as when he claims the transformation of the Thugs into useful tent makers as one of the striking achievements of the East India Company's rule.[45] But in that *Memorandum* where there are listed "some of the most important achievements of a Government of which perpetual striving towards improvement is the vital principle," there is more than an echo of the doctrine of *Representative Government*, that progressiveness is the mark of a good form of government and that progressiveness is a great deal more than efficiency and orderliness.[46] James Mill would have been satisfied when the Indians had learned businesslike habits; J. S. Mill, only when they had reached the point at which they would spontaneously have begun to develop their own capacities for themselves.

Mill's career at East India House was mostly uneventful. W. T. Thornton's brief memoir of his chief is mostly devoted to personal reminiscence, including the appalling story of the—incidentally, hideously ugly—inkstand that his assistants vainly tried to present to Mill on his retirement.[47] And Eric Stokes spends more time on justifying his own comparative neglect of Mill's career than on that career itself.[48] He says, rightly enough, that Mill's interests were much wider than those that the job involved and that he was in any case not inclined either intellectually or temperamentally to lay down the law in the way his father had done. It was also true that the internal reorganization of the company had done much to lessen the influence that had been exercised through the examiner's office in the heyday of James Mill's tenure there. The company's commercial functions had been taken away from it in 1833, and it was thereafter exclusively concerned with the task of governing the Indian empire; accordingly, directors took a much more intense and continual interest in the details of decision making, so it was no longer possible to commit them to policies in the way James Mill had managed to do.[49] Nonetheless, at the very end of Mill's career there was a brief period when he swung all the weight of an office described as "equal in importance if not in dignity to that of a Secretary of State" against the proposed Government of India Bill.[50] This defense of the company produced a number of documents, including four pamphlets published by the company[51] and the *Petition*, with its biting opening antitheses:

> Your Petitioners, at their own expense, and by the agency of their own civil and military servants originally acquired for this country its magnificent empire in the East . . . The foundations of this Empire were laid by your Petitioners, at that time neither aided nor controlled by Parliament, at the same period when a succession

of administrations under the control of Parliament were losing to the Crown of Great Britain another great Empire on the opposite side of the Atlantic.[52]

The interest of all these sources for our present purposes is that they all reiterate the same argument about the causes of good government in India and, almost as importantly, the same doubts about the absence of proper checks to misgovernment under the new proposals.

Mill never tired of expressing his belief that good government relied on the expression of a variety of opinions; questions had to be looked at from several angles rather than one, expert advice had to be sought, public opinion had to be heard, and obstacles had to be erected in the way of folly and wickedness. In Britain, it was public discussion that acted as the great check against misgovernment; but in the case of India, "the only means of ensuring the necessary discussion and collision of opinions is provided for within the governing body itself."[53] This was achieved primarily through the division of authority between the Board of Control and the Court of Directors, the former answerable in the end to Parliament, the latter representing the continuing administration of the country and independent of Parliament's good and ill will.[54] The ability of the court to initiate policy, subject to being overridden by the president of the Board of Control, meant that knowledge and political accountability struck a rarely achieved balance; this, of course, has wider implications for the role of the civil servant in relation to his politically appointed ministerial master, implications that Mill draws both in *Representative Government* and elsewhere. Thus, the *Petition* comments on the new proposals: "To believe that the administration of India would have been more free from error had it been conducted by a Minister of the Crown without the aid of the Court of Directors, would be to believe that the Minister, with full power to govern India as he pleased, has governed ill, because he has had the assistance of experienced and responsible advisers."[55] Mill's emphatic insistence on the need for the expertise of skilled and experienced administrators was further supported by his distrust of what political accountability was likely to amount to in practice; questions about the welfare of India would become weapons in party competition for office, with the result that concern for the interests of India or the security of Indian government would "be secondary to the one important question, whether one man, or another much the same as he, shall sit for a while on the Treasury bench."[56] The contemporary doubt whether politically appointed ministers with little prior knowledge and short tenure in a department are in any condition to head their offices successfully was certainly shared by Mill.[57] But Mill's real scorn was directed at the proposal that the new president of the Board of Control should govern India through a council chosen by himself. Mill's objection amounts in essence to the argument that a man who chooses his own advisers thereby chooses the advice he receives, and that advice so chosen is not advice at all, but a prop to some preexisting prejudice. The absence of independent voices is described as "the most fatal blow which could be struck against good government in that country,"[58] while the power of the president to ignore his council without giving reasons or allowing for appeal was characterized thus: "Your Petitioners cannot well conceive a worse form of government for India than a minister with a council whom he should be at liberty to consult or not at his pleasure, or whose advice he should be able to disregard without giving his reasons in writing, and in a manner likely to carry conviction . . . Any body of persons connected with the minister which is not a check, will be a screen."[59]

Mill did not claim that the good results that he ascribed to the current arrangements owed much to deliberate contrivance; what he argued was that since the system worked as well as it did, it ought to be replaced only by a form of government that contained similar provisions for constitutional checks and for independent advice that could not be ignored or overridden in silence. In *Representative Government*, he reiterated his gloomy view of the new arrangements.[60]

Now, anyone skeptical of the influence of ideas upon the course of events will be quick to remind me that even the ambivalent and qualified attitudes that I have ascribed to Mill failed to get a hearing in 1858, since Mill and the company ended up on the losing side; and we have little or no evidence of what effects Mill's criticisms had on the subsequent activities of the government of India. This is true enough, and I should not wish to make any extravagant claims on Mill's behalf. Rather, I should see his influence as one stream of thought that contributed to the increasingly important view of the civil servant as to a large extent his own master, a view that stressed the qualities he brought to his work that were largely lacking in his political masters—the men Mill described as "exciting the mirth of their inferiors by the air with which they announced as a truth hitherto set at nought and brought to light by themselves, something which was probably the first thought of everybody who had ever looked at the subject, given up as soon as he had got on to a second."[61] This belief in expertise, in the independent opinion, and this faith in the man who can press a view of his own without fear or hope for his own position are all to be found in writers other than Mill and in other utilitarians too. The really distinctive overtones in Mill's account are those that come from his suggestion that administrators should contribute in their way to the wider culture of their society, and these are to be found in *Representative Government* and his occasional essays. For all that, Mill's service in the East India Company served to strengthen rather than weaken these convictions.

Mill's only public pronouncement on the subject of civil-service reform was the letter to Trevelyan alluded to earlier. Assessing its importance is complicated by two factors. The first is that the fact that Trevelyan was very obviously canvassing support—even if he sometimes failed to get it when he expected it[62]—might be thought to make it harder to guess whether Mill had unspoken reservations about the proposed changes. It is doubtful whether he did, both because he was extremely harsh on Jowett's proposals about testimonials[63] and because he was at that time in a particularly uncompromising frame of mind after his marriage to Harriet Taylor.[64] The other doubt is raised by Packe's claim that Mill had roused himself to write the letter only for the sake of Harriet.[65] So consistent is the letter with everything Mill said on related topics, however, that there is no reason to suspect it reflects anything other than long and firmly held opinions. Mill was enthusiasm itself so far as the proposal to open the civil service to examination went: "The proposal to select candidates for the Civil Service of Government appears to me to be one of those great public improvements, the adoption of which would form an era in history. The effects which it is calculated to produce in raising the character both of the public administration and the people can scarcely be over-estimated."[66]

But Mill's support of the measure contains several elements that are not run-of-the-mill arguments for efficiency, and it is on these that we ought to concentrate. Mill was quite happy to accept Stephen's charge that what Trevelyan was doing was creating "statesmen in disguise."[67] We have already seen how concerned Mill had been to secure the independence and authority of those who administered India. Here he supported Trevelyan's concern that "the most experienced officers of a department ought not to be so engrossed in disposing of the current business as to have neither time nor strength to attend to the general objects concerned with their respective duties."[68] Consequently, Mill supported the distinction that Trevelyan drew between the mechanical tasks of the clerks and the genuinely intellectual administrative work. Indeed, as compared with the proposals advanced, Mill's only strictures were on the requirement of testimonials, where he attacked the "terrible principle brought in by the truly inquisitor-like proceedings recommended by Mr Jowett."[69] Jowett was quick to withdraw the implications Mill had seen: "I should object as strongly as Mr Mill to the proposals contained in the paper relating to the examinations, if I understood them as he does."[70] Mill's spikiness may well have owed a lot to the horrors surrounding his recent marriage; but it probably owed something to his usual radicalism and dislike of social distinctions of the kind that the apparatus of testimonials from clergymen or tutors would have tended to preserve. For one thing that was quite clear to Mill was that no consideration of social class ought to stand in the way of recruitment by merit. He dealt with the usual objections to open admission very curtly:

Another objection is, that if appointments are given to talent, the Public Offices will be filled with low people, without the breeding or the feelings of gentlemen. If, as this objection supposes, the sons of gentlemen cannot be expected to have as much ability and instruction as the sons of low people, it would make a strong case for social changes of a more extensive character . . . If, with advantages and opportunities so vastly superior, the youth of the higher classes have not honour enough, or energy enough, or public spirit enough, to make themselves as well qualified as others for the station which they desire to maintain, they are not fit for that station, and cannot too soon step out of it and give place to better people.[71]

Mill's characteristic contribution was his stress on the measure's educational impact, on the "extraordinary stimulus which would be given to mental cultivation by the effect of the national recognition of it as the exclusive title to participation in so large and conspicuous a portion of the national affairs."[72] In this, of course, Mill differed from someone such as Chadwick, whose concern was much more straightforwardly for efficiency and honesty even if it was combined with a traditional animus against the aristocratic connection. Mill hoped for results at two different levels. The first was in the universities, where he joined forces with Jowett in supporting the reform of government as a step toward reforming the universities. In Mill's view, the universities were national endowments that had for centuries failed to serve any national purpose, but had rather served to cement the alliance between a particular religion and a particular social class in the interests only of unjust privilege. If the English civil service was to be opened to unrestricted competition, there would be more room in public service for the first-rate man, and the universities would have more incentive to turn out first-rate men. Mill seemed unmoved by Stephen's belief that first-class men would be much too good for the jobs they were called on to perform—that it was a matter of putting a racehorse between the shafts of the brewer's dray. Obviously, there was a clash of principle here, with Stephen thinking of civil servants as little more than clerks, whereas Mill envisaged a much more independent and demanding role for them. Mill foresaw a process of reinforcement whereby more demanding work would call forth a better class of person to perform it. There is, too, a nonutilitarian streak to be observed in all this. In his early twenties, Mill had begun to absorb Coleridge's ideas about the "clerisy," the class of enlightened leaders in moral and intellectual matters. Three dissimilar streams converged here. There was the old utilitarian belief in an education that amounted to something near a benevolent indoctrination; there was Mill's more emotional response to Coleridge's emphasis on tradition and culture and the need for a class of persons who could be the repositories of that culture; and there was the historical analysis supplied by the Saint-Simonians, who saw society as being in a "critical," or what we might now call an anomic, condition and who looked to an elite that could use its authority to re-create an organic unity. The universities, were they to perform their true functions, would produce many of the members of this clerisy. We might say that Mill almost reverses the switch of meaning between the medieval and the modern usage of the term "clerk" when he assigns some of the functions of the clerisy to the higher civil servant. The only immediate moral I wish to draw from the varied sources of Mill's ideas is that it reinforces the point made at the very outset concerning the complexity of anything that we might want to call the utilitarian view of the social and political world. Later, I shall call on this evidence in saying something about the relationship between Mill's concern for progress and his views on bureaucracy.

The other aspect of Mill's concern for education focused on a lower level of attainment. In our concern with the development of the "administrative" class in the English civil service, it is all too easy to forget that the Northcote-Trevelyan Report anticipated that examination criteria would be applied to all civil-service posts—presumably in much the way that they are applied to those posts in the civil services of the United States that are termed "merit" or "civil service" posts as distinct from those filled by election or patronage. Mill was not one of those who poured scorn on the idea of examining tide-waiters, watermen, postmen, and the like; an educated civil service might very well make more impact at that level, where everyone would be re-minded of the paths open to a measure of intelligence and application. Many of Mill's opinions are hinted at when he writes: "A man may not be a much better postman for being able to draw, or being acquainted with natural his-tory; but he who in that rank possesses these acquirements has given evi-dence of qualities which it is important for the general cultivation of the mass that the State should take every fair opportunity to stamp with its ap-probation."[73] Mill was always concerned with devices for diffusing educa-tion among the lower classes, and hence always anxious, as here, to support a measure that might increase the respect felt for education and that might tend to raise the image of public service among those usually lacking in public spirit.[74]

One of the interesting things to emerge from the letters written to Trevel-yan is how little the debate addressed itself to anything resembling the de-bate of recent years over the individualist and collectivist strains in govern-ment. There is little or no sign of antagonism between individualists and collectivists, and practically no general discussion of the merits and demerits of greater governmental intervention in social and economic life. Trevelyan alluded to the "great and increasing accumulation of public business" very much as if it was a familiar part of the political landscape.[75] The reforms were intended to handle this business more effectively, but there is no sug-gestion of a new role for government. We may, of course, argue that there were great changes in progress of which the actors were unaware; but if this is so, it does not suggest that we should look for any accompanying doctri-nal change. Moreover, I should like to stress that the connection between thought and action is such that the fact that our actions are different pro-vides no evidence that the justifying theory we hold has altered at all. The same physical theory explains why bricks fall just as readily as it explains why balloons do not; the same moral framework may enjoin interventionist policies at one time, and condemn them at another. One reason why utili-tarianism is a *general* moral theory is precisely that it is not tied to particular injunctions such as hostility to the Corn Laws or dislike of the aristocracy. As a general theory, it allowed its adherents to frame arguments appropriate to new situations; but because it was a theory, these form more than a series of ad hoc responses. So I want to conclude this essay by turning to *Representative Government*, not so much to show what are the utilitarian prescriptions for our ills, but more to show how these ills appear when they appear as ills to a utilitarian. To say it again, this is not "the utilitarian theory of the state" that we are explicating, merely a few utilitarian dilemmas.

Although I have said, and stand by having said, that there was no such debate in progress as the debate between individualists and collectivists, a distinction worth introducing at this point relates to the substance of that argument. Mill was aware of the danger of a benevolent oppression in democracy in a way that was foreign both to Bentham and James Mill, and almost as foreign to enthusiasts for spiritual community like T. H. Green. Mill was afraid of the stifling of individuality, a deadening of initiative, especially in moral and intellectual matters; and it was this fear of social oppression more than the fear of political oppression that dominated *On Liberty*.[76] When discussing the matter in that essay, Mill drew two different lines along which we might oppose governmental interference. One ground for resisting is that the activity in question is simply not the business of society at large—not, at any rate, in the sense that society has any right to coerce people into some particular line of conduct; the other ground is that although the action does fall into the domain of public business, the odds are that government, being clumsy and expensive, will do more harm than good by intervening, at any rate coercively.[77] These are very different kinds of objections, for the former is an absolute moral prohibition on control and coercion, while the latter is technical only. Mill, however, takes great care to leave room for governments to act noncoercively, for example, in collecting and circulating information, offering advice, and helping private efforts—in other words, there is no antipathy to collective action as such except when it is collective coercion.[78] This means that Mill's views, to some extent, cut across the usual line of debate. For instance, he was emphatic that the state ought to intervene very strenuously in making parents responsible for the health, education, and welfare of their children, but adamant that neither government nor society at large was entitled to inquire into the religious beliefs of teachers, members of Parliament, and so on. Apropos of the usual arguments about collectivism, we ought, on this evidence, to be careful to distinguish the libertarian argument about the undesirability of governmental activity in some areas of a sacrosanct kind from the utilitarian argument about probable ineffectiveness of government activity. Mill, on this reading, was both more and less a collectivist than his father and Bentham had been—more in his wanting government to take a kind of cultural lead that they never expected of it, but less in that he attached, as they did not, a positive value to doing things for oneself wherever possible. Strictly speaking, there is not much place in utilitarianism for this sort of argument for the intrinsic merits of self-rule.[79] It was a notion imported into utilitarianism from outside—Mill's sources being Coleridge's concern for self-culture and Humboldt's enthusiasm for untrammelled self-expression.[80]

Now, one argument that bears on the above really does seem to have occupied Mill and Trevelyan alike, and this was the endless nineteenth-century debate about aristocracy versus democracy. It is obvious enough that much nineteenth-century debate centered on the problems of admitting to governmental positions persons who were gentlemen in neither origin nor manner. Trevelyan's leanings toward aristocratic principles have been misrepresented, but there is undeniably a concern for the aristocratic virtues in what he wrote.[81] There are many issues here rather than one; some of them relate to matters of lifestyle and whether the leisured and cultivated lives of the aristocracy were to be sacrificed to the perpetual pushing and scrambling that marked the existence of the urban middle class; others were issues of good management, issues that became particularly prominent when the Crimean War revealed the extent of maladministration in both the civilian and military services.[82] Some issues were raised in a spirit of pure moral indignation against the corruption and jobbery that marked aristocratic control; but some of the indignation could well have been synthetic, masking the fact that the opposition was less to the fact of jobbery than to the particular distribution of its spoils.

The tension between democracy and aristocracy appears in utilitarian theory as an ambivalence about the role of expertise vis-à-vis public opinion and elected governments. There are good grounds for adopting a utilitarian view that resembles the one offered in James Mill's *Essay on Government*, in which the expert simply decides on the most efficient way of realizing the will of the legislature. This omnicompetent body makes its will known, and the only question is that of how to put its will into effect. With a sleight of hand that no one has ever regarded as remotely convincing, James Mill equated the will of the electorate with the general interest—thus reducing the role of the expert in securing the general interest to a narrowly technical one. But when J. S. Mill came to write *Representative Government*, he saw democracy in no such simple light. In his view, democracy was liable to stagnation, to dead and oppressive conformity, and thus unlikely to make the kind of progress that he saw as the end of good government. What the people wanted and what they would have wanted, had they been wiser, could by no means be presumed to be the same thing; and Mill's mind was constantly drawn to ways in which democracy could be saved from itself and made to avail itself of superior talents. This preoccupation was displayed in Mill's addiction to proportional representation and a variety of fancy franchises.[83] But the activities of the civil service vis-à-vis the legislature provided another opportunity to serve the same ends. Mill's legislature was to be a debating body, not a legislating body;[84] after debating issues, it was to hand down instructions on matters of legislative importance, but it was not to try to draft legislation itself.[85] Drafting was a matter for expertise, and only a legislative commission could tackle the task properly. The legislature might approve or disapprove, or send back for alterations, but it was not to be allowed to amend. Permanent officials were thus given an elevated role, for they would have to go far beyond mere compliance with instructions if they were to translate necessarily general principles into the detail of legislation. It is, of course, true that concern with legislative ability is a continuing utilitarian trait, and one found even more in Bentham than in J. S. Mill—Bentham's major interest was always in the creation of a legal code, and it was only toward the end of his life that he turned from the legal question of how legislation was to be framed to the political question of who was to frame it. But it is only in J. S. Mill that this concern is harnessed to the desire to use whatever means were available to pursue progress in the face of the dangers of democracy.

Clearly, Mill's approach presupposes a good deal of authority among the civil servants whose task it is to advise ministers in their work. Trevelyan, too, emphasized the need for men "occupying a position duly subordinate to that of the Ministers who are directly responsible to the Crown and to Parliament, yet possessing sufficient independence, character, ability and experience to be able to advise, assist, and to some extent influence those who are from time to time set over them."[86] We have already seen Mill's skepticism about the newly arrived minister's capacity for business; and as a corrective, he advocated setting up a ministerial cabinet—a thing often suggested since—which would guide and advise the minister. But true to his standing concern for the antagonism of opinions, this was not to be a cabinet appointed by the minister himself, but a council of permanent independent advisers.[87] We need not recapitulate the arguments he employed in favor of such a device when defending the government of the East India Company, for he himself described the arrangements he had in mind as being very like those formerly obtaining in the government of India, arrangements that seemed "destined to perish in the general holocaust which the traditions of Indian government seem fated to undergo, since they have been placed at the mercy of public ignorance, and the presumptuous vanity of political men."[88] Throughout *Representative Government*, variations on this theme constantly recur; so much so that there is less need to dwell on them than on the fact that Mill was concerned to point to the infirmities of the best form of government, and not to argue that some other would be better. Mill maintained that in spite of everything, representative democracy was the best form of government, even though it is perhaps more interesting for our purposes that the second-best governments were those aristocracies that had virtually been bureaucracies, such as the one that oversaw the Venetian Republic. Even these were, taken overall, inferior to a well-constructed democracy; but as a rational being, he thought it folly not to try to obtain the advantages of other modes of government and to lessen the infirmities of the chosen mode.[89]

In all this, Mill's elitism was in tune with that of Trevelyan; but Mill perhaps went further in adhering to the principle that this was to be an elite of merit, not one chosen by birth; even in *Representative Government*, the old-fashioned radical prejudice crops up in statements to the effect that the characteristic concern of aristocratic regimes is to secure a steady supply of jobs for the friends of the regime.[90] And it is hard to imagine that Macaulay's commendation of the way the young Charles Trevelyan sat on his horse would have struck much of a chord with the utterly unathletic Mill.[91] Such qualities were simply not relevant to government, in much the same way that Stephen's charming pleas for the rights of the intellectually mediocre were out of place in the serious business of government service. The point, I think, is of more than biographical interest, for it shows up a certain weakness in the utilitarian dislike of the aristocracy and in Mill's hopes for its replacement by an aristocracy of talent. There is some cause to suppose that moral, intellectual, and spiritual leadership owe rather more to the qualities of leadership as such than Mill ever imagined. In other words, there is what we might call an intellectual cavalry, with dash, energy and initiative, which are not qualities simply reducible to intellectual ability. To hope to find many of these men in the civil service, or indeed in any routinized occupation, is perhaps asking too much. Stephen may well have been right in doubting that this was their natural arena.

To sum up, then, what I hope I have argued is this. There is no such thing as *the* utilitarian view of bureaucracy, either in the advocacy of more rather than less government or in pressing the claims of expertise against those of public opinion—and vice versa. It is not even the case that there is a single account to be given of the nature of expertise; utilitarianism shifts ambiguously between depicting the expert as a man who knows what will maximize the general welfare and who ought therefore to be allowed a free hand to manage our lives, and depicting the moral arena as one in which free beings make what claims they can on the right to tell experts (who possess a wholly factual kind of knowledge) what goals to pursue and what policies to implement—and here, of course, there is no question of the existence of "moral expertise." Behind these ambiguities lie the following considerations: to be a theory of any degree of generality, a moral theory like utilitarianism must be able to capture and explain moral attitudes that were not initially couched in utilitarian terms. So utilitarianism tends—as do religious creeds and any other ethical systems—to stretch the notions of pleasure and pain in order to accommodate what began as other values. This, I should emphasize, is not to say that there is nothing distinctive about utilitarian ethics, any more than the observation that Aristotelian and Newtonian physics both explain many of the same phenomena would support the argument that they were indistinguishable. What, indeed, I hope that this essay has shown is how the reformer's problems appear when they appear in a distinctively utilitarian guise.[92]

Mill and Rousseau: Utility and Rights

IN THIS ESSAY I attempt two rather different things. The first is to elucidate some differences between rights-based and utilitarian defenses of democracy; the second is to illustrate my account of these differences by reference to Mill and Rousseau. The account I give of Mill and Rousseau, however, is to some extent subversive of the account I give of the differences between rights-based and utilitarian justifications of democracy, and the resolution of this apparent contradiction forms the conclusion of this essay. I begin with a few remarks about recent treatments of Mill and Rousseau, to set the scene for what follows.

Since the early 1960s, the names of Mill and Rousseau have often been coupled. They have been seen as theorists of "participatory democracy," defenders of a classical ideal of citizen virtue and public spirit who could still teach us something about the point of democratic government.[1] The invocation of their names was part of a revolt against an excessively "realistic" style of theorizing that owed much to Joseph Schumpeter on the one hand and to the first students of American voting behavior on the other.[2] "Democracy" was defined, in terms drawn from the practice of British and American politics, as "that institutional arrangement for arriving at political decisions in which individuals acquire the power to decide by means of a competitive struggle for the people's vote."[3] When most people most of the time turn out to know little about politics beyond the name of the party they propose to vote for—they know little about the policies of their party, they have few views about the issues of the day—this need not impugn the democratic credentials of the political order; so long as teams of would-be decision makers present themselves to the voters, and incumbents leave office quietly in the event of defeat, we have a stable democratic order. Indeed, it was plausibly argued that the political quiescence of the common man was all to the good; he could not be expected to master complexities in the way professional politicians and administrators did, and if his views were allowed to determine policy too directly, policy would surely be too simple, too crude, and too clumsy. His proper task was to register a general satisfaction or dissatisfaction with the professionals in government, and this he could do through the ballot box every four or five years.[4] Some darker fears were raised by the contemplation of a more active citizenry. The common people were less tolerant, more authoritarian, and more prone to anger and resentment than were the better-off, better-educated, more practiced political classes; their direct entry onto the political stage would cause disasters of a kind, even if not on a scale, familiar from Nazi Germany.[5]

Mill and Rousseau seemed to offer grounds for optimism in the face of these anxieties and this "realism." It was true that the demands they made on the ordinary man—and ordinary woman, so far as Mill, though not Rousseau, was concerned—were much greater than the demands the "realists" made on the American voter. But this did not mean that Mill and Rousseau were simply wrong about "democracy." Mill and Rousseau were critics of reality; the political sociologists had simply endorsed it. If present-day voters fail to live up to the standards of democratic citizenship set by Mill and Rousseau, we may criticize the voters and the present political system rather than Mill and Rousseau.[6] Of course, if we could show that nobody *could* meet the requirements of Mill and Rousseau, we should be obliged to admit that their ideals were unrealistic; but both Mill and Rousseau have a great deal to say about the training citizens must get if they are to meet their requirements, as well as about the social and economic system that their political ideal presupposes.[7] If these views are well founded, current practices may properly be condemned as not fully democratic, but there is no reason to despair of the common people.

Even if their political ideals are not fully realizable—if the modern nation-state is simply too large and too elaborate for intelligent political participation by the mass of the population—they may provide us with participatory and democratic ideals in other areas of life—in the school, factory, or office, for instance.[8] With regard to Rousseau especially, we may well think that the price he would want us to pay for political participation is too high, that he would deny us the tolerance, the variety, and the prosperity of modern liberal societies; but we may also think that much of what he wanted is acceptable elsewhere.[9]

This is not the only interpretative possibility, however. Further reflection on the contrast between the demands made on the citizenry by Mill and Rousseau on the one hand and by modern writers on the other may make us doubt whether Mill and Rousseau were unequivocal democrats at all. They too recognized that the time, patience, commitment, strength of character, and the rest that we seek in those who devote their whole lives to political activity cannot be found in everybody. "Were there a people of gods," says Rousseau, "their government would be democratic. So perfect a government is not for men."[10] In practice, authority will and must gravitate toward a small number: "It is unimaginable that the people should remain continually assembled to devote their time to public affairs, and it is clear that they cannot set up commissions for that purpose without the form of administration being changed."[11] The whole people cannot devote its time to discussions of legislative and administrative detail; inevitably, some specialization will occur, and the people at large will play a more passive role in public affairs. For all human purposes, an element of aristocracy is required in government, and of the three sorts of aristocracy he distinguishes—the natural, the elective, and the hereditary—Rousseau says firmly: "The first is only for simple peoples; the third is the worst of all governments; the second is the best, and is aristocracy properly so called."[12]

That Rousseau defends elective aristocracy as the best form of government seems, moreover, to put him in Mill's company in this reading as firmly as did the "participatory" reading first suggested. For Mill's *Representative Government* is in many respects an extremely "elitist," or aristocratic, work; the duty of the average man and woman is not to try to govern themselves directly, but to elect those who will govern better than they could themselves. Mill, of course, goes further in insisting that even when we have elected our representatives to Parliament, they, too, should exercise a great deal of self-restraint and should avoid interfering with the detail of administration: "There is a radical distinction between controlling the business of government and actually doing it."[13] What is essential to representative government is that by law and by the positive morality of the state in question, the people, through their deputies, *can* dictate what the administrators may do. Government is, if you like, practically aristocratic, though morally democratic; since this aristocracy is answerable to the people through the electoral system, it is properly characterizable as an elective aristocracy.

This view of Mill and Rousseau as defenders of the same system of elective aristocracy will strike many readers as suspect. For it does not take into account one large contrast between them. Mill's treatise is entitled *Considerations on Representative Government*; like his father, Mill regarded representative institutions as one of the most important political inventions of the modern world. They bridged the gap between our desire to have the same grip on our governors as the citizens of Athens and Rome had on theirs, and our sense that large, complex, pluralistic societies simply cannot put the clock back and adopt the institutions of the city-state.[14] But Rousseau denies that the people can have representatives:

> The deputies of the people, therefore, are not and cannot be its representatives: they are merely its stewards and can carry through no definitive acts. Every law which the people has not ratified in person is null and void—is, in fact, not a law. The people of England regards itself as free; but it is grossly mistaken; it is free only during the election of members of parliament. As soon as they are elected, slavery overtakes it and it is nothing.[15]

The premise from which he deduces this result is that

> sovereignty . . . cannot be represented; it lies essentially in the general will and will not admit of representation: it is either the same, or other; there is no intermediate possibility.[16]

The reply to this appears between the lines in what follows. The outline of the answer, however, is simple enough. There is a strong case to be made on Rousseau's side, and one that is all the stronger if we insist on taking his talk of "the will" quite seriously and literally. For then it must be true that no law is law—that is, it has no morally binding force—except to those who have actually assented to it. My assent cannot be given by anyone other than me; the community's assent cannot be given by any body other than the community. To this, it might be replied that Rousseau is by no means clear in his use of the concept of the will and that little in the way of popular participation is required for the general will to be exercised. Until we have become clearer about the role of deliberative assemblies in Rousseau's scheme, we cannot be sure that he and Mill are wholly at odds, since we cannot be sure that what Rousseau says cannot be represented is anything that Mill thinks can be. But it is time to turn to the general problems of rights-based and utilitarian theories of democracy in order to show how this problem arises.

Democracy and Rights

A rights-based theory of democracy must be concerned above all else with questions of legitimacy and authority rather than with consequentialist questions. That is, a defense of democratic institutions in terms of rights must claim that a democratic government is uniquely legitimate rather than that a democratic government is more likely than any other kind of government to maximize utility. That this is the central issue for democratic theories founded on a doctrine of rights emerges both where writers think they can show that democratic governments are legitimate and where they despair of doing so. Thus, Ronald Dworkin derives the legitimacy of the liberal democratic state from our fundamental right to be treated with "equal concern and respect";[17] and Robert Paul Wolff, though he fears that the anarchist has the last word and that no government is legitimate, thinks that only "unanimous direct democracy" is compatible with individual moral autonomy.[18] We shall see a little later that Rousseau does think that there is something special about democracy, but not that it is the only legitimate government—indeed, we shall see that Rousseau thinks that governments are legitimate or illegitimate only at secondhand. What is legitimate or not is the legislative power and its laws. This is enough to ensure that Rousseau is in the mainstream of the argument connecting a concern for rights with a defense of democracy, since the question we can frame is this: "Under what conditions can I be obliged to obey laws, consistent with my natural right to perfect freedom?"

The obvious reply to this is that laws are (morally) obliging if they are made by a person or a procedure—or by persons acting under the terms of a procedure—that we have ourselves authorized. Each person starts with the right to act as he chooses, subject only to not infringing that right in others—infringing that right in others would presuppose that we already possessed the right to dictate how others should act, and the whole point of a natural-rights theory is to deny that such a right exists by nature. If we all possess authority over ourselves and over nobody else, political authority must be the result of compact or quasi compact. If authority over me exists only by grant from me, the binding force of law and the authority of those who make it must be traced back to my consent. To the extent that democracy is a form of polity in which either the laws, or the power to make laws, are assented to by everyone, democracy is uniquely legitimate.

It is clear that Rousseau began from these premises: "Since man has no natural authority over his fellow, and force creates no right, we must conclude that conventions form the basis of all legitimate authority among men."[19] Making others do what we wish is infinitely far from having the right that they should do as we say, and Rousseau mocks writers like Hobbes and Grotius who try to derive authority from de facto power. But the question that the natural-rights theorist faces is this: "How do we consent, and to what?" On the face of it, the answer must be that first we consent to there being a political community of which we are members—in effect, there is a club, and we are its members, bound by its rules. The sense in which what there is is not a state, or possesses no sovereign, if we do not all consent seems to be only that a political community that has de facto control over those within a given territory can treat as members only those who have consented to its authority over them; others under its control may be treated as harmless strangers or, if necessary, as enemies. Only members stand in relations with the community that raise questions of legitimacy. It is not that my refusal to recognize the British state, say, automatically deprives it of legitimacy; but it does mean that its dealings with me do not raise questions of legitimacy. However it treats me, I cannot complain that its acts are *ultra vires* (beyond its authority). This does not mean that it has no moral obligations toward me at all, though. It has duties under the law of nature, but not under the laws of its own constitution.

Thus far, we might find ourselves in the company of Hobbes and Locke as much as of Rousseau; and we should find ourselves in the company of untutored common sense too. States are artificial legal communities constituted by the allegiance of their members. Laws are morally binding on all those and only those who accept the state's authority, or, to put it more stringently, only those who accept the state's authority can treat its say-so as a sufficient reason to regard its laws as morally binding. Others must look to other considerations.[20] That the state does not, in practice, inquire into the consents of those to whom it applies its laws is easily explained; so long as the laws are required for the safety and well-being of the people, it is right to insist that all those whose obedience is needed should obey them. To require nonconsenters to obey is not tyrannical; indeed, it is a mild demand, since the state could, without displaying a merely neurotic fear of subversion, claim that the absence of their consents makes it reasonable to suspect that they will evade the law when they can, and makes it reasonable to impose fiercer penalties and a narrower scrutiny on them than on citizens.[21]

None of this, however, yields the conclusion that the only legitimate form of government is democracy. Indeed, since we have been keeping company with Hobbes, it seems that the argument thus far must legitimate absolute monarchy as readily as democracy.[22] The way in which it does so is clear enough: once we have consented to there being a state, the positive constitution of that state is whatever we unanimously declare it to be, and the law thereafter is whatever the constitution entitles us to call law. Thus, if we agree to be one political community and lay down that whatever the king-in-Parliament declares to be law is law, thereafter we are morally bound to take as the rule of our actions whatever the king-in-Parliament lays down.[23] If we are to tie consent to democracy in the required fashion, we need some way of avoiding these Hobbesian conclusions. The obvious way to do this is to deny that we can hand over the power to make law in such a comprehensive way. That is, we must deny that we can renounce in perpetuity the right to decide whether a law is legitimate. Hobbes, in effect, claims that once we have authorized the sovereign to make law, whatever he makes is genuinely and bindingly law. The test for the legitimacy of law is the test for the legitimacy of the lawmaker; if we made him sovereign by our consents, he is and remains sovereign. Rousseau's view—the view of anyone who wants to argue for something other than an absolute monarchy—is that the people must ultimately be sovereign; even if there is a temporary dictatorship, its authority exists only by concession and the concession is revocable.[24] The grounds for this view are to be found in the initial question; only if people are responsible moral agents can there be any point in asking whether governments are legitimate and their laws morally compelling. Hobbes's answer destroys the point of the question by asserting that people were once able to legitimate a government but that in doing so they lost the power to do so again. But ex hypothesi, it is just because we cannot have lost that power that we are able to ask the question.

So we reach the position that some sort of continuing consent to law is required; to put it more dismayingly, we reach the position that some way of preserving unanimous support for the laws is required.[25] This conclusion is dismaying because it seems unlikely that we could operate anything but the smallest and simplest of groups on a consensual basis like this. It is this that leads Wolff to concede the case to the anarchist; if these are the requirements of legitimate legislation, they cannot be met.[26] There is perhaps more room for maneuver than he supposes, however. At all events, what seems to connect democracy with unanimity is an interpretation of the nature of majority voting that is owed to Rousseau and that is not obviously fallacious.

Law requires the continuing consent of every member of a community if it is to be valid law. This is not, of course, to say that laws must be proposed by everyone, but that they must be assented to by everyone. We may leave their preparation to a small number of people, but we cannot leave their ratification to this small number; law is the command of the general will, and unless ratified by the general will, it is invalid.[27] The general will is by definition one will and not several, so the dictates of the general will cannot be anything other than unanimous; the interesting question is then what procedures reveal the dictates of the general will. If it can be argued that voting procedures of the sort we normally associate with democracy do, uniquely, reveal the general will, we may then claim that we have reconciled the demand for unanimity with the exigencies of everyday life. Since I do not think that Rousseau was an unequivocal or wholehearted democrat at all, I do not want to suggest that the argument I offer now is completely his or the only argument he offers. As I shall show later, Rousseau's twin tests for the general will—voting, on the one hand, and the tendency of the legislation in question to promote the general interest, on the other—pull in different directions. But there is an argument of a respectable sort to connect majority voting, unanimity, and the criteria for legitimacy, and it owes something to him.

The voting test is a procedural test: hence its connection with the individual's will. What we suppose is that individuals all will their continuing membership in a political community founded to protect everyone's interests. They need a procedure to make decisions about what is in everyone's interests; the question is what it is to be. It is important to stress that what everyone votes on is the question of what will promote the interests of everyone; only if everyone votes on that question can we accept that where things go badly, this will be the result of ignorance rather than wickedness.[28]

What makes majority voting attractive is this. If we ask questions like "What penalties for murder, fraud, or burglary would be in the general interest?" we should be unlikely to achieve unanimity. People who genuinely try to answer such questions with an eye to the welfare of everybody and not just of themselves will still disagree with one another. We expect, however, that although there will be nothing close to unanimity at this first stage, the decision to which the community, or the assembly, comes at this point will subsequently receive unanimous support. Once the decision has been taken, the question each person asks himself or herself is no longer what he or she independently thinks is for the best, but whether he or she should support the measures decided on. In short, if we are eager to achieve unanimity, what we adopt is a majoritarian procedure for taking what we might call provisional or prima facie decisions, although what would make them really binding was that they were, or could properly be, endorsed unanimously. But the claims of the procedure depend on our belief that the procedure has been used properly, that is, that those who were in the majority were attempting to answer the right question in a disinterested spirit.

If we are to remain at the level of an argument from procedure, we must claim that what majority voting achieves is the giving to each voice its fair and equal share in determining the outcome. I have no right to use any procedure whatever to try to grab a greater share of the general prosperity for myself; that is, I have no right to treat voting as a kind of moderated fight in which we are all out for what we can get for ourselves. It is only if I am trying to answer the right question that I can claim that my moral standing is impugned if my view is not taken exactly as seriously as that of anyone else. But if I am asking the right question, then my opinion must carry as much weight as anyone else's. It is worth noticing that in one interpretation, this argument is an argument against seeking unanimity, though on another, unanimity retains its attractions. That is, if our aim was to give each person equal influence on an outcome, anything other than simple majority voting seems to give an unfair degree of influence to the minority.[29] At its extreme, a unanimity rule would mean that the one person whose consent was necessary for a law to pass could exercise over its passage as much power as the whole of the rest of the society. If we are engaged in a rather different enterprise, something other than a simple majority is more defensible. If voting is like voting by members of a jury, the pressures for something better than a bare majority become obvious. The point of demanding something better than a simple majority is partly that if there is a question with a genuine answer being asked, we are more likely to find an overwhelming majority in the right than a bare majority; even if we are somewhat skeptical about the objectivity of the answer we are looking for, an overwhelming majority among disinterested voters is morally persuasive. If we are in a tiny minority, and we trust the serious intentions of the majority, we are likely to agree that the odds against our being right are so high that we must go along with the majority view.[30]

It is time to turn to a utilitarian view of these issues; but I must draw attention to what I have left dangling here. In Rousseau's employment of an argument much like the one I have just sketched, the question that voters are to ask is not exactly whether "the people approves or rejects the proposal, but whether it is in accordance with the general will, which is their will."[31] Because the general will is an objective entity, the connection between voting and the general will is not the connection between voting and procedural fairness we might infer from much of the above; it could be argued that a measure manifestly in the general interest is manifestly required by the general will, and that voting is, at best, the most reliable way of discovering whether something is in the general interest. There may well be other means, and if they are reliable enough, democratic procedures lose their peculiar attractions. It is on this point that we shall ultimately have to rely to show what departures from both democracy and a strictly rights-based theory of government Rousseau makes.

The argument from utility to democracy is briefer; it is essentially an external argument in the sense that there is no attempt to connect the legitimacy of a government with its possessing a democratic constitution. Indeed, in my view, utilitarian political theory has no place for the notion of legitimacy, strictly speaking. Whether a government is the lawful government of a territory is a factual question, that of whether it gets a habitual obedience from the overwhelming bulk of the population of that territory. A person in that territory knows which body of persons possesses sovereignty by applying that test. For himself, he has to make up his own mind whether and in what way the lawfulness of the government affects his duty to obey the laws it promulgates. A good utilitarian always seeks only one thing, which is the maximizing of the general utility, and in the light of that he makes up his mind how much claim on him the laws have. If he is a twentieth-century utilitarian and has been reading R. M. Hare, he will be scrupulous about not taking unfair advantage of other people's compliance with the law, too.[32] But the existence of government is a fact external to the concept of duty with which he works.

What, then, justifies democratic government? The answer is that only a government that is answerable to the whole population through some such device as periodic elections can be relied on to govern in the general interest and not in the interests of the members of the government alone.[33] A crude version of this doctrine is argued in James Mill's *Essay on Government*. Its premises are that each of us needs security of person and property in order to have either the prospect of happiness for ourselves or an incentive to work and cooperate with others. This requires the creation of government in order to organize the power to suppress those who would otherwise invade the persons and properties of the rest of us. The creation of government, however, poses a problem just as it solves one; since we need government to fend off the results of selfishness, what is to stop those who possess the power of government from employing it to exploit their subjects? James Mill's answer is that since only power can check power, the only acceptable form of government is one in which the community has the power to dismiss its rulers.[34] The way to do this in a modern society is by electing representatives who may be turned out if they govern us badly.

In this account of democracy, as much as in a rights-based theory, the acceptability of the people's vote as a way of determining policy and law depends upon everyone casting his vote with an eye to the interest of the public rather than with an eye to his own private interest.[35] There is, of course, a decided difficulty about this requirement, at any rate in the context of James Mill's *Essay*. The premises that make democracy necessary appear to make it inconceivable—we must have democracy because we cannot trust our rulers to govern disinterestedly, but democracy is acceptable only if we can trust the voters to vote disinterestedly. On the face of it, if virtuous voters are obtainable, we might hope for virtuous rulers, and if we may not do so, it suggests that virtuous voters are not obtainable.

James Mill's reply to this is obscure, but in essence it amounts to supposing that the people at large do not suffer from the same temptations as their rulers; power corrupts, rather than human nature. But what this all suggests is something quite important. For James Mill, the value of democracy is that it secures that the government is answerable to a body whose interests are identical with the general interest. We can now draw two inferences from this. The first is that if we were able to find a government that, for reasons other than the restraints imposed by elections, pursued the general interest, it would be as good as a democratic government. The implications for the British in India hardly need to be spelled out.[36] The other is that we do not need anything like universal suffrage to achieve the effects James Mill wants. So long as the electoral body is large enough to stop "sinister interests" from gaining too much influence, it is large enough to ensure that its interests and the general interest agree. It is from this observation that James Mill drew his notorious inference that women could safely be left off the electoral rolls, as could young men (those under forty, that is) and the propertyless.[37] The point is simple enough: in the utilitarian view, governments exist to protect our interests, and so long as our interests are protected, we can have no reason to participate in government. Because questions of legitimacy are not at issue, there is no pressure to ensure that each person has a voice in making decisions; because outcomes, assessed by the principle of utility, are all that is at issue, procedural issues are not directly relevant and individuals are not supposed to be concerned about the connection between outcomes and their own consents.

Doubts about Democracy

I began by saying that Rousseau and Mill threatened to upset my account of the connection between rights and democracy, on the one hand, and between utility and democracy on the other. I now turn to explicating that threat—in essence, by showing Rousseau to be a nostalgic republican, but less a democrat than I first suggested, and by showing Mill to be more a democrat and more concerned to argue that democracy has special claims on our allegiance than I have hitherto suggested that utilitarian theory allows.

Rousseau has already been quoted to the effect that elective aristocracy is the best form of government, and yet I have also invoked him to argue that a writer obsessed, as he was, with questions of legitimacy is pushed toward defending democracy. Now, one thing that is worth noticing is that Rousseau is explicit that government is not founded on a contract, though the legitimacy of law is.[38] What Rousseau has in mind is that there is no pact of obedience and protection between subject and ruler; rather, the sovereign legislates as to the form of the government, and then those who are to fill the appropriate niches are chosen.[39] Rousseau is much exercised by the problem of reconciling the choice of personnel with what he has earlier said about the generality of law and the requirement that laws should not refer to particular persons; and this gives democracy one rather peculiar claim to be special: "It is, indeed, the peculiar advantage of democratic government that it can be established in actuality by a simple act of the general will. Subsequently, this provisional government remains in power, if this form is adopted, or else establishes in the name of the sovereign the government that is prescribed law; and thus the whole proceeding is regular."[40] That is, all that could be the object of an acceptably general law is "that there should be a government of such and such a form"; appointment to office is a governmental act, and we seem to face the paradox that we need a government in existence to bring a government into existence. In the unique case of a democratic form of government, the people constitutes itself the government in the act of deciding that there should be a government of that form. Rousseau thinks there is nothing extraordinary about the people switching from legislation to executive action, and cites the way in which the House of Commons can act as a committee of the whole house and then report back to itself.[41]

The upshot of this, though, is that although democracy occupies a special place, other forms of government may be constituted as legitimately as it; all governments get their legitimacy by grant from the people, but it is a matter of prudential calculation what sort of government to create by such a grant of authority. At this point, Rousseau is actively hostile to democracy, for democracy is more riven with factions than any other form of government, demands tremendous public spirit and self-control in its citizens, and will work only if the state is small, economic equality is maintained, and issues are kept simple so that the ordinary citizen can understand them, vote on them, and administer the laws he has helped to make. These observations are in line with the claims made by Montesquieu and others. They suggest that for all practical purposes, the best form of government is elective aristocracy; although Rousseau follows Montesquieu in thinking that large countries need monarchs, and that large countries with hot climates are all but doomed to despotic governments, it seems that there is some scope for choice in constitution building and that where there is, elective aristocracy is what is wanted.[42]

This raises the question of the role of the people under such a regime. It is unclear to me how we should integrate Rousseau's remarks about the Roman Republic into the main argument of the *Social Contract*; however, I suppose that we should not simply leave Rousseau's arguments about legitimacy and his borrowings from Machiavelli's *Discorsi* to jangle against each other. If not, we reach, I think, the following view. Republican governments are the best form of government; they maximize the number of citizens, and they achieve liberty. That is, they are ruled by law, not by the whim of one man or one class; and they are ruled by their own laws. Moreover, their laws are the reflection of the general will. Now, in saying this, we are not claiming that the ordinary man plays an active political role; we are not claiming that he is to initiate legislation or take part in discussions of the merits of legislation; nor are we arguing for *la carrière ouverte aux talents* (careers open to the talented), for social mobility, or for an open, democratic society in the twentieth-century sense.[43] The general will is realized, less because of what anyone wills than because the society is one with a clearly defined common interest and because those who wield the initiative do so in the interests of the whole society and not of themselves alone. Rousseau's talk of the will is slightly deceptive—or, perhaps, "will" is not an altogether apt rendering of *volonté*. At all events, a society possesses a *volonté générale*, not by virtue of acts of the will of individuals, but by virtue of being a coherent community with enough shared interests to enable it to function. It follows that a law that is in the interests of all members of the society, treating all of them fairly, in accordance with policies that would make the average person as happy as possible over the long run, is what the general will requires. Whether we have the wit to see it is a separate question.[44]

This raises the obvious question of why republican Rome seems almost uniquely desirable as a political solution. The answer is that the system of mutual checks, the place allowed for leadership, the happy match of the economic and political circumstances of the country, and the high state of citizen morale all conspired together to ensure that for a very long time at least, the government did invariably act in the general interest. The people played their proper role in such a system: they acted as a check upon corruption.[45] For the people to play this role, they needed to be properly organized too: "It is impossible to be too careful to observe, in all such cases, all the formalities necessary to distinguish a regular and legitimate act from a seditious tumult."[46] The Roman people could play their role of checking the ambitions of their rulers only because they were provided with wise leadership. Given wise leadership, the people at large are more or less infallible in their opposition to corruption, since they do not have the ambitions that would lead them to try to make alliances to subvert the constitution, and if affairs are simple, their lack of sophistication is not likely to lead them into being bamboozled. Indeed, Rousseau suggests that the unsophisticated are likely to see through wiles that would take in the educated.[47]

Republican Rome was not a democracy; it was a mixed popular government in which birth and wealth were given advantages, but not so many advantages that a few rich men could outvote the rest of the population. It was not a democracy in twentieth-century terms or in Rousseau's. There was no commitment to formal political equality, no thought that formal civil rights needed to be complemented by equality of opportunity or "welfare rights." It was a government in which the people played an indispensable but relatively passive role. Whether it was a government that has any twentieth-century analogy or any twentieth-century message is arguable. On the whole, admirers of it are likely to stress what we have lost rather than to suggest how we might recapture it; and since Robespierre, most commentators have taken a cautious view of the prospects for a revival of republican virtue.[48] The only points I want to emphasize, however, are these: Rousseau's conception of the general will appears not to require democracy, and if we could show that the average citizen of the modern stare is not hopelessly corrupted by affluence, his political passivity need not alarm Rousseau. The absence of occasions for plebiscitary endorsement of the constitution might worry him; but if we could display a system of checks and balances working with tolerable efficiency, we might find Rousseau prepared to accept more of the modern state than we should expect at first sight.

If Rousseau is less a democrat than my initial account of rights-based defenses of democracy suggested that he ought to be, J. S. Mill turns out to be rather more a democrat than my account of the relatively loose connection between utilitarianism and democracy suggested he ought to be. I do not wish to deny that there are strongly aristocratic strains in *Representative Government*; that some men and women are simply better than others is not a proposition Mill flinches from. What I want to suggest is that Mill does what I denied that utilitarians could plausibly do—that is, take seriously the thought that democratic governments are uniquely legitimate.

The primary claim made for representative government by Mill is that it is the most progressive form of government; it makes more demands on its citizens than any other, and these demands are educative. It makes as much use as possible of existing abilities and promotes as much as possible the development of new abilities. On the face of it, this is a utilitarian argument, even if one that stresses the development of character as much as the satisfaction of more obvious interests. But it is a utilitarian argument that makes the possession of a capacity for self-government central.

Thus, if we turn to Mill's discussion of benevolent despotism, we find him arguing that it "is a radical and most pernicious misconception of what good government is" to suppose that "if a good despot could be ensured, despotic monarchy would be the best form of government."[49] On the contrary, says Mill, a good despot would simply deprive his subjects of energy, intelligence, and public spirit; and a mild despot would prepare the way for a less mild one by making his subjects too passive to resist. To suppose that a good despot might preserve the spirit that democracy produces is incoherent; it can be done only by giving people the right to discuss public issues, to organize, to protest, and all the rest. This, then, raises the question of whose will is to prevail if the despot and public opinion are at odds; if public opinion prevails, we have an inadequate constitutional monarchy, and if not, we have a sham that cannot achieve the advantages of a government whose subjects enjoy genuine liberty.[50]

Can there be circumstances in which democracy is not a good thing? For Mill, the answer is certainly yes; quite apart from temporary dictatorships in advanced societies, "despotism is a legitimate mode of government in dealing with barbarians, provided the end be their improvement, and the means justified by actually effecting that end."[51] But when people are sufficiently advanced to be able to manage their affairs by discussion between free and equal citizens, then only one form of government is legitimate. The arguments in favor of forms of government of a nondemocratic kind presuppose that democratic governments have a special status; all other forms of government are warranted to the extent that they inculcate the necessary self-discipline, public spirit, good order, and the rest to allow democracy to operate. The argument was employed at its clearest when Mill set out to justify the East India Company's management of Indian affairs; the company's record, said Mill, was one of improvement. He freely admitted that it was a despotic government in that it was neither chosen by the Indian people nor directly answerable to them. He justified this by a principle that offered a new and different version of a "good despot" from that discussed above; the East India Company itself ran on the principles that ought to animate a democracy—answerability and antagonism of opinions—but in the Indian context, its role was to put itself out of business by teaching its Indian subjects how to govern themselves.[52] Once India could practice self-government, the East India Company's rule would be illegitimate.

Representative government, then, is defended on the grounds that it is self-government; persons at a certain level in human development are, essentially, sovereign agents who have a right to govern themselves and whose rights are violated when they are kept in leading strings any longer than necessary. The same message is reiterated in many of Mill's essays; the essay *The Subjection of Women* is a long argument to the effect that the moral equality of women and men means that women must enjoy the same legal and political liberties as men. Moreover, since the argument relies on the assumption that no people that has attained liberty will sell it at any price, the conclusion must be that a society in which men and women are equal will also be one in which every man and woman will have an equal vote in political matters.[53] In *The Principles of Political Economy*, workers' control emerges as the only form of industrial organization compatible with the modern workers' striving after citizenship and self-government. There may in the future be some peculiarly feeble or obtuse laborers who will be content to work for a capitalist employer, but for the most part, assumes Mill, self-respect will forbid it.[54] This is consistent with, indeed it rests on, Mill's belief in the superiority of some men and women to their fellows. The point, rather, is that self-respecting men and women will obey those whom they choose to govern them, especially since they will choose them on the ground of their superior ability to see what the general interest requires or their superior sense of where progress lies; they will not obey those who lay claim to authority on the grounds of birth or wealth.[55] A final point that needs to be brought into the account is that Mill thinks of representative government as, above all else, government by discussion. Conflicting opinions must be sought and argued through; a constant lively questioning of what is done is what lies between a genuine representative democracy and the tyranny of the majority.[56]

If this is an accurate account of Mill, it strongly suggests not only that democracy is a good form of government because it secures the compliance of governments with the people's wishes, but also that it is a quite special form of government because it is, uniquely, one in which individuals are treated as fully responsible adults, with duties to their country and rights to the whole range of civil and political liberties. Only in such a system can they rightly feel that the government is their government.[57]

Rights versus Utility

I began by admitting that Mill and Rousseau would provide a certain amount of trouble for my account of the differences between rights-based and utilitarian defenses of democracy; for, on my account of it, rights-based theories should be concerned with legitimacy rather than consequences, democracy should be defended as uniquely legitimate, and other forms of government accepted, if at all, very much as a *pis aller* (last resort). Rousseau, it goes without saying, is a rights theorist. Conversely, utilitarian theories may give us good consequentialist grounds for approving of democracy, but there is no attempt to argue that democratic procedures are themselves special for anything other than consequentialist reasons. J. S. Mill, it goes without saying, is a utilitarian. Yet Rousseau seems to prefer something other than democracy; Mill seems to be more deeply committed to democratic procedures than pure utility warrants. Either they employ their own moral schemes oddly, or I have misrepresented the resources of the two theories.

The answer to this challenge is not altogether simple, but in essence it involves pointing to the utilitarian and prudential elements in Rousseau's theory of government and to the role of individual rights in Mill's utilitarianism. Some of this has been done already, but we can now summarize the results. As far as Rousseau is concerned, we have to bear two things in mind: the difference between the sovereign and the government on the one hand, and the twofold nature of the general will on the other. The nature of sovereignty is the nature of law, and Rousseau says firmly: "I therefore give the name 'Republic' to every state that is governed by laws, no matter what the form of its administration may be; for only in such cases does the public interest govern and the *res publica* rank as a *reality*. Every legitimate government is republican."[58] In this sense, a constitutional monarchy is a republican form of government, but an absolute monarchy not. If a state is governed by laws so that there is nowhere in it merely personal power, it is, for Rousseau, a republican government and it can appeal to the legitimacy of its authority in dealing with its subjects.

Governments, therefore, are merely ministers of the law, creatures of the constitution; we seem to have a doctrine that is what one might call a constrained version of Hobbes. The constitution is legitimate if we all consent to it; the government exercises legitimate power if it is operated in accordance with the constitution; the difference between this doctrine and Hobbes's is that the constitution cannot give absolute, arbitrary, and irrevocable power to anyone. But so long as the government is governed by a constitution, it need not be democratic in form. Moreover, Rousseau's account of why government is instituted at all is heavily indebted to the utilitarianism underlying Hobbes's account. People have conflicting interests, and they have shared interests; conflicts of interest make government necessary, and shared interests make government possible.[59] Competing traders have conflicting interests in the outcome of their competition; they share an interest in the maintenance of order and the administration of a sensible system of property law. So long as the law is concerned with their common interests and not concerned to favor one over the other, the law articulates their common will. Legitimate governments are those that promote the welfare of the anonymous man. Rousseau's emphasis on equality and simplicity can be seen as ways of uniting a broadly utilitarian goal with individual commitment; a government that favors nobody, sacrifices nobody to anyone else, and operates in a generally benevolent way will, in the long run, do as much as it can for the average man. But a society in which there are great inequalities is one in which few people will have a close identification with the average man. This is why Rousseau's desire for a good deal of uniformity is not only, even if it is quite largely, a nostalgic and sentimental plea for the ancient Romans.

Now, if it is true in addition that what makes the general will a general will is not so much the number of people who will it as the object to which it is directed, we come close to saying that a government that operates according to the rule of law and is concerned always to promote the welfare of all its subjects to the extent that it can do so without sacrificing any of them to the rest is a legitimate government. Whether its form is democratic or aristocratic or even monarchical is not essential; what it aims at and how it does it is essential. This, to be sure, weakens the contractual element in Rousseau's theory to the point where it is equivalent to Kant's understanding of the social contract:

> It is in fact merely an idea of reason, which nonetheless has undoubted practical reality; for it can oblige every legislator to frame his laws in such a way that they could have been produced by the united will of the whole nation, and to regard each subject, in so far as he can claim citizenship, as if he had consented within the general will. This is the test of the rightfulness of every public law. For if the law is such that a whole people could not *possibly* agree to it, it is unjust.[60]

What we are left with is the hypothetical contract, an intellectual device that reconciles utility and justice by encouraging us to ask whether legislation is such that we should have assented to it in ignorance of how it would affect us individually; the pursuit of the general welfare on terms fair to all is what ought to emerge from such a thought experiment.[61] To the extent that there is still in Rousseau's work a decided favoring of something more participatory than this, it comes not from the bare argument from legitimacy, nor from the analysis of the concept of a general will, but from a commitment to achieve the civic liberty of the classical republics rather than from a commitment to have a republican—that is, a constitutional—regime at all.[62] As a defender of democracy in the modern world, Rousseau would need to be taken seriously but cautiously.

The case of Mill is rather different. For Mill's defense of representative government raises, rather, the question whether he does not slip from utilitarian to rights-based arguments or, more generally, whether he does not tailor his utilitarianism to make democracy special—in particular, by crediting people with a desire for self-government and improvement that means democratic politics produces a special degree of utility. There is no short answer to this question. Moreover, it is a question that bears as much upon the understanding of *On Liberty* as on the understanding of *Representative Government*. All the same, something along the following lines seems to catch the sense of what Mill requires. To argue from what he terms "abstract right" would commit us to a doctrine about legitimate authority that invoked the idea of a social contract, and such an idea is unhelpful.[63] All the same, even if societies are not founded on a contract, the scope of legitimate authority may be understood as if they were; what men and women would not rationally contract into cannot be a legitimate form of authority. Employed as it is employed in *On Liberty*, this subverts the "tyranny of the majority" by insisting that however social rules are made, there are some things they cannot be made about at all. And this, in turn, is a way of discovering what rights people ought to have recognized.[64] The difficulty with this argument is obviously that it seems to rest on something more than utility alone, since what it appears to invoke is something closer to the injustice rather than the disutility of ignoring some voices in the determination of the law. In many places in his work, Mill lays it down as an axiom that modern society is impossible except on terms of equality. This, of course, gives us a rights-based account of why the burden of proof now rests with those who wish to limit voting rights or to restrict access to office; what is less clear is that it gives us a utilitarian account.[65]

At this point, all one can do is point out that Mill's utilitarianism possesses an unusual but not unpersuasive property, that of giving an account of the conditions under which committed utilitarians would recognize one another as possessing rights that no utilitarian considerations ought to override. In essence, we can admit both the suggestions offered above—that Mill appeals to consideration of rights and legitimacy, and that his utilitarian arguments presuppose something close to a desire for self-government among those whose welfare is at issue—but deny that this amounts to a weakening of his case. For his case would be that what we might call the tailoring of his account of utilitarianism to justify democracy is better described as a discovery about the full resources of the doctrine of utility. The simpler version of utilitarianism espoused by James Mill would leave little room for the thought that democracy is uniquely legitimate, and its justification of democracy would be external and consequentialist alone, in the way we saw before. A more developed utilitarianism has a more complex view of the individual and his rights and a more elaborate view of what motivations he acquires in the appropriate political environment.

I hope, to sum up, that this at any rate suggests that the claim that rights-based defenses of democracy are distinctive, partially nonconsequentialist, and concerned with legitimacy, while utilitarian defenses are the reverse, survives the examples of Mill and Rousseau. For, on my view of it, each employs the language of individual rights in a context where legitimacy is at issue and where democracy emerges as a special solution to problems of legitimacy, and each allows utilitarian considerations to make a difference to what institutional arrangements we practice—though they do so in very different ways, since it remains true that Rousseau's ethics are fundamentally the ethics of natural right and Mill's are fundamentally utilitarian. I shall not try to decide whether they are unequivocal democrats, nor whether their defenses of citizenship have an obvious purchase on our present anxieties; I hope, indeed, that I have shown how rash it would be to plump for simple answers and how cautious we must be in invoking the shades of Mill and Rousseau in a twentieth-century context.

Bureaucracy, Democracy, Liberty
SOME UNANSWERED QUESTIONS
IN MILL'S POLITICS

MILL'S *AUTOBIOGRAPHY* was intended to provide the reader with the authorized version of Mill's life. It was the life of the John Stuart Mill who had been born the son of James Mill, the author of *The History of British India*, and nobody whose interest lay in anything other than the education he had received first from his father and then from Mrs. Taylor was encouraged to read it. At the outset, Mill says: "The reader whom these things do not interest, has only himself to blame if he reads farther, and I do not desire any other indulgence from him than that of bearing in mind that for him these pages were not written" (*Collected Works* [hereafter cited as *CW*] 1:5). There are many reasons for lamenting Mill's preoccupation with paying his debts to his father and Harriet Taylor. On this occasion, my regret is that Mill was reluctant to unbutton himself about issues about which he might have changed his mind between his precocious youth and the years of retirement during which he published *On Liberty, Considerations on Representative Government*, and *The Subjection of Women* along with *Utilitarianism, Auguste Comte and Positivism*, and *An Examination of Sir William Hamilton's Philosophy*.

When writing about Mill's contribution to the development of utilitarian ethics, we might wish that he had said much more about the way his essays "Bentham" and "Whewell's Moral Philosophy," together with the final chapter of *A System of Logic*, underlay or did not underlie *Utilitarianism*. For my purposes in this essay, it would have been interesting to know more about what Mill thought about the bearing of the way India was governed on the way the United Kingdom should be governed; about the extent to which he had grown out of the anxiety about moral authority that permeated his youthful essay "The Spirit of the Age"; and about the extent to which he felt that he had achieved a stable balance between a utilitarian concern with benevolent management and an "Athenian" concern with the self-assertive, self-critical, engaged, public-spirited, but independent-minded citizen (Urbinati 2002). In the absence of Mill's answers to my questions, I offer speculative answers on his behalf. But the best I can say is what Thucydides said of the speeches he put into the mouths of Greek statesmen and generals in his history of the Peloponnesian War on those occasions when he had neither been present nor obtained firsthand reports: "In the way I thought each would have said what was especially required in the given situation, I have stated accordingly, with the closest possible fidelity on my part to the overall sense of what was actually said" (Thucydides 1991:13 [i.e., 1.22]).

India and Empire

India illuminates, sometimes in alarming ways, Mill's views on many subjects: peasant proprietors, the nature of progress, the governance of dependent states, the ethics of coercive intervention in the affairs of other societies for liberal reasons, and the limits of the doctrine that we may not coerce other people for their own good. I here discuss only Mill's views on the government of India and their implications for his views about empire, progress, and pluralism. Then I move on to the issue of authority and the difficulty of knowing quite what Mill's final assessment was of the condition of modern society: whether we suffer from a deficit of authority, a surfeit, or, more plausibly, from a deficit of the right kind of authority and a surfeit of the wrong kind. I end by doing what I can to balance Mill's deep conviction that man for man, the Athenian was a better citizen than the Victorian Englishman with his equally deep conviction that the making of law and the administration of public business were best left to experts.

First, India. Mill's account of his time in the East India Company is not dismissive, but it is brief and not suggestive of any great passion for the work. If it was not faute de mieux, it was certainly not the center of his interests; its merit was that it gave him a reasonable income for work that was a great deal better than drudgery and not too onerous. He had initially been destined for a career at the bar, which would have given him a much larger income and no more work than the company. But his father was appointed to a senior permanent position in the company's London offices in 1819, and appointed his son to a clerkship in the company in 1823, when John Mill was sixteen. He remained there for thirty-five years, retiring when the company was wound up in the aftermath of the Indian Mutiny of 1857. He disapproved of the dissolution of the company and refused to serve on the successor council, but his loyalty to the company does not appear to have been very great. He says in the *Autobiography*, "I do not know of any one of the occupations by which a subsistence can now be gained, more suitable than such as this to anyone who, not being in independent circumstances, desires to devote a part of the twenty-four hours to private intellectual pursuits" (*CW* 1:85). His position at India House was highly suitable to his requirements; he worked from ten to four, and during much of that time he was free to write essays and portions of his books rather than drafts of the instructions that were to go to officials in India. He goes on to say that he had

> through life found office duties an actual rest from the other mental occupations which I have carried on simultaneously with them. They were sufficiently intellectual not to be distasteful drudgery, without being such as to cause any strain on the mental powers of a person used to abstract thought, or to the labour of careful literary composition. (85)

Mill's position was in the office of the examiner of India correspondence, a somewhat odd title for the man who ensured that the East India Company was able to manage the affairs of the subcontinent effectively. By the time J. S. Mill joined it, the East India Company was operating a "contracted out" form of government on behalf of the government of the United Kingdom. It lost its last commercial functions in the 1833 charter renewal. Earlier, the company had had a checkered history; it had never made money, but its individual employees–the company's servants—had made a great deal. Until the late eighteenth century, individuals could trade on their own accounts; the profits this allowed, together with the "presents," or bribes, they received from Indians hoping for favors, enabled young men to accumulate quantities of wealth that astonished and outraged their compatriots: having grown up on the history of the subversion of the Roman Republic by men who had grown rich on the plunder of the East, their critics feared—or said that they feared—that the "Nabobs" would return from India, buy seats in Parliament, and exercise a corrupt influence on British politics.

In Mill's day, it was still possible to make a great deal of money in India, but this was not because company employees traded on their own accounts or took bribes. It was rather because the hazards of working in an unhealthy climate were such that in addition to the already substantial income that a lawyer, for example, might make in England, there was a substantial risk premium for working in India. Otherwise, anyone wanting to make a great deal of money had to do it by working for someone other than the company, whose civil and military servants benefited from the cheapness of life in India more than from the size of their incomes. What Mill worked for was a curiosity, but it was in essence an arm's-length administrative mechanism of the British government, the virtues of which Mill defended at the time of the 1853 renewal of the charter, in the last year of the company's existence, when he was fighting to prevent its extinction, and in *Considerations on Representative Government*, when he was contemplating the best way of governing colonies (CW 19:562–77, esp. 577).

Mill's views on empires and the British Empire have been much discussed in recent years.[1] They aroused little interest until recently, and there is much to be said for this neglect. Mill was not a very interesting theorist of the imperial project and does not show to advantage in his casual comments on the subject. The center of his attention was mid-Victorian England, and when it was not, it was the France of Guizot and Tocqueville, Louis Blanc, and Auguste Comte, of philosophers such as Victor Cousin and adventurers such as Napoleon III. He could not but take some interest in imperial adventures both French and British, partly because of his detestation of the foreign policies of Lord Palmerston and Adolphe Thiers in the late 1830s and early 1840s and perhaps more because once he had absorbed Coleridge's ideas about nationality in the mid-1830s, he was forced to pay attention to issues of national identity. Mill acknowledged that nations were held together by sentiment and that one of the most powerful of these sentiments was the fellow feeling created by a common political history; and one element in fellow feeling might well be pride in our forebears' achievements. Among those achievements was the acquisition of an empire, and Mill writes as though it is incontestable that the possession of an empire adds to Britain's prestige in the world, although he does so in an arm's-length fashion (see, e.g., CW 19:564–66).

Recent readers have been more startled than they should that Mill was unembarrassed that Britain possessed an empire and that many Britons were pleased by this. Mill's unembarrassment, however, was not the same thing as enthusiasm for, or deep interest in, Britain's imperial possessions. He was interested in colonization in the context of the English settlement of New Zealand and Australia, but as a contribution to resolving the population problem in Britain and Ireland, not as a contribution to national self-esteem. Territorial expansion for its own sake was not something in which he saw merit, and it is worth remembering that until late in the nineteenth century, the conventional British view was that a trading nation such as Britain needed bases for refitting its naval vessels and revictualling its crews, not the encumbrance of unprofitable territories. It was a characteristic trope in Mill that he allowed the French more latitude in expressions of national pride in their empire than he allowed the British. The British had evicted the French from North America and India and ought to be neither surprised that the French felt aggrieved nor dismayed that the French wished to acquire a new empire. But Mill's tone of voice was that of someone who acknowledged a forgivable human failing, not that of someone who himself felt surges of national pride at the contemplation of imperial glory. It was the same tone of voice in which Mill's godson Bertrand Russell criticized the foreign policy of the British government in 1914. Germany was playing "catch up" and might be forgiven a degree of obstreperousness and self-assertion impermissible in the British.

Contrasting Mill's attitude to India with Tocqueville's attitude to Algeria is instructive, although less so than it would have been if they had corresponded on the subject. Tocqueville was not merely less squeamish than Mill about the violence of the conquest but almost exultant about it; as Mill did not, Tocqueville came from a family that were *noblesse de l'épée* (nobility of the sword), and he lamented, as Mill would not have known how, the fact that he was too frail to take up a military career. Tocqueville's two brothers served in the military, as did his distant cousin and close friend Louis de

Kergolay, with whom he corresponded about Algeria. Mill was concerned with good government, not national glory. His discussion of the government of dependent territories in *Representative Government* is a concise defense of the proposition that it is possible to achieve good despotism, but that such a government is likely to be achieved only when the despotic government is drawn from somewhere other than the country over which it is exercised: "Under a native despotism, a good despot is a rare and transitory accident: but when the dominion they are under is that of a more civilized people, that people ought to be able to supply it constantly" (*CW* 19:567).

The argument is simple. Ordinarily, Mill thinks benevolent despotism is a contradiction in terms; and in a country capable of self-government, despotism is intolerable. Benevolent despotism in that context is even worse than nonbenevolent despotism on the principle of "damn braces, bless relaxes"— for a government to nanny its citizens when they are capable of governing themselves is worse than simple oppression leading to rebellion. The argument for despotism applies where an alien power governs under conditions in which the governed cannot provide good government for themselves. The puzzle is how an unaccountable government is to be kept honest. Unaccountable governments habitually descend into something like kleptocracy. There was no question of relying on British settlers to observe the decencies. Like most nineteenth-century British liberal writers, Mill was concerned about the tendency of settlers to become savage and exploitative; if English settlers in India were not to treat Indians with contempt and exploit them mercilessly, they had to be held in check by government. This sharpens the puzzle: if settler governments are unashamedly exploitative, how is an alien government to be made to behave better?

Mill's argument, whether in *Representative Government* or in explaining the virtues of the East India Company in the *Morning Chronicle* in July 1853 or, before that, in giving evidence to the House of Lords committee on the renewal of the company's charter was always the same.[2] The government on the ground must be carried on by persons trained to the job but answerable to an authority in Britain. For the sake of fostering self-government, Mill envisaged more and more of the senior posts within the Indian administration inside India being occupied by Indians over a period of years; and for the sake of fostering simple efficiency, he was pleased that by the time he retired, the mixed system of patronage and examination that had prevailed since 1805 was giving way to a more purely competitive system—it was no accident that Sir Charles Trevelyan, the joint author of the Northcote-Trevelyan Report of 1854, which launched the modern British civil service, cut his administrative teeth in India. It is often observed that Mill never saw India, with the implication that he can have known nothing about the country whose affairs he was helping direct; but Mill's role was that of drafting questions and advice for the directors to send to the people who knew India and were working there. Nor was Mill drafting for people who did not know the country firsthand. The rules governing the composition of the board of directors required a steadily increasing number of its members to have served at least ten years in the administration of India in India itself. It was not news to the London office that it was inevitably at the mercy of its in-country staff in the short term; but the directives that were sent were agreed to by experienced people, were frequently broad-brush statements of policy and principle, and often took the form of retrospective approval or disapproval of acts taken by local officials.

One may think Mill's view of the ease of achieving good government for dependent territories was Pollyannaish; he may have been readier to believe that good intentions would translate into good practice than he should have been. But Mill knew that good intentions allied to ignorance would cause trouble. He was, for instance, adamantly hostile to letting missionaries get their hands on the Indian educational system. This was not because he was hostile to Christianity or because he had a deep respect for the native culture of the subcontinent, but because he thought it was politically dangerous. Whereas we might think religious freedom would be enhanced by allowing any religion whatever to set up schools, Indians would believe that the schools were part of a plot to overthrow Hinduism and establish Christianity in its place. After the mutiny, the last thing any rational person wanted was to excite that fear. Mill may have been overoptimistic about the virtues of the East India Company, but he was not gullible (CW 19:570).

Progress

Mill's argument for the right way to govern an empire was simple. Governments that are unaccountable to their subjects were despotisms; that was true by definition. Colonial governments were unaccountable to their subjects and were therefore despotisms. The question that could not be settled by definition was whether the British government could ensure that India was governed by a good despotism. The answer was that the government could, but not by allowing a lot of ignorant members of Parliament or vote-seeking ministers to occupy the role of despot. Governing through a "double government" in which people with an interest in the local welfare could filter ministerial views and ministers could ensure that those people were of reasonable probity and intelligence was the way to achieve good despotic government.

The justification of despotism for the short run was progress over the long run, and that meant, inter alia, progress toward rendering despotism obsolete. Mill's readiness to announce that a good stout despotism was sometimes the best route to achieve progress strikes different readers differently. Some like the abrasiveness of the approach; others flinch, fearing that Mill overlooked the obvious fact that it is easier to install good stout despots than to ensure that they remain good and produce progress. Mill offered a short and highly selective list of candidates for the title of good despot, not all of whom provide persuasive evidence. Peter the Great, Elizabeth I, and Charlemagne are, in different places, offered as having had a better understanding of their people's needs than the people themselves had. This may be true enough; it is likely to be true under many sorts of regimes that the rulers of a society have a better understanding of affairs than do their subjects; but it is not obvious that the despotic qualities of Mill's heroes were essential to whatever good they did their people. In the case of Peter the Great, it is all too plausible that it was the despotic and absolutist aspects of his government that ensured social and political progress were not sustained. Conversely, it is not obvious that Elizabeth exercised a truly despotic authority. She declared herself "an absolute princess," but she frequently had to persuade a skeptical Parliament to grant her the resources to govern with at all.

Mill's argument is one from the occasional necessity for violent and irregular methods, for it was not only despotism that Mill advocated as an intrinsically undesirable but sometimes inescapable means of progress. In an interesting letter on the Polish insurrection of 1863, addressed to the editor of the *Penny Newsman*—his old friend Edwin Chadwick—Mill argued that almost any country in eastern Europe would benefit from revolution. He admitted that the Emancipation Decree of 1861 by which the czarist government had emancipated the serfs had been a step forward; he went on to point out that it had secured the serfs' personal liberty without doing anything for their access to the land to which they had once been enserfed. The French Revolution had secured the ownership of the land they worked for French peasant proprietors, and a Polish revolution would be wholly justified if it did the same for Polish peasants. Mill was not impressed by military glory, and he had no taste for violence for its own sake, but he found it easy to sympathize with violent insurrection from below.[3] The point is worth making only because his views on despotism have attracted attention in a way that his views on revolution have not, and it is easy to think that the point at issue is Mill's "elitism." It is not; the point is rather one about the permissibility of violent shortcuts when more deliberative methods are unavailable.

Mill's conception of progress needs more discussion than it will receive here. For our immediate purposes, the discussion here serves only to raise the familiar question whether progress for Mill is convergent or divergent. The answer is that it is both; but it is not both for all sorts of progress. More importantly, there are several forms of progress that need to be disentangled but also to be re-entangled in due course. In the case of India, which in this respect is very like the case of Ireland, there is a substratum of practical advancement that is the precondition of other sorts of progress, although once a virtuous circle is established, practical advancement becomes the means of practical advancement as well. When Mill set out to defend the East India Company against dissolution, he produced a memorandum of the improvements in the condition of India that the company had made over the previous three decades. Many of the improvements were infrastructural:

docks, roads, and railways. Others were legal and institutional. Inducing Thugs to become tent makers might be thought to have been both infrastructural and psychological ("Memorandum of Improvements," *CW* 30:91ff.). The point, viewed in the long term, was to create a country where there was an adequate infrastructure and a citizenry well adapted to use it to make themselves prosperous.

Down that track lay Indian self-government and the extinction of the company. Did that imply cultural convergence and the extinction of a distinctively Indian culture? Mill was neither an Orientalist in the sense of having a great sympathy for, and understanding of, Asian cultures at large and Indian, or Mogul, or Hindu culture in particular, nor a Westernizer in the sense of thinking that the sooner Indian superstitions were stamped out, the better for everyone. The remarks at the beginning of *Representative Government* provide most of what evidence there is about his views. The machinery of administration could be assessed against settled and uncontroversial standards of efficiency. Room for discussion about the quality of administration was limited to means-end issues; where there are specific problems, there are solutions on which rational people will converge. Culture comes into the equation only because there are many cultural influences on our willingness to seek the most efficient solution and our promptness in adopting it. Mill retained enough of his father's suspicion of "sinister interests" to know that some social groups had rational—even if corrupt—reasons to oppose efficiency; but in the context of a broader theory of progress, it was rather the aptness of a whole culture for improvement that he focused on. The checkered history of well-meaning efforts in the field of economic development attests to the importance of the subject. That checkered history does not undermine our belief that there are standards of efficiency of a cross-cultural kind. A sense of the complexity of social change may make us more generous toward cultures that sacrifice efficiency to other goals, but that is a separate issue.

Modes of government allow more room for divergence because there is more room to suit ourselves. Even there, Mill hardly looks at possibilities other than some form of what we call liberal democracy and he more fastidiously called representative government. He contemplates the possibility of a modernized Venetian form of government incorporating aristocratic and bureaucratic elements, but he mentions it very much in passing. Representative government was not "democracy," because it played down the role of simple-majority voting, both where the election of representatives was at issue and in the operations of Parliament. Mill perhaps ought to have opened the field rather wider, because one could imagine many possibilities opening up for people who had become the full-fledged, responsible, self-disciplined, imaginative, and cooperative persons that Mill hoped that we might eventually become. Jefferson's preferred system of "ward republics," which is to say, a federation of small direct democracies handling most of their needs themselves and delegating upward only those powers it was essential for a larger government to possess, is not representative government in Mill's sense, but it would be attractive to citizens of the kind he hoped for. Whether it could work only in an agrarian economy is another matter; Jefferson thought farmers were the only reliable republicans, but the obvious retort is that he was simply wrong. Mill's ideal system of economic self-government founded on worker cooperatives would be a natural counterpart to a system of ward republics and would not be constrained by technology ("Chapters on Socialism," *CW* 5:703ff.).

Seeking a divergent view of progress in Mill, however, involves stepping outside *Representative Government* and digging into the ambiguities of *On Liberty*. This is not the place to do more than note the familiar tension. Mill offers two justifications for freedom: one in terms that would readily fall under the rubric of a natural right to do as we please so long as we do not interfere with the exercise of that right by others except in self-defense, the other in terms of the need to encourage experiments in living, which is to say, in terms of progress. Then the question arises whether those experiments lead to one answer to the question of what is the good life for man. It is plain that they do not lead to one answer in any literal sense, because Mill takes it for granted that human beings are so varied that the good for one of us is not in all respects—or is only at a very high level of generality—the good for others of us. What experiments tell us is what our own individual nature is and, therefore, what the good for us individually is. The sense in which that yields one answer is that it supposes that there is a single, determinate answer to the question, "What is the best life for me?"

Progress is—in this view—a matter of becoming increasingly clear about the good for each of us and being increasingly able to realize it. This is not a process that we should expect to be very rapid; Mill observes wryly that since what Comte, following Saint-Simon, described as the "critical" phase of European cultural and social history had lasted for eight centuries, the return to a "natural," or "organic," state in which there were universally agreed standards of judgment was not to be expected in the near future—pace Comte's belief that he had inaugurated it (*Auguste Comte and Positivism*, *CW* 10:263ff.). It is not surprising that Mill's essay *Auguste Comte and Positivism* is the other face of *On Liberty*. The question before us, however, is whether Mill's view of moral progress, in the sense of progress toward a more complete understanding of our own and, therefore, the general good is a convergent or a divergent conception. The answer is quite unclear to me; Mill seems never to have posed the question to himself in that form and therefore seems to have seen no need to answer that question precisely.

We can press answers on him, but we cannot know whether he would have assented to them. One possibility is that because Mill had an objective conception of good, there is a genuine fact of the matter about what the good for each of us consists in; the fact is different for different people because what is good for one of us may not be so for another, but for each of us there is a fact of the matter. The other is that Mill's emphasis on creativity and imagination means that at some point the facts of the matter give out; as in painting, there are objective or near-objective standards such that any informed observer could distinguish a mere daub from a genuine painting, but where invention takes over, there is a diversity of routes leading in different, noncompeting directions, not all of which can be pursued, but along any of which there is something that practitioners and observers agree is progress—or the arrival at a dead end. Talk of the competent observer brings us to the issue that lies beneath the surface of *On Liberty* and *Representative Government*. This is the question of authority.

Authority: The Anxieties of "The Spirit of the Age"

Because there has been a long tradition of complaining about the way Mill tended to revise his work by qualifying bold initial statements into statements hedged about with "may be," I am reluctant to wish that he had concentrated on turning "The Spirit of the Age" and the essays on Bentham and Coleridge into a full-length work on the culture of modern society. We know that he regretted that he had not been able to make headway with the unformed science of "ethology," and it is clear that progress with it would have been both a condition and a result of pursuing the anxieties and intimations of the essays of his late twenties and early thirties. But there is a freshness and an unguardedness—visible also in his *Essays on Some Unsettled Questions in Political Economy*—that to a considerable extent disappeared from the later works in which Mill attempts to provide a settled view. Too often, what he gained by making his views less vulnerable to criticism was lost by making them less thought-provoking.

"The Spirit of the Age" was an unfinished series of articles written for the *Examiner* in 1831. It was a time of upheaval in Mill's life as well as in British and French politics. He had fallen in love with Harriet Taylor, had been vastly excited by the French Revolution of 1830, had encountered the Saint-Simonian missionaries, and was in the full tide of rebellion against the narrower kind of Benthamism. So the idea that this was an age of unsettled opinions, contestable standards, and deep uncertainty about what the future might hold was something he did not merely believe but also deeply felt. This is so even though Mill's politics were astonishingly untouched by the years of Sturm und Drang. He retained his father's contempt for the political competence of the English landed aristocracy and wrote as though it was obvious that their political ascendancy was over. Only in reviewing the second volume of *Democracy in America* did Mill concede anything to the legitimacy of a landed class, but even then it was more nearly a matter of conceding the Hegelian claim for an agrarian culture than urging the political merits of a landed aristocracy (CW 18:153ff.). We are so accustomed to thinking of Mill as an "aristocratic liberal" that we sometimes take our eye off the fact that as the child of an archetypally aspirant middle-class striver, he grew up as the protégé of aristocrats whose aim was to take the government of Great Britain out of the hands of Tory landowners and put it into the hands of virtuous public servants from the middle ranks of society. James Mill's *Essay on Government* was as hostile to neglectful mill owners and industrialists as to landed aristocrats, but the only heroes of the essay were the virtuous middle ranks (James Mill 1978, 53–98).

What strikes all readers of "The Spirit of the Age," however, is Mill's anxieties about the absence of intellectual authority in the modern world. Some of these anxieties are, to all appearances, a straightforward reiteration of Saint-Simonian themes: we live in a critical age and suffer from the loss of the security that characterizes organic or natural periods. There is an interesting undercurrent of a more private kind. Having fed himself the medicine of Wordsworth, Shelley, and Goethe as a prophylactic against the depression of his mental crisis, Mill needed a coherent account of the moral or psychological authority of the poet. Mill avoided the trap of treating poetry as merely an expression of emotion and settled on the view that poets intuited truths that philosophers could subsequently elaborate; the social philosophy that was needed by the modern age was "poetic intuition plus logic." How this was to work in practice was never quite explained, but it survives as an aspect of *Utilitarianism* and, in *On Liberty*, in the insistence on the role of the individuals who perceive new human possibilities.

Because Mill was inclined to see himself as the importer of Parisian intellectual insights for the benefit of the excessively practical English, it is difficult to get a concrete sense of what he hoped a more organic condition of English society might yield. The general answer is obvious enough: there would be a consensus on the (nature of the) answer to questions about the good life and, by extension, on the (nature of the) answer to questions about the duty of individuals to society; this would sustain a hierarchy of intellectual authority, because a consensus on the nature of the answers we sought would—as in the sciences—sustain a ranking not only of suggested answers but also of the capacity of different individuals to provide them. Just as, in the sciences, a neophyte can understand why a given answer is the right answer, even though he is quite incapable of reaching it for himself, so in these conditions, a cultural, moral, and political neophyte could understand why a given answer was right, even though he is incapable of reaching it for himself. Just as in the sciences, too, the proper attitude of the neophyte would be to embark on a process of understanding in greater and greater depth the answers he was given, initially with no idea of overturning them, but regarding their exploration as an apprenticeship in self-understanding and social understanding.

The disanalogies between moral and political judgment and scientific inquiry need no emphasis here; what needs emphasis is the fact that all his life, Mill wrote as though there were no such disanalogies but fought for causes that presupposed that there were many. It is this that links Mill's concerns to

Isaiah Berlin's criticisms of the Enlightenment faith in the sciences of man, but also makes it hard to say anything illuminating about what Mill and Berlin had in common. Berlin always insisted that the kind of consensus at which science aims is not to be looked for in cultural and ethical matters, but Mill was ambivalent. "The Spirit of the Age" is sufficiently unfinished to look very different to different readers; some have thought it authoritarian, whereas others have thought it intelligently nuanced and to be preferred to *On Liberty* (Himmelfarb 1963, vii–xx).

The difficulty is to know about what, if anything, Mill may have changed his mind between the one work and the other. Mill could have written these very different essays without changing his mind on fundamentals. He might have believed first and last that mankind was fated eventually to be of one mind about the good life and the ends of human existence. As we have said, they would not believe there was only one version of the good life, because they would understand the open-ended diversity of individual natures. Still, they would be of one mind about how to think about the good life, their beliefs about the good life would be well founded, and some among them would be better judges of the worth of different lives than would others, and we would happily defer to their judgment. It remains entirely possible that at the outset Mill thought it more urgent to reach that terminus and believed in addition that it was not far distant, whereas later he thought it less urgent to reach it and that it was very far distant indeed (CW 10:263ff.).

Authority and *On Liberty*

That indeed is what I think the truth is. There is one further element in the case. Another thing about which we might feel that we would like to know a lot more is what changes occurred in Mill's understanding of the role of "the mass"—or public opinion, the majority, "society," or however we describe the starting point for a rational discussion of the way in which large numbers of others have an impact on the individual by virtue of their numerousness. Mill's exploitation of his French resources was a matter not only of borrowing extensively from the Saint-Simonian view of history as a process driven by ideas and involving the decay and re-creation of orthodoxies, but also of borrowing a French understanding of the conflict between the mass and the individual. Tocqueville's understanding of *individualisme* in *Democracy* was not borrowed from Mill, but it is not dissimilar to the condition that Mill described in "The Spirit of the Age" in which individuals who are at a loss to know what to do with themselves and seek in vain for a settled doctrine about how to live turn in on themselves and lead self-centered but unsatisfactory lives (CW 22:227ff.).

Conversely, the Saint-Simonians not only taught Mill about the need for association, as Tocqueville also did, but persuaded him as well that history was increasingly being driven by mass phenomena, the famous tendency for masses to predominate over individuals that he announced in "Civilization" (*CW* 18:117ff.). We now have the ingredients for the argument that it is possible in a mass society for there to be, at the same time, too much and too little authority. Public opinion exerts a pressure on individuals by way of the unofficial social sanctions of ostracism and disapproval, and the more official sanctions associated with the law and with differential enforcement of and access to the law; an individual who does not follow the rule of thinking like everyone else will find himself under acute psychological pressure. Mill was emphatic that the tyranny to be feared was not the tyranny of proletarian insurrection but that of a form of mutual psychic policing that came all too easily to the Victorian English middle classes. At the same time, mere pressure does not supply genuine authority; it can supply an alarming simulacrum of it, because a person who internalizes these sanctions acquires an inner censor that dictates his behavior. An inner censor is what real authority supplies as well; so the crucial abilities we need are the ability to distinguish the real from the fraudulent and the ability to distinguish rational acquiescence from simple fear. That mass society makes these abilities impossible to acquire is the chilling thought behind *On Liberty*, and the fear that unites Tocqueville, Mill, and Nietzsche. Authority, the real thing, allows us to follow someone else's lead with our eyes wide open and our brains fully engaged. Merely being too frightened to think for ourselves is not an acknowledgment of authority but simple submission to the tyranny of opinion.

Because Mill's sociology was an eclectic construction from a variety of different sources, he rarely provided a detailed account of how these deplorable processes operated. This poses a problem, not of supplying the missing account of these pressures and their operation, for that is easy enough, but of providing a persuasive account of how these pressures can be resisted and on what basis real authority can be erected. The aspect of Mill that some readers admired as a kind of Stoic bleakness—the icy, aristocratic aspect that Charles Kingsley saw and admired even as he flinched from it—is an argumentative and theoretical weakness. It appears that individuals have only their own resources to rely on, and society's tyrannical pressures can be held back only by the force of arguments that, if Mill himself is to be believed, society is not likely to heed. It is easy to see how attractive he and Harriet Taylor must have found the image of lonely defiance that *On Liberty* exudes, as well as the thought that they might be among the few individuals who are the origin of all great advances. The emotional attraction of the position does nothing to hide its weaknesses. What Mill required was a sociological theory of the open society so that he could explain what sorts of association encouraged boldness and imagination and would sustain their members against a conformist wider society. As it is, he leaves too much on the individual's shoulders.

The Englishman's Agora

Mill's need for a sociology of the progressive society is obvious in light of his hopes and fears for modern liberal democracy—representative government. Mill was convinced that, man for man, the citizens of Athens were more politically competent than his contemporaries. Given all the many things one might say against Athenian politics—its vulnerability to superstitious terrors, the domination of politics by family feuds, the incapacity of the Athenians to create the stable federal system that would have saved them from subjection to the Kingdom of Macedon and its Hellenistic and Roman successors, the skittishness of the Athenian populace as described by Thucydides, and its taste for exploitative imperialist adventures—this was a contestable judgment, but it was not a foolish one. The Athenian citizen faced responsibilities greater than those of the modern citizen: he voted for war or peace, and when he voted for war, he put his own life directly at risk. The judicial murder of Socrates and the frivolous expulsion of Aristides were not the only ways in which Athenian opinion expressed itself; they were remembered because they were the exception. Ordinarily, the need to persuade the *ecclesia* of the validity of what one was saying was an exercise in taking public responsibility of a kind that the modern world provides little of for anyone other than a handful of professional politicians. In the sophists, it may have given rise to a breed of spin doctors who would teach people appearing in the courts to make a bad case look better and to make an opponent's case look worse, but the energies that democratic politics liberated in Athens were astonishing to contemporaries and remain astonishing still.

But by the time Mill wrote, all the commonplaces were well established. From Polybius onward, the inferiority of Athenian democracy to the Roman mixed constitution was taken for granted; from Montesquieu onward, the thought that democracy could be practiced only in very small units was widely accepted, only disturbed by the cleverness of Madisonian federalism and the utopianism of Jeffersonian ward republics. And after Constant's essay on the contrast between ancient and modern liberty, enthusiasts for the *juste milieu* (happy medium) could comfort themselves for the dreariness of parliamentary politics with the thought that it was the price we had to pay for avoiding the more alarming features of ancient, more participatory republicanism. Constant himself, of course, was not anxious to go down that track; like Mill, he thought that a committed liberal should want both the liberty of the ancients and that of the moderns.

Mill was acutely aware of the benefits of rational administration. But this was not to put himself wholly at odds with classical Athens, where activities such as the building and equipping of the fleet were confided to the hands of professionals whose judgment was very widely accepted. Whether to go to war was for the people at large to decide; who to employ and where to find the best timber were jobs for those who knew what they were doing. The greater breach was not so much at the level of orderly management as in the sphere of legislation. Mill was horrified at the way Parliament drafted legislation on the floor of the house; his own ideal was, in effect, that Parliament should assent to the principle of legislation: trained lawyers draft legislation to give effect to a principle, and then Parliament considers the results and agrees or not (CW 19, esp. 428ff.). Given that the members of Parliament imagined by Mill had already been filtered by a voting system that awarded extra votes on the basis of education and had survived the rigors of a single-transferable-vote electoral mechanism, one would have thought that they were about as competent a body of representatives as any legislative assembly has ever possessed. To give them the power to say no more than yea or nay to what was proposed by expert draftsmen was to tilt the mechanism of representation a very long way from direct democracy of the Athenian kind. The practicality of Mill's proposals is not the point; the British legislative mechanism at present places on parliamentary draftsmen the burden of trying to give effect to what they frequently, although privately, regard as the incoherent and half-formed views of cabinet ministers, and of assisting ministers in patching up the larger errors of phrasing or the most disliked elements of legislation as a bill winds its way through committee.

The difficulty with assimilating Mill's wish to give the task of drafting legislation to experts to the present system in Britain is that the British system works as it does because British governments are elective dictatorships, a one-party government that can get its own way except in very odd circumstances and can therefore resist all amendments to a bill. Mill disliked parties, even though he voted almost straight down the Liberal Party line in his three years in Parliament. Mill's ideal version of parliamentary government is hard to visualize, but it seems that a chamber elected for its personal merits on Mill's elaborate franchise would form something more like a deliberative jury than a body in which government and opposition benches faced each other in the familiar way. Policy would be put to it, although it is not absolutely clear by whom, and upon it being agreed that a given policy was to be pursued, legislation to give it effect would be devised, brought back, and voted up or down. Although it is very different from the British parliamentary system as it has evolved, it is not difficult to see how such a system could work. With a little imagination, it is the Athenian or Florentine system: one could have a directing committee, elected (or chosen by lot) from the body itself or separately; its task would be to produce policy and present it; such a committee could have members specializing in different tasks—a secretary for the navy, foreign affairs, or whatever—and would certainly need a chair. It would be more like the U.S. system of government than the British, except that legislation would be introduced by the cabinet and civil service rather than by members of Congress.

Balance or Incoherence

If that catches some of Mill's intentions, we can defend Mill against the charge of incoherence. Mill's support for ways of engaging individuals in the direct governance of their own neighborhoods suggests that a jury model of citizen engagement might be a plausible implementation of liberal democracy. We do not volunteer to serve on a jury but perform—more or less willingly—the social duty that we are required to perform when we are picked out by lot.

It would be easy to run city planning committees in the same fashion; they would—as Mill knew—need efficient permanent officials to present options and implement the policies on which they decided. Indeed, almost all local politics could operate on such a basis; there are few technical issues that require much education to grasp; all the interesting questions occur at the margins, where it is a matter of coordinating one locality's decisions with another's. That is where Mill's dictum—following Bentham—of "centralize knowledge, localize power" will not quite do what we want. There is, after all, no point in building efficient sewers in my locality if yours—your locality and your sewers—will not cooperate.

Coordination is why we need representative government. When Mill describes his version of market socialism, he does not raise these difficulties because he does not imagine government playing a substantial role in the management of an economy. So far as the economy goes, the market provides all the coordination that is needed. The market can govern the interplay between productive and distributive enterprises once government has set some guidelines and the framework of appropriate property rights. That, however, leaves untouched the question of coordinating governmental action. The market is not in general an effective mechanism either within or between different localized governments, because so much of government is a matter of attending to public goods that the market will not provide or of coping with market failures, such as by ensuring that the cost of negative externalities falls on those who cause them and that the creation of positive externalities brings some reward to those who create them. Mill shows a considerable nontechnical understanding of these issues in book 5 of the *Principles*, but does not tie the discussion into his account of the cooperative future.

We can imagine Mill subscribing to a great variety of alternative political arrangements, and he did not spell out which of them he wanted above all others. What he wrote in his later years was quite closely matched to the interests of his readers and to immediate issues confronting British politics, so we should not complain that we cannot find fully described accounts of utopia. There was inevitably a good deal of tension between Mill's wish to see his countrymen and countrywomen acquire the self-reliance and public spirit of the Athenians, on the one hand, and the unpropitious conditions in which they were going to have to do it, on the other. There was also a less inevitable but an evidently unresolved tension in Mill's mind between self-government for its own sake, which may include a great deal of trial and error, and rational public administration, where the elimination of error is an important objective. There is also a tension, which has not been explored at all here, between the intentions of schemes such as Thomas Hare's system of proportional representation and those of systems of choice by lot that marked older sorts of democracy. The one place where there is no tension at all is between Mill's admiration for the life of the agora and his admiration for the virtues of the East India Company. Individuals have it in them to be both passionate and efficient, and a political system should find room for both passion and efficiency. How it is to do it is as much a question for us as for Mill.

References

Himmelfarb, Gertrude. 1963. Introduction to *Essays on Politics and Culture*, by J. S. Mill. Edited by Gertrude Himmelfarb. New York: Doubleday.

Mill, James. 1978. "Essay on Government." In *Utilitarian Logic and Politics*, edited by Jack Lively and John Rees. Oxford: Oxford University Press.

Mill, John Stuart. 1963–91. *The Collected Works of John Stuart Mill*. Edited by John M. Robson. 33 vols. Toronto: University of Toronto Press.

Thucydides. 1991. *The Peloponnesian War*. Indianapolis: Hackett.

Urbinati, Nadia. 2002. *Mill on Democracy: From the Athenian Polis to Representative Government*. Chicago: University of Chicago Press.

19

Bertrand Russell's Politics
1688 OR 1968?

IF BERTRAND RUSSELL is remembered in the United States by anyone other than formal logicians and analytical philosophers, it is almost certainly as a ferocious critic of America's role in the Vietnam War, and on account of the energetically anti-American stand he took at the time of the Cuban missile crisis. The violence of his rhetoric during those years opened wounds that have not since healed. When my account of Russell's politics was published, Hilton Kramer deplored the whole book in his *Wall Street Journal* review because I was not as wildly hostile to Russell's stand on Vietnam as he thought proper. Sidney Hook's much more kindly review chided me nonetheless for not opposing John Stuart Mill's defense of liberal interventionism to the high-pitched anti-imperialism of Russell's last years.

That Russell's last writings were unfair, that they verged on the hysterical, and that they employed a rhetoric he would earlier have thought preposterous it is hard to deny. Nor did he entirely deny it himself. When scolded by a writer in *Tribune* for the "unsociological" quality of his writings on nuclear disarmament, Russell replied that he had earlier devoted a good deal of time and thought to the sociology of contemporary politics, but now he felt as though he was watching "a man dropping lighted matches on heaps of TNT," and just had to act as best he could. Elsewhere, he said over and over that even if logic were one of the greatest achievements of the human mind, it would have no point if mankind blew itself to bits.

Still, there is no denying that what came out under his name during the middle and late 1960s was very extraordinary. I say "what came out under his name" because there is every reason to suppose that much of it was written by other people. In content, and even more importantly in style and grammatical carelessness, it reads like the standard outpourings of the student Left of the time and not at all like the immaculate and stylish prose in which Russell had previously couched his views—however outrageous those views may have seemed at the time. *War Crimes in Vietnam*, for instance, offers this characteristic "anti-imperialist" trope: "The people of Vietnam are heroic, and their struggle is epic; a stirring and permanent reminder of the incredible spirit of which men are capable when they are dedicated to a noble ideal. Let us salute the people of Vietnam."

Russell had years earlier written an essay that was intended as a prophylactic against just such guff. "The Superior Virtue of the Oppressed" was a lighthearted assault on the idea that the victimized are always right. In Russell's account of the matter, the resonances of which for contemporary eastern Europe are all too obvious, the deepest wish of the oppressed is commonly to throw off their oppressor in order to victimize somebody else. That does not mean that victimizing them is therefore all right, but it does mean that we ought not to sentimentalize them. Had Russell applied his own analysis to the case of Vietnam, he ought to have argued that North Vietnam was yet another deeply unpleasant communist autocracy, that the Vietcong were certainly brave and ingenious, but were also cruel and brutal, in the interest of causes with which he had no sympathy—but that none of this justified the Americans in risking world peace by making war in Vietnam. The argument against the American presence was not a matter of some high-flown principle of nonintervention, but an argument of expediency. The United States could do little good to Vietnam, but it could do a great deal of damage to the American political system. There is something very odd, not to say disheartening, about the anti-Americanism of Russell's last years; even if he was simply interested in lending his fame and prestige to young people battling in a good cause, he ought surely to have insisted on better terms for the use of a name as good as his.

Many Americans, however, remember an earlier Russell, one who starred in a small courtroom drama that led to his losing the professorship at the City College of New York to which he had been appointed in 1940. On that occasion, Russell was assailed by respectable America, and liberal philosophers including John Dewey and Sidney Hook did their unavailing best to defend him against the forces of unenlightenment. At the end of the 1930s, Russell found himself in an embarrassing position; he had no university position, and had for years made his living by a combination of journalism and lecturing that he very much disliked. Though he could never have made a satisfactory professor, whether in a British or an American university, he hoped for some such position to be offered to him. After a series of visits to Chicago and Los Angeles, he was finally offered a post at City College, resigned from a temporary appointment at the University of California, and made ready to take up the new job.

At this point, his old enemies fell upon him. He had long been regarded as a menace to good morals by Catholics, more generally by enthusiasts for female chastity, by the foes of birth control, and by believers in the sanctity of marriage. First, the Episcopal archbishop of New York, William Manning, wrote a circular letter to the press denouncing the appointment as a threat to the morals of the young. Catholic journals joined in the hue and cry. Then the mother of a CUNY student, a Mrs. McKay, brought suit against the city Board of Education, alleging that the appointment was *ultra vires* (beyond its authority) because Russell's teaching (in logic and the philosophy of mathematics) was, among other things, "lecherous, libidinous, lustful, venerous, erotomaniac, aphrodisiac, irreverent and narrow-minded." Astonishingly, the court found in her favor, and the appointment was quashed.

Since Mrs. McKay had brought suit against the Board of Education, Russell had not been a party to it and could not defend himself. The board behaved cravenly, and would not appeal the decision, in spite of the urgings of the American Association of University Professors and of educators across the country who feared that if this sort of thing could happen in relatively liberal New York there was no knowing what might happen elsewhere. If Dewey had not induced Albert Barnes of the Barnes Foundation to hire Russell to lecture on the history of Western philosophy, he would have found himself unemployed and unemployable, three thousand miles from home with no hope of crossing the Atlantic in wartime, with a wife and young child to support. It is not surprising that Russell was thereafter a bit sharp about freedom of speech on American campuses.

For our purposes, what is most interesting is the way Russell managed to combine two views not ordinarily found together. He detested many, perhaps even most, of the characteristic features of American life and yet thought that the United States ought to be the self-conscious, unabashed leader of the Western world; indeed, from 1946 to 1948, he argued that the United States ought to use its (then) monopoly of nuclear weapons to force the Soviet Union to disarm, to get Russian troops out of Eastern Europe, and, at his most ambitious, to exercise a world hegemony that would eventually lead to some form of world government. How he arrived at what seems on the face of it to be the paradoxical position that the United States is both intolerable and the only hope for the human future provides much of the substance of this essay. But perhaps the first thing to observe about it is that it does complicate any simple picture of Russell as just anti-American, as just an elderly hanger-on of the movement for nuclear disarmament and the anti-imperialist movements of the 1960s.

Russell used to joke that he could not be accused of being anti-American when his first and last wives had both been Americans—Alys Pearsall-Smith and Edith Finch, respectively, both of them from the high-minded Philadelphia academic upper-class that Russell somehow enjoyed and disliked, mocked and abused, and yet fell in love with. In fact, his relations with his first wife give at least one clue to the anti-American side of his work. Though he fell madly in love with Alys Pearsall-Smith when they were brought together by his elder brother Frank, during the whole marriage he was driven wild with irritation at her middle-class habits. What one might have expected him to pass over as mere nervous good nature, he felt to be intolerably vulgar. It is significant that when he embarked on an affair with Lady Ottoline Morrell, which ended his first marriage and set him on the path of personal and social emancipation that he never left thereafter, he remarked that it was a tremendous relief to be in the company of someone genuinely aristocratic, with whom real uninhibited laughter and enjoyment were possible. America, for Russell, never quite recovered from the disadvantage of being the land of the Pearsall-Smiths.

All this is historically explicable enough. Russell was born in 1872, the second son of a somewhat eccentric Liberal, Viscount Amberley (the third son of Earl Russell), and his wonderful wife, Kate Stanley. His birth was a radical event; he was delivered by Elizabeth Garrett Anderson, then unable to practice as a doctor but soon to lead the movement that brought women into medicine as something other than nurses and midwives, and eventually to give her name to the best-loved hospital in London. He was born into two ruling families—the Russells and the Stanleys—who were unusual among the English aristocracy in welcoming intellectuals into their midst. Gilbert Murray thus became a cousin by marriage some years later. In addition to the advantages of birth, he had the symbolic advantage that one of his godparents was John Stuart Mill, who had campaigned with his parents for the extension of the vote to women, for the rearrangement of the laws of property to the benefit of agricultural tenants, and for a league of nations. Mill, of course, died when Russell was only some seven months old, and his impact was not felt until Russell was eighteen. Then Russell read Mill's *Autobiography*, came across the passage where Mill remarks that the first-cause argument for the existence of God is invalid because it only provokes the further question "What caused the First Cause?" and promptly lost his faith. The story seems so nearly a parody of the inner life of the rationalist philosopher that one would not credit it but for the fact of a contemporary entry in Russell's (secret) diary recording the event.

Both of Russell's parents died before he was four, and he was brought up in the household of his paternal grandmother, Countess Russell. She was by this time in her late fifties; his grandfather, Earl Russell (Lord John Russell, "finality Jack" of the First Reform Act), was twenty-three years older than she, and died in 1878, when his grandson was only six. So it was his fierce, strict grandmother who inevitably had most influence over him. He could never quite make up his mind how much he hated her.

He was appallingly lonely, stuck away in the large grace and favor house in Richmond Park that a grateful nation had bestowed on his grandparents. Visitors were agreed that it was no place for a small boy. Worse still, his older brother Frank showed early signs of the talent for getting into matrimonial trouble that eventually resulted in his being the last peer to be tried, literally, by a jury of his fellow peers—they sent him to jail for six months for inadvertent bigamy in 1912. Frank's career at Winchester persuaded Countess Russell that Bertie was better off at home, where she could keep an eye on him, and at home he stayed until he was seventeen.

The regime had its advantages. Round his grandmother's table assembled Liberal luminaries by the score; few fourteen-year-olds were brought up to entertain Mr. Gladstone after dinner, even though Russell complained that he spoke only one sentence and that was to wonder why the excellent port had been served in a claret glass. Irish Home Rule was hotly debated—friends like John Morley were enthusiastically pro–Home Rule, while Russell's Stanley grandmother was fiercely anti. Countess Russell was puritanical, devout in whatever ways a Unitarian can be devout, but not particularly interfering in her management of the succession of governesses and tutors that looked after the boy's education. Whatever Russell's miseries, his mind was taken care of.

Moreover, by the time Russell was of an age to take an intellectual interest in the world, Frank had begun to bring home interesting friends, among them the American philosopher George Santayana and scientists such as John Tyndale. There were, however, some deep wounds. One was that his grandmother was terrified of the streak of madness that ran in the family—not absurdly either, for Russell's own elder son, John, the fourth Earl Russell, was mentally ill for much of his life, and one of John's daughters committed suicide in her early twenties. When Russell wanted to marry Alys Pearsall-Smith, his grandmother used the threat that they would produce mad children as an argument against marriage, but she had obviously dwelt on the matter before. What made it more corrosive was that there was a suggestion that somehow sexual passion and lunacy were closely allied. His aunt Agatha had been engaged, had been forced to break it off because she suffered from delusions, and was now more or less mad—and Uncle William had spent most of his life in a hospital. What could one infer from that? Russell recorded a pathetic dream he had while the argument over his marriage to Alys was going on; he dreamed that his mother was not dead but locked up in a madhouse. It is tersely recorded, but it makes one wince. It is no wonder that Russell's *Autobiography* sends, as one might say, very mixed signals. Sometimes, he writes that his childhood was happy enough, sometimes that all that kept him from suicide was the urge to learn more geometry.

The effect of going to Cambridge after this was what one might expect. Intellectually, it was like going to heaven. One might think anything about anything, and nobody would disapprove—though they might try to argue one out of it. On the other hand, it was almost as socially narrow as the background he had come from. Moreover, the entire social and political tone was what he would afterward have dismissed as decidedly precious; it was the background to Bloomsbury, and Russell and Bloomsbury got on very badly. Still, all his life, the effect of it stuck. He always thought that the goods that G. E. Moore's *Principia Ethica* celebrated as absolutely good in themselves—beauty and personal friendship—really were among the very greatest goods, even though he added to them something one may suppose that Moore took for granted too, the thought that the knowledge of abstract, universal truths such as those of philosophy, mathematics, and logic was one of the great glories of human existence. What Kenneth Blackwell has labeled a "Spinozistic ethics of impersonal self-expansion" was thereafter Russell's creed; unlike Spinoza, he did not think it a dictate of reason, nor did he think one could derive one's duties from it with the lucidity of the lemmas of a geometrical theorem; still, it was what held together virtually everything he wrote thereafter on ethics and politics.

As that suggests, it was a doctrine at some distance from everyday political life. Russell always wavered, sometimes inclining toward the view that for everyday purposes, a rough-and-ready utilitarianism had to serve because it was impossible to tell what impact political action would have on those exalted and ultimate ends to which it was appropriate to direct our individual allegiance. At other times, he was much more prepared to invoke those ideals directly; as we shall see, this was generally when some kind of international catastrophe threatened them with the gravest damage—as in modern warfare. To the extent that this implied something recognizable as a political theory in the ordinary sense, it was simply that some political system or other was required as a shelter for almost any human good; these human goods required more than that, for they required a government properly sensitive to the needs of private life, to the pursuit of knowledge, and to the creation of art and other sorts of beauty—a government attuned to what he called in a letter to Ottoline Morrell "the spark of the divine" in each of us. But not very much follows from this. Certainly, a liberal political theory of some sort, but one that has little that is decisive to say about economic policy or about many other issues of the nitty-gritty of policy making. It is a view that inclines one to caution about the positive contributions of government. Governments can certainly do much damage, but it is less clear that they can do very much directly to aid these ultimate values.

Later, he advocated a form of guild socialism in his *Principles of Social Reconstruction* (1916), based on a dichotomy between the "possessive" and "creative" impulses that he understood to be fundamental to human nature. This picture of human nature suggested to Russell that private property and capitalist economics made for competition, divisiveness, and, in the last resort, war, while an emphasis on satisfying work, political participation, and educational and sexual liberation made for peace, happiness, and an emotional security that was not merely conservative and narrow minded. Though the *Principles* is, to my mind, the best thing Russell wrote on politics, it is not unkind to observe that it operates at a high level of abstraction and that its tone owes a great deal to the exigencies of World War I and Russell's own activities on behalf of the No-Conscription Fellowship. Indeed, the slenderer volume of lectures *Political Ideals*, which gave an abridged version of the *Principles*, was published in the United States under the title *Why Men Fight*.

At times of something other than the exaltation of the battle against the forces of darkness, Russell's political loyalties so far as Britain was concerned tended to settle in a "lib-lab" mold. That is, he thought it impossible to achieve the Liberal program of Asquith and Lloyd George except through the medium of the Labour Party, and at the same time was fearful that the Labour Party would have too little regard for intellectual distinction and too little awareness of the need to tolerate unpopular opinions for the sake of progress and variety. His mature position was summed up in his Reith Lectures (1948)—the first series to be given and, in many people's view, one of the very best—published as *Authority and the Individual*. He took it for granted that in the middle of the twentieth century, governments needed the capacity to preserve not only civil order in the simple military sense but also economic order; they needed to be able to reproduce an intelligent and skilled workforce; they needed, in short, to be able to manage a complicated modern society. This implied at least a social democratic government. But after the experience of Hitler and Stalin, we all know that the search for managerial efficiency can exact far too high a price. Efficiency easily becomes liberticide, and even benevolent despotism is despotism. What falls short of despotism may nonetheless be intolerably boring. "Give me the old days," he quotes an old Indian as saying. "It was dangerous, but there was glory in it." Sober Russell was Russell reminding everyone that the task was to reconcile society's need for authority for the sake of order with the individual's need for liberty for the sake of his or her pursuit of the ultimate goals.

Liberal democratic sobriety was not Russell's most characteristic style. The rest of this essay is devoted to the less sober aspects of his ideas—some of which were sparked by his horror at modern warfare, others by simple irritation and anger at modern society, as represented usually by the United States as most recently encountered. His interest in politics began early; his family assumed that he would go into public life or at any rate that he would start in the diplomatic corps and migrate to active politics in due course. This vision of his future he rejected fairly energetically, though he stood for Parliament three times in seats he knew there was no risk of winning.

His first interest in theoretical issues in politics was evoked by the Marxism of the German Social Democratic Party; his first published work was *German Social Democracy* (1896). The real Russell came to life more visibly in 1901, and then completely in 1914. When the Boer War broke out in 1899, Russell found himself questioned by foreign friends and colleagues who could not see the justice of Britain's war against Paul Kruger's Boer Republic of the Transvaal. To them, it looked like simple bullying by a strong imperial power directed at a bunch of possibly obnoxious and certainly amazingly ignorant but otherwise apparently harmless Afrikaner farmers who happened to have stumbled on the world's richest seams of gold.

Russell's response was, by later standards, very odd. He was entirely hostile to the British Empire and at the same time a firm imperialist. His arguments were characteristically Russellian—acute but counterintuitive. He scorned all forms of militarism, the full-fledged Prussian variety more than the dilute British form, but for none of them did he feel anything but loathing. British imperialism threatened to turn Britain into a militarist state indistinguishable from the kaiser's Reich and was therefore to be deplored. Yet he took it for granted that the spread of European influence was a good thing and that most of Africa and Asia would progress faster under European tutelage than under its own steam. European domination was the way to make progress; the only policy issue was how to carve up Africa tidily and peacefully rather than messily and by warfare. The British were absolutely entitled to squash the Boer Republic; "Je suis utilitaire," he wrote to the mathematician Louis Couturat, and in that light he argued that justice lay with the advanced nations whenever they encountered the less advanced. In World War I, he employed the same line of reasoning to argue that wars of self-defense were not justified if it was a matter of war between two civilized powers, but that the conquest of uncivilized nations was entirely acceptable. Who, he asked in a tone that one would hardly risk today, can regret the passing of the American Indian? It was doubtless bad luck for the American Indian that the white man had triumphed, but viewed from a global perspective, it was all to the good.

In fact, he had scarcely produced this defense of the British case than he turned against it. From his *Autobiography* one might almost be led to think that he simultaneously fell out of love with Alys, was turned into a mystic by his experience of the shocking loneliness of Evelyn Whitehead in her painful heart attacks, and became a "pacifist" under the combined impact of these events. Rereading his letters shows a much slower process taking place; it also shows that he never became what he would have called a pacifist. That is, he never departed from the view that violence was not absolutely evil, and never held that war was never justified. What he held was that war was justified only to the extent that it promoted the ultimate values of European civilization. These were the values discussed already; in that light, it is easy enough to see that wars between civilized countries are very unlikely to pass the justificatory test, while wars against uncivilized societies will have a much easier time.

There were instances of something closer to principled anti-imperialism before World War I, but the only striking example was his detestation of British and Russian policy toward Persia. There, he thought, there was a developed democratic movement and a developing political culture. For the British to agree to a carve-up with the autocratic Russians—like all good liberals, Russell loathed czarist Russia for its own sake and the Soviet Union as a nastier version of its czarist parent—was the betrayal of British liberal values. For the Russians simply hanged or murdered without trial such of the local democrats as they could lay hands on, and this they did knowing the British would not interfere.

Still, it took 1914 and the outbreak of European war to bring out his activist nature. From the moment war was declared, he threw himself into opposing it. He wrote endlessly against it in whatever journals would still open their pages to him; he organized meetings of the Union for Democratic Control in Cambridge until his college barred their rooms to them—provoking G. E. Moore to suggest that the college chapel ought also to be closed, since it was full of people saying they worshipped the Prince of Peace.

He lectured widely, giving as lectures what became *Principles of Social Reconstruction*. When conscription was introduced, he promptly became a full-time organizer for the No-Conscription Fellowship led by Clifford Allen; it cost him his lectureship at Trinity, even though the move was violently deplored by the young men of Trinity on active service. They took the admirably high-minded view that they were fighting to preserve the liberties of independent people like Bertrand Russell, not to gratify the patriotism of dim and elderly fellows of Trinity.

Eventually, it landed him in jail when he rashly wrote in the *Tribunal*—the magazine put out by the No-Conscription Fellowship—that after the war was over, he expected Britain to be policed by the American army, which would be employed to put down strikers in Europe as they had traditionally been in America. This was held to be "insulting an ally," and he duly got six months, reduced on appeal to six months in the "first division"—that is, in a large cell, with no duties, meals brought in, a fellow prisoner to clean the room, and endless books. Though it had a certain comic side to it, it was effectively the end of his career as an academic and the beginnings of his extraordinary career as a nomadic journalist, lecturer, popular broadcaster—and deeply influential part-time philosopher.

The discrepancy between his violent antipathy to the war and the philosophical underpinnings of that antipathy is still something to puzzle over, and not altogether different from the discrepancy between the violence of his opposition to the war in Vietnam and the pragmatism of the political theory that he claimed to base it on. In a series of essays titled "Justice in Wartime," which appeared in the *Atlantic Monthly* during 1915—they were intended to sway American opinion against the war—he argued, as he always did, that pure pacifism was implausible. War was justified if its consequences were good enough, and not unless they were. Self-defense was not an argument; if one were to be held up by a highway robber, one would not be right to shoot him dead to preserve one's purse or even one's life—though one might if one had an overwhelmingly important mathematical discovery to communicate to the world. Nations had to be held to the same standard. It was certainly wrong of Germany to violate Belgian neutrality, but once it had done so, launching a war was a bad response. It would destroy European civilization, and that was an evil that nothing could exceed. This line he held through thick and thin; he engaged in an acrimonious debate with T. E. Hulme, who was deeply enraged that the Russell he had once admired for professing a heroic view of the world was now apparently ratting on it. No, said Russell, he stood by his old view; he merely thought that killing millions of young men was a perversion of these values.

This was the attitude that led him in 1946 to advocate the compulsory pacification of the world by nuclear blackmail. In 1918, his experience of war and wartime politics did much to persuade him that mankind was collectively all but mad and that he individually was inept as a practical politician. He repeatedly claimed that he longed to return to pure philosophy, but could never stand the atmosphere of the traditional universities. So although he spent much time with old Cambridge friends and attended meetings of the Apostles with some regularity, he drifted away from that setting. He had discovered a considerable talent as a popular lecturer and writer; now, having given away the rather substantial fortune he had inherited at twenty-one, he had to turn that talent into cash. The need to do so grew more urgent when he married Dora Black, some twenty years his junior, and promptly begot two children; the need became even greater when they opened Beacon Hill School in Hampshire, which ran at a chronic loss and needed all the help Russell's lecture tours and occasional writings could give it.

This interwar phase of Russell's life produced a curious sort of semipolitical intervention in public life. It is one that induces a good deal of ambivalence; on the one hand, Russell usually fought for good causes—birth control; religious, racial, and political toleration; a more egalitarian society; livelier educational systems; and so on—while on the other, he did so by relying on simple cleverness and a gift for dazzling phrases to carry him over complexities that a writer more respectful of his readers would have acknowledged. "What fools they must be, to take us so seriously," he remarked to Max Eastman, after a public debate between the two of them; Eastman recoiled from the remark and never forgave Russell for it.

Whatever one's ambivalence about it all, it is hard to regret the talent that turned out more than fifty "penny dreadfuls" as he used to call them, including *Marriage and Morals*, which won him the Nobel Prize for Literature in 1951. Along with *The Conquest of Happiness*, *Sceptical Essays*, *Popular Essays*, and *Unpopular Essays*—so called, said Russell, because a reviewer had objected that *Popular Essays* contained several sentences that even an intelligent five-year-old might find difficult—they formed a library of dissident ideas that excited more teenagers and alarmed more parents and schoolteachers than one can count. Speaking for myself, the discovery of Russell in 1956 when I was just sixteen remains one of the aspects of my education for which I remain most grateful.

Nor did Russell always wait to turn his work into penny dreadfuls. For several years he wrote little columns for the Hearst newspapers; he could dictate 1,500 words to a secretary in one go, with never a mistake, and always had something quirky and unlikely to say. Moreover, he never compromised his views. "Who May Wear Lipstick?" is not Russell the erotomaniac discoursing on the means of sexual attraction, but a deft little piece of mockery denouncing American local school boards for forbidding female employees from wearing makeup. Nor does he engage, as radicals of a later age might have done, in elaborate appeals to First Amendment rights of free expression and all the rest. He observes that it would do children a lot of good to be taught by cheerful, warm, and friendly young women, not by a lot of frumps. All his life, he feared that the relentless pressures of respectability deprived most women of the capacity of uninhibited thought. Many of his arguments for a more liberated outlook on sex were drawn less from a concern for sexual happiness—though that certainly moved him—than from a concern that the constant policing of young women was terribly bad for their brains.

The disquieting thing, as suggested above, is how much he disliked doing it all. Instead of cherishing a genuine and publicly useful—even if, in the great scheme of things, a rather minor—talent, he always fretted that he was not advancing the frontiers of pure philosophy. Between Russell the political essayist and the Russell who communed with the eternal verities, there was not merely an emotional chasm but positive hostility. The tension made for a political flightiness that could often be alarming. His daughter, Katherine Tait, suggests in her memoir of her father that he had "an essentially religious temperament." Given his lifelong detestation of all organized religion, it is hard to go along with that in any simple way; still, there is evidently something in it. Whatever his motives for going along with Ottoline Morrell's florid mysticism in the years of their grand affair, he evidently found it no trouble to do so. He had already written "A Free Man's Worship" and the other essays that make up *Mysticism and Logic*. His utilitarianism was always skin-deep, and something wilder and less calculable was always waiting for expression.

In that vein, he easily dropped into a rhetoric that suggested the choices before us were simple, vast, and to be taken on pure moral conviction. Harold Macmillan was "more wicked than Hitler" because he would not agree to immediate unilateral nuclear disarmament; *Has Man a Future?* offered the choice between heaven on earth and a radioactive ash heap. The thought that mankind might somehow muddle along between both extremes seemed not so much rhetorically less powerful, though it plainly is that, as intellectually less inviting. One extreme example that again shows Russell's ambivalence about the United States in a striking light is the transformation of his views about the morality of war between 1936, when he wrote *Which Way to Peace?* and his postwar advocacy of nuclear blackmail.

In 1936, he was straightforwardly defeatist: Hitler was certainly a menace, and the Nazis were certainly disgusting. Anti-Semitism he hardly mentions, and after the war regretted having failed to take it seriously as a genuine driving force of Nazi policy. In 1936, he took something close to the usual appeasers' position. The Germans wanted to regain their place in the sun; in that case, the British should give them as many colonies as they wanted. They were no use to the British and might as well encumber the Germans— or indeed the Americans, who would probably purchase the British West Indies for a "good round sum in dollars." The larger question was what to do about British reactions to German aggression and invasion. Russell's reply was that the only possible response was passive resistance. Noncooperation and an attitude of contempt for Nazi views and projects would soon induce the occupiers to give up and go home.

The grounds of this view were what one might expect. In the age of the bomber, civilization would lie in ruins within days of the opening of air war.

Gas and high explosives would kill thousands, and reduce everyone else to gibbering incapacity. At a time when the British had used bombs only against villagers in Afghanistan, in Iraq, and occasionally in Sudan, it was easy to project their panic to a city like London and imagine the results on a vast scale. That the actual course of events was so different, both in Britain and in Germany and in Japan until the use of the atomic bomb, does not entirely discredit him. What is harder to accept is the dichotomous style that suggests that domination by Hitler would not be too bad, while resistance would be the end of absolutely everything.

Russell never liked *Which Way to Peace?* He never allowed it to be reprinted. He backed away from it, and from the company it brought him into, almost as soon as he had written it. When the war actually came, his never very latent British patriotism boiled up. He desperately tried to get back to England to lend what aid he could to the war effort. He saw that Hitler was an infinitely nastier proposition than he had supposed—not merely a German nationalist of a familiar kind, but a moral nihilist whose aim was to destroy precisely the values by which Russell thought political policies were to be judged. But he had always thought Stalin as obnoxious and dangerous as Hitler. Russophobia was never far from the surface in Russell; among the many reasons why World War I was intolerable was the way it brought France and Britain into alliance with Russia. During World War II, he told Gilbert Murray that he thought Stalin at least as evil as Hitler. As the war ended, he turned to thinking of ways in which Soviet Russia could be contained.

In 1946, in the American magazine *Cavalcade*, he proposed that the United States should in effect blackmail Russia into disarming. This was not because he thought the United States particularly a model for Western society; as always, he thought American politicians vulgar, hysterically anticommunist, hypocritical in their religious professions, and largely contaminated by greed and racism. Still, America was a liberal democracy, whereas the Soviet Union was entirely opposed to the values of liberal democracy; moreover, America was not bent on world conquest and Russia was. Quite what he had in mind remains somewhat mysterious. In later years, he claimed never to have made the proposal; when it was pointed out that he plainly had done so, he claimed he had never been serious; but that is hard to believe, since he made the suggestion several times and in various places over a period of three years. Moreover, the idea is not wholly at odds with Russell's way of thinking. He was not, as he said, a pacifist on principle. He was a consequentialist. Even nuclear warfare had to be treated in that framework.

Sometimes it seemed that he thought that the mere threat of nuclear war would suffice to induce Russia to disarm. But Russell understood better than most what nuclear weapons in their then state of development could and could not do, and he knew that limited nuclear attacks would be unable to halt the Red Army or bring Russia to its knees overnight. So he more usually envisioned Russia refusing to disarm, refusing to open its military sites to inspection, refusing to forswear the attempt to develop nuclear weapons itself. In that case, there would have to be war. Sometimes he optimistically envisioned a quick nuclear war, as when he speculated that "it would not be difficult to find a *casus belli.*" More often, he accepted that it would be more protracted. What World War III would be like was hard to say, but he thought that it might well kill five hundred million people and set European civilization back for five centuries. This, however, was a price worth paying to save European values.

It is hard to assess such ideas. At one level, they have the slightly mad logic of the thought that it had been necessary to destroy the town of Hue in order to save it from the Vietcong. To kill half a billion people and push Europe back five centuries is a strange way of advancing European values. One would have to be very certain indeed that all the alternatives had been carefully thought out and rejected before one started thinking along those lines. In a way, it is an example of something close to the religious mode of thought that I have suggested came naturally to him. Heaven and hell were the only alternatives worth contemplating; that Europe had to pass through a half millennium of purgatory in order to reach heaven and escape hell was not unthinkable. The oddity is to bolt such a way of thinking onto the rationalist, consequentialist forms of political argument that came equally naturally to him. It is no wonder that many American readers of Russell in the last twenty years of his life wondered quite what he had against them when he swung from the cool rationalism of the case for restraint in American foreign policy in a dangerous world to a rhetoric more reminiscent (though twenty years in advance) of the Ayatollah Khomeini's denunciations of the Great Satan.

What is one to make of it all? Three things perhaps. In the first place, the Russell whom one might describe as the heir of 1688 and the Whig Revolution was a vastly useful liberal influence. Liberals tend to suffer from a shortage of rhetorical vigor and a lack of vital energy. Russell's astonishing refusal to grow old and behave respectably was a useful counter to that depressing characteristic of liberal politics. His workaday politics were curiously, but usefully, Whig, liberal, and democratic socialist all at once. The need to combine respect for an aristocracy of intellect with the benefits of the welfare state is a genuine need and one he could state better than most as the possessor of an aristocratic intellect who had given all his money to good radical causes in his youth. His dislike of Marxism, even as he still recognized its rhetorical power and the ills it fed on, was useful when he first broached it in 1896, more useful in 1920 when he wrote *The Practice and Theory of Bolshevism*, and entirely up to date in the 1950s. His violent attacks on American foreign policy in the 1960s ought not to blind us to the fact that the last political statement he wrote was a condemnation of the Soviet invasion of Czechoslovakia in August 1968. All his life, he was more nearly right than most people about the effects of both the policies he approved of and those he loathed, though one result is that when people now-adays read Russell's books of the 1920s on education, marriage, sex, and social policy, they seem models of elegant prose but politically rather tame.

In the second place, there was about him an antipolitical streak. This was not 1688 but 1968, when there was a demand for new visions, for the total reconstruction of everything. In this vein, he did not contribute to politics, though he certainly contributed to the vividness with which those who were totally hostile to the existing order set about attacking it. Most of the time, he saw quite clearly that it was not something one could ask from politics; but he also, and to my mind rightly, saw that it was a side of human life that one needs to protect—to find a political framework within which people can pursue these quasi-religious intimations and find some ultimate value in their lives. As is evident, I am cautious about all this and mistrustful of the effects of confusing salvation and political action. Still, it must be said both that this was a powerful strand in Russell's intellect, temperament, and po-litical style, and that it is hard to see how people would be motivated to take part in politics at all if they were not to a degree propelled by such passions.

And lastly, there was the side of Russell that it is impossible not to like—the Socratic gadfly, whose aim is not to rally us to a cause but simply to stir up our grey cells. That he did wonderfully well, not just in his popular work but also in his more academic writing too. There is a lovely phrase in his essay "On Denoting" in which he accuses Alexius Meinong of failing to preserve the sense of reality that should accompany even the most abstract work, and somehow he managed to convey that sense in his abstract work—and in his potboilers, the converse, the sense that there was also a higher and nobler realm of intellectual light whose rays might, if we were lucky, some-times illuminate everyday life. His ability to make hard thinking and sur-prising conclusions attractive to such a wide audience is one that anyone with pretensions to teach must surely find it as hard not to envy as it is im-possible to emulate. But we can at least take in it the sort of pleasure Russell evidently aimed to give.

Isaiah Berlin
POLITICAL THEORY AND LIBERAL CULTURE

Introduction

THE VIVIDNESS OF the life and personality of the author whose more narrowly intellectual contributions are under discussion would not usually present a problem for the commentator (Ignatieff 1998). The case of Isaiah Berlin is rather different. Bertrand Russell led a vivid life and had a striking personality, but the academic treatment of his work prescinds from these, concentrating on the austerities of his contributions to formal logic and on his less formal analyses of problems in metaphysics and epistemology. The relationship between Berlin's personal history and his intellectual contributions is more intimate than that, however. Because Berlin practiced the history of ideas in a highly personal and imaginative fashion, the student of his analyses is also a student of his sensibility. This is not an unusual state of affairs in more literary subjects, in which we take it for granted that an understanding of the work involves an understanding of the interaction between the author's sensibility and experience, and criticism of the work properly roams back and forth between the author's experience and its subsequent transformation into art. Philosophers who do not write their autobiographies are commonly immune from such scrutiny. The exceptions prove the rule: Mill's *Autobiography* and Russell's; St. Augustine's *Confessions* and Rousseau's. These works invite a more personal and more intimate scrutiny from the reader—though Mill himself strenuously denies this (1981 [1873], 4). They do not merely assert and defend a doctrine but display a sensibility and a temperament; the cogency of their arguments demands discussion, and so does the quality of their sensibility.

Here, then, I tread cautiously. I allow myself some biographical background and then drop Berlin's philosophical work out of sight as irrelevant to our present purposes. I then move to Berlin as a historian of ideas, a student of distinctively Russian social and political themes, and a defender of a distinctively pluralist, anti-utopian liberalism. The division is artificial in the extreme, and the issues raised in each area of discussion are inextricably intertwined. The not particularly liberal Machiavelli is invoked in aid of a liberal moral pluralism, as is the much more liberal Russian Alexander Herzen. Much of the apparently more formal argument of even such essays as Berlin's inaugural lecture, *Two Concepts of Liberty* (1958a), is carried by the invocation of historical figures with whom Berlin carried on those astonishing transhistorical conversations that his friends, students, and lecture audiences all over the world were allowed to overhear.

A Little History

The *Guide Michelin* starts its readers on their journeys with a short introductory account of the history of the region, its people, its culture, and its way of life. Isaiah Berlin was born in Riga, Latvia, in 1909. Owing to an accident at birth, he had a permanently damaged left arm; whether he might otherwise have had athletic tastes and abilities may be doubted, but in any event, his favored place was the sofa rather than the mountain track. His upper-middle-class family was Jewish; his father was a descendant of the founder of the Lubavitcher sect, but the immediate family members were thoroughly Europeanized, and their tastes were musical and literary. A comfortable life was disturbed by the First World War, which provoked anti-Germanism and anti-Semitism; the family moved to Petrograd in 1916 and there encountered both the Russian Revolutions of 1917. Although they suffered no violence, and not much deprivation, the family saw what might happen after the Civil War of 1920–21 and made their way to England. Mendel Berlin, Isaiah's father, was a timber merchant with commercial ties to Britain, and he thought well of British schools.

Arriving with little English in a wholly strange environment, the twelve-year-old Berlin thrived. A suburban preparatory school, in the English sense of the term, was followed by public school, also in the English sense; from St. Paul's, where he followed the traditional classical syllabus, Berlin went to Corpus Christi College, Oxford. He made many friends, and his flair for conversation was a great resource in so doing. Late-1920s Oxford was both snobbish and mildly anti-Semitic, but it sheltered a society that was less attached to its social prejudices than to cleverness and charm. Both of these the young Berlin had in abundance.

To those who know them and their reputation, any account of All Souls College, and any account of the pleasures of a prize fellowship seventy-seven years ago, is otiose. For those who do not, it perhaps suffices to say that Berlin's situation combined the intellectual pleasures of a professorship at the Institute for Advanced Study with the social pleasures of a lifetime membership at the Century Club enhanced by an introduction to all the other members. Berlin was the first Jew to be elected to All Souls and was duly congratulated by the chief rabbi and invited to dinner by Lord Rothschild (Ignatieff 1998, 62). Intellectually, the 1930s were the time of logical positivism's bracing blasts of scientism and skepticism; the Oxford environment was not particularly hospitable to importations from Vienna, but among Berlin's friends were A. J. Ayer, who had come back from Vienna full of Rudolf Carnap and Moritz Schlick, and Gilbert Ryle, who had a clearer grasp of where the Ludwig Wittgenstein of the *Tractatus* had been and where the later Wittgenstein was now going. Berlin's closest intellectual companions were John Austin and Stuart Hampshire, neither of them imbued with the belief in science that drove the logical positivists, but each in his own way entirely disaffected from old-fashioned, intuitionistic Oxford philosophy, though each in his own way a great admirer of Aristotle (Berlin 1973).

Berlin wrote several deft, acute, and accurate essays on the logical positivists' favorite pieces of analysis—of sentences about the past and sentences describing physical objects in the world around us—but although these showed great philosophical talent, they did not offer any insights into what else he might do (Berlin 1978a). Berlin's own account of his development suggested that his philosophical career was essentially a prewar matter. This is not entirely accurate. It is true that his essay "Verification" dates from 1939, but *Concepts and Categories* (1978a) includes the chastely titled "Empirical Propositions and Hypothetical Statements" (1950), in which he showed that categorical statements about the past and the external world cannot be reduced to hypothetical statements about what we would experience under various conditions, as well as the seminal essay "Equality" (1956a). The one piece of work from the 1930s that does offer such an insight is *Karl Marx* (Berlin 1996 [1939]). This was commissioned for the Home University Library in 1935 but delivered only in 1939. Berlin read very widely for it and was one of the first non-Marxists to take seriously Marx's youthful enthusiasm for the philosophy of Hegel and Hegel's critics, such as David Friedrich Strauss and Ludwig Feuerbach. Marx's economics did not interest him in the least, however, and the book as a whole is a series of reflections on the sort of temperament that leads its possessors to embrace utopian, determinist schemes of social improvement. (I return to Berlin's treatment of Marx below.)

Berlin's career was less interrupted than kick-started by the outbreak of the Second World War. It took him to New York for the Ministry of Information, whence he was poached by the Foreign Office for the Washington embassy. From there, he sent back streams of dispatches to his masters in London (Nicholas 1981). It was partly this close contact with the makers of American foreign policy that reshaped his life, but more importantly, it was his postwar encounters with Russian poets, novelists, dramatists, and other intellectuals in the winter of 1945–46.

Just what happened is hard to recapture, but it evidently persuaded him of two things. The first was that he was, after all, a Russian intellectual, for all his years in Oxford, and the other was that Stalin's attempts at the destruction of Russian cultural and intellectual life were appalling, not only because of the cruelty and thuggishness involved in all of Stalin's actions, but also because there had been a vitality, vividness, and originality in Russian literature and political thinking from the 1840s onward that was un-matched in the West (Berlin 1998, 198–254). At a personal level, it was his encounters with Anna Akhmatova and Boris Pasternak that persuaded him of this; at a more—but not very—austerely intellectual level, it was his read-ing of Alexander Herzen and Ivan Turgenev.

High Tide

From 1950 onward, Berlin was important in British academic life and more broadly in British culture as a lecturer for the BBC and as a general commen-tator on political and intellectual life in the context of the Cold War. Berlin wrote nothing about the Holocaust and little about German anti-Semitism as such. He was a Zionist and a good friend of Chaim Weizmann, who was the first president of Israel and the subject of one of Berlin's most heartfelt *éloges* (Berlin 1958b). His cousin Yitzhak Sadeh (born Isaac Landoberg) was a noted general in the Israeli war of independence, and Berlin recalled him with immense affection. He described Sadeh as "a huge child" who did more for Israel than his exploits on the battlefield alone might suggest. In Berlin's words, he "introduced an element of total freedom, unquenchable gaiety, ease, charm, and a natural elegance, half bohemian, half aristocratic, too much of which would ruin any possibility of order, but an element of which no society should lack if it is to be free or worthy of survival" (Berlin 1998, 89–90). Berlin wrote interestingly about Moses Hess's slow and reluctant movement from assimilationism to a liberal Zionism not wholly unlike his own (Berlin 1959b). And he wrote the most unlikely short double biography of all time when he discussed Karl Marx and Benjamin Disraeli as exemplars of mid-Victorian London Jewishness (Berlin 1970). Still, it was Stalinist to-talitarianism, not Nazism, that concerned him. His interest lay in the way in which the rationalist and reformist impulses of the Enlightenment, some-times in perverse combination with the anti-Enlightenment forces of Ro-manticism, had produced millenarian and totalitarian movements that had set back the cause of liberal, pluralist, humanitarian progress by a century and more. It was in arguing on behalf of a pluralist, indeterminist, open-ended liberalism that he invoked the memory of those figures in the history of ideas that he particularly made his own.

Let us begin by asking a slightly odd question: why did Berlin invoke these figures at all? To put it another way, if Berlin wished to argue that values are many, not one, that the future is open, not closed, and that the quest for utopia is more likely to arrive at hell than heaven, why did he need help from the dead? These are philosophical questions, or perhaps in the case of the last thought, a matter of political prudence, that he could have argued on his own behalf and without appealing to anyone else for support. Of course, to say this is to gesture to the essays in which he did argue the case with less historical reference. Viewed as an essay in "pure" political philosophy, *Two Concepts of Liberty* (1958a) would seem heavily encrusted with historical allusion, but it is manifestly not an essay in the history of ideas. "From Hope and Fear Set Free" (1964) is similarly light on historical reference, and such essays as *Historical Inevitability* (1954) argue against determinist theories of history with relatively little further reference. The answer to the odd question must go back to Berlin's treatment of Giambattista Vico (Berlin 1976).

Berlin was seized by Vico's concept of *fantasia*. To argue about Berlin's understanding of Vico's concept is fruitless here, though others have done so profitably in different contexts (Pompa 1975). The point here is Berlin's use of the idea as he understood it. Essentially, Berlin took over Vico's thought that human society was historical, that an understanding of the human mind was to be sought by an active effort of positive, imaginative re-creation, and that understanding the moral and political concepts by which we make sense of our existence, both individual and collective, is a historical activity.

This last point, incidentally, suggests that Berlin's own account of having abandoned philosophy in favor of the history of ideas is misleading; as Bernard Williams observed (personal communication), the truth is rather that he abandoned the idea that philosophical analysis is always concerned with the timelessly valid explication of concepts. The logical positivist ideal of philosophical analysis was that it would eventuate in a definition that would hold true forever. But in Berlin's version of *fantasia*, the concepts of political philosophy are the reflection of transitional, even if not necessarily transitory, attempts by human cultures to grasp their moral and political experience and to mold it as they desire. The other aspect of *fantasia* that provides the clue not so much to the content as to the dazzling rhetorical form of Berlin's work in the history of ideas is its emphasis on reenacting past thought as it was thought by past thinkers. I have elsewhere perhaps overused the image of Berlin taking his hearers to a party in the Elysian Fields; but the thought that conveying a full understanding of another writer is like bringing the reader into the physical presence of that writer is, with due allowances made, hard to escape.

Here is Berlin's account of the kind of knowledge that, he believed, Vico had identified.

> This is the sort of knowing that participants in an activity claim to possess as against mere observers: the knowledge of the actors as against that of the audience, of the "inside" story as opposed to that obtained from some "outside" vantage point; knowledge by "direct acquaintance" with my "inner" states or by sympathetic insight into those of others, which may be obtained by a high degree of imaginative power; the knowledge that is involved when a work of the imagination or of social diagnosis or a work of criticism or scholarship or history is de-

scribed not as correct or incorrect, skilful or inept, a success or a failure, but as profound or shallow, realistic or unrealistic, perceptive or stupid, alive or dead. (Berlin 1969, in 1978b, 117)

That description opens up the reason why Berlin so often invoked long-dead allies in making the case for pluralism, liberalism, and open-endedness. In effect, thinking our own way through the dichotomies of pluralism-monism, freedom-authoritarianism, and indeterminism-determinism is one side of a conversation with writers who happen to be dead. It is one facet of imagining our society set against others so as to illuminate the virtues and vices of each. To know why we believe in—if we do believe in—negative liberty, for instance, is to know what we would want to say to Pericles about his beloved Athens, and what we would want to say to Benjamin Constant (1988 [1819]) about the contrast he drew between the liberty of the ancients and the liberty of the moderns. Seen in that light, Berlin's handling of the figures about whom he wrote becomes easy to understand.

Consider one of the most famous essays, "The Originality of Machiavelli" (Berlin 1972a, in 1978b, 25–79). The "originality" of Machiavelli is itself an interestingly ambiguous topic. Taken in a simple, literal sense, originality is producing ideas—about life, morality, politics, or whatever else—that were unprecedented, unheard of, not previously ventilated by other thinkers. By that definition, Machiavelli might plausibly be said to have been unoriginal. He himself claimed that although his method was novel, what he was doing was reminding the rulers of the "Christian states," whose "proud indolence" he deplored, of truths about successful political practice that had been known to the ancients and forgotten by themselves.

When we consider the general respect for antiquity, and how often—to say nothing of other examples—a great price is paid for some fragments of an antique statue, which we are anxious to possess to ornament our houses with, or to set before artists who strive to imitate them in their own works; and when we see on the other hand, the wonderful examples which the history of ancient kingdoms and republics presents to us, the prodigies of virtue and of wisdom displayed by the kings, captains, citizens and legislators who have sacrificed themselves for their country—when we see these I say more admired than imitated, or so much neglected that not the least trace of this ancient virtue remains, we cannot but be at the same time as much surprised as afflicted. (Machiavelli 1992 [1531], 90)

Another understanding of the concept of originality, however, gets us to a different result. We think of individuals as originals if we react to them with surprise, astonishment, and even something akin to shock; it is not that every single component of their thought and behavior is, taken separately, unprecedented, but that the ensemble strikes us with a certain awkwardness and unassimilability. Machiavelli has, of course, always been treated as a shocking figure. *The Prince* was the first book to be placed on the index of works that Roman Catholics were forbidden to read; and it was so thoroughly banned that even priests who wished to preach against it were required to obtain special leave from their bishops to read the work they were about to assail.

It was this unassimilable quality that attracted Berlin's attention: "There is something surprising about the sheer number of interpretations of Machiavelli's political opinions. There exist even now over a score of leading theories of how to interpret *The Prince* and *The Discourses*—apart from a cloud of subsidiary views and glosses" (Berlin 1978b, 25). Berlin's interpretation did not exactly deny the plausibility of, say, seeing Machiavelli as somehow the begetter of Italian nationalism, as Italian commentators of the nineteenth century, such as Pasquale Villari, had done; rather, as his remarks about Vico's interpretive methods suggest, Berlin implied that that was not a particularly illuminating insight into the extraordinariness of Machiavelli. As to what would provide a deeper insight, Berlin was not concerned to add a twenty-fifth or twenty-ninth interpretation to all the rest. His interpretation was intended to answer a present-centered and essentially philosophical question, and thus to deepen the present-day reader's encounter with Machiavelli. Of course, a man who observed that he preferred the city to the salvation of his own soul was a devout patriot. Machiavelli certainly had a strong sense of Italian identity; that is, he had a strong sense that the Italians were not like the French and Spanish who so often trampled through his country. To think of him as a nationalist was, however, unlikely to prove deeply illuminating; much of the intellectual interest of nineteenth-century nationalism lies in the fact that it was very unlike the patriotism and localism of previous ages.

So when Berlin offered his picture of Machiavelli as a moral pluralist, this was to tell us something about how we can read him rather than to tell us much about how his contemporaries might have read him. They, to be sure, found him difficult in somewhat the same way we do. Nonetheless, his superiors in the Florentine diplomatic service did not find him unreadable, merely somewhat too enthusiastic for overly subtle plans and schemes. By the same token, his friends were surprised that he spent so long in his study of an evening, dressed in the robes of a councillor, locked, as it seemed to them, in conversation with long-dead sages, generals, politicians, and other heroes. They could not, however, think of him as committed to an alarming form of moral pluralism. That was a way of conceptualizing the world that they did not possess. Berlin's writing, then, offers us a Machiavelli who is original in standing out against what Berlin thought of as the great hope of all European philosophy, the hope of demonstrating that beneath (or above or beyond) the chaotic flux of experience there lay a realm of order and harmony where conflict was once and for all dissolved. That was the realm in which reason and desire, impulse and conscience, and all the goods that a person might pursue would be shown to coexist, and indeed to imply one another. Berlin thought, though he never did much to prove, that the Platonic ambition to uncover a timeless truth in which all values would be reconciled was the dominant urge in European thought. Machiavelli was interesting not because he set out to show that Plato was wrong and that no such reconciliation was to be had, but because he simply took it for granted. The fact that he made a devastating philosophical point without taking the trouble to do so overtly was what made him philosophically unplaceable.

What Berlin wished to extract from Machiavelli was, however, a simple and slightly brutal point. This was that there is no overarching harmony in this world, that different moral universes and different cultural attachments are compelling, even equally compelling, but irreconcilable. Machiavelli did not argue that the values of tough, patriotic little city-states were superior to those of Christian self-abnegation; nor did he argue only that the self-abnegating were likely to make poorer soldiers and less aggressive statesmen than their classical predecessors. He certainly argued the latter, and we may guess that he believed the former. What was more off-putting was his insistence that his readers had to choose. If they wished to avoid the heat of the kitchen, they should retire to the monastery. Once they had decided to enter the kitchen, they should learn to endure the heat. Two exemplary little tales, one in *The Prince* (1992 [1531]) and one in *The Discourses* (1975 [1531]) make this clear. In the first, Machiavelli commended Cesare Borgia for the cleverness with which he had first used a particularly nasty aide, Remirro de Orco, to subdue the Romagna, and then had ordered him murdered in order to appease the population and convey the impression that the cruelties of Remirro de Orco had nothing to do with Cesare Borgia. From the second, Machiavelli drew the moral that men do not know how to be truly good or truly wicked. Giovanpaolo Baglioni had the chance to kill Pope Julius II, and in the process make himself master of the whole of central Italy. He drew back—not, as Machiavelli was at pains to insist, because he was an admirable character. He was certainly a parricide, an indulger in incest, and in general an object of loathing to almost all who knew him. What he lacked was the nerve to do something that everyone would have found astonishing as well as appalling.

This is part and parcel of the extraordinary casualness with which Machiavelli referred to *crudelita* and *terribilita* as part of the "virtue" (*virtu*) of heroes such as Hannibal. It is not that Machiavelli thought of cruelty and the ability to terrify one's subordinates as intrinsically good or attractive. He took for granted the everyday estimate of human action, and was in that sense not a moral innovator or a moral subversive. Leo Strauss's (1978) indictment of Machiavelli as a teacher of evil is less an indictment than one might suppose; on the one hand, he taught men that they must do evil to achieve good ends in the political arena, but on the other, he did not suggest that that somehow makes the evil less evil. Under indictment, the political innovator who does evil for the safety of the state will argue not that he has done no evil, but that he did evil so that good might come. He will not expect his soul to be saved, only his city.

The peculiarity of Berlin's capture of Machiavelli for the pluralist cause is threefold. The first peculiarity is perhaps something of a quibble. Berlin was a pluralist; Machiavelli was more nearly a dichotomist. That is, he was not so much concerned to agree that there were many ways of life, each of which seemed good to its own practitioners, as to show that the moral values officially promoted in his own time and place were inimical to the welfare of the society that promoted them. What he pointed to was not pluralism but a head-on conflict between secular, political values and otherworldly values. The upshot was not that saints and generals inhabited different worlds but that a society of saints would be preyed upon by anyone who cared to do so. The reason why one might dismiss this point as quibbling is that Berlin does not deny it. To deepen the point: there cannot be a meeting of minds between the two sides of the conflict. It is no good telling the self-abnegating saint that he will fall prey to the brigand and the pirate; he knows it already. Nor is it any good telling Hannibal that he has behaved with brutality; he knows it already. The very currency in which they are willing to deal ensures that they will reject each other's calculations.

The second peculiarity about Berlin's appropriation of Machiavelli is that, whatever Machiavelli was, he was not a liberal. I shall recur below to two familiar anxieties about Berlin's pluralism, namely, its connection to liberalism and its difference from relativism, so I shall say almost nothing on this point here. Still, it is worth recalling that Machiavelli's conception of freedom was not the liberal conception of freedom. In the terms that Constant (1988 [1819]) made famous, Machiavelli was concerned with "the liberty of the ancients" rather than "the liberty of the moderns." Hobbes almost made the point a century and a half before Constant when he distinguished between the freedom of the city and the freedom of the person (Hobbes 1968 [1651]). That is, Hobbes thought Machiavelli and the enthusiasts for republican liberty were concerned with the city's independence from outside interference; the individual might, as Hobbes insisted, be less interfered with in a loosely governed despotism such as the Ottoman Empire than in Lucca (Hobbes 1968 [1651]). This is not quite right. Machiavelli was in fact concerned with the liberty of the individual as well as the independence of the polity. Above all, however, he emphasized the citizen's immunity from the predatory activities of the upper classes, and not Hobbesian or liberal laissez-faire. What counted as liberty was not license to do whatever we want so much as it was freedom from the arbitrary, selfish, corrupt, and greedy whims of those whose power outran their self-control. The Romans, in this view, possessed individual liberty; rich men did not dare to affront the honor of the wives of their social inferiors, and nobody's property or person could be considered fair game. This was tough, tightly constrained republican freedom.

The third irony of Berlin's use of Machiavelli is that Machiavelli was willing, in a way that no twentieth-century writer could sensibly be, to envisage warfare as a permanent way of life. That states were, at best, in a state of suspended hostility to one another did not cause him any particular anxiety. The prince addressed in *The Prince* is encouraged to avoid the self-civilizing process that contemporary manuals on princely conduct urged; he was advised to confine himself to hunting, since that was an enjoyable way to learn the lay of the land in a way that he would need in time of war. The twentieth century has certainly been a time of war, but it has also, for that very reason, been a time when the desire for peace has been stronger than at any other time in human history. Liberalism is, on the whole, a pacific, even if not exactly a pacifist, doctrine, and one would wonder at the invocation of Machiavelli in the pluralist cause if that invocation were to carry any acceptance of Machiavelli's bellicose enthusiasms. Of course, the truth is that it does not.

Why, then, is it worth dwelling, in this mildly obsessive fashion, on this one instance of Berlin's invocation of an entire gallery of historical ancestors and instances? The reason is simple enough. It is not surprising to find Berlin invoking John Stuart Mill's *On Liberty* in his essay on Mill and the ends of life (Berlin 1959a). Mill was insistent that the ends of life were many and varied and perhaps even "contradictory." It is not surprising to find Berlin appealing to Montesquieu; Montesquieu's pluralism is most famously sociological and political, but it would be strange to deny that he had an eye both for the importance of social pluralism as the reinforcement of the separation of powers and the moderate liberty of a state such as eighteenth-century Britain, and for the sheer variety of moral attachments and preconceptions that different societies and peoples exhibited. It is far from surprising to find Berlin invoking Alexander Herzen as the touchstone of liberal sensibility. By the same token, whatever one's anxieties about the sharpness of the line between relativism and pluralism, and whatever one's confidence about Johann Gottfried von Herder's place on one side or other of that line, there is nothing surprising in Berlin's attention to his work. He was perhaps the earliest articulate critic of the Enlightenment's belief in the unity of human nature, and of the unity of the goal toward which anything we might call progress must be tending. But what is astonishing is Berlin's ability to find in Machiavelli—an archaic thinker, a deliberate throwback to a vanished world, and a decided skeptic about anything we might dignify with the title of human rights—an ally in the metaphysical battle between the monists and the pluralists.

Russian Thinkers

It is time to say a very little about Berlin's Russian allegiances. If simple incapacity did not deter me from attempting to say much on this theme, the tremendous eloquence of Berlin's account of Herzen, Vissarion Belinsky, Turgenev, and his own contemporaries such as Pasternak would render any commentary unnecessary. A feature of Berlin's treatment of all historical figures was that he wrote as if they were present in the room and in full flood. This has one slightly discouraging effect, which is that Berlin's work is not treated as seriously by historians of ideas as it might be. Because he did not draw much of a distinction between those elements of his account that were supposed to be taken absolutely straightforwardly as contributions to a strictly historical account of the subject and those that were supposed to open a way into another mind for beginners (or the merely puzzled), the more dogged sort of reader can become impatient. The one field where this is not true is in his treatment of nineteenth-century Russian writers. Although here too Berlin relied on what one might call the direct as opposed to the contextual approach; the fact that the writers who most interested him were part of the twentieth-century political struggle between communists and liberals within and without the Soviet Union meant that any account of them and their ideas involved taking sides in what might vulgarly be called the great debate over whose fault the Russian Revolution really was. Oddly enough, Berlin was on the opposite side of one of his oldest and best friends, Leonard Schapiro, on the question. Schapiro held that the chronic tendency of the Russian intelligentsia of the nineteenth century to seek total solutions had laid the foundation for the contempt for individual rights that was such a marked characteristic of the Bolsheviks and then the Communist Party of the Soviet Union, whereas Berlin thought that what one might call the 1848 intelligentsia displayed an ambivalence about means and ends and about the compatibility of individual emancipation and social order that were strikingly modern in themselves and in some form central to the liberal imagination (Kelly 1998). As Aileen Kelly has argued, Western commentators throughout the years of the Cold War tended to use "intellectual" as a term of condemnation; since the Soviet Union was not entirely inept in recruiting the intellectuals of both actual and recently emancipated colonies for nationalist, anti-American, and anti-British political movements, it is not hard to see why they did so. Moreover, Stalinist propaganda was quick to attempt retrospectively to recruit radical nineteenth-century intellectuals as forerunners of modern communism. In a manner of speaking, Berlin's aim was to rescue writers such as Herzen from this embrace by people whom he would have loathed; writers on the other side were less inclined to dispute with Stalin the title to their memory but were more inclined to explain why they had rendered themselves vulnerable for such a takeover (Malia 1961).

The most famous of all Berlin's essays on Russian thinkers is the least relevant to this argument. *The Hedgehog and the Fox* (Berlin 1978c [1953]) explored the head-on conflict between Tolstoy's passionate conviction that he was called to give the world a unified moral vision and put all his rhetorical and literary talents behind it and his complete inability to see the world in such a unitary fashion. The title, as the whole world knows by now, comes from a fragment from a Greek poet, Archilocus, to the effect that the fox knows many things, but the hedgehog knows one big thing (Berlin 1978c [1953], 22). Tolstoy, in this view, was a fox who drove himself mad by trying to be a hedgehog. His genius was to be a fox, and it is that ability to see the world in a fragmentary but aesthetically coherent fashion (to the extent that art confers unity) that makes a novel such as *War and Peace* a masterpiece. Conversely, readers of *Anna Karenina* are not infrequently moved to complain that the novel is artistically damaged by Tolstoy's determination that the adulterous Anna shall come to a bad end. However that might be, my point is that in this one essay, Berlin's anti-monism is not a political doctrine, nor much freighted with metaphysics, but rather an insight into Tolstoy's increasingly fragile grasp on reality in his old age. It is of course a moral, metaphysical, and political doctrine elsewhere and often.

The more central essays, from the standpoint of politics, are Berlin's discussions of Herzen and Turgenev. Here I must admit to an uncertainty. Ignatieff (1998) maintains that it was Turgenev to whom Berlin felt closest. This strikes me as less than entirely persuasive because Berlin's (1955, 1956b, 1968) accounts of Herzen seem to me more deeply felt, less apologetic, and far more convincing than the picture of Turgenev that he presents in *Fathers and Children* (Berlin 1972b). But this raises the question, convincing about what? If Berlin's liberalism is at least as much a matter of sensibility and attachment as it is a devotion to theories of freedom, human rights, political democracy, and the usual subject matter of political philosophy, what sensibility does that liberalism invoke, and to whom might it be most passionately and unswervingly attached? In *Fathers and Children*, Berlin devoted much of his energy, as had Turgenev, to the task of explaining to the young and enraged that the elderly liberal is not merely cowardly, not merely unable to give up his comforts. The liberal is torn between two distinct impulses; the first is to side with the violent indignation of the young and to assist in their destruction of the existing order; the existing order is, after all, always sufficiently replete with injustice, cruelty, oppression, and the rest to justify any amount of destruction; but the second impulse is the opposite. The existing order contains as much of civilization as we possess, and its cruelties can be palliated or even eliminated in due course, as can many of its injustices. The liberal cannot help noticing that people filled with indignation about the existing brutalities and injustices might be likely to commit a number of brutalities and injustices themselves, perhaps out of a failure to hit only and exactly the right targets for attack, perhaps out of a regrettable tendency to get carried away by zeal, and perhaps, worst of all, out of acquiring a taste for violently dispatching their enemies.

Ignatieff (1998) suggests that the identification with Turgenev that is visible in Berlin's Romanes Lecture of 1971 represents a liberalism under attack. That is true enough, but it marked something of a retreat from the more exuberant liberalism that Berlin had earlier derived from Herzen. Whether Herzen was in any straightforward sense a liberal is a large question that we may decently duck on this occasion. We can agree that he was a populist, a socialist, and sometimes a revolutionary, and still say that he possessed what Berlin considered the archetype of the liberal sensibility. For Herzen's creed was the importance of rescuing individuals from every form of oppression, including the oppression of duty, sociability, and solidarity. Even to call it a creed is something of a mistake, since creeds were another of the oppressions that Herzen was eager to battle. When he described himself as waging "a little guerilla war" against all restraints on individuality, he meant it. Herzen knew that this was a reckless way to think and that one might easily be led into contradiction and confusion; but when praised by Dostoevsky for writing dialogues in which Herzen himself was always being driven into corners by his interlocutors, he replied, "But that is the point." More than a few of the building blocks of Berlin's liberalism were explicitly part of Herzen's anticredal creed: the antipathy to distant goals that might be made the excuse for vast sacrifices of present happiness; a skepticism about abstractions, even including freedom, justice, democracy, and the nation; an insistence on the importance of small, concrete happinesses; a preference for the empirical and felt over the theoretical and rational.

Liberalism and Pluralism

Finally, what of the theoretical structure behind Berlin's liberalism? Is it proper that he should be remembered as the theorist of negative liberty and the writer who showed that pluralism and liberalism were natural allies? No short answer can be persuasive, and what follows is inevitably dogmatic. Berlin wrote a good deal in defense of a certain sort of liberalism, though not all of it was in an academic vein. Thus, *On the Pursuit of the Ideal* (Berlin 1988) was a mildly polemical attack on utopian thinking, delivered to a large audience who had come to see Berlin receive the Agnelli Prize for contributions to European ethics. Essays such as *John Stuart Mill and the Ends of Life* (Berlin 1959a) were partly about their ostensible subject matter—in this case, John Stuart Mill and the inconsistency between Mill's official utilitarianism and his actual passion for individual freedom—and partly about the nature of freedom and a liberal society. The individual thinker illuminated the larger topic, and the larger topic framed the individual thinker. The discussions of Vico and Herder, like the lectures on Romanticism, were part of a larger strategy of casting doubt on some of the cherished beliefs of the Enlightenment, though always in such a way as to preserve many others.

What this means is that Berlin's liberalism is not like that of, say, Rawls (1971, 1983). Whereas Rawls deduced or at least derived the two principles of justice that for him define the basic framework of a liberal social, political, and economic order, Berlin supported a kind of liberalism with essentially cultural and historical arguments. Although he was, of course, concerned with human rights, he never thought it plausible to define liberalism in terms of its attachment to rights, save insofar as an attachment to rights is both instrumentally a way of enhancing freedom and expressively a way of insisting on the importance of freedom as a central human good. Berlin, like Herzen before him, was content to agree that the liberal's passion for individual freedom is historically, geographically, and culturally local, without thinking that this in any way impugns liberal ideals. That the individual with whom liberalism is concerned is a historical novelty does not diminish the appeal of freedom, any more than the fact that we were born rather recently and will not live forever excuses an unconcern with living happily and decently while we are alive. To say, as commentators sometimes do (Gray 1995), that Berlin's liberalism is not "Enlightenment liberalism" is both true and misleading (Kocis 1989, Galipeau 1994).

To the extent that the Enlightenment is identified with the view that morality is timeless, rationally derived, known a priori to be valid (or true), universal, and therefore no more culturally variable than mathematical truth, Berlin was a critic of the Enlightenment. He did not deny that human nature is in many ways uniform; Shylock's famous question, "If you prick us, do we not bleed?" is as powerful a question as Shylock supposed. Still, Berlin agreed with the Romantic critics of the Enlightenment that talk of "Man" in the abstract was unhelpful and that what we encounter is human beings in an almost infinite variety. The insistence on this point was what Berlin found congenial in Marx's work; what he rejected was the semireligious faith in the existence of an ultimate solution to all of humanity's ills. Again, then, if utopianism is a feature of Enlightenment thought, Berlin's anti-utopianism is anti-Enlightenment.

What is not anti-Enlightenment is Berlin's hostility to irrationalism. Berlin's antirationalism was not irrationalism; he had, one might think, a great dislike of the cruelty that so often goes along with irrationalism. He could not but think that Maistre was a precursor of fascism, and that was almost the end of the matter. He was not much concerned to dissect Maistre so as to distinguish the rationalizable, Burkean elements in his thought from the violently theocratic and irrationalist ones; it was as though the latter aspect of Maistre struck him so forcefully that argument began and ended there (Berlin 1990). If what we are offered is antirationalist but not antirational, contextualist but not narrowly local, what sort of liberalism is it, and how is this cultural and historical account of it sustained by such relatively abstract essays as *Two Concepts of Liberty*?

The answer is not easy to sustain, but in outline it is simple enough. Berlin's inaugural lecture was not, appearances to the contrary, concerned to distinguish between two concepts of liberty, let alone to defend one against the other. The lecture was more nearly a broadside against everything Berlin deplored and a gesture in favor of all the things he wished to defend. There is not, and cannot be, one concept of liberty that holds together the Stoic conception of the freedom available to the slave whose self-control makes him freer than his master, the Hegelian-Marxian thought that freedom is the consciousness of necessity, the supposed collectivist conception stemming from Rousseau's thought that a person is free when obeying the *moi commun* ("communal I"), and the several other "positive" conceptions that Berlin presented to his hearers. Conversely, the several glosses on negative liberty that he offered did not identify one negative conception, let alone one that could neatly be set against one positive conception. Therefore, the conclusion to draw is not that *Two Concepts* was confused but that it was doing so many different things at once that even its author was not wholly in command of the plot. That may sound either frivolous or faintly insulting, but it is not meant to be so; if Herzen was prepared to argue against himself in the hope of illuminating a truth that could not be gained by simpler means, there is no reason why Berlin should not have been doing the same thing.

This, however, brings us to one of the standard cruxes. If Berlin was arguing for a kind of liberalism suited to a pluralist culture such as our own, why did he not confront more directly the difficulty that all commentators have pointed to, namely, that pluralism is not particularly the natural ally of liberalism? That there are conservative varieties of pluralism is not news. The Ottoman Empire's millet system suffered non-Muslim communities to survive and, up to a point, flourish. David Hume's defense of a conservatively understood balance of powers within the British constitution was not, in Berlin's sense, liberal, since it privileged order over liberty. It certainly advocated as much liberty as order would allow, and defended a secular, tolerant, accommodating society as good for both commerce and individual happiness. It was not, however, a pluralism that simultaneously claimed that values were multiple and that freedom was somehow special. Berlin seems to have contradicted himself in a way that Hume did not.

In fact, appearances are again deceptive. Berlin's thought was culturally local. Once we have a society in which individuals are capable of feeling stifled by having to accommodate themselves to the prevailing norms simply in order to keep the peace, pluralism implies liberalism. This is what one might call the liberalism of nonsuffocation; it is the liberalism implied in Herzen's revolt not only against the czarist police but also against all the overbearing calls to acknowledge our duty in which nineteenth-century political writing was so rich. It is not so much philosophically grounded as culturally and psychologically grounded. The distinction between positive and negative liberty then turns into several distinctions, all of them doing a good deal of work. The refusal of the "retreat to the inner citadel" that characterizes Berlin's rejection of Stoicism is an affirmation of the modern confidence in our ability to act on and in the world. The rejection of the Rousseauian wish for a liberty that we can share only with fellow citizens is an affirmation of Constant's liberty of the moderns. The insistence that liberty is not justice, not equality, not democracy is Berlin's way of reminding us that we may have all of these and still be oppressed in the ways Mill and Herzen identified. The repudiation of an account of being one's own master that equates it with the control of our lower selves by higher and enlightened selves is Berlin's way of defending the empirical, here-and-now individual and his or her aspirations against anyone else's attempt to second-guess them. In some situations, pluralism would not support liberalism because these aspirations would be unattainable or would not be conceptually coherent. Where they are coherent, attainable, and deeply rooted in our sense of ourselves, the connection holds.

This will not reassure critics who have thought that Berlin was doing an orthodox kind of political philosophy. The objection that liberty is always one thing, subject only to different understandings of what obstacles we wish to be free *from* and of what we wish to be free to *do*, is familiar (MacCallum 1967, Gray 1980), but it is beside the point. For one thing, it is not an entirely successful analysis of liberty—not all obstacles from which we may wish to be free are obstacles to freedom; for another, it only deflects the argument onto the question whether a purported obstacle really is an obstacle. The Stoic insists that no conventionally characterized obstacle is one; the Stoic's critic insists that most really are. More importantly, Berlin's case rested on the assumption that conventional philosophical analysis could not make a sufficient moral or political difference. It could perhaps help us see what might make such a difference, but it did not change anything itself. Whether Berlin was offering an unconventional philosophical analysis or engaging in a polemical exercise of another kind entirely may not matter very much; locating the difference between academic philosophical analysis and Berlin's work matters rather more. In so doing, the secondary literature is of limited use; the one indispensable aid is Hardy's (1997) meticulous bibliographical work.

References

Berlin, I. 1939. "Verification." *Proceedings of the Aristotelian Society* 39:225–48.
———. 1950. "Empirical Propositions and Hypothetical Statements." *Mind* 59:289–312.
———. 1954. *Historical Inevitability*. Auguste Comte Memorial Trust Lecture 1. Oxford: Oxford University Press.
———. 1955. "Herzen and Bakunin on Individual Liberty." In *Continuity and Change in Russian and Soviet Thought*, edited by E. J. Simmons, 437–99. Cambridge, Mass.: Harvard University Press.
———. 1956a. "Equality." *Proceedings of the Aristotelian Society* 56:301–26.
———. 1956b. Introduction to *"From the Other Shore" and "The Russian People and Socialism,"* by A. Herzen, vii–xxiii. London: Weidenfeld and Nicolson.
———. 1958a. *Two Concepts of Liberty*. Oxford: Clarendon.
———. 1958b. *Chaim Weizmann*. London: Weidenfeld and Nicolson.

———. 1959a. *John Stuart Mill and the Ends of Life*. London: Council of Christians and Jews.

———. 1959b. *The Life and Opinions of Moses Hess*. Lucien Woff Memorial Lecture. Cambridge: Heffer. Reprinted in Berlin (1978b), *Against the Current*.

———. 1964. "From Hope and Fear Set Free." In *Proceedings of the Aristotelian Society, 1963–4*, 1–30. Oxford: Blackwell.

———. 1968. Introduction to *My Past and Thoughts*, by A. Herzen, xiii–xxxvii. London: Chatto and Windus.

———. 1969. "A Note on Vico's Concept of Knowledge." In *Giambattista Vico: An International Symposium*, edited by G. Tagliacozzo and H. V. White, 371–77. Baltimore: Johns Hopkins University Press. Reprinted in Berlin (1978b), *Against the Current*.

———. 1970. "Benjamin Disraeli, Karl Marx, and the Search for Identity." *Transactions of the Jewish Historical Society of England* 22:29–49. Reprinted in Berlin (1978b), *Against the Current*.

———. 1972a. "The Originality of Machiavelli." In *Studies on Machiavelli*, edited by M. P. Gilmore, 149–206. Florence: Sansoni. Reprinted in Berlin (1978b), *Against the Current*, 25–79.

———. 1972b. *Fathers and Children: Turgenev and the Liberal Predicament*. Oxford: Clarendon.

———. 1973. "J. L. Austin and the Early Beginnings of Oxford Philosophy." In *Essays on J. L. Austin*, edited by G. Warnock, 1–16. Oxford: Clarendon. Reprinted in Berlin (1998), *Personal Impressions*.

———. 1976. *Vico and Herder*. London: Hogarth.

———. 1978a. *Concepts and Categories*. London: Chatto and Windus.

———. 1978b. *Against the Current*. London: Chatto and Windus.

———. 1978c (1953). *The Hedgehog and the Fox*. London: Weidenfeld and Nicolson.

———. 1988. *On the Pursuit of the Ideal*. Turin: Giovanni Agnelli Foundation.

———. 1990. "Joseph de Maistre and the Origins of Fascism." In *The Crooked Timber of Humanity*, 91–174. London: John Murray.

———. 1996 (1939). *Karl Marx*. 4th ed. London: Harper Collins.

———. 1998 (1980). *Personal Impressions*. London: Pimlico.

Constant, B. 1988 (1819). "The Liberty of the Ancients Compared with That of the Moderns." In *Political Writings*, edited by B. Fontana, 307–28. Cambridge: Cambridge University Press.

Galipeau, C. 1994. *Isaiah Berlin's Liberalism*. Oxford: Clarendon.

Gray, J. 1980. "Negative and Positive Liberty." *Political Studies* 28:507–26.

———. 1995. *Isaiah Berlin*. London: Fontana.

Hardy, H. 1997. "A Bibliography of Isaiah Berlin." In I. Berlin, *Against the Current*, 2nd. ed., 356–89. London: Pimlico.

Hobbes, T. 1968 (1651). *Leviathan*. Harmondsworth: Penguin.

Ignatieff, M. 1998. *Isaiah Berlin*. London: Chatto and Windus.

Kelly, A. 1998. *Toward Another Shore*. New Haven, Conn.: Yale University Press.

Kocis, R. 1989. *A Critical Appraisal of Sir Isaiah Berlin's Political Philosophy*. Lewiston, Me.: Mellen.

MacCallum, G. 1967. "Negative and Positive Freedom." *Philosophical Review* 76:312–34.

Machiavelli, N. 1975 (1531). *Discourses on Livy*. London: Walker, Routledge.

———. 1992 (1531). *The Prince*. Edited by R. M. Adams. New York: Norton.

Malia, M. 1961. *Alexander Herzen and the Birth of Russian Socialism*. New Haven, Conn.: Yale University Press.

Mill, J. S. 1981 (1873). *Autobiography*. Vol. 1 of *The Collected Works of John Stuart Mill*, edited by J. M. Robson. Toronto: University Toronto Press.

Nicholas, H. G. 1981. *Washington Despatches, 1941–1945*. London: Weidenfeld and Nicolson.

Pompa, L. 1975. *A Study of the New Science*. Cambridge: Cambridge University Press.

Rawls, J. 1971. *A Theory of Justice*. Cambridge, Mass.: Harvard University Press.

———. 1983. *Political Liberalism*. New York: Columbia University Press.

Strauss, L. 1978. *Thoughts on Machiavelli*. Chicago: University of Chicago Press.

21

Popper and Liberalism

IT IS CLEAR to all readers of Popper's work that there is some sort of natural affinity between the account he gives of the rationality of science and his commitment to political liberalism. The object of this essay is to explore the nature of that affinity. The claims I make about it are initially very uncontentious and hardly go beyond Popper's own words; I end, however, by making the more contentious claim that Popper's account of scientific rationality is itself in a broad sense political and that what sustains his commitment to some awkward epistemological views is his liberalism. That is, it is not so much that his philosophy of science supports his liberalism as that it expresses it. This is not a claim that I imagine Popper himself would accept; indeed, I imagine that he would be extremely hostile to it. Nonetheless, I should perhaps say at this point that it is not a claim made in any very hostile or critical spirit. Defenses of liberalism, like defenses of science, are almost doomed to waver somewhat between the thought that it is the *process* that justifies the result—a political decision or an accepted theory—and the thought that it is the *result* that justifies the process.

Since one of the things I wish to explore here is what kind of liberalism it is that Popper espouses, I shall follow his recommendation that we should avoid starting with elaborate definitions of our subject matter (Popper 1962, 2:17). So I start by observing only that liberalism must, whatever else, place a high value on liberty and equality. It is true that Ronald Dworkin has recently tried to persuade us that liberalism is concerned only with equality; but even he concedes that there will be liberal and nonliberal conceptions of equality and that the liberal conception of equality will be characterized by its concern for individual autonomy (Dworkin 1978, 127ff.). So I think we shall come to no harm if we start from the thought that liberals are concerned to achieve as much liberty and equality as may be.

Now, Popper remarks in his autobiography that he long ago came to the conclusion that although equality might be a good thing, it was excessively costly in terms of liberty (Popper 1976, 36). But here, it is clear, the sort of equality he has in mind is something like equality of wealth or income. In *The Open Society and Its Enemies*, Plato is attacked for his inegalitarian views not, of course, because he defends inequality of wealth or income, for in these terms Plato's guardians are worse off than the rest of the population of the republic, but because he defends a kind of political elitism that is at odds with the sort of equality to which Popper *is* committed (Popper 1962, 1:94ff.). That is, there must be at least an equality of basic rights; we may not wish to try to secure that the most energetic and the least energetic end up with the same amount of wealth or the same annual income, but we shall almost certainly want to start by giving everyone the same rights to acquire wealth or income, and we shall certainly want to give everyone the same political rights and immunities (256–57).

In accordance with another of Popper's own claims, we can agree that most liberals will see that these are values that we cannot pursue as "absolutes." If, say, freedom was understood as the absence of authoritative control over our behavior, there is a strong case for saying that the creation of "absolute" liberty by abolishing all such control would be self-destructive by virtue of permitting the strong to tyrannize the weak without restraint. Similarly, if we were to start with the notion of equality as absolute equality of wealth or income, we should soon find that any attempt to create *that* equality would be destructive of other sorts of equality—in particular, the need to police whatever system of achieving equality we dreamed up would destroy any sort of equality of power (Popper 1976, 36–37). The idea that we can have absolute equality in the sense of equality in everything and in all ways is seemingly absurd, as is the idea that we can have absolute liberty; creating some equalities threatens others, just as leaving some liberties alone threatens the survival of others.

In this view, then, liberals will try to secure as much liberty and equality as possible; sometimes equality will strengthen liberty, and sometimes it will be in competition with it, just as sometimes liberty will reinforce equality and sometimes not. The kind of political equality that is enshrined in democratic procedures will, under favorable conditions, assist in the preservation of liberty by restraining rulers from trying to control every aspect of their subjects' lives, but under unfavorable conditions, it may simply replace the tyranny of one man by the tyranny of the majority. There cannot be any conceptual demonstration that if only we pick the right conception of liberty and equality, we can secure that there is no competition between them and that we can have all we want of both—properly understood (cf. Dworkin 1978, 123–26). Or, more guardedly, any attempted demonstration of this compatibility is no use; we shall not know until after the event whether a given political choice embodied the right conception.

Given this minimal characterization of liberalism, it is easy to show how many of Popper's concerns have been central to the concerns of mainstream liberalism. Consider *The Poverty of Historicism*. The object of that work is to show that social prophecies of the kind embodied in Marx's social and political theory are no part of a rational program of scientific research. The idea that it is the task of the social sciences to uncover the laws of history is attacked with a variety of weapons, but chiefly with the claim that the "laws" on offer—say, Marx's "law of increasing immiseration"—have not been laws at all, but trends (Popper 1961, 115–16). They have not been properly framed universal hypothetical statements, but extrapolations of conjunctions of singular statements. The defender of Marx might argue that this is by no means a fatal objection. If a trend could be shown to be properly grounded in true laws and the appropriate initial conditions, it ought in principle to be possible to show that the trend would continue—in some appropriate fashion—for an indefinite period. There are, perhaps, two slightly different ways of explaining why this will not do. One might be to construe laws as Mill did, as asserting that whenever A, then a, unless something interferes; human affairs, of course, amount to a continuous attempt to interfere with what would have happened but for the interference, so there will be very little predictive power to be had from laws of this sort in social matters. Of course, we can sometimes predict how people will interfere, and make allowances for it, but we cannot do so at anything beyond short range. A man setting a booby trap engages in ad hoc predictions about how people will try to interfere with the workings of his device; but he cannot hope to predict how long it will take for them to get wise to everything he does—all he knows is that since they will be trying very hard, he himself had better keep innovating. A second way of putting the point, perhaps truer to Popper's own formulation, is to say that a law of the form $(x)(Fx \rightarrow Gx)$ may hold *so long as* people do not know of it; once they know of it, or perhaps even once they know of something else on which this law's holding depends, the law becomes false (vi–vii). Again, the man setting the booby trap illustrates the point; the generalizations about the way people set out defusing a device on which he has hitherto depended turn out not to hold once their knowledge increases. The little semiformal demonstration of the impossibility of determinism that prefaces later editions of *The Poverty of Historicism* makes the central point: we cannot predict what we are going to discover in future, but we do know that what we shall do depends on those discoveries (v–vi).

It is in tracing the bearing of these arguments upon traditional conceptions of liberalism that we begin to see what sort of liberal Popper is. For in the liberal tradition, we may discern two distinctive approaches, one most clearly espoused by Mill, one most clearly espoused by Kant; and these would yield rather different interpretations of why the arguments of *The Poverty of Historicism* matter so much. Suppose there were some people, social scientific experts, who did possess the sort of far-ranging knowledge of society's operations that we currently do not suppose they could actually have. What authority would this give them? On the difference between Kant's reply to this question and Mill's reply to the same question hang the two different liberalisms at stake here.

Kant's answer is unequivocal; such knowledge would not give its possessors authority over us. Their position vis-à-vis us is rather like that of a "civilized" country proposing to colonize some "primitive" people. However enlightened we may be, we have no right to colonize other countries (Reiss 1970, 21). However much our experts may know, they have no right to our obedience unless we give them that right. In Kant's formulation of the point, he appeals to the idea of a social contract, not as a historical fact, since he knows as well as his successors that no such event took place, but as an Idea of Reason—a methodological device to remind us that we can obey with a good conscience only those authorities to whose rule we could have consented in the appropriate circumstances (79). Popper's hostility to "the myth of the origin" is such that it is hard to guess whether he would have much sympathy for what Kant was trying to do; at least, he would certainly want to rewrite Kant's appeal to a hypothetical contract in noncontractual terms. But there is much in Popper to suggest that he would at any rate be sympathetic to the thought that each individual possesses a sort of moral inviolability that limits anyone else's claim to authority over him.

Now, Mill, who was perhaps a more consistent liberal than a utilitarian, can accommodate something like Kant's restrictions on the grounds of authority only by appealing to liberal ideals rather than individual rights, and at some cost to the supposed utilitarian foundations of his liberalism. That is, Mill's claim was that a sufficient disparity in knowledge between ruler and ruled did amount to a license for despotism (J. S. Mill 1914, 73). Colonization was morally quite acceptable so long as its aim and effect were the improvement of the subject population. He was at least tempted by the appeal to expertise that ran through all of Comte's work. To get back to something like liberal principles, Mill resorted to history; once a society was "civilized," its people were improvable by argument; once people were improvable by argument, the difference between more and less informed ceased to matter. All claims to knowledge are fallible—a view plainly congenial to Popper's criticalist account of science—and those who claim to know more than the rest of us are to be trusted only as far as they are willing to subject themselves to criticism from wherever it may come (80–81). Whether Mill's appeal to fallibility is consistent with his generally inductivist approach to the growth of science is a moot point, but one we can leave on one side here.

More crucially, Mill had to appeal to the *ideals* of liberalism to defuse the claims of the knowledgeable. Liberty is one of the liberal's supreme values: he therefore minds very much about the way in which the less knowledgeable obey the more knowledgeable. They must be led with their eyes open; they must give the best assent they can: unforcedly, freely, and on the basis of such information and argument as they can be given. To this extent, Mill might even have held that Popper's appeal to "piecemeal social engineering" was dangerously misleading as an account of the politics of the liberal state. For it is characteristic of the inert, nonhuman material out of which bridges and automobiles are built that it has no view of its own, no values of its own, and could neither give nor withhold its assent to anything proposed for it. But what makes us human is precisely that we do have our own values, our own views, and a taste for self-government rather than heteronomy (J. S. Mill 1914, 114ff.).

Although I think that Popper's liberalism is much more nearly Kantian than Millian, it cannot be said that the texts are absolutely conclusive on their very faces. For Popper does not develop an elaborate account of rights in the way that Hayek, for instance, does; even worse, from my point of view, Popper's clearest view is that the best defense of the political decencies is a kind of negative utilitarianism. That is, the constitutional problem is not Kant's problem—how to reconcile the freedom of each with the collective authority of all—but a problem more familiar in James Mill's *Essay on Government*. Since those who hold in their hands the power to do the good things we desire from government also hold in their hands the power to do evil, how can we design institutions to minimize the evil (James Mill 1957, 50)? To the extent that this implies any very determinate position in political morality, it is that of a general humanitarianism, and a reminder that the miseries of the least significant member of society are miseries nonetheless and therefore to be taken account of. At first sight, it is the negative case that is doing all the work: like Isaiah Berlin, Popper is frightened of theorists who believe that if only the right leader and the right doctrine coincided, everything would go perfectly (Popper 1962, 1:120). Like Berlin, he thinks there are no indisputable criteria for leadership, no special knowledge or special qualities of character to which they can lay claim. In this sense, liberalism is the product of skepticism even more than of a theory of inalienable rights, or of a commitment to the ideals of liberty. Nonetheless, I think the beginnings of the positive case for liberalism are also to be found here—a positive case that is built up along with Popper's description of the practice of scientific research.

But one feature of the skeptical case also suggests the Kantian affiliation of Popper's politics. Popper insists on the logical distinction between facts and decisions—his version of Hume's famous distinction between *is* and *ought* (Popper 1962, 1:60–61). This makes him more nearly Kantian than Millian on the connection between knowledge and authority. Mill seems to envisage superior minds knowing more than the rest of us not only about economics and sociology but also about what constitutes true elevation of character and the like. He is at least insecure about whether there can or cannot be moral experts, and this has given his critics a field day, with the more energetic claiming that his liberalism was the defense of an authoritarian secular enlightenment (Cowling 1962). Kant, however, had no doubt that moral ideals were something that each person had to accept for himself. Technical advice could be proffered ad lib, and if we were sensible, we would take the best advice we could get. But it was tyranny of the worst kind to force others to adopt our conception of their good or to force upon them our moral ideals.

It is central to Kant's thought that the state enforces external rules, which can be obeyed without further moral consideration, and that the authority of the state is limited to enforcing these. It is why property rights matter so much to Kant; through property rights and their cognates, we can deal with each other coercively but at arm's length (Reiss 1970, 135). I promise you my bicycle for your stamp collection; once you have handed over the stamps, I must hand over the bike; if I do not, you may properly force me to. What you and the state may not do is demand that I hand over the bike in any particular state of mind. It is my external performance only that is subject to control. This marks a concern to distinguish what is public, nonmoral, subject to law, and external from what is private, internal, and moral. There is no such concern in utilitarianism; one of the oddities of Mill's *Liberty*, indeed, is that there is no mention of the distinction between public and private.

If this is right, the Kantian flavor of Popper's liberalism is not accidental. Further evidence for this comes in the conjunction of his uncertain attitude to democracy and his negative utilitarianism. Popper's defense of democracy is odd in that it is not based on what one might call the positive moral attractions of the democratic formula. Against Plato, with his contempt for the ordinary man, and his mystical faith in the qualities of the guardians, Popper certainly defends democracy, in the sense that he defends the rights of the common man to a say in the government of his country, and attacks the guardians' claims to any such moral and intellectual infallibility as their authority is supposed to rest on. Moreover, says Popper, if the common man does not have the power to throw out rulers he wishes to throw out, he will be mistreated; all experience shows the truth of Lord Acton's dictum about the corrupting effect of power (Popper 1962, 1:136–37).

The justice of this as an attack on Plato is, of course, open to dispute. If one makes the first concessionary step of agreeing that Plato's intellectual universe makes sense, then the claim that experience shows that power corrupts will not seem quite such a knockdown argument; Plato's reply is that, of course, power has always corrupted in the past because philosophers have not been kings and kings have not been philosophers. To my mind, this response really shows something else—that Popper was right to launch a wholesale attack on Plato; the aim cannot be to show the internal incoherence of Plato's case, but to show that this whole approach to politics is misguided from the ground up. Then, the defense of democracy can be made in the casual way Pericles makes it in *The Peloponnesian War* (Popper 1962, 1:77). In essence, it is the old claim that the wearer of the shoe knows whether it pinches; not everyone can aspire to formulate policy, but what everyone can do is say whether the policies dreamed up by others are painful in their consequences.

There is more to it than that, of course. For one thing, what Popper and Pericles are eager to defend, and what Plato hates, is variety, vivacity, experiments in living. What Plato denounces as mere ignorant and childish running about after one fancy after another, Popper and Pericles praise as an attractive and enjoyable feature of the life of democratic Athens. As a defense of democracy in the narrow sense of the rule that decisions should be taken by some sort of majority vote, this would all be irrelevant, of course;

but Popper is not concerned to defend that rule, since he knows as well as the next man that it can produce ugly results and paradoxical ones. The defense is more nearly a defense of toleration, what you might call a democratic view of cultural and moral issues, to the effect that the ordinary man has a right to live as he pleases within the limits of the law, and so long as he neither disturbs the peace nor prevents others exercising a similar freedom (Popper 1962, 1:186–87).

If this is plausible, it reinforces the point that this is a Kantian liberalism, since Kant's defense of the individual's rights is couched in very much the same terms. It offers a limited defense of democracy in suggesting that individuals have a right to a say in the affairs of their country, and, more importantly, that they are not likely to preserve their other rights unless they have some such say.

Primarily, however, it is a defense of individual rights, and only secondarily a defense of a decision-making formula—which is one reason why Popper is more a constitutionalist than a democrat, just as Kant was. The thought that this is the right lineage of Popper's views is not unduly disturbed by observing that Popper and Pericles side with Mill in defending experiments in living (J. S. Mill 1914, 115). For Kant was every bit as concerned as Mill to defend such experiments. Kant's conception of the hidden point of history, it may be recalled, is that the goal of history is the development of all human faculties to their highest point. Of course, there is no empirical proof that this is the point of history; it is another of the Ideas of Reason that we employ to make sense of human experiences. We might be anxious about the difference between Mill's defense of variety for its own sake and Kant's notion of a historical task; but, of course, it is axiomatic in Kant's system that we have a right to harmless enjoyments—we would not have assented to a government that could curb them—and it is implicit in his slightly awkward relation to his scholastic predecessors that he believes that the universe can contain as much good as possible only if it is as varied as possible too.

But it is at this point that Kant's liberalism and Popper's view of science begin to touch. Kant's defense of an evolutionary but nonutopian picture of human history partly rests on the claim that out of the crooked timber of humanity no straight thing is made; but mostly, it rests on the view that nature sets us a series of problems, the solutions to which set us new problems, and so indefinitely on. Kant's view that "progress" is the goal of history is a sort of transcendental hypothesis, in something of the same way that Popper's conviction that increasing verisimilitude is the goal of science is a transcendental hypothesis. And one implication of this is that each individual who shares in the growth of knowledge or the development of human capacities may contribute only a little to the development of the whole species, but can, nonetheless, find a meaning to his life in so doing (Reiss 1970, 42–43). One ought not to be unduly surprised that two thinkers who adamantly reject the "bucket" theory of the mind and insist on the active role of the intelligence in interpreting experience should share more than epistemological allegiances.

If we place experiment, social progress, and fallibility at the center of our politics, we have good reason to support a strenuous constitutionalism, which guarantees each man the maximum liberty consistent with the liberties of others. Democracy—in some sense other than conferring absolute power upon a majority—is one expression of this sort of constitutionalism, since anything other than equal political rights seems to flout the view that everybody has the same claim as everybody else not to be under anyone else's control without good reason. There is, of course, a more obviously utilitarian case to be made for democracy too, namely, that unless people can voice their views, even a well-meaning government may be ineffective for lack of information about what people want. But we must recall Popper's view that the problem of government is not to secure that good men have the information to do good, but to secure that the nonrulers can throw the rascals out. Democracy, conceived as a device for the circulation of elites, is an answer both to the question of how to select competent rulers—by getting rid of the less competent ones peacefully—and to the question of how to retain power to throw the rascals out (Popper 1962, 1:124–25). The reason why I mention the consistency of this defense of democracy with the "elite theories" of writers like Vilfredo Pareto and Gaetano Mosca is to further draw out the affinity between Popper's conception of democracy and his conception of science. In science, the essential is that no hypothesis can be protected by an appeal to authority. It does not follow that every scientist is equally good at testing old hypotheses or equally imaginative in suggesting new ones—let alone at carrying out tests of new ones. What does follow is that the merits of a hypothesis are a matter of what happens to it under test, not a matter of who suggests it. In a democracy, not all ideas are equally good, and many policies are quite silly; nonetheless, we ought not to restrict the right to propose policies, and we must always remember that the merits of a policy are independent of the social or academic status of the proposer of it.

The way Popper's defensive view of democracy and constitution building place him in the Kantian tradition emerges even more clearly when we turn to his negative utilitarianism. His defense of this ethic is not elaborate or sophisticated—he has nothing much to say to the observation that a moral theory devoted to misery minimization would prescribe an unexpected and painless death for the whole of the human race. But this, too, is significant. Mill, whose *On Liberty* claims in passing that governments do best when they stick to harm prevention, is aware that his official theory of government holds that governments ought to do whatever maximizes the general welfare; he sees that he needs to claim that liberty is an essential element in happiness, and that misery is more readily identified and more easily dealt with, if he is to square negative utilitarianism in practice with positive utilitarianism in theory (J. S. Mill 1914, 132–33). Hence the complexities in his case that have irritated and excited critics for a hundred and thirty years.

Another view of the matter achieves the same results less awkwardly. Kant held that we simply had no business *making* other people happy. Governments might hinder hindrances to the search for the good life; but that was all (Reiss 1970, 134). Of course, all this becomes very much less simple when we probe it, and the line between hindering hindrances and positively promoting happiness in a paternalist fashion is harder to draw than it looks. All the same, the point of the doctrine is clear enough. Whereas Mill starts from the view that governments may legitimately do anything that promotes the general welfare, and then erodes that view in order to find room for individual liberty, Kant credits us with a right of self-defense and allows governments to do only those things that help us to help ourselves without attacking others.

I do not wish to exaggerate the definiteness of Popper's case here, nor the clarity of its lineage. Popper is plainly at one with Mill in thinking that one reason for pursuing a negative utilitarianism is shortage of information. We are much more readily able to discover what makes people unhappy than what makes them happy, and on the whole, what makes people unhappy is more uniform than what makes them happy; it is, also, quite often easier to cure. (This is, of course, very far from being universally true, and it is simple enough to think of exceptions.) Painters, poets, and pianists all suffer from cold and hunger, but a piano is no use to a painter, nor an easel to a poet. The state may properly engage in the provision of a range of basic welfare services, but is ill advised to do much more. It is not a major concern of Popper's to draw sharp lines around the proper tasks of the welfare state, and it would be wrong to try to extract too much from his argument (Parekh 1982, 146–53). All the same, it is perhaps worth noticing that the slightly blurred argument here, and the uncertainty about quite what tradition the argument belongs to, is characteristic of writers who have made much more of it than Popper. Hayek, for instance, sometimes employs utilitarian arguments against welfare-state utilitarianism—or welfare-state "liberalism," in the American sense of the term; and sometimes, he employs arguments of a more strictly rights-based kind (Hayek 1944). In one view, the ambitious state fails in its purposes because its information is inadequate and its techniques clumsy; on the other, positive steps to maximize social welfare involve illegitimate coercion in forcing members of society to part with goods and services they do not choose to part with, and for purposes other than self-defense.

I conclude, then, that Popper's liberalism is more nearly in a Kantian than a Millian mold, that it is a genuine liberalism in defending constitutionalism above a populist form of democracy, and that even where it is eclectic in its sources, it is classical liberalism in its concern for individual inviolability (Popper 1962, 1:99–104). I turn finally to the task of showing that the connection between Popper's defense of liberalism and his view of science is partly a matter of instrumental and sociological arguments, but in part is simply a matter of pointing out the liberal virtues of the ideal scientific community. The instrumental case is relatively straightforward. Science seems to entail an open society, and an open society is indispensable to science. That is, if we manage to establish the scientific enterprise in any solid form, its achievements are sure to have an impact on society at large. We cannot believe one thing at work and another at home; we cannot study biology in the lab and heal ourselves with witchcraft at home. The degree to which conceptual incoherence is cheerfully tolerated by many people may be much greater than the out-and-out rationalist would like to believe, and the contents of our minds are not entirely transparent to us—whence, of course, Popper's own insistence on the need to institutionalize the pressure to think clearly and articulately. All the same, there will be a steady pressure to square the beliefs of society at large with the findings of science. This, however, is just what makes an open society: beliefs are not locked solid, rendered immune from investigation and challenge. If we live in a society with a flourishing scientific community, we shall find ourselves in a society with a pressure toward openness (2:217–22).

This, again, is a view that Popper seems to share with both Kant and Mill, and it is, of course, a contestable view; we are familiar with colleagues who seem to subscribe to one cosmology in the laboratory on weekdays and to another in church on Sundays, and no doubt there were physicists who were committed Nazis and no worse physicists for it. My own view is that a closed totalitarian society would stagnate scientifically after two generations and would never do better than replicate work done elsewhere—but that is a hunch rather than a testable sociological hypothesis. What one can surely say is that no closed society can allow its scientists to chase hunches wherever they may lead; if the license to hunt is implicit in science, closed societies cannot practice science. Conversely, it is at least arguable that science needs an open society as background. The willingness to challenge established theories, the ability to go out on a limb without undue anxiety, the combination of eager questioning and patience to wait for answers, all seem to require the social training provided in a liberal society. The scientific community is one full of people who have passionately held convictions but who need to resist the temptation to close ranks or shut up dissenters; the better the training in self-restraint provided elsewhere, the better the science. Again, the argument is contestable. Writers like Kuhn (1962), who emphasize the closed and authoritarian nature of scientific communities, cannot be lightly dismissed. The violence of Popper's reaction to Kuhn suggests that he cannot bear to entertain the thought that liberalism and science may be systematic enemies rather than allies (Popper 1970, 51–59).

Kuhn, of course, represents himself as a modified disciple of Popper, but the point is still the same. Even if Kuhn's claim is only that scientists need to organize themselves in a more hierarchical and authoritarian fashion than

Popper supposes if they are to carry out the eminently Popperian task of rigorously testing their conjectures about nature's laws, science would cease to be the natural ally of liberalism. Kuhn emphasizes that among scientists, ideas are not accepted regardless of who puts them forward; only some people are authorized to change the current orthodoxy, and then in ortho-doxy-conserving ways. If that is inescapable, we must accept that the habits of free speech and open discussion that characterize liberalism will be irrel-evant to science. Conversely, if great stress is laid on the difference between what scientific claims mean to professional scientists and what they may fail to mean to laymen, the idea that there will be a sort of leakage from science to society at large that forces laymen to adopt new ideas and new ways of thinking will also be false.

In the argument between Popper and Kuhn, one could pursue a concilia-tory course by pointing out that Popper stresses what Kuhn never denies—that nature tests our hypotheses, whoever devises them—and that Kuhn stresses what Popper never denies—that scientists need tenacity as well as a willingness to change their minds, that some attempts to protect hypotheses against premature falsification are justified, and that a scientific community needs some taken-for-granted ways of deciding where to direct its efforts (Kuhn 1962, 231ff.). Still, the story I wish to advance is at odds with this conciliatory intention. It starts with a familiar epistemological point. Many of Popper's critics have complained that once Popper's account of the pro-cess of conjecture and refutation is deprived of any residual empiricist or positivist elements, Popper can no longer tell us what hypotheses are tested *against*. Popper insists on a correspondence theory of truth and also insists that there can be no statements that are simply known to be true by virtue of corresponding to the facts. The earliest version of Popper's account of science seemed to suggest that the asymmetry between justification and fal-sification was important because we could know beyond doubt that some singular proposition was true, and use this as bedrock in testing general claims. This view is now said not to be Popper's own. All statements are re-visable; all statements are interpretive; and general statements may be saved by numerous different strategies, some of which are quite justified.

The claimed virtues of science now become rather harder to elucidate because the idea that scientific progress amounts to increasing verisimilitude is now more than ever an Idea of Reason in the Kantian sense, and the way is open for a much more "sociological" account of science. That is, once it is accepted that we have a great deal of choice about what statements to ac-cept or reject as part of the corpus of science, the pressure is on us to give an account of what amounts to good and bad choosing. The "scientificity" of scientific doctrines becomes a matter of the process by which they are cho-sen rather than a simple matter of their factual truth. The obvious instru-mental view that the goodness of the process of choice is simply a matter of the effectiveness with which the process eliminates false beliefs and replaces them with truer ones cannot be sustained in any simple way once all ties with empiricism have been cut. At best, the claim that what the progress of science achieves is theories that are increasingly true to the facts becomes a metaphysical hypothesis, a heuristic maxim: "Act as if it were true that theories mirror facts." At worst, Popper finds himself in the company of critical theorists such as Jürgen Habermas, whose notion of truth is parasitic on what people would agree to say under conditions of freedom to say what they liked, equal ability to contribute to the consensus on what to say, and some sort of pressure toward reaching such a consensus (Habermas 1970, 360 ff.). It is going too far to suggest that Popper has arrived at the point of saying that the discoveries of science just are what the ideally liberal scientific community agrees to say they are, but it is not an exaggeration to suggest that he is under the same pressures in that direction as writers like Habermas have been.

I will not try to show what the consequences of this might be for Popper's defense of objectivity, though I cannot forbear remarking that the sort of tension I have pointed to seems to account for the critical anxiety that Popper's appeal to "World 3" induces. I shall end by emphasizing what I take it to show. It is not just that Popper espouses a rather Kantian liberalism; and it is not just that he thinks that the scientific frame of mind nourishes, and is nourished by, an open, liberal society. It is that the same Kantian picture of what it is like to try to make sense of the world that permeates his philosophy of science means that the bedrock reason for approving of science as an activity is that it is intellectual inquiry carried on by liberal means. To put it another way, it is the politics of scientific inquiry that makes it admirable, and the defense of political liberalism is not so much supported by an appeal to science as it is simply another part of a seamless web. This conclusion remains an uncomfortable one to square with Popper's hostility to what he thinks of as subjectivism, and I do not seek to disguise that. I will, however, say that it is not uncongenial to Kant's defense of the Enlightenment, with its cry of "*sapere aude*," and not uncongenial to Popper's own defense of the Enlightenment and his hostility to the irrationalism of Wittgenstein's later philosophy, with its defense of forms of life and its claims for the inescapability of current and local habits of belief (Reiss 1970, 54).

Postscript

I am grateful to Bryan Magee, John Watkins, and seminars at Oxford and Reading for their reactions to earlier versions of this essay. In two respects I feel that I have not been able to do justice to them. Watkins thinks Popper mistaken in relinquishing the "empiricist" elements in falsificationist methodology, and thus that I follow too readily down a road that leads nowhere. My only response is that I am impressed by the similarities between Popper's problems and those of Kant and think the comparison illuminating. I am inclined to share Watkins's doubts about Popper's antiempiricism—but that would have been a different essay. My question here was not so much whether that antiempiricism was right, but whether the connections I suggest between Popper's philosophy of science and his political liberalism would hold up if (or even if) his antiempiricism were right. Christie Davies (after the Reading seminar) suggested that I should have been sharper about the distinction between a liberalism founded on humanitarian concern and one founded on rights. He instances debates over abortion as occasions where one kind of liberalism is worried by the conflict between the rights of the mother and those of the unborn child, whereas the other worries only whether humanity to unwilling mothers carries unacceptable costs in other directions. I agree, of course, that these different forms of political argument have characterized debate in Britain and the United States. But Popper is not a natural-rights theorist nor simply a rule-of-thumb utilitarian, so too sharp an insistence on the distinction would have meant pressing his writings for answers to questions they do not raise. I am inclined to say that like Kant, Popper defends legal, constitutionally guaranteed rights not because we just do have (natural) rights, but because they are the legal expression of something like Kant's principle of the inviolability of the individual. I must, however, admit that I am not sure that I could infer from what Popper has written on particular issues what he might say on those about which he has not written.

References

Cowling, M. 1962. *Mill and Liberalism*. Cambridge: Cambridge University Press.
Dworkin, R. 1978. "Liberalism." In *Public and Private Morality*, edited by Stuart Hampshire. Cambridge: Cambridge University Press.
Habermas, J. 1970. "Towards a Theory of Communicative Competence." *Inquiry* 13:360–75.
Hayek, F. A. von. 1944. *The Road to Serfdom*. London: Routledge and Sons.
Kuhn. T. S. 1962. *The Structure of Scientific Revolutions*. Chicago: University of Chicago Press.
Mill, James. 1975. *Essay on Government*. Indianapolis: Bobbs-Merrill.
Mill, J. S. 1914. *Utilitarianism, Liberty, Representative Government*. London: Dent.
Parekh, B. C. 1982. *Contemporary Political Thinkers*. Oxford: Martin Robertson.
Popper, K. R. 1961. *The Poverty of Historicism*. 2nd ed. London: Routledge and Kegan Paul.
———. 1962. *The Open Society and Its Enemies*. 4th ed. 2 vols. London: Routledge and Kegan Paul.
———. 1970. "Normal Science and Its Dangers." In *Criticism and the Growth of Knowledge*, edited by I. Lakatos and A. Musgrave. Cambridge: Cambridge University Press.
———. 1976. *Unended Quest*. LaSalle, Ill.: Open Court.
Reiss, H., ed. 1970. *Kant's Political Writings*. Cambridge: Cambridge University Press.

PART 4

Liberalism in America

22

Alexis de Tocqueville

Introduction

ALEXIS DE TOCQUEVILLE (his family name was Alexis-Charles-Henri Clérel) was born on 29 July 1805 in Paris, and died on 16 April 1859 in Cannes. In a short and not wholly happy life, he wrote two of the most important works to grace the discipline that has since come to be labeled political sociology. When he wrote them, Auguste Comte had barely coined the barbarous but indispensable word "sociology"; nonetheless, Tocqueville was aware that he was engaged in something novel and was not embarrassed to claim that the novelty of American political experience demanded a new political science. What Tocqueville wrote might also be described as "philosophical history"; it was not a philosophical analysis of the concept of democracy, nor a simple narrative of the origins of American political institutions, but a form of political theory that used historical evidence to teach general lessons about the prospects for politics in the present.

In spite of the novelty of Tocqueville's own work, the genre went back at least as far as Machiavelli's *Discourses on Livy*, and Tocqueville's work stands comparison with anything in the genre. *Democracy in America* was an immediate success in England, France, and the United States; *The Old Regime and the Revolution* was an equally immediate success in France when it appeared in 1856. Under the Third Republic, it was rather soon submerged beneath more patriotic, more populist, and, in due course, more Marxist accounts of the origins of the Revolution. So far as French intellectual life is concerned, Tocqueville's virtues were "rediscovered" by Raymond Aron some forty-odd years ago—an episode that left Americans remarking that they had never lost sight of them—but he has, so to speak, come fully into his own in his native country only during the past twenty years as the liberal interpretations of the French Revolution offered by François Furet and Pierre Rosanvallon have gained ground and Marxist interpretations have lost credibility[1]

As we shall see, both *Democracy in America* and *The Old Regime and the Revolution* were written for French readers rather than British and American ones. *Democracy in America* might have had any number of subtitles along the lines of "and why equality is consistent with liberty in America and probably not in France." It remains true, however, that *Democracy in*

America has until recent years fallen into the hands of the British and the Americans, and that even *The Old Regime and the Revolution* was for many years more highly regarded by American political sociologists as a contribution to the theory of revolution than by French historians as a contribution to the history of the Great French Revolution.

We must begin by placing the author in his times and among his family. Eleven years before Alexis's birth, Tocqueville's father, Hervé, had narrowly escaped death at the hands of the Revolution. Hervé had recently married the granddaughter of Lamoignon de Malesherbes, the statesman and lawyer who defended Louis XVI at his trial; during the Terror, the revolutionaries duly took their revenge on Malesherbes, his family, and his friends. Before the Revolution, Malesherbes had enabled the Encyclopédistes to publish their work, but past services to the Enlightenment counted for nothing in the Terror. In December 1793, Hervé and his new wife, together with his in-laws and many friends of the family, were taken up and imprisoned. Malesherbes was executed along with Louise's father and other members of the family; Hervé and Louise might have met the same fate if the Terror had not ended with the fall of Robespierre and their release from jail. Hervé was twenty-one; when he emerged from prison, his hair was white, while Louise was permanently neurasthenic and a lifelong sufferer from migraines. At the outset of the Revolution, Hervé had been mildly liberal and reformist, hoping that the Revolution of 1789 would install a constitutional monarchy along the lines of the government established in Britain by the Glorious Revolution of 1688. This was the hope of many English admirers of the Revolution at the time. It had never occurred to him that reform involved breaking with the monarchy; after their encounter with the Terror, Hervé de Tocqueville and his family remained staunch royalists. The impact of his father's sufferings on the future author of *Democracy in America* has always puzzled commentators. The younger Tocqueville was not a simple royalist, nor a wholehearted democrat. He was an aristocratic liberal. What he felt was an attachment to the prerevolutionary monarchy along with an affection for the democracy he saw in America.

This might or might not have been an entirely coherent political attitude, but it certainly set him at odds with the bourgeois "July Monarchy" of Louis-Philippe and with the bourgeois republic of February 1848. His dislike of the July Monarchy was a family characteristic. There is no evidence that Hervé conspired against the First Empire or plotted with the exiled court of Louis XVIII; nonetheless, he was known to be devoted to the Bourbon monarchy. The defeat of Napoleon and the Bourbon Restoration allowed Hervé to claim his due as a loyal servant of the exiled monarchy, and he duly served as prefect of several departments, including the Oise, Moselle, and Somme, and finally Seine-et-Oise, where he enjoyed the life of a courtier-administrator and happily attended Charles X at Versailles and Saint-Cloud. He gave up the post when he became a member of the House of Peers in 1828, and left politics for good in 1830 when Louis-Philippe was installed during the July Revolution.

Hervé died at the age of eighty-four in 1856, only three years before his youngest son. His wife had died twenty years before him, in 1836; she was only fifty-four years old, and her youngest son described her as having died "after twenty years of misery."[2] The frailty and melancholy that were so marked in Alexis were probably inherited from her. Hervé was politically clumsy, and his career was marred at least as much by his own impulsiveness as by the ill will of his rivals and superiors, but he was a robust and self-confident figure. His wife did not share his vigor and self-confidence, but she shared his politics, taking if anything a more intensely royalist and Catholic stand than he.

Alexis was the third son; his relations with his older brothers were not always smooth. Indeed, the oldest of them, Hyppolite, born in 1797, irritated him intensely both because of his political antics and because of a certain silliness that infected all his activities; Edouard, born in 1800, had more of Alexis's sobriety and melancholy, and they generally got on well. The one occasion for prolonged coldness in their relations was the Revolution of 1848 and the subsequent accession of Louis Bonaparte, subsequently Napoléon III. Edouard and his wife were, in Tocqueville's eyes, much too frightened by the 1848 Revolution itself, and then consumed by the fear of socialism that led so many of the French middle class to hail Louis Bonaparte as their savior and to ignore the criminality and corruption of his government. This seems a harsh view, especially in light of Tocqueville's own *Souvenirs*, elegant and vivid as they are; they too might be described as irrationally fearful and exaggerated. Still, Tocqueville was clear that it was Louis Bonaparte who was to be blamed for extinguishing French liberties and that cooperation with him was impossible after his coup d'état in December 1851. When Edouard stood for the Assembly in 1852, there was a good deal of tension between them. It did not last, although Tocqueville's most recent biographer suggests that the "fact that Edouard was so roundly defeated by the official candidate probably helped smooth over this difference of opinion."[3]

Tocqueville's boyhood and youth were apparently happy. He was at first educated by the Abbé Lesueur, a fiercely illiberal nonjuring priest who had been Hervé's tutor twenty years before and who then went on to play the same role to all three boys. He was fonder of Alexis than of his brothers, and was thought by many observers to have been especially indulgent to Alexis. The latter's intellectual success, both as a student at the lycée, and in later life, suggests the Abbé's benevolence could hardly have done him much harm. Tocqueville was a passionate young man; his family suppressed scandalous details, but he fell violently in love with socially unsuitable young women and had to be persuaded by his friends that marriage to them would be a mistake. Acquiescence in their good advice was evidently reluctant.

When he became famous after the publication of the first volume of *Democracy in America* in 1835, he celebrated by marrying Mary Mottley, a middle-class Englishwoman some six to nine years older than himself, and an entirely unsuitable match from which his family had been trying to dissuade him for years.

It was not a wholly happy marriage, but it was, after its fashion, a wholly successful one. Husband and wife were passionately attached to each other, and if he occasionally threw plates at her when exasperated by the slow pace at which she ate her dinner, she did not let it disturb her. The story goes that when this happened, she responded only by asking the servant for another slice of paté. The two unhappinesses of their life together were their failure to have children—he was tubercular, and that may have made him sterile—and their failure to see eye to eye on religion. Mary Mottley had, of course, been brought up as an Anglican, but she converted to Catholicism before marriage and became extremely devout. Tocqueville appears to have lost his faith in his teens; he read the philosophes and found his belief damaged beyond repair. He retained something of the philosophes' deism, and a belief in the immortality of the soul, but he could no longer accept the claims of the Catholic Church nor believe in the literal truth of Christianity. This was for him an extremely serious matter. Not only did it mean that he was forced to be less than frank with his much loved "*bébé,*" the Abbé Lesueur, it cast a somewhat odd light on his claims about the role of religion in sustaining liberty and the rule of law in the United States.

Unlike John Stuart Mill, his greatest student and interpreter, who had been brought up agnostic and who thought Christianity doomed to disappear in a more rational and more secular age, Tocqueville lamented his own loss of faith and thought the loss of Christian conviction was fraught with danger for society generally. These were anxieties he could not share with Mary. As a matter of kindness to her and duty to his society, he attended church regularly, and on his deathbed took the last rites. But his anxieties and interior disbelief he shared only with others, such as Madame Swetchine, a Russian *emigrée* some twenty years older than himself who was fascinated by mysticism and was able to speculate as he did on the inscrutability of divine purposes. It was not only Mary to whom he could not be entirely frank. One effect of the French Revolution was to persuade the nobility that they had been wrong to encourage the skeptics of the Enlightenment and that their fashionable agnosticism had been one of the causes of their undoing in the Revolution. After the Restoration, a devout Catholicism was the invariable accompaniment of loyalty to the throne. Tocqueville had no intention of challenging these loyalties, and therefore had to keep silent about the extent of his disbelief in their metaphysical foundations.

He frequently said that he loathed philosophical speculation, and it is certainly true that *Democracy in America* and *The Old Regime and the Revolution* eschew overt discussion of such issues as the plausibility or implausibility of the doctrine of the rights of man. They are the works of a moralist, but not of a moral philosopher. Nevertheless, his most notable quality was, by his own account and in the view of all observers, a constant restlessness of mind. It was a quality that did his political career no good. One of the most important qualities in a politician—especially a politician in the highly personal and strikingly corrupt political system of 1830–48 France—is the ability to suffer fools gracefully. Tocqueville lacked that ability to an almost pathological degree. He was not a snob, but he had a very acute sense of what it was about the manners and social style of the aristocracy that set them apart from the commercial middle class. Fawning, pandering, even passing the time of day with people he regarded as culturally, intellectually, and politically null was beyond him. He wanted to get on with the next matter that preoccupied his restless intelligence, and they knew it and resented it.

The outline of his career is briefly told. He began his career as a junior magistrate at Versailles; it was here that he made friends with Gustave de Beaumont, his companion on the great journey to America and a lifelong friend and ally. He had studied law in Paris in the mid-1820s, and was appointed to the post of *juge auditeur* in April 1827. The main interest of this position for the development of the ideas of the future author of *Democracy in America* is that it reinforced Tocqueville's belief in the centrality of legal institutions and of attitudes toward the law in shaping the politics of modern societies. One of the many ways in which, he later thought, the old regime in France had weakened its own position was by its centralization of the legal system on Paris and its erosion of the common law in France. The other interesting feature of the post was that it provided the ostensible reason for the visit to America that Tocqueville and Beaumont made in 1831—to investigate the prison system of the United States, a task that the two colleagues in fact fulfilled so well that their report, the *Système pénitentiaire*, became a considerable resource for French prison reformers years after both of them had left government service.

Tocqueville's time at Versailles was not disagreeable, even though it took him some time to make friends with his colleagues. Among other things, it left him time to attend Guizot's lectures on the history of civilization, delivered between 1828 and 1830, and his notes suggest that Guizot's conception of the purpose and method of this broad-gauge account of a whole culture rubbed off on him not only when he set out to write the history of the Revolution and its antecedents, but equally when he set out to characterize the democratic culture of the United States. The fall of Charles X and the installation of Louis-Philippe brought his career as an aspirant judge and administrator to an end. He was happy enough to see the back of Charles X, whose attempt to govern extralegally had brought its just reward; but he was loyal to the Bourbons, did not think much of Louis-Philippe, and was suspect to the new regime. He bit the bullet and swore loyalty to the new king, as all his fellow magistrates were required to do, but remained an object of some suspicion to his superiors. When he and Beaumont applied for leave to visit America, permission was a long time coming, and they were told to make the trip at their own expense.

Still, on 2 April 1831, they set sail from Le Havre, arriving in New York on 11 May. We shall look at their journey in a little more detail below. When they returned, early in 1832, neither took up his former employment. Beaumont was dismissed in May 1832 after refusing to serve as prosecutor in a political case, and Tocqueville resigned in protest. *Du système pénitentiaire aux États-Unis et de son application en France* was written nonetheless; it was largely the product of Beaumont's pen, with Tocqueville supplying notes and criticism. It secured the Montyon Prize in 1833, which did something to pay the costs of the journey to America, and it secured Beaumont's election to the Academy of Moral and Political Science in 1841. It is scarcely discussed in the literature on Tocqueville, and to a modern eye may be interesting for its unflinching acceptance of the harshness of the American prison systems it describes rather than any more elaborate reason.[4]

The publication of the *Système pénitentiaire* was followed two years later by that of volume one of *Democracy in America*, and Tocqueville was instantly famous. He wanted to capitalize on his fame by entering politics, though he detested most of the things that a successful political career would involve. In 1837, he stood for the Chamber of Deputies and lost; in 1839, he was elected for his home district of Valognes, and was to be safely reelected until the July Monarchy was overthrown by the revolution of February 1848. He was also, and in many ways more happily, engaged in local politics from 1842, serving on the local council of the district of La Manche and acting for a time as its president. He was a modestly successful oppositional figure; though he admired Guizot as a historian, he loathed him as a politician. Tocqueville was more successful as a journalist in the pages of *Le Commerce* than as a deputy. He cast longing eyes at the English scene, where progressive conservatism of the type he espoused was successfully practiced by Sir Robert Peel, and felt acutely the contrast with France.

The year 1848 brought out something less than the best in Tocqueville. He was elected to the Constituent Assembly, charged with drafting a new constitution after the fall of Louis-Philippe and Guizot, but he was not much in sympathy with even the modest reformism of the revolutionaries. Where John Stuart Mill defended the revolution against Lord Brougham, and for the rest of his life stood by the very mild socialism briefly aspired to by Louis Blanc, Tocqueville saw red revolution, expropriation, and bankruptcy in every proposal. The not very remote cause of the 1848 revolutions all over Europe was failed harvests and economic crises, and many workers in both the towns and the countryside were close to starvation. Tocqueville was a rigid adherent of the classical orthodoxies in economic matters, much closer to Nassau Senior than to Mill, and therefore convinced that governmental intervention to relieve mass distress would always do more harm than good. The Parisian workers rose against such brutal policies in June 1848, and Tocqueville's friends shot them down.

The results were not what he had hoped for. General Cavaignac, who had led the forces of law and order in the June Days, lost in the presidential elections of December 1848 to the adventurer, Louis Bonaparte. For a few months of 1849, Tocqueville was sufficiently reconciled to the new prince-president to serve as his foreign minister, but when the Barrot government was dismissed in October of that year, Tocqueville left office more or less willingly and was careful to do nothing that suggested he wished for reinstatement. The coup d'état of 2 December 1851, in which Louis Bonaparte seized power, was the final straw. Tocqueville, along with many members of the Legislative Assembly, was arrested and held for several days—and then released rather apologetically. Apologies made no difference. He withdrew absolutely from politics and occupied himself with writing *L'ancien régime et la révolution*, the book in which he settled accounts with the tendency of French republics to turn into caesarist despotisms. It is a poignant contrast between nineteenth- and twentieth-century despotisms that the Emperor Napoleon III neither prevented the publication of a work that the meanest intelligence could see was a roman à clef as well as a work of disinterested history, nor took any steps against its author. By the time the book was published, Tocqueville was unwell; so was Mary, and their lives were increasingly dominated by illness. Although he hoped to continue the story of the Revolution to the accession of the first Bonaparte, he could not, and died in April 1859 with his second masterpiece unfinished. Mary survived him by five unhappy and tedious years.

*   *   *   *   *

Tocqueville's journey to America was definitively described and analyzed almost sixty years ago by G. W. Pierson in a book of immense charm and good humor.[5] The book is not uncritical, however. The subtext of the account, friendly toward Tocqueville as it is, is that Tocqueville went to America to prove a thesis. Pierson quotes a jibe against Tocqueville by one of his French critics: *il a commencé à penser avant d'avoir rien appris*. He had thought it all out before he had learned anything about it. The question is what assumptions he brought with him to America. There seem to have been several, though their sources are not always easy to uncover, and some of Tocqueville's most interesting views were original with him. In particular, the thought that John Stuart Mill took from Tocqueville and made the centerpiece of the argument of *On Liberty* seems to have been freshly minted. This was the thought that the "tyranny of the majority" to be feared under democracy was not to be understood in the terms that Madison had feared it—lower-class exploitation of the propertied classes in the form of projects for the cancellation of debts, artificially low interest rates, and the like, nor even in the form in which Jefferson, who coined the phrase, had understood it—a proneness to religious intolerance and a violent and coercive invasion of private life. For Tocqueville, the new form of tyranny was especially insidious because it was not violent and coercive, but subtly invasive, causing each of us to side with the majority against himself or herself. This is the theme that increasingly permeates the second volume of *Democracy*, and it has had an impressive afterlife in twentieth-century commentators.[6]

For the most part, Tocqueville's views were those one might expect in a liberal of French rather than British upbringing.[7] On the whole, the British and the Americans had found it easy to think of governments as institutions to protect the natural rights of their citizens, and thought that the great desideratum was a form of constitution that prevented governments from violating these rights and forced them to protect them. The ten amendments to the U.S. Constitution that form the Bill of Rights give a clear idea of what these fundamental rights were supposed to be, and the whole arrangement of the Constitution rests on a theory about the importance of the separation of powers and a system of checks and balances in making sure that governments did not violate the subjects' rights. The British constitution was more elusive and harder to describe, but it was not unreasonable to think that it too displayed the virtues of the separation of powers and allowed for an intricate system of checks and balances. Tocqueville moved in a different universe.

He was more nearly a disciple of Montesquieu and Guizot. That is, he emphasized social as much as—or even rather than—political checks and balances; it was the way ideas and aspirations were diffused among the different social and economic groupings that explained what political and economic aims they would pursue and what institutions they would establish and operate, and with what success. Although Montesquieu was the most famous exponent of the doctrine of the separation of powers, in which he located the success of the British form of government in maintaining liberty, the thrust of his work was toward emphasizing the social underpinnings of the formal institutions of government. In this, Tocqueville followed him, so much so that he pays rather little attention to the formal separation of powers that is, to a British eye, so striking a feature of the American political system, and much more to the question of what social groups might or might not sustain an antimajoritarian outlook. Tocqueville was not trapped by his intellectual borrowings. In particular, it took a decided leap of the imagination to decide that what was practiced in America was a successful form of democracy. The thought that federalism was the key to practicing republicanism or democracy in a large nation state was not original with him; both Montesquieu and Rousseau had thought as much, and it was a key element in the argument of the *Federalist*. Until the U.S. Constitution was in place, this had been very much a theoretical suggestion, and it took some boldness on Tocqueville's part to announce to a European audience that it worked so well in practice. To the extent that Tocqueville stood by this view, it gave Europeans some grounds for optimism. The conventional, Montesquieuian view of democracy had been that it was a form of government possible only in small city-states, whose inhabitants could be made to live austere and virtuous—that is to say, public-spirited—lives in which the pursuit of private gain would be subordinated to the military and political well-being of the polity in which they lived. It was taken for granted that this was not a live option for more than a very few eighteenth-century European states. Even Rousseau, who sometimes thought that Geneva came as close to emulating these ancient ideals as it was possible to come, hardly suggested that democracy was a live option. He thought an elective aristocracy much more plausible as a form of republican government, and would have been astonished by Tocqueville's claim that in America the people really ruled.

The French Revolution seemed to many commentators to prove Montesquieu's point. It had been impossible to re-create the Roman citizen by dressing the modern Parisian in a toga; the violence and disorder of the Terror was testimony to the inaptness of the ideal as well as to the degree of disillusion its failure had provoked. The success of the federal republic might suggest that the device of federation could secure republican institutions in the absence of such a degree of republican virtue as Montesquieu had suggested a republic required. Perhaps America had shown that modern inventiveness was up to the task of proving Montesquieu wrong, or at any rate incomplete. Perhaps it showed that the demand for political equality was so irresistible that whatever the French Revolution suggested, the future lay either with a liberal regime built on the assent of the masses or an illiberal regime built on their deluded or coerced support.

From the same sources, Tocqueville would have gained another insight to take with him and to bring back modified in some respects and confirmed in others. The British and American conception of equality before the law was only one of many conceptions of equality; it, indeed, was perhaps the only conception of equality that was consistent with preserving the social pluralism on which Montesquieu had thought that ordered liberty must depend. Equality of condition, that is, an equality of social standing and economic position, was inimical to freedom. The image it conjured up was that of oriental despotism, in which all were equal before and beneath the sultan's throne. The English had contrived to control the danger of despotism inherent in monarchy without falling into the chaos that attended ancient attempts at popular self-government, but this was the work of an essentially aristocratic form of government and depended on the population at large recognizing that social inequality was the price of liberty and willingly paying that price. The American experiment posed an intriguing question— how, in light of Montesquieu's assumptions about what preserved liberty and what threatened it, had the United States contrived to preserve its citizens' liberty while at the same time achieving a greater equality of condition than any nation in Europe? Was this achievement stable, or merely a passing but unstable balancing of two opposing forces, one of which must in due course predominate?

As a liberal and an aristocrat, moreover, Tocqueville was deeply concerned with other issues implied by these large questions. Could a country long cherish liberty without an aristocracy, or was there a crucial difference

between a country like France, which had achieved liberty by violently revolting against its aristocracy, and a country like America, which had
achieved liberty by taking its ingredients from England and finding that they
grew even better in transatlantic earth? Few of these were questions Tocqueville thought he had answered before he saw America. Nor, as a matter of
fact, did he take all his ideas to America and bring them back intact. The
astonished tone of much of volume one of *Democracy* is more than a literary artifice. Nor did the thoughts he brought back from America remain
unchanged after his return. Sophisticated recent commentators have analyzed the impact of political events in France on Tocqueville's original ideas
and have shown how his increasing disillusionment with French politics in
the late 1830s, as well as the reflections provoked by his visits to Britain and
his correspondence with British economists and political commentators,
was reflected in the increasingly apprehensive tone of the discussion of the
culture of democracy in the second volume of *Democracy*.[8]

Democracy marked a decisive break with a genre of travel writing that
was popular at the time and for a good many years afterward. It also reinforced one preexisting feature of such writing. English writers had already
begun to produce unkind accounts of their stays in America, even though
the most famous had not yet appeared when Tocqueville and Beaumont arrived in New York in the spring of 1831. The most notorious member of the
genre was Mrs. Trollope's *Domestic Manners of the Americans*, published
the following year, 1832, and perhaps the best-selling contribution, Charles
Dickens's *American Notes* of 1842. But one of the most unlovable had just
come out; this was Captain Basil Hall's *Travels in North America in the
Years 1827 and 1828*, a work of such mean-spirited and reactionary unkindness toward the very Americans who had made Hall and his family so
welcome that American commentators a century later wrote of it with real
anger.[9] Tocqueville and Beaumont were to write in a wholly different style,
not concerned to make fun of the obvious differences between the manners
of polished French society and the rough-hewn ways of the American frontier, but to establish what made American society work as it did. In their
sympathy toward the Americans, they were, however, following an equally
established though different tradition. It was not only that the American
colonists, in rebellion against their British rulers, had needed and obtained
the assistance of France in securing their independence. There was a French
tradition, dating back to the writings of Hector St. John de Crèvecoeur, that
praised the American colonist as a man of purified morals, sharp wit, and
democratic instincts who might revive the glories of the ancient republics in
the newest of new worlds. Four years before Tocqueville and Beaumont set
out on their journey, Chateaubriand's *Voyage d'Amérique* of 1827 wove the
latest variation on the theme. It was impossible for a Frenchman of any
political stripe not to wonder whether a republic on the scale of a modern
nation-state could be sustained, whether there was something about the
Protestant origins of the New England colonists that made them peculiarly

apt for democratic citizenship, and thus whether America was the place where French aspirations might be fulfilled.

*   *   *   *   *

The visit itself was, as everyone has observed, lopsided in the attention it paid to different parts of the United States. In particular, the travellers saw next to nothing of the real South. They were doubly innocent about it, since they spent little time either there or in Virginia; intending to stay longer in Charleston and then to visit James Madison, living in retirement near Charlottesville, in the end they could not. The result was that they saw next to nothing at first hand of the operations of the slave-based plantation economy of the southern states, and had only a fleeting glimpse of the curious mixture of coarseness and aristocratic refinement that set the South culturally apart from the northern states. Nor did they encounter the Virginian upper class that had led the American Revolution. In consequence, it might plausibly be said that what they got was a view of Yankee America, a society whose puritanism, egalitarianism, and attachment to local democracy were not entirely typical of the whole country. Tocqueville acknowledges in his introductory pages that there were two American types, the New Englander and the Virginian, but goes on to claim that the former dictates the national style.

The journey fell into several distinct phases. From 11 May to 30 June, they were largely in New York and the Hudson Valley; July and August were spent in an extended journey to the then northwestern frontier, that is, as far as Detroit and the Michigan Peninsula, from which they returned to Boston by way of Lower Canada, that is, French-speaking Canada; the fall, from early September to mid-November, was again spent on the East Coast, in Boston, Philadelphia, and Baltimore, from where Tocqueville and Beaumont set out for the Mississippi, down the Mississippi to New Orleans, and back across the south to Washington. This allowed them a month, from 18 January to 20 February 1832, to see Washington and once again New York.

The journey was full of incident; they had the misfortune to strike the worst winter in memory, and what ought to have been an easy journey down the Ohio River and then down the Mississippi turned into a struggle across frozen ridges, a near escape from death by drowning, and another near escape from death by pneumonia. The Mississippi was frozen all the way north from Memphis. Modern English and American readers should perhaps remember three things about the journey that do not emerge clearly in *Democracy* itself. The first is how very thoroughly Tocqueville saw North America through French eyes, not English eyes; his letters and diaries reverberate with the sentiments of a man who was acutely aware that the French had decisively lost out to the British on the North American continent only seventy years before. There had been no very obvious reason why the French could not have consolidated their possessions along the St. Lawrence and established themselves all the way down the Mississippi, so checking British expansion. In 1831, the United States was still very sparsely settled any-where more than two or three hundred miles from the Atlantic seaboard, and Illinois and Kentucky were frontier states. The great flood of immigra-tion that swept across the Mississippi and onto the Great Plains was a dozen or more years off, and Tocqueville can hardly be complained of for looking back to 1763 rather than forward to the results of the Irish Famine and the failed revolutions of 1848.

A second thing is that Tocqueville's picture of the character of the Ameri-cans is colored by his sense of the contrast between the English national character and the French. The bleak, self-controlled determination of the English made them unlovable but highly successful colonizers. The French, by contrast, were more likely to melt into the local landscape, establish themselves in villages that reminded them of home, and struggle no further to impose themselves on the new terrain. One of his simplest arguments against social analyses that overemphasized the importance of the physical environment was to point out the difference between French settlers, who would put up with all sorts of privations rather than leave the places in which they had settled, and English settlers, who would abandon their exist-ing habitations for the least chance of improving their lot. National charac-ter mattered a good deal more than American geography. The most striking characteristic of Tocqueville's intelligence was its ambivalence, and his abil-ity to admire the British without much liking them is one more example of it. He thought his own France needed an imperial project to improve na-tional morale, and approved of the French conquest of Algeria as such a project. In North America, he lamented the failure to secure French Canada and wondered whether there might somewhere be a leader who could in-spire the French Canadians to rise up against the British and take their free-dom. Since they greatly outnumbered their oppressors, there was every rea-son why they should do so.

The third thing was Tocqueville's interest in the half-castes he encoun-tered in the near Midwest and on the Canadian border. These *bois-brulés* or *métis* aroused his curiosity for much the same reason that the contrast of French and English national character did. The French had always found it relatively easy to accept people from different cultures; as the jargon of the 1980s had it, they had no fear of the Other. The English were great bound-ary maintainers; they feared contamination from alien cultures and there-fore set up tremendous taboos against sexual relations with Indians and made the social position of "half-breeds" intolerable. The French took it for granted that sexual attraction operated across cultural and linguistic barri-ers, and were correspondingly more tolerant of the results. Whether any of this was true, generally or locally, it seems impossible to say. Tocqueville remained all his life fascinated by the question of what was or might be in-herent in a given racial type as opposed to what was or might be inculcated by education—in the broad sense of education for which the unlovely term "socialization' was later coined—and he was a good friend of Arthur de Gobineau, sometimes called the father of scientific racism, and a man whose career in the diplomatic service Tocqueville went out of his way to promote. Tocqueville himself was not at all what later generations have meant by a "racist"; his ironical and cautious intelligence was not easily to be pressed into the task of ranking different human groups as inevitably and unchangeably better and worse. Moreover, his indignation at the effects of European colonization on the American Indian peoples, who had been displaced, robbed of their land, corrupted by booze and trinkets, and destroyed by European diseases, was entirely unfeigned. He was simply fascinated by the combined effect of whatever it was that essential human nature contributed and the social and physical environment working on it.

The shortcomings of the journey as a preparation for a synoptic account of the United States are obvious enough, but later writers have often seemed to complain more about Tocqueville not seeing places that had not been built and events that had not occurred, or else about aspects of the journey that reflected Tocqueville's theoretical convictions rather than his inadequacies as an empirical observer. Industrial America was perhaps slighted and so, for that matter, were the men who ensured that commercial and financial matters were conducted with tolerable efficiency; but one might equally reply that the industrial giant that America would become by the time of the Civil War had scarcely begun to stir. Tocqueville's interest in economics was always conditioned by his belief that it was the effect of economic life upon *les moeurs*—that untranslatable term embracing custom, moral attachments, and standards of etiquette and social esteem—that really mattered. In fact, he met numerous people with commercial and financial interests, and was deeply impressed—both favorably and unfavorably—with the commercial spirit of the country; and he observed more than once that Americans were peculiarly receptive to the attractions of commerce and industry. More attention to merchants, bankers, and manufacturers and their opinions would not have made much difference to the book he was going to write. It was the American national psyche that he had come to analyze, not American industrial, agricultural, and financial technique.

* * * * *

The reception of *Democracy in America* was all that an author could have desired. "I see you have written a masterpiece," said Tocqueville's publisher upon the publication of volume one, and readers generally concurred. The second volume was less universally admired, but the two together were agreed by most critics to represent a stunning achievement in explaining to Europeans what the new civilization the other side of the Atlantic was like; critics were also struck by Tocqueville's insistence that what was happening in America was part of the same process that was making European societies more egalitarian.

The enthusiasm of John Stuart Mill was one of the major reasons for the book's success with English-speaking readers. It struck a chord in Mill that it could hardly have done in anyone else. For Mill read *Democracy* at a point in his life where he had broken with the radicalism of his father and Jeremy Bentham and was looking for a new social and political vision. Mill, in essence, had come to reject the utilitarians' belief that all social ills could be cured by a Parliament elected by popular vote, together with a rational, disinterested, uncorrupt administration to implement the policies that such a Parliament would enact. Under the impulse of such writers as Thomas Carlyle, Samuel Taylor Coleridge, and William Wordsworth, and reflecting on his own experiences as a young man, Mill had come to think that the limitations of democracy were greater than his father and Bentham had realized. He had accepted even before he read Tocqueville that in the modern world, public opinion was increasingly powerful and that even governments that were not democratic in form would increasingly become so in substance. Unlike many of his contemporaries, Mill was not particularly anxious about the possibility that pressures for an expansion of the suffrage or for making government more answerable to the middle and lower-middle classes would result in mob rule or mere chaos. What he feared was that it would result in a dreary, barren, narrowly businesslike society. It was, so to speak, the cultural consequences of universal egalitarianism that he feared. His one complaint against Tocqueville when he read the first volume of *Democracy in America* was that Tocqueville talked of the effects of "democracy" when he meant only the effects of equality. Democracy considered as a form of government had merits that were detachable from the dangers of generalized egalitarianism.

The surprising thing is less that Mill should have so admired the book than that its continued vitality in the Anglo-American world should have been so great. A few American critics in the nineteenth century complained over the next two decades that Tocqueville made a great show of discovering things that all Americans knew already; others complained that he had ignored the Americans' own reflections on their political system. For the most part, however, they were quick to recognize that Tocqueville's English critics, other than Mill, had frequently used him as a weapon against the extension of the franchise to the large majority of the British population that was still unenfranchised, and they therefore applauded the friendliness of his analysis. Whereas British conservatives used his criticisms of America as reasons for not extending the reach of democratic institutions in Britain, Americans used his relatively cheerful assessment of their condition as a prop to national pride and self-confidence.

Of course, later writers expressed the perfectly sensible view that as time went on, the United States had changed rather dramatically—the whole continent had been occupied, there had been a civil war, and the country's culture had been transformed by vast waves of immigration from Ireland, Germany, eastern and southern Europe, and then from Asia and Spanish

America. The anglophone culture of Puritan New England was not just one element in a more kaleidoscopic picture—it was a rather small element.[10] Tocqueville was not unaware of the existing influx of immigrants from the heart of Europe, but it was certainly easier to see the United States as a branch of the English project in 1831 than it was seventy-five years after. Odder, however, was the way *Democracy* became once more a text for our times, both in the aftermath of World War II and again some twenty-five years later. In David Riesman's classic study of "other-directed man," *The Lonely Crowd*, Tocqueville's fears were brought up to date. Tocqueville had feared that each single individual would be so confined by his domestic affections and attachments that he would have no psychological resources to resist public opinion and the ideas of others, but would regard public opinion as the only test of truth, virtue, and propriety. Riesman, unlike Tocqueville, was not enthusiastic about the kind of inner direction represented by Puritanism; it was too driven, and too repressive for modern tastes. Riesman looked for a more modern sort of autonomy as an ideal—the sort of character who was driven neither by conscience nor by public opinion, who was not driven at all.

The more narrowly political implications of Tocqueville's work were stressed by Ralf Dahrendorf in the mid-1950s; his anxieties were more directed at his native Germany than at the United States, but the sociological views that he found alarming were American. In those years, many sociologists emphasized the virtues of "consensus" and were anxious to stress the blessings of social and psychological integration. Dahrendorf reached back to Tocqueville's emphasis on the "antagonism of opinions" as a way of combatting the tyranny of the majority, and reminded American readers that their own tradition had resources that too many modern sociologists had neglected. Tocqueville's view that men might be lonely in the midst of crowds has worn almost better than his more directly political anxieties. Richard Sennett's essay *The Fall of Public Man* makes the point that citizens who do not know how to present themselves in public and who concentrate too narrowly on their domestic concerns will wake up to find that the political system has fallen into the hands of crooks and manipulators and that they are doomed to live under yet another variant of the quiet despotism that Tocqueville feared.

*   *   *   *   *

Democracy in America is not an entirely easy book to describe and analyze. A large part of the difficulty stems from Tocqueville's decision to write two very different books. The first volume is essentially an account of American democracy in operation. It focuses on what everyone would conventionally describe as the features of democratic government—federalism, the respect for rights, the role of lawyers, and the obsession with the rule of law, political parties, and the relations among localities, states, and the federal government. It is very much a sociologist's and a moralist's account in that the moralist focuses on the problem of the tyranny of the majority, and the sociologist not only asks about the role of formal institutions in reducing the dangers of majority tyranny but goes on to talk about the role of social equality in promoting political equality, the role of religion, the role of education, and so on. True to the tradition stemming from Montesquieu, Tocqueville touches on the role of the physical environment in sustaining American institutions, while arguing that—to quote the heading of a famous section of chapter 17—"The laws contribute more to the maintenance of the democratic republic in the United States than the physical circumstances of the country, and the customs more than the laws" (2:319–23).[11]

In volume two, Tocqueville raises his sights dramatically. Volume two tackles the larger question of the impact of democratic institutions upon a society's entire culture. American habits and institutions illustrate the theses that Tocqueville puts before the reader, but the focus is—to a much greater extent than in volume one—on the prospects for any modernizing and therefore, in Tocqueville's eyes, democratizing society. The two volumes also read rather differently. Mill's reviews pick up the difference in an almost exaggerated form. His first review leaves the author and the reader optimistic about the prospects of a democratic political order, even if Mill suggests few grounds for optimism about the culture of the sort of society that sustains a democratic politics. Until the Civil War changed his mind, Mill copied Tocqueville's unkind characterization of American men as "dollar hunters" and American women as the breeders of dollar hunters.

Mill's second review, five years later, was the most conservative essay he ever wrote and came nearer to defending the continued existence of relations of superiority and dependency between landowners and peasants than one would have believed possible in an essay written by Mill. Just as Mill's essays were visibly written by the same intelligence, the two volumes that provoked him are visibly written by the same man with the same anxieties throughout. Tocqueville's concern with the tyranny of the majority persists throughout, and volume two ends with a consideration of the kind of despotism to which democracies are prone, an observation that would not have been out of place in volume one. Still, it would not be wrong to suggest, as Mill did, that the first volume is primarily a treatise on politics, and the second primarily a treatise on democratic culture. One can see without straining very hard that a man of Tocqueville's fastidious, critical, aristocratic temperament might well have felt much less happy about the culture of a bourgeois society than he did about the more narrowly political arrangements in such a society. One can also see that readers who enjoyed the first volume because of its vivid descriptions of American institutions and behavior might feel that the second had lost that liveliness in turning aside from the description of an exotic society to broad questions about issues that prefigure *L'ancien régime's* obsession with centralization and the concentration of power in governmental hands.

To the extent that a one-sentence summary of so complex a work makes any sense at all, we may borrow from Tocqueville: a tendency to equality of condition is operating in the world, one so irresistible that we must ascribe it to divine influence; we can see what this process entails for America, where it has gone further than anywhere else, and we must ask what it means for Europe. To set the question in such a light relies, as we have seen, on the Montesquieuian thought that in most societies where equality has existed on a large scale, this has been equality before the throne of a despot. *Democracy in America* explains why this is not the American condition, and inquires whether such good fortune can be expected to persist. The philosophical cleverness of the work lies in the thought that when "the people" rule, the potentiality for despotism is as great as in other systems of government. James Mill had famously observed that when the people govern themselves, they cannot try to govern themselves against their own interests; Tocqueville pointed out that when the people rule, the position of each person is that he is ruled by all the rest, and that if they form a compact, self-sustaining mass, united in opinion and outlook, they will overbear each of their number quite as effectively as any oriental despot might. There are innumerable variations on this thought spread over the two volumes, but it is perhaps true to say that between the first and second volumes there is something of a transition from the fear that each individual will find himself impotent in face of a spontaneous consensus and the fear that a popular leader might arise who uses the overwhelming support of the masses at his back to govern like a despot even if he observes the constitutional proprieties.

J. L. Talmon coined the expression "totalitarian democracy" to describe the situation of the popular dictator who could govern in the name of the whole people but without concern for the rights of his subjects. Although Tocqueville anticipated nothing worse than what actually came to pass with the rise to power of Louis Bonaparte, first as "prince-president," then as the self-proclaimed Emperor Napoleon III, his picture of what one might call an "unofficial" democratic totalitarianism is one that has chilled many twentieth-century readers.

The analyst of *Democracy* is inhibited by two opposed features of the work. On the one hand, Tocqueville provides chapter headings that amount to a running summary of the book and make an analysis redundant, while on the other, both volumes are so full of asides, diversions, and changes of tone that one comes to feel that any summary leaves out so much of interest that it traduces the character of the book. As every commentator observes, the introduction is the key to everything that follows; like most introductions, it was written after the rest of the volume that it summarizes, and tells us much about what the author thought he had accomplished: "Among the novel objects that attracted my attention during my stay in the United States, nothing struck me more forcibly than the general equality of condition among the people. I readily discovered the prodigious influence that this primary fact exercises on the whole course of society; it gives a peculiar direction to public opinion and a peculiar tenor to the laws; it imparts new maxims to the governing authorities and peculiar habits to the governed" (1:3). Equality of condition did not mean identity of wealth or occupation or similarity of day-to-day existence; the trapper on the frontier led a very different life from that of the merchant in Boston, Philadelphia, or New York. Nor did it mean that at any given moment incomes were even roughly equal. It was an equality perhaps more obvious to a French aristocrat than to most observers; it was equality of status, a total absence of unearned or inherited deference, a complete unwillingness to acknowledge oneself any man's social inferior, and it went along with an absence of the old aristocratic urge to incorporate oneself as a landed, or territorial, ruling class. The erosion of accepted differences of status was what Tocqueville thought would spread over Europe as well and what he described as "a providential fact," adding, "It has all the chief characteristics of such a fact: it is universal, it is lasting, it constantly eludes all human interference, and all events as well as all men contribute to its progress" (1:6).

Readers familiar with *Democracy* will know that Tocqueville seems to draw back from this in volume two. In chapter 20 of the second book, "How an Aristocracy May be Created by Manufactures" (1:158–61), he follows Adam Smith in suggesting that as the division of labor advances and manufacturing thrives, the individual worker becomes increasingly stunted. A man who spends his working life making heads for pins becomes something less than fully human. Between him and the owner of the business a great gulf opens up. But then Tocqueville begins to vacillate; rich manufacturers do not really form a social class; they have no sense of a common interest and a common purpose, and their fortunes are too evanescent to found a real aristocracy. Still, he concludes, turning round once more, if a new aristocracy arises, that will be its source. He would no doubt have thought "robber baron" an apt term for those who amassed vast fortunes fifty years later.

That *Democracy* was written for Frenchmen emerges very early on in the introduction, when Tocqueville outlines the reasons why democracy in France has not been accompanied by the rise of liberalism but by a constant tendency to despotism. Essentially, his thought was, and remained, that before the Revolution, the French monarchy had increasingly suppressed all competing sources of authority. This left a sort of vacuum, so that when the Revolution overthrew the monarchy, the new government inherited a society devoid of the checks and balances that would make for liberty. The villain was the centralization of all administrative functions and the consequent weakening of civil society's capacity for self-help and self-maintenance.

Tocqueville was at least as interested in the cultural tone of an egalitarian society as in its origins. The French experience was not reassuring; whereas noble and serf were separated by a vast gulf, they nonetheless felt nothing degraded in their relationship, but in the modern world, the proximity of social classes to one another creates more envy, more bitterness, and more antagonism. The American experience, in contrast, suggests that democracy in the sense of equality of condition is not always the enemy of liberty. Equality of condition will perhaps inevitably be the enemy of glory, better at reducing misery than at creating public splendor, more apt to give everyone some education than to throw off tremendous flashes of genius; but these may all be acceptable trades.

Because the first volume of *Democracy* was avowedly devoted to the political institutions of the Americans, it is not surprising to find Tocqueville beginning with a rapid sketch of the origins of New England and an account of its present social condition. Nor is it surprising to find that Tocqueville argues that what allows liberty and equality to coexist in America is the fact that the conception of liberty the Puritans brought with them to America was a distinctively Christian conception, not mere "let alone" nor a liberty that might turn into license, but a capacity to conduct ourselves by a law we freely accept. The fainthearted might worry that an extended quotation from Cotton Mather tells us little about public opinion in 1831, but Tocqueville's insistence that it is a view that finds its way into the legal system and into the culture of lawyers, judges, and legislators may persuade us that a view that has its roots in a particular religious vision can readily find its way into secular institutions.

On those institutions themselves, Tocqueville's commentary is a mixture of observations that retain much of their interest, and observations that are now entirely out of date. Among the latter, many of the observations on the U.S. Constitution have been superseded by changes in that document, such as those providing for the direct popular election of senators. His belief that the ties among the states might weaken has been contradicted by the twentieth century's experience of a greatly increased role for the federal government and a consequent weakening of the role of the states. His belief that the presidency was an office of next to no importance was being falsified as he wrote by the vigor of President Jackson, and is now wholly out of date. Defenders of Tocqueville's perceptiveness as an observer can reply that he at least noticed that the most likely route by which the presidency would gain in importance would be through the president's leading role in foreign relations. In the 1830s, there was little else for the president to concern himself with, but this could not and did not last.

Among the discussions that remained relevant even after their obvious institutional relevance had gone, one might cite Tocqueville's discussion of the New England system of township government and his insistence on the localism of American politics. Changes in institutional arrangements have somehow not made a corresponding difference in citizens' attitudes; and any foreign observer is still struck by the way voters and politicians alike take next to no notice of the tastes, interests, and beliefs of the rest of the country in asserting the claims of their locality. Such a localism persists in American politics in an age when the federal government has grown to a degree that nothing in Tocqueville's experience could have suggested. Indeed, Tocqueville thought that the dissolution of the country by each state going its own way was not unlikely; the cementing of national unity by the forces of the railroad, the interstate highway system, and the demands of the modern industrial economy were unpredictable and unpredicted.

To the modern reader, the first volume hinges on the discussion of the power of the majority and the various ways in which it does and does not amount to a tyranny. Tocqueville held a skeptical, or perhaps we should say a "realistic," view of the relationship between the written Constitution and the actual exercise of power. Madison had caustically described proposals for a Bill of Rights as proposals to erect "parchment barriers" against tyranny. Tocqueville had much of that skepticism. In all societies, there must be some ultimate repository of power. Even if there was a constitution that governed the operations of the political system, there was still a force somewhere that would either reinforce its constraints or override them. In any case, when Tocqueville wrote, part of the federal government was elected by indirect means as a barrier against the direct exercise of the will of the majority, and it was only the federal legislature and executive that had such restraints. State and local government was more simply majoritarian. Since, he thought, internal affairs were almost entirely in the hands of state governments, it was there that he had to look to see the absolute sovereignty of the majority in action. And there he thought he saw it clearly: "The very essence of democratic government consists in the absolute sovereignty of the majority; for there is nothing in democratic states that can resist it. Most of the American constitutions have sought to increase this natural strength of the majority by artificial means" (1:254).

One skeptical view has always been that no matter what the nominal form of government, public opinion dictates how it operates. Tocqueville did not need to argue along those lines, since the various state governments that he considered tied the legislature and the executive very firmly to the expressed wishes of the electorate. Legislatures had extensive powers, and were commonly elected for very short terms, often for no more than a year. The result had to be that there was something close to direct majority rule. Tocqueville had the same doubts that most European observers entertained about the instability of American opinion; a long footnote comments caustically on the way the majority in Pennsylvania first emancipated Negro slaves, then ensured by intimidation that they could not vote or exercise their other civil rights—thus showing that the majority might pass what laws it liked and then violate them too. But this all leads to the central theme: "It is in the examination of the exercise of thought in the United States that we clearly perceive how far the power of the majority surpasses all the powers with which we are acquainted in Europe" (1:263). Because Americans deferred so completely to the majority, it had only to become clear that the majority had formed a view for dissent to cease. Kings threatened their subjects, intimidated them into a desired external compliance, and left their minds free. But, said Tocqueville, "I know of no country in which there is so little independence of mind and real freedom of discussion as in America" (1:263).

Was everything lost, then? The answer was plainly not. The great American talent was for decentralization and self-help. This meant that for much of the time, Americans did without government entirely and hardly bore upon one another so continually as to exercise very much of a tyranny over one another. Then, too, the legal-mindedness of the country helped. Lawyers had a certain aristocratic tendency that worked in an antimajoritarian direction: "Men who have made a special study of the laws derive from this occupation certain habits of order, a taste for formalities, and a kind of instinctive regard for the regular connection of ideas, which naturally render them very hostile to the revolutionary spirit and the unreflecting passions of the multitude" (1:273). Tocqueville argued that the tendency of American politics to recruit lawyers to large numbers of official positions beside the more narrowly legal was likely to reinforce their influence over the public mind; the fact that the American legal system inherited the English common law added another, perhaps more double-edged reason for their ascendancy over the layman—not merely was common law arcane, it was also the embodiment of tradition. To the degree that lawyers played a prominent role, one could expect them to resist direct majority rule.

The mitigation of majority tyranny might seem a small, even if an important, part of the maintenance of a liberal democracy. Tocqueville set out the positive supports of democracy under three headings: "I. The peculiar and accidental situation in which Providence has placed the Americans. II. The laws. III. The manners and customs of the people" (1:288). The first embraced what later became a familiar American obsession with the role of the frontier in allowing liberalism to coexist with majority rule. It was not an accident that Tocqueville placed his anxious reflections on the horrors of American slums in a footnote to the discussion of the frontier; in essence, his view was that it was American prosperity that saved the day and that prosperity was a product of the continent's endlessness. As restless explorers poured out of the East on their way to the frontier, they left a labor shortage that offered immediate prosperity to the incoming immigrant and a safety valve for those who might otherwise form the revolutionary mobs that upper-class French observers had to fear. The laws that he considered most important were the constitutional provisions that made America distinctive. But not only were the manners and customs of the people the most important cause of the success of American democracy, but Tocqueville's view of them was also somewhat startling. The thought that the Protestantism of the Pilgrim Fathers was a good foundation for democratic politics was not surprising; it is something of a cliché to see the dissenting meeting and the township as cognate institutions. Tocqueville gave the case a particular twist in arguing that Puritanism supported individual independence rather than a taste for equality. He looked, however, to Catholicism as the religion of the future. Partly, this was in the belief that Protestantism was likely to become lukewarm and thus gradually to lose its grip on the American mind. Partly, it was in the belief that the connection between Catholicism and antidemocratic forces in countries such as France was essentially accidental. Where, as in the United States, the church faced nothing like the plebeian anticlericalism it faced in Europe, its emphasis on the equality of all believers and its insistence that the only difference in status that it cared for was the distinction between the priest and the laity made it a force for republican and democratic ideals. To these religiously based forces, one had to add the secular force of the generally high level of practical education and practical intelligence. It was when he had cause to praise the shrewdness, the understanding of political institutions, and the general understanding of the rights and duties of the citizen that Tocqueville's real affection for the Americans he had met on his journey shone through.

One of the most striking portions of the first volume of *Democracy* is the last chapter, in which Tocqueville considered the relations between the "three races that inhabit the territory of the United States" (1:331). Tocqueville said rather interestingly that it was an excursion from his main theme— democracy. Yet he could not simply turn his back on the two great horrors of the American scene, black slavery and the gradual extermination of the American Indian. To repeat an earlier observation, we ought not to exaggerate Tocqueville's humanitarian inclinations, nor ought we to ignore his readiness to see the French conquer and occupy Algeria in the most brutal fashion. He had what is perhaps rarer today, a bleak sense of the moral frailty of most of mankind: "If we reason from what passes in the world, we should almost say that the European is to the other races of mankind what man himself is to the lower animals: he makes them subservient to his use and when he cannot subdue them he destroys them" (1:332). Tocqueville's account of the destruction of the Indian population is matched by his account of the horrors of slavery. The Indian is driven out of everywhere he might inhabit; as the European settlements advance, so the game on which the Indian depended disappears, and even where he is not driven out by force, he is driven away by famine. Should the Indian turn to agriculture to support himself, the lands he cultivates become the object of the greed of the European, who then finds one device or another to take them and once more drive the Indian further and further away. This has only one foreseeable terminus: the total destruction of the aboriginal inhabitants of the country.

Slavery was a different matter. The black population of the United States was increasing rather than decreasing. But this placed the states that practiced slavery in a dilemma. The slave states were essentially backward and sluggish; the existence of slavery stigmatized hard work and innovation by associating labor with slavery, and innovation with the destruction of a bastard form of aristocratic agriculture. On the other hand, they could not easily abolish slavery; too much of the value of slave owners' estates was bound up in the value of the slaves, and if emancipated, the slaves would be entirely unfit for membership of a largely white society. Tocqueville put his finger on what has turned out to be the crucial issue: classical slavery involved only the unfreedom of the slave, so that a Greek or Roman slave might well be the equal of his master in intellect, knowledge, and imagination. All he needed was emancipation. Black slaves would remain blacks after they had ceased to be slaves. The white, especially the white English, hostility to the colored races would be as great after emancipation as before. Slavery had to come to an end, since it was an atrocity unimaginable in the enlightened nineteenth century, but however it came to an end, whether by emancipation or by a black uprising, it would be a continuing problem, to which Tocqueville saw no solution.

The discussion of the plight of Indians and blacks was a coda or excursion from the main theme of the first volume of *Democracy*. Volume two can hardly be called an excursion, since it is rather more in the nature of a distillation of Tocqueville's thoughts on the cultural consequences of democracy, in which the underlying anxieties about the chances of further revolutionary outbreaks and further despotic episodes keep returning to color the argument. Indeed, one might suppose that in 1833–34, when he was writing the first volume, Tocqueville had it in mind that he would complement his discussion there of the causes that mitigate the tyranny of the majority with the melancholy and eloquent chapter at the end of the second volume, titled "What Sort of Despotism Democratic Nations Have to Fear" (2:316). Nonetheless, if the second volume is not an excursion, it does not so much add to the first volume as deepen some of the insights that Tocqueville sketches there in order to enforce the moral he wanted to draw for European nations contemplating their future.

To this observation there is one large exception, and that is the stress that Tocqueville places on the nature of American family life, on the role of women in American life, and on the good and bad features of what we have come to think of as "middle-class morality." Tocqueville's first thought on arriving in New York was that unmarried American women were very much freer than their French counterparts, but that once they married—according to their own inclination—they were removed into a domestic setting in which their only task was to admire their husbands. Since the salon was not an American institution, he did not say this as lamenting the absence of the intellectually sophisticated Parisian drawing rooms, but to observe that American morals were purer than French. Married women were not expected to flirt or to make themselves attractive to men to whom they were not married, and the fact that marriages were founded on mutual affection in the first place made clandestine affairs less attractive. Tocqueville was not sentimental here either, however. He saw that the attractions of the domestic hearth were reinforced by the ferocity of public sentiment against adultery: "In a country in which a woman is always free to exercise her choice and where education has prepared her to choose rightly, public opinion is inexorable to her faults. The rigour of the Americans arises in part from this cause. They consider marriage as a covenant which is often onerous, but every condition of which the parties are strictly bound to fulfil because they knew all those conditions beforehand and were perfectly free not to have contracted them" (2:205–6).

The three large themes that might be extracted from the second volume of *Democracy* are obvious enough. The first is the quality of intellectual and cultural life in an egalitarian society; the second, the stability or proneness to revolutionary upheaval of such societies; and the third, Tocqueville's final and most distinctive thoughts on democratic despotism, or what one might term quiet totalitarianism. Themes such as the place of religion in public life, the effects of centralization, the American enthusiasm for creating and belonging to a multitude of public and political associations, all reappear from the first volume, of course, and generally in such a way that the first volume's suggestion that the Americans had done well enough to give Europeans some grounds for hope is a good deal undermined. Thus, he says rather fiercely, "I am of the opinion that, in the democratic ages which are opening upon us, individual independence and local liberties will ever be the products of art; that centralization will be the natural government" (2:296). The thought is a simple one. As rulers and ruled become more similar in their tastes and ideological affections, the sympathy between rulers and ruled becomes stronger. Egalitarians tend almost automatically to prefer uniform solutions to problems; governments always do. When these two tendencies run in harness, the way is paved for a steady increase in the centralization of administration.

Tocqueville's view of the cultural consequences of egalitarianism come as no surprise to a modern reader, although some of them have been overtaken by unpredictable events. Thus, when he considers intellectual life in America, he observes, as many have done since, that Americans are plainspoken in everyday life but descend into an extraordinary pomposity and rhetorical inflatedness in their public speech. He had earlier complained that Americans tended to address him as if he were a public meeting, but his usual estimate of Americans was highly favorable. Like most people, Americans spoke foolishly on topics they knew nothing about, but unlike most people, they were immensely well informed about their own society. Their readiness to tolerate pomposity and inflation reflected, thought Tocqueville, a need for something to compensate for the pettiness of their usual concerns. Discussing rhetorical inflation in general, Tocqueville worried that American poetry would become empty, bombastic, and sprawling. It is easy to believe that he would have disliked Whitman had he lived long enough to take an interest in his work, and that he would have been confirmed in his view by American landscape painting in the style of Albert Bierstadt.

Tocqueville does not confuse form and substance. When mocking the eloquence of Congress, he observed mildly that Americans "show their long experience of parliamentary life, not by abstaining from making bad speeches, but by courageously submitting to hear them made" (2:92). The more interesting and complicated observation was that intellectual life in general in the United States was marked by a concern for practicality and by a generally high level of matter-of-fact competence, not by the productions of genius, nor by the creation of things that would appeal to refined taste. So fiction would, he thought, turn out to be a trade in which authors would engage in the same frame of mind as the manufacturers of anything else. Science and literary culture otherwise was not a high priority; Americans could leave the English to supply their needs, and if they could, why not do so? The sinister side of this was not the low level of public taste so much as the potential for a kind of intellectual despotism. If there was no general acknowledgment of excellence, there might be a tendency to demand of everyone that they conform their beliefs and the expression of their beliefs to whatever everyone else believed and said. That was consistent with the promotion of a great deal of variety in unimportant matters, and Tocqueville was neither the first nor the last observer of American social and intellectual life to think that it simultaneously displayed great variety and changeability but was, for all that, extremely monotonous.

The Americans struck Tocqueville as an extraordinarily restless people. The question was whether they were also a revolutionary one. The war by which they had secured independence from Britain, he absolutely did not consider to be a revolution. His idea of revolution was the modern, sociological idea—large-scale and sudden social change accompanying political upheaval, not only the unconstitutional transformation of the government narrowly considered. Tocqueville's reason for thinking that Americans were not going to be revolutionaries is one that Aristotle offered a very long time before, and twentieth-century sociologists discovered all over again a hundred years later. The thought is that revolutions may take place either to reduce the inequalities of wealth, power, and social status between the lower classes and the ruling class or else to reinforce those inequalities and make them harder to remove. The first kind of revolution will be launched from below, and the latter will be launched from above. The first is the classic example of a populist uprising, the latter an oligarchical coup to forestall any such uprising. Americans were almost universally sufficiently well off to feel no need to engage in the first, and were so rarely members of a traditional ruling class that they had no urge to engage in the second. In a society in which most people had something to lose, and in which fortunes once made were not likely to persist for more than one or two generations, the prospects of gaining very much from upheaval were too slight to tempt anyone to engage in revolution to improve his circumstances. The thought that stability requires such a distribution of wealth and income that most people have enough and few have too little or too much is sometimes referred to as aiming at a "lozenge-shaped" distribution; and many people have thought during the past fifty years or so that Western democracies have become increasingly stable because that is the sort of distributive pattern they have achieved. One might admit the skeptical counter that the distribution is shaped less like a lozenge than an eccentric pear, with its top stretched out an immense distance, but the larger point would remain untouched.

Finally, then, Tocqueville's reconsideration of what sort of despotism a democracy might produce ends in a memorably disturbing paragraph. Tocqueville's fearful second thoughts about the moral of his American experience led him to think that the "individualism" of Americans would lead not to each individual being able to think for himself or herself and to carve out his or her own view of the world, but to a desperate isolation. "Lost in the crowd" of other individuals, we run the risk of having no resources except domestic ones and of becoming absolutely dependent on government and public opinion for emotional, intellectual, and, finally, economic support. It was this movement toward mass society that posed the greatest threat—not, of course, to Americans in particular, and probably to Americans least of all, but to every egalitarian society. This it was that Mill picked up from Tocqueville and naturalized as the theme of *On Liberty*. It is this, too, that links Tocqueville and recent writers such as Friedrich von Hayek as critics of the welfare state.

No later writer, however, produced a more plangent account of what was to be feared than did Tocqueville himself. His description of a soft totalitarianism could hardly be bettered:

> After having thus successively taken each member of the community in its powerful grasp and fashioned him at will, the supreme power then extends its arm over the whole community. It covers the surface of society with a network of small complicated rules, minute and uniform, through which the most original minds and the most energetic characters cannot penetrate, to rise above the crowd. The will of man is not shattered, but softened, bent, and guided; men are seldom forced by it to act, but they are constantly restrained from acting. Such a power does not destroy, but it prevents existence; it does not tyrannize, but it compresses, enervates, extinguishes, and stupefies a people, till each nation is reduced to nothing better than a flock of timid and industrious animals, of which the government is the shepherd. (2:319)

It hardly needs saying that this vision of the dangers of democracy has exercised the imaginations of innumerable critics ever since. It is perhaps worth saying that part of its power springs from the twentieth century's experience of the totalitarianisms of Nazi Germany and Stalinist Russia; both of those hideous regimes were avowedly in some sense democratic and egalitarian, even though each of them glorified leaders and leadership all the way through the ranks of the military, the party, and on to the supreme leader at the head of all the rest. Their egalitarian and democratic elements were just those that so alarmed Tocqueville—the resentful insistence that nobody was any better than oneself, the urge to be part of one common popular mass—and as everyone points out, they surpassed anything he feared in their capacity to sustain dictators of the most brutal and ferocious stripe. Twentieth-century Russians and Germans would have had cause for gratitude had they seen nothing worse than Napoleon III. One might think that the fact that the liberal democracies had emerged victorious from their hot wars with Nazism and Fascism and their Cold War with Soviet communism would cast some doubt on Tocqueville's political sociology, first as suggesting that quiet totalitarianism was not a live option, since whenever it appeared it was violent and bloody, and second as suggesting that liberal democracies had less to fear than he supposed, since they remained so completely different from their major competitors.

This, however, is where what makes Tocqueville hard to describe and to analyze makes him hard to resist. For what survives any amount of criticism is Tocqueville's critique of the very ordinariness of modern society. His shrewd insights into the factory-like production of modern literature unnerve us; his wistfulness about the capacity of aristocratic societies to pursue grandeur rather than mere comfort embarrasses us. Even when he ends *Democracy* by trying to rise above the scene he has depicted in order to balance the comfort of the many against the glory of the few, one feels that everyday middle-class existence has been found wanting by a fastidious taste against which there is no appeal. This is not to suggest that we cannot in fact defend ourselves and stand up for the liveliness, variety, and interestingness of the culture of modern democracies. We do not have to be intimidated by Tocqueville's aristocratic style and sensibilities. Nonetheless, they provide a permanent and, it must be said, a fruitful and useful countercurrent to the natural tendencies of an egalitarian society in which the principle of *vox populi vox dei* must always be in some risk of overstepping its proper bounds in the realm of politics and economics to invade the realms of our private tastes, our religious convictions, and our hopes for human progress.

23

Staunchly Modern, Nonbourgeois Liberalism

Introduction

THE TITLE OF this essay is, of course, a gentle tease at the expense of Richard Rorty's well-known essay "Postmodernist Bourgeois Liberalism," an essay that is itself something of a tease at the expense of the harder Left's attack on middle-of-the-road social democrats and their concern for human rights and nonviolent change.[1] I have a nonteasing purpose, however, and that is to emphasize (as, of course, Rorty himself does) that Dewey's own conception of his social and political theory was that it expressed the self-understanding of modern society—"modern" being no more precise in its denotation than "postmodernist," but certainly meaning at different times both the society that lived off and built on the scientific revolution of the seventeenth century and the society that came into existence with the capitalist Industrial Revolution of the eighteenth and nineteenth centuries.[2] Dewey's beliefs about the demands of modernity provide the part of my framework that deals with modernity.

As to "nonbourgeois," I want to emphasize in a way that many commentators on Dewey do not that he was a keenly class-conscious writer. I do not mean that he advocated the politics of class war; quite the contrary. He was, rather, gloomily conscious that the class-divided nature of capitalist societies—sometimes seeing this as a matter of owners versus workers in a more or less Marxist or Weberian style, sometimes seeing it as managers versus the managed in a way more akin to C. Wright Mills—meant that his view of the ways in which modern society opened up novel possibilities of self-expression and social advance was constantly at odds with the immediate facts. One of his many jokes against himself was the observation "I am very skeptical about things in particular but have an enormous faith in things in general."[3] In social theory, this meant that the organic unity of thought and action, efficiency and free expression, that was latent in modern society was constantly frustrated by conflicts based on misunderstanding and disorganization. What class division pointed to was not the need for a Marxian revolution but for something closer to guild socialism and a system of devolved workers' control.[4] His belief in the need for industrial democracy as a complement to political democracy provides at least one nonbourgeois element in the framework I use. I should emphasize that this is not entirely at odds with Rorty's essay, though I think Dewey would have thought that "bourgeois" covered too great a multitude of sins to be entirely at home praising bourgeois democracy, and Rorty is far less optimistic about the possibilities of anything resembling workers' control in the context of twenty-first-century capitalism.

Dewey's views about the peculiar form of freedom available in the modern world make him a liberal. I say this while agreeing, and indeed emphasizing, that until quite late in the day, Dewey's organizing concept was "democracy" rather than "liberalism"—that is, from the very beginning of his discussion of social issues, back in 1888, Dewey thought in terms of the character of a democratic community rather than in terms of the liberal repertoire of individual rights and immunities.[5] When he turns to discussing liberalism in so many words, it is largely in order to argue that American liberalism must be updated, must turn away from laissez-faire, and must be redefined as "intelligent social action."[6] Nonetheless, Dewey's conception of democracy is emphatically a conception of liberal democracy; its origins lie in the ideas of T. H. Green, whose liberal credentials have never been impugned, and its guiding ideal is the strengthening of the organic interconnection of individuals on the basis of freedom and equality. I cheerfully admit that if we define "postmodernism" in terms of the renunciation of the search for "foundations," and "bourgeois" in terms of the educated middle-class audience for views like Dewey's, we can, stretching a point, talk about postmodernist bourgeois liberalism—but I rather hope we shall not want to.

The mode of analysis I employ is genealogical. I do not mean this in an elaborately Nietzschean or Foucauldian sense, but literally—that is, Dewey is here treated against the intellectual background out of which he emerged, because it is easier to understand any writer by seeing where he or she comes from and what assumptions he or she has brought with him or her and has kept or abandoned along the way, and Dewey is discussed, to a degree, in the political context in which he wrote, because some element of contextual understanding is necessary to make sense of what his ideas meant in their own time. It is oddly difficult to do either of these things with any degree of persuasiveness. Assessing just how much baggage he carried with him from his Hegelian youth is difficult because he was obsessed with an issue that hardly bothers us, and yet is one that makes some difference to understanding just what he was up to. That is, his autobiographical sketch "From Absolutism to Experimentalism" gives us Dewey's version of his intellectual progress—an escape from the Absolute. When Russell teased him, none too gently, about the residually Hegelian elements in his thinking, Dewey would angrily insist that he had indeed escaped from Absolutism and that the charge was preposterous. But Russell's charge was not that Dewey wished to revive the Hegelian Idea or Notion; it was that Dewey shared Hegel's belief that thought uncovered an organic unity in the world, that the world was a world replete with meaning and not just with cause-and-effect connections (which were themselves anyway to be understood as resting on the meaningfulness of experienced reality as a field of causal forces), and that the empiricist's sharp divisions between fact and value, religion and science, art and utility, misrepresented a reality that presented itself to us as a seamless whole. Of course, Dewey was also insistent that he was an "infinite pluralist" as well and that the world was, so to speak, remaking itself as a differentiated unity. Antidualism was quite other than a form of monism. Dewey would also have objected to the suggestion that one is tempted to make: that he was an "experimental Hegelian."[7] He had briefly espoused such a position in the 1880s, arguing that it was empirical evidence in the field of psychology that took us to the understanding that the world was dependent on a Self, so he knew what he had repudiated.[8] What is less easy to decide is how he understood these other "organic" commitments; but it is at least clear that there was more to Dewey's metaphysics than the naturalism of W. V. Quine or other successors.[9]

Understanding the connections of his work to matters of the day is not intellectually difficult; the problem is that we have an abundance of Dewey's writings but very little autobiographical evidence with which to illuminate their purpose. That is, a great deal of Dewey's output from the time he moved to New York, and especially after 1914, just is commentary on current politics. This is often politics of a fairly domestic sort. For instance, he wrote against proposals to allow religious instruction in school or to reduce the "progressive" elements in education or to close down art classes and so on, all of which were topics on which Dewey could speak with the authority of the nation's greatest educational theorist, the longtime president of a teachers union, a founder of the American Association of University Professors, and a sponsor of the American Civil Liberties Union. He also wrote on politics on the grand scale—the American entry into World War I, the Versailles Treaty, and, while he was chairman of the People's Lobby, on the early New Deal policies of Franklin Roosevelt—and on much of that one may reasonably have some reservations about his credibility. What is harder to come by is nonpublic thinking on his political positions. There is an overabundance of prepared material—articles, letters to the editor, and statements of position—but a great shortage of private statements. This makes it hard to see quite how Dewey's political responses tie into his philosophical thinking. As we shall see in conclusion, one thing that happened to Dewey during the 1930s was that he became convinced that he ought to have paid more attention to the importance of the individual; but it is extremely hard to know quite what he meant and equally hard to know what he wished he had said differently earlier in his career.

Although the explanatory tactics here are historical—to show how Dewey employed the intellectual machinery he had constructed by about 1904 to understand the politics of the next forty years—the point of the story is not historical at all. The point I wish to make may surprise some readers, since I claim both that Dewey's work is of great importance and that it is unsatisfactory in crucial respects. Deweyan liberalism is, in my analysis, very close to the only philosophy of liberal democratic politics that a twenty-first-century reader is likely to find credible. This is not to withdraw any of the skepticism already implied and later spelled out a little about Dewey's contributions to the politics of the day; in particular, it is not to deny that his thoughts on the "outlawry of war" were muddled, incoherent, and laced with wishful thinking, and it is not to deny that his most serious essay on democratic politics, *The Public and Its Problems*, is maddeningly evasive and equally laced with wishful thinking. It is to say that Dewey provides a philosophical basis for twenty-first-century liberalism; or, if you do not like the term "basis," that he provides a uniquely persuasive philosophical gloss on the convictions and commitments of the twenty-first-century liberal. Readers sometimes complain that Dewey's account of twentieth-century politics is shrouded in mist. In the account of the matter offered here, the fog in the photograph sometimes reflects the wobbling hand of the photographer, but is more often a clear representation of a foggy world. Since we all know perfectly well that no philosophical theory can preempt the messy processes of politics and policy making, and indeed that modern liberalism is committed to taking the messiness seriously, we ought not to ask for a clarity that we cannot have at any price we are ready to pay.

What is Dewey's claim on our attention? Dewey, uniquely, ties the concerns of Jefferson, Tocqueville, Mill, and writers of a Millian persuasion to a philosophy that escapes the pitfalls of both empiricism and classical Hegelian Idealism. The persuasiveness of contemporary writers such as Charles Taylor and (to a lesser degree) Jürgen Habermas owes a great deal to what they share with Dewey—in particular, to the thought that our moral and intellectual horizons are not closed by our social attachments but are, in ways that it is hard to elucidate, nonetheless bounded by communal understandings, and that a modern ethics and politics must be individualist at the same time that it must be understood as the product of a particular culture and time, outside which the very idea of the overwhelming importance of individuality would make no sense[10] It is by now not much disputed that the so-called liberal–communitarian debate was nothing of the sort and that the parodic picture of liberalism offered in Michael Sandel's *Liberalism and the Limits of Justice* served only one valuable purpose, that of forcing liberal political theorists to say more clearly than they had bothered to before just what the sociological and cultural assumptions of their theory were. Once we see that any liberalism must be simultaneously communitarian and individualist, we can work out more delicately in what sense it is true, as Sandel and Taylor have surely persuaded us, that persons would not have selves at all but for the ways they have been shaped by their backgrounds and upbringing, and yet, as Dewey emphasizes, and Taylor's *Sources of the Self* surely persuades us too, that persons fully attuned to the modern world must pursue the project of individual authenticity and social progress that we call liberalism.[11]

Idealism and Naturalism, 1880–1900

From a purely philosophical perspective, the most interesting years of Dewey's life came between about 1882 and 1899, when he moved gradually through and out of neo-Hegelianism and into the naturalism that was his trademark. Here, there is no room to do more than sketch those parts of this progress that bear on the present topic. But one extraordinary feature of his career is how soon he seized upon the field that became his life's work. It needs to be stressed here not for biographical reasons but as contextual evidence for the claim of this essay that Dewey was *primarily* a philosopher, not a political commentator propping up his political enthusiasms with philosophy. He graduated from the University of Vermont in 1879 at the age of twenty; he was at something of a loose end until he took up a job teaching in Oil City, Pennsylvania, in a high school run by a cousin. But while he was there, he wrote and sent off to the *Journal of Speculative Philosophy* the essay "The Metaphysical Assumptions of Materialism," which he hoped would decide whether he should pursue a career in philosophy. The piece—at this distance in time, it is almost unreadable—was well received by the editor, W. T. Harris, and Dewey's career was set.[12] Dewey's first philosophical allegiances were to an intuitionism that was commonplace in the late nineteenth-century United States and was what he had been taught by H.A.P. Torrey at the University of Vermont; it was (oddly, perhaps, but certainly beneficially for Dewey) not shared by W. T. Harris, nor by G. S. Morris, who taught him at Johns Hopkins, both of whom were Hegelians rather than followers of James McCosh, the president of Princeton University, or Sir William Hamilton. Dewey's attachment to intuitionism dissolved very rapidly. By the time he came to write an article on what he called "Intuitionalism" for an encyclopedia of philosophy during the 1890s, he had come to believe that intuitionism was little more than Christian platitudes propped up by wishful thinking. It was not so much philosophy as the assurance that anything we minded about enough had an objective correlate in the real world—a quick way to God, freedom, and immortality. But this was reason conscripted into the service of orthodoxy, unrespectable in motive and argument alike. Dewey's education did him more good than one might have expected it to, however. The piety and conservatism of teachers like Torrey and the university's president, Matthew Buckham, ran off him like water off a duck's back. Indeed, his education had the unintended effect of making him take empiricism and naturalism seriously because it left him a great deal of time to read the British periodical journals to which the University of Vermont subscribed. There he came across John Morley, the Stephens (Leslie and James Fitzjames), H. S. Maine, Henry Fawcett, Henry Sidgwick, and an intellectual life not circumscribed by the conventions of Congregationalist New England.

It seems to have been these writers, rather than his philosophy teachers, who sparked his interest in philosophy; it was certainly they who persuaded him that the political options were wider than his teachers supposed. President Buckham was a good citizen but one who believed that all that was needed for social reform was already embodied in the Christian Gospels and that men needed no more than a change of heart to induce them to accept those Gospels as a guide. Radicalism seems to have alarmed him and puzzled him in more or less equal measure. Dewey liked Torrey and continued to study German and German philosophy with him after he graduated; but his verdict on Torrey, too, was that he had hidden his light under a bushel. His constitutional timidity stopped him from pressing arguments to their conclusions—and Dewey cited the telling anecdote of Torrey remarking that, philosophically speaking, pantheism was the only plausible doctrine and was incredible only in the light of revelation.

For Dewey's final philosophical stance, it was not a course in philosophy that mattered most at all. Dewey seems to have acquired the belief that naturalism and organicism were consistent with each other by reading Thomas Huxley's *Physiology* in his junior year. Fifty years later, in the autobiographical sketch "From Absolutism to Experimentalism," it was Huxley's *Physiology* that he said was the crucial model for successful understanding. He was never tempted by atomistic forms of empiricism; he never subscribed to ethical individualism in the social-contractarian sense, nor to the hedonist individualism that underlay Benthamite utilitarianism, but he was always ready to be a naturalist.

The path led through T. H. Green and Hegel. The importance of Green is almost impossible to overstate—even though Dewey himself always had reservations about Green that one imagines he must in part have imbibed from G. S. Morris. Morris's grasp of the history of German philosophy was sufficient for him to teach Dewey that Green was a Fichtian rather than a Hegelian. For all that, Deweyan conceptions of the good of the individual, and Dewey's "democratic" allegiances all his life, had a strongly Greenian flavor. Under the influence of Green, he suggested some remarkable intellectual possibilities. The most astonishing and most dazzling of these was his vision of the eventual transformation of Christianity into democracy:

> It is in democracy, the community of ideas and interest through community of action, that the incarnation of God in man (man, that is to say, as an organ of universal truth) becomes a living, present thing, having its ordinary and natural sense. This truth is brought down to life, its segregation removed; it is made a common truth enacted in all departments of action, not in one isolated sphere called religious.[13]

The thought was that the church would eventually cease to exist as a separate institution—a typically Deweyan thought—and would realize itself by dissolving back into the wider community. Eighty years later, a similar fascination with the idea of the *Aufhebung* (transcending) of state and civil society in the communist utopia was something of a commonplace among readers who had rediscovered the humanistic Young Marx, but in Dewey's oeuvre, the thought stands out because it comes with no account of its pedigree. Its flavor is not unlike that of much else of Dewey's thinking; for instance, in his account of the way the school is to be an aspect of the community's transmission of its own self-understanding rather than a separate institution. But for someone from a Congregationalist background, it was a bold move to suggest, even in passing, that the church should wither away when the Christian message came to fruition in the lives of a democratic people.

The specific attention to Christianity here, however, points to another important feature of Dewey's work. He always insisted on the religious quality of the democratic faith; however sociological his understanding of philosophy, he never doubted that democracy rested on "faith in the common man" and that that faith was a religious faith. The sense in which it was to be at once religious, philosophical, naturalistic, and scientific is one that takes some elucidation—but unless one accepts that that is what Dewey offered, one underestimates his reach. Dewey soon concluded that Green was an inadequate philosophical guide; he suffered from the Kantian tendency to divide the empirical selves that we fully were from the universal self that we aspire to be but can never wholly become. Dewey's antidualism repudiated even such a vestigial duality and insisted that we were already one with the universal and that we could rest securely in the sense that the world was not inimical to human aspiration. This was transformed into a reliance on our communal nature by the time he wrote *Human Nature and Conduct*, but the sentiment is much the same:

> With responsibility for the intelligent determination of particular acts may go a joyful emancipation from the burden of responsibility for the whole which sustains them, giving them their final outcome and quality. There is a conceit fostered by perversion of religion which assimilates the universe to our personal desires; but there is also a conceit of carrying the load of the universe from which religion liberates us. Within the flickering inconsequential acts of separate selves dwells a sense of the whole which claims and dignifies them. In its presence we put off mortality and live in the universal. The life of the community in which we live and have our being is the fit symbol of this relationship.[14] [Hence his distaste for the "lachrymose" quality of Russell's *Free Man's Worship*.]

Although Dewey's autobiographical essay "From Absolutism to Experimentalism" gives a general sketch of the transformation, it is more difficult to see on the ground. His famous essay "The Reflex Arc Concept in Psychology," however, deserves the place it has in all accounts of Dewey.[15] He wanted to repudiate *both* the idea—very prominent in his earlier *Psychology*—that the study of any empirical phenomena led inexorably to the conclusion that the world was mind, *and* his earlier belief that the only alternative to that metaphysical idealism was atomistic empiricism. But even when Dewey had lost faith in his argument that the world was essentially a Self, the thought that we could understand an organism by building up a system of stimulus-response connections remained incredible. The essay on the reflex arc argued, as Dewey always argued thereafter, that stimulus-response connections made sense only because they were embedded in an organism whose whole constitution was oriented to something like self-maintenance in a problematic environment.

"Experimentalism" was a label Dewey preferred to "instrumentalism," largely because he was less willing than William James to scandalize the believers in truth; "instrumentalism" suggests that truth is what it is good to believe, while "experimentalism" suggests only that a major part of all thinking is forming plans or projects for dealing with the world. Dewey's critics were never satisfied that he had given an answer to their questions about the relationship between our thoughts and the world to which those thoughts referred. They were clear that he did not believe in truth as correspondence to fact; but did he think that beliefs were true only to the extent that the world was as we believed it to be? Dewey's refusal to divide experience into subjective sensation and belief on the one side and objective fact of the matter on the other thoroughly irritated them. All the same Dewey insisted that all beliefs needed to be tested in experience, and that experience was not in any sense merely subjective. It was, so to speak, the experienced world. One has to be delicate here; although he was less scandalous than James, Dewey was less an "objectivist" than C. S. Peirce. While he was helped to stabilize his own ideas on "warranted assertability" by Peirce's 1878 paper "The Fixation of Belief," he set no store by the thought that there would be a final convergence on beliefs that, by virtue of that "end of the day" convergence, one would know to represent "objective" reality. So far as he was concerned, the progress of human understanding would be indefinite and perhaps infinite. Dewey was not hostile to the notion that truths were established, and he certainly was hostile to wishful thinking. Rather, we should take seriously the fact that the search for truth was problem driven and (perhaps most crucially) take seriously the injunction to turn from "the problems of philosophy" to "the problems of men" and look for fruitful kinds of cultural criticism rather than hope that a new philosophical wrinkle would resolve the dilemmas that had held up our predecessors.

What this means for Dewey as liberal and democrat is easy to list, but not easy to articulate as the connected philosophical argument he meant it to be. Dewey was best known—after 1899 and the publication of *The School and Society*—as the great theorist of the school as an institution central to a democratic society.[16] A characteristic production, it suggests a good many of the reasons why he was simultaneously regarded with near veneration by the mildly progressive and assailed with some fierceness by both the conservative and the more wildly radical. Much of what he thought about education might appeal to any reader, philosophically inclined or the reverse: for example, the claim that the school must itself be a community in which children learned to respect the rights of others while they learned to claim their own, his fastidiousness about balancing leadership from the instructor and intelligent acceptance of that leadership by the children, and his insistence that education had to become livelier and more interesting, less a matter of rote and more a matter of lived experience. Both friends and enemies, in fact, could seize upon such statements; those who think Dewey conceded too much to vocational education in the sense of job training will read those concessions into his defense of the practical, while those who think he conceded too little will read impracticality into his insistence that the meaning of the practical must be elicited by reflection—when what the enthusiasts for vocational training usually wished the schools to produce was quick and obedient workmen. According to taste, one could side with those who thought he conceded too much or too little to rote learning, to the authority of the teacher, and to almost any feature of applied pedagogy one cares to name. It is built into the "philosophy of the *via media*" that it should be vulnerable to those who want the brisker and simpler extremes[17]

The deeper interest of Dewey's educational views, at any rate for us, lies in the philosophical doctrines that all this embodied. In 1894, he sketched, in an amazing twenty-page letter, a syllabus for the Laboratory School that worked through practical and theoretical tasks and linked the tasks to the changing seasons, in a sort of Hegelian spiral; this unity of theory and practice, and the ascent to deeper understandings through seeing the practical implications of theory and the theoretical questions raised by practice, were supposed to carry the child through the various stages of school and beyond. It embodied one of his many antidualisms—in this case, the claim that there is no ultimate division between theory and practice—and was an image of his later understanding of science: that science properly was not the piling up of mathematical abstractions but the achievement of an increasingly organic understanding of the meaning of events. Whether six-year-olds really understood the full interest of the fact that metal rusting and food cooking are examples of the same oxidization process, one might wonder, but the thought is a fertile one. In practice, in the Laboratory School, Dewey's teachers taught in what a British observer fifty years later might have thought was an enlightened but not an astonishing fashion. Children would spend their first morning at school making boxes for their pens and pencils, and then go on to consider the geometry of what they had created; the sandbox would provide both recreation and an opportunity to think about three-dimensional geometry, the different properties of different materials, and so on. None of this was to be hurried; it is noticeable that Dewey balances his insistence that play must be shaped and directed by an adult understanding of where the child is heading with such statements as this:

The first [stage] extends from the age of four to eight or eight and a half years. In this period the connection with the home and neighbourhood life is, of course, especially intimate. The children are largely occupied with direct social and outgoing modes of action, with doing and telling. There is relatively little attempt made at intellectual formulation, conscious reflection, or command of technical methods . . . Hence in the second period (from eight to ten) emphasis is put upon securing ability to read, write, handle number etc., not in themselves, but as necessary helps and adjuncts in relation to the more direct modes of experience.[18]

Or, to put it somewhat uncharitably, a long time was spent on socialization before the three Rs were inflicted on the kids.

In fact, as everyone noticed, Dewey wrote next to nothing thereafter about the details of curriculum issues or pedagogical tactics and strategy. As I have said, pedagogy is subordinate to social theory, and social theory is subordinate to what one might call the *Lebensphilosophie* ("philosophy of life") of the modern world. This is not a complaint; Dewey was a philosopher, not a professor of pedagogy—except during the ten years at the University of Chicago when he was indeed professor of pedagogy as well as the head of the Department of Philosophy. The role of the philosopher was not so much to spell out ways in which students might be taught more or more enjoyably as to elucidate the place of education in the experience of the community. The opening paragraph of *School and Society* is an obvious illustration; in his first breath, Dewey insists on discussing education as a community concern, not an individual one: the community must treat all its children as devoted parents treat their individual children, and a society in which their education turns on a competitive struggle between parents seeking the best for their children one by one is a society in disarray. What he then goes on to discuss is not the mysterious quality that makes each child both typical and a unique individual—something to which Russell, for instance, comes closer—but the social background that sets the problems of modern education, such as urbanization, industrialization, the factory, the city, and the slum.[19]

The Mature Doctrine

Democracy and Education, published in 1916, was the culmination of such thinking. That book, he later said, "was for many years that in which my philosophy, such as it is, was most fully expounded," though he went on to observe that his philosophical critics had taken no notice.[20] It was certainly true that the conception of democracy to which the discussion of education was attached was philosophical rather than political; Dewey made almost no reference to institutions such as the vote, nor to such central liberal institutions as accessible law courts and an uncorrupt police and judiciary. The book makes many references to two basic liberal values—freedom and equality—and Dewey took it for granted, as he always had, that all arrangements in a democratic society should foster freedom and equality and that all its benefits and opportunities should be available to members of the society on a free and equal basis. Nonetheless, what made democracy democracy was, he said, "organic communication." Hilary Putnam has lately written admiringly of Dewey's "epistemological" justification of democracy; but what is striking is not so much that Dewey thinks of democracy as "organized intelligence," which he certainly does, as that he *defines* democracy in communicative terms. Democracy is less a political concept in this account than a social one, and its everyday descriptive meaning has been transmuted into something altogether richer; a democratic society is (though this is a thoroughly un-Deweyan thought) one in which the essence of sociability is actualized. A democratic society is one in which we can reveal ourselves to one another more deeply and more comprehensively than ever and, therefore, come to understand ourselves adequately in the process. There is no such thing as an adequate but solipsistic self-understanding; all self-understanding implies an actual or potential interlocutor, and only a thorough training in explaining oneself to others will provide the basis for any sort of skill in explaining oneself to oneself.[21] For any of this to happen, we have to be educated in such a way that we are self-aware and adept at communicating with our fellows; and for that to happen, we have to share an education with them. Here was the essence of Dewey's emphasis on making the school continuous with the community. The common school was thus, to put it in the simplest way, the basis of a democratic morality; but that slightly pious way of putting it is un-Deweyan, because by this time the usual notion of morality had also suffered a sea-change.

Readers of *Human Nature and Conduct* will remember that an ethics of rules and prohibitions, sanctions and requirements, was not what Dewey had in mind at all. Dewey's ethical pragmatism had, by the middle of the second decade of the twentieth century, become a democratic Aristotelianism, if that is not too sharp a contradiction in terms. Dewey starts from a double departure from what Bernard Williams has abused as "the institution called morality."[22] For him, the crucial point was that ethics was not primarily an individual matter; since that is a misleading formulation, one might better say that he thought that beginning with an image of ethical inquiry as a matter of the single individual searching for principles to guide his conduct, or scrutinizing his conscience for its judgments on his behavior, was to start in the wrong place. Ethics begins and largely ends in social practice and socialized habit. In other ways, this was not an anti-individualist argument. It is obvious enough that ethical decisions are made by individuals; they draw upon a common stock of solid judgment about what a satisfactory life in a satisfactory community is like, what behavior it requires, which questions are settled, and which open, but it is individuals who draw upon these resources when they engage in decision making. So the second innovation was to play down the separateness and distinctiveness of *moral* requirements, to remind us that ethics is a form of practical reasoning and that all forms of practical reasoning have much in common; they are not divided by nature into prudential, ethical, and aesthetic forms. (Indeed, though this is by the way, the division of theoretical and practical reason is by no means natural.) They all have a strong means-ends quality, and their goal is always—in formal terms—the satisfactory resolution of a problematic relationship between the organism and the environment. Ethics, like most interesting aspects of experience, is a form of problem solving. It is a general axiom of Dewey's account of experience and inquiry that without a problem, the organism would not think at all and would, in Dewey's analysis, scarcely have anything one could call an experience of the outside world. This is not to say that the problem is always what the layman would call a practical one; Dewey's analysis of the painting of Cézanne and Matisse is an analysis of problem solving, but the goal is a form of experience that he calls "consummatory," and the problem thus to enhance that experience rather than attain a further goal.[23]

Dewey's contribution to moral theory is, up to a point, to slide it toward the use of the concept of healthy functioning as its main organizing notion and away from treating either adherence to principle or the pursuit of utilitarian goals as such a notion.[24] Not to belabor the point, a radical and secular reinterpretation of Green might take one a long way toward such a position. A democratic society, in this view, is a healthy society; surprisingly, in view of Dewey and Russell's quarrelsome relations, the similarities with the views of Russell's *Principles of Social Reconstruction* are striking, though I know of no direct evidence that Dewey read the *Principles*, and I am sure that he would have found too much of the lachrymose tone of *A Free Man's Worship* in the text. But the emphasis on education, the secular religiosity, and the organic account of successful psychological functioning are strikingly alike.

War and Depression

If this picture is generally accurate, we can see why Dewey was, by 1914, an unusually persuasive philosophical voice. He was optimistic about the potential of society and fiercely critical about the distance between its potential and its actuality. The capacity to be optimistic in general and discontented in particular is one that Americans have always valued very highly. Dewey had it in the most developed possible form. He had a Ruskinian sense of the importance of work in human life that fit into the American self-image readily enough, but with the radical suggestion that work as actually engaged in in the factory or on the stock exchange frustrated the real purpose of work in the moral life and created ugliness rather than beauty. It was not surprising that he voted for Eugene Debs in 1912 but for Woodrow Wilson in 1916: an ideal socialism that closed the gap between utilitarian production and artistic creation was obviously a goal to pursue, but not to the neglect of the here and now. The ideal school was a long way off, but he could easily believe his daughter and Randolph Bourne when they told him "that the 'Gary Plan' put into operation by William A. Wirt in Gary, Indiana, was proof that . . . Dewey's philosophy could be put into practice on a large scale in the public schools."[25] And so it went, more or less across the board. The outbreak of World War I was the beginning of disillusionment.

The war severely damaged Dewey's poise. It is easy to overlook this, since he published *Democracy and Education* in the middle of the war, but before the entry of the United States, and ended the war by writing *Reconstruction in Philosophy* and *Human Nature and Conduct* with apparently undiminished confidence. But he was overtaken by events in the course of the war. He must, by war's end, have had grave doubts about his own response to Bourne's attacks on his views; and his reactions to Versailles and the rise of irrationalist politics in the twenties and thirties were inept. His defense of the "outlawry of war" movement was a pure case of willing the end and refusing to will the means, while *The Public and Its Problems* was infinitely less persuasive a defense of democracy than Walter Lippmann's two assaults, *Public Opinion* and *The Phantom Public*, had been criticisms.

Dewey's views, it is easy to say in hindsight, were ill adapted to the strains of war, a point that Bourne made with all the ferocity of disappointed discipleship. The vision of society in its "normal" state as a problem-solving organism did not assert, but nonetheless suggested, an evolutionary process in which ordinary social habit would suffice for everyday activities until some shock or crisis jolted us into rethinking our habitual behaviors. But this suggested that society was a unity within which the kinds of strains that were revealed by the "Americanization" programs of the war were invisible; Dewey wanted assimilation but not a "melting pot"; immigration presented the United States with problems of assimilation that might be difficult, but in the long run gave the nation its unique vitality. With the war, it became less easy to believe that American society, jolted out of its everyday existence, would respond imaginatively and productively to new demands. One can see Dewey getting stuck when responding to such militaristic proposals as conscripting all male school students as military cadets; he was, one imagines, simply hostile to it, but in order to oppose it, he largely had to stick to the issue of localism versus nationalism and object to its antifederal aspects. On the other hand, he remained more optimistic than not, and his "What Are We Fighting For?" of 1918 was characteristically upbeat in suggesting that for all the risk of postwar chaos and of a world divided into warring imperialist blocs, the message of the war was the priority of organization over property, the need to employ every able-bodied person when emergency arose, and the ability of nations to cooperate across national divides. If these lessons were incorporated in the peace, there would be a world "made safe for democracy and one in which democracy was firmly anchored." At this stage, early in

1918, he was optimistic about the possibilities of something like the League of Nations, too; indeed, he was sure that only under such a league would the world become safe for democracy.[26]

Nor was the war calculated to show pragmatism at its best, at any rate for anyone as intrinsically pacific as Dewey. For, in a situation in which it seemed obvious that American self-interest narrowly construed lay in keeping out of the European conflict, espousing absolute neutrality, and offering good offices as a mediator while the conflict was on and economic aid in reconstruction when it was over, Dewey would swallow neither the idea of an American alliance with the "antimilitarist" powers—czarist Russia looking particularly implausible as a specimen of that class, and imperialist France and Britain looking hardly more persuasive—nor the sort of realism that would have enjoined giving the cold shoulder to Britain. Dewey was reduced to arguing that the war demanded action, but it appeared to be action in general rather than action to achieve some particular end. Bourne was later to profess tremendous shock and outrage at Dewey's eventual espousal of the U.S. entry into the war on the Allied side, but it was not a surprising result. Once one was committed to the thought that a "cold neutrality" was intolerable, and that the United States had to somehow be active but not active militarily, one was a long way down the slippery slope. For as the war went on, it became harder and harder to see what activity was possible that would not eventually drag the country into the war. But it was not an attractive result, even though Dewey said, once it had happened, that he hoped that the result of engagement would be to speed up social development in the United States.

A good deal of Dewey's commentary while the war was on was unpersuasive, though this aspect of it was not, and in fact became commonplace about World War II. But his reactions to the illiberal, militaristic, chauvinistic, and antisocialist doings of the government, universities, mobs, and the press were deeply depressing. His first thought was that American illiberalism was "puppyish"; the country was not used to fighting major wars (itself an odd thought from someone whose father had served in the Union army), and so people got boisterously aggressive when pacifists protested.[27] He nearly lost the twenty-year friendship of Jane Addams by making silly remarks about the pacifists' lack of moral fiber, and did not much appease her by insisting that she did not lack moral fiber but most of her fellow pacifists did.[28] The activities of the president of Columbia University, Nicholas Murray Butler, who sacked dissident faculty without the least pretence of going through the procedures established for such purposes, woke him up to a degree, but whereas Charles Beard resigned from the university, Dewey limited himself to resigning from the disciplinary committee that had been slighted by his president. Late in the day, he saw that the effect of the war on American intellectual life really was disastrous, and said so boldly enough. Still, he seems even then not to have protested against such monstrous actions as the ten-year sentence imposed on Eugene Debs, nor thought that Wilson's refusal to commute it was as vindictive as it obviously was.

Once disillusioned, he swung to extremes. He opposed the Versailles Treaty on entirely decent and rational grounds, but also opposed American membership in the League of Nations and became a propagandist for the "outlawry of war" movement launched by Salmon Levinson. This proposed to make war an international crime, but as all its critics observed, it lacked any means to enforce the world's judgment of the criminal's misdeeds. Lippmann and others kept urging that only a system of collective security would be effective in repressing warmongering, but Dewey's response was that it was "contradictory" to employ war to put down war, an argument that, applied to domestic politics, would suggest that it was contradictory to give police the means forcibly to restrain muggers and murderers. His isolationism remained unwavering until Pearl Harbor; as late as 1940, he wrote an essay entitled "Whatever Happens, This Time Keep Out," which argued, rather as Russell's *Which Way to Peace?* had done, that the democracies would only lose their own civil liberties by embroiling themselves in war. Dewey had more than a touch of the traditional American contempt for the politics of the European states; World War I was an imperialist squabble that had lured America into what was falsely billed as a war for democracy, and his was very much a case of once bitten, twice shy. Once the war was on, he wrote nothing on its conduct or on the postwar settlement; interestingly enough, his most active contribution was to try to disillusion his countrymen about the Soviet Union: alliance with it might be needed to win the war, but this was a far cry from requiring us to think that Stalin was anything other than a murderous tyrant and the Soviet Union anything other than a slave society. That, on the whole, seems well judged, but it cannot be said that international relations were Dewey's strong suit.

Non-Marxian Radicalism

Nonetheless, Dewey's ideas about the demands of a modernized liberalism were as rational as anyone's could be. He swallowed too much of a too-simple class analysis and a too-simple materialism, and was thus ready to blame an ill-defined capitalist culture for just about everything he disliked, but he was steadily anti-Marxist, thinking that neither revolution nor violence was an effective means for the ends radicals had in mind. In this, he was much like Russell once more, as he says in his contribution to "Why I am Not a Communist." Unlike Russell, he had solid philosophical reasons for holding that view; because he refused to draw a sharp distinction between means and ends, it was easier for him than for Russell to insist that evil means corrupted the ends they were supposed to serve. The fundamental thought of most of his 1930s writing was that liberalism needed to be modernized. There were new threats to liberty, and therefore there were needed new forms of organization to overcome these threats. This is the argument of both *Individualism Old and New* and *Liberalism and Social Action*. It is often rather thin, but it is never silly nor hysterical. Nor is it vulnerable to charges of wishful thinking. The worst that one might have claimed a quarter century ago was that all of Dewey's opponents had died and that his work was therefore rather unsurprising. He had spent his energy attacking Marxist revolutionaries to his left and laissez-faire conservatives to his right, and in 1975, say, one might have thought both of them sufficiently discredited by events. After the Reagan counterrevolution, one might reasonably think differently. Even had there not been a Reagan counterrevolution, there is still some vitality in Dewey's implicit criticism even of the non-laissez-faire liberalism of theorists like John Rawls. Dewey complained that Lippmann, himself a critic of laissez-faire, failed to see what new liberalism demanded; that is, Lippmann's conception of freedom was too narrowly political. It did not look for freedom in the workplace as well as the polling booth. This is a charge that one might launch against modern non-laissez-faire liberals who are rightly impressed by the difficulties of squaring industrial democracy and civil liberties but who are too quick to renounce the former.

His view of politics was even then frequently inept; defending Dewey against the charge that he underestimated the novelty and effectiveness of the New Deal is a thankless task. It can be done: there is something to be said for the thought that Roosevelt's unprincipled willingness to try anything that would dig the United States out of the slump was not an example of Deweyan experimentalism but simply thrashing about. But to hold this view in the way Dewey did involved much more than pointing to a methodological crux. Dewey, for instance, believed as firmly as anyone that capitalism was simply doomed; nor was this the belief that capitalism defined just in simple nineteenth-century laissez-faire terms was doomed; rather, it was the belief that the capitalism of large, modern, government-assisted and government-regulated corporations was also doomed. Whether one ascribes the survival of this economic form to Roosevelt, Keynes, or the military buildup to World War II and the subsequent Cold War, its survival is hard to dispute. Against this sort of disproof by history, philosophical arguments must look thin.

All of this is without regard to his actual political good works. Here we may think the People's Lobby not particularly impressive, Westbrook notwithstanding, and Dewey's persistent hope for a third-party breakaway led by people like the Republican senator George Norris simply misguided. And one might wonder how to evaluate the adventures into which Sidney Hook led him; the Trotsky trial in Mexico City was a heroic adventure, and the Congress for Cultural Freedom a good idea in the late thirties, whatever it turned into after the war. But, Dewey's constant defense of liberalism in education was always admirable, and even if a great deal of what he wrote in the thirties and forties is of more or less antiquarian interest, one never feels embarrassed on his behalf.

Conclusion

In the end, the point we must cling to is that Dewey was a philosopher rather than a political activist; Dewey's philosophy is in all sorts of ways practically minded, and it is in some ways antiphilosophical; that is, it largely eschews what Dewey thought of as metaphysical inquiries, and it never allows the traditional formulation of philosophical issues to dictate present analysis. His claim that philosophy was a form of cultural criticism—in fact, the criticism of criticisms—conveys a sense of what he was after. Nonetheless, the obvious contemporary figures with whom he is to be compared would be Jürgen Habermas and Charles Taylor.

Dewey's conception of the demands of modernity is strikingly like Taylor's discussion of the ethics of authenticity: there is a form of individualism in ethics that is simply inescapable, but it is inescapable because we learn it in a particular sort of society, not because one could not imagine a different world, nor because it reflects a deep metaphysical loneliness or alienation from our fellow creatures.

Toward the end of his life, Dewey said that he wished he had emphasized the role of individuals in social and political life more than he had done; he felt that he had understated the role of individuals in innovating, and underestimated their role in reforming social and intellectual practices of whatever sort. One can hardly quarrel with his own assessment of his ideas, but it is not clear that he had very much for which to apologize. His argument had never been that reason works behind the backs of individuals, and for that kind of Hegelian teleology, he had no taste at all. It had always been that individual projects embody social resources; the individual must either be sheerly unintelligible to himself and to others or must appeal to a stock of concepts and a view of the evidence that he shares with others in his society. The modern project puts upon individuals the burden of making choices about the use of those resources that former societies may not have done, and certainly offers fewer transcendental comforts than the moral projects of earlier ages. But this is not to say that the society supplies the modern project with no resources; the point of an essentially comforting philosophy like Dewey's is to say what those are.

24

Pragmatism, Social Identity, Patriotism, and Self-Criticism

IN THIS ESSAY, I discuss the connection between Dewey's educational ideals, his philosophy more broadly, and his account of American identity. I contrast Dewey's ideas with those of some other pluralist writers of the period of World War I, not to say a great deal about these other writers, but to render Dewey's ideas more distinctive in their American political context. I should draw attention to a contrast implicit in what follows, but one I cannot here spell out in the detail it deserves. The contrast is between Dewey's conception of identity and that of German philosophy of the 1920s and 1930s. The contrast is interesting inasmuch as it is sometimes said that Dewey and Heidegger held similarly nonfoundationalist views of philosophy, held similarly skeptical views about traditional metaphysics, and in a sense agreed that philosophy had become the criticism of culture. The interest of the comparison, however, is that they were wholly at odds about what followed from this.

Just as Heidegger regarded Germans as a peculiarly philosophical people with a cultural mission to twentieth-century humanity, so Dewey, one might say, regarded Americans as the bearers of a special philosophical revelation; but the revelation was the antithesis of Heidegger's, for it was the revelation that there was no deep truth about the world or man's relations to Being. It was the success of Americans in *constructing* an identity and a world in which they could be at home that Dewey's pragmatism celebrated. Philosophically, this was what one might not implausibly describe as a "technological" view of our psychic and political situation and, therefore, the polar opposite of Heidegger's view of what philosophy taught about the mission of the German people and German culture.

The contrast could be elaborated at length. Whereas Heidegger and his followers detested modern science and its technological fruits, Dewey celebrated modern science and looked for a humane, nonexploitative form of social technology to build a better world. Whereas they thought of mankind as "thrown" into the quotidian world, forgetful of Being, Dewey thought of mankind as the builders of their own being, certainly looking for satisfactions deeper and more lasting than those that the utilitarians had spoken of, but insisting that here or nowhere is where we must build our new Jerusalem. Heidegger moved between two dramatically different views of politics: first hoping that a führer in politics might realize the vision of the philosophical führer that he aspired to be, and then wholly abandoning the political realm in favor of a quietist attachment to poetry and art. Dewey never deviated even momentarily from the view that liberal democracy was the only tolerable political creed in the modern world. He never thought that philosophers should turn their backs on politics. He never believed that they could do so, since philosophy inescapably reflected the political conditions of its creation. Yet this did not mean that the philosopher was more than a good citizen among other good citizens. In particular, he resisted any idea that we should look for a philosopher king and hand him absolute authority when we had found him.

For the purposes of this essay, however, the central contrast is ideological rather than personal. It is the contrast between a view of personal, social, and political identity that is forward looking, pluralist, this-worldly, and, in a broad sense, "constructivist" on the one side, and a view that is backward looking, unitary, otherworldly, and, in a broad sense, essentialist on the other. The German attachment to a conception of themselves as a "primordial" people, like the Greeks of the classical age but quite unlike the mongrelized English or French, was the sort of account of identity that Dewey deplored. But this is very far from being a contrast between Americans' and Germans' views of themselves; it is no part of this essay's case that Dewey embodied the American vision and Heidegger the German vision. In many ways, Dewey's views were always a minority taste in the United States. The contrast lies more importantly—more importantly for someone whose interests lie where Dewey's lay in American politics—between different understandings of American identity. Having set out these accounts of American identity, I shall end somewhat paradoxically, for I shall end by suggesting that Dewey showed that we might do better to stop thinking about identity altogether, that he offered a way for Americans to be more secure in their identity by not taking the concept of identity seriously.

Pragmatism is often said to be peculiarly American; this is usually said by way of abuse, and has often been a complaint based on the vulgar idea that pragmatism is the philosophy of utilitarianism and big business—this was the charge leveled by Bertrand Russell and later by Julien Benda, for instance. It was much resented by Dewey, and quite properly, for he was an unrelenting critic of American capitalism; and even in his mild, prepragmatist, Idealist young manhood, he had insisted that the achievement of political democracy was both a nonstarter and a morally inadequate goal unless it was accompanied by a "democracy of wealth." Marxists denounced pragmatism for much the same reasons and induced the same irritated reaction in Dewey. It is, even on its face, a slightly mad complaint to make against Dewey. It would be almost equally absurd as a complaint against C. S. Peirce and William James, however. Peirce was anything but an efficient manager of his own and others' affairs, while James denounced the cult of bigness and complained memorably about the "bitch-goddess success." My reading of pragmatism characterizes it as American only in the sense that it is a distinctively late or post-Hegelianism originating in the United States; but the affinities of pragmatist social theory with the ideas of L.T. Hobhouse, Émile Durkheim, and, more recently, Jürgen Habermas are not difficult to spot. I have argued elsewhere, and I shall argue here, that pragmatism is "modern" and "North Atlantic" rather than uniquely "American." Certainly, Dewey drew conclusions about the peculiar fate of twentieth-century Americans from these more universal premises, and he was a devout, unreflective believer in American exceptionalism. Nonetheless, his intellectual focus was on modernity rather than on "being American."

Not all objectors to pragmatism have thought that its objectionable features reflected the essence of American culture. In the 1910s and 1920s, an American version of Russell's complaint was leveled against Dewey, but this complaint was that Dewey's pragmatism accepted the bad, capitalist, conformist surface of American culture and failed to do justice to its livelier and more oppositional depths. Lewis Mumford and Waldo Frank, in much the same frame of mind in which Randolph Bourne had assailed Dewey's support of the U.S. entry into World War I, denounced what Mumford called "the pragmatic acquiescence," a phrase that caught their common conviction that pragmatism was a philosophy of means rather than ends and that it took an unexamined conception of its ends, such as they were, from the surface of American capitalist culture.

The thought of these cultural critics was that pragmatism was disabled by its relentless emphasis on practice and "adjustment" from giving an adequately critical account of its relationship to the surrounding culture. In that view, pragmatism's overemphasis on the "practical" left pragmatists unable to stand back from their times in order to criticize them as savagely as they demanded. This is a sharper and more interesting criticism than the misdirected attack on pragmatism as an ideological prop to capitalism. These complaints and rebuttals raise a doctrinally interesting question that the work of Hegel many years before Dewey, and the work of our own contemporaries like Michael Walzer and Charles Taylor today, also raises: how far can we be as emphatic as the pragmatists were, and as Walzer and Taylor today are, about the social debts of social critics—about what Hegel posed as the demand that we find the rose in the cross of the present—while still stressing their role as critics? In what sense is it true that we must find our ideals in our existing social setting?

There are thus three themes in this essay. The first is the background of Dewey's discussion of "Americanization" and American identity, which I sketch briefly by rehearsing some of the anxieties of Randolph Bourne, Herbert Croly, and Horace Kallen, against which Dewey's views become clearer and more intelligible. I suggest here that Dewey offers a philosophical rather than a simply sociological account of national identity in a culturally pluralist society and try to say to what that amounts. My second aim is then to raise some questions about how far Dewey's pragmatism, with its emphasis on the sociality of thought and individuality, can sustain a loyal but critical stance toward our "own" society. I argue that Dewey's pragmatism is a form of "naturalized left-Hegelianism" that sustains the same project as Habermas's defense of modernity and, on the same basis, of a communicative account of the self. It is, for that reason, less American than "modern," less midwestern than mid-Atlantic. American identity, therefore, is to be understood in terms of a modern rather than a more local identity. It thus appears that the "society" from which we derive our ideals and in terms of which we criticize local cultural, economic, and political practices is not the here and now of any particular nation-state, but the latent community of self-aware and productively intelligent persons that any particular state shelters only partially. Modernity is inescapable; Chicago is rather easily escapable, and the 1915 United States hardly less so. My third aim is to end self-destructively or perhaps on a note of self-transcendence: I shall argue that we should *not* ask questions about American (or any other) "identity," even though I agree that the inhabitants of the United States should devote themselves to the realization of the American project—as one local and admirable instance of the project of modernity. I claim that this is, in fact, Dewey's argument, too. This essay thus combines history, philosophy, and lay sermon—a mode practiced with some success by all the writers I discuss here.

Ambivalence about "Americanization"

Herbert Croly's *The Promise of American Life* is often described as the manifesto of Progressivism, but this is not wholly apt. When it was published, in 1908, the Progressive movement had already achieved most of the reforms for which it was known: improved city government, meritocratic civil service recruitment, and anticorruption measures. Croly was more plausibly described—by Theodore Roosevelt—as a theorist of "new nationalism." New nationalism was not nationalism at all in the European sense; it had nothing to do with trying to make the nation coextensive with the ethnos; nothing to do with blood, race, and soil; and except for one unguarded remark, nothing to do with the thought that the nation gave military expression to a particular culture. It was an essentially liberal nationalism. Its guiding thought was—as its title suggested—that the United States existed more as a promise than as a fact; hence, that there was indeed a project of Americanization yet to be accomplished, though not the project that nativists and anti-immigrant groups proposed. They wanted to impose an image of Americanness on new arrivals and to shut out those whom they thought unfit for that treatment. He thought that the vast territory of the United States had yet to be permeated by an American culture, economy, and politics. That there was in existence a project of this sort, he did not doubt, but American life was a promise, not a manifest destiny. The outcome of American social, political, and economic history was anything but manifest. Most importantly, the fulfillment of the promise was threatened by the nature of the promise itself. The promise was a promise of individual emancipation, and it was an egalitarian promise; its aim was to allow each individual to realize himself or herself in this new and astonishingly open environment. It thus bypassed questions of identity by assuring everyone who came to this new nation that he or she could make of himself or herself whatever the heart desired. But how the American was to know what to desire or how the promise was to be fulfilled was another matter.

Croly's argument throughout *Promise* was that the individualism of a rights-based political system had thus far thwarted the achievement of the goals that the founders had set out, a thought in which he anticipated the so-called communitarians of the 1980s by seventy years. The founders had, as every American schoolboy knew, split over the question of the national government's role in controlling and promoting economic activity and the development of the vast unexplored hinterland of the thirteen states. Croly's genius as a publicist was to coin the thought that we must "pursue Jeffersonian goals by Hamiltonian means." The villain of American political life was Andrew Jackson, who had treated the ideal of equality as the principle that every snout should have equal access to the public trough, and the only political leader adequate to American life had been Abraham Lincoln, who alone saw how to employ the entire force of the federal government in pursuit of an ideal of equal membership of the American people. An individualism that asked only to be left to one's own devices was morally obnoxious and increasingly at odds with the industrialized and urbanized place that late nineteenth- and early twentieth-century America had become. Croly had been brought up in a Comtist household and had been a student of Josiah Royce at Harvard; *rugged* individualism would have been repudiated in both places, though it was only from Royce that he could have learned that the life of personality was a moral goal.

An interesting and complicated aspect of Croly's work, in light of Dewey's semi-socialism, was his reaction to the tensions between capital and labor that were a marked feature of American economic and social life in the last years of the nineteenth and the first years of the twentieth centuries. Where many critics of capital hankered after a return to the agrarian simplicities of the eighteenth century or wanted the breakup of the new corporations, Croly followed in the track marked earlier by the work of Edward Bellamy: the new corporate forms were a response to the need for the organization of production and should not be destroyed, but nationalized. The struggling trade unions that had been hampered by means both legal and extralegal and had found themselves constantly in the middle of the most violent conflict with the employers should neither be destroyed nor be encouraged to wage class warfare; they should be understood as the latent form of a national organization of labor. When Croly looked at the way the contemporary railroads conspired to fix their charges, he did not suggest trust-busting to force competition on the railroads, but a national railroad system.

That still leaves the question of what sort of nation was this project to sustain. What was American about American life and its promise? How did Croly's "new" nationalism relate to the nationalism with which Europeans are all too familiar? The answer is surprisingly hard to come by. At one level, there is no difficulty; the slogan "Jeffersonian goals by Hamiltonian means" sums up the project in a simple though mildly vulgar fashion. But *Promise* does something difficult and perhaps slightly incoherent. Croly told Americans that the American state was fifty years behind the times and absurdly slow to attend to tasks that European states had long been performing. But he wanted, in the process, to emphasize the need for a distinctively American form of national consciousness. The United States was not to play "catch-up," but to overleap its time. Still, the image of what the United States might be was European in one important respect: Americans had to bring their own energies to achieving a national culture whose character was modeled on what Croly admired about France and Germany.

Croly was, thus, not a theorist of the peculiarity of American identity in quite the same way as Bourne, Kallen, and Dewey—all of them good friends at various points and all of them contributors to Croly's *New Republic*. He was not a pluralist in the ways they were. Croly's vision of American nationality emphasized the thought that the American nation would become more a nation as the activities of the state become more intense and more adequate to the needs of society. What matters about that thought is essentially negative: Croly did not raise the question whether the strikingly multiethnic and multicultural quality of the United States ought to be brought into the center of his picture of American life and its ambiguous promises. He was not a theorist of the melting pot nor a conservative inclined to complain about the hyphenated quality of the Americanness of new immigrants. Nor was he simply a believer in the old picture of the United States as a branch operation of the English *mission civilisatrice*. Not forced assimilation, the melting pot, or multiculturalism, but the interesting thought that the American contribution to national identities ought in some fashion to be the creation of a modern nationalism in the country that of all great nations had thus far been able to avoid thinking of itself in such terms. The terms of this argument, however, were functionalist rather than pluralist. This is worth emphasizing here because Dewey, too, was as much a functionalist as Croly about the relationship of the state to social life, but was a much more deeply committed pluralist about the nature of that underlying social basis. If nothing else, that set Dewey a more difficult task than Croly when the time came for him to explain in what sense the United States could be *e pluribus unum*, could build a common life out of strikingly diverse elements.

The discussion of pluralism occurred some seven or eight years after the publication of *Promise*. It took place in the context of the panic-stricken

"Americanization" campaigns that were sparked by the outbreak of World War I. Although the United States was not involved and initially seemed unlikely ever to become involved, the almost-immediate effect of the war was to raise questions about the loyalties of the vast flood of immigrants that had poured into the country between 1880 and the beginning of the war. This caught Croly and the friends who were about to work on the *New Republic* entirely off guard. I say only a very little about Dewey, Kallen, and Bourne in this connection, since our subject is not the war, but what the war provoked—Americanization. Descriptively, Dewey is the least interesting of the trio because he is the least concrete; Kallen later and rightly observed that Dewey was a less compelling observer of cultural diversity than Bourne. Analytically, and theoretically, he was more ambitious and more complicated than they, and he raises more puzzling questions than they. It is simplest to follow the argument in three set-piece discussions: Randolph Bourne's "Transnational America," published in the *Menorah Journal* in 1916; Horace Kallen's "Democracy versus the Melting Pot," published in two installments in the *Nation* in 1915 (though his postwar "Americanization" in *Culture and Democracy*, where the essay is reprinted and expanded, is in some ways even more striking); and John Dewey's "Nationalizing Education," published in the *Journal of Education* in 1916.

Their interests and views overlapped but were not identical. Bourne was a cultural critic in a way that Dewey hardly could have been; he was interested in popular culture in a way Dewey was not, and he was violently hostile to the humdrum existence of the American lower middle class in a way that Dewey would have thought snobbish. Still, he was a student of Dewey's and a great admirer until they quarreled over America's entry into the war. Like Croly, Dewey, and Kallen, Bourne agreed that what the United States offered its new arrivals was above all freedom—emancipation from an old life, and opportunity to do what they could in a new world. What Bourne feared was that immigrants had found only an "external" freedom; they were for the first time able to do as they liked, but they did not have the internal and expressive freedom that could come only from living out their own cultural life. In other words, they got their freedom only on terms, and the terms were acquiescence in the dominant culture of the country they entered. Bourne was a sharp critic of the monolithic quality of existing "English" culture: "The Anglo-Saxon element is guilty of just what every dominant race is guilty of in every European country, the imposition of its own culture on the minority peoples." No liberal-minded person wanted this monolithic result, as Bourne took for granted. He slyly observed that the most purely Anglo-Saxon and untouched part of the country was the South; and writing for a Jewish journal, he could take it for granted that his readers did not think of the South as a moral ideal. To drive the point home, he asked them to compare the southern states with Wisconsin, where a combination of German culture and "outwardly and satisfactorily American" habits prevail.

This led Bourne to the claim that haunts observers of American life still as they look at the effects of migration on migrants from the poorer regions of Latin America and Asia. America, said Bourne, knows how to *de*culturate but not how to *ac*culturate. This was not a wholly original thought with Bourne. Although Bourne's interests lay in literary and other forms of culture in a way that Dewey's did not, it was still true that Jane Addams and John Dewey had observed in Chicago during the 1890s that deracination had happened, but not a corresponding process of reracination. Much of Dewey's educational theory, formulated as it was under the impact of those years in Chicago, reflected a concern for what you might call the reracination of urban children and migrant children alike. Although Dewey was by no means reactionary, nor a conservative filled with nostalgia for rural life, he nonetheless believed that compared to an urban child, a farm child had an easier time growing up—learning the rhythms of life, the skills of the farmer, and, along with these, the emotional and moral attachments that made farm life so satisfying. The urban child, thought Dewey, had a much harder time of it; industrial life had a much less visible unity and coherence, the linkage of production and consumption was more indirect, and much of daily life was conducted out of sight and far away. It was for that reason that he so emphasized the role of the school in socializing the urban child into an understanding of his or her society's material existence and so emphasized the need to integrate work and play at school.

Dewey was nothing like as eloquent as Bourne about the conditions of the unintegrated adult. One might, for all that, complain that Bourne's statement of *how* the multicultural, or, as he said, "transnational," life was to be led was decidedly thin: the goal must be "the good life of personality lived in the environment of the Beloved Community," said Bourne, and it was the task of the younger intelligentsia of America to give an account of it. It is obviously not to be laid against Bourne that he fell victim to the influenza epidemic that ravaged the United States and most of the rest of the world at the end of the war. All the same, this gesture toward the notion that Josiah Royce had put into circulation, as though it was as usable by radical young intellectuals as it had been by the much more conservative Royce, raised more questions than it answered. Thin as this vision was, it made it quite clear that as against European nationalisms and European cultural unity, the American promise and the American task was to develop unity in pluralism. America's distinctive contribution to the world was to be a coherent cultural pluralism.

Horace Kallen, too, struck some convincing blows during a very rough time, though he was neither as philosophically imaginative as Dewey nor as culturally imaginative as Bourne. His essay "Democracy versus the Melting Pot" was a head-on assault on the political aspect of Americanization. By 1915, it had long been a complaint against the newcomers to the United States that they refused to assimilate, refused to give up their original languages, eating habits, religions, and the rest of it; they were, it was said, "hyphenated Americans" rather than real Americans. Italian-Americans or Jewish-Americans were not good enough for the advocates of 100 percent Americanness. It was hyphenation that Kallen defended against the enthusiasts for a monolithic America. Critics of unfettered immigration also objected to the squalor of immigrant communities and to the way the presence of immigrants allowed unscrupulous employers to drive down wages and force their workers to work in hideous and unsafe surroundings. Kallen claimed that this kind of humanitarianism was skin deep, that what troubled the critics of immigration was "not really inequality; what troubles them is *difference*."

Kallen argued that the fact of being an immigrant community—or a community of immigrant communities—was what set the American political agenda. Radical pluralism was the only hope of the Left. The socialist wish to use the power of the state to reduce economic inequality made sense in Europe but much less sense in the United States, where the entire political culture was against it. Socialist ideals were beside the point in the United States: the interesting line of cleavage on the liberal side of politics lay between people who thought the problem was the battle between monopolistic captains of industry and old American ideals of equal opportunity (so that the issue was only that of getting immigrant workers into decent jobs with decent pay and conditions) and those who thought that change, even that sort of change, hung on accepting cultural pluralism as a fact of life to live with and make something of—Kallen, of course, belonged to the latter persuasion. He did not oppose meliorist class-based politics, but insisted that they must be practiced differently from anything offered by Woodrow Wilson on one side or his socialist critics on the other. Kallen felt some ambivalence about "Americanness." He took up the conservative complaint against hyphenated Americans and turned it into a term of praise. German-Americans, Jewish-Americans, Irish-Americans were all of them entirely acceptable Americans. The interesting question is how long a productive balance between the two sides of the hyphen can be preserved; if it is only a transitional state that will give way to something more monolithic, how much attention does it deserve? If it is what makes American identity distinctive but is doomed to perish, what should we think of "American-American" identity?

A few years ago, Michael Walzer followed in Kallen's footsteps and gave a cheerful account of American identity as such a hyphenated identity, later embodied in his *What It Means to Be an American*. In Walzer's view, much like Kallen's, the cultural attachments of hyphenated Americans lay to the left of the hyphen, and their political attachments to the right. So long as hyphenated Americans subscribed to the political rules, they might lay their cultural allegiances where they chose. This is the note struck by Kallen in his optimistic moments. But Kallen also shared the anxieties of Bourne and Croly, Dewey and Jane Addams. He feared that the necessities of everyday life would steadily erode immigrants' attachments to the languages, religions, cultures, and family life they brought with them and provide nothing with the same richness and depth in return. If the common elements of American life—the English language, mass media, public school education, and an unspecific spirituality—are used only for instrumental reasons by groups that need to get on in the world, immigrant communities will lose the attachments that gave their lives shape before and will be no better than illiterate in the adopted culture.

Dewey was less anxious than Kallen and Bourne—than Croly, too, for that matter—because he had more confidence that twentieth-century America could weave a new culture out of the ingredients it had acquired from elsewhere and had generated from within in the previous two and a half centuries. Its relations with the cultures of Europe and Asia would no doubt be intricate, but that was the nature of the modern world and not something to be flinched from. One point worth bearing in mind is the need to keep some grip on the facts about cultural loss and gain. Those of us who have derived pleasure from the literary criticism of Lionel Trilling and Harold Bloom will surely wish to say that the United States has, at any rate, *permitted* the offspring of immigrant European Jews to do great things with English writers. Too much discussion of simple deculturation ignores the reality that people who lost the cultural resources of deprived eastern European villages acquired in due course the resources of the whole English-speaking world. By the same token, the villages doubtless lost something with the departure of their brightest inhabitants, but lost far more from the economic and political changes that swept through their world in the first half of this century. Moreover, the immigrants whose deracination was lamented may well have had a pretty tenuous attachment to the culture of their native countries. The children of former peasants almost certainly became more literate in English than they had been in their native tongue, and the children of already cultivated aliens added another culture to the ones to which their parents were attached. Dewey was probably right to devote about as much attention to the children of the American cities as to migrants.

When Dewey contemplated the issue of Americanization, he distinguished good and bad nationalism, very much as Bourne had done before him: good nationalism would create a distinctively American culture and be consistent with internationalism; bad nationalism would repress internal differences and be bellicose. Dewey was, of course, perfectly aware that in real life the phenomenon of nationalism does not come so neatly labeled. His philosophy was, after all, built around a refusal of what he described as "apart thinking." That, however, allowed him a useful opening; bad nationalism was a form of apart thinking, dividing the world into ourselves versus foreigners, the loyal versus the disloyal, and so on. A characteristically Deweyan touch was his claim that American nationality was actually constituted by democracy; an undemocratic America would be a contradiction in terms. This was a doubly elegant stroke; on the one hand, it meant that American ultranationalists, who were prepared to use undemocratic means to enforce one national character, literally did not know what they were doing, since an undemocratic nationalism destroyed just what it sought to create, and, on the other, it meant that democrats need not fear a proper American self-assertion. A second Deweyan stroke was his insistence that the hyphen is "good when it attaches, bad when it separates." This was an obvious implication of Dewey's deepest methodological allegiances and his hostility to "apart thought." Separating what ought not to be separated was the characteristic vice of philosophers: mind *versus* matter, ethics *versus* prudential calculation, logic *versus* empirical inquiry were some of the dichotomies he tried to subvert. Now, as we see, he could apply it to political attachments. By this time—1916—Dewey was the world's most famous educational theorist; it was anxiety about the misuse of the educational system for polemical and propaganda purposes that led him to write this essay and others in defense of pluralism in American education.

The role of education, Dewey argued in "Nationalizing Education," was not to inculcate one canonical image of American identity, but to foster mutual respect among the diversity of cultures and peoples that make up the American people. As to how to do it, he had nothing very surprising to say, as he himself was at some pains to emphasize. It was not, after all, an arena in which very astonishing ideas were to be looked for; what was needed was a commitment to a humane pluralism. So far as curriculum and pedagogy are concerned, Dewey suggested, plausibly enough, that one obvious way ahead was to teach a view of American history that stressed the positive contributions to American society of the successive waves of immigrants. Eighty years later, this seems absolutely right, even though it raises some exceedingly awkward questions about just what tone we must adopt in encouraging this mutual exchange of narratives. "Immigration" is not exactly what happened to Africans who were brought to America as slaves, and even Dewey would have been hard put to find a wholly convincing way of telling the story of the African American contribution to American history in such a way that it was neither a tale of passivity and victimization nor a Pollyannaish celebration of the successes of the downtrodden.

The object, however, was clear. Other nations formed their conceptions of national identity around descent, commonality of blood, language, or residence. They defined their position in the world by contrast with their neighbors and (generally) enemies. American identity was not so formed. It was future oriented rather than past oriented; it could not be based on commonalities of kinship, residence, or even—initially—language, since no such commonalities existed. It had to be formed out of a conscious intention to combine for the purposes for which the United States was an apt setting. Hence, Dewey's view that the classroom would be a plausible setting for the various tribes that make up the American people to bring their contributions to the common table. I mention now what I shall argue later, that if identity is essentially a backward-looking concept, Dewey's forward-looking conception of philosophy suggests that what others interpret as identity, he has reinterpreted as a commitment to a particular conception of the future. In short, American identity is a question of the American project.

484 • Chapter 24

Sociology and Philosophy

If our evaluation of these ideas turned on the liveliness of their accounts of the multiplicity of cultures that migrants brought to the United States, Bourne would surely catch our eye. If we were concerned only with giving a cogent defense of moderate pluralism, Kallen would bear off the prize—he did not fear the cultural incoherence that hyphenation brings with it, and he had a lively common sense and a splendid hatred of oppression and bullying, a combination that can take one a long way. To see why Dewey is the most philosophically interesting of the four writers I have mentioned, one must understand that Dewey tried to do something harder than Bourne, Kallen, or Croly. Dewey believed in Americanization and in multiculturalism simultaneously. That is, he believed it was possible to create an American identity that was distinctive and yet not at odds with the plural cultural resources on which it would draw. He found it possible to believe this because he understood all forms of identity as the production of relative unity from plural ingredients, and individual personal identity as an interpersonal and indeed a social construct. This allowed him to escape the usual questions about identity; and it gave him not only an antiessentialist sociology, but also a communicative and plural ethics.

Dewey followed George Herbert Mead in thinking that the "I" emerges only by distinction from the "Me," and that getting clear about this difference is an achievement of which we are capable only in a social setting. Individuality is a social achievement. Only a merely biological identity is a gift of nature, even though it is an important fact that biologically differentiated individuals are experiential centers that can come to reflect on and to "own" their specific streams of consciousness. That is, all sentient creatures experience the world, but only humans "have" experiences. But identity in any interesting sense is an accomplishment, and perhaps a pretty intermittent one; Dewey was an anti-Cartesian who held that for the most part, thought occurs without a thinking ego. Once he turned to social interaction, Dewey anticipated by eighty years Habermas's move from a problematic of the subject to a problematic of communication. The interesting consequence is that Dewey demands more unity from American identity than many pluralists, while he insists as fiercely as they that this must be a unity in plurality. The idea that Americans can happily be nothing more than hyphenated Americans thus will not satisfy Dewey. But he thought the image of a melting pot was actively repulsive. What he wanted to do, as a good, though lapsed, Hegelian ought to have wanted, was to give an account of unity in difference.

What is sociology in Kallen and Bourne is thus philosophy in Dewey. That is a simple claim. Its elucidation is more difficult. The first element in that elucidation is to take seriously the fact that Dewey thought *Democracy and Education* was his most important book. He maintained that it was for many years the fullest exposition of his philosophical position that he had produced, and that his critics had failed to understand this. It made the argument (much resisted by philosophers) that all philosophy is the philosophy of education. The proper method of philosophy is genetic and naturalistic, and its aim is to sophisticate our understanding of how we acquire the mature problem-solving competencies of intelligent adults in a great variety of contexts. Which is to say that it inquires into how we have been educated, and it must have at least an implicit concern with how we might be better educated than we are.

This is unexceptionable, but raises a question that leads to the second elucidatory point. How do philosophy and democracy relate to each other? The two most distinguished philosophies of education in Dewey's eyes were Plato's defense of the need to train "guardians" to act as good shepherds of their uncomprehending charges, and Rousseau's insistence that we must protect young Émile from a society that has been corrupted by the growth of the arts and sciences. Dewey's educational philosophy was avowedly intended as a response to Plato and Rousseau. He wanted neither shepherds nor social isolates, but members of a community. That this was to be a democratic community involved a difficult move. He defined democracy not as a matter of voting systems or political mechanisms, but in social terms, namely, as "organic communication on free and equal terms." Deep, free, and unfettered communication was the essence of social interaction, so in a fashion oddly reminiscent of the young Marx, we find Dewey explaining democracy not merely as the essence of the political, but as the essence of the social. Dewey thus explains both moral growth and the nature of democracy as functions of our capacity for "associated living"—neither an elite of shepherds nor a scattering of isolated, uncontaminated individuals. Education allows us to draw on our own resources and those of the whole society in order to open ourselves to one another and indeed to ourselves. This is the moral perspective that underlies Dewey's view that the only goal of moral action is "growth," just as it underlies his view that the moral motive is always the enhancement of personality.

The third clue to Dewey's purposes is his emphasis on modernity; we live, like it or loathe it, in the modern world. Just where "the modern world" is is never quite clear in Dewey, since its indicia range from the achievements of the scientific revolution of the seventeenth century to the disorganization of the capitalist industrial world of the nineteenth. But the nature of modernity is easy enough to discern: social and geographic mobility, economic and moral individualism, subjectivity, secularism, a faith in the capacity of science to resolve the problems that beset our world, and, on the downside, the thing that Dewey was perhaps most anxious to cure, a sense of being abandoned by God, or, in another jargon, a sense of "alienation." The one thing Dewey never added to this list separates him from many of his contemporaries: the conviction that our sexual anxieties are deeper and more fundamental than all others was one he never accepted.

How did Dewey integrate his account of modern identity and his account of the stresses of modernity? The answer is that his entire career was an attempt to do it; both his more arcane philosophical work and his political journalism preach his vision of how to make ourselves at home in the modern world by making the world fit to be our home. "Modern society" is the fundamental analytical category of this enterprise; "democracy" is the cultural—and then, by inference, the political—character of such a society. America is not the only home of modern society, but it has a privileged position in one respect. It is where the modern condition is least obscured by everything else we have inherited. This is not an unmixed blessing: in the 1930s, Dewey wished that the United States had possessed a Labor Party like the British Labour Party so as not to have to submit to the distracted lunging and retreating that he thought Franklin Roosevelt engaged in during the implementation of the New Deal. Still, it was only a passing hankering, for his considered view was always that the politics of the Labour Party would not work in the United States. Nor did he regret this. Class politics seemed to him to be bad for a society, so he would not have thought the United States would have done better to inherit the British class system even if it had brought the Labour Party with it.

Modernity is, however, a philosophical as much as a sociological concept, because the investigation of modern thought is a philosophical activity—it is a large part of the social criticism of social criticisms that Dewey decided philosophy had now become. The implication for a pluralist conception of the social world now becomes clearer, but it still remains hard to make fully articulate: against his Hegelian youth, Dewey repudiates the search for an Absolute; but in the spirit of that youth, he hangs on to the aspiration after a society in which fully transparent self-understanding and communication are possible. Such a world does not obliterate differences of perspective and contribution, but it possesses a kind of unity in which devotees of a cheerfully empiricist and sociological pluralism might take little interest. In that sense, Dewey really was a theorist of Americanization, since he wanted to identify the American project with the achievement of a novel form of emancipation, one that did not threaten to leave us deracinated even while it enabled us to think more coherently and scientifically about just what sort of soil we were rooted in.

The New Deweyans

Since the mid-1980s, arguments over "identity" and "difference" have spread into every area of American political discussion. Their original academic home was commonly in literary theory rather than political theory, but issues of cultural attachment came to have considerable political resonance during the 1980s. In Canada, there has been the perennial issue of Quebec's "particularity" and the new demands of Inuits and other aboriginal peoples. In the United States, old anxieties over immigration have revived, but they have now been linked to a new despair over the difficulties of the African American poor. A new assertiveness on the part of women, and more marginally on the part of gays and lesbians, has made up in intellectual passion for anything it has lacked in political consequence. From the perspective of such cultural conflicts, the philosophical defense of human rights offered by conventional liberalism, whether John Rawls's or Robert Nozick's, seems sociologically unsophisticated. The most interesting account of these strains, however, has not been offered from either of the extremes—that is, by writers defending an "old" universalist liberalism against the theorists of difference or by the defenders of the "new" politics of difference themselves. The most interesting response is Richard Rorty's claim that the existence of cultural diversity is a brute fact about our sort of society, but that it should not, for all that, be allowed to subvert the politics of the "old" liberalism.

In a 1993 essay in the *New York Times* and in a longer and more considered earlier essay, "Two Cheers for the Cultural Left," Rorty has argued that the American academy is *American*, that the professoriate has a patriotic duty to articulate the "uplifting stories" of traditional American historiography. This distresses critics on the left, against whom, of course, this claim is directed. Dewey had a good many resources with which to deal with the difficulty of finding a position from which to acknowledge an American identity—or rather to finesse the question of its existence and its character—while retaining a critical stance toward American practice. Rorty has fewer. The critics' question is simple enough: how do we give sufficient weight to the less uplifting elements in the American narrative, and how do we square our belief in the rights of all manner of people who do not feel that theirs has been a particularly "uplifting" story with the patriotic and friendly wish that the American story should be their uplifting story, too? My view, for what it is worth, is that the late twentieth-century United States needs a large dose of old-fashioned social democracy, and that this would do much more to make the "uplifting story" acceptable than any number of stories about stories; this was, of course, Dewey's view, too.

The American project, to which Dewey was devoted, is the project of making the uplifting story come true. It is a story about the possibility of combining cultural plurality with political unity, allowing the widest opportunity the world has known thus far but somehow escaping anomie and alienation, and so familiarly on. One virtue of Dewey is that he does not divert the defense of the American project through anxieties about American identity. Identity is an unnecessary intervening step in the argument from the virtues of the American project to its claim on our allegiances. I share Rorty's irritated conviction that prosperous American professors should speak more kindly of their country's ambitions—and as harshly as is proper about its failure to live up to them. But as a resident alien who is anything but an alienated resident, I emphasize in conclusion that it is not because Rorty's readers are Americans that they should join in, but because the project is rationally and morally compelling, and they happen to be geographically well-positioned to promote it, and they are supported by the taxes and tax concessions of large numbers of people whose consent to what the intelligentsia gets up to was never asked, and they ought to feel some reciprocal obligation.

2 5

Deweyan Pragmatism and American Education

Introduction

THIS ESSAY HAS three purposes: to show the connection between John Dewey's pragmatism and his ideas about education; to link his conception of philosophy with his views about the character of modern society in general, and modern American society in particular; and to draw some lessons from these two discussions. I do not do this under these headings. I begin with the difficulty that many readers have in knowing quite what Dewey wanted to say about philosophy, education, and many other subjects, and then turn to an account of his educational ideas. I mostly concern myself with his early writings—that is, what he wrote during the ten years he was in Chicago and in the years immediately after that. The reason is that on education, these were the years of his greatest inventiveness, and thereafter he mostly defended himself against misunderstanding. On his politics, I focus, for what I think are good reasons, on his thoughts about American nationalism in the context of World War I. I end, very briefly, with an account of what I think we may learn from those World War I thoughts.

Dewey and Difficulty

Dewey is said to be a "difficult" writer. Such accusations are hard to refute: if readers find an author difficult, he is difficult, at any rate for them. Dewey's difficulty is not captured by that simple thought. Dewey is not so much difficult as elusive. In the ordinary sense, his prose is not difficult; he uses no technical jargon and no stylistic tricks. The problem he presents is that he was always groping for an appropriate vocabulary in which to express novel and unconventional ideas. The traditional vocabulary would not do: he strenuously tried to break out of every orthodoxy with which he was presented. He called himself an "instrumentalist" until he thought the term misleading and preferred "experimentalist." He did not want certainty, did not suppose that anything he wrote captured the absolute truth, and later in life came to think that the purpose of philosophy was rather to enhance experience than to catalogue its features. For all his antipathy to philosophy as traditionally understood, however, he was sure that he was a philosopher; if described as "an educator," he would respond irritably.

Nowhere in Dewey is there an answer to traditional philosophical questions such as "Does the world exist independently of our perception of it?" and "To what does the word 'I' refer?" He thought the unanswerability of such questions showed not that they were deep but that we were muddled.[1] Philosophical problems are "got over" rather than solved. That, however, tells us little about how we get over problems, or whether some ways are more effective than others. In the case of Dewey's writings on education, what is clearest is mostly negative. For instance, his reputation as an enemy to high standards and classical values—the complaint of conservative critics in Britain as well as in the United States—is clearly undeserved; but his positive views on classical values are less clear. A man who observed at his seventieth-birthday celebrations that his favorite reading was Plato was not an enemy of high standards or of a serious engagement with the classical tradition. Still, no one reading Dewey can learn whether Dewey thought teenagers should or should not learn calculus, foreign languages, Latin and Greek, or European history; he barely even discusses the question of when elementary schools should insist on children learning the three Rs.

One might expect Dewey's ten years in Chicago to cast light on his views on such practical matters. These were, after all, the years of the Laboratory School. In fact, his work with the school tells us little. In 1894, Dewey was a new boy in a new university; he was thirty-five years old and not well known, and had been appointed only reluctantly by President William Rainey Harper after a search for someone grander. As chairman of the Department of Philosophy, Psychology and Pedagogy, he was more preoccupied with raising the funds to keep the school going than with its curriculum. Before it opened, he wrote interestingly about what such a school could do, but in high-level philosophical terms, not in the terms that come naturally to a teacher planning a school week, let alone a lesson. Once the school was in operation, it had a principal and teachers of its own, and Dewey was not responsible for its day-to-day operations. As its name suggests, the Laboratory School was supposed to be a laboratory for students of social psychology. Funds had first been set aside for a more orthodox psychology laboratory; when there was no need for it, the funds were spent on the school. In any event, the school became a site for pedagogical demonstration where visitors could see something of Dewey's ideas about elementary education in operation, as the familiar label of the "Dewey school" suggests. For all that, it is not only later generations that have difficulty knowing what was "Deweyan" about it; visitors often thought it was some sort of a Froebel kindergarten.[2]

Dewey was a great success as the theorist of, and the publicist for, a new approach to education, but he was a prophet without much honor in his own land. Reading and sending off endless querulous memoranda on the administration of his department occupied much of his working life. The Laboratory School was a constant source of anxiety because it had no endowment and only a small subvention from the university. It was expensive. Personal care was lavished on the students, and this required a generous ratio of teachers to pupils; creating a suitable environment for small children meant specially made chairs and tables and apparatus for the children to play on. The school in its original incarnation was always on the brink of extinction for purely economic reasons. In short, we cannot argue directly from what happened in the school to what Dewey's educational theory must have been, nor is there a simple deductive argument that links Dewey's philosophy to the school's practice. One has to turn to Dewey's writings about education to know what his philosophy of education was.

Pragmatism and the Educational Visionary

An important, even if seemingly unlikely, feature of Dewey's pragmatism was that it resolved the tensions that had driven him to reject his mother's Congregationalist piety. Brought up in Vermont, Dewey experienced New England Protestantism as a creed that separated man from God, heart from mind, ethics from both science and poetry. His initial enthusiasm for the work of T. H. Green, the English Hegelian moral philosopher, waned when he came to think that Green's conception of the universal self in which all individual selves are to become members itself replicated the "apart thinking" of his mother's Protestant Christianity. He briefly turned to Hegel, but soon decided that Hegel's insights into the essentially cultural character of human thought and action should be divorced from a philosophy that aspired to the Absolute. Long after neo-Hegelianism had become a minority taste, Dewey assailed our hankering after the Absolute. *The Quest for Certainty*, *Experience and Nature*, and *A Common Faith* all argued that we could have the sense of belonging to the world—of being at home in it, and of somehow sharing in a cosmic purpose—that Hegel's devotees got from his work, without aspiring to see the world through the eyes of the Absolute. Whether pragmatism really resolved Dewey's problems is a question I here evade. But there is no doubting the continuity between Dewey's Hegelianism and his pragmatism, nor the usefulness of pragmatism for Dewey's somewhat dilute religiosity.

A characteristic display by Dewey the visionary is the little essay "My Pedagogic Creed." It nicely displays the elusiveness I have in mind; it is written as a lay sermon rather than a proposal for curriculum review, and is clearer about the importance of education than about just how children are to be taught and just what. Dewey's aims as a teacher of teachers, or perhaps one might better say as a provider of moral and intellectual frameworks for teachers, were pitched at a higher level than curriculum reform. "My Pedagogic Creed" was Dewey's first famous statement of his educational convictions; he wrote it in 1896 for the *School Journal*, and it is so replete with striking statements of the religious character of all true education, and with equally striking statements of the centrality of the school to social progress, and the centrality of the educational experience to all social understanding, that anyone writing about Dewey's views must be tempted to leave the job to Dewey.[3] After explaining the place of the school in rationally organized social change, elegantly rebutting the forced contrast between an individualism that lets the child run amok and a collectivism that stifles him, Dewey ends with this declaration: "I believe that in this way the teacher always is the prophet of the true God and ushers in the true kingdom of God."[4] As Lawrence Cremin observed, it was "little wonder that American educators came to view this quiet little man with the dark mustache as a Moses who would eventually lead them toward the pedagogic promised land!"[5]

Dewey's comfort with the language of "uplift" suggests the continuity of interests between his younger, straightforwardly religious self and his later liberal and pragmatist self. His philosophy of education was part of a worldview that smoothed away sharp oppositions and showed readers a strikingly optimistic vision of the future. Education was "the art of giving shape to human powers and adapting them to social service"; so defined, it was "the supreme art," a claim calculated to jolt readers who remembered Aristotle's claim that politics was the highest art. Children came into the world neither as tabulae rasae upon which teachers might write whatever they chose, nor as limbs of Satan, whose wills must be curbed to make them "apt for society," as Hobbes once put it; they were bundles of intellectual, emotional, and moral potential, ready but not predestined to turn into useful and happy adults. As he did two decades later in *Democracy and Education*, Dewey took the chance to display his vision of the way individual and society might mesh. He asserted his belief that

> the individual who is to be educated is a social individual, and society is an organic union of individuals. If we eliminate the social factor from the child we are left only with an abstraction; if we eliminate the individual factor from society, we are left only with an inert and lifeless mass. Education, therefore, must begin with a psychological insight into the child's capacities, interests, and habits. It must be controlled at every point by reference to these same considerations. These powers, interests, and habits must be continually interpreted—we must know what they mean. They must be translated into terms of their social equivalents—into terms of what they are capable of in the way of social service.[6]

This was the educational creed of a progressive, but not exactly the creed of a "progressive educator." "Progressive education" later came to be a label for an educational theory that overemphasized the importance of teaching what interested the child, and overemphasized the child's responsibility for what went on at school. Dewey was utterly hostile to progressive education so described. He feared that his emphasis on the need to take the child's abilities and interests seriously had been taken as a license to abandon teaching entirely. "Child-centered" education had come to mean that it did not matter what the teacher did. For any such view, he had complete contempt. His views were "teacher centered."

Politically, his position was decidedly progressive; his educational views presupposed that the school was an engine of social progress. Anyone less optimistic about social progress might have thought him naïve; Bertrand Russell observed that nobody ought to teach who did not have a profound feeling for the reality of original sin. Dewey had no such feeling. He knew there would be a need for a minimal amount of repressive discipline, but the need did not bulk large in his views. He thought that the integrated child would be a happy child, that virtue was both its own reward and the path to true happiness. A well-run school works with the grain of infant nature.

An aspect of Dewey's pragmatism that has lost none of its force in the intervening hundred years is its acceptance of the restlessness of modern society. In 1896, Dewey insisted that "it is impossible to foretell definitely just what civilization will be twenty years from now. Hence it is impossible to prepare the child for any precise set of conditions."[7] The only adequate form of preparation was that every pupil must be put "in complete possession of all his powers." Only by making children the masters of what is already part of "the funded capital" of society and by giving them the ability to acquire what will be unpredictably added to it in the future do we prepare them for the world after school. In a general way, this is plainly *the* liberal view of education; if it seems banal, that is a sign of how far we have moved away from a belief in producing factory fodder or in instilling political acquiescence in a lower class whose destiny is to take orders and do the world's work.

Nonetheless, the reader of Dewey's work is surprised by the minor place that the details of the curriculum occupy in Dewey's account even of the Lab School and its purpose. In *The School and Society*, what he writes about is the place of the school in a democracy and the role of the school as an agent of social progress, not such down-to-earth issues as what mathematics to teach eight-year-olds. There are barely a dozen pages of curricular matter in the hundred-odd pages discussing educational principles and describing the Lab School. Dewey opens *The School and Society* by observing that until recently, education took place at home because life was lived around the home. In the countryside, the connection between earning a living and everyday life was visible and immediate. Children were socialized into becoming useful participants in the household and village economy: "There was always something which really needed to be done, and a real necessity that each member of the household should do his own part faithfully and in co-operation with others."[8]

The modern city broke that bond between the child, his upbringing, and his finding a useful place in society. Dewey was fastidious about not giving a one-sided account:

We must recognize our compensations—the increase in toleration, in breadth of social judgment, the larger acquaintance with human nature, the sharper alertness in reading signs of character and interpreting social situations, greater accuracy of adaptation to differing personalities, contact with greater commercial activities. These considerations mean much to the city-bred child of today.[9]

The change posed a question: "How shall we retain these advantages and yet introduce into the school something representing the other side of life—occupations which exact personal responsibilities and which train the child in relation to the physical realities of life?"[10] There are several things to be said about this question. One is that Dewey saw elementary education—education up to the age of thirteen—as a moral training and not a purely intellectual training. Indeed, "purely intellectual" would have been a term of abuse. There are two extremes from which Dewey has always been attacked: on the one side as someone who has an inadequate view of the need for discipline, order, and instilled habit, and on the other as a theorist of the manipulation of children into docile membership of the corporate order.[11] Both are infinitely far from the truth. The skeptic must start not from Dewey's desire that the powers of the child should find their natural fulfillment in life in a democratic society, but from his belief in such a natural harmony. What separates Dewey from more skeptical liberals is his assumption that something close to complete harmony can be realized by intelligent action.

A second thing to notice is the light that Dewey's starting point casts on his concern with "manual training." A familiar complaint against Dewey is that his emphasis on learning by doing was a recipe for preparing children to go on to vocational schools. American schools, like their British counterparts, put the brightest children into academic streams and the less bright into vocational streams; bright children would go on to be prosperous and well-rounded members of the managing classes, while the less bright would be less prosperous members of the managed nonelite. So all discussion of manual training tends to raise the unlovely specter of an educational system that takes the existing division between managerial and manual work and reproduces it in the classroom. Dewey knew that. He thought that if there were an adequate system of trade schools, manual training in the elementary school would be an acceptable way of getting children to acquire the dexterity, discipline, and work habits that trade schools could turn into the skills needed for wives and mothers on the one hand and manual workers on the other. Characteristically, he went on to insist that to think of practical training in this way was "unnecessarily narrow," adding, "We must conceive of work in wood and metal, of weaving, sewing and cooking, as methods of living and learning, not as distinct studies."[12] All children were to acquire practical skills, as a moral imperative, even if only some of them would earn their living by using them.

Agricultural societies focused on farm and village showed the child the entire process by which life went on; nobody could turn a switch and have electric light. To get light, they had to kill animals, render tallow, and make their own candles. The school had to show children the complexities of the modern world that has replaced that lost world, but Dewey did not propose to do it by telling them about the way industry and commerce worked. Swamping children with information in their early years was worse than useless; it bred superficial understanding and sapped the ability to concentrate. The children had to work their way through an activity from beginning to end. At the Lab School, the children grew wheat in a corner of the schoolyard, ground it, and learned to make bread; when slightly older, they learned about metal smelting and built their own furnace. To learn chemistry, they cooked, and to cook, they learned chemistry. This was how to acquire a hands-on understanding of the world. Dewey's pragmatism insisted on the practicality of knowledge, and here was the theory in practice. The vice of philosophers traditionally had been to think of all knowledge as spectatorial; Deweyan education started from the view that knowing was a form of engaging with the world.

A third feature of Dewey's discussion was his passionate belief that the educational process had to make adequate ties with every aspect of the life around. In a chapter titled "Waste in Education"—an odd location for what he discussed—Dewey leaped in one bound from the concept of waste to that of organization, and then spread his wings on the topic of what organization meant for the school. He read his audience a sermon on the theme "All waste is due to isolation. Organization is nothing but getting things into connection with one another so that they work easily, flexibly and fully."[13] The details of the picture do not matter. The frame of mind does. For "organization" took on a decidedly supermanagerial tone in the argument. The school was a spiritual entity. As a philosopher obsessed by the "meaning" of events, Dewey emphasized that the school was a network of meanings rather than a collection of spaces in which children read, cooked, played, painted, and whatever. The "organization" Dewey had in mind was an emphasis on the school's ties to the whole social environment; cooking in the school kitchen linked the child to home and to the countryside where food was grown, and thus to the school's own physical environment; sewing in the textile room tied the school both to the home and then out to the world of business and industry.[14]

The School and Society was vastly popular; its popularity was a function of its combination of great clarity in general orientation and openness of argumentative texture. Dewey insisted over and over that schooling is part of life, not just a preparation for it; that children must use all their energies at school, not just intellectual ones and not just manual skills; that something of vast importance was happening in the school, since this was where the next generation was growing and everyone knew that it was vastly easier to form children adequately than to have to reform them when they were teenage delinquents. All this was good news, and appreciated by his readers. One might complain that it did not yield very obvious conclusions about just what to teach and just how to teach it, but Dewey had headed off his critics in advance; the distinction between how to teach and what to teach was another of the separations that he deplored. Form and content, style and matter, were to be adjusted to each other as we came to better understand what successful teaching was all about. We know that it is not about handing over slabs of undigested fact, and we know it is a mistake to send the young out into the world primed with information but with no skills of processing and evaluating it; beyond that, *experientia docet* ("experience teaches"): people must experiment, report on their experiments, and hope to agree on good practice.

Dewey himself was ready to exploit even theories that he did not accept. He told the story of a visitor asking to see the kindergarten section of the Lab School and being told there was none. Then the visitor

> asked if there were not singing, drawing, manual training, plays and dramatizations, and attention to the children's social relations. When her questions were answered in the affirmative, she remarked, both triumphantly and indignantly, that that was what she understood by a kindergarten, and that she did not know what was meant by saying that the school had no kindergarten.[15]

Dewey agreed that what the school gave children between the ages of four and thirteen did "carry into effect certain principles which Froebel was perhaps the first consciously to set forth."[16] But he was not a disciple of Froebel. Froebel could not give a sensible account of the role of play in early education, because he lived in an authoritarian society to which such playful activities were anathema.[17] Dewey thought Froebel had had to give elaborate metaphysical justifications of the symbolic value of childish play-acting because he had to detach school activities from the outside world in order to protect the child against the everyday world.[18] The American child, as opposed to the Prussian child, had an inalienable right to the pursuit of happiness, and his activities at school needed no metaphysical defense. His everyday desire for play could be part of the process of leading him gently toward adult life. Froebel's kindergarten methods were more useful when detached from Froebel's philosophy.

The same attitude marked Dewey's approach to Johann Herbart. Herbart was best known for the slogan that "ontogeny recapitulates phylogeny," a misleading and distracting slogan in biology, and worse in its effect on the social sciences; what it means, literally, is that the growth of the individual takes place in stages that mirror the development of the species. What it meant in schools was that the curriculum was supposed to be governed by the individual child's gradual movement from an infancy in which he or she mimicked the mental and social relations of primitive peoples to an adult life in which he or she was a full member of a fully civilized community. Dewey wrote several papers disputing this as a picture of child development.[19] Yet the curriculum of the Lab School took something like it as a model; as a critic noticed, "In the ordered progression of theme activities from preliterate man to modern society there were patent vestiges of the very recapitulation theory Dewey had attacked before the National Herbart Society."[20]

But teaching children about the growth of human culture in an evolutionary fashion, and sophisticating the children's grasp of increasingly abstract material, made good sense independently of Herbart. Dewey's thought was simply that children should be gradually weaned from their homes and the emotional and intellectual stimuli that home provided and on to a more abstract, more impersonal intellectual and social diet. It would have been possible to teach children history and social studies by starting with modern society and working backward, but it takes little imagination to think of some reasons to prefer children to know a little about Neolithic man and a lot about the contemporary world rather than a little about New York and a great deal about prehistory.

On the plausibility of Dewey's picture of child development, opinions have always varied. Practicing infant teachers might think that Dewey had his eye too much on where children were going next and not enough on the joys of the particular stage they had reached. Academically minded readers may flinch at how long it was before the children of the Lab School were supposed to settle down and learn some of the three Rs. What cannot be denied is that the gradual shift from what others would have denoted as play to what others would have denoted as "real work"—neither of which Dewey would have so labeled—was always controlled by a clear idea of the child's destination. It was not nostalgia for a vanishing rural past that made Dewey start six-year-olds on small-scale farming, harvesting, and cooking, but rather his belief that these were basic activities of human existence, and ones that children understood some part of by the time they reached school.

The homeliness of Dewey's manner and the homeliness of his examples are misleading about the intellectual thrust of the syllabus he suggested. He did not think that all knowledge is applied knowledge, nor that all learning was to be assimilated to farming or washing the dishes; rather, he passionately believed that ideas made sense only as solutions to problems and that educationalists had neglected this fact. He saw his own contribution as suggesting ways of putting children into situations where they would grasp the problems to which increasingly sophisticated ideas and academic skills were solutions. Dewey steered a delicate path between simpler views that were not wholly wrong but, in his eyes, missed the point. When he started writing about education, two opposed positions much in the public eye were the Herbartian emphasis on *interest* and the emphasis of his old mentor W. T. Harris on *effort*. Dewey thought the Herbartians' emphasis merely sugared the pill of a set curriculum, while Harris's emphasis on effort would create students who were either passive or rebellious. The point of Dewey's complicated argument about setting children problems and teaching them to think was that he believed that under those conditions they would be as interested as the Herbartians wished them to be and would make the effort that Harris and his colleagues so rightly stressed.[21]

All these arguments are, so to speak, "precurricular," and Dewey's little pamphlet *The Child and the Curriculum*, too, is not a discussion of the curriculum, but a plea for the abolition of sharp separations in methods of teaching where there should be none in the process of learning. The slogans of "discipline" and "interest" that opposed sides hurled at each other, one thinking to defend "the subject" and the other to defend "the child," reflected an analytical distinction inflated into a false vision of the world. Of course children must learn something in particular, of course there was a particular direction in which they needed to be led, and so of course they needed to master the disciplines of learning; but to master anything in such a way as to have really been educated by it was a matter of absorbing it and turning it to one's own purposes, and this was a matter of our own interest. The only discipline worth having was self-discipline, and the only interest worth gratifying was an interest capable of being sustained over a long enough run to enable us to learn a subject matter thoroughly.

This lesson was spelled out for two hundred pages in *How We Think*. It was published in 1910, six years after Dewey left Chicago, but was essentially a "Chicago" work. It offers exactly what Dewey intended, a guide to teachers who are puzzled to know what counts as intellectual progress on the part of their students and when they are in the presence of it. Practically oriented though it is, it still contains a good deal of philosophical provocation. The observation that "primarily, naturally, it is not we who think in any actively responsible sense; thinking is rather something that happens in us" is both true and shocking; the further suggestion that to say "*I* think" is to announce an achievement is in the same vein.[22] Talking sense to teachers did not require Dewey to abandon his philosophical revolution.

Dewey was addressing himself to teachers who found themselves bombarded on all sides with panaceas; he refused to add to their number. He made good sense philosophically credible and morally uplifting, an achievement not to be sneered at. He refused to accept that teaching was to be left either to muddling through or to the flair of the individual teacher. There was a problem, or rather a set of problems—catching the child's attention; providing materials for thought; getting the child to think consecutively, coherently, organizedly, self-propelledly, and relevantly; and watching always for how this contributed to what was to come next—and such problems were not soluble simply or by some trick; but they were not soluble at all by people who failed to identify them in the first place. As Dewey put it, the problem was to find "the forms of activity (a) which are most congenial, best adapted, to the immature stage of development; (b) which have the most ulterior promise as preparation for the social responsibilities of adult life; and (c) which *at the same time*, have the maximum of influence in forming habits of acute observation and of consecutive inference."[23]

Once we set up the issue like that, a heavily scientific education must look tremendously attractive, the more so to the extent that children themselves can devise their own experiments, build their own equipment, cooperate in designing and running their own projects, but still have to answer to someone else for the results. Yet even the reader who thinks Dewey has loaded the scales in favor of his view that good education is permeated with the scientific outlook must admit that the contrast between lugubrious modern discussions in which scientific education is assumed to have the one and only purpose of assisting the country in international trade, and Dewey's vision of a training that is simultaneously moral, social, and intellectual is all in Dewey's favor.

One puzzle that this emphasis on problem solving presents is whether Dewey's approach slights training in the humanities. Dewey's stress on problem solving, on the social basis of knowledge, and on education as a form of social training seems to make science central to education and looks likely to turn history and geography into applied social science as the study of how societies conceived as problem-solving organizations adapt to their environment by adjusting themselves to its opportunities and demands and adjusting it to their needs and techniques. Where in this is a love of poetry, art, or music for their own sakes? Where is the cultivation of the eye and ear and a sense of rhythmic aptness? Where, even, is mere curiosity about the past? Dewey always believed that human beings had a natural urge to celebrate, commemorate, dance, play, sing, and paint, and had no difficulty in encouraging these as school activities. The difficulty lay in giving an account of their developed state, accommodating the not uncommon sentiment that Mozart operas are not "good for" society but possess a special sort of value that gives a point to human existence. Throughout the 1930s, Dewey defended art education in elementary schools as an essential, not a "frill," and he knew what he was in favor of. The question of how it would fit into the schema he offered teachers was another matter.

A modern reader must see most of Dewey's ideas in *How We Think* as common sense; but it was Dewey who made them so. *How We Think* was addressed to working teachers; a large part of the teacher's trade in 1900 lay in conducting "recitations," when, as the name suggests, children had to "recite their lessons" and teachers "heard" them. Dewey saw that unless they were conducted very well, they were diseducative:

> To re-cite is to cite again, to tell over and over. If we were to call this period *reiteration*, the designation would hardly bring out more clearly than does the word *recitation* the complete domination of instruction by rehearsing of second-hand information, by memorizing for the sake of producing correct replies at the proper time.[24]

When foreign visitors to the United States encounter multiple-choice tests, they usually share Dewey's sentiments about reiteration.

When Dewey was writing, the better-trained teachers had got beyond recitations and were accustomed to drawing up lesson plans along lines laid down by Johann Herbart. Herbart had claimed, as Dewey represents him at least, that

> there is a single "general method" uniformly followed by the mind in an effective attack upon any subject. Whether it be a first-grade child mastering the rudiments

of number, a grammar-school pupil studying history, or a college student dealing with philology, in each case the first step is preparation, the second presentation, followed in turn by comparison and generalization, ending in the application of the generalizations to new and specific instances.[25]

Suppose the lesson was to be a lesson on rivers—to take Dewey's example; as "preparation," we would begin by getting the children to talk about streams and rivers they had seen, or about water flowing in gutters, and explain the purpose of the lesson; "presentation" would then involve the formal presentation of films, photographs, models, perhaps a visit to look at rivers. Comparison and generalization are the stages by which the inessential features of the phenomenon are stripped away so that a solid sense of what we are supposed to know about rivers is left. Finally, this knowledge would be anchored by being applied to new cases, so children who knew about the Thames would go on to write about the Hudson. Dewey was in a dilemma vis-à-vis this Herbartian orthodoxy. He did not want to say that teachers should walk into class and play it by ear, but he did want to say that the five-stage schema was too pat, too neat, and in crucial ways misleading. He did not want to exaggerate the difference between his own view and the Herbartian, but he thought the Herbartian schema implied that imparting concepts and information for their own sake was the sum total of instruction. What was lacking was the purpose of instruction, the need to solve a problem.

Dewey offered his own five-stage schema, though he cheerfully admitted that it was never followed in all its steps and that it was only a rough abridgment of how we think. Dewey's five stages of what he called "the complete act of thought" were "(i) a felt difficulty; (ii) its location and definition; (iii) suggestion of a possible solution; (iv) development by reasoning of the bearings of the suggestion; (v) further observation and experiment leading to its acceptance or rejection; that is, the conclusion of belief or disbelief."[26] Dewey's informal analysis is interesting because it suggests how difficult it is to map the process that Dewey so plausibly describes by a formal logical analysis. The fourth step in particular, in which we convert a hypothesis into an explanation whose relevance to the phenomena is articulated and made obvious, is exceedingly hard to formalize, though logicians have labored to create a "relevance logic" for many years.

Dewey thought that his five-stage scheme overlapped Herbart's scheme, but brought out more clearly something central to the educational process. The crucial difference comes at the beginning. Dewey's children begin with a problem; the Herbartian schema begins with a teacher's lesson plan and the goals she was supposed to announce to the class before she started the lesson. Dewey's children acquire information on their way to solving a problem; information is assimilated in the process of thinking their way through to a solution. The Herbartian scheme does not exclude the idea that we think about what we learn, but it does suggest that thought is incidental to information acquisition; Dewey insists always and throughout that acquiring information is incidental to problem solving. Not emphasizing this made the Herbartian scheme misleading.

Guessing how much effect Dewey had on American education is difficult. His admirers often suggest he had rather little effect; one might parody their argument as the claim that since public education is still terrible, Dewey cannot have had much effect. His detractors sometimes seem to believe that he single-handedly debauched a fine system—which, seeing that he first wrote about education at a time when no more than 7 percent of the population had a high school education and less than half of all children got even five years of schooling, is perhaps an exaggeration. Dewey himself was never sure which of his ideas were capable of large-scale implementation in the American public school system and which would be hard to implement outside the Lab School. The Lab School taught classes of eight and ten, while most public schools had classes of forty or more.

Among the reasons why Dewey's influence was never likely to be as great as critics and defenders have claimed, three stand out. They are simple but conclusive. One is that Dewey schools are very expensive: they need small classes, a lot of equipment, and elaborate arrangements so that teachers can spend time and attention rethinking what they are doing. Dewey's vision of the school as a place of experiment was, it must be remembered, not a vision of an "experimental school" in the sense of a place where eccentric, novel, or surprising things went on, but the vision of a place permeated by the experimental spirit. It could be run only by teachers who were able to get together to discuss their goals, their techniques, their successes and failures, and prospects for change.[27] The second is that Dewey schools are appallingly demanding of their teachers. Dewey may have assured teachers that they were doing God's work, but God's work is notoriously hard work. Since Dewey's educational philosophy was so determinedly teleological—at every stage, the child was seen as a creature about to embark on the next stage of growth—the teacher could not concentrate only on the child's current attainments and interests. Every encounter with a child was a chance to see how the moment might be turned to advantage in giving the child a grasp of arithmetic, languages, physics, chemistry, biology, geography, history, and whatever other skills we wish him or her to acquire. There never were many teachers colleges capable of turning out teachers with that range of skills, and given the rates of pay for primary teachers, not many people with the ability to learn what this demanded were going to volunteer to become teachers. The third is that it is unclear just what a "Deweyan" school is. Enormous numbers of people believe they attended one, but the schools they attended are exceedingly diverse. Since Dewey himself was not much interested in secondary education, and thought that by the time students attended college their mental habits were pretty well fixed, it is not surprising that there was little consensus over what a Deweyan allegiance meant at any level above the first few years of elementary school.

Dewey's Americanism and Ours

Having argued that Dewey's educational theory was, in the ordinary sense of the term, less a theory of education than a theory of the place of education in the politics of modern society, it remains to situate Dewey a little more firmly in the politics of his own time and ours. Dewey was a lifelong socialist, though a socialist of a liberal, guild socialist stripe. He was an inveterate democrat, though "democracy" as he understood it was a far cry from anything yet achieved in the United States or anywhere else. Without entirely ignoring those attachments, I here focus on his ideas about how we can build a modern democratic nation from diverse, plural—in the modern terminology, "multicultural"—ingredients. Dewey came to maturity during the 1880s and 1890s, a time when the industrialization of the American economy was in full flood and when enormous numbers of immigrants from Ireland, Germany, Scandinavia, and eastern and southern Europe were pouring into the country. The Chicago he encountered in 1894 was a city where barely a quarter of the inhabitants had two American-born parents.

Many Americans reacted to the arrival of these strangers with fear and distaste. Some denounced hyphenated Americanism; they did not want a country full of "German-Americans" or "Jewish-Americans," but 100 percent Americans. "Racism" in those far-off days was more commonly an attitude toward new kinds of European migrants, Polish Jews and southern Catholics in particular. Black Americans were below the horizon of consciousness in the northern states, to which, after all, the majority of immigrants went. Dewey was an American nationalist, but one of a peculiar stripe. He had no doubt that the United States was in some sense "special," though he was even more sure that it was a general truth that human beings needed to acquire a sense of individual identity within a stable society with which they could identify. To the extent that American nationalism was an acceptable moral stance, it was because the United States was engaged in a moral undertaking that could properly engage the allegiances of a serious person. This distinguished it from European "blood and soil" nationalisms. These issues came to a head during World War I, when anti-German fury disfigured American politics and "Americanism" became xenophobia. In an essay titled "Nationalizing Education," written in 1916, Dewey distinguished good and bad nationalism in much the way that his contemporary Randolph Bourne had done a year before in his famous essay "Transnational America": good nationalism creates an American culture and is consistent with internationalism, whereas bad nationalism represses internal differences and is bellicose. A very Deweyan touch was the claim that American nationality is constituted by democracy; a second was his insistence that the hyphen in designations of hyphenated Americans is good when it attaches, bad when it separates.

Unlike contemporaries who thought that the affirmation of American unity in the context of World War I entailed the suppression of other identities, Dewey was a good Hegelian to the extent of thinking that American unity had to be a differentiated unity. To seek a unity built on the suppression of difference was to turn our backs on the possibilities of cultural and political growth. America was an organism whose potentialities were only now beginning to reveal themselves. This was one of the ways in which Dewey brought together his ideas about modernity and democracy with his ideas about education. If it was not true that unity built on repression was just impossible, it was certainly true that it was both a waste of the energies that the excluded could bring to modern America and a denial of the ideals of personality that lie at the heart of the American commitment to democracy. As for education, it was, as Dewey's critics often complained, concerned to achieve "growth" in the individual. The individual's growth was ideally a facet of the community's growth. Critics complained that Dewey would never say just what growth consisted in; but that was no oversight on his part. Neither the individual nor society was growing toward a fixed, predetermined goal. Education must enable us to rethink our goals, always in cooperation with our fellows in a democratic society. The belief that we can do so may strike some readers as utopian, but it was at the very heart of Dewey's social and educational theory, just as our very partial success in doing so was one of the things that made him an acerbic critic of American society almost until the day he died.

This allows Dewey to speak to the recent arguments over "identity" and "difference" that have been such a feature of American intellectual life. Demands to have our "identities" respected and our "differences" acknowledged have made their way into the classrooms of America at every level from kindergarten upward. The debate represents a reversion to the ethical standards of Dewey's youth. From the perspective of the theorists of "difference," the philosophical defense of human rights offered by the conventional liberalism of John Rawls and Robert Nozick is sociologically unsophisticated and inattentive to the needs of groups and communities as well as individuals. But it would have seemed so just after World War I, had it come to the notice of an audience that took it for granted that "personality" and "community" were the poles of debate. The one respect in which we differ from our predecessors is that we are less confident that the circle can be squared and that plural identities can be made consistent with an overarching national identity.

It is at this point that Dewey's educational politics might decently be revived. For Dewey's conception of identity—as an achievement rather than a brute fact—usefully reminds us to take absolutely seriously the antiessentialism that so many postmodernist critics preach but do not practice. Indeed, we might do well to let the notion of identity have a holiday and focus instead on the concept of a project. So conceived, American identity can again be what Dewey thought it ought to be, something defined as part of the great experiment that Dewey had in mind: the attempt to build a society that would exploit all the resources of modernity and allow all its members to feel both that they were contributing to a common project and that what they contributed was distinctively theirs.

Conversely, the various more localized identities to which people are properly attached can be emphasized without the sense that they trap their bearers—"I am a black American, so how can I be an expert on Shakespeare?" has more than once been heard—or that they swallow up their bearers' lives. A gay racing driver may or may not pilot a Formula One car in a distinctively gay fashion, but if he is to stay alive on the track, it is the project of getting to the checkered flag quickly but safely that has to preoccupy him. The virtue of Deweyan experimentalism is that it teaches us to look for ways in which we can be all the things we are, and encourages us not to believe that there is characteristically only one and that it must trump all the others all the time. There are surely many ways of providing an education that attends to that thought; but not all the kinds of education that we at present offer our children do so very well.

26

John Rawls

ACADEMICALLY RESPECTABLE PHILOSOPHERS are generally obscure figures. They have specialisms just as natural scientists have; they are known to their colleagues in those specialisms and to few besides—just as natural scientists are; they beaver away like their colleagues in chemistry and physics; and like everybody else, they are variably nice to their families and friends. They are almost never known outside their own subject; and they almost never go in for public pronouncements on the great issues of the day. Bertrand Russell used to do it, and was held to have ruined his reputation as a result, even though he used to go to some lengths to maintain that when he wrote on political issues it was "not as a philosopher." "I wrote," said Russell, "as a human being who suffered from the state of the world" (Schilpp 1943, 730). Nonetheless, the picture most people now have of the engaged philosopher owes a great deal to Russell.

This makes it all the more surprising that John Rawls's long and intricate book should have caught the attention of so many people outside the world of professional philosophers. *A Theory of Justice* is 550 pages long; it is written with tremendous clarity and care, but there is nothing about it to provoke instant excitement. Its clarity puts it in a different universe from the suggestive murkiness of Foucault, Gadamer, or Habermas; there is no suggestion that enlightenment can be achieved only after a prolonged groping in the dark. But unlike Russell, say, who was his equal in clarity but who enlivened his driest work with a constant crackle of humor, Rawls writes with Puritan plainness and sobriety, and also unlike Russell, Rawls has neither been jailed for his opinions nor been accused of fomenting revolution; he has not fired off letters to presidents nor torn up his party card. His views are controversial, but he is not himself a controversialist.

Yet since *A Theory of Justice* appeared in 1971, it has sparked off more argument among philosophers, and has been more widely cited by sociologists, economists, judges, and politicians, than any work of philosophy in the past hundred years. Its first major review (Hampshire 1972) announced that it was the most significant work in moral and political philosophy to have appeared in a century; comparisons were made with Henry Sidgwick's *Methods of Ethics*—the book that may be said to have created modern moral philosophy—and with John Stuart Mill's *Utilitarianism* and *On Liberty*. Commentary on Rawls quickly attained the status of a "Rawls industry"; but not even the most hostile critic ventured to suggest that these initial estimates of Rawls's importance were exaggerated. As we shall see, writers such as Robert Nozick ask some very awkward questions of Rawls. Nonetheless, Nozick begins his scrutiny of Rawls's theory with the following tribute:

> A *Theory of Justice* is a powerful, deep, subtle, wide-ranging, systematic work in political and moral philosophy which has not seen its like since the writings of John Stuart Mill, if then. It is a fountain of lovely ideas, integrated together into a lovely whole . . . It is impossible to read Rawls' book without incorporating much, perhaps transmuted, into one's own deepened view. And it is impossible to finish his book without a new and inspiring vision of what a moral theory may attempt to do and unite; of how *beautiful* a moral theory can be. (Nozick 1974, 183)

It is true, and I will try to explain why, that Rawls's impact has been greater in America than elsewhere; but the astonishing thing is the way in which a sober-sided Harvard professor should have caught the intellectual imagination of such a wide audience. Part of the explanation is no doubt that large numbers of readers had been waiting for the book for thirteen years—ever since Rawls had suggested in an article in the *Philosophical Review* ("Justice as Fairness"; Rawls 1958) that the way to develop a theory of justice was to ask ourselves what arrangements we would have agreed on if we had been devising the basic political and economic institutions of our society via a "social contract" made under conditions that guaranteed that contract's fairness. But the impact on nonphilosophers is hardly explained by that. Let me suggest what does explain it.

A *Theory of Justice* is a book about rights. American liberals have long been accustomed to arguing about rights, in part because of the place that the Supreme Court has in American politics, and because of the possibility of appealing to rights enshrined in the Constitution of the United States. Battles over capital punishment, like battles over school desegregation thirty years ago, are fought out in the courts as much as in Congress, and they are fought out by asking whether, say, the right not to be subjected to "cruel and unusual punishment," which is enshrined in the Eighth Amendment, or "the right to the equal protection of the laws," which constitutes the Fourteenth Amendment, means that capital punishment is unlawful or that all children have a right to attend the same schools.

A *Theory of Justice* sets out to discover what rights we have against one another; it sets out to find these rights from first principles—rights against our government, such as the right to a fair trial or the right not to be forced to fight in an unjust war; civil and political rights, such as the right to vote and the right to choose our own occupation; and economic rights, such as the right to protection against poverty and exploitation. What is distinctive about it, and what accounts for its wide influence, is that in doing so, it defends what one might for shorthand call "American welfare-state liberalism"—the view that governments must open up to their citizens the widest possible range of civil rights and economic opportunities. It argues that any government that fails to conduct itself on democratic lines, fails to open up economic opportunities, or promote the welfare of its least advantaged subjects, violates their moral rights and has no claims to their allegiance. The boldness of these claims is obvious. Welfare-state liberalism turns out—if *A Theory of Justice* is right—to be a great deal more than merely the political platform of the New Deal Democratic Party, and something quite other than a political program that happens to appeal to the so-called New Deal coalition of Jewish liberals, labor leaders, and black civil rights activists. It turns out to be a form of politics that is uniquely just and uniquely rational. The plainness of Rawls's prose perhaps makes it harder to see just how ambitious a project he was embarked on, but there is no doubt in my mind that it was that which accounts for its impact on the liberal audience that took it up. And the ambition has touched at least two noteworthy subsequent attempts to provide a grounding for modern liberalism (Dworkin 1978; Ackerman 1980).

The intellectual support for liberalism was all the more welcome because welfare-state liberals are an intellectually hard-pressed group. They are traditionally abused from the left by socialists who think they hardly begin to understand the real problems of a capitalist society, and hemmed in on two sides by different sorts of conservative. In the American setting, it has been the conservatives who have been the more vociferous—no doubt another reason for Rawls's appeal to American liberals, who must often have felt that the conservatives had always seemed to have the best of the arguments about rights.

On the one side, paternalist conservatives have always argued that if a government is—as they agree it is—obliged to look after the needy and entitled to use tax revenues to do so, it is entitled to set the terms on which it does so. A paternalist government should decide what books we may read and what religious views we may profess, and should extend its interest in our welfare to our moral welfare as much as our physical well-being. The argument is spelled out by George F. Will in *Statecraft as Soulcraft* (1984) in avowed opposition to Rawlsian liberalism and to the more familiar American conservatism that owes more to Herbert Spencer than to Edmund Burke. Will stands on the Burkean claim that society is a contract for more than material purposes: "It is a partnership in all science; a partnership in all art; a partnership in every virtue, and in all perfection" (Burke 1961, 110).

If the liberals try to argue that although the government has every right to spend its tax revenues on the hard-up, it has no right to police our libraries and our bedrooms, they find themselves facing conservatives of a different sort, who argue that the only defense against interfering governments is complete laissez-faire. I cannot here settle the vexed question whether such enthusiasts for laissez-faire are best described as conservative; F. A. von Hayek has often denied that he is a conservative and has said that he is a liberal *pur sang* ("pure-blood"); and some English conservatives would repudiate Hayek's "free-market liberalism" precisely because they agree that conservatism is about tradition and paternalism, not about individual liberty and free choice. But here the speech of the vulgar must be our guide; the defenders of laissez-faire are frequently, and reasonably, regarded as conservative because they treat the growth of the welfare state and government regulation of the economy as a series of more or less disastrous moves away from an earlier and more golden age of minimal government. If some defenders of universal laissez-faire would be better described as "anarcho-capitalists" than as conservatives, the public perception of them is sound enough, since they stand up for the capitalist economy to which conservatives are committed and regard governments that tax their subjects in order to pay for a welfare state as engaged in a form of official robbery.

Theorists of this persuasion stake everything on liberty and understand individuals as essentially the proprietors of themselves and their abilities, free to dispose of their "property in their own persons" (Locke 1967, 305) as they see fit. The resulting social theory is agreeably simple and uniquely calculated to keep government at arm's length in all spheres of life. Everyone must fend for himself with whatever property in his own talents he has been given by nature and whatever other property he can lawfully acquire; no doubt the rich ought to be charitable to the poor, but governments must not try to run a welfare state, for just as censorship violates a man's right to put what he likes into his own mind, so a welfare state violates a man's right to do as he likes with his own property. Small wonder that liberals often look wishy-washy and insecure, faced with the certainties of energetic paternalists on the one hand and the cool clarity of the descendants of Herbert Spencer on the other. *A Theory of Justice* promises relief by showing the liberal's position to be the consistent outcome of an argument from more or less uncontroversial premises. If its arguments are sound, liberalism is not a patched-up compromise between conservatism and socialism, but a distinctive creed with solid foundations.

A Theory of Justice asks us to engage in a thought experiment. Rawls asks us to imagine ourselves trying to arrange social and economic institutions in the company of others whose consent we have to obtain—in short, he asks us to imagine that we are drawing up a social contract. But there is one crucial feature of this situation: we are to imagine that we know nothing about our tastes, talents, and interests and do not know what social and economic position we shall occupy, nor in what society we shall live. This feature is what Rawls calls "the veil of ignorance" (Rawls 1971, 136–42); the thought is that an acceptable theory of justice ought to tell us what rights we possess by telling us what rules we *would* have drawn up to govern the way we cooperate with one another if only we had known none of those things that usually get in the way of complete impartiality.

In setting up his theory in this way, Rawls has "returned to Grand Theory" thrice over. Against those philosophers, dominant in the 1950s and 1960s, who restricted philosophy to the analysis of concepts, Rawls has set philosophy back on the path followed by his predecessors like John Stuart Mill. *A Theory of Justice* stands up for controversial political positions. Rawls's views are not extravagant or extreme, but they are certainly controversial. For instance, he holds that elected officials are under an altogether stricter obligation to obey the laws and uphold the constitution under which they were elected than the rest of us are (Rawls 1971, 112, 344)—a view that President Nixon flouted in practice, and, more interestingly, that his defenders objected to as a matter of theory. Rawls offers a defense of civil disobedience that would make politically motivated disobedience a much more acceptable part of our political life than either the U.S. Supreme Court or the English judiciary seems likely to contemplate (363–68). And his views about the subservience of economic institutions to "social justice" place him firmly on one side of what is currently the most fiercely contested dividing line in politics in Britain today.

A Theory of Justice has also returned to *grand* theory in setting itself the task of providing a systematic and comprehensive theory of justice, starting from minimal first principles and ramifying out into principles to cover every case. This goes directly against the most common tendency in recent moral and political philosophy, which has generally argued that there is little room to systematize our ideas about social and political values and that all we can do is to "trade off" one social value against another in an intuitive way (Barry 1965, 3–8). Rawls has tried to produce a theory of justice that will rank the components of justice in a determinate and rationally supported way. The similarity between Rawls's work and that of Kant extends not merely to the way they both espouse a "hypothetical" social contract theory (cf. Rawls 1971, 12, and Reiss 1972, 73–87), but also to the almost "architectural" quality of the resulting theory, with its hierarchical structure of the principles of practical reason, first principles of right, and their personal and institutional implications all neatly labeled and rationalized (Rawls 1971, 109).

Rawls's third return to grand theory is perhaps his most surprising one: the intellectual apparatus that Rawls has called upon to sustain all this is the theory of the social contract. To go back to contractual ways of thinking is, in the most literal sense, a return, for while the social contract provided the theoretical framework in which Hobbes, Locke, Rousseau, and Kant all wrote in the seventeenth and eighteenth centuries, it is usually supposed that the theory was dismantled by Hume—and the wreckage was buried by Bentham in the early nineteenth century (Hume 1963; Bentham 1949). It is a mark of the distinction of Rawls's work that none of his critics is prepared to stand up and say that *A Theory of Justice* is simply archaic. They are unanimous in accepting that Rawls has at least uncovered *something* that the crude dismissals of Bentham and his fellow utilitarians hid from sight.

The reason behind Rawls's appeal to contractual ways of thinking is his perception of the central weakness of the commonest—that is, broadly utilitarian—ways of thinking about social welfare. Many people think at first sight that it is obvious that the only way to run a society is to maximize the welfare of its inhabitants. Rawls points out that this is at odds with our views about justice. There will be many occasions when we could increase the total welfare of society if we were willing to sacrifice one person for the benefit of all the rest—but most of us would think the sacrifice of an innocent simply unjust. The fundamental principle to which Rawls is committed is that nobody is merely a means to the ends of society at large; to put it differently, he insists on the *separateness* of persons, on the fact that we are not simply units of account in working out the total welfare. It is this separateness to which contractual ways of thinking do justice and other ways of thinking do not (Rawls 1971, 27).

It is this emphasis on the need to secure each individual against any temptation to sacrifice him or her for the general good that explains the place of two distinctive features of Rawls's theory. The first of these is how he makes the rules governing the distribution of our fundamental freedoms take absolute priority over all other social rules; this, the principle of "the priority of liberty" (Rawls 1971, 244ff.), causes all sorts of difficulties for Rawls, but it faithfully reflects one of the theory's crucial motivating ideas: that a theory of justice is in part a theory about the absolute impermissibility of coercing people in various ways. The second feature, that for which Rawls is best known, is his attempt to exploit the so-called maximin principle, familiar from game theory, in explaining what "fair shares" from the results of any cooperative enterprise must look like. It is a well-known theorem in game theory that when playing against an opponent in conditions of uncertainty, the best strategy to adopt is that of ensuring that the worst outcome of the game is as good as possible. We should play in such a way as to minimize our maximum losses or to maximize our minimum gains, whence the abbreviated tags of maximin or minimax. It is a disputed question whether this analysis *does* apply in the context of Rawls's own analysis of justice. Behind the veil of ignorance, when we are trying to draw up terms for a social contract, we are not really playing *against* anyone. The justification of maximin is that our opponents are trying to ensure that we end up with the worst outcome; it is this that makes it rational to ensure that their success is as painless to us as possible. We shall shortly see what this implies for Rawls's theory; but here we should notice how well Rawls's defense of his maximin conception follows from the thought that a theory of justice has a substantial defensive component. If questions of justice arise in the context of cooperative enterprises, as Rawls says, they also arise only against a background in which it is likely that those with whom we cooperate are unwilling to let us have more than they have to to secure our cooperation. It is a theory of justice for people in competitive conditions.

A person who is fearful that others may wish to sacrifice him for their benefit and who is asked to construct a set of rules for governing their conduct will look most attentively at what happens to the worst-off person in the society whose rules he is thinking of. It is this that makes the most attractive principle for distributing the fruits of economic and social cooperation something like the following: distribute the benefits of cooperation in such a way that the worst-off person does as well as possible. If nothing is gained from an unequal distribution, things should be equally distributed; but if an unequal distribution would make things better for the worst-off person—perhaps by creating incentives that make everyone much more prosperous—then an unequal distribution is better than an equal one, and among all the possible unequal distributions, the best is that which makes the worst-off person as well off as possible. (The intuitive thought is simple enough: If I do not expect to become a doctor, or if there is no way of telling whether I shall become one or not, there is no reason for me to vote for an economic system in which doctors get high salaries, unless I think that this will improve medical services and benefit nondoctors. But if I do expect this to improve medical services and so to benefit me, even if I turn out not to be a doctor, it would be silly to vote against high salaries for doctors simply because I knew I might not turn out to be one.)

This principle is what Rawls calls the "difference principle." It is clear how it resembles the principle of "maximin"—the principle of maximizing the benefits to you of the least favorable outcome of a competitive game. Nonetheless, it is not obvious that this is what rational contractors would choose in a condition of ignorance. It is vital to Rawls's own formulation of his theory that they should choose his maximin conception; and, equally, his utilitarian critics have perceived that it is a point in favor of utilitarianism if the theory of rational choice leads to it even in Rawls's own schema. It is at any rate hard to see why Rawls's contracting parties should be so adamantly opposed to thinking about anyone but the worst-off person. Since nobody has any reason to suppose that he or she is going to be the worst-off person, it is irrationally cautious to choose rules that are exclusively determined by the aim of making the worst-off person as well-off as possible. If we turn out not to be the worst-off person, we may have made unreasonably large sacrifices of our welfare for the sake of the worst off. On the face of it, the principles that ignorance would dictate would have a strong utilitarian component—that is, if we were rational, self-interested, willing to keep our promises, but otherwise uninterested in other people's welfare (the conditions Rawls lays down) and ignorant of our future talents and place in society, we would vote for rules that would make the average person as well-off as possible. We might be a shade more cautious and vote for rules that had an "insurance" component and made sure the worst-off person did not do too badly. But we would have no reason to vote to make the worst-off person as well off as possible if this threatened to take a large slice out of the welfare of the average person. To argue for maximin, Rawls either needs some independent reason for supposing that extreme caution is part of rationality—which means going well beyond anything obtainable from game theory—or needs to appeal more directly to our moral intuitions.

It seems to me—though not, it must be admitted, to most of his critics—that Rawls does the latter; in effect, he appeals to what one might call the psychology of the moral outlook to suggest that nobody who cared much for justice would be able to look the worst-off person in the eye and say that the society he lived in was just, if all he could point to was the fact that the average standard of well-being was high. There is more than a hint of Rousseau rather than Kant in this, and it is a far cry from the view defended by Nozick that all I need ever say to the worst-off person is that I used only what I had a title to and therefore never violated his rights (Nozick 1974, 225–26).

But this principle is, for Rawls, subordinate to another and more important one. This is the principle that all members of society are to have the greatest freedom consistent with a like freedom for all. Here, there is no question of distributing benefits unequally. It is a matter of giving everyone a number of absolute immunities against the tyranny or coercion of others and a number of positive political rights in addition. The right to a fair trial, to freedom of speech, to freedom of occupation, and to vote all belong in this category of rights to the most extensive liberty consistent with a like liberty for all (Rawls 1971, 60). This principle takes what Rawls calls "lexical" priority over the difference principle; that is, before we may think about economic matters, we must first attend to these civil liberties (61). Even if we could make the worst-off person better off by curtailing civil liberties—by abolishing elections for the sake of economic stability, say—we must not do so, for doing so would violate the personal integrity that it is the whole point of this theory to respect.

This is a good point at which to see how Rawls's account of our civil liberties extends into a defense of civil disobedience as a proper element in the political process, for this is the aspect of his theory that seized the attention of many Americans in the bitterest years of the Vietnam War. Rawls gives an account of how justice requires governments to be democratically elected and to govern with due respect for the convictions of the minority; law has no claim on us at all unless it is made by due process. But even if a government is properly constituted and generally governs according to both the letter and the spirit of the law, any political system will have lapses from grace. This poses the problem of how we are to behave if a government violates our considered convictions about what constitutes tolerable policy or legislation. Even under a just constitution, citizens who are concerned about the justice of the government they live under will think that their ultimate duty is to preserve the rule of justice and that this takes priority over the obligation to obey any particular law or command. There cannot be any duty merely to obey every rule or every order handed down by their government. Citizens who are sincerely convinced that some act of government violates justice in a serious way certainly may and sometimes must disobey the law as a way of calling attention to the violation and asking for reconsideration.

To do this they must act nonviolently, and they must be ready to submit to whatever legal penalties there are for breaking the laws they break. It is important to see that it can be only in some political systems that civil disobedience is possible—that is, only in some societies will there be a consensus on what governments ought and ought not to do, and only in some societies will there be such a universal anxiety that people should be able to obey the law in good conscience that what the disobedient are doing will make the right sense to their opponents. Only where the rest of us are desperate not to trample on the consciences of others will civil disobedience make much sense. Gandhi, for instance, thought that no matter what the appearances, the British really shared his followers' sense of justice and could be civilly disobeyed. Rawls never quite says whether America is the scrupulous sort of place he has in mind or whether it had ceased to be so during the Vietnam War. But at a time when the government seemed to be fighting an open war against the Vietcong and a covert one against its own young people, Rawls's reminder of the creative place of dissent in our politics and his insistence that the good citizen owes disobedience as well as obedience to his government was both a noble and a healing gesture.

Not only do questions of civil liberties take priority over questions of welfare, but they also play their part in dictating how the difference principle is to be implemented. So it is not surprising to find Rawls insisting that when we implement the difference principle in economic matters we must make sure that all positions are open to everyone on the basis of equal opportunity (Rawls 1971, 61). That is, the civil liberties that take priority over everything else represent the idea that each person has a basic moral equality with everyone else—the positive face of the proposition that no one is to be merely a means to the ends of others—and since that is so, the only fair terms on which access to positions of advantage can be distributed are those that permit equality of opportunity.

What is surprising in Rawls's theory is not so much what it asserts as what it denies. The main thing it denies is that we should try to distribute income and wealth according to desert. Most people would think that desert is the central notion in justice; Rawls sweeps it aside. People's successes and failures spring from characters and talents they have done nothing to deserve (Rawls 1971, 103–4). They are certainly entitled to whatever income they earn by doing the jobs to which they have been appointed; but this entitlement rests only on our having observed the rules of appointment and performance, not on desert—much as I am entitled to occupy the house I have bought in a fair market, regardless of whether I deserve it. It is only the system of rules under which I gain my entitlements that is subject to further question—the question whether they work for the greatest benefit of the worst off.

Again, Rawls's account of justice has no room for the thought that even if we do not deserve our talents, we still have a right to what we can get from exercising them simply because they are ours. As he puts it, from the standpoint of justice, our talents form part of a common social pool; it is the task of the theory of justice to discover what rights each of us should have over the results of using those talents. To put it another way, Rawls treats property rights as entirely a matter of convention; neither "our" abilities nor what we can get for their exercise "belongs" to us by natural right. About all kinds of property right we must ask: what conventional rights would the theory of justice require us to create? Rawls's theory does not merely support the thought that those who are asked to contribute by way of taxation to the operations of the welfare state have no right to complain about the use of "their" income; it supports the more radical thought that it is not in any deep sense "their" income at all. Many people do not much like the idea that we have no such basic ownership of *any* of our talents, and Robert Nozick for one has made a great deal of play with the grimmer implications of a wholesale denial of such a proprietorship (Nozick 1974, 206–7). For instance, it is as much an arbitrary matter that an intelligent, energetic, and good-looking woman has those agreeable qualities as that Henry Ford II happens to be born the son of Henry Ford; but do we suppose that the intelligent, agreeable, and good-looking woman is either to be deprived of her advantages or else forced to use them in such a way as to benefit the worst off—say, by marrying a man who is (again through no fault of his own) boring, lethargic, and ugly and therefore much in need of a boost to his level of well-being? Indeed, Nozick asks, where does this leave Rawls's insistence on our not being mere means to the ends of others? What is left of me if all my qualities and aptitudes are simply part of the social pool?

Rawls has many resources for disarming his critics. To Nozick, he can properly reply that external property belongs in a morally less serious category than do our own abilities, and these in a less serious category again than do our personal affections. Moreover, the transfer of external property, particularly in the form of money, from one person to another can generally be relied on to do some good. To have someone married to you by force destroys just about all the value of the marriage relationship. To account for such obvious points, there is no need to resort to the thought that we have proprietorial relationships to our personal qualities, talents, and the like.

On more straightforward economic issues, Rawls is equally well placed to fight off critics who claim that he licenses something like the continuous interference of a socialist command economy. Although he often claims that justice is consistent with an economy run on welfare-state capitalist lines *or* on welfare-state socialist lines—since property rights are not part of our basic rights, there is no overriding argument in favor of the private ownership of things like construction companies, railways, or department stores— the theory of justice rules out most of socialism as currently practiced. We cannot have direction of labor except in a military emergency. Since Rawls claims that we can restrict freedom for the sake of freedom but not for the sake of prosperity, the priority of liberty straightforwardly rules out a command economy. Since the same principle dictates that we must give people open access to occupations, most directive planning is ruled out too. Market socialism is consistent with Rawls's theory, but it is a socialism that no socialist country practices and that no country with a capitalist "social market" economy seems tempted to try (cf. Ryan 1984). Moreover, even if the private ownership of businesses is not demanded by Rawls's theory, the private ownership and unconstrained multiplication of consumption goods plainly are, since only thus can people have secure freedom of choice of lifestyle. This, too, is at odds with the practice of most socialist regimes.

It is no part of my argument that Rawls is safe from his critics just because he is not a committed socialist. What the previous paragraph does show, however, is that Rawls is safe from those critics who maintain that what purports to be a defense of liberalism actually collapses into a wholesale collectivism; and it is part of my argument that it is a virtue of Rawls's theory that it leaves open the question whether socialist economic arrangements are consistent with a proper concern for justice and liberty.

This, of course, is not what his critics on the left believe. They do not form a monolithic group, so I cannot pretend to sum a general view. But there are what one might call two representative objections to the theory. The first is the objection that it leaves out too much of the real force of egalitarianism. In Rawls's view, there is no limit to the degree of inequality in society that is "just"; so long as inequalities are necessary to make the worst off as well off as possible—or, rather, better off than the worst off would be in any other system we might reach—their extent is neither here nor there. No one brought up on writers like R. H. Tawney (1932) would accept that. Genuine egalitarians want to close the gap between the best off and the worst off even if in worldly terms the worst off do somewhat less well than they otherwise might as a result. It is not clear to me how hard this criticism bites on Rawls's theory of justice. It must do so to some degree, since Rawls's theory explains the place of equality in economic life as a feature of the self-interest of the worst off and cannot therefore treat equality as a moral and political value with a life of its own. But it may not bite hard, since by the time Rawls himself has argued for the virtues of a society in which envy can have no place, he has begun to sound a good deal more like Tawney himself (Rawls 1971, 536ff.).

Rawls's Marxist critics, on the other hand, have less difficulty in establishing their distance from him. Marxism takes almost the polar opposite of stances at all levels. Methodologically, Marxism is hostile to "rational man" theories and hostile to "state of nature" theories; against Rawls, all Marxists argue that he performs the characteristic sleight of hand of apologists for capitalism by building in to human nature the features of competitors in the capitalist marketplace. Thus, it is not a truth about human nature that we need to be offered incentives to develop our talents, but a truth only about men in competitive conditions who will give nobody anything for nothing (Lang 1979, 123ff.; Macpherson 1973, 87ff.). But only by building in such false assumptions can Rawls motivate his theory. The retort, of course, is that the record of Marxist attempts to run society on other assumptions about human nature has been so depressing that it seems safer to believe that human nature is more or less as Rawls's theory supposes it to be, and that the picture of men building a decent society on the basis of mutual advantage before they go on to create relationships of a more fraternal and altruistic kind is politically prudent as well as morally compelling.

Morally (if one can use that term of a Marxist view), Marxism and Rawls's theory are equally at odds. There is no room in Rawls's theory for such a notion as "alienation"—the idea that men have created a world that now oppresses them as an alien power demands a theory of history and a philosophy of human nature quite at odds with the world of prudent calculators in a timeless bargaining situation. There is room in Rawls's theory for the other concept on which Marx's condemnation of capitalism rests, the concept of exploitation, but Rawls would not analyze exploitation in the same way, and the result would be very different from Marx's own concept of exploitation. Rawls would think of exploitation as a matter of well-placed bargainers driving iniquitous bargains with poorly placed bargainers, while Marx tried to show that exploitation occurred not in exchange, but in production. Again, the morality appealed to by Rawls is individualistic and supposes that the significant actors on the moral stage are individuals who mind about the conscientiousness of their actions; Marxists look rather to classes and consider the extent to which their actions promote their interests and the purposes of history, and place more store by solidarity than by justice. To say whether Rawls has adequate defenses against all this is quite impossible. It is even truer here than it usually is that the issues at stake go so deep that they involve the adoption or rejection of something like an entire weltanschauung rather than a particular theory. What one can say is that insofar as Rawls claims that the ultimate test of his theory lies in its appeal to the reflective intuitions about justice that he takes all his readers to share, the conviction of highly intelligent and open-minded Marxists that they share no such thing is at any rate disturbing.

Even if one is neither a conservative nor a Marxist, one may have doubts about the solidity of the theory. One important doubt is about the priority of liberty over other values, and about the doctrine associated with it, namely, that liberty can be restricted only for the sake of liberty. In a general way, it is easy to see Rawls's point—liberals would hardly be liberals if they were willing to sell their freedom for a 2 percent rise in gross national product. On the other hand, liberals would hardly be liberals if they thought that a commitment to democracy entailed that we should institute majority rule tomorrow afternoon in a society where we knew for certain that the first thing the majority would do would be to pass anti-Semitic legislation and the second thing would be to pass a law restricting voting rights (Rawls 1971, 228ff.).

But Rawls goes further than that, and in doing so surely makes a mistake. The thought that liberty can be restricted only for the sake of liberty hardly survives reflection on the criminal law: it is not for the sake of the liberty of my fellows that my freedom to hit them on the head is curtailed—it is for their safety—and it is not for the sake of their liberty that my freedom to steal their goods is curtailed either (Hart 1975). Conversely, Rawls himself agrees that there will be conditions when the absolute priority of liberty makes no sense; if people are so hard up that they cannot use their freedom, then we may curtail liberty for the sake of making their freedom more valuable to them by increasing their prosperity. At this point, one may feel that the theory is beginning to lose its simplicity and elegance and that we are slipping back toward the view that all we can do is trade off various values against each other—Rawls, like a good liberal, is insisting that we exact a high price for losses of liberty, but not doing anything more distinctive than that.

In short, Rawls's theory offers a large and tempting target to critics. People who dislike the methodology complain that we cannot find out what our rights and duties are by asking what they would have been if they had been created by contract. Critics on the left complain that the attempt to make civil rights sacrosanct in a way that economic welfare is not ignores all those countries where survival, let alone comfort, demands tough, illiberal governments that can force birth control, efficient irrigation, sensible farming methods, and the other requisites of development upon a backward population. Critics on the right who care less for the Third World than for the rights of Westchester County either conspire with the Left to argue that the various emergency clauses that Rawls allows to override the absolute priority of liberty can be invoked so often that they let governments do anything they like, or else throw up their hands in horror and refuse to believe that Rawls is so wicked as to think that we do not deserve our riches and do not really own our own abilities.

But reading Rawls is a particularly salutary experience for British readers. British politics is unaccustomed to a strenuous insistence on people's rights—our liberalism does not rest on the thought that people have absolute freedom of religious profession, free speech, and the like, but on the thought that it does more harm than good to push dissenters around; and our welfare arrangements rest on a vague feeling that we ought to be nice to those worse off than us. To come across a writer arguing for 500 pages that even if it did do some good, we *must* not push dissenters around and that regardless of our feelings about them, the hard-up have a *right* to be as well off as possible is a useful shock to our insular and excessively casual modes of thought.

Further Reading

Before the publication of *A Theory of Justice* (1971), Rawls had written several articles that were much discussed; in addition to "Justice as Fairness" (1958), there was "The Sense of Justice" (1963a), "Constitutional Liberty and the Concept of Justice" (1963b), and "Distributive Justice" (1967); since the publication of *A Theory of Justice*, Rawls has contributed to a symposium on the book in the *Journal of Philosophy* (1972) and has expanded some of its arguments in "Fairness to Goodness" (1975) and in his Dewey Lecture, "Kantian Constructionism in Moral Theory" (1980). His reply to Hart's doubts about the "priority of liberty" comes in "The Basic Liberties and Their Priority" (1982).

The critical literature is enormous; there is a ten-page bibliography of articles from the period 1971–76 (Fullinwider 1977). Happily, fourteen of the most interesting of them are reprinted in the anthology by Daniels (1975). There are book-length studies of Rawls by Barry (1973) and Wolff (1977). But the impact of Rawls is visible in most recent work in political theory, for instance, in that by Miller (1976), Dworkin (1978,) Fried (1978), and Walzer (1983). The study by Nozick (1974) remains the best route into the strengths and weaknesses of Rawls's work as well as an outstandingly interesting book in its own right.

Much of the work on Rawls has been concerned with the coherence and validity of the attempt to derive rights from a contractual framework, and has been highly critical. Scanlon (1982) attempts to rescue the insights of contractualism; a balanced essay by Hart (1979) is in the same vein. Lastly, it should be noted that Parfit (1984) defends utilitarianism by conceding Rawls's claim that the separateness of persons would be an argument against utilitarianism and then proceeding to argue that persons are not, in a deep sense, separate after all.

References

Ackerman, B. 1980. *Social Justice in the Liberal State*. New Haven, Conn.

Barry, B. 1965. *Political Argument*. London.

———. 1973. *The Liberal Theory of Justice*. Oxford.

Bentham, J. 1949. *"Principles of Morals and Legislation" and "A Fragment on Government."* Edited by W. Harrison. Oxford.

Burke. E. 1961. *Reflections on the Revolution in France*. New York.

Daniels, N. 1975. *Reading Rawls*. Oxford.

Dworkin. R. 1978. "Liberalism." In *Public and Private Morality*, edited by S. Hampshire. Cambridge.

Fried, C. 1978. *Right and Wrong*. Cambridge, Mass.

Fullinwider, R. K. 1977. "A Chronological Bibliography of Works on John Rawls." *Political Theory* 5:561–70.

Hampshire, S. 1972. "A New Philosophy of the Just Society." *New York Review of Books*, Feb. 24, 1972, 38–39.

Hart, H.L.A. 1975. "Rawls on Liberty and Its Priority." In *Reading Rawls: Critical Studies of "A Theory of Justice,"* edited by N. Daniels, 230–52. Oxford.

———. 1979. "Between Utility and Rights." *Columbia Law Review* 79:828–46.

Hume, D. 1963. "Of the Original Contract." In *Essays*, 452–73. Oxford.

Lang, W. 1979. "Marxism, Liberalism, and Justice." In *Justice*, edited by E. Kamenka and A. Erh-Soon-Tay, 116–48. London.

Locke. J. 1967. *Two Treatises of Government*. Edited by P. Laslett. Cambridge.

Macpherson, C. B. 1973. *Democratic Theory: Essays in Retrieval*. Oxford.

Miller, D. 1976. *Social Justice*. Oxford.

Nozick. R. 1974. *Anarchy, State, and Utopia*. New York.

Parfit, D. 1984. *Reasons and Persons*. Oxford.

Rawls, J. 1958. "Justice as Fairness." *Philosophical Review* 67:164–94.

———. 1963a. "The Sense of Justice." *Philosophical Review* 72:281–304.

———. 1963b. "Constitutional Liberty and the Concept of Justice." In *Nomos 6: Justice*, edited by C. J. Friedrich and J. W. Chapman. New York.

———. 1967. "Distributive Justice." In *Philosophy, Politics, and Society*, 3rd series, edited by P. Laslett and W. G. Runciman. Oxford.

———. 1971. *A Theory of Justice*. Cambridge, Mass.

———. 1975. "Fairness to Goodness." *Philosophical Review* 84:536–64.

———. 1980. "Kantian Constructionism in Moral Theory." *Journal of Philosophy* 87, no. 9: 515–72.

———. 1982. "The Basic Liberties and Their Priority." In *The Tanner Lectures on Human Values* 3, edited by S. McMurrin. Cambridge.

Reiss. H., ed. 1972. *Kant's Political Writings*. Cambridge.

Ryan, A. 1984. "Socialism and Freedom." In *New Fabian Essays on Socialism*, edited by B. Pimlott, 101–16. London.

Scanlon, T. M. 1982. "Contractualism and Utilitarianism." In *Utilitarianism and Beyond*, edited by Amartya Sen and Bernard Williams. Cambridge.

Schilpp, F. 1943. *The Philosophy of Bertrand Russell*. New York.

Tawney, R. H. 1932. *Equality*. London.

Walzer, M. 1983. *Spheres of Justice*. New York.

Will, G. 1984. *Statecraft as Soulcraft*. New York.

Wolff. R. P. 1977. *Understanding Rawls: A Critique and Reconstruction of "A Theory of Justice."* Princeton, N.J.

PART 5

Work, Ownership, Freedom, and Self-Realization

27

Locke and the Dictatorship of the Bourgeoisie

IT IS A COMMONPLACE, but true, that the two terms on which Locke rests the greatest weight of doctrine in the *Second Treatise* are "consent" and "property." It is with the second of these terms that we are here concerned, and in particular with the use which Locke makes of his doctrine that "the great and *chief end* therefore, of Mens uniting into Commonwealths, and putting themselves under Government, *is the Preservation of their Property*."[2] There has been a good deal of criticism leveled at Locke's account of property from one direction or another. Complaints of wild and absurd individualism[3] contrast with assertions of his collectivist leanings.[4] Complaints about his obsession with history that never happened[5] contrast with assertions of his intense interest in, and the great importance to his theory of, sociology, history and anthropology,[6] in as genuine a form as the seventeenth century knew them. Here we shall concentrate on a different issue, namely, on the extent to which it is true that Locke's account of property, and his resultant account of natural rights, political obligation, and the proper functions of government, form an ideology for a rising capitalist class. My question is, how far does what Locke says in the *Second Treatise* substantiate Macpherson's[7] thesis that he was providing—perhaps no more than half-consciously—a moral basis for the dictatorship of the bourgeoisie?

One initial clarification of the scope of my discussion of this question is needed. Macpherson uses a good deal of material from outside the *Second Treatise* to substantiate his view of it. Indeed, his working assumption seems often enough to be that we should look for Locke's political theory outside the *Second Treatise* and then see whether previously ambiguous passages in that work (numerous enough in anyone's reading) will square with the theory obtained elsewhere. This may be a method appropriate to a historical inquiry into Locke's political intentions; it may yield the historian a coherent and convincing answer to the question of what Locke *really meant*. Here, however, I take the alternative path of attempting to find within the *Second Treatise* alone some coherent doctrine of political right and obligation, based on what Locke says there about property. Such an account may perhaps be in danger of refutation by the historian as an account of what Locke intended. It is in less, even no, danger of contradiction from such a quarter as an account of what Locke said. And in case this is thought too small a claim, let me point out that we usually hold people to what they say rather than to what they may suppose to follow from what they meant to say.

The essence of Macpherson's account is that Locke intends to supply the moral basis of that stage of economic advance that we have called the dictatorship of the bourgeoisie; this is a state of unrestrained capitalism, brutal in its treatment of the laboring classes and ruthless in its destruction of traditional values, of all social ties that impede the advance of the propertied classes. Locke is thus arguing for nothing less than the rightful absolute power of the propertied classes, for a morally justified tyranny of the employers over the employed. Indeed, the laboring and the unemployed classes have their rights so ruthlessly eroded that their status is to be subject to civil society without being full members of it; they are in it but not of it. The state of nature that Locke envisages must therefore be such that these elements of the bourgeois state follow from it. Crediting Locke, as no one has done before, with a logically rigorous deduction of civil society from the state of nature, Macpherson argues that everything in the state of nature conceived by Locke was put there by him for the purpose of generating some feature or other of bourgeois society. The misery, the viciousness, and the instabilities of the resulting society are attributed to "contradictions" put into the state of nature by Locke. I need not emphasize how different is this Locke from the one we have met before.

I

The twin pivots upon which Macpherson's account turns are the premises he ascribes to Locke of the natural proprietorship of one's own labor, and the dependence of freedom and morality, and hence of citizenship, upon the possession of rationality. These are, of course, important elements in Locke's political theory; to Macpherson, they account for the whole of this theory. They are central, vital, and closely connected. Rationality is evinced by (sometimes it seems that Macpherson is saying it is identified with) the ability to acquire goods and go on acquiring them up to the limits set by the law of nature. A rational man is one who obeys the law of reason, and the law of reason is in turn the law of nature, and this is the will of God. Given such a gloss on what it is to be rational, the argument clearly runs that it is morally excellent to accumulate, that success in accumulating is a moral virtue, and hence that the man of property is of greater moral worth than the man without property. In the state of nature before the invention of money, the title to property is given by labor, for in the state of nature, each man is originally the unconditional owner of his own labor. This doctrine is, on Macpherson's account of it, an important and indeed a decisive break with medieval attitudes to labor and property, which were concerned to emphasize the obligations of a man to society and to his fellows, not his rights against them. So the rational man sets about accumulating property, and because his right to it is derived from his absolute right to his own labor, this right is absolute, too. According to Macpherson: "If it is labour, a man's absolute property, which justifies appropriation and creates rights, the individual right of appropriation overrides any moral claims of the society. The traditional view that property and labour were social functions and that the ownership of property involved social obligations, is thereby undermined."[8] Thus Locke secures the right to unlimited accumulation.

But in the state of nature before the invention of money, there are two limitations upon the exercise of this right. The first is that "enough and as good" must be left for others (Locke, *Two Treatises*, secs. 27, 33, 35), which one may call the sufficiency limitation. The second is that nothing may spoil in the hands of the person who gathers it: "As much as any one can make use of to any advantage of life before it spoils; so much he may by his labour fix a Property in. Whatever is beyond this, is more than his share, and belongs to others. Nothing was made by God for Man to spoil or destroy" (secs. 31, 37, 38, 46). This we may call the spoliation limitation. There is a third apparent limitation imposed by the labor criterion of ownership, namely, that a man must mix his labor with whatever he appropriates (see, for example, sec. 27). This limitation lies at the heart of what one might call "radical" labor theories of value, where the intention is to deny any title to property other than the title of manual labor. The obvious similarity between Locke's premises and those of all labor theorists leads many writers to suppose that he shares, or at any rate should have shared, this conclusion; but as we shall see, it is an important part of Macpherson's case that Locke never intended such a limitation at all.

The two initial limitations are transcended by the invention of money. They are not broken or cast aside; rather, the sort of conditions under which they are applicable no longer obtain. The invention of money is seen by Locke as the discovery of "some lasting thing that Men might keep without spoiling, and that by mutual consent Men would take in exchange for the truly useful, but perishable Supports of Life" (sec. 47). Although a man may by purchase acquire more land than he can use the immediate product of, he still leaves enough and as good for other men. It is true that this is not enough *land* and as good as that appropriated—though Locke seems at times to want to argue that even this is true—but rather that the standard of living is at least as good as before for everyone else (secs. 37, 41). That is, even when all the land is appropriated, the general standard of living is improved for everyone, even for the landless, because the invention of money has enabled the rational capitalist to apply his skills and labor to land and raw material that were formerly of little or no value to mankind. Locke puts a good deal of stress on this: "For I ask whether in the wild woods and uncultivated wast of America left to Nature, without any improvement, tillage or husbandry, a thousand acres will yield the needy and wretched inhabitants as many conveniences of life as ten acres of equally fertile land doe in

Devonshire where they are well cultivated (sec. 37)." Besides this transcending of the sufficiency limitation, there is now no risk of infringing the spoliation limitation.

For money does not decay, so however much of it a man has, he has no fears of it perishing uselessly in his possession. A man may heap up gold and silver ad infinitum: "He might heap up as much of these durable things as he pleased; the exceeding of the bounds of his just Property not lying in the largeness of his Possession, but the perishing of anything uselessly in it" (sec. 46). As for the third limitation, Locke never meant it to hold. The crucial point about Locke's calling labor a form of property is not that it is a peculiar and sacred form of property, but that being property, it is alienable; in the state of nature as elsewhere, men must be supposed free to exchange their labor for subsistence or for a wage. (Indeed they must, if Locke's fantasy of a prepolitical market economy is to make any sense.) In his support, Macpherson quotes Locke's equation of "my" labor with the labor of my servant. The passage runs: "Thus the Grass my Horse has bit; the Turfs my Servant has cut; and the Ore I have digg'd in any place where I have a right to them in common with others, become my *Property*, without the assignation or consent of anybody. The *labour* that was mine, removing them out of that common state they were in, hath *fixed* my *Property* in them" (sec. 28). The only meaning that such a passage will bear indicates that Locke never doubted that one man could appropriate the labor of another and thus become the owner of it. "My" labor includes the labor of anyone I employ; hence, the requirement that we mix "our" labor with whatever we appropriate imposes no limits on the right to appropriate.

Given that it is morally excellent to accumulate property, whether consumable or durable, but particularly the latter, and given that the invention of money enables such accumulation to go on indefinitely, certain consequences for Locke's political theory may be drawn. Macpherson not only goes on to draw them, but also holds that Locke drew them too and, further, that Locke regarded them as the most important parts of his theory. The first is that Locke's wide definition of property as "Lives, Liberties, and Estates, which I call by the general Name Property" (sec. 124) is not the one usually adhered to, and is not the one involved in the crucial sections of the *Second Treatise* dealing with the limits on the authority of any government and with the right of the people to rebel against governments which they find oppressive.[9] In these passages, says Macpherson, "property" means what we normally mean by the term, and refers particularly to property in fixed capital goods. From this it follows that "the people" to whom Locke entrusts the right of rebellion cannot be the whole population, but must be the propertied classes only. The grounds of revolt are comprised under the heading of the government failing to preserve the property of its citizens; since very few people have any property, only this small number have any right to rebel. Laborers without property are in any case not fully rational—as demonstrated by the fact that they have no property—and therefore have no claim to full membership of civil society: "While the labouring class is a necessary part of the nation its members are not in fact full members of the body politic and have no claim to be so . . . Whether by their own fault or not, members of the labouring class did not have, could not be expected to have, and were not entitled to have full membership in political society."[10] As something less than full members of political society, they are objects of administration rather than citizens.

This part of Macpherson's case is a crucial one, and my criticism of Macpherson's interpretation of Locke is largely concerned with this part of his account. An added merit Macpherson claims for his account is that it disposes of such riddles as Locke's basing obligation upon consent. If "the people" are in fact the propertied classes, then they will readily give their consent to whatever the legislative enacts, since what it enacts will always be in their class interest, and the interest of the class against the rest of society is more vital to each member of it than is his own interest against other members of his class. The state has thus become a committee for managing the common interests of the bourgeoisie. Naturally, this also solves the clash between the individualist and collectivist elements in Locke's thought. To behave as an extreme individualist is to behave as a successful capitalist, and this is to achieve moral excellence; it is, however, a form of moral excellence only possible at the expense of those against whom one competes successfully, and of those whose labor one uses to enrich oneself. Hence, what is needed by the individualists is a strong government that will hold the ring for their competition. Its strength is no threat to them, since it is a blatant instrument of class rule; the tough capitalist does not require protection from his fellows. According to Macpherson: "The individuals who have the means to realize their personalities (that is, the propertied) do not need to reserve any rights as against civil society, since civil society is constructed by and for them, and run by and for them."[11] The propertied class has a coherent, cohesive interest in maintaining its position vis-à-vis the laboring classes. Individual rights thus disappear: the laboring classes have none, the propertied class needs none. Similarly, the oft-noted analogy between Locke's civil society and a joint-stock company takes on a new aspect. Locke "would have no difficulty in thinking of the state as a joint-stock company of owners whose majority decision binds not only themselves, but also their employees."[12] The only shareholders in the firm are the board of directors. The workers are employed to maximize the wealth of the firm, but have no say in the running of the company. Thus, the domination of the state by the rising bourgeoisie is complete; its goals are their goals; its machinery is their machinery; its decisions are their decisions. Their power over the laboring proletariat is absolute, and it is rightly so.

II

Macpherson supports this account of the ideological Locke with a good deal of quotation from the *Second Treatise*; but it will be appreciated by anyone familiar with that work and the variety of interpretation to which it has given rise that no conclusive argument emerges from these quotations alone. The establishing of Locke as a capitalist lackey rests heavily, therefore, on his economic writings, in which his attitude to the laboring poor and even more to the unemployed is indubitably severe. Similarly, Locke's disparagement of the rationality of the poor is drawn from *The Reasonableness of Christianity*. In the light of a theory drawn from these sources, it is not difficult to put the appropriate gloss on the ambiguous passages of the *Second Treatise*. (All my objections to Macpherson are based on the unambiguous passages to which I fear he pays less careful attention.) About these outside sources, I am skeptical. For one thing, they cover a period of forty years, and one may doubt both Locke's consistency over that period and his remaining interested in precisely the same problems for so long. For a second thing, *The Reasonableness of Christianity* was largely written to point out that the detailed disputes of sects were beyond the scope of *anybody's* reason, and its moral hardly seems to be that the working class is peculiarly irrational. It may be an ungracious response to so exciting an account as Macpherson's, but the impression made by his welding together of all this disparate evidence into a tough, lucid, and consistent theory is that of an interpretative tour de force rather than of a natural or convincing account of Locke.

Confining ourselves to the *Second Treatise*, there is ample room for doubt about Macpherson's account, and some plainly unambiguous statements by Locke that flatly contradict it. On the issue of rationality, for example, it is true that this is Locke's basis for knowledge of the moral law and hence the basis for being able to obey it. But it is quite incredible that Locke intends us to believe it is the property of one class only, or that he thinks it is chiefly displayed in the acquisition of capital goods. It is stated explicitly by Locke that very nearly all men are rational enough to know what the law of nature requires of them, though most men are little enough inclined always to obey it: "The *State of Nature* has a Law of Nature to govern it, which obliges everyone; and Reason which is that Law teaches all mankind who will but consult it" (sec. 6; cf. sec. 12). The problem is not that some people have not the ability to know what the law requires of them, but that they will not take the trouble to think that they are morally obliged to do, or if they do take that trouble, they will not take the trouble to do what they are morally obliged to. The reason, in general, why the law of nature is not enough is human selfishness and not human intelligence. In fact, the only qualification Locke places on the general possession of rationality is that of age or mental defect: "We are born Free, as we are born Rational; not that we have actually the exercise of either; Age that brings one, brings with it the other too" (sec. 61.). The only persons other than the young who are not qualified by rationality are "Lùnaticks and Ideots. . . . Madmen" (sec. 60), who hardly seem to be coextensive with the whole class of the laboring poor whom Locke is said to have written off as nonrational. Moreover, this statement by Locke comes only one chapter after the account of property rights in which the erosion of the rationality of the propertyless is supposed to have occurred. The total absence of any sign that Locke was sliding into the doctrine that is said to be his considered opinion leaves us with no grounds for supposing that the mere absence of property in the sense of capital goods is sufficient to deny citizenship to persons who, by all normal tests, are sane and rational when they reach years of discretion.

Moreover, there is a good deal of confusion in Macpherson's account of what is supposed by Locke to be the distinctively rational feature of capitalist accumulation. There is initially a good deal of confusion in Locke too, but Macpherson does not so much clear this up as ignore it in favor of a doctrine that he attributes to Locke, apparently for no better cause than that it is the doctrine that a moralizing capitalist ought to have held. The only consistent line for Locke to take is fairly simple, and the elements of it are at least hidden in the account of property rights he does give. The will of God, which he identifies with the law of nature and the demands of reason, requires all men to be preserved as far as possible. The man who appropriates land, employs his skill upon it, and thus enriches mankind is thereby obeying the demands of reason, that is, he is being rational. This is Locke's argument in a number of places. He refers initially to the right that each man has of preserving all mankind (see, for example, sec. 11)—a "right" that is better termed a duty. He argues that the man who encloses land and works it confers a benefit upon mankind; almost everything required for a civilized existence is due to the skill and effort that men have lavished upon the raw materials supplied by nature. In one passage he begins with the assertion:

> I think it will be but a very modest Computation to say, that of the *Products* of the Earth useful to the Life of Man nine out of ten are the *effects of Labour*. (sec. 40)

Just how modest he thinks this computation to be appears soon enough:

> Nay, if we will rightly estimate things as they come to our use, and cast up the several Expences about them, what in them is purely owing to *Nature*, and what to *labour*, we shall find, that in most of them ninety-nine out of one hundred are wholly to be put on the account of *labour*. (sec. 40)

And a moment later the proportion becomes 999 parts in 1,000 (sec. 43). The invention of money allows this process to be carried to the lengths typical of a developed economy. Thus the laborer, along with society generally, benefits from the activities of the capitalists. And this is the rationale of capitalism.

But, what is the incentive for the capitalist himself? According to Macpherson, Locke holds that capitalists develop their personalities in capitalism; but Locke says nothing of the sort, and in any case, it is both an unconvincing and vacuous account of the matter. What does it amount to beyond the assertion that people who want to become capitalists gratify their wish if they do become capitalists? Locke in fact is confused. At one point he suggests that nothing more than a fanciful liking for gold is at the bottom of it—but the rationality of piling up prettily colored stones and metals is not clear. The value of money, of course, is a fancy value, not in the sense of being a fanciful value, but in the sense of being an agreed or conventional value. But Locke does sometimes equate this with having no value at all. When he refuses to allow the conqueror the right to the conquered's territory, he excludes money thus: "For as to Money, and such Riches and Treasure taken away, these are none of Natures Goods, they have but a Phantastical imaginary value: Nature has put no such upon them" (sec. 184; cf. sec. 46). This clearly confuses conventional value and no value at all. The explanation of the good sense of capitalism that Locke hints at elsewhere, which makes a sound case, had three elements in it. The first is that men have come to have more wants than nature gave them; they desire more than they absolutely need; clearly, the day laborer living at the English subsistence level is much better off than the Indian king living at a high standard for a savage; a rational man will clearly join in this better consumption—an explanation of the inducement to become a capitalist that Macpherson rejects, but that makes good sense. But on occasion, Locke identifies the desire of having more than we need with simple greed and suggests that the premonetary state of nature was a golden age (sec. 111). In which case, the capitalist is not merely not rational, not morally excellent, but positively corrupt. (Macpherson's defense that the condemnation of greed applies not to the capitalist but to the propertyless who covet the capitalists' goods is clever, but is impossible to reconcile what Locke says about the earliest governments ruling a simple society.[13] It is the whole state of society, not that of a single class, that Locke commends or disapproves of, and he clearly places the arrival of greed at the time of the invention of money [sec. 108].) The second element is one that we have already discussed, namely, the argument that the capitalist is morally bound to promote the well-being of society; and Locke tends—as we noted in the case in which he terms a duty a "right"—to equate being bound by reason with wanting to do what reason tells one. So for Locke, doing what is right can be something the capitalist gets out of being a capitalist. The third element is Locke's suggestion that a man will want to provide for other people to whom he feels an obligation or perhaps for those to whom he simply wants to give his goods. Giving away is a recognized form of use (sec. 46).

Of these three elements, only the first is a genuine prudential consideration that would allow us to say that the capitalist was being rational in the prudential sense rather than in the moral sense. It is plainly the account that Locke ought to have taken to match his conventionalist account of money. For if money has a conventional value within some society or other, then the whole point of getting rich is to be able to share the advantages of that society's economy to an increased extent. It seems that Macpherson confuses further what Locke confuses sufficiently. The only consistent line to be found in Locke is that capitalism is rational—morally—because it is a step to the betterment of society, and that being a capitalist is rational—prudentially—because it enables one to enjoy a greater share of the betterment. A man's share in the greater social product is both his incentive and his reward. But so simple a doctrine as this is far indeed from fulfilling the requirements of Macpherson's theory.

This becomes clearer when we examine Macpherson's curious assertion that property rights are absolute because labor rights are so. The labor theory of proprietorship has been much misunderstood by Macpherson. It begins not as a theory of proprietorship but as theory of identification.[14] Locke says of the diet of the Indian: "The Fruit, or Venison, which nourishes the wild *Indian*, who knows no Inclosure, and is still a Tenant in common, must be his, and so his, i.e. a part of him, that another can no longer have any right to it, before it can do him any good for the support of his Life" (sec. 26). But the sense in which food must belong to a man before it can do him any good is a biological one—namely, he has to eat it; and the sense in which an Indian's nourishment is *his* is a logical one—namely, that we can identify nourishment only by identifying the man nourished. This is not to talk of rights at all, and particularly not to talk of absolute rights. It is a very dangerous way of talking, for it swiftly confuses the "his" of identification with the "his" of ownership or rightful possession. Thus, there is a perfectly good sense in which "the *Labour* of his Body, and the Work of his Hands we may say, are properly his" (sec. 27). But this sense needs elucidating. In one sense, it is bound to be "his," since it is a truth of logic that only *he* can do *his* laboring, and in this sense, whomever he labors for, it is still "his" labor. But this does not establish that the only person entitled to benefit from his labor is himself. It is, moreover, impossible to reconcile Locke's concern for the rights of wives and children with the right to be absolutely selfish that Macpherson ascribes to Locke's natural man.

The confusion may be as much Locke's fault as anyone's, but it is fair to point out that Locke never talks of an "absolute" right to anything at all. Customarily accepted moral obligations are not mentioned—or not often—but this might well be because Locke took them for granted, not because he did not accept them. Locke's concern, after all, was to defend men against royal force and robbery, and this is not a category that includes the demands of friends and family. The point of Locke's initial account of the right to goods given by labor is surely negative. He is faced with the question of how undifferentiated goods become the exclusive property of some one man; and the answer is that where there is plenty for everyone, acquisition and ownership need not be distinguished. If a man acquires something without breaking the laws of nature in the manner of his acquiring it, that is enough. The answer to the question "Who has it?" serves as the answer to the question "Whose is it?" Macpherson's emphasis on the absence of obligation to society is odd in view of the fact that at this point, the conditions that create social ties do not exist at all; and the minimal obligation of leaving enough and as good for whoever may chance along is surely some sort of obligation, while obligations to one's family presumably exist at this rudimentary stage too. And Locke says clearly enough that when a man enters society, he has his social title to his goods on society's terms (sec. 120)—a pre-echo of Rousseau. This, after all, is Locke's consistent line: we enter society to protect our property, so we must be prepared to contribute our fair share of whatever is required for this defense, and society must judge what it needs for the successful performance of its functions. If property includes life, limb, liberty, and possessions, then some pay taxes, but all forgo their natural liberty, and all are liable for the defense of the country from enemies external and internal (secs. 128–30).

If we are correct in arguing that talk of "absolute" property is seriously misleading and that no sort of absolute ownership is involved in life, liberty, or goods, on all of which there can be claims, then there seems less reason than ever to suppose that Locke restricts the meaning of "property" to fixed property in goods or to suppose that he is engaged in an attempt to deprive the proletariat of all political rights for the benefit of the employing classes. The only essential characteristic that property possesses is that property is that of which a man cannot be deprived without his consent; for example, Locke says of the rights of the conquered under the conqueror: "Whatsoever he grants them, they have so far as it is granted, *property* in. The nature whereof is, that *without a Man's own consent* it *cannot be taken from him*" (sec. 195). And elsewhere, it is the absence of this characteristic that removes a possession from the position of actually being a man's property: "For I have truly no *Property* in that, which another can by right, take from me, when he pleases, against my consent" (sec. 138). This characteristic applies for Locke to all goods both bodily and mental, except one's own life, which one cannot dispose of by contract, but which one can lose the right to by a sufficient breach of the natural law. It is significant that Macpherson's view of the power exercised over the propertyless is that of Locke; it is despotic power, absolute and arbitrary, a power that Locke explicitly contrasts with political power. And it is crucially important to notice that the only case of despotic power allowed by Locke, and hence, by inference, the only case he allows of a man without property, is power over the renegade against reason and society:

> *Despotical Power* is an absolute, arbitrary power one man has over another, to take away his life, whenever he pleases. This is a power, which neither Nature gives . . . nor Compact can convey . . . but it is *the effect only of Forfeiture*, which the Aggressor makes of his own life, when he puts himself into the state of war with another. (sec. 172)

Of political power he says in the next paragraph:

> (By *Property* I must be understood here, as in other places, to mean that property which men have in their persons as well as goods.) *Voluntary Agreement gives . . . Political Power to Governours* for the benefit of their subjects, to secure them in the possession and use of their properties. (sec. 173)

And this power is immediately contrasted with power over the propertyless:

> And *Forfeiture* gives the third, *Despotical Power to Lords* for their own benefit, over those who are stripp'd of all property. (sec. 173)

And finally he sums up:

> *Paternal Power* is only where minority makes the child incapable to manage his property; *Political* where men have property in their own disposal; and *Despotical* over such as have no property at all. (sec. 174)

This seems to me conclusive enough against Macpherson's thesis that "property" is to be read as if it referred only to property in goods. An obvious consequence, however, that we must draw is that if we accept Locke's wide reading of property as *bona civilia* ("civil goods"), or "life, liberty, health, and indolency of body; and the possession of outward things such as money, lands, houses, furniture, and the like" (sec. 3, editor's note), then it is clear that we must accept the whole population who have reached years of discretion as being the "people" for the purposes of entrusting them with the right of revolution. That Locke did so is shown clearly by what he considers as a possible objection to his doctrine: "To this perhaps it will be said, that the people being ignorant, and always discontented, to lay the foundation of Government in the unsteady opinion, and uncertain humour of the people, is to expose it to certain ruine" (sec. 223).

His reply does not matter: what is important is how this contradicts Macpherson's picture of Locke. Locke is hardly likely to think it a plausible criticism of the rising capitalists that they are ignorant or unsteady of opinion or uncertain of humor. One verbal point that might lead one into accepting Macpherson's account is Locke's talk of "deputies" and "representatives"; it is easy enough to slip into thinking that this involves electing MPs—and of course no one suggests that Locke is advocating universal suffrage. But if we recall that Locke counts a monarch ruling without a council, or a permanent oligarchy, as legislatives in precisely the same sense as the English king-in-Parliament is a legislative, it becomes clear that to be represented is not necessarily to have voted (sec. 138). Macpherson may still be willing to argue that the laborer is not a "full member" of civil society—but the trouble here is that Locke talks only of members, and never distinguishes between full and any other sort of membership. The passage Macpherson rests his case on is an oddity, and is anyway concerned with distinguishing the status of foreigners residing in a country from that of genuine subjects:

> And thus we see, that *Foreigners*, by living all their lives under another Government, and enjoying the priviledges and protection of it, though they are bound, even in conscience, to submit to its administration, as far forth as any Denison; yet do not thereby come to be *Subjects or Members of that Commonwealth*. Nothing can make any man *so*, but his actually entering into it by positive engagement, and express promise and compact. (sec. 122)

Here it is the foreigner who is being contrasted with the member or subject; Macpherson's contrast is between the laborer who is a subject but not a member, and the propertied man who is both, a contrast of which the text is innocent. The obligation that the laborer and the foreigner incur, they incur along with the capitalist, for they have all given their tacit consent by enjoying property: "Whether this his possession be of land to him and his heirs for ever, or a lodging only for a week; or whether it be barely travelling freely on the highway" (sec. 119).

If this puts the laborer on a level with the foreigner, it does so only by putting him on a level with his employer too. Locke never solves the problem of why a man's first country is thought to be his only country, but it is surely implausible to suggest that he anticipated Marx in holding that the proletarian has no country, only a class. It would be a foolish doctrine for Locke to hold, since it would have involved him in releasing laborers from the obligation to defend their country against external enemies, and would have meant that they could not be held guilty of such crimes as treason. We cannot but conclude that if laborers can be said to have a property—and we have seen no reason why they cannot be—then they are members of civil society. They receive benefits and accept corresponding obligations. They may pay no taxes, but they lend their labor and their strength to the defense of their society against enemies internal and external: "The *Power of Punishing* he wholly *gives up*, and engages his natural force (which he might before imploy in the execution of the Law of Nature, by his own single Authority, as he thought fit) to assist the executive power of his society, as the law thereof shall require" (sec. 130; cf. 136). Men allow society to regulate their lives, their liberties, and their possessions; all who have need of protection for any of these things can receive it from civil society and thereby become obliged by its rules. The state exists not for a class but for all who are willing and able to use it on equitable terms.

III

Although Macpherson's theory about Locke's doctrine is thus falsified in so many details, it still presents a challenge to any critic. For its overall coherence and interest is extremely impressive, even though its foundations are shaky; and some of the detail—for example, the exposition of Locke's defense of unequal property rights—is superior to anything yet produced on Locke. All discounting made of the ideological overtones that Macpherson hears in every word of Locke, the force of Macpherson's account challenges one to produce some alternative picture that fits the text better than his, but that takes notice of what is most valuable in his account. Let us then agree that the chapter "Of Property" is intended to justify the achievement of the capitalist and the reward he reaps. As we argued above, the simplest argument for this is based on God's will that all mankind should flourish. Given fair distribution, the greatest social product is the will of God and the dictate of reason. Locke never argues explicitly that the distribution is fair, though the elements of the argument required are there. They lie in the insistence that even the worst off in modern society is better off than he would be outside it, a thesis backed up by the ubiquitous American Indian; these latter, it will be remembered "have not one hundredth part of the Conveniences we enjoy: And a King of a large and fruitful Territory there feeds, lodges and is clad worse than a day Labourer in *England*" (sec. 41). And they lie too in the suggestion that it is the superior ability and greater efforts of the capitalist that lead to his greater wealth: "And as different degrees of Industry were apt to give Men Possessions in different proportions, so this *Invention of Money* gave them the opportunity to continue and enlarge them" (sec. 48). And perhaps, finally, in the suggestion that even now there is some surplus land left "in some inland, vacant places of America" (sec. 36). Thus, the capitalist is worthy of his profit; that he is worthy of all his profit Locke does not argue; perhaps his laissez-faire inclinations were not so strong that he thought it was true; perhaps they were so strong that he thought it needed no proving. The basic point, however, is simple enough: since all men have profited by entering a market society, there is no cause for complaint if some men have done better than others.

But, here we part company with Macpherson. In Macpherson's account, Locke now proceeds to pile political oppression on top of inequality of possessions. A more convincing picture is that of Locke moving from the negative point that the laborer and the capitalist were not at odds to the positive task of showing that they have a shared interest, a common ground of political obligation, and a common right to see to the maintenance of their interests. It is indubitable that both are bound by the law; therefore the law must give something to them both, in return for which they are bound to obey it. And it is this something that Locke calls "the Preservation of their Property" (sec. 124) or else "the mutual *Preservation* of their *Lives, Liberties and Estates* which I call by the general Name, Property" (sec. 123). A common interest requires one term to describe it, even though the most disparate things come as a result to shelter under the name of "property." All the inhabitants of a well-governed and well-organized country benefit from its government—even resident foreigners—so they all have a share in something; and whatever it is that they have a share in, Locke calls property. Peace and security are also said by Locke to be the ends of government; men enter civil society "by *stated Rules* of Right and Property to secure their Peace and Quiet" (sec. 137). All men require peace and security to lead tolerable lives, so all men have as much property as requires government for its preservation. It is, of course, odd to talk of all the things that society protects as property, but the effect is surely not that of setting up a bourgeois dictatorship so much as of finding some common interest shared by both the proletarian and the bourgeois in a state that must often have seemed to give nothing except to those who were rich and powerful enough to need nothing from it.

And the importance of giving the proletariat and the bourgeoisie a common interest is surely that their interests are opposed to absolute monarchy; nothing could be clearer than that the target of the *Second Treatise* is not the peaceful and docile proletariat, but the doctrine that a monarch has an absolute and, more particularly, arbitrary power over his subjects. This is a recurring theme of the whole treatise, which might indeed have been subtitled "A Treatise against Arbitrariness and in Favor of Relevance in Political Power." A large part of the chapter "Of the Dissolution of Government" is a defense of regicide as a last measure against a king who claims to have an absolute and arbitrary authority over his people (secs. 232–39). Despite the occasionally lighthearted manner in which he discusses the question of how we are to join reverence with a knock on the head, Locke commits himself to views that abundantly explain why he did not wish to be known as the author of the work during the lifetime of James II. Locke's bitterest attacks are always on absolute monarchy, as when he says:

> Hence it is evident that *Absolute Monarchy*, which by some men is counted the only Government in the world, is indeed *inconsistent with Civil Society*. (sec. 90)

or that:

> Absolute, arbitrary power, or governing without *settled standing Laws*, can neither of them consist with the ends of society and government. (sec. 137)

or that:

> *Absolute Dominion*, however placed, is so far from being one kind of civil society, that it is as incompatible with it, as slavery is with property. (sec. 174)

It seems quite incredible that anyone should not take it as an attack on the pretensions made by James II (or those that he was suspected of being about to make) to the position of a recipient of divinely granted power, and thus to freedom from all human law and control.

Locke's target is arbitrariness rather than absoluteness; he goes into some detail about martial law, which allows summary execution for disobedience even to lethally dangerous orders, but which will not allow a general to touch one penny of a soldier's goods; the reason given by Locke is this: "Because such a blind Obedience is necessary to that end for which the Commander has his Power, *viz* the preservation of the rest; but the disposing of his Goods has nothing to do with it" (sec. 139). Locke generalizes the argument that authority is limited in its scope to what is necessary to secure the ends for which the authority is set up to cover the case of Parliament, the monarch, and any other sort of authority. All rights are limited by the ends they are meant to secure, and the right to our obedience vested in our rulers is in exactly the same case. Royal authority, in other words, depends not on the person of the monarch, but on the good of the society. The quarrel is not between bourgeoisie and proletariat, but between king and people. No doubt the people are but rarely justified in revolution; but there is no question that they have the right to rebel in extremis.

Even in this reading of Locke, his theory is still a bourgeois one. It is beyond doubt a bourgeois mind that envisages all rights as property rights; it is also, more importantly for the political philosopher, a perceptive sort of confusion that leads to such an identification. For "property" is not an inapt general name for the class of rights and obligations that enter into social theory—quasi-contractual rights and duties as they are. For in many ways, property rights, in the ordinary sense of "property," are paradigms of the rights that are exchanged and protected by contract. But only a bourgeois mind could fail to see that they are paradigmatic rather with respect to procedure than with respect to the importance of the ethical values involved. They are paradigmatically contractual, but they are not the most important contractual rights. But this still goes no way toward justifying Macpherson's attributing to Locke a ruthless, dictatorial program of class domination. In the joint-stock company that is Locke's state, all men are shareholders. Some men hold shares of life, liberty, peace, and quiet alone, while others hold shares of estate as well; these latter may receive more of the benefits and play a greater part in the running of the state, but there is no reason to suppose that in the eyes of God or Nature (or even in the eyes of John Locke), their shares have a peculiar importance. Few or no practical conclusions follow readily from Locke's account of political obligation; Macpherson's conclusions follow even less readily than the more egalitarian and humane ones that have been drawn in the past.

Hegel on Work, Ownership, and Citizenship

HEGEL IS so much a writer whom every commentator turns to his own purposes that some initial account of my purposes is, I fear, not to be avoided.
What follows is in part a matter of explication de texte, though my aim is
not primarily exegetical. What I hope to do is to show Hegel combatting
both a utilitarian and a strictly Kantian account of the connections between
work, ownership, and citizenship, with the ultimate aim of showing how
various tensions that commonly beset theories of property bedevil Hegel's
account also. This is partly a contribution to understanding Hegel, but
partly a contribution to arguments about property rights today. For example, there is a tendency for writers today to describe such things as job security and the ability of trade unions to influence management decisions as
"new property" rights; but there is a strong case for saying that they are not
property rights at all, but rights of a different kind, which demonstrate that
non-property-based substitutes for property rights can readily be created or
can evolve.[1] A man who has tenure in his post—say, a university teacher of
a certain rank—does not *own* his job; he cannot sell to anyone else his right
to the job, he cannot bequeath his position to his son, he cannot stipulate,
even, who should succeed him. In all these ways, his position is quite different from that of, say, Montesquieu, who did own his position of *Président à
mortier* at Bordeaux in the straightforward sense that the post had been sold
by the Crown; he could sell it himself or leave it by will, and the new owner
would have the same property right in it.

Hegel certainly saw the importance of the distinction between owning
one's job and having security of tenure during good behavior; indeed, he
argued that the transition from medieval to modern constitutional arrangements necessarily brought with it a transition from private ownership of
public positions to crown appointment on the basis of qualifications and
performance: "It is only in an external and contingent way that these offices
are linked to particular persons, and therefore the functions and powers of
the state cannot be private property" (*PhR*, sec. 277).[2] As so often, the unti-
diness of the English came in for reprobation: "In France seats in parliament
were formerly saleable, and in the English army commissions up to a certain
rank are saleable to this day. This saleability of office, however, was or is still

connected with the medieval constitution of certain states, and such constitutions are nowadays gradually disappearing" (*PhR*, sec. 277A). All the same, Hegel stretched the notion of property in other contexts in much the same way that theorists of the "new property" do. Thus, the family exists in part to look after family possessions; the "family, as persons, has its real external existence in property" (*PhR*, sec. 169). This "property" is then widened to include anything that amounts to "means"—Hegel calls them *Vermögen*, which Knox translates as "capital" to avoid the misleading connotations of "estate"; I incline to think that "resources" might be the better translation, for reasons that will emerge almost at once. When Hegel is well into the discussion of what property a family possesses in civil society, he counts both skills and security of income as forms of *Vermögen*, as when he remarks: "In the corporation, the family has its stable basis in the sense that its livelihood is secured there, conditionally upon capability, i.e. it has a stable capital" (*PhR*, sec. 253). To which the reply might well be that while we might generally agree that a man's abilities were part of his "resources," we would not describe a man who owned no property as "a man of means," no matter how great his skill; nor would we want to say he was a man of property even though he could guarantee that those skills would find employment.

The point is not one of merely jurisprudential or antiquarian interest—arguments about the existence or nonexistence of a "new class" in socialist states have often hinged on the question of what to count as property. For we might find a class of functionaries who have the de jure right as well as the de facto power to control the use of state-owned property in the means of production, and at a certain point we might be puzzled whether to say that they did or did not own them.[3] To say that the property in question is "state-owned" begs the question, of course, against saying that the "new class" owns it, too; clarity seems to dictate that we should say that what we have is a class that has the powers over investment and employment that formerly depended on ownership, but that these powers now depend upon bureaucratic position or party rank or whatever. Since the "new class" has not got the crucial legal capacity, that of alienating the state's property to new owners at will, it does not have property rights in the state's property. One might then conclude, as Trotsky did, that the so-called new class cannot be a class after all, since a class is only such in virtue of its ownership or nonownership of the means of production.[4] Or one might conclude instead that whether a group of people constituted a class was a question that ought to be detached from the question of what they owned; it might plausibly be argued that what we had always been interested in was power, and that once power and property were divorced, as they were in the Soviet state, nothing was to be gained by insisting on tying classes to ownership. What is new about the new class is just that its power depends on its access to the state and its apparatus of coercion and indoctrination, not on its ownership of anything.[5] Or one might suggest that the concept of property needed stretching to include the new case; sufficient control over the state's resources, in effect, amounts to ownership of them. So if some official or other could secure that he both derived an enlarged income from, say, his management of a chemical plant and that he could dictate the terms on which people worked in that plant and could dictate both the terms on which he left his post as manager and the succession to his position, he would be to all intents the owner of the plant.[6] Of course, all such arguments are bedeviled by further problems about the extent to which what is being alleged is that individuals in the new class have taken the means of production back into de facto private ownership as opposed to the new class having collectively taken the state's property into joint—that is, exclusive of everyone else's—possession, without there being any question of individual members of the class having more than a share in the proceeds. Hegel would have sided with anyone who argued that the concept of property was open textured; at any rate, he certainly held that there was no distinction between a right to ownership and a right to the whole and entire use of something (*PhR*, sec. 61). So, no doubt, if the members of the "new class" either jointly or severally get the entire use of the Soviet Union's means of production, then the "new class" owns them, whatever the law says; if the law says something else about the legal title, the law is a dead letter.

Still, this is to run ahead of a proper exposition of Hegel's case. To take this at a proper pace, something must be said about the intellectual context of Hegel's exposition. This amounts to a recapitulation of themes associated with four authors: Locke, Rousseau, Kant, and Hume. It goes without saying that although Hegel in effect stalks Kant throughout the *Philosophy of Right*, the other three writers appear by implication rather than in their own persons. The themes I have in mind are these: in the work of Locke, we find an account of the right to property that rests that right on human labor and that further depends on the claim that everyone has a right to his own person, a property in his person; this right is a natural right, depending on no convention for recognition, and it follows that there can be private ownership of particular things in a state of nature.[7] Hegel sets out to deny most of this account; to some extent, he intertwines his objection to what we may call Lockean naturalism with objections to a very different sort of naturalism, namely, that which treats the laws of an organized political society as if they are natural, organic products, but here it is only the distinctions that he makes in opposition to Locke that concern us.

Rousseau is important not as a theorist of natural law but because Rousseau's *Discourse on the Origins of Inequality* provided one of the most rhetorically compelling cases against private property that the eighteenth century possessed. The true founder of civil society and the great author of all our ills was the man who put a fence round a piece of land, declared "this is mine," and found an audience credulous enough to believe him; had his hearers retorted, "The goods of the earth belong to all, and the earth itself to nobody," all the evils of civilized life would have been averted. Nor was

Rousseau impressed by the argument that without property rights nobody would have had any inducement to work harder and live better; in Rousseau's account, the idle savage was a happier man than we, and the smiling fields of wheat to which the apologists for private ownership of the land were accustomed to point were fields that had been watered by our sweat.[8] Hegel's relationship to this dystopian tradition was interesting and awkward; he did not deny outright that there was a great deal of misery and injustice attributable to the existence of private property. He did not even try to argue that civilized man was happier, healthier, and better fed than the idle noble savage; he claimed instead that reason required that things should have owners. To put it less strikingly, Hegel's conception of freedom as the goal of human history was a conception that required that men lived in a constitutional state, where they had a certain sort of equality of rights as citizens; the having of rights hinged upon the existence of property because men could not act in the world as free agents unless they had the right to possess and use mere things: "A person has as his substantive end the right of putting his will into each and every thing and thereby making it his, because it has no such end in itself and derives its destiny and soul from his will. This is the absolute right of appropriation which man has over all 'things'" (*PhR*, sec. 44).

Kant had already taken a not dissimilar route in justifying private property.[9] He had taken Rousseau's anxieties to heart and agreed that human history presented a grim spectacle if looked at in the terms Rousseau had set. Yet if it was viewed as a sort of education, a roundabout route to the development of human faculties and to the universal rule of reason and justice, history was a process with which rational men could identify after all. But Kant's conception of what it was for individuals to have rights against one another was altogether too abstract and too individualistic for Hegel. Kant's emphasis on the coercive element in law, his stress on the independence of each individual, together with his willingness to include some rather odd relationships within the sphere of possessory rights, antagonized Hegel. Kant's picture of individual independence, although not founded on traditional natural law, inevitably led to the doctrine of the social contract. The way in which a system of rights integrated men into society, the way in which recognized social roles gave men their moral ideals and ambitions—what Hegel called *Sittlichkeit*—was thereby misrepresented by Kant, although, of course, his central offense, that of reducing our relationship with the state to a contractual relationship, was one that Kant committed with innumerable others.

Hume stands here for the entire utilitarian tradition. In that tradition, the role of property rights is simple, though the working out of that role is not. The starting point is the observation that human wants exceed what nature willingly supplies; this is partly a brute fact about the meanness of nature, but partly a result of the way in which human wants change and expand, so what once satisfied them soon fails to do so. In consequence, we have to work and adapt nature in order to satisfy our wants; but work is, in itself, unpleasant, and we engage in it only in order to reap the reward of more and pleasanter things to consume. As rational creatures, we shall not work if there is no prospect of enjoying the results of our efforts; so some way of ensuring that our efforts are rewarded is needed if there is to be any incentive to effort. Property rights are, in essence, rights to dispose of things and efforts; they are not "natural," since they exist only insofar as they are recognized, though they are certainly natural in the sense that human and non-human nature together explain why all societies from the very simplest have rules about property. The fact that these are not natural rights distinguishes utilitarian theories from a theory like Locke's; individuals are the source of labor, but they are not naturally its proprietors. That the most effective way of exploiting human effort and natural resources is by giving everybody a right to his own efforts—that is, a right to choose whom to work for and so on—and by enforcing property laws much like those of eighteenth-century England is a claim of the utilitarian theory. There may well be times and places when utilitarian considerations would support slavery or some sort of common rather than private ownership.

The heart of the doctrine is that the justification of property rights is that they foster economic cooperation at the degree of efficiency possible at a given time and place. Government exists primarily to defend such rights. The existence of government sets problems, however, for governments acquire power, which may tempt its possessors to act in ways that undermine the goals government is set up to defend. The utilitarian theory of government, especially as presented in James Mill's *Essay on Government*, is the theory of how to avert these unpleasant side effects. Hume, on the whole, looked to the power of the landed gentry to restrain the crown, whereas James Mill looked to universal suffrage to restrain both the landed gentry and the crown.[10] Of a concern with citizenship, there is something in Hume and almost nothing in James Mill; nonetheless, the theory of political rights can be sketched swiftly enough. Persons whose interests are identical with the general interest should possess enough power to prevent persons whose interests are hostile to the general interest from acts hostile to it. A working class content to follow middle-class leaders might have the vote; middle-class property owners should certainly have it. Workers who were likely to pursue their short-term gains by expropriating the possessing classes had better not have the vote.[11] There were, of course, no pure exponents of what I here offer as the utilitarian theory, though James Mill comes close. Hume was more influenced by classical notions of the senatorial virtues than the ideal type utilitarian would have been.[12]

Hegel was emphatically antiutilitarian; he did not remark, as Nietzsche was later to do, that man cares nothing for happiness, only the Englishman wishes to be happy—but he came close to it. We have already seen that he would not tackle Rousseauist critics of civilization on the ground of utility, and this was a general rule. He was unimpressed by utilitarian arguments in principle; happiness was too indefinite a goal with which to rationalize a legal system; the utilitarian conception of happiness as a surplus of pleasures over pains was in addition inadequate, since happiness, as opposed to a string of sensations, demanded some judgment about a whole life; finally, the ordinary man's pleasures were essentially heteronomous, a matter of trying to keep up with the Joneses. Over and over, Hegel insisted that the rationale of a system of rights is freedom, not happiness; it might be prompted into existence by the need to satisfy one or another impulse, but its goal was freedom. This, of course, meant also for Hegel that its basis was essentially rational, since it is only if the will is determined by reason that it can be determined at all and yet be free. The difficulty here, as more generally, is to see in what sense a system of law in which there is a good deal that is accidental, local, and arbitrarily chosen can nonetheless be a dictate of reason.[13]

One further preliminary observation about the argumentative context of Hegel's account of property is needed. There is a sense in which the whole of Hegel's philosophy is a possessory philosophy, and a sense in which the whole of Hegel's philosophy is obsessed by a kind of work. In the *Economic-Philosophical Manuscripts*, Marx offers a famous rewriting of Hegel's *Phenomenology of Spirit* in which he says that Hegel was right to see work as the essence of history and to see the appropriation of the products of work as its central task, but that Hegel was an idealist who thought of work only as the work of the mind, that is, thinking, and who thought of the products of work only as the products of thinking, that is, ideas. That the central question of philosophy is that of how we may appropriate our own products Marx thought of as a position he shared with Hegel.[14] Now, there is an undeniable charm to this interpretation; there is certainly a sense in which the *Phenomenology* describes a process of creation, loss, and retrieval; and it is certainly true of Hegel as a stylist that he plays on the imagery of the German language. Objects, or *Gegenstände*, are, so to speak, standing out against us, as if opposing and resisting us; concepts, or *Begriffe*, aid us to seize them and grasp them, to hold them and therefore subdue them. The question remains, however, of the extent to which this illuminates Hegel's own thinking—we can agree that he came to provide Marx with an apt starting point, and that he provides Alexandre Kojève with an exciting topic for his lectures, but does this suggest that work and appropriation are the hidden key to Hegel's own philosophy?[15] It is hard to believe that they are; there is certainly a sense in which the wider philosophical concerns haunt the *Philosophy of Right*, but that seems to be almost as far as it goes. That is, there is no suggestion that work plays a peculiarly important role in our philosophical mastery of the world; there are a couple of small jokes at Kant's expense about the way in which work and consumption both deny the reality of thing-in-itself (*PhR*, secs. 44R and 44A), but this is intermingled with an attack on philosophical realism, too, and there is no suggestion that Hegel intended anything very substantial to follow from these observations.

The starting point of the derivation of property rights is the claim that the object of right is freedom; rights are derived from free will, not from their serving needs. The first and fundamental rights are those of persons, and persons exist in the first place as property owners. It may seem odd to start from this end of the doctrine of rights; most modern writers would begin with some sort of statement of basic human rights, which everyone was supposed to have and to recognize in others, and then derive property rights, if at all, after some process of deciding which basic rights were of primary importance. Thus Ronald Dworkin lays down a right to equal concern and respect as *the* basic right, and from this deduces the political institutions of liberal democracy—the right to equality in voting, for instance—as a political corollary, and, to a more limited extent, the institutions of the market—as a device that treats all wants indifferently—as an economic corollary. The right to property has to come in, to the extent that it comes in at all, as a result of, or as a means to, securing equality of concern and respect.[16] Now, Hegel is evidently not engaged in a process of the same sort; property rights do not in any obvious sense provide the premises from which one can deduce political or other rights. It seems, rather, that Hegel's aim is to start from what we might call the minimum characterization of a person; this minimum characterization is as someone capable of distinguishing what is him from what is not or, in Hegel's terms, capable of externalizing his will. This minimal, and thus abstract, personality allows two crucial distinctions to be made: between myself and other persons, and between myself and what I can have an effect upon. Thus, the first rights are rights to control external things; they are assertions of the right of my will to determine the behavior of things and demands for the recognition of this right (*PhR*, secs. 39 and 40). So eager is Hegel to insist that this first right of the will over external things is the basis of rights that he repudiates the familiar Roman-law distinction between *jus ad rem* ("right to a thing") and *jus ad personam* ("right against a person"): "To be sure, it is only a person who is required to execute the covenants of a contract, just as it is also only a person who acquires the right to their execution. But a right of this sort cannot for this reason be called a 'personal' right; rights of whatever sort belong to a person alone. Objectively considered, a right arising from a contract is never a right over a person, but only a right over something external to a person or something which he can alienate, always a right over a thing" (*PhR*, sec. 40R). My will cannot occupy another person; hence, Hegel sees in a right a relationship of occupancy between a person and a thing that other persons are called on to acknowledge. This is contrary to the utilitarian tendency to say that all rights are *jus ad personam* on the ground that *jus ad rem* is simply a right good against an indefinite number of persons as opposed to a right good against some specific person or persons. And this is important because it makes the relationship of *possessing* important in a way it simply cannot be for any utilitarian writer.

The obvious question that this raises is why Hegel thinks that the relationship between the will and the thing is of such central interest; in a way, the simplest answer is that it is one instance of the relationship between mind and nature, and that Hegel's philosophy is predicated on the urge to eliminate the independence of seemingly brute and alien stuff by showing that everything is an aspect of mind. But this answer is too simple; the basic philosophical task is itself so difficult to render intelligible that assimilating Hegel's social philosophy to it is to explain the less obscure by the more obscure. The account that one might try to give is something like this. In the search for freedom, we distinguish ourselves from objects in the outside world, which interact with each other merely in a mechanical, causal fashion; we use, alter, make, consume, and control things. In doing this, we also alter the status of those things; they cease to be objects with no point or purpose and come to reflect and embody our purposes. The world literally takes on human purposes. The doing of this both presupposes and demonstrates that we have a right to do it; or, rather, it makes it clear that the suggestion that we do not have a right to do it is incoherent. Only if there were already a will like our own opposing our will would we have no right, which is why we cannot, in principle, make slaves out of other persons (*PhR*, secs. 57R, 57A). Ex hypothesi, what makes things merely things is that they are will-less and not self-owned (*PhR*, secs. 44, 52). Whether there is also some suggestion that the world of pointless things in some sense needs to be owned it is hard to say; in a philosophy so permeated with Christian reminiscences as Hegel's, it would not be surprising to find echoes of the view that the world itself shared in the Fall and that its better nature is to be elicited by our efforts. When Hegel says that a thing has no ends of its own and "derives its destiny and soul from [its owner's] will" (*PhR*, sec. 44), the redemptive tone is marked.

Hegel does not, as Locke did, derive the right to property from the right to the use of our own bodies. Rather, he puts on a par our occupation of our own organism and our occupation of things outside it. To be more accurate, what he does is argue as follows: our own bodies are in one aspect things like other things, and although it is true enough that my existence as a moral agent hangs upon the continued operation of a particular body, nonetheless it is only really *my* body insofar as I put my will in it (*PhR*, sec. 47). My body answers to my control only so long as I choose to control it (*PhR*, sec. 48). Hegel has the good sense to see that this line of reasoning has to be treated with care; there is a difference between theft and assault, and the person who hacks off my hand and runs away with it has not stolen my property but has injured me. Because we feel in our bodies, says Hegel, there arises a distinction between personal injury and damage to property (*PhR*, sec. 48R). What this threatens, however, is to assimilate human beings and animals, since animals certainly possess their bodies to the extent of controlling them and feeling in them. Hegel avoids this assimilation by agreeing that animals possess themselves—that is, they have de facto control of themselves—but he claims that they are not objects to themselves. Paradoxically, he expresses this by claiming that animals are external to themselves, where one might suppose that the obvious point was that they do not see themselves as external objects in the way humans do. As worryingly, Hegel also seems to think that this leaves room for slavery; persons who do not have the appropriate sort of possession of themselves can be the property of other men. If they withdraw their wills from themselves, they are occupable by the wills of others. In fact, Hegel is ambivalent on the subject. As one might expect in view of the role played in the *Phenomenology* by the "dialectic of lordship and bondage," he thought that slavery was justified at a particular point in human history, but he was unwilling to go as far as to claim that slavery might be right. As did Rousseau, he held that the blame for a man's enslavement lay with him as well as with his master:

> The wrong of slavery lies at the door not simply of enslavers or conquerors but of the slaves and the conquered themselves. Slavery occurs in man's transition from the state of nature to genuinely ethical conditions; it occurs in a world where a wrong is still right. At that stage wrong has validity and so is necessarily in place. (*PhR*, sec. 57A)

This, however, goes beyond Rousseau in limiting the claim to a particular point in ethical evolution. Again, however, its interest lies less in that than in the way in which Hegel's case is fundamentally antiutilitarian; once humanity has reached a certain point of culture, then it is absolutely wrong to enslave anyone just because the institution of slavery is inconsistent with that developed moral consciousness. Taken in the abstract, slavery is not a matter for utilitarian calculation but for prohibition outright; even when it was in place, it was "right" only in the thinned-out sense in which a necessary evil may be said to be right.

Hegel's distance from a Lockean view of our property in our own persons extends further than this, however. Locke's account of property rights in oneself was essentially defensive; property was that of which we might not be deprived without our own consent. Our lives and liberties were our property only in this negative sense; there was certainly no suggestion that since our lives and liberties were our property, we might alienate them at will. We could not sell or give ourselves into slavery, and suicide was an infringement of God's prerogative, for it lies in his hand, not ours, whether we should live or die. Hegel evidently wishes to tie property rights much more tightly to the right to alienate than did Locke, and he cannot safely count life and liberty as part of our property, since he, like Locke, wants to deny that we can alienate these at will. Yet the first moves he makes include the claim that our bodies, on which our lives depend, become ours when we put our will into them. In essence, what Hegel does is to deny that personality itself, religious liberty, and the like *are* really external in the requisite sense: "I may abandon as a *res nullius* ["nobody's property"] anything I have, or yield it to the will of another and so into his possession, provided always that the thing in question is a thing external by nature" (*PhR*, sec. 66). From which it follows that

> those goods, or rather substantive characteristics, which constitute my own private personality and the universal essence of my self-consciousness are inalienable and my right to them is imprescriptable. Such characteristics are my personality as such, my universal freedom of will, my ethical life, my religion. (*PhR*, sec. 67)

The upshot of this might well be to conclude that lives and liberties simply are not property in any useful sense of the term, but if we draw this conclusion, there is some difficulty in hanging on to Hegel's claim that it is as property owners that persons first exist.

What is equally distinctive in Hegel's development of the right to property is the treatment of the relation between work and acquisition. Evidently, in any developed legal system there will be many ways of acquiring property rights other than by working; gift, bequest, and transfer by contract or by purchase are obviously all of them relevant. For simplicity's sake, we can distinguish between rights acquired by transfer of whatever sort and rights by original acquisition. The suggestion of a great many writers is that there is only one principle of original acquisition, and that is acquisition by labor. Locke's claim that mixing our labor with unowned things gives us ownership of them, subject to our not preventing others from doing the same thing and subject to our making proper use of them, is no doubt the best known.[17] But a version of the same doctrine is a feature of Robert Nozick's *Anarchy, State, and Utopia* and a commonplace of nineteenth-century radicalism.[18] It is a doctrine that has many internal difficulties and obscurities, one class of which involves the grounds of the claim that labor gives a title, and another related class of which involves the extent of the rights thus claimed. Sometimes Locke seems to suggest that it is a matter of justice to give him who takes pains to get something the thing he takes pains to get; sometimes he seems to suggest that because there is something new that was not there before, it self-evidently belongs to him who brought it into existence. Again, it is not clear whether Locke thinks that a man who clears the waste should have a bequeathable freehold in the land he has cleared or whether some more limited right—say, a longish lease with a right to compensation from his fellows when he vacates—is what is got.[19]

Hegel follows Kant in avoiding these anxieties by denying that the title springs from labor; rather, it springs from the will to possess. This is not to deny the role of labor, for it is no good merely wishing that one were the owner of whatever it is. The object must be occupied: "Since property is the embodiment of personality, my inward idea and will that something is to be mine is not enough to make it my property; to secure this end occupancy is required" (*PhR*, sec. 5). Here we find a characteristic difficulty in Hegel. For there are two sorts of claims about occupancy that we need to balance. Hegel says that being able to mark something as ours is the way that most clearly demonstrates the mastery of things by mind; and this is evidently true in the sense that a conventional mark, simply because it is conventional and not natural, must preserve the difference between mind and matter particularly acutely—we alter the destiny of a thing without, so to speak, lowering ourselves to its physical level; it was mine, it is yours, its destiny has switched tracks without my or your embroiling ourselves with it. Yet Hegel also stresses the role of forming things. Now this, which is the Roman-Law doctrine of *specificatio*, sticks to the same line of argument. Working on things changes their forms, showing that the way in which they were initially and naturally presented is to be negated: "To impose a form on a thing is the mode of taking possession most in accordance with the Idea to this extent, that it implies a union of subject and object, although it varies endlessly with the qualitative character of the objects and the variety of subjective aims" (*PhR*, sec. 56R). To the question of the extent of the right that we get over things, Hegel insists that we do not own only the difference we make to things; what we own is the things themselves, and we own them outright. This seems to settle the matter decisively in favor of the view that for Hegel, ownership is absolute in the sense not only that somebody or other is always to be identified as *the* owner—which is, in essence, the Roman-law as opposed to the common-law view of ownership—but also that the owner has full and complete rights of disposal over the object owned.[20] This seems to commit Hegel to holding that the very concept of property implies freedom of testamentary disposition, and that insofar as we stand in relation to our own selves as owners to owned, suicide and self-destruction are implicitly licensed by the very concept of property. Yet Hegel denies that we have the right to commit suicide; we may sacrifice our lives for something higher than mere existence, so that we may lose them in a war, say, (*PhR*, sec. 70A) if and when the state demands it, but he emphasizes that even the Roman hero in committing suicide is acting against his personality, not in accordance with its rights.

We ought not, therefore, to be surprised that Hegel did not think that unlimited freedom of testamentary disposition was part and parcel of the right to property: "The recognition of a man's competence to bequeath his property arbitrarily is likely to be an occasion for breach of obligations and for mean exertions and equally mean subservience; and it also provides opportunity and justification for the folly, caprice and malice of attaching to professed benefactions and gifts vain, tyrannical and vexatious conditions operative after the testator's death and so in any case after the property ceases to be his" (*PhR*, sec. 179R). Whether Hegel intends to distinguish, as he might, between rights of alienation during one's lifetime and rights of testamentary disposition is not entirely clear, for the remark on bequests occurs during the discussion of the family, and by then there has already occurred one of the several baffling shifts that Hegel makes, from the claim that property is essentially private and individual property to the claim that what we "own" as members of a family is in some sense family property (cf.

PhR, secs. 46, 170, 171). The whole issue is further confused by the fact that Hegel's most famous remark about the way in which "restrictions on ownership (feudal tenure, testamentary trusts) are mostly in the course of disappearing" as being "not in accordance with the concept of property" (*PhR*, sec. 63A) occurs in a context where it is the right of a family to sell or pawn its goods that is at issue. So whereas one might assume that restrictions on testamentary freedom were a feudal relic, whether they affected families or individuals, and that outright ownership was the only true form of ownership, the subsequent discussion seems to imply that the preservation of the family justifies restrictions at least on the making of wills; and whereas one might have tried to argue that Hegel thought that an individual without family ties might leave his property to whom or to what he wished, while the family man must not consult only his own whim in these matters, the context in which the point is made suggests that Hegel's distinction is between feudal and modern property law, not between bachelors and husbands and fathers.

Having begun to pursue Hegel on such points, we may broaden the scope of our anxieties a little. The case we have so far been making is that Hegel's account of property rights is one that seems to stress their "expressive" dimension: we express our status as free subjects by occupying mere objects. Again, there is an expressive aspect in the picture of work; things we transform by our efforts come to express our purposes in the world. They form, as it were, a record of our intentions and actions, and this is why, although work is not a title to ownership of the unique kind Locke claimed, it is a very complete way of occupying things, closing the gap between us as subjects and things as objects. There are some corollaries of all this that are of considerable interest, although we cannot pause for them now: Hegel's account of the ownership of ideas, for instance, offers a way into discussions of copyright quite different from utilitarian considerations about offering incentives to writers and inventors who would be deterred by unchecked plagiarism. Again, he says little on the vexed topic of the difference between the work of the innovative artist and the everyday labor of the manual worker, but he offers hostages to more romantic theorists in the same tradition who would distinguish between *labor* and *work* along the same lines by claiming that work involves the transcendence of mere nature, as mere labor does not.[21]

What is more important is that Hegel's picture of the abstract individual making his mark on the world by owning it and working on it already contains the seeds of a slide toward something different. This different thing is the claim that as we fill out the conception of freedom that grounds the *Philosophy of Right*, so we come to a more and more complete freedom, because what it is that is free is less and less the abstract individual and more and more the citizen of the rational modern state. But as we pursue this course, various troubles arise. A very familiar one is that there seems a near contradiction between Hegel's account of the way in which feudal restrictions on property are vanishing (*PhR*, sec. 63A already cited) and his defense of those restrictions as something that makes the landed aristocracy fit to occupy political office (*PhR*, sec. 306).[22] Nor is it enough to cite his observation that if it were not for the political purpose served by such restrictions, they should be abolished as mere restrictions (*PhR*, sec. 306A); for that reduces Hegel's account to the perfectly decent but entirely commonsensical claim that restricted property rights may have useful indirect effects, for example, if they mean that elder sons of landed families will be guaranteed an income that will allow them to take part in political life without anxiety about making a living. What Hegel seems to be committed to is the development of the concept of freedom in such a way that something implicit in our free use and transformation of the world in our barest guise as property owners is more adequately revealed and realized in our activities as members of families, participants in the economic life of civil society, and citizens of a rational state. Much that Hegel says about life in a modern society makes entirely adequate sense; but it makes, so to speak, common sense. This is, I think, not true of the initial exposition of the right to property, much of which captures an important human aspiration and much of which suggests ways of analyzing everyday phenomena that are not themselves everyday ways. The same thing seems to me to be true of Hegel's account of the alienation of property, which again hangs on the thought that if we could not dispose of what we had once acquired and, so to speak, restore it to its unoccupied status, we should be trapped in and dominated by the natural world after all. Whether this image is persuasive to all of Hegel's readers is dubious, no doubt, but at any rate the stress on the individual's mastery of the world and on his ability to read the success of his purposes in the world is a stress that many of his readers have responded to. The difficulty is to discover whether this stress remains once we move from abstract right to the realm of *Sittlichkeit*.

Some doubts have already been ventilated in the context of the family. Hegel argues as if once there is a family, property is the family's property and the head of the family is its administrator and supervisor; but since not all families do have property in the usual sense, Hegel also broadens out the notion of property to include anything that is a part of the family's means of survival. Now, one can agree that between mere arbitrary behavior and genuine freedom some distinction needs to be drawn; one can also agree that the shaping of the will needs a moral context, that of the family inter alia, in order that we should acquire steady aims toward which to direct our actions and so on. But this should not lead us to gloss over the extent to which someone who supervises a family's property really is supervising its property and not his own; conversely, if it is his by legal title, but he feels that the family's claims upon it limit his freedom to treat it as he wishes, this is hardly an extension of his freedom. A person may certainly find that the existence of family ties provides a framework without which his work and his stewardship of his own or its property would be aimless. But he may not, and there is nothing to be gained by evading the fact that the initial account of man's relationship to the unowned thing suggests an exuberance in the mastery of nature that is quite at odds with the patient labor of the salaried, commuting paterfamilias of contemporary folklore.

The problem evidently gets more acute once we contemplate civil society. In one sense, we are back where we started, for civil society is the market-place; it is where we turn up with what we have got and see what we can get with it and for it. We come onto the stage as owners of our skills, our labor, and our property in the narrower sense, and we do our best to maximize our take (*PhR*, secs. 183, 187). Here we are certainly individuals, and we relate to one another as property owners. But we are, by this stage of the argument, concrete, particular persons, and to say that we are in civil society is to say that we are selfish persons not by choice and not because this is the final account of what we are, but because in the modern world, we have to get our living by coming to the market economy. Such an economy presupposes that people may buy and sell what they have got; it operates only because they can do so and because they treat one another as means to their own ends. It is here that the problems of deriving Hegel's results by conceptual expansion really begin. We can tackle the problem from perhaps three angles. The first is the difficulty that arises when we see that Hegel begins to suggest that collective interdependence is a form of property; the second is the difficulty that arises when we press the claim that work is a way of occupying things with our will and confront the division of labor; the last is the familiar difficulty of squaring what Hegel says property is with what he says about the various social classes that arise in civil society.

The simple point that one needs to make is that although it is, of course, true that the person who has nothing but his labor to sell must indeed rely on the fact that there is an interdependence between each and all, it is stretching the notion of capital a good deal to refer to "the complex interdependence of each on all" as "the universal permanent capital which gives each the opportunity, by the exercise of his education and skill, to draw a share from it and so be assured of his livelihood" (*PhR*, sec. 199). It is not that Hegel is not making a number of perfectly plausible points here. He is, as the first part of section 199 shows, intrigued by how each person's pursuit of his own well-being becomes a means to the well-being of others, and he is certainly right that their needs provide us with opportunities we should not otherwise have. It is not unduly fanciful to suggest that Hegel's readiness to follow the line of reasoning from individual ownership to market interdependence is to be explained by the extent to which mind subordinates mere things. If we take our eyes off the individual's success in permeating any particular thing with his purposes and look instead at the extent to which a society's environment now reflects the impact on it of the interplay of everyone's purposes, the transition from one sense of property to the other is not hard to follow. Yet it obviously raises the question whether the total effect of social interaction *is* a result with which we can identify. The result of the "invisible hand" may be in one way a result we approve of, but if it is the doing of the invisible hand, it surely has lost some of the charms that the doings of more visible hands may be said to possess. Hegel's own position is, notoriously, one that many people have refused to accept; he seems to want to admire the doings of the invisible hand while also insisting that only the visible hand of the state is ultimately satisfactory. But quite how the workings of the invisible hand are to be embedded in the self-conscious and rational control of society by the state is not clear.

The same problem arises with work and the division of labor. Treated as a claim about the need to acquire new skills as more and more elaborate wants emerge, Hegel's argument is unexceptionable. Again, treated as part of an argument against Rousseau's praise of the idle savage, Hegel's insistence on "the element of liberation intrinsic to work" (*PhR*, sec. 194), his characterization of work as "practical education" (*PhR*, sec. 197), and his defense of the skilled man "who produces the thing as it ought to be and who hits the nail on the head without shrinking" (*PhR*, sec. 197A) all make good sense. They also hide a problem. The problem is whether the self-expressive aspects of work really are consistent with the division of labor. One can see why Hegel's own account is not in serious trouble here; since his conception of the will is a rationalist one, he can, so to speak, move back and forth between a view of the will that suggests that individual mastery of a whole task is what is wanted and a view that suggests that an understanding of and an endorsement of the process to which one contributes a small part is even better. But does it make sense to say that the man who performs some small task in an elaborate process really comes to *occupy* the thing that forms the end result of the process? Should not the metaphor of occupation be given up, and would we not be clearer if we admitted that some of the satisfactions available to, say, craftsmen in a preindustrial setting simply cannot be had at a later stage of the division of labor—even if we then went on to explain how something like them might be found in other settings?

Last, then, one needs to show how the same problems spill into Hegel's account of the formation of social classes. It ought not to pass without mention that Hegel's account of the class system that founds the modern state is a very reputable piece of sociology. One may complain, as I am about to, that it is rather loosely derived from anything he has to say about property rights and work, but it can hardly be denied that the divisions to which he called attention were more important until long after 1848 than the division between owners and workers that Marx insisted was the only one worth attending to. Hegel's division between classes is a cultural rather than an economic distinction; he writes as if it is based on property, but in reality the question on which the distinction turns is one about the way in which people relate to the sorts of resources that give them a living. Thus, the agricultural class is not divided into owners and farmworkers, or into large landowners and three classes of peasants; rather, the agricultural class is defined by its attitude to the land from which it gets its living and by the naturalness of its behavior (*PhR*, sec. 203). This provides Hegel with one of the rare occasions when he is forced to characterize some actual state of affairs as contrary to nature: "In our day agriculture is conducted on methods derived by reflective thinking, i.e. like a factory. This has given it a character like that of industry and contrary to its natural one" (*PhR*, sec. 203A). He appears to have thought that this was largely an English vice, and that the patriarchal, God-fearing and trusting character of agrarian life was not much disturbed in Prussia at any rate. Again, the business class, embracing the activities of craftsmen, industrialists and their workers, and merchants is defined by the way it treats what it creates. Members of the business class regard their property as assets; a man may be in cotton today and wheat tomorrow, but always he is trying to make the most of his assets. It is not inappropriate to describe this as treating one's property reflectively or formally. For what matters is not what it is, but what it is worth; and equally, the worker who treats his time and his abilities as interesting not in themselves but in terms of what they will fetch on the market may be said to display the same attitude. Once Hegel tackles the third of his classes, all suggestion that its importance is how it relates to its property has gone; for the third class in Hegel's system is the class of civil servants. They are distinguished by the fact that their interest lies in the promotion of the general interest. So far from there being any suggestion that their resources are their property, Hegel insists, as we saw earlier, that they must be appointed by the crown and must make their way by promotion on merit.

We must avoid the temptation to go on at length about the class system and about the curious stratum that is half in and half out of the classification, namely, the *Pöbel*, what Knox translates as a "rabble of paupers" (*PhR*, sec. 244). The simple points that I wish to make here are only two. The first is that the very good sense of Hegel's account of what social divisions we need to understand undermines any suggestion that a division along lines of property alone makes much sense; but the price of accepting common sense here is again that the claim that class divisions can be developed out of basic conceptions of rights over things is decreasingly persuasive. It may be said that the complaint is ill founded, and that all we can do is follow Hegel in two inquiries, the first being into the preconditions of the state and the second being into the variety of ways in which the search for rational principles of self-direction yields its results. To fight off such a reply would be a lengthy task, and in any case unnecessary, since I do not wish to deny that Hegel is indeed doing this. But what I do want to say is that we have had two shifts from the starting point of the argument about the will's expression in the outer world: we have shifted from the recognizable individual human subject to something that is either a collective subject such as society or else is not so much a subject as a role—so that we might say that a doctor realized his will qua doctor by doing the duties of a doctor conscientiously, without this bearing on the question of what satisfaction Smith or Jones would get from doing the job of a doctor. The second simple point I want to make is that Hegel lays himself wide open to just such a critique as Marx later launches against him: he suggests that whatever it is that a class masters is its property, though he retreats because he evidently does not want to say that whatever keeps civil servants alive is their property. Marx is working in the same framework when he asserts that what Hegel reveals is that the bureaucracy has in some sense "appropriated" the state; political life has become the property of the civil service and its masters. One may flinch at Marx's claim that political life can be property—though we would not usually flinch at saying that a group had "monopolized" it—but one could hardy flinch at his seizing on Hegel's apparatus for his own purposes.

What, then, ought one to say by way of conclusion? Perhaps something like this. Hegel's account of property is engaging and persuasive in all sorts of ways; viewed sociologically, as on the whole it has not been viewed here, the theory picks up some of the social and psychological consequences of different sorts of property rights very acutely, and in ways that most instrumental and utilitarian accounts do not—the way in which people identify with what they own, for instance, or the likelihood that a mercantile and industrial bourgeoisie will regard the state in contractual terms only unless various corporate institutions are created to breed patriotism and public spirit in them. It is persuasive in linking work to self-expression, catching the way in which people want something like a record of their effects on the world, not just an income. It requires us to pay attention to the way in which both working and consuming in any developed society are processes with a high symbolic content. We do not eat just food; we eat "cheap cuts" or buy "the cereal that caring mothers give their children" or whatever. The richness and the complexity of economic relations are well caught by the way Hegel tackles his subject. In distinction both to the classical economists, who could not see how governments might manage civil society without wrecking it, and to the Marxists, who shared their blindness, Hegel has at least a few suggestions about the extent to which a capitalist economy is manageable by an effective state with adequate authority. Viewed philosophically, the theory is part of two enterprises: one, an account of how we come to be rational and free agents by becoming citizens of the modern state, and the other an account of how the world itself comes to be rational by being drawn into civilized intercourse.

I have complained that the internal coherence of these projects is not all that it might be; sometimes, forms of control that do not seem to have anything to do with property are talked of as if they are property, and sometimes not; nor is there any adequate account of how individual control of the environment and social control of the environment tie into each other. Perhaps as alarmingly, there is a tension between reason and self-expression such that it is never quite clear whether we are being asked to believe that the satisfaction yielded by the daily round is akin to that of the artist's unpredictable creative spurts. There is no attempt to demonstrate that social control of the world is as impressive as the artist's control of his materials;

whether Hegel thought that Berlin was as impressive a testimony to Prussia as the *Moses* or the *Pietà* were to Michelangelo is undecidable, but it is a question raised by the form of analysis. This sounds grudging, but it is not. In a thinker with lesser aspirations than Hegel's, we should gratefully accept most of what Hegel has to say about rights of ownership and their place in the world; we might think that modern sociologists had taken it all in and that we had nothing much to learn from Hegel, but we should hardly complain of his account on those grounds. It is only because of Hegel's apparent determination to reveal a coherence quite other than the limited coherence accountable for at the sociological level that one complains. It is perhaps much the same experience as Marx had: Hegel offers to show us that the whole world is satisfyingly *ours*, but he cannot. Unlike Marx, I do not claim to have any idea of what it would be like for the world to be like that; but then, anyone who did have would owe it to us not to spend his time wrestling with Hegel as I have just been doing.

Utility and Ownership

ANY THEORY OF RIGHTS ought to have something serious to say about rights of ownership. Property rights may not be the most important rights we have—supposing that we can draw a clear line between property rights and other rights. Nonetheless, one can hardly imagine a sociology that did not concern itself with the causes and consequences of the distribution of titles of ownership; and one can hardly imagine a normative jurisprudence that was unconcerned to lay down the proper duties and powers of owners. There are three ways of taking property rights seriously that I shall here have in mind: they do not exhaust the possible approaches to the subject, but they cover enough of them, I think, at any rate to show what is at issue in any account of the nature and purpose of ownership. The first of these is the doctrine that there are natural rights of ownership and that taking any sort of rights seriously must start from a conception of individuals as "self-owning." Thus, much of Robert Nozick's criticism of John Rawls's account of justice boils down to the objection that Rawls supposes that society originally owns all the talents of all its members, and also that this supposition is at odds with taking seriously the rights of individuals over themselves.[1] What it is for individuals to have rights over themselves is explained by reference to individuals owning themselves in something like the "liberal conception of ownership" explicated by A. M. Honoré.[2] In this view, individual rights are either natural or else created by contract between individuals who are essentially proprietors.

The existence of natural rights of ownership is denied by both of the other two ways of thinking about property that are at issue here. Both of these positions see property rights as essentially artificial creations, essentially the creatures of the law, and as dependent for their moral weight on instrumental considerations. The second of our three views, then, accepts that individuals have rights that are in an important sense "natural," or at any rate "nonartificial" and certainly nonlegal; what property rights individuals may be granted by the law is constrained by the rights they have before the law, and what rights individuals ought to be granted by the law may—depending on the full development of the theory of rights in question—be more than merely constrained. If our theory of rights yields rights to welfare or even rights to employment, we may find that the best way to embody these rights in positive law is by giving people proprietary rights of some sort or other.

More plausibly, however, we are likely to find that such considerations would simply limit the freedom of owners to do what they liked with their property—welfare or employment rights would plausibly constrain owners of capital from dismissing their employees or paying them whatever wages the market would allow them to pay, rather than yielding anything resembling "job ownership."

The third of our three views, and the one to which most of what follows is devoted, is the utilitarian account of property rights. This normative theory of property rights is distinctive in that it is not merely insistent that property is essentially the creature of the law, justified or not for instrumental reasons, but that those instrumental reasons do not themselves involve references to rights. The justification of property rights is, in general, a matter of showing how a system of legally defined and enforced rights and duties best promotes the general welfare; there will be all sorts of questions raised by an attempt to show which system is optimal from a utilitarian standpoint, but these will not be questions about the protection of people's natural rights. Now, in what follows I shall be concerned to argue that a utilitarian account of property rights is generally able to take property rights with all the seriousness they deserve; this is quite a different matter from saying that traditional utilitarianism can take all rights as seriously as they deserve, but I shall also argue in passing that property rights are not basic rights of the kind utilitarianism is commonly said to misrepresent. My view is that the utilitarian rejection of rights as a fundamental component in morality does create problems at the point at which a utilitarian's liberal intuitions come into conflict with the demands of the general welfare; but the rights that these intuitions seem to presuppose are not property rights.[3] As always in this area, J. S. Mill presents us with some difficulties, since he did want to show that utilitarianism was deeply committed to the existence of *moral* rights; but here I confine myself to defending the consistency of his claim that all property is the creature of the law with his defense of individual liberty in *On Liberty*.[4] I reach my conclusion slightly episodically by tackling four familiar issues in the theory of property: the problem of "initial appropriation" of unowned things, the state's rights of taxation and compulsory purchase, the legitimacy of slavery, and whether we "own" our bodies. But before tackling these issues, I begin by making five fairly obvious points about a utilitarian account of property rights in order to show that these episodes are episodes in one theoretical story.

I

Part of the importance of the utilitarian account of property rights, both in its historical impact and now, lies in its disconnection of the defense of property from appeals to liberty. There are, as we shall see, various ways in which this disconnection is effected. The first, which goes back to Hobbes at the latest, is the disconnection of the analysis of property rights from the defense of traditional republicanism and its account of the role of property rights in maintaining civic liberty.[5] Traditionally, the defense of republican government was the defense of civic liberty; this, for instance, is the whole point of Machiavelli's *Discorsi*, a work that takes it for granted that one thing a constitution maker must attend to is the regulation of property to preserve liberty.[6] This was not an archaic concern by the time Bentham discussed property rights in his *Principles of the Civil Code*.[7] Rousseau acknowledged his debt to Machiavelli in the *Contrat social* and, perhaps even more clearly though inexplicitly, in the provisions of the *Economie politique*.[8] Jefferson, too, knew that his defense of the small proprietor belonged to a classical tradition, and the Scottish social theorists of the eighteenth century are interesting just because they live in two intellectual worlds, one of them concerned with civic virtue and civic liberty, the other with progress and prosperity. But "liberty" in this sense means nothing to the utilitarian theory of property. Or, to put it more moderately, it cannot be the central concern of the utilitarian theory, and even if it becomes an important concern of some utilitarians, it cannot become so in quite these terms. To Bentham, as much as to Hobbes, "freedom" consisted in the silence of the laws, not in those laws that did exist being self-imposed under a republican constitution.[9] If you were concerned to re-create some of the characteristics of classical republican politics, there were, no doubt, various things you might well be advised to do about property; but none of them were best described as creating liberty. This conceptual point about what "liberty" *is* was, however, made with the casualness it was partly because neither Hobbes nor Bentham had any time for the republican virtues anyway. It is noticeable that when J. S. Mill came to defend producer cooperatives as incorporating the best of private proprietorship and socialism, he revived the classical emphasis on self-government and broadened the concept of liberty to include virtue as part of freedom.[10] I will not labor the point further, since I have tried to spell it out at some length elsewhere.

II

The second aspect of the disconnection between property and liberty is better known, and is more to our present purposes. This is the insistence that there is no natural right to property and that in whatever ways the property laws of a state may be misconceived, or its taxation and welfare policies, too, it is not in violating a man's natural liberty to do what he chooses with his own. There is no such thing as natural ownership, and whatever natural relationship you may establish with things external to you does not amount to ownership until the law makes it such. Since all the property rights you *could* have would be created by the law, whatever rights you do have are simply what the law says they are. Whatever laws there are about property do not diminish your liberty by removing a former right of ownership.

Now, this claim must be understood quite carefully. It is not the claim that the law cannot abridge your liberty at all. For Bentham, as for Hobbes, the whole point of law is to abridge liberty for the sake of making more useful the liberty it leaves us with. The laws protect us in our use of the liberty they leave us by restraining others from interfering with us; that is, they remove the liberty to interfere with one another in various areas in order to allow us to live more securely and more contentedly. In the state of nature, there would be liberty to seize what you could, liberty to hang on to it, liberty to defend yourself against attack, but also liberty to attack others, liberty to seize what they had got, and so endlessly on. It is this useless liberty that the law abridges. And what that useless liberty does *not* achieve is the creation of a property right in whatever you succeeded in seizing and holding.[11]

In Bentham's account of these issues, it sometimes seems that his attachment to legal positivism stems from the view that duties are logically prior to rights. That is, Bentham holds that rights exist only when there is some power capable of laying upon others the obligation to refrain from interfering with us. For my de facto possession to ripen into de jure ownership, I must be the beneficiary of a rule backed up by sanctions that essentially says to others that under such and such conditions, they must not interfere with my use and control of whatever it is. My rights in the thing are the shadows cast by your duty to allow me to exercise my abilities unimpeded.

But, of course, there are two distinct issues here: one, whether some rights defy such analysis; the other, whether duties imply positive laws. There is, I think, one kind of right that Bentham's account has great difficulty in dealing with. This is the right to decide one's future conduct that one can transfer to another by a promise made to him or her. Suppose I promise a friend to accompany her to the cinema; once I have made the promise to her, I have transferred to her the right to say whether I shall or shall not go. This seems to presuppose that in the absence of any such promise, I had just such a right as I transferred; and this right seems not to be the shadow of anyone else's duties, but rather to be the basis on which their duties are to be understood. It is, on the face of it, a general right to liberty, on the one hand, and a power to bind ourselves by transferring that right, on the other.[12] If promising becomes intelligible only as a means of our having this kind of underlying right, Bentham's program of eliminating rights from the foundations of morals runs into difficulty. This, however, does no great damage to the program of giving a utilitarian account of property rights, since there is no reason to construe promises as if they are a transfer of property.

The point can be enforced by turning to the writer who talks of our having a property in our own persons, and in the process we can see the second point at issue, namely, that it can be perfectly plausible to argue that there are natural property rights, even if rights are the shadows of duties—or, less aggressively, even if rights are secondary to duties and duties are the creatures of law. Locke's talk of "having a property" in ourselves is very far from implying that we are our own property; we are, he says, the property of the God who made us. Locke's account of our capacity to make promises to one another is an account of how men have a limited sovereignty over themselves, limited because it is granted by God for his reasons.[13] In relying on such a case, Locke takes it for granted that duties are prior to rights. All the same, men have some elaborate property rights in the state of nature; the reason is clear enough. God requires us to go about his business; we must therefore have the powers that we require for the fulfillment of those duties his business lays on us. It is not just that many of our rights can be explained in relation to other people's duties—that my right to life, for instance, is to a large extent the shadow of your duty not to kill me except in self-defense; it is also that I have a duty to preserve myself, and therefore a right to do so. My quasi-legislative capacities to make something mine and to make it yours by transfer are not understood solely as shadows of your duties of nonintervention; rather, they are powers I must have if I am to make the most of God's endowments. What rights I have in the state of nature become intelligible in the light of a rational understanding of God's purposes, which is why Locke thinks it is clear that the requirement that we must not let anything perish uselessly in our possession is a distinct requirement from that of leaving as much and as good for others. "Spoiling" is a matter of God's purposes rather than human whim.[14]

In the same way, my right to positive aid from others as well as to noninterference stems from others' duties to God. They are obliged to preserve all mankind as much as may be where their own preservation comes not into competition; this means that they have a duty to preserve me if I am likely to perish otherwise. I do not merely have a right that they not impede me in looking for food elsewhere than among their goods; I have a right to some portion of those goods too.[15]

It is thus clear that in any simple fashion the view that duties are prior to rights does nothing to show that there could not be *natural* property rights; conversely, the view that rights are prior to duties and that there are moral rights as well as legal rights does nothing to show that there are natural *property* rights. But there does lurk here a view that Bentham ought to have found congenial, although so far as I know, he does not embrace it. In essence, he could have argued that duties are prior to rights, that duties are imposed by law; Locke believed this, believing as he did that obligation depended upon the will of a superior. Locke, therefore, believed quite consistently that under natural law, with a divine lawgiver, men had rights in the state of nature. Once God was dead, natural law was dead, natural duties were dead, and natural rights were dead. A secular natural-law theory is simply incoherent, and a secular natural-rights theory is therefore incoherent too. Against a writer like Nozick, the argument still has some force.[16]

III

A third feature of the utilitarian account of property then becomes clearer; this is the view that the nonexistence of a system of property rights enforced in law is not an infringement of anyone's rights, not itself a restriction of their liberty, and not straightforwardly an injustice to them. Any positive system of property rights will, as we have seen, certainly restrict their liberty; in an instrumental but nonutilitarian view, a positive system of property rights may also infringe rights, though it will not infringe property rights—for example, the legal enforcement of slavery does not violate the slave's ownership of himself, since he has no such ownership by nature, but it does, in this view, violate something like his right to equal treatment as a moral personality among others.[17] To do this to him is to perpetrate an injustice against him. But the absence of a system of property rights seems, on the face of it, to leave everyone at liberty to manage as best they can; this does no injustice to anyone and violates no rights.

One thing that a more elaborate utilitarianism will, however, want to say about this is that the absence of a system of enforceable property rights is, at least, a missed opportunity to do a lot of good. The interesting question is, what is the best account of the good undone? Take a society in which there is no adequate patent law, say; any utilitarian view of ownership will agree that an inventor here lacks an incentive to develop an invention properly—no man will sow where another will reap. This will mean that society at large does not benefit as it might from his talents. Mill, I think, would have gone further than that; given his view of liberty as enlargement of choice as well as absence of coercion, it is plausible to say that we should increase the freedom of the inventor by creating property rights in the forms covered by patent law; therefore, one form of good left undone in their absence would be the creation of liberty. Again, it seems plausible that Mill might also have held that the primitive notion of justice ties individual deservings to individual doings; the absence of natural ownership rights is not the same thing as the absence of natural deserts, and even if patents are not the only way to secure natural deserts, they may be such an obvious way that it would be right to say that their absence constitutes an injustice, or certainly a failure to secure justice.[18]

Once there is a legal system of some sort in operation, the justice with which it distributes benefits and burdens among different classes of person will interest the utilitarian as much as anyone else.[19] In that sense, the nonexistence of some particular sort of property right against a background of the existence of many such rights will certainly raise questions of justice, because the burdens of abstaining from other people's property will be imposed on everyone, but only some people will get a reasonable quid pro quo for that abstention. The difficulties of giving a persuasive account of the place of these distributive questions occupied Mill a good deal and can perhaps be left to one side here, since they relate to the utilitarian treatment of rights and justice generally rather than to the utilitarian treatment of property rights in particular.[20]

Still, it is worth noticing what follows for the extinction of a given property right. Since the right is not a deliverance of natural liberty, it is a mistake to complain that the proprietor's liberty has been reduced. Rather, he has had a privilege or an immunity removed. Nonetheless, considerations of justice do enter into the case, though less as rock-bottom considerations than by way of the principle that expectations legitimately acquired ought not to be frustrated without good cause and on equitable terms.[21] This requirement is met readily enough if the proprietor gets some form of compensation for what he loses. Suppose a mine owner buys his mine in good faith, and some years later has to give it up upon nationalization. There is no injustice in this and no important direct loss of liberty—there may well be important issues about the concentration of power lurking in the background, but these have to be taken care of separately; what the coal-mine owner cannot fall back on is any cry equivalent to "It's *my* coal mine." What he can properly do is complain if the terms on which his ownership is abolished impose undue burdens on him.

IV

A fourth feature of utilitarian accounts of property is that they face a characteristic problem, that of reconciling security and equality. The most famous discussion of this is Bentham's own, but in one guise or another, it has run through the literature ever since.[22] Because the utilitarian is not moved by claims such as Robert Nozick's to the effect that there can be no place for redistributive action in a world in which everything comes into existence already attached to an owner,[23] the forward-looking nature of utilitarian justifications of any distributive arrangement means that the utilitarian is always wondering whether existing rules for the distribution of the society's stock of resources could be improved.

On the face of it, an equal distribution of goods is likely to best serve utility. If goods generally possess diminishing marginal utility, and people have much the same tastes and psychology, then as a rule of thumb, equal shares maximize total utility. But the essence of ownership is surely security. The point of having a property right in something is that I can control what happens to it, whether or not it gives me much, or indeed any, utility at that point. The benefit to society of having rules that secure people in their control of things is obvious enough. A man will not sow where another may reap, and the social cooperation needed for anything more elaborate than small-scale sowing and reaping is unimaginable unless there are rules allowing people to plan ahead and to rely on others performing in due season.

The world would simply not be used efficiently in the absence of such rules.[24] It does not follow that those rules have to be exactly like those of full private ownership in our sense—communal ownership and longer or shorter leases would be sensible enough, or family ownership plus trustee discretion—but they do have to provide certainty and security.

The conflict between security and equality then develops inexorably. Productivity demands security, that is, laws that do not change quickly, rights that can be relied on no matter what. But the process of production will steadily create increasing inequality as the clever and fortunate do well and the rest less well. At any given moment, there would be an increase in welfare if we were to divide up everything equally; but to do it would set at risk the environment of security and predictability that we rely on to create the wealth to redistribute in the first place. To put it simply, the utilitarian has to discover what distribution of the golden goose's eggs deters the goose from laying.

The dilemma itself compels no particular resolution. Moreover, as all discussions of the disincentive effects of taxation reveal, the argument is clouded with special pleading as well as bedeviled by the obvious problem that what deters people and what does not depends a lot upon what moral, political, and other beliefs about the world they hold. Bentham and James Mill argued in a way that has recently been popularized by Hayek and that rates security very highly indeed.[25] Over the long run, the only way the state can maximize overall welfare is by creating private property rights and then policing a laissez-faire economic order. This, moreover, appeals even to the more egalitarian sort of utilitarian; it might be true that at any given moment the worst-off person *now* would benefit from an equal division of the social stock, but over any long run, the worst-off person in the laissez-faire order will be better off than the worst-off person in any other system. Bentham in practice did not stick to quite such a rigorously "hands-off" position. Since there is nothing in the utilitarian calculus to forbid the sacrifice of one sort of gain for another, Bentham was not tempted to suppose that we should never tamper with expectations at all. The crucial point is to avoid frustrating the sort of expectations we ought to arouse. If my father cannot pass on his property to me now, I, having come to expect to get it, will feel frustrated; had he been told when he acquired it that *I* would not be able to pass it on, there would have been no frustration—he could have satisfied his expectations, I would satisfy mine, and my unborn children would have no expectations in the case.[26] The general position adopted by Bentham seems to be that the government may properly encumber property with taxes and restrictions from a future date in order that persons in the future take possession knowing what they are getting, and people in the present do not stand a loss at once. Compared with a theory that is wholly committed to the *rights* of owners, this is casual about the loss of the ability to decide exactly what shall happen to one's property; a utilitarian sufficiently impressed with people's attachment to the distant future might be more tender to the desire to tie up one's property, but this would be a matter of political psychology rather than direct moral theory. The crucial point is simple. As against the theory that holds that all redistribution is illicit because what it is proposed to distribute already has owners, the utilitarian holds that the artificial device, which is what a legal system is, can be constructed in whatever way we choose; but the importance of creating and satisfying stable expectations means that it is almost certainly wrong to attempt anything more than slowly operating methods of redistribution.

V

In all this, there is one point we have skirted but not confronted. This is the claim that for society to establish rules regulating property rights, society must claim something like initial ownership of the property thereafter confided to private hands.[27] The fifth and final point that needs to be made about the utilitarian theory of ownership is that its conception of rights is quite at odds with this view. There is a sort of natural affinity between the utilitarian justification of property rights—in general and in particular—and the legal positivist view that what property rights exist at any time and place is a factual matter to be settled by inspection of the local legal system. The conceptual question of what property is is divorced from the question of what property rights there ought to be; and an implication of this is that the utilitarian simply denies that the state must claim ownership in order to create ownership. Once there is a legal system, it is, of course, true that *individuals* do have to own things before they can transfer them. It does not follow that the relationship between the state and the individual is, in positive law, the same, and it does not follow that the relationship between society and the individual is, in morality, a shadow of the legal relationship between individuals. When the state claims the power to tax, to take by compulsory purchase, and all the rest of it, this need no more rest on claims of ownership than I have to claim ownership of my neighbors' houses in order to have the right to pull them down in the event of their threatening to set my house on fire.[28]

What this means is that the utilitarian theory of ownership is, in the last resort, not very bothered about ownership at all. Ownership is to be analyzed as a bundle of rights, and the bundle can be unpicked in various ways and reassembled as we choose. To wonder who *really* owns a vast corporation like Imperial Chemical Industries, since the rights to income, rights to control the day-to-day operations of the company, and all the rest of it are scattered among so many different people—and since the shareholders who own the company do not in any simple way own the company's property—is not an anxiety that comes naturally to utilitarians.[29] To suppose that things *must* have owners is habitual with Kant and Hegel but alien to the utilitarian tradition. In the utilitarian view, ownership is a convenient device, but one whose functions could largely be replaced by other sorts of rights, and it would be no lacuna in a legal system if many things were simply unowned and were dealt with in quite different ways.[30]

To insist that the state has no right to alter ownership rights except by the grant of such a right from the owners is, in effect, to start from the prejudice that only rights can generate rights and that rights are essentially proprietary in nature. This, however, is an odd view to take; its oddity comes out in interesting and curious ways in Nozick's *Anarchy, State, and Utopia*, where the distinction between offenses against the person and offenses against property is simply collapsed—all are illicit boundary crossings.[31] Anyone tempted in that direction, as was Kant, who wished to grant the state the same range of economic powers that most utilitarians would wish to, then has the awkward task of justifying the introduction of a fictional communal ownership of the earth as a starting point and a fictional contract empowering the state to regulate subsequent private ownership in appropriate ways.[32] The awkwardness is so extreme that it makes the utilitarian view of the conventionality of property rights and their dependence on the activities of the state all the more attractive in comparison.

VI

These considerations can be fleshed out a little more by taking four issues in which the arguments alluded to so far have been put to work. The first of these is the proper way to treat "original acquisition"—the question of what rights persons can plausibly claim over unowned things. The second is the question of the legitimacy of slavery. The third is whether the state's right to tax is equivalent to a right to impose forced labor upon its subjects. The last is whether we own our own bodies. The point of taking up these issues is that they show up neatly the differences between utilitarian and natural-rights theories, and show in addition that even when utilitarianism perhaps cannot deal with everything a natural-rights theory can deal with, we need not resort to natural rights of ownership. At two points at least these are issues that embarrass utilitarians whose liberal instincts and utilitarian arguments pull in different directions. Mill is often accused of incoherence in arguing that people ought not to be allowed to sell themselves into slavery; it seems to be a breach of his own prohibition of paternalistic legislation; he seems to depart from strict utilitarianism in just assuming that there is nothing to be said for slavery; and he cannot give a coherent account of the individual's rights over himself or herself—if the individual is sovereign over himself in what harms nobody else, how can he not have the right to sell himself into slavery?[33] Again, when utilitarians are accused of being willing to sacrifice one person for the welfare of another, an example often employed against them is what one might call "compulsory transplanting." What is the objection to killing an innocent person in order to distribute his or her bodily organs among sick patients who would otherwise die for lack of them?[34] As we shall see, the utilitarian is not without resources to answer this question, but the natural-rights theorist is, at first glance, perfectly equipped—he simply says that our bodies are ours, not part of a publicly available stock of medical resources.

The rights a person can claim over unowned things are the subject matter of Locke's theory of property most famously, but they must occupy any theorist's attention. In Locke's account, the crucial and contested claim is that a man who acquires something by catching it, picking it, drinking it, or whatever, mixes his labor with it and in the process makes it his.[35] The question is whether a utilitarian like Mill, who is sympathetic to the thought that individuals have moral rights as well as legal ones, is forced to concede that people's moral rights amount to ownership. The answer seems to be no. On the doctrines of *On Liberty*, what a person may do with an unowned object depends on just the same considerations as govern a person's rights generally; that is, he may do what he likes so long as he does not threaten harm to others. Does this mean that when he picks an apple from a tree, he comes to own it? The answer cannot be straightforward, depending as it does upon prior assumptions about what the central elements of ownership are. But suppose we agree that since picking the apple harmed no one, he was permitted to do it; we can then go on to agree that once he had picked it, it would then be an unwarranted interference with his liberty to stop him eating it. The more interesting question is what happens if he tries to pass it on to someone else. If his taking and eating harmed nobody, it is likely that giving it to someone else will harm nobody, and that he ought not to be prevented from doing it.

Is this, however, a transfer of property rights? I think it is not. That is, the new possessor's right to noninterference comes from the fact of his de facto possession and the general rule that whatever he does ought to be tolerated unless it does harm to others. Similarly, if the previous possessor imposes restrictions on what can be done with the apple—suppose he insists that the new possessor eat the apple himself rather than pass it on in turn—these restrictions are intelligible as the result of a promise made to the former possessor rather than as features of the property in question. One could envisage many of the incidents that attach to property and run with it as restrictive covenants being mimicked by a string of promises, and promises to exact further promises, but these would still be matters of personal rights, not real rights. The obligation to exact a promise from whomever we pass the apple to is an obligation holding us to the particular person to whom we made the promise only.[36]

The temptation to say that a person who takes an unowned thing must become its owner seems to stem from two things. The first is that because we identify actions by their doers, we cannot but agree that it is "his" or "her" taking that alters the status of the thing taken; it was *his* taking that moved it from a state where nobody had it to a state where he had it. The temptation then is to think that he has mixed what was his with what was nobody's and thereby made it his too. It should not be a strong temptation, though, since the sense in which our actions are ours is not much like the sense in which a car is ours.[37] The second temptation lies in the idea that a person who takes an unowned object does so with the intention of becoming its owner, rather as the king of Spain took possession of the New World from his study in Madrid with the intention of thereafter controlling its destiny. This is fundamentally the way Kant and Hegel tackle the issue.[38]

The objection to tackling the issue in this way is that it simply begs the question by presupposing what it tries to explain. It more or less ends by asserting that a person who takes an unowned thing asserts a sovereignty in it that has to be acknowledged as a corollary of the principle of respect for persons. There are two things a utilitarian might wish to say in response. The first is that utilitarianism can give a perfectly sensible account of why first occupancy ought generally to be treated as a step toward legal ownership; asking what conventions would maximize utility, we are likely to end by thinking that ceteris paribus, we should confirm the title of those in possession, those who have mixed their labor, and so on.[39] The second is that no utilitarian would accept respect for persons as a fundamental principle; it is altogether too like the doctrines of "abstract right" that Mill deplored. The idea that people establish themselves in the world as owners of external things would have struck him as an implausible derivation from an implausible principle. It might be argued that someone who held an instrumental theory of property rights, but who held that individuals had some rights— perhaps a right to equal concern and respect among them—that were not conventions established for instrumental reasons, might be more inclined to think that the rights one might have over unowned things did amount to ownership. Even so, there is no great pressure in this direction.

VII

I turn now to the question of slavery. Rights theorists have had various views about the institution. One extreme view, associated with Grotius, and perhaps with Nozick, is that since we begin by being the outright owners of ourselves, we can give that ownership to anyone we choose; once the transfer has taken place, we no longer own ourselves, of course—we are owned by whomever we have transferred ourselves to.[40] His or her ownership of us, like anyone's ownership of anything, is a matter of tracing how he came by the title; since we once held it and transferred it to him, he has a good title. The other extreme view is that slavery is incoherent; it presupposes that the slave is both mere thing and full-fledged person, and he or she cannot be *that*. The rights essential to personality cannot be transferred, either because, as in Locke, we do not hold them in the absolute way we hold rights over things, or because, as in Hegel, there is felt to be some incoherence in basing the right to extinguish our personality on the fact of that personality.[41] Neither view looks to the utilitarian advantages of slavery versus other economic arrangements; both look to one question only, which is whether slavery necessarily violates the slave's rights in such a way that even a voluntary act of the would-be slave cannot make him a slave.

The utilitarian cannot go along with those who think that slavery is conceptually illicit. On the positivist account to which utilitarians subscribe, slaves exist if some legal system or other provides for their existence. The only question is whether it ought to be possible to own another human being and whether a person who tries to sell herself or himself into slavery can be held to the terms of any such agreement. It is, for all that, true that before Bentham turns to discuss the issue at any length, his first step is to condemn the defenders of slavery by inquiring if they would be happy to change places with slaves—no doubt a good question, but dubiously utilitarian in spirit.[42] The more interesting response is offered by Mill in his discussion of perpetual contracts, in which he, perhaps a bit contentiously, links slavery and marriage. The difficulty Mill is in is obvious enough; if people are to be allowed to do whatever they wish so long as they do not damage the interests of others, we seem to be committed to letting them sell themselves into slavery—or marriage. But Mill denies that society ought to enforce any perpetual contracts of this kind. The way he presents the case, moreover, suggests that he, too, may have thought it an awkward one—a paternalistic interference with free choice, but justified in terms of the enlargement of freedom rather than in the usual paternalistic terms of the interference being "good" for the person interfered with in terms which he or she might not appreciate.[43]

A more accurate view dispels the air of paradox. The defense of leaving people to do as they choose is not based on the thought that they "own" themselves and can do as they choose with all their various pieces of property, themselves included. There is no natural ownership, whether of ourselves or of others. What a person who wishes to be a "slave" can do is promise to do whatever he or she is asked to do by the person he nominates as the "owner." He cannot be a real slave in the absence of a legal system that recognizes servitude as a legally enforced condition; he cannot do more than set out to behave slavishly. With that, we ought not to interfere—except by engaging in those activities that Mill groups under the general heading of exhorting and entreating; more crucially, we ought not to side with his "owner" if he changes his mind about the whole business and decides to stop behaving like a slave. This seems to meet the case—it is not that we stop people doing what they naturally can, but that we decline to provide institutional sanctions to make them go on doing it. It may be compared with the case of suicide; we ought not to prevent someone's committing suicide—under appropriate restrictions about making sure that he or she knows what sort of choice he or she is making. It does not follow that we are obliged to assist anyone to do away with himself. To do the latter is to limit our own freedom of action; perhaps we are so convinced that a given person's life is a misery that we do feel we ought, say, to lend him our gun to make a quick job of it, but this will be a matter of particular cases, not a matter of a general obligation to help someone to realize his choices no matter what. If I think him or her mistaken, I am under no obligation to help.[44]

One possible argument to show that Mill is still in trouble would be to claim that the obligation on the rest of us to enforce a perpetual contract stems from the fact that it is a promise like any other. If in general we think we ought to enforce the rights people get from others in virtue of being the beneficiaries of promises, why ought we not to enforce this promise—what grounds are there for saying that the "owner" gets no rights, no matter what promises the "slave" makes? It plainly is not like the case in which what I promise is something I have no right to do, such as the case in which I promise you that I will murder someone else. I have the right to act slavishly, and I promise to do just that. The reply, I take it, is that for a writer such as Mill, the way in which promises are to be understood is as a social device; promising is a device for enlarging the scope of choice. Promising belongs in an institutional framework that society offers to its members for the better conduct of their affairs. The rationale for it is in part libertarian, that is, it is partly out of a concern that people should be able to make arrangements facilitating future but as yet unknown projects that we mind so much about promising. But this rationale is at odds with enforcing self-enslavement.[45]

This, of course, is to stick within the framework offered by rights theorists who raise the question whether we have the right to enslave ourselves. On the rather wider issue of how to respond to arguments about "respect for persons" that rule slavery out of court as a morally tolerable institution, Mill's position is impeccably utilitarian. That is, he thinks that slavery was once justified as the only way of allowing enough economic advance to promote human progress generally. Once civilization advances, it is clearly intolerable. But in the nineteenth-century context, he still argues that although slavery is quite wrong and ought to be abolished, the owners of slaves should get proper compensation; there is no suggestion that their complicity in an illicit institution rules out a claim to compensation.[46]

VIII

Armed with the utilitarian view that property rights are entirely conventional, we can give a straightforward account of the state's right to tax, expropriate, or otherwise dispose of the property of individuals. The utilitarian's commitments to both individualism and collectivism balance out quite elegantly here. In a manner of speaking, the ultimate beneficiary of our efforts and the world's resources ought to be the community at large, or "all sentient creatures";[47] yet because the community exists only as discrete individuals, the only satisfactions there are are satisfactions of particular individuals. We must be tender to individuals for the sake of the whole collection of individuals. Therefore, in principle, governments may create and extinguish titles of all sorts and tax at any rate they choose.[48] But three sorts of consideration ought to animate them in making up their minds about what property rights to recognize and what taxation policies to adopt. The first is the need to keep up incentives, to avoid depressing initiative, and the like. This, we have seen already, may lead to a cautious policy about trying to redistribute resources; but it may leave plenty of room for maneuver about what we tax—we may go gently on earned income but have a large accessions tax on the grounds that this would increase the incentive to *earn* an income and does not much reduce incentive in general by making it less easy to give wealth to the already wealthy.[49] This is the place in utilitarian theory in which an answer comes to the recently popular question whether taxation is not the same thing as forced labor. The reply is that in this view it is not. Certainly, taxation is a forced contribution to social costs—even if we approve of all the measures the government takes, we have no choice whether to pay our contribution to its expenses. But not all forced contributions are forced labor, and the utilitarian knows why corvées cause social unrest in a fashion income taxes usually do not. An income levy is much the least painful way of extracting taxes—tithes are worse, and labor duties worse yet. Moreover, viewed in the utilitarian framework, there is no particular anxiety about the status of taxation generally; it is not that we have a property right in our incomes and then reluctantly hand over some portion to government. Morally, as opposed to legally, there is no reason to think that we do have that sort of right to our pretax incomes; rather, we are entitled to some share in the net proceeds of social collaboration, even if the simplest way of organizing the business is a way that gives more comfort than it ought to the nonutilitarian.

The second consideration is the need to do justice to different classes of person. Here, once more, we have to take it on trust that utilitarianism possesses an adequate account of justice; if it does, we must recognize that in addition to the considerations of incentive and the like just mentioned, we must take care that fairness is not neglected, either in the allocation of tax burdens or in compensating those whose property rights are extinguished. But all this is bread and butter to social theorists like Mill, who took considerable pains with his evidence to parliamentary committees on just such topics.[50] The last consideration is perhaps the most interesting. If the utilitarian justification of property rights is to enlarge choice and create security, it may be that we ought to break up the property rights characteristic of a capitalist economy based on individual private property and the joint-stock company for much the same reasons that animated the putting together of those bundles of rights in the first place. For instance, we may want to divorce the ownership of capital assets from the right to appoint managers; we may want to divorce the right to receive an income from shareholding from the right to receive a share of capital gains; and we shall certainly want to insist on separating the state's right to insist, say, that any firm above a certain size is run as a workers' cooperative from any suggestion that the state should try to monopolize the right to decide prices and output in the manner of a command economy.[51] But what is above all to be noticed about what all this implies for the utilitarian theory of ownership is that when a rights theorist might begin by asserting that people just *are* originators of value, creators of moral worth in the world and the begetters of their own projects—all of which requires expression in the appropriate ownership institutions—the utilitarian is content to say that although people are not essentially anything of the sort, this is what, with luck and good social design, they may become—and a rational justification of property rights justifies those rights that that progress requires.[52]

IX

I turn last to the suggestion that if we do not start with a doctrine of self-ownership, the utilitarian is driven to treat as serious moral proposals ways of treating people that we all know to be simply wrong. The thought experiment of the argument for compulsory transplant surgery is a good example. We suppose a ward in which two men are dying, one for lack of a suitable kidney, one for lack of a suitable heart, say; to the news that no spare parts are available, they reply that they are—all the doctors need do is kill some unsuspecting donor and save two lives for the price of one.[53] It is, I think, clear that no sensible utilitarian would give the suggestion houseroom, for reasons familiar to all insurance companies—it creates a moral hazard in that it gives people an incentive to ruin their own organs, since they stand to benefit from transplants if they are ill and they stand not to be used for spare parts if they are not fit to be so used.[54] But some writers appear to think that this misses the point. The difficulty is to decide what that point is. One suggestion is that because the donor's organs are *his* organs, it violates his rights to take them. Even if all we did was take a pint of his blood and leave him to recover quietly after we had done so, it would still violate his rights, just because it was *his* blood and not ours.

It seems to me that there is not much to be said for trying to explain the illicitness of treating people as resources in terms of property rights—except perhaps negatively in recalling that we are not one another's property. But it is not because we are each our own property that we are not one another's property. We draw a sharp line between theft and assault, and a theory of rights that blurs the distinction is unattractive. It was precisely because we cannot be injured except in our own bodies that Kant had to go to such lengths to explain the nature of property in terms of our being "injured at a distance" by mischiefs done to it.[55] It seems peculiarly unattractive to make the case the other way round—to explain injury as a sort of theft close to. Another consideration in the same vein is that whatever one thinks about rights in general, property rights are at least often through and through artificial; but rights over our own bodies come as close as anything can to being natural rights. Even to walk down the street presupposes that I have the right to move my legs in the appropriate fashion. It is hard to see what rights would be like at all if they did not include rights over one's body—but it is not hard to see how there could be such rights and no property rights.

In short, if there is something distasteful about such a suggestion as the compulsory transplant surgery, it seems to be for two reasons. The first is moral. The idea treats people as mere means to an end, treats them as resources. I do not think that utilitarianism can do very much to accommodate the idea that this is intolerable; this is one reason why many writers have thought that an instrumental theory of property rights was correct, but resisted the thought that the best instrumental theory is utilitarian. All the same, utilitarianism can do a good deal to embrace the same conclusions as the theorist of a right to respect as a person would reach. If people just do passionately mind about not being treated as objects, even for benevolent purposes, that launches the utilitarian case for treating people's own wishes with extreme tenderness.[56]

The second reason that may underlie this desire for being the controller of our own fates is more nearly metaphysical. It is the consequence of our human embodiment that for each of us, *this* body is special; we and it are so closely bound up with each other that we cannot coherently see ourselves as both selves and mere collections of parts. It is quite unclear to me how far one can press this point, and equally unclear to me how much metaphysical baggage utilitarianism has to carry or jettison. Happily, this does not matter, since the only point I have to make in conclusion is that these considerations do not affect the analysis of property rights. If an inability to give an account of the categorical imperative in its various guises is a defect in utilitarianism as a complete system of ethics, it makes no difference to utilitarianism's capacity to give a persuasive account of property rights. As we have just seen, there may be some rights—the right not to be sacrificed, say—for which utilitarianism cannot offer a very compelling rationale. But such rights are not property rights. Of those rights that are genuinely property rights, utilitarianism gives the plainest and most compelling account we have.

Maximizing, Moralizing, and Dramatizing

TOWARD THE END of *The Presentation of Self in Everyday Life*, Erving Goffman writes, "The claim that all the world's a stage is sufficiently commonplace for readers to be familiar with its limitations and tolerant of its presentation, knowing that at any time they will be able to demonstrate to themselves that it is not to be taken too seriously."[1] The object of this essay is to ask, how seriously is too seriously? Since one perfectly plausible answer to that question is offered both in *The Presentation of Self in Everyday Life* and in *Frame Analysis*—an answer that reminds us that what goes on on the stage is not *real*—some justification is needed for making more fuss than that about so-called dramaturgical explanation. If we know why we should not take the dramatic analogy too seriously, do we need to take it seriously at all?

The justification for doing so runs something like this. A large part of social science requires us to explain why actors act as they do in the situations in which they find themselves. To explain their behavior is to reconstruct what Karl Popper terms "the logic of the situation."

This, again, can plausibly be represented as explaining their behavior in relation to their doing what is, in some sense yet to be explained, "the thing to do."[2] It is a commonplace of recent sociology that the concern of traditional sociologists with social structure, with invariant relationships rather than varying personnel, often led to the assumption that "the thing to do" and the actor's belief that it was indeed "the thing to do" could be read off from some universally agreed description of the social role occupied by the actor. Hence, one mode of explanation by situational logic would simply be that of discovering an actor's role and inferring what it required him to do on a given occasion. To understand what an agent did would simply be to understand what role he was filling. There are, no doubt, far more questions raised than answered by such a claim. It tells us nothing about why a given society recognizes the roles it does; it does not suggest any way of discriminating between those bits of activity that are role fulfilling and those bits that are not. All this is commonplace.

Appeals to roles leave out questions of motivation in particular. That is, at one level, we may suppose the question "Why did Smith shoot himself after he had been slapped by the pork butcher?" is answered when we are told that Smith was an officer in a crack regiment. To be slapped by a social inferior with whom it was impossible to settle the matter by dueling would be to be dishonored; only suicide could restore his honor and that of the regiment. But what we do not know is why he was so committed to the code that he was willing to accept death rather than dishonor. This suggests that if we want to know why someone does what he does, we must look to the goals he is seeking and to his beliefs about their rewardingness to himself. The assumption underlying the demand is the belief that men do what they find it most rewarding to do—even if, to paraphrase G. C. Homans, they find the damnedest things rewarding.[3]

This assumption provides the general structure of an answer to the question about an actor's motivation for doing what, as we say, "the role requires" him to do. The answer to the question of why Smith shot himself is that he found death more rewarding than dishonor, or that, of all the actions available to him, death by his own hand was the most rewarding. This still leaves unanswered the question of why he finds death the most rewarding of the available options; nonetheless, we should have no trouble, in principle at least, in providing a genetic account of how he came to feel that he would rather die than live dishonored. The structure of explanation would be to assume that what was done was the most rewarding thing to do, and then to answer questions about how it can have been such in the individual's socialization. Sometimes we are unlikely even to be tempted to invoke the role a person occupies when explaining his behavior in maximizing terms. The man who is dying of a painful disease and who therefore shortens the process by taking an overdose of sleeping tablets is quite readily represented as calculating that if the returns on being dead are zero, the returns on dying slowly and painfully are negative, so the rational choice is to be dead sooner rather than later.

There is some tendency for writers to oppose role-filling and returns-maximizing models, as if the fact that one account talks about "officers" and the other about Smith, Jones, and Wilkinson placed them in competition. Of course, this is not so. There is much to be said about an excessive reliance on the concept of a role or, relatedly, on the concept of a norm, and about the dangers of assuming that men will just do what they think they ought, or what their role requires; and there is much to be said about the dangers of tautology in the returns-maximizing model, as well as more sophisticated things about which elements of a theory of motivation we can safely agree to be tautological and which elements we must at all costs preserve as vulnerable to empirical test. Still, the immediate point is simply to observe that there are both actors and roles, that *Smith* is an officer and that *an officer* is what Smith is.

It is this insistence on preserving both aspects of the role-filling and returns-maximizing model that lets in the third view of how to determine what "the thing to do" is. We accept both premises of the previous models; there are roles with rights and obligations attached to them, and rights and obligations do provide reasons for action and can, therefore, feature in the explanation of why an actor did what he did: but there are also agents who are individual, flesh-and-blood creatures who are not bundles of rights and duties and who have goals, wants, wishes, purposes of their own. Explanations of social behavior must accommodate both persons and parts, just as an explanation of a game of chess needs to accommodate not only the rules that lay down what moves each piece can make, and what counts as victory and defeat, but also the aims of the players, their skills, their temperaments and so on. The sociologist may, perhaps, rest content with giving a structural description of a society's role structure—and no one reading Siegfried Nadel could be in any doubt about the importance and the difficulty of so doing.[4] But, if we want to explain what happens during some strip of social interaction, we need both roles and actors, both the recognized rights and obligations and the hopes, fears, skills, and weaknesses that the actor brings with him in filling his roles.[5] It is an insistence on this that seems to mark out the "dramatistic," "dramatic," or "dramaturgical" approach to the study of social interaction.[6] (I am not sure that anything hangs on which of these expressions one adopts.)

I now broach the question that will haunt what follows, even though little of what follows tackles it explicitly. This is the question whether the dramaturgical model insists on the theatricality of social life merely in the sense of insisting that people fill roles just as persons act parts in a play; that they can, therefore, cease to fill them, can at all times fill them with more or less commitment to the standard goals and purposes that the roles appear to presuppose; that they can, at least sometimes, stand back from their own performance of the role and ask themselves why they are bothering to go on with it when they could be doing something more interesting or more agreeable; that they can take advantage of the role to indicate to others that they are not quite the people they seem from the performance they are putting on.[7] That is, it is the question whether the crucial element in the dramaturgical picture is that cluster of insights that goes under the general heading of "role distance." Or is the crucial element the claim that style is the man? That is, that we leave out the aesthetic dimension of social life at the risk of misunderstanding much of what goes on; that when people put on a good performance of some social part, this is not simply a device for leaving in other people's minds the impression that they are peculiarly estimable or admirable, nor necessarily to plant in other people's minds false beliefs about the terms on which they are prepared to cooperate in the projects of others, to exchange benefits with them, or whatever. Is it, perhaps, the claim that the only way in which we can accommodate the twin pressures of social life, on the one hand, and of our private selves, on the other, is by turning that process of accommodation into a work of art, into a project that is better understood by poets, playwrights, and novelists than by a cost-benefit analysis or the functionalist analysis of roles?

Antoine de Saint-Exupéry was very fierce about a young man who pulled on a pair of white gloves before blowing his brains out.[8] Was he complaining of the "theatricality" of the gesture? If he was, are we to infer that there is a distinction between serious matters and matters susceptible to dramatic renditions; or are we to infer that serious matters are susceptible to dramatic rendition precisely because theatricality is a vice that destroys good drama and only good drama?

So much by way of introduction. I now want to say something—though I do not know how to say enough—about the peculiarities of rational explanation and about the role of reconstructions of "the thing to do" other than the role of explaining an action or series of actions. To do this, I take a brief look at the perhaps overworked problem of accounting for voting behavior in the terms proposed by Anthony Downs's *An Economic Theory of Democracy*.[9] All this leads on to the suggestion that if the world both is and must be rather short of people who are rationally maximizing values—either returns to themselves or some other value[10]—it is no wonder that social scientists should turn their attention to some of the nonmaximizing activities in which people are engaged, such as staging social dramas or planning their lives as works of art. This remains nothing better than a suggestion, for reasons that become sufficiently obvious when we turn to some recent accounts of the phenomenon of suicide (and of Émile Durkheim's *Suicide*).

It would be pointless to adduce as an explanation of an action the good reasons for doing it unless we accepted something like "the principle of rationality,"[11] which Popper calls "false but indispensable" to the social sciences. Yet as Popper's characterization of it suggests, it is a strange principle; it can hardly be a generalization from particular cases, for all the familiar reasons about the impossibility of identifying the explanandum in particular cases without already presupposing the principle. Thus, we seem to be left to read the principle as a conceptual truth or as a heuristic principle. That is, we might construe the principle of rationality not as saying that by and large men do the thing to do, but as the conceptual claim that what a (rational) action *is* is what an agent does because it is (in some sense or other) the thing to do; to read it thus would be to take it in something like the way Kant takes the principle of universal causality. Or we might treat it as a heuristic principle, which tells us not to give up trying to find reasons for a piece of human behavior, not to rest content with any explanation that does not show how what happened was at least subjectively the thing to do. People who are skeptical about heuristic interpretations of such principles might reflect on the work of, say, R. D. Laing, in which the principle is adopted in very unpromising circumstances in order to try to render the behavior of schizophrenics intelligible.[12] The attraction of this is that it brings back into the fold of human actions events that would have to be taken otherwise as things which merely *happened* to the schizophrenic patient.

If the rationality principle is not a conceptual truth or a heuristic principle, it is hard to know what else it might be. As an empirical generalization about men generally doing the right thing, it is pathetically false, in view of the unfortunate human proneness to error. If it is to be read more narrowly, as it would be, for instance, by many sociologists when they claim that rational behavior is common in economic matters but not in social life generally, then "rational" is clearly being interpreted much more narrowly than it is here—either in such a way as to fulfill Max Weber's account of *Zweckrationalität* or in some sense as equivalent to Vilfredo Pareto's account of logical action.[13]

What this means is that, in one view, to show that an action was in any sense "the thing to do" just is to show that it was the rational thing to do, for showing that it was the thing to do is rationally to explain it. In the other view, to show that it is the thing to do is to render it intelligible; to show that it is the *rational* thing to do is to go one step further. There is no easy way to tell what hangs on the choice of a more or less restrictive account; if we want to insist on the significant differences between explanations in relation to people's goals and knowledge, on the one hand, and straightforward causal explanations, on the other, presumably we shall have no objection to the wider usage; if we want to insist on how differently the artist, poet, or priest shapes his means to his ends from the way the entrepreneur and engineer shape theirs, we shall presumably want to narrow the notion.

Downs's *Economic Theory of Democracy* illustrates some of the problems we are faced with here. Downs's book expands on a suggestion implicit in Joseph Schumpeter's *Capitalism, Socialism, and Democracy* to the effect that political parties and voters can be understood as if they were firms on the one side and consumers on the other.[14] Voters spend their votes to secure the greatest possible flow of utilities from the policies that political parties will implement if they gain office. Political parties are assumed to have only one aim, that of securing power by selling their policies to as many voters as possible. Initially, Downs credits all parties with much the same omniscience that the theory of perfect competition assumes in orthodox economics, but the analysis gets exciting only when real-life phenomena analogous to brand loyalty and information costs are allowed to intrude. The best-known crux, however, arises when we make only the assumption that voting is an activity with opportunity costs; because once voting is allowed to have costs, Downs sees that it is very hard to explain why people vote *at all*. The rational voter operates with some estimate of what difference it will make to his overall utility if one party rather than another should win; what he then has to work out is whether the chance that his vote will make all the difference between the "right" and the "wrong" party winning, multiplied by the difference it makes for the "right" party to win, is a larger sum than the cost of voting rather than doing any of the things he would rather do. Now, it is evident that in a large electorate, the chances that any given individual's vote will make all the difference are tiny; the value of the voting act, therefore, is tiny also, since it is unlikely that the party differential is so enormous that it would make a serious difference to the result. Hence, if voting has any cost at all, the voter will not vote—not if he is rational, that is.

Downs begins his book by suggesting that the only point of a theory is to predict what happens, and therefore commits himself to the view that the only proper course of action when we are faced with such a divergence between what the theory demands voters should do and what voters actually do do is to junk the theory. One would suppose, therefore, that Downs would simply throw out the hypothesis that voters are acting to maximize their utility flow. In fact, he does not do so. So strong is the grip of the theory that he looks round for something other than the party differential to supply the voter's payoff. Thus, he suggests that the voter is not just voting for the party that offers him the better deal, but also voting to sustain democratic government too. If fewer than a certain number of voters turn out, democracy will collapse; the voter, therefore, has to consider the costs to himself if the whole system were to collapse. This, in essence, is a way of pushing up v (the utility of an outcome) to compensate for the smallness of p (the probability of its occurring under specified conditions). And like other arguments addressed to self-interested persons in order to induce them not to free-ride, it is bound to fail if the odds against their individual contribution being decisive one way or the other are very high. The odds against any single voter's participation or abstention being decisive are so enormous that the self-inflicted costs of abstention are bound to be very low, no matter how much the individual may dislike the prospect of the collapse of democracy.[15]

Now, here two avenues open up that we ought to keep distinct. The first is that which leads us to investigate what decision rules people do use, in order to see why they make decisions that pure utility maximizers might not make—supposing they were infallible in their estimate of the probabilities attaching to the various outcomes. In essence, we should stick to the view that people act self-interestedly, but look more closely at how they do so, in order to see whether they are, perhaps, satisficers rather than maximizers, or whether they are intendedly maximizers but have curious views about probability. Now, along these lines there are many interesting results we might want to investigate. For instance, the phenomena of football pools and insurance companies suggest two things—that when we are faced with the prospect of really large losses, we overestimate the danger of their occurrence and thus accept odds that a true utility maximizer would not, and that when we are faced with a really large gain, we are prepared to gamble a small amount at odds that the utility maximizer strictly ought to reject. Downs might, along these lines, have argued that voters will overestimate the possibility of system collapse, or else that there is a threshold below which they do not count costs at all and would happily vote in the same frame of mind as they would spend fivepence on a lottery ticket. But Downs takes the second line, which is to treat as sacrosanct the assumption that men are utility maximizers, and to then look round to see *what* yields them a utility. Downs tinkers with the payoff to the voter by suggesting that the pleasures of a satisfied conscience make it worth the voter's while to go and do his duty and vote. It is, of course, an empirically well-confirmed view that people's disposition to vote at all correlates much more closely with the strength of their sense of "citizen duty" than with their perception of the differences between the parties. This certainly suggests that the first version of Downs's theory is less likely to hold water than the second version.[16]

But, of course, once we allow "doing one's duty" to feature in the desires of the agent, we run into exactly those troubles that Thomas Babington Macaulay so enjoyed pointing out to James Mill.[17] The theory that men maximize their flow of utility loses its explanatory stuffing. We begin with the belief that when rational behavior is thought to be utility-maximizing behavior, we can find some simple constraints on the sort of thing that will yield men a utility—such as money income. We then find ourselves baffled, because if men were acting to maximize money returns, say, they would not vote at all. Now, when we stand by the notion that they must be maximizing something or other, we end up with a different theory and a different empirical task. We do not have a predictive, falsifiable, and, indeed, falsified theory; what we have is an analytical framework into which we try to fit a rather different predictive theory, if we can find one.

Faced with the failure of utility-maximizing models to do as much as they promised to tidy up the explanation of choice, one can see why people have been attracted to alternative models, such as the dramaturgical. But it can hardly be said that the model has received what one might take to be a definitive statement, or to have been spelled out in such a way as to achieve consensus on what its scope and limits are. The situation is not helped by the fact that the writer with whom the model is most frequently associated, Erving Goffman, has more than once done his best to get out from under its shadow. That is, a good deal of *Frame Analysis* is devoted to denying that everything is a piece of theater; Goffman insists that events in everyday life have *real* consequences in a way that events depicted on the stage do not, and he spends the bulk of a particularly engaging chapter elaborating the devices by means of which we make sure that what happens on the stage is not taken to be part of real life.[18] The topic is not an easy one to keep clear; but a small start might be made if we were careful to distinguish between *pretending* and *depicting*. It is important that the actor who plays Othello does not *pretend* to be Othello in anything like the sense in which the con man pretends to be a gas-meter reader; his playing of Othello is not at all intended to mislead anyone into supposing that he *is* Othello, whereas it is the essence of the con man's activity that he should induce us to believe that he really is the gas man, and just as it is an essential part of the fraudulent claimant's activities that he should be taken to be the very same person as the legitimate heir. It is an important consequence of Goffman's analysis of, for instance, the occasion when a member of the audience leaped onto the stage and began to attack the "hero" of *Look Back in Anger* that whatever sort of suspension of disbelief it is that the theater requires, it cannot be one that requires us to think that we are really seeing Othello strangle Desdemona.[19] The proper response to Othello's strangling Desdemona would be to stop him.

Now, it is certainly true that in the world that Goffman shows us there is a great deal of pretending going on. People are constantly pretending to be acting in good faith when they are not, pretending to competences they do not possess, and pretending to commitments they do not feel. At any rate, one aspect of the notion of role distance—though not, perhaps, the most important—is its reminder of the way we often pretend to be more at ease in a given task than we are, the way we try to mislead others about our ability to perform the task at hand with something to spare. To that extent, it may be thought that the element of deception is crucial and that "putting on a show of doing" is the central notion in dramaturgical analysis. This, I think, is to chase too hard in only one direction. For the notion of depiction, which is more obviously dramatic in its connotations, has a role to play. We do not need to suggest that a man who plays the role of surgeon is only *pretending* to be a surgeon; what he really is is a surgeon all right. But, we might well want to say that what he does qua surgeon also depicts what a surgeon does, in spite of the obvious awkwardness of saying any such thing. The awkwardness is, of course, that it seems odd to say that a thing might be both itself and a picture of itself; but there is no particular awkwardness in saying that a given piece of behavior might be both that piece of behavior and a picture of pieces of behavior of that sort. A cricketer who plays an admirable cover drive both plays that particular drive and displays an image of the good cover drive. So in this view, we ought not to be unduly alarmed by the suggestion that a given activity is both the real-life activity of saving lives by surgery and an exemplary picture of what it is like to do the job conscientiously, efficiently, skillfully, and so on.

Nor does the argument end there; we might go on to claim that it is just because the activity can be seen as an image of that sort of activity that it allows room for considerations of style, for an aesthetic dimension. That a man fills the role at all is not usually a question of style; to *be* a surgeon at all is mainly a question of ability, or qualifications, or what he usually does to the patients confided to his care. Doing the job is a technical matter; but the surroundings in which the job is done offer the chance to do it *in style* rather than *merely*. In something like surgery, style is very much the man—bound up with how an individual manages the demands on him; but it is also an element in the role, in the sense that an account of the style in which a role can be filled is one of the things we would want to know about any role before we felt we understood it. It would be a thin knowledge of cricket that did not include the insight that Wally Hammond was, and Ken Barrington was not, a stylish player.

This is by no means all there is in Goffman's accounts of "strips" of social interaction, and a worrying aspect of Goffman's habitual offhandedness about his theoretical commitments should be broached now before we push on to take a closer look at dramaturgy. This is the ambiguity between a disposition to see "what is going on" as something played as a drama, and a disposition to see it as a game in the game-theoretical sense, a game in which we are standardly beset by something like prisoner's dilemma problems and in which we are constantly trying to get as much as possible for ourselves out of an essentially fragile cooperation with others. In this second reading, the importance that Goffman attaches to the control of information about ourselves has a much more obvious explanation than it would on a more committedly dramaturgical view. It is the object of each of us to convey an impression of himself that will make the terms of cooperation more favorable to himself. On this view, the surgeon who does his job stylishly is not concerned to make the terrors of dying and of causing death more bearable by distancing them in an aesthetic framework, but to secure his dominance over the rest of the surgical team, to induce in them the belief that he is vital to the success of the operation and that to secure his cooperation, they have to yield to him. Or, more generally, what the actor is up to is trying to rig the social terms of trade by engendering the appropriate beliefs in everyone else. This, of course, requires what Goffman always insisted on, the essential gap between agent and role. Everyone in everyday interaction knows that social life is possible only if everyone is kept sweet enough to be willing to do his bit in the social undertakings on which we all depend; so everyone is watching out for signs that other people are reliable or unreliable, competent or incompetent. A feature of Goffman's work that is apt to offend people is the apparent implication that we spend so much time either sneaking a look at the shortcomings of others or trying to tart up the image we ourselves present. A good many of his readers protest that they rarely, if ever, think about putting themselves over to an audience and never, or at least very rarely, entertain doubts about the sanity, sexual normality, good temper, or whatever of their associates. If they are outraged and are also attracted to one of the contemporary versions of Marx, they may insist that these anxiety-ridden phenomena are typical of a society whose values are corrupted by commodity production, and where, therefore, we worry incessantly about what price our virtues will fetch and about whether we shall be sold a pup by others. I am not at all sure that anything so sinister ought to be read into it all; though it does appear that there is a genuine puzzle about the generalizability of Goffman's work, a genuine puzzle whether what he says is true of Americans and not of the British, as Michael Banton suggests,[20] or whether it is true of advanced industrial societies and not of simpler, preindustrial societies. The only question at issue here is whether we should treat his account of social interaction as a story about how we rig the market or as a story about how we engage in putting on a good show.

In *The Drama of Social Reality*, Stanford Lyman and Martin Scott suggest that they have something of the same anxieties about Goffman's theoretical commitments.[21] But they regard themselves as thoroughly committed to the view that life really *is* theater. The question then arises to what are they thus committed, seeing as G. H. Mead and Freud are invoked along with Goffman to explain what the dramaturgical standpoint is, even though Goffman is then dismissed as not a full-fledged dramaturgical theorist. The obvious considerations on which they draw are such things as our ability to rehearse *in foro interno* (literally, "in the inner court") what we are going to do before we do it—but that in itself scarcely seems enough, since the mere fact that I work out a calculation in my head before I write it down will qualify as an instance of rehearsing what I am going to do without tempting many of us to see it as the rehearsal of a drama. Again, they seem to suggest that in all aspects of social life we follow a script; but for the reasons suggested above, it is not clear whether this is a script or a game plan, whether it is a script containing technical instructions or the lines in a tragedy. I am following a text when I follow the instructions in the car's handbook and change a wheel; but Goffman's insistence that there is a difference between changing a wheel on the road and changing a wheel in a play still makes one want to say that even if the two activities looked like each other, we are miles from showing that all life is theater.

It might be said that changing a wheel is not a social interaction, being a matter merely of the driver and inanimate matter locked in combat; but merely introducing another character to assist one in following the instructions does not seem to alter the analysis much. More plausibly, we might say that only where we do what we do in front of an audience, real or imagined, is there room for the theatrical analogy to operate. Thus, where it is not simply me, or me and a mate, wrestling with the beastly wheel, but me representing myself to some audience or other in the guise of "one who is wholly incompetent, but through no fault of his own," we might say I am putting on a little drama. But at just this point the ambiguity we noticed above comes back: can we not equally well say that what I am doing is telling people that my imposing upon them the burdens of assisting me is not the result of a flaw in my character or of mere idleness? If we can, we are back where we were with the question of how we are to distinguish an insistence on social life as a drama from an insistence on attending to the ways in which people set out to secure a definition of the situation, either cooperatively or in competition with each other.

There is one hint that might suggest that the attractions of the emphasis on aesthetic explanation rest on something other than the false claim that all the world is really a stage. The suggestion stems from Freud's concern with art, and at best it surfaces briefly in the analysis offered by Lyman and Scott. The hint is that the enjoyment that we get from art, which lies at the root of all aesthetic activity, is to be explained by the role of artistic transformation in making the pains and anxieties of life more bearable. In Lyman and Scott's account, it sometimes looks as if it is Freud's *theory* that is the drama, with id, ego, and superego playing parts in a tragicomedy;[22] the more interesting notion is that within the theory, ego is to be recast, not as an economic calculator trying to maximize psychic gratification in a dangerous world, but as a poet or dramatist making life bearable by giving it a unity that is not itself explicable in economic terms. That is, even preserving the claim that in some sense the task of the ego is to adjust the dealings between the organism and the environment, the claim would be that the nature of this adjustment was essentially rather than contingently to be understood by invoking considerations appropriate to the evaluation of a work of art. It is a striking claim, and it goes much beyond anything to be elicited from, say, Mead's observation that behind the social Me there lies the personal I; for it is a claim, however inexplicit, about how the I shapes what happens to the Me, and about why the I is prepared to put up with all sorts of misadventures to the Me so long as they are organized in the right way.

Still, this is no more than a speculative throwaway. If we go back to our earlier anxieties, there is one further issue to settle before ending with a confession of bewilderment. It is sometimes said that dramaturgical explanation must be parasitic on other sorts of explanation in the sense that what goes on in the theater is already parasitic on what goes on in the nontheater. There are two rather different points to be made. The first is that some versions of everyday behavior depend for their effect on being copies of what goes on in a film or in a play or whatever; the surgeon who puts on the manner of Gary Cooper for some particularly grim operation is plainly borrowing from the realm of the theatrical in the strictest sense. But this is not to say that the dramatic qualities of real-life behavior depend on our lifting the script from a drama—what goes on in plays, films, and the rest is a heightening and a concentration of what goes on elsewhere. But, second, there is certainly a sense in which dramaturgical explanations are parasitic on other explanations. In any case in which a dramatic explanation is in place, there is some other explanation in place as well. The woman who commits suicide and represents herself as having been truly brokenhearted, therefore, may be said to be performing the last lines of a tragedy of blighted love.[23] But we have two explanations pinned to one action here. The reason for committing suicide might be to make a coherent ending to an otherwise intolerably muddled existence; but the misery that needs resolving is a misery in its own right. The woman may be engaging in a *dramatic rendering* of "I am really brokenhearted," and the half-intended impact of her death may be to ensure that the blame for it falls squarely on the man who jilted her; but none of this would make any sense unless being brokenhearted was already understood to provide adequate reasons for putting an end to oneself. If we invoke the analogy of the drama only to suggest that her suicide was a saying as well as a doing, the passing of a message as well as an act of self-destruction, the burden of the explanation falls as much on those motives to which she is drawing attention as it does on the dramatic presentation of them. To get extra mileage out of the dramatic analogy, we have to suggest an explanation of why only a drama will put across the message; otherwise, the drama is not merely, as it must be, parasitic on the other account of motivation, but also thoroughly uninformative.

This point is important and general. When Lyman and Scott apply their talents to the analysis of Shakespeare's most famous plays, the result is oddly unimpressive. They may be right to suggest that what *Antony and Cleopatra* is in part concerned with is the rise of bureaucratically rational administration; but what we want to know is why should Shakespeare write a *play* about a phenomenon that is handled so differently in, say, Talcott Parsons's *The Social System*?[24] The distinction this rests on, between the message and its vehicle, is one that is crucial to the anxieties I have expressed about separating out the information-passing account of behavior from a genuinely dramaturgical account. When Durkheim attends to moments of social effervescence and explains how religious rituals enforce, symbolically, the moral relationship between individuals and society, one feels inclined to ask why *this* way of telling the individual these things is *the* way to do it. Even in Weber's account of *wertrational* behavior, something of the same difficulty recurs; a given action is thought to be the only possible way of expressing a particular value or of driving home the point of a given way of life. And we are left anxious about the way the values and the expression of them are connected, and left to look for some account of how a mode of expression is or is not adequate to what it has to express.[25]

A last look at three sorts of suicide, in the light of the anxieties of what has gone before, may sum up the doubts of this essay, even if it will not lead to any conclusions. The three cases we might contrast are a man killing himself to avoid dying of a painful, wasting illness; a captain going down with his ship, having been forced to scuttle it; and the jilted woman who drowns herself. It does not seem at all difficult to account for the first in value-maximizing terms; the only awkwardness is posed by the values of the man's society and the extent to which they restrain the pursuit of self-interested goals of this sort. The man certainly *has* good reasons, in self-interested terms, to take his own life, but according to the local norms, he may have good reasons not to do so. I do not have anything to say about when a man will take as his reasons for acting one set of reasons rather than another, but it is obviously a topic of central importance in accounting for rational explanation.[26]

The second case is analyzable so simply that it explains why role theory has been the object of some derision; that is, we might simply adduce in explanation the convention or norm that disgraced captains go down when their ships go down. If we want to know why Jones chose to drown, we simply point out that he was a captain who had been forced to scuttle. We have, as was suggested at the beginning of the essay, a problem that is the converse of that which the first case presented. That is, the first case raises the question of how norms constrain the acceptance of self-interested reasons; here we have the question of how self-interest constrains the acceptance of altruistic norms. The captain has a good, selfish reason for not going down with his ship, but he does not take it as his reason for action.

Although, as suggested just a little earlier, it is the third case that raises the question of how to apply dramaturgical concepts, it might be argued that they are at home here too. For what is it to go down with one's ship except to end one's career in style, to leave the stage in the grand manner? This is not, of course, to say that there is any room here for such a notion as role distance, for the thing about the captain is he does not distance himself from the role—he identifies himself with it so completely that he never thinks of doing anything but going down with his ship. But the suggestion raises the question whether the role of captain is sustained by the opportunities it offers for *displays* of heroism and so on.[27] And one then has to decide how an act's heroism refers to its "desirability characteristics": is heroism to be explained simply as a function of altruism, endurance of pain, and so on, or as a feature of the show a hero can put on in front of an appreciative audience?

In the third case, there is no temptation to suggest that the woman played a role, so long as roles are thought of as bundles of rights and duties, though if we want to run the dramaturgical model for all it is worth, we may well say that "Sheila, the jilted woman" is a part, a dramatis persona. But just as we worried earlier about the tendency of dramaturgical images to boil down to stories about how behavior conveys information—getting a certain definition of the situation established and so on—here we may end up feeling that she has not put on anything interestingly analyzable as a drama, but has done something, part of the point of which was to establish *why* she had done it. What she was up to was, in part, telling us why life seemed to her to be so intolerable.

All of this raises far more questions than it answers, and this in spite of the fact that innumerable issues have not been raised at all, although a full analysis would require their resolution. Thus, nothing has been said about distinctions between rituals, dramas, different kinds of games, interior monodramas, and so on; nothing has been done to resolve the doubts of those who think that all this suggests that the only sort of theater ever devised is the naturalistic drama of recent western European culture. Again, nothing has been done to spell out the differences between those theorists who insist on our need for an audience to appreciate our activities and those who insist on our need to retreat "backstage" and put on consolatory shows in private. Indeed, the upshot of what has gone before is perhaps this only: first, to raise the question whether, in appealing to the dramatic or stylistic component of social behavior, we have invoked a distinctive kind of explanatory framework for activities otherwise misunderstood or merely noticed what was noticed before the Flood—the importance of impression management; and second, to raise the question of the indispensability of particular symbols, particular modes of passing information, and so on— the question, perhaps, whether in this area, the medium and the message are distinguishable.

The Romantic Theory of Ownership

THIS ESSAY has a purpose and a theme, but I am rather conscious that it has no very straightforward conclusion. The purpose is to draw attention to the characteristic concerns and claims of those I pick out as "Romantic" theorists of work and ownership; the theme is that what they have in common is best highlighted by a contrast with instrumental and utilitarian accounts of these matters. The absence of a straightforward conclusion reflects the fact that there is no one thing that Romantic writers either saw or failed to see that writers in another tradition would either have failed to see or could not have helped seeing. There are Romantic writers who are ardent socialists— in my view, the youthful Marx was one such—and there are utilitarians who think that the utilitarian argument favors common ownership rather than private ownership; conversely, there are Romantic writers—Kant, for instance—who are as committed to the institutions of bourgeois society as were Bentham or James Mill. What I argue below is not that there were particular conclusions about the gains and losses of work, or about the legitimacy of private ownership, to which Romantics came and instrumentalists did not, but that the route by which they got to their conclusions was very different, and that this fact casts doubt on the idea that they were quite the "same" conclusions.

Before making out my case, there is a preliminary duty I should perform: this is to disembarrass myself of my title. There is a convention among writers on Romanticism that the first observation to be made is that "Romanticism" is a very vague word and that figures who are now called Romantics would have resented the label very much indeed. I am quite happy to follow the convention. My subject matter might well be called "will-based" theories of work and ownership, since it is on working and owning as expressions of the free will that both Kant and Hegel concentrate. But even that more reticent title would create its own difficulties; one might wonder to what extent Hegel's account of civil society really does rest on the will of the individual, seeing how many constraints the individual finds in his environment.[1] It is true that Hegel seems to justify civil society because it allows for the expression of the abilities and characters of persons who are attuned to life in a market society; but these characters and abilities do not look very *willed* much of the time. Still, this is not a reason to despair of finding some characterization of the "Romantic" tradition that emphasizes the will, the will as the expression of character, and social institutions and activities as ways of "fixing" or objectifying that will in the outside world. However constrained Hegel's workers and owners become, Hegel's account of their existence begins with the need of the free will to objectify itself; no utilitarian could begin anywhere other than with the need for food, drink, and shelter. Anyone who still finds the word "Romantic" objectionable as applied to Kant, say, or to Marx will lose little by reading it as "expressive" or "will-based."

Instrumental and Utilitarian Theories

If the Romantic theory of work and ownership is to be understood by contrast with an instrumental account, our first need is a brief summary of that instrumental account.[2] The elements are these. Work is in itself a disagreeable necessity, forced upon us by the multiplicity of human wants and the meanness of nature. Human beings are more vulnerable than most animals because their wants are more varied and because their wants are changeable over time. The boa constrictor sleeps off its lunch; the human being wonders about the possibilities of gastronomic innovation. It is a moot point whether this is a "natural" feature of human beings: Hobbes ascribed it to our constantly changing physical state, while Hume, recognizing that competition made it worse, saw it as a more nearly pure social phenomenon.[3] At all events, scarcity exists because our desires to consume outrun what the environment naturally offers. Work is needed to increase the supply of things for consumption; since work is an evil, nobody will do more of it than is needed to satisfy whatever wants are in question. This is not to say that all work is of equal unpleasantness. All that is involved is the claim that work is a cost incurred in order to secure a benefit and that the benefit is to be measured in terms of a flow of consumables.

How do these truisms create a basis for property rights? By reference to incentive and security. If we move from individual calculations of how much effort it is worth expending to questions of social welfare, we can see that property rights are essential to social cooperation. An individual may naturally possess his own labor and what it produces in the sense that nobody else has, as a matter of fact, the ability to make him work other than as he chooses or to take from him what he has created. But this is not a property *right*; no titles to his efforts have been allocated, and there is no procedure for enforcing such an allocation. If he is to cooperate with anyone else, some sort of recognized title to a portion of the results is essential: without security for the end result, neither party has an incentive to make the initial effort. Even where it is a matter of an individual deferring consumption rather than cooperation, property rights are needed; if I leave apples on the tree, or if I propose to employ some of them for planting new trees, I have no incentive unless I have security for my enjoyment of the end product. Rules for allocating and securing titles so that people may be got to work efficiently are what the utilitarian and instrumental view would call property rules.

Marxist critics have sometimes seen in this argument a tendency to beg the question whether a person has a natural, prior property in his own labor and thus to read back into a presocial state the peculiar position of the proletarian who owns his own labor and nothing else. The illicitness of this is obvious; Aristotle, for instance, could never have derived property rights from a prior property in one's own labor, because it was too obvious to him that a slave was owned by somebody else and hence that his labor was so owned as well. But the utilitarian is in no difficulty. He does not start with any view of men as having rights over their efforts. A man's labor is "his" only in the sense that it is he who labors; in this sense of "his," it is no more his property than his headache is his property. Because, in this sense, his labor cannot be anyone else's, it cannot be his in the proprietary sense either.[4] The question whether there *ought* to be slavery or free labor is a utilitarian question to be settled on utilitarian grounds. Men have no natural rights at all; when Bentham dismissed them as "nonsense on stilts," he spoke for a tradition. Men are neither self-owning by nature nor slaves by nature; there may be very good arguments for having rules about property that make it impossible for one person to own another;[5] and there may be very good reasons for treating employment as a contract between the provider of wages and the supplier of labor; but, whether such rules do exist is a question of what the actual rules of an actual legal system are. The question of whether they *ought* to exist is a question whether proposed rules will induce men to employ their abilities and the resources of nature as productively of consumable things as possible.

This raises the question of what sort of rights property rights are.[6] Here the answer must be given dogmatically; above all, they are rights to exclude others from the control and use of whatever it is that is at issue. This is not a complete account of property, since we also need to include duties owed to others in respect of what one owns. For property rules such as *my* car is the one that *I* must keep in a roadworthy state, or it is *my* cow's damage that I must pay for if she should stray into your field, the degree of control allowed by the law is indeterminate; we should not deny that something was my property just because I could not leave it to whomever I wished, but we might seriously wonder whether I had anything worth calling a right to exclude others from use or control if my own rights to control were excessively restricted. There will be cases in which the owner would very much wish to divest himself of ownership and yet could not without this leading us to say that he is not really the owner. In the utilitarian tradition, it is generally assumed that the crucial powers that an owner must have for ownership to serve its purposes are those of alienation and the creation of lesser interests in his property that he can exchange for money or money's worth.

By the same token, the utilitarian allows that these rights may be exercised over anything that can be controlled, used, and disposed of. Nothing is intrinsically unownable, and there is no repugnancy to appropriation in anything. It would be silly to create ownership of, say, individual, uncaught, indistinguishable fish; and it would be wicked to allow one man to own another, but in neither case is there any conceptual awkwardness about the idea of owning these things. Again, land is in no way "special"; its status as "real property" is a holdover from feudal arrangements and is of no theoretical interest. Indeed, a utilititarian's chief concern with land amounts to anxiety about the existence of freehold ownership; the utilitarian who sees the point of property rights as being their tendency to encourage the best use of resources is ready to encumber property with obligations—land ought to be kept in good heart, for instance, and title should be dependent on its being so kept. Morally speaking, therefore, the landowner is never more than a lessee from society at large. Such considerations conflict, to be sure, with the basis of property rights in other ways; security is essential to incentive in most utilitarian accounts, and security is impaired if society is too quick to remove a bad farmer. But the resolution of such conflicts is just what a full-fledged utilitarian theory of property is intended to provide.

The history of utilitarian arguments about property is quite largely a history of arguments about security and rewards. The crucial argument is one that is recurrent in Bentham's work. The point of property rights is to encourage the direction of effort to resources for the production of (eventually) consumables. Yet the security of tenure and the availability of contractual arrangements on which the value of the institution depends mean that those who work hardest may end with very little, and those who own much may live well without effort. Questions of justice aside, this raises two questions: the first is whether this distribution of rewards is stable, the second whether it is efficient in maximizing well-being. The obvious answer is that if those who do the work get too little of the rewards, they will eventually bring down the system; it also seems clear that the principle of diminishing marginal utility is true enough for a wide class of goods to suggest that their value is maximized if they are distributed equally. Since the losses of the better off are more than compensated for by the gains of the worse off, transfers from richer to poorer are generally justified. But to make them erodes the security that is the essence of property. The early utilitarians argued, as their successors have often done, that the short-run gain from distributive upheaval would be wiped out by disincentive effects over the longer run. Arguments from "secondary" utilities tend in the same direction; if there are property rights, then there are the pleasures of expectation—my pleasurable anticipation of the pleasures of owning my father's estate, say. Conversely, the misery of disappointment must be reckoned among the evils of tampering with property rights; not merely am I worse off than if I had my father's estate, but the sense of deprivation is itself a distress.[7] The one argument that no utilitarian can or will employ is that society has no right to envisage such redistribution because all the goods whose redistribution is contemplated already belong to someone and are not available for redistribution.[8]

Writers like Bentham, as much as writers like Godwin, see owners as essentially stewards.[9]

The Romantic Alternative

Utilitarianism does not find the possessory relationship intrinsically interesting, either as a matter of morality or as a matter of social psychology. Here lies the heart of the contrast with Romanticism. The young Marx and Moses Hess claimed that our attitude of *having* prevents us from truly appropriating the world and making it our true property.[10] Max Stirner claimed that if I take my goods and chattels seriously, I cannot possess them but must be possessed by them; even Hegel claimed that it was central to my proprietorship that I should show that the thing I possess is inessential to me.[11] And the connection between work and possession is not a contingent tie, or a tie resting on the civil law for its existence. Because possession is less a matter of one's having something de facto in one's hands than a matter of having established a certain relationship with whatever it is, work is often seen as the only way to establish such a relationship. It is important not to exaggerate; Stirner makes one's playful dealings with things essential to owning them, and there is always a strain in the argument that assimilates work and artistic creation and thus narrows the gap between work and play. Still, it remains true that Romantics hold that possession is an achievement and that an activity to which "work" is a plausible label to apply is the most satisfactory or only means to that achievement.

It may seem perverse to locate the starting point of this tradition in Kant's philosophy of law; his bleakly puritanical moral philosophy and his search for eternal principles of morality and epistemology seem at odds with the characteristic Romantic enthusiasm for self-expression and the equally characteristic sense of historical change that romanticism brought into social thought. Nonetheless, it is where we must begin. Kant's derivation of property rights starts from the thought that what property rights are are rights of control; control rather than use is the essence of ownership. So Kant rejects use as a title to property, and he rejects labor as a title, too—on the grounds that labor rearranges existing matter and does not create ex nihilo. All that is left is the will to possess; to own something is to will to possess it, and to display the will to possess it in a way that demands recognition from others.[12]

The thought is actually simple enough. If I own something, then whoever uses it without my leave wrongs me; but he does not wrong me in the way he would if he struck me a blow and injured me. I am, as it were, wronged at a distance. To explain this, Kant distinguishes two sorts of occupancy of things by the will—physical and rational. Rational occupation is readily distinguished from physical occupation: I may sit on a park bench I do not own, and I may own a shirt I send to the laundry and am not at that point occupying. To own something is to bring it under the control of my will in such a way that I can defeat subsequent attempts by others to bring it under the control of their will. This is not a matter of power; it is a matter of rights, in that my initial occupancy claims respect even if I am in no position to enforce it.

Before showing how, in Kant's view, this is possible, we should note two things. Although Kant's notion of property as a matter of rights of excluding others is much like the utilitarians' notion, the way the argument runs already implies that owning is a matter of a human will taking possession; it therefore already excludes slavery as a possible form of property: persons cannot be owned, even though Kant is prepared to admit a very curious sort of external possession of children, wives, and servants, a view that none of his critics have ever much liked.[13] Kant did follow Locke in admitting that slavery might be a legitimate punishment for evildoers, but like Locke, he held that it required some positive act of evildoing before a man could lose his civil personality and so become an ownable object. But the thought is clear enough: what defeats appropriation is that something is already occupied by the will of an agent, and what defeats the appropriation of a person is that he is necessarily occupied by his own will. The other point is that this allows a new view of natural rights. Kant thinks that rights require social recognition, so he cannot accept traditional accounts of natural rights. All the same, natural rights now have a place as the presuppositions of non-natural rights. The natural ownership of ourselves and our abilities that we find in Locke, say, reemerges in the thought that unless our wills were ours, we could not become proprietors of external things by taking them into our possession.

One might say that all Kant seems to be doing is endorsing some of the basic ideas of most legal systems; initial occupancy of something unowned is a good title in most systems, and Kant endorses it. When I fence a piece of ground, it is my control and my intention to exercise that control in the future that counts, not my present or future use. The interest of Kant's case lies elsewhere, though. For he brings back the importance of work and use, almost more impressively than if he had founded title on them. Kant obviously agrees that we must work to eat, and that if there were no ownership, the incentive to labor would be impaired, but he gives work a role apart from the production of consumable useful things. Work, so to speak, *fixes* our ownership of the world. Willing to possess is the bare bones of proprietorship; full ownership demands that the world should conform to and reflect our purposes.

The thought that dominates Kant's philosophy of history, though not his legal theory in its narrowest sense, is that history exists to develop human abilities to the utmost; its goal is perfection rather than anything describable as welfare.[14] Work is essentially educative. The obduracy of nature and the diversity of human wants are not to be complained of, for they spur us to develop our talents. To do this, we must treat our talents as forms of property; we must "thingify" them, treat them as assets to make the most of. The thought could be paralleled by the utilitarian claim that prosperity is increased by giving people the right to sell their own efforts and abilities at will, but it is not that argument. The utilitarian argument treats doing well as the goal; for Kant, the need to do at any rate better is what spurs us on, but the point is to develop human abilities and to do so in a community governed by rational laws and a strict sense of justice.[15] And all this, of course, rests on a thoroughly nonaggregative moral view; as opposed to the utilitarians' preoccupation with making the greatest use of what lies to hand by way of talents and materials, Kant's philosophy stresses the value of each person's enterprise and each person's freedom as an owner.

He was acutely aware of what he could not guarantee. The development of humanity was not a process that implied that each and every person would develop. In a world where stokers are in demand and poets are not, my capacity for verse might be stunted. It is the history of the species that we are to admire, not any individual life, and Kant seems to have recognized that this might be scant consolation to many of us. Again, Kant's ideal of a society of independent owners and producers engaged in exchanges that threatened nobody's freedom looks modest enough; but he knew that for many people, the reality would be dependence on an employer and little scope for individual initiative. He seems, rashly, to have hoped that the collapse of feudal restraints on property would reduce this dependence, but he was aware that many people would neither find self-expression in work nor fix their purposes in the world through ownership.

Kant's bleakness on this point interestingly matches his bleakness over questions of our knowledge of the world. His epistemology leaves us ignorant of "things-in-themselves," and confines us to knowledge of their appearances; his social theory also leaves our relationships with others oddly external. We do not share lives; exchange and work leave each of us untouched in his inner freedom. Even though the terms of his discussion of the purposes of history are very much those of the Romantic tradition, he leaves each of us detached from history—we are not merged with our culture, but stand aside, able to look at it and question it. Rights protect each person's independent sphere of action from interference by others; we are tied to others exactly to the extent to which we choose to tie ourselves.

Hegel

It is in Hegel's work that Kant's bleakness is transcended. The greater expansiveness of Hegel's thought is, again, something that can be seen both in his theory of knowledge and in his social theory. Hegel allows the human mind to grasp things-in-themselves as well as mere phenomena, and he makes an account of social and legal rights the basis for an account of how we share in the lives of one another—and, of course, in so doing he seems much more thoroughly to be working in the Romantic spirit.

One first point ought to be made; Hegel's philosophy is sometimes thought to be entirely about work and ownership.[16] The thought is that *The Phenomenology of Spirit* gives an account of the way in which mind creates an external reality that is then an obstacle—misunderstood, endowed with a will of its own, operating according to material forces that are essentially unintelligible, and thus alien—and that, after various vicissitudes, mind then appropriates as its own creation. One might say that knowledge in all this is a sort of ownership, and that only what we have made can be fully possessed or fully known. Now, although there is something in this, it is something that must here be ignored. For although this possessory image of knowledge is important, it is also true that work and ownership themselves do not play a very important part in Hegel's *philosophy*. That is, Hegel certainly thought of them as important social phenomena, and is interesting on them, but he did not think that work in the usual sense had any direct epistemological or ontological implications. There is one small joke against naïve realism in *The Philosophy of Right*, when Hegel suggests that the sheep's consumption of grass shows that not even sheep believe in the self-subsistence of material objects. It is a terrible argument against naïve realism, but it does show how little Hegel wanted to found his epistemology on social theory.[17]

The main lines of Hegel's account of property rights are very like Kant's in that he begins with the right of the free will to externalize itself. Put less opaquely, this amounts to saying that the idea that we are free agents makes little sense unless we are free to do something; what we do makes a difference to the physical world, so we must have the right to control it, alter it, and dispose of it in the exercise of our freedom. The thought that we might not be able to appropriate things is incoherent, for what can prevent us? The appropriating will can be forestalled only by another such will, and things have no such will of their own. Savages may think that trees have souls: we know better. Moreover, the world needs an owner; it has no value or point until it is given one.[18] It is this that Hegel expresses in the claim that human beings bring the principle of negation into the world; even the sheep negates the grass, showing that mind may turn matter to its own purposes.

Armed with this equipment, Hegel proceeds fairly predictably. How we bring things into our possession is partly a matter of convention, but partly something with a natural foundation, so our ability to grasp things founds our control. Like Kant, Hegel treats the presence of a prior will as defeating ownership; but animals do not have this sort of will, and human beings may not have—though Hegel is evasive on the legitimacy of slavery, saying that it had a place only when wrong was still right.[19] In any developed society, there can be no two ways about it. Again, he argues that I must have the right to alienate my abilities, not all of them and forever, since that would be slavery and the alienation of myself, but at any rate any one of them and for periods of time. It does not take much imagination to see the opening this leaves for Marx and other radicals.

Work is important not so much because it uniquely entitles one to property, nor because people need to be induced to work, but because work is a more complete negation of the world than mere taking. The more that mere stuff is permeated by human will, the more humanized and the more thoroughly appropriated the world is. We no doubt work because we want the end product, but this instrumental motive is not the point of the activity—the point is the activity itself. This suggests, as most commentators agree, that the paradigm of work here is not routine activity, but artistic creation. But it is important not to go far down this path; Hegel agrees that there are continuities, but he is also eager to defend the routine and the efficient.[20] The man he admires is the craftsman who knows his job.

But the crucial stress is that on the fixing of the will in the world, and it is that which causes the characteristic tensions in Hegel's account of these issues. To put it simply, there is a tension between what one might call a natural, psychological interpretation of this view and the more rationalistic, philosophical interpretation. On the natural interpretation, the attraction of a view like Hegel's is that it picks up the rather common aspiration to have one's work reflect one's own abilities, the desire that what we do should be a record of our achievements. Hannah Arendt, distinguishing work from mere labor, emphasizes the way in which a man's works are the sort of thing you can put on a shelf or see in the street; the aim of work is to create *a work*, a record of our doings.[21] The more rationalist interpretation rests on the view that what is rational is the work of a whole society, a whole culture, even of "Mind" or "Spirit." Work and ownership make sense not as expressions of the aims and desires and abilities of particular individuals, but as articulations of the life of the whole community. That Hegel presses in this direction is beyond doubt; he sees rights, for instance, less as Kant saw them, as barriers behind which each individual can get on uninterfered with, than as powers that enable each person to fulfill his social role; the restrictions on a father's ability to disinherit his children, for instance, is not seen by Hegel as a loss of freedom by the individual, but as a way of making the paternal role effective. We appear in *The Philosophy of Right* not so much as Tom, Dick, and Harry, but as role bearers in a system whose rationality is a property of the whole system.

But if this is so, there is a serious problem here. For the attractions of Hegel's account seem to spring from the way it picks up what is genuinely a Romantic emphasis on self-expression. If we then dilute this appeal, we are in some difficulty with the idea that anything like self-expression is achieved. We may, of course, admire the rationality of the way the whole social system is organized; Hegel admired the operation of the invisible hand detected by Adam Smith, and we might—though most critics do not—admire the way the society described by Hegel had allocated social roles to people. It is not at all clear that what we would then admire is the way those roles reflected the wills of those people, for we would surely think that it was rather that those people had been given wills that reflected the duties imposed by their roles.

There are, certainly, satisfactions of a characteristically Hegelian kind to be had; the nonnaturalness of social life, for instance, is a theme of which he never tires. The reflective person, contemplating his world, must be aware of the extent to which the world is permeated with human ends, so little in his surroundings owes its presence to the arbitrary operations of blind nature. The world reads us an object lesson in its availability to us because what we see is so much evidence of what we can do with it. As Marx was later to insist in *The German Ideology*, even what we call "nature" is by now a residual category—it refers simply to what we have so far left alone, not to something with autonomous powers or quasi rights of its own. In a way, Hegel is a critic of twentieth-century environmental ethics ahead of his time. It is not that we should plow up every inch of soil, and it is not that we should consume everything that we can; it is simply that any concern for an environment is a concern for what we can get out of it. But it cannot be too fiercely insisted on; this does not entail that the satisfactions of the triumph over the brutely material are ones that each individual can have. If one thinks that the Hegelian account seems to start by offering us something of the sort and then backs off into offering us only the triumphs of the species—which is where we saw Kant obliged to leave us—this will seem a deficiency. If one thinks that this takes an altogether *too* individualist, or too simple-mindedly individualist, view of what is on offer, it will not seem anything of the sort.

Marx and Carlyle

The tension I have outlined can be nicely illustrated from two quite famous sources. The more famous is Marx's assault on Hegel, the less famous Carlyle's statement of the gospel of work in *Past and Present*. Marx essentially turns Hegel's weapons against himself and attacks Hegel for failing to deliver on his own promises. Thus, in his critique of Hegel's *Philosophy of Right*, Marx complains that Hegel's account of politics just contradicts his account of the nature of property rights; Hegel first says that it is the essence of property that it is disposable of at will, and that it is the property of an individual, but then ends by praising such antique devices as the entail as an aid to political stability. Is this not an admission that property cannot be squared with the needs of society?[22] More importantly, the *Economic-Philosophical Manuscripts* demolishes the justification of private property in the very terms that were supposed to support it. Ownership does not make the world less alien but more; once something is property, it must be treated as the market dictates, not as we choose. Because there is a market, things come to dominate us, not the other way about. Of course, a factory does not literally tell its owner what to produce, but it is certainly true that unless he produces what will make him the maximum profit, he will go out of business.

Similarly, the process whereby we come to see our abilities as ownable things to be made the most of is one that rebounds upon us; we have to sell our labor to whoever will buy it, and since he has no interest in it except in what it will yield in profit, the pressure will be on to reduce our abilities to those sufficient for the simplest machine-minding tasks. Marx's hostility to the division of labor in the *Manuscripts* comes out of the same logical stable. Because our ability to work and to express our individuality in work is the central fact about us as human beings, the way that we are reduced to working in the fashion and at the pace dictated by current machinery is simply inhuman. Now, the plainest utilitarian might have agreed with Marx that the effects of existing systems of property ownership and their effect on the sort of work people did were in various ways deplorable—hours of work were excessive, wages were too low, the imminence of starvation for many people was greater than could be be justified by any view of incentive, and so on. What he could not have said, and what Marx did say, is that men in these conditions were *alienated*. The standards by which alienation is judged are Hegelian standards; it is the humanization of the world—the bringing of things under human control, the creation of a world that reflects and embodies human needs and abilities—that sets the framework for Marx's denunciation. Neither individuals nor society fix their intentions in the world under a regime of private property and the division of labor.[23]

Even in Marx's account, though, the tensions persist. Marx does come out clearly enough for the view that if the world is to be truly ours, private property must be abolished. More worryingly, he extends the concept of appropriation and, with it, the concept of work to the point that it seems at times as though he wants to say that the enjoyment of the world is a form of working on it, as if the eye of the perceptive spectator contributes to the beauty of a painting by making it more than a mere assemblage of paint and canvas. Then the beauty of the paintings is a property appropriated by the appropriate sense; this, then, is a form of human and not private property. But even if this is an acceptable way of glossing Hess's claim that *having* stops us from owning the world, it still leaves some of the tensions between individual achievements and social organization untouched.

Marx claims that free production is production in accordance with the laws of beauty; this and his attacks on the division of labor seem to imply that he thought that craftsmanship and work that approached artistic creation were the only possible human forms of work. But he later denounced craft idiocy, so whatever it was that he favored it can hardly have been skilled craft labor in the usual sense; yet if one tries to imagine kinds of work that have some utilitarian point and satisfy those who perform them, it is hard to see what, other than skilled work of this sort, we can have in mind.

The difficulty, then, is to see how this sort of work can survive the growth of large productive enterprises and how we can combine an elaborate technical division of labor with satisfying work. Of course, we can appeal to the satisfactions we found Hegel offering, though not so much those of the intellect satisfied by the understanding of social intricacy and interdependence as those of the flesh and the emotions—for whatever else Marx wants, he certainly wants us to enjoy the results of social cooperation. This is a good start, and we can go further; Marx plainly envisages that work will be shared out by some democratic process of decision making when it ceases to be dictated by the market, and we may all welcome this—if it can be had—as an advance. But although Marx can engage the utilitarian along these lines, if what is at issue is competing ways of maximizing the utility of output while minimizing the effort that output costs us, this is not the same satisfaction as that which the workman feels in the job well done. We may all agree that the work we do is what we ought to do, and that it has been parceled out justly and rationally; what that does not show is that the work will be satisfying as self-expression.

Marx, like Hegel, has to lose the empirical individual in the collective subject if human work and human appropriation are to be made universally available. Moreover, in Marx's first thoughts about this, the whole idea of real or human appropriation reveals its implausible face. When we talk about a man tending a garden, we normally know what we mean when we distinguish the worker from the owner or say that the man working in the garden owns it too. We can readily distinguish owner, and worker, from the spectator, who looks at the garden and enjoys it. If we start saying that the spectator who admires it is the true, human proprietor, we stray into nonsense. What seems to be at issue is a perfectly plausible attack on, say, cupidity, and in this context we may well say that it is a mistake to want to own something as opposed to wanting to enjoy it; we might cheerfully agree that the owner who thinks of nothing but his ownership of the garden "gets less out of it" than the spectator who likes the flowers and the trees. But to treat this as an elucidation of the concept of appropriation seems an error. What makes private property an internally incoherent institution, if anything does, is that an institution whose point is to allow individual and social control over the world ends up by defeating both. The suggestion that what we call property therefore is not property, but that something else—namely, enjoyment—would be is a needless addition. It is not surprising that Marx dropped all such talk almost at once and turned upon Moses Hess with a vigor that suggests Marx may have been embarrassed by ever having learned the idiom in the first place.

If the ambivalence between individual and species success is one standing difficulty, the other great difficulty is the role of the will. I have skirted round the obvious problem that what one theory might call "self-expression" and the imposition of the will, another might treat as self-abnegation and the humbling of the will; I have hinted at the possibility in arguing that Hegel tinkers with the identity of those who get their satisfaction in work and ownership—it is not that individuals are *restricted* in what they can do when they become fathers, but that they become fathers and then *un*restrictedly do what fathers do. Whether this rewriting of the identifying description of an individual is a legitimate move in taking away some of the tension between a methodologically individualist and a methodologically holistic or structuralist social and moral theory is a large question, and not to be settled here.

An issue that is, again, not to be settled here, but that certainly must be raised here is the question of the extent to which various disputed elements of Romanticism in its everyday sense are consistent. In particular, much of what has gone before has raised the question of the extent to which a rationalist account of the will and its fixing in the world through work and through the institutions of private property is at odds with the idea of self-expression in artistic creation. It is worth at any rate noticing that many artists, whether painters, novelists, musicians, or whatever, resist the thought that their art amounts to any sort of work of art that needs to be brought into existence; novelists are surprised by what their characters do, painters are startled by the posture adopted by their figures and so on. To the extent that the Romantic conception of work assimilates work to artistic creation, there must be some doubt about the connection between work and the will and, by the same token, between work and control over things. In a sense, one might almost claim that everything I have said about the way the Romantic theory of work and possession stresses the lifelessness of mere things is pregnant with problems for the assimilation of work to art; for much art, things must be allowed a life of their own.

A final glimpse of Carlyle's gospel of work will illustrate these points. In *Past and Present*, Carlyle introduces the man who ought to be—but in many ways fails to be—an industrial hero, one Plugson of Undershot, a cotton manufacturer. Plugson is a man who is genuinely going to master nature; the pages are thick with the metaphors of military conflict and military organization. Cotton defies human will; it will not clothe men's backs unless it is picked, ginned, spun, woven; the industrial army is rallied for a fight with cotton, and cotton is duly worsted, or licked into calico at least.[24] The captain of industry is a captain just because he can lead us into a battle with nature—though Plugson is duly condemned because his relations with his troops are mediated by the callous cash nexus and not by the brotherly relations of the band of heroes they truly are.

Here it is immediately clear why we can speak of will and its imposition; the resistance of nature is even to be welcomed in providing the better battle. The implications for theories of ownership are not much spelled out by Carlyle, though plainly the general message is "to the probable victor the means of production." But this exuberant and expansive will to conquest is not all there is here; the foot soldier in industry learns patience and self-discipline, and here work shapes the will that it expresses too. Unlike Hegel and Kant, Carlyle envisages hierarchies of expression almost from the first. But there is yet more to it. For Carlyle also offers a different image of the relationship between man and nature that is implicit in work, though without much suggestion that it might be at odds with that involved in the Plugson epic. For when he speaks of agricultural work, Carlyle hymns the amount of unassuming, humble labor that has turned wasteland into a green and smiling world. Here we are not looking at men beating nature into submission so much as men coaxing the hidden possibilities of nature out of the tangle in which they are hidden. This is not a story of foe against foe, rather one of siding with nature's better self.

This links up with our anxiety about the assimilation of work and art. It is plausible to suppose that the workers who unlock the smiling fields hidden in the waste are doing something of the same sort as Michelangelo when he liberated the prisoners from their marble. He did not scare them into the open, but helped free them; Plugson's military sortie against recalcitrant cotton fits no such picture, though it does fit our intuitive ideas about what the triumph of the will might be like.

What, then, ought we to conclude? I hope that nobody will wish to conclude only that the Romantic theory of work and ownership is a chaos of unresolved problems. For, it is worth recalling that as the history of orthodox economics shows, the utilitarian varieties of social theory are full of problems of their own. Rather, what these tensions show is what the range of problems is that a Romantic theory must tackle—it must concentrate on the nature of the will, on the nature of self-expression; it needs to concern itself with the extent to which different temperaments may find their expression in different sorts of work; it needs to concern itself with the way in which disposability and restricted disposability of property assist in the creation and expression of valued forms of character. We cannot conclude that the justification of private property or the abolition of private property will emerge as the obvious implication of adopting this approach; all we can suggest is what the argument will be fought over.[25] But we can also see ways in which a tradition of argument like this will couch its disputes in terms whose emotional and political overtones are radically different from those of the utilitarian tradition. One *can* envisage cost-benefit calculations suggesting that a revolutionary transformation of the mode of production is essential; and one can envisage Romantic arguments in defense of the mixed economy. But it is hardly an accident that there are few utilitarian revolutionaries, nor that Hegel's successor was Marx.

Justice, Exploitation, and the End of Morality

THIS ESSAY is a small contribution to two large subjects. The first large subject is that of exploitation—what it is for somebody to be exploited, in what ways people can be and are exploited, whether exploitation necessarily involves coercion, what Marx's understanding of exploitation was and whether it was adequate: all these are issues on which I merely touch, at best. My particular concern here is to answer two other questions: whether Marx thought capitalist exploitation unjust and how the answer to that question illuminates Marx's conception of morality in general. The second large subject is that of the nature of morality—whether there are specifically moral values and specifically moral forms of evaluation and criticism, how these relate to our explanatory interests in the same phenomena, what it would be like to abandon the "moral point of view," whether the growth of a scientific understanding of society and ourselves inevitably undermines our confidence in the existence of moral "truths." These again are issues on which I only touch if I mention them at all; the questions I try to answer are the following: what does Marx propose to put in the place of moral judgment, and what kind of assessment of the horrors of capitalism does he provide if not a moral assessment?

Marx and Morality

It is a feature of Marx's work that he seems at one and the same time to be dismissive of morality and yet full of what most people would describe as moral indignation (Lukes 1985, 4–5). Take perhaps the best known of all Marx's prophecies:

> Along with the constant decrease in the number of capitalist magnates, who usurp and monopolize all the advantages of this process of transformation, the mass of misery, oppression, slavery, degradation and exploitation grows; but with this there also grows the revolt of the working class, a class constantly increasing in numbers, and trained, united and organized by the very mechanism of the capitalist process of production. The monopoly of capital becomes a fetter upon the mode of production which has flourished alongside and under it. The centraliza-

tion of the means of production and the socialization of labour reach a point at which they become incompatible with their capitalist integument. This integument is burst asunder. The knell of capitalist private property sounds. The expropriators are expropriated. (Marx 1976, 929)

It is hard to deny that terms such as *usurpation, slavery, degradation,* and the like are terms of moral condemnation, and implausible to think that Marx employs them in less than a wholehearted way. Cohen's claim that whether Marx knew it or not, he attacked capitalism for its injustice rests on the plausible point that Marx uses terms such as "rob" and "usurp" in their plain sense and does not, so to speak, bracket them or place them in quotation marks; Marx condemned theft, not "theft" (Cohen 1983, 443). Yet Marx's skepticism about ethical appeals is well known. When he wrote to Engels about his address to the International Working Men's Association, he observed, "I was obliged to insert two phrases about 'duty' and 'right' into the Preamble to the Rules, and also about 'truth, morality and justice' but these are placed in such a way that they can do no harm" (Marx and Engels, 1962a, 139). In the *Communist Manifesto,* Marx mocks the believers in eternal moral truths and seems at least to suggest that the Marxist conception of ideology relegates ideals of all sorts to an epiphenomenal status:

> When people speak of ideas that revolutionize society, they do but express the fact, that within the old society, the elements of a new one have been created, and that the dissolution of the old ideas keeps even pace with the dissolution of the old conditions of existence.
>
> When the ancient world was in its last throes, the ancient religions were overcome by Christianity. When Christian ideas succumbed in the eighteenth century to rationalist ideas, feudal society fought its death battle with the then revolutionary bourgeoisie. The ideas of religious liberty and freedom of conscience merely gave expression to the sway of free competition within the domain of knowledge. (Marx and Engels 1962b, 1:52)

The task, then, is to see whether Marx has a consistent position on all this.

The starting point is Marx's antipathy to writers who stressed the role of ideas—moral and other—in social life; it has two sources, neither of them particularly surprising. In the first place, Marx's so-called materialist conception of history is very largely an "anti-idealist conception of history." Marx, writing in opposition to his former friends and colleagues, was eager to insist, as he had done in his critique of Hegel's *Philosophy of Right,* that what happened in social, economic, and political life was not to be explained as the result of an Idea implementing itself (Marx, 1975, 60ff.). Greater economic equality was not caused by Equality manifesting itself in the phenomenal world. Demands for justice did not arise because Justice embarked on a campaign of self-realization. Whether Marx was right to think that his Idealist contemporaries believed in the efficacy of the Ideal in quite so literal a fashion is not a question we need pause for, though we ought to recognize

602 • Chapter 32

the passion with which he assaulted all appeals to *verités eternelles*. It is enough to see that a man who denies that ideas owe their effectiveness to the operations of the Idea is not denying that ideas make an important difference to what happens. Marx, indeed, tended to overestimate the importance of ideas—intellectuals usually do; a man who thought ideas had no impact at all would hardly have spent twenty years in poverty and ill health writing *Capital*, nor would he have been so concerned to destroy the erroneous views that, as he thought, the Lassalleans put into circulation in their Gotha Program. All Marx seems to have believed was that for ideas to make a difference, they had to be *somebody's* ideas and to make a difference to how they acted. Moral ideas may make a difference, but not in virtue of reflecting the demands of Morality; they make a difference by making a difference in the way individuals behave. As Cohen emphasizes in another context, when norms are cited in a causal explanation, it must be by way of how adherence to those norms affects behavior (Cohen 1978a, 217–25).

Second, however, Marx evidently believed that moral demands were intrinsically dubious in a way that other kinds of practical demands were not. There are two or three different things at stake. The first is that Marx thought that in politics, mankind is mostly moved by self-interest; so where people profess ideals, they will act against them under the impulse of self-interest, or they will interpret them so as to reconcile them with self-interest. It is thus inept to ask people to do for purely altruistic reasons anything very much opposed to their interests. Ethical socialists were asking employers and members of the ruling classes to behave "justly" or "fairly," with no reason to suppose this would affect their behavior.

The second point is not a matter of sociological but of philosophical skepticism; although it is harder to elucidate, it is intellectually more fundamental. Marx followed Hegel in disbelieving in the existence of a realm of the *ought* that stands opposed to the *is* (Marx and Engels 1975, 37). Hegel's objection to the Kantian picture of a noumenal realm of values that contrasted in all ways with the phenomenal realm of the merely factual strikes a chord with many twentieth-century readers. It starts from the objection that occurs to many readers on first taking up the *Groundwork of the Metaphysics of Morals*—if men are moved in fact by phenomenal desires but are supposed, as a moral matter, to be moved by the moral imperatives of the noumenal self, it is impossible to see how the noumenal self gets the necessary grip on the phenomenal self. The point is not restricted to the most impressive or serious aspects of morality; an opening batsman who is going out to face what Len Hutton aptly called "the nasty short-pitched fast stuff" in the fading light may reasonably feel fairly frightened, but he cannot quell his fears by issuing himself with injunctions to be brave or not to be frightened. Unless he already desires to be an unflinching opening batsman, nothing will come of addressing any number of imperatives to himself. In putting forward this view, Hegel and Marx were anticipating views recently defended by Philippa Foot and Bernard Williams, both of whom have argued that all reasons, moral reasons included, can *be* reasons only for persons who have preexisting aims to which those reasons are relevant (Williams 1981; the same thought runs through Williams 1985).

Third, Marx also thought, as many other writers have done, that there was something epistemologically dubious about moral judgments, or, more mildly, that they were not on all fours with factual judgments. A man who, when it is raining, *believes* that it is raining will best explain his beliefs by appealing to the fact that it *is* raining; the truth of what he believes features in the best explanation of the fact that he believes it. Marx's theory of ideology may—though I think it does not—imply that the truth of a belief is never an adequate explanation of our holding that belief. In the case of moral beliefs, however, Marx certainly holds that we are always to look for an explanation of someone's moral beliefs elsewhere than in their truth. His sociological analysis of morality, though utterly undeveloped, at least implies that "morality" belongs with law as part of the machinery by which class-divided societies preserve order in the face of conflicts of interest. The features that Kant ascribes to morality—its coercive character and its independence of self-interest above all—reflect in a mystified fashion the social function of the institution of "morality."

Exploitation

It is in this perspective that what follows is written; before plunging into the main topic of exploitation and justice, I should say that the above sketch of Marx's position is not intended to preempt discussion of a familiar view (put forward as persuasively as I have seen it by Steven Lukes in his *Marxism and Morality*) to the effect that Marx had no time for the morality of rights, obligation, and justice, but espoused what one might call an ethics of liberation (Lukes 1985, 27). I think that this is a misleading way of stating the case, and one that does some violence to Marx's insistence that he preached no ideals, not even that of liberation. To my mind, the interest of Marx's stand on the status of morality is this: he repudiates any suggestion that his condemnation of capitalism rests on ethical or moral considerations, and he looks forward to the day when we shall dissolve all forms of appraisal in the one category of the "practical." I shall argue for this view at the end of this essay, however, and do not mean to beg it now. For the moment, I want only to rest on the familiar fact that Marx both appears to condemn capitalism as unjust and immoral and to repudiate moral assessments as practically futile and intellectually worthless. It is to the dissolution of this paradox that I now turn.

The best recent discussion concludes that Marx thought that capitalist exploitation was unjust; some writers who hold this view go on to claim that Marx had what can properly be characterized as a theory of "needs-based" justice, epitomized in the famous slogan "from each according to his ability, to each according to his needs" (Elster 1985, 229–31; Geras 1985, esp. 60–65). I do not suggest—some writers have done so, however—that Marx thought that capitalist exploitation was just; my claim is that Marx thought that it was not in an absolute sense just or unjust, because there is no such sense. On Marx's account, capitalism was and had to be just in appearance according to prevailing notions of justice, but it was and had to be unjust in reality according to those same prevailing notions. The assertion of a gap between appearance and underlying mechanism is a familiar feature of Marx's analysis of capitalism (Cohen [1971] usefully explains why), but it raises the question whether Marx believed that capitalist exploitation was *really* unjust. This turns out to be a bogus question because it presupposes what Marx denied, that there is a transhistorical standard of justice that can be applied to the case. His position is not unlike that of the post-Copernican astronomer who readily speaks of the sunrise and who yet understands the nature of the phenomenon quite differently from his Ptolemaic predecessor. The astronomer denies that the question "Does the sun really rise?" has a firm answer, and Marx in the same way denies that the question "Is capitalist exploitation really unjust?" has a firm answer. The proper response is neither yes nor no, but an account of why we talk about the world in the way we do. Marx's denial of eternal moral truths, and of *justice eternelle* along with them, makes the status of his own distributive principle (first enunciated in so many words by Louis Blanc, apparently) "from each according to his ability, to each according to his needs" problematic. Is it a principle of socialist justice? My answer is that it is not—or, to put it differently, that Marx certainly thought it was not and had compelling reasons for so thinking.

The question of exploitation arises for Marx in the following way. It is apparent that in precapitalist societies, a lot of unpaid labor is done by, say, peasants working their lords' fields three days a week, or by slaves working at the absolute pleasure of their owners. If we ask how the surplus product generated in such societies finds its way—is *ausgepumpt* ("pumped out"), in Marx's graphic term—from the laborers to their superiors, a story about the exploitation of the direct producers comes naturally. Those who produce the product work for nothing; they perform unrequited labor for their feudal superiors or their owners or whomever. But we might say that the question whether they are *exploited* needs a further premise in addition to the premise that they perform unrequited labor. This is that they perform this unrequited labor on an unjust basis; this proposition may be supplied by, or run in conjunction with, another premise, namely, that this labor is *forced labor*.

It is debatable whether the fact of coercive extraction is an indicator rather than a constituent of injustice. In the view that it is a constituent, we begin from the premise that seizing goods or labor from another is prima facie unjust, either because it is a violation of the proprietorship of the victim or because it is an unwarranted invasion of his freedom. The contrast between coerced and uncoerced labor marks the distinction between a gift, which raises no questions of justice, and forcible taking, which does raise such questions. In the "indicator" view, it is some other notion of justice that explains the injustice of the taking; the fact of coercion is itself explained by appeal to the unlikelihood that the victims would consent to unjust treatment. If we were to set as the criterion of justice the view that the laborer should receive goods equal to the market value of his efforts, it would be neither here nor there whether workers were forcibly parted from the difference between that standard and what they actually got. If they were induced by some sort of religious enthusiasm to accept an exploitative bargain, it would still be exploitative. We might, however, expect to find that most exploitation was backed by coercion just because ideological blandishments work badly if they have to work on their own. My own view is that Marx is not absolutely clear on this, but that his settled position is that it is the coerced quality of the labor that is objectionable. In any view, we may certainly say that when one man labors unrequited for another, and does not do so voluntarily—that is, when he is not giving his efforts as a gift—the question of injustice is raised. Marx was impressed by the way capitalism's apologists pointed to the contrast between the visibly coercive nature of feudalism and slavery and the contractual nature of capitalism, and to the contrast between the visibly unpaid nature of slave labor or feudal services, on the one hand, and the paid labor of the worker under capitalism, on the other, as the features that make capitalism nonexploitative and intrinsically just. To their apologia, he had two powerful replies. The first is that within slavery and feudalism there was a standard of justice that slavery and feudalism appeared to meet (Marx and Engels 1962b, 426, 429 [*Wages, Prices and Profit*]).

The slave owner was entitled to the product created by the slave because the slave was the property of the owner; there was no more question of the slave having entitlements over the product than of the plow or the spade he wielded having entitlements over the product. Since the slave was the owner's slave, so was the slave's labor and so was the slave's product. With his functional account of moral ideas, Marx was committed to the thought that in some sense the slave system had to have a legitimating theory that allowed it to survive; if slaves more or less met the conditions the theory demanded—were captured in war, were foreigners rather than former citizens, or whatever it might be—the social order could operate smoothly enough. It goes without saying that slaves do not like being slaves; but the point of all theories of justice is to allow us to think that what people do not like doing, they may rightly be compelled to do if the coercion simply enforces just entitlements. Mutatis mutandis, the same story applies to feudalism; the theory of justice required is not one that turns the direct producers into the property of the exploiting classes, but one that depicts them as related in a hierarchical system of mutual obligation and benefit. Once again, there must not be too great a gap between the legitimating theory and the apparent operations of the society; Marx seems to think that this presents few problems until the social system is ripe for dissolution.

A qualification to my denial that Marx holds an absolute standard of justice must now be made. Marx is in no doubt that the standards of right that emerged as slavery gave way to feudalism, and as feudalism gave way to capitalism, were "higher" standards. He is, in this, a good pupil of Hegel, holding as Hegel did that the perception that "men as men are free" is one of the achievements of the modern world. This is not, however, because Marx thinks that at the end of the road lies a state of affairs in which we know what justice really is and finally create a society that realizes justice. At the end of the road lies a society that has left justice behind. To see this, we need to move on to the question of how Marx's account of the operations of a capitalist economic system relates to his ideas about justice and exploitation. The basic elements of the story are the same as before, but their employment is interestingly more complex.

The concept of exploitation features in Marx's second reply to the apologists for the capitalist order; its technical role belongs to Marx's account of the generation of surplus value and thus to part of the explanation of the capitalist's profit, but that account also demolished the apologists' understanding of how the capitalist was entitled to his profit. Marx faces a problem that baffled his predecessors. If the capitalist buys all his inputs at full value and sells his product at no more than its full value, where does the "extra" come from that the capitalist can pocket as his profit? That he has to pay full price for his inputs is guaranteed (on average) by the existence of competitive markets; anyone dissatisfied by his offered price can move elsewhere. By the same token, he can ask no more (on average) than the full value of his output. Marx hits on the solution when he decides that what the capitalist bought from the worker was a special kind of commodity, namely, "labor-power." Labor-power is special because it is the one commodity that, when it enters into production, creates more value than went into its production (Marx 1976, 270ff.). "Labor-power" is the worker's capacity to work, and when the capitalist buys it, what he buys is the right to set the worker to work for whatever time it is the labor contract lasts and to appropriate whatever value the labor actually done adds to the other inputs.

The question arises whether the worker is "robbed." The difficulty is that Marx appears to say both yes and no. The worker certainly does unpaid labor; as Marx insists, only a part of the worker's time is used to repay the cost of his subsistence, the rest going gratuitously to the capitalist. But Marx equally insists that the capitalist acts "with full right"; the fact that he gets a better deal out of the worker than the worker intends or understands is neither here nor there—any more than it is when you sell me a horse you believe to be ill-tempered and feckless and I turn it into a Derby winner (Marx 1976, 301). One way of resolving this apparent contradiction is to beat one's way through Marx's vast oeuvre looking for a definitive view. The difficulty with that approach is that it is easy to impugn the status of much of what Marx wrote, and we are still left to decide which texts represent (what would have been) his considered position. The other way is to put together what appears to be the most coherent account that is tolerably consistent with what he said over many years; this is what I shall do now.

So we must revert to the question of how we are to decide on the justice of the process whereby the worker sells his labor-power for its full value—which is, roughly, subsistence wages—but gives surplus value to the capitalist. Bourgeois justice is based on the thought that everyone ought to receive a return equal to his or her contribution; this is the principle of market exchange, that equals exchange for equals, and it displays the kind of equality and impersonality to which bourgeois society aspires (Marx 1976, 280). There is no space here to go into the interesting question of how this standard relates to another basis for the capitalist's assertion of a right to his profit, namely, his insistence that his capital is his, just as the worker's labor-power is the worker's, and whatever happens after the bargain is struck makes no difference to the legitimacy of the bargain. Marx certainly takes this claim seriously, as we have seen. The obvious thought is that Marx intends, first, to employ this kind of argument ad hominem against socialists who found their socialism on the idea that workers *own* their labor, and second to show how vulnerable capitalism is to an inquiry into its origins. If capitalism began in forcible expropriation, the current generation of capitalists cannot claim that the resources they control really are "theirs." If the system began in robbery, it must go on being robbery, just as it would be only an elaborate form of robbery if I stole £50 off you by first seizing your bicycle and then selling it to you for £50 (Elster 1985, 222–23). Quite how the attack on the pedigree of current titles of ownership bolts on to the ad hominem demonstration of capitalism's injustice is hard to say. For my purposes, it is enough to notice that at least it provides Marx with yet another opportunity to insist that what the workers ultimately want is not justice but the abolition of private property.

"Equals for equals" is a very different standard from that which underpinned slavery and feudalism: under capitalism, "freedom, equality, property and Bentham rule" (Marx 1976, 280). At the level of exchange, claims Marx, this principle did, generally and on the whole, govern proceedings. Some employers cheated their workers, paid them with dud coin, made them buy their food in the employer's shop and then watered the milk—but these were exceptions, and the existence of profit did not depend on the existence of crooks. Indeed, magistrates and judges from the same social class as these criminals were perfectly ready to use the law against them. Social stability demanded that most people believe that justice was enforced, and justice had to be enforced to induce that belief.

At the level of exchange, where the operations of capitalism were visible to the untutored eye, equals exchanged for equals. There was a known standard, and wages revolved around it. The worker whose employer would not pay the going rate could leave and work elsewhere; the employer could truthfully say that he could not pay more than the going rate—if he did, his prices would rise, he would lose his trade, and he would go out of business. There was thus no question of exploitation being a matter of personal wickedness on the part of capitalist employers, a fact Marx insists on when he explains how capitalists appear in the pages of *Capital* only as the bearers of capitalist relations (Marx 1976, 92). Some capitalists were decent, good-natured men, and some were perfect brutes who abused their wives and children along with their employees and their servants. That was beside the point. The point was that qua capitalists, they were all locked into the same exploitative relations with their employees, and that their relationship had to be, and was, compatible with bourgeois standards of justice at the surface, unreflective level.

It is important to take this insistence on detaching the question of surface justice from the moral evaluation of individual capitalists at its proper weight. In part, it amounts to nothing more than Marx's reminder that the task of the social scientist is not to judge but to explain—we do not rebuke Odysseus for his superstitions, for he could not be expected to rise above the intellectual level of the age, and we do not rebuke capitalists for behaving as their position in the economy forces them to behave. If it is true that in the usual sense of freedom, capitalists, having more resources than their workers, are therefore much freer than they, it is also true that Marx sees all of them so caught up in the workings of the capitalist economy that he regards it as futile to ask whether the capitalist is "free" to cease being a capitalist. Marx does not suppose that capitalists wish to injure their workers, and he does not suppose that capitalists have eccentric views about the desirability of overwork, bad housing, and bad food; what they suppose, and largely correctly, is that they cannot under capitalism do anything about it.

Marx's impatience with moralizing is more than an insistence on that point. It reflects, if it is not itself an argument for, his holistic view of the social and economic order, both his explanatory holism and his evaluative holism. It is a requirement of capitalist production relations that the transactions that appear as an exchange of wages for work should be compatible with conventional ideas about justice, and however we are to explain the origins and acceptance of the bourgeois conception of justice, its interest for Marx is almost wholly exhausted by its role in the system. Marx's interest in justice does not descend to the level of injustices done to or perpetrated by individuals, even though, as the long extracts from the Blue Books and elsewhere in *Capital* make clear, it is the effects of the capitalist system upon individual welfare—overwork, fear, destroyed health, destroyed family life, pervasive misery—that make capitalism repulsive (Marx 1976, 370–416). In explanatory terms, it is the abstract and impersonal nature of the capitalist system that is distinctive. Individual capitalists are but the agents of capital, which governs them—more comfortably, to be sure—just as it governs the workers. Marx's thought is exceedingly hard to set down simply, but it is at least that whereas the systemic properties of the whole society depend upon the thoughts and actions of its individual members, they also confront individual members as an external fact (Giddens's [1976] concept of "structuration" is intended to accommodate this double perspective). It is worth writing in terms of "the capitalist mode of production" only because it is simultaneously a network of individuals interacting according to their own aspirations and beliefs as well as a system that dictates to those individuals what aspirations and beliefs to adopt.

The heart of the analysis, in Marx's own eyes, lies in the analysis of the productive system. He was full of contempt for economists who distinguished, as Mill did, between the laws of production and the laws of distribution (Cohen 1978a, 108–11). He had even more contempt for "distributivist" socialists who thought that all the ills of capitalism could be cured by tinkering with distributive mechanisms in the name of "fairness" (Marx and Engels 1962b, 2:21 [*Critique of the Gotha Programme*]). In Marx's account, production determines the distributive system. So it is not surprising to find that Marx looks for the truth about the exploitation of the laborer in production, not distribution. Marx claimed that the surplus was *created* in production, not distribution; it was only realized in exchange. It is not because goods are bought at less than their value or sold at more than their value, but because a surplus appears in the course of production that the capitalist can appropriate a profit. The process is simple enough; the capitalist buys his inputs, including labor-power, then sets them to work; all inputs other than labor-power simply add their existing value to the output. When labor-power, bought at its full exchange value, is turned into labor—which is a use value—the divergence between what goes into the worker's labor-power and what the laborer can add to the product's value appears, and there is the surplus value waiting to be appropriated (Marx and Engels 1962b, 1:430–31; Marx 1976, 268–70).

The merits of this account as an account of the generation of profit are not very great; happily, they are no concern of ours here. Three aspects of the account are important, however. In the first place, Marx's account locates the source of profit only in "living labor"; the great contrast that Marx insists on is that between capital considered as "dead labor" and the worker's activity, which is "living labor" (Marx 1976, 1006–08 [appendix]). The metaphysical horror of capitalism is that dead labor sets living labor to work; and the worker's efforts go toward reinforcing the power of dead labor over him. The driving force of capitalism, says Marx, is capital accumulation; dead labor demands constant additions to its strength, and neither the worker nor the capitalist can resist it. This is in part a matter of imagery and rhetoric, but it is important imagery and rhetoric, since it is the natural embodiment of Marx's sociological perspective on the capitalist economy. What Marx says is that capital itself appears like a vampire, death in life, sucking the lifeblood of its victims. The sociological holism of his explanatory theory generates an evaluative (but not a moral) holism, for the implication is that capitalist society is "inverted" and the curious combination of slavery and freedom embodied in capitalism results in a society where the absolute freedom of everyone to buy and sell in the market is at the same time the enslavement of everyone by an impersonal, even a dead, force.

A second and equally important, though less dramatic, feature of the argument is that it shows how Marx can both assert and deny that capitalist exploitation is consistent with justice. In buying labor-power, the capitalist does not violate the rule of "equals for equals"; in *using* labor-power, he does (Marx and Engels 1962b, 1:429). "Robbery" does take place, but it does not take place where any previous critic thought it took place. This, incidentally, is one reason why Cohen cannot be quite right in arguing that Marx's theory of exploitation can be detached from the labor theory of value (Cohen 1978b). Under capitalism, the surplus exists only as surplus *value*. With rents in kind, forced labor, or the ownership of slaves, the workers' forced contributions to the wealth of the exploiting classes is based directly on the products of their labor, but capitalist exploitation works at all only because the way in which it works is veiled by its expression as the appropriation of value rather than things. It is nonetheless true for Marx that exploitation is always the same thing, namely, the forced performance of unrequited labor. But Marx's contrast between what goes on visibly in exchange and invisibly in production now shows why there is no straightforward answer to the question whether capitalism is unjust; the elaborate but only satisfactory answer is that capitalism is in contradiction with itself, forced to produce in ways that violate the principle of justice that it is simultaneously forced to profess.

It must be noted that Marx is not, as some commentators have thought, arguing that capitalism is just by its own lights and unjust by socialist lights. Insofar as capitalism is unjust, it is unjust by capitalism's own lights, not by some socialist standard of justice. Indeed, there are no socialist standards of justice. For the third thing to observe about Marx's analysis of exploitation in the production process is that it leads on very naturally to what he says in the *Critique of the Gotha Programme* about the fatuities of the Lassalleans and the true contrast between capitalism and socialism.

The Lassalleans had demanded a fair day's pay for a fair day's work and had propped this demand up with the claim that since labor was the only source of value, the laborers were the only people entitled to share in it (Marx and Engels 1962b, 2:18–20). Marx regarded this as utter nonsense; the value of whatever is produced depends on much more than the labor that goes into it, and in any case, under any system of production, the total product will have all sorts of claims on it—for depreciation, research, new investment, and the education of those too young to work and those too old or too ill to work. To suppose that "the whole product of labor" is there to be consumed at will by the laborers is completely absurd. Moreover, appeals to a fair day's wages compound the folly by supposing that there could be such a thing as fair wages; the only rational demand is for the abolition of wages. And it is to this that Marx turns his attention.

In doing so, he makes his famous distinction between the lower and the higher stages of socialism, arguing that under "stage one" of socialism, "bourgeois standards of right" will prevail in the sense that what workers receive will vary according to their contribution to the social product; only under "stage two" will society be governed by the principle "from each according to his ability, to each according to his needs." The interesting issue concerns the status of stage one. In stage one, workers are paid in proportion to their contribution; and at this stage, we find that exploitation ceases and (bourgeois) justice is achieved. For in the absence of capitalists, nobody can take home an income simply because he happens to own the means of production; the workers as a whole get the whole product—over a lifetime, of course, not in the wage packet each week. For between what they get through the social wage—education, pensions, sick pay, and so on—and their ordinary wages, they get everything there is to be had. That is one purpose of getting rid of the capitalists (Marx and Engels 1962b, 2:22–23).

But as between one individual and another, justice requires that those who contribute more should receive more. As Marx says repeatedly, equal right creates unequal results; returning what is contributed means that those who contribute more get more (Marx and Engels 1962b, 2:24). Thus, over a lifetime, the more productive receive more than the less productive, though neither loses anything to the unproductive classes, who have now been expropriated. Marx plainly regards this stage as a second best; so do writers such as John Roemer and Jon Elster, who are committed to "individualist" accounts of justice and might therefore be expected to regard it as the end of the road to justice. In fact, all three concur in their skepticism about the idea that greater contributions entitle those who make them to greater rewards. Elster and Roemer are partly motivated by skepticism about the whole idea of desert, and partly by the thought that those who do the most productive work frequently have the most interesting occupations and therefore hardly need added reward. Marx does not go into details, but seems to hold something of the same view as Rawls—that desert may well be illusory, but that differential rewards are an economic necessity. It is worth stressing that it is only because of economic necessity that "bourgeois" justice still gets a look in.

After that stage, we reach the end of the road. Here, in my view, there is no justice because there are no rights. There is, however, a principle for distributing work and resources, the famous principle of "from each according to his capacity, to each according to his need." This is not a principle of justice in Marx's eyes—or mine—because it does not ground claims of right. There is no question of its imposition on the members of a communist society; there is no question of anyone being forced to work on these terms. Not only is it not a principle of justice, but it is not a moral principle at all. It will be understood by everyone not as a moral principle, but as a practical or rational principle. It does not have the mystified standing of what are nowadays passed off as moral principles; that is, people who adopt that principle will understand that they have chosen it because it expresses the way of life they wish to live, not because it is a "dictate of morality."

Skeptics will not wish to take my word for it that this is Marx's view. They may be persuaded if they consider what Marx says in his early *Critique of Hegel's Philosophy of Right*. In that essay, Marx defends two views: first, Hegel is quite wrong to suppose that the modern state is a rationalized constitutional monarchy, and second a truly democratic society would abolish the state entirely. The status of this second claim is exceedingly unclear, but there seem to be two elements in it: first, there would be no distinctively "political" institutions in such a society, and second, social decisions would not issue in "law." These two thoughts are connected; Marx thought that republican theory, as found in writers like Rousseau, emphasized the public-spirited role of the citizen and the general-interest-directed nature of the state precisely because the actuality of bourgeois society was competitive, individualistic, and directed at private interests only. The Rousseauist state had to be simultaneously a moral ideal and a repressive reality because it demanded the sacrifice of men's real interests for the sake of imposing an external order on the war of all against all that raged in civil society. Paradoxically, Marx came to think that there was a hidden harmony to be elicited in capitalist society—production was cooperative and social—even though he held as strongly as anyone that in practice, bourgeois society was riven with conflict. This allowed him to think of the institutions of a socialist society as, so to speak, emanations of the collective life of that society, not as something imposed in the name of a political morality. That rational institutions *are* such emanations was something else he learned from Hegel; as a very young man, he seems to have thought that law might be this even in his own Prussia. Thereafter, he held the view we always associate with his name—the view that law is essentially coercive and class interested, but that a society free of conflict would have rules that were noncoercive and, by our present standards, not really "rules" at all.

An illustration is his treatment of representation. Real representation is a matter of real needs; so the butcher and the baker are my real representatives—they mediate between nature and me. Political representation is illusory; there cannot be any such process as that of licensing another person to bear my moral or political will and commit me against my actual empirical will. There can, and under any conceivable scheme would have to be, some way of delegating decision making. The authority such decision makers would have is not moral or political authority. It is, so to speak, only as much authority as the facts and our wishes between them will generate. It would be a practical matter, and their authority would be in the same sense only a practical authority. They would serve my need to delegate decision making in the same way the butcher and the baker serve my need to delegate the process of getting food.

Critics of Marx have often mocked his apparent belief in the possibility of a society in which there was simultaneously absolute freedom of choice for every individual and absolute unanimity in collective decision making. It is certainly true that he offers not even a sketch of the decision-making process by which the freedom of each is to be reconciled with the decisiveness of all. It is equally true that he owed his readers some account of the process, since it is plain that the two chief planks in his account of socialism are its concern for individual freedom and its commitment to a form of economic rationality that transcends the "anarchy of production." I do not have anything to add to this argument, except for a suggestion about the proper framework for its conduct. That framework is holistic and historicist, and is roughly as follows. Like Hegel, Marx sees history culminating in freedom and reason; capitalism is, in some ways, the most perverse of social and economic orders just because it offers so much liberty, in the sense of laissez-faire, and demands so much rationality, in the sense of means-ends calculations, and yet operates under the sway of blind necessity. It is this latter fact that is decisive. Marx contrasts what one might call our mastery of nature with the social system's mastery of us. This is Marx's naturalized version of the Hegelian notion of alienation, and it is what underlies the Marxian conception of freedom. It is a concept that makes sense only in a holistic context, one in which the subject of history is the human species; the mechanisms of alienation are capable of reconstruction in individualist terms, however, and the species' misfortunes fall, of course, upon individual human beings (Marx 1975, 189).

At this point it is possible to put the argument together. The horrors of capitalism are, of course, horrors—misery, overwork, ill health; they are not, however, moral horrors. That is, they are not be laid at the door of anyone's wickedness or misbehavior, and they lead to no conclusions about who is to blame. Nobody is guilty of the crime of constructing capitalism. They are, so to speak, natural disasters like cancer or consumption, plainly disastrous but not the results of wickedness. This is wholly consilient with the view that we are the victims of capital, not masters of our productive abilities; it is also consilient with the view that freedom and necessity are compatible where the necessity is that of the natural connection between means and ends—and that they are not compatible when the contrast is between being constrained by needs you would rather not have as opposed to needs that stem from goals you choose. In saying this, I am not conceding that Marx does, after all, have a moral view, one founded on freedom. It is not a moral view; freedom is not an ideal, and we are not morally obliged to seek it. Like freedom from ill health, it is a natural good, and its pursuit is a practical, not a moral, imperative. This is not to say that *very* much hangs on whether we follow my view or that put forward in Lukes's *Marxism and Morality*; I do, however, think that my view has the advantage of lining up more exactly with what Marx said and with what motivated him. Against Lukes, my reading makes it more intelligible that Marx should insist so vigorously that the communists preach no ideals (Marx and Engels 1965, 47). It also makes Marx an interesting precursor of, for instance, Bernard Williams. Like Williams, Marx denies the existence of specifically and specially *moral* considerations; though he does it in different terms, he also—following Hegel—sees the difference between Greek, or more specifically Aristotelian, ethics and modern forms of ethical thinking in the impact of nonteleological natural science and in a resulting ability to analyze the judgments made with so-called thick concepts into a descriptive and an evaluative component (Williams 1985, 143–45). What Marx adds is a sociological hypothesis about why we have the mystified concept of "morality"—I readily concede that what Marx omits is a careful account of where the boundaries lie between "moral" and non-"moral" evaluation.

Is it worth insisting on the extreme position I have been pursuing? It is not a question to which a wholly conclusive answer can be given, but there are some considerations I find very persuasive. It might be said that Marx leaves open exactly what Bernard Williams leaves open, namely, the debating of alternative conceptions of the good life, "ethics" even if not "morality." This, however, cuts across two distinctively Marxian concerns. In the first place, although Marx was avowedly attracted to the Greek world in something of the same way that Schiller was, he was insistent that mankind had grown out of that stage of life. If we try to say that Marx had an "Aristotelian" conception of ethics as opposed to a Kantian conception of morality, we have to acknowledge that Marx himself would have insisted that in the modern world, one could not be an Aristotelian without qualification. In the second place, Marx's concept of the practical goes beyond Aristotle in supposing that we might conflate *all* separate forms of assessment in the one category of the practical. Critics of Marx as well as enthusiasts for the intellectual bravado with which he conducts his case will surely wish to emphasize the divergence of his case from common sense as well as from Aristotle.

Similarly, it might be argued that Marx's insistence on the need to move beyond assessments of justice and rights makes him some sort of utilitarian. Here again, I think Marx's insistence that decision making under socialism would not issue in rules, would not involve concepts such as blame, would not rely on inner sanctions such as the conscience, pulls him so far away from moral theory as ordinarily understood that we do better regarding both moral theory and an accurate grasp of intellectual history to emphasize the difference between Marx's enterprise and anything more orthodox. Indeed, I think we ought to side not only with Bernard Williams's sharp contrast between morality and ethics but also with Geoffrey Warnock's earlier insistence that it is intellectually coherent to deny the claims of morality and that writers such as Nietzsche did so (Warnock 1971). On my reading, Marx did not do that; rather he bracketed the claims of morality and went on to characterize capitalism and its alternatives in different terms. That leaves it an open question whether he was wholly wise to do so; I hope I have suggested that he was not, but I should emphasize that I have certainly produced no conclusive arguments against his enterprise.

One last point needs to be made. There is one sense in which Marx might be said to have an ethic. The imperative to rise up and overthrow capitalism is a practical, not a moral, imperative. Nonetheless, if it is to be followed, there are various qualities of mind and character that men must possess if they are to do it. The sick patient who is either cowardly or self-deceived may in a sort of way know that he must have a painful operation or submit to a disciplined course of medical treatment, but he will not be able to bring himself to do it or will always find some half-believed reason for not doing so. So with the proletariat; what it needs above all else is a combination of intelligence, vitality, and courage. Sentimentality and self-indulgence will do no good—as Marx told Wilhelm Weitling with some heat as far back as 1846 (McLellan 1973, 157). These are what one might call military virtues; they are, again, instrumental rather than moral, but no harm is done by calling them virtues. As always with Marx, and with many other thinkers for that matter, there is some question whether he does not in fact value the qualities of cis-revolution man so highly that he really has less enthusiasm for the trans-revolutionary than he claims to have. Anyone who has spent any time in an art museum will remember the contrast between many artists' detailed and enthusiastic treatment of this world and the inferno, on the one hand, and their insipid depictions of what purports to be paradise. That, however, is another topic and one that would take us very far from the narrower topics of this essay.[1]

References

Buchanan, A. E. 1982. *Marx and Justice*. London: Macmillan.

Cohen, G. A. 1971. "Karl Marx and the Withering Away of Social Science." *Philosophy and Public Affairs* 1:182–203.

———. 1978a. *Karl Marx's Theory of History: A Defence*. Oxford: Clarendon Press.

———. 1978b. "The Labor Theory of Value and the Concept of Exploitation." *Philosophy and Public Affairs* 8:338–60.

———. 1983. Review of *Marx*, by A. Wood. *Mind* 92:440–45.

Elster, J. 1985. *Making Sense of Marx*. Cambridge: Cambridge University Press.

Geras. N. 1985. "The Controversy about Marx and Justice." *New Left Review* 150:47–85.

Giddens, A. 1976. *New Rules for Sociological Method*. London: Hutchinson.

Lukes, S. 1985. *Marxism and Morality*. Oxford: Clarendon Press.

Marx, K. 1975. *Early Writings*. Harmondsworth: Penguin.

———. 1976. *Capital*. Vol. 1. Harmondsworth: Penguin.

Marx, K., and F. Engels. 1962a. *Selected Correspondence*. Moscow: Foreign Languages Publishing House.

———. 1962b. *Selected Works*. Vols. 1 and 2. Moscow: Foreign Languages Publishing House.

———. 1965. *The German Ideology*. London: Lawrence and Wishart.

———. 1975. *The Holy Family*. In *The Collected Works of Marx and Engels*, vol. 4. London: Lawrence and Wishart.

McLellan, D. 1973. *Karl Marx: His Life and Thought*. London: Macmillan.

Roemer, J. 1982. *A General Theory of Exploitation and Class*. Cambridge, Mass.: Harvard University Press.

———. ed. 1986. *Analytical Marxism*. Cambridge: Cambridge University Press.

Warnock, G. J. 1971. *The Object of Morality*. London: Methuen.

Williams, B.A.O. 1981. "Internal and External Reasons." In *Moral Luck*, 101–13. Cambridge: Cambridge University Press.

———. 1985. *Ethics and the Limits of Philosophy*. London: Fontana.

Wood, A. 1981. *Karl Marx*. London: Routledge and Kegan Paul.

3 3

Liberty and Socialism

THIS ESSAY will at best contribute only a little to one small corner of its subject. Nonetheless, it seems to me that since the late 1970s, political theorists have sufficiently changed their minds about the nature of freedom and its institutional implementation to justify another look at what might otherwise seem a pretty tired subject. I shall concentrate on two issues, one to do with property and the other with education. The first is whether the abolition of private property rights in the means of production would in itself be an assault on freedom: it is sometimes claimed that it would be such an assault that socialism simply cannot be defended on libertarian grounds.[1] Some defenders of socialism, as well as its critics, accept this conclusion and think of socialism as the search for justice, welfare, or fraternity at the expense of freedom—or "bourgeois freedoms."

I argue against this view, but agree that there are various liberties, such as the freedom of occupational choice and freedom of choice of lifestyle, freedom of association and other political liberties, that are, up to a point, protected by the existence of private property in liberal capitalist regimes, and that would need institutional safeguards under socialism. This is not to say that the existence of private property is by itself sufficient to protect them; one need think only of fascist regimes of the fairly recent past to see that it is the liberal rather than the capitalist character of the regimes that matters. But just as I take it for granted that it is the way that political institutions allow us to use our private property that secures the connection between private ownership and some liberties, I take it for granted that the way in which public ownership or "no-ownership" is institutionalized will make all the difference to whether a socialist regime will be, on balance, more or less free than a comparable capitalist regime. Unlike many socialists, I think that there is a good case for supposing that the regime of private property is sometimes a serious and reasonably successful attempt to institutionalize liberty; unlike all defenders of capitalism, I do not think that this rules out the claims of socialism to be an even better institutionalization of the same value.[2]

The second issue is whether a "no-ownership" regime would allow room for greater or lesser intellectual freedom, for a more or less libertarian educational system. I argue that there is *room* for more freedom, though again I take it for granted that everything depends on institutional arrangements.

I am therefore entirely at one with Peter Archer in thinking that serious socialism must be concerned with constitutional issues, and especially with issues of decentralization, on the one hand, and the protection of individuals against maladministration, on the other.[3] Many writers have relied heavily on the belief that under socialism, various unpleasant features of the world as constructed at present will disappear and that this will enable us to have more freedom. Bertrand Russell, for instance, and even to some extent his godfather, John Stuart Mill, let alone Karl Marx or William Morris, have all claimed that once socialism is instituted and there is less greed, less envy, less selfishness, and less competitiveness, there will be no need to curb the aggressors or to limit the freedom of the aggressed upon so that they may better be defended against their enemies. I do not dismiss this claim, of course, but it is one I do not wish to rely on here; here I want to make as few assumptions as possible about changes in human nature under socialism and to argue about freedom as currently conceived in liberal capitalist societies. If my case holds up on these "minimalist" terms, it obviously does even better if the optimistic views of Marx and Russell are right. My main claim is that if there is to be liberty in education under socialism, there will have to be a positive effort at decentralization by central governments and local authorities, and that in the absence of the private-property-based liberty for anyone to open a school if he or she can finance it, there will need to be some corresponding access to public resources by self-help groups.[4]

Throughout what follows, I accept that a system can be socialist and tyrannical, or socialist and libertarian; that is to say, I shall not try to define a tyrannical system as nonsocialist just by virtue of its being nonlibertarian. So far as I am concerned, a society is socialist if the powers that in capitalist societies are vested in private hands via the ownership of the means of production are vested in public bodies of one sort or another, or, perhaps, are possessed by nobody.[5] That is, a system in which workers' cooperatives own their means of production but individual members are not shareholders who are able to sell their shares to someone else would be socialist; so would a system in which central or local governments own the means of production and lease them out to workers, or own the means of production and simply employ the workers as wage laborers. It would be socialist whether it is governed by a one-party state or a multiparty state, whether there is much freedom of speech or none.

If a society's economy is organized on the basis of public rather than private ownership of the means of production, it is socialist. I say this without denying that there is room for dispute about the importance of formal property rights versus de facto control. People who describe the Soviet Union as a "state capitalist" society are, in my view, wrong but not silly; they are wrong, because it confuses the issue to suggest, what is avowedly not true, that the power and privilege of the Soviet political and managerial elite amounts to "ownership" of the resources from which they benefit; they are not silly because it is obviously true that as far as the power to secure benefits for oneself, straightforward political control is every bit as good as ownership, and perhaps because their behavior is also like that of their capitalist counterparts. By the same token, I do not think that political and economic institutions alone are needed; a more generally libertarian culture is obviously essential—again, something on which Mill, Marx, and Russell were agreed, and rightly.

To show that socialism may be more consistent with liberty than capitalism is, we need to begin by showing that the existence of private property is not entailed by a concern with liberty. To do this, we need to begin with a brief look at the concept of liberty. In spite of the eloquent and persuasive arguments put forward by Isaiah Berlin's *Two Concepts of Liberty*, I do not think that there are two concepts of liberty. In one view there is only one, and in another view there are probably three; in the current jargon, we might say that there is one concept and three conceptions, but I would rather say that there is one concept and three views about when we are free.[6]

There are three prominent views about when freedom is achieved; one of these we might call the negative theory, and two of them the positive theories of liberty. The one concept of liberty is that we are free when our actions are really our own—the positive concept of liberty, that of a man being "his own master" or his own man, is, to my mind, not a concept of liberty but the concept of liberty itself.[7] The negative theory about liberty is, then, the view that what a man needs in order to be his own master is simply not to be coerced by other men. I am my own master and my actions are my own if I am not coerced into acting one way rather than another. One aim of a theory of liberty must be to give an adequate account of the grounds of legitimate coercion, an aim that evidently involves begging or, better, answering some awkward questions about such things as what constitutes a threat, what constitutes harm, what constitutes punishment, and so on. In this view, one aim of Mill's *On Liberty*, much like Berlin's *Two Concepts of Liberty*, is to justify a particular conception of what those grounds are and to explain what damage it does to misconceive them.[8]

The first of the two "positive" theories of liberty emphasizes the importance of the range of choices actually open to someone, arguing that the enlargement of options is an enlargement of liberty. In this way, the old question about whether the poor man is really free to eat at the Ritz receives what may look like an evasive answer, but what is probably the best one we can give. (One may feel happier with an evasive seeming answer after reflecting that Tawney referred to the right to eat at the Ritz if one could afford it as a "formal" freedom, which is surely quite as evasive.) Eating at the Ritz is an option for him, but barely so; he would have to save what is, by his lights, a large sum of money and therefore forgo many other things in order to do it, even though he is not forbidden to eat at the Ritz and would not be forced not to eat there if he did save up. But a bigger income would make him freer because it would enlarge his range of choice, would make eating at the Ritz a more genuine option.

The second positive claim about liberty is that its essence lies in self-government. This, of course, is a claim that goes right back to the origins of arguments about freedom and invokes perhaps the most obvious contrast of all, that of the slave and the free man. The slave is the paradigm case of the man whose acts are not his own, whose own say-so cannot bind him, on whom others cannot rely because his future performance is not within his own sovereignty. The free man may be bound by laws, and they may be pretty stringent. His freedom is also not entirely his individual possession, since to play his part in the government of his community he has to rely on the conventions and habits of allegiance of his fellow citizens; but since these conventions, laws, and habits stem from their own wills, they do not limit their freedom.[9] There are many variations on this theme, but the thing they have in common is that they regard having some share in the government of oneself as constitutive of liberty properly speaking. Commonly, writers in this tradition will agree quite readily that a robber who cannot be coerced into obedience, or a rich man who can evade the law, are *free* from restraint and in that sense are free to behave badly; but this does not bear on whether they possess "liberty."

It is worth distinguishing this "political" conception of liberty from theories of "self-mastery" and the like. Theories of self-mastery seem always to rely on some picture of a divided self, with a higher or better or more rational self mastering the lower or worse or more animal self; the imagery is as old as the political conception of liberty—at any rate, Plato seems to trade on it in the *Republic*. But it belongs to a different intellectual universe and a different range of concerns. In the self-government conception of liberty I have just sketched, there is no particular suggestion that people's selves are chronically, often, sometimes, or ever "divided."

The crucial claim is only that a man is free when the decisions that bind him are ones he himself takes. This conception of liberty is quite sufficient to generate the paradox on which the Stoics traded when they claimed that the slave could be freer than his master. The slave did not necessarily "retreat to the inner citadel" and say to himself that since he could not get what he wanted, he would train himself to want nothing; rather, he pointed out to his master that no matter what the master got up to, it was up to him, the slave, to decide whether to take any notice or not. This would, of course, demand a considerable readiness to put up with pain, but not necessarily any attempt to train oneself not to suffer. Autonomy is intact so long as the slave can, so to speak, distance himself sufficiently from what happens to him to go on saying, "You may offer me all these inducements to obey, but it is I who decide whether to take any notice of them." It is, I think, a point in favor of my view that freedom is a matter of being one's own master that it will in this way illuminate the paradox in the Stoic conception of freedom without making the fatal error of confusing the free slave with the happy slave. There is no paradox at all in the idea that someone might prefer slavery to freedom and might be a contented slave; the paradox lies in the thought that the person who, by one standard, plainly does have a master plausibly claims, by another standard, not to have one.[10]

It is now time to show that liberty in these three forms does not uniquely prescribe private ownership of the means of production. This is not an easy task, and I do not expect to carry complete conviction at all points. Indeed, since my case is that the libertarian virtues of either a private-property or a common-property regime depend on the way they are institutionalized, I am deliberately putting the burden of carrying conviction on shoulders other than my own. What I want to do is defend the view that in comparing socialism and capitalism, there can be a serious argument about which is, in principle, more favorable to liberty. There can, of course, be many other comparisons—of their success in achieving justice, equality, prosperity, or whatever; what I am anxious to do is to scotch any suggestion that in comparing socialism with capitalism, we are arguing about sacrificing some or a lot of liberty in return for some or a lot more equality, security, justice, or whatever. This is by no means to slight these goods, though I confess that my enthusiasm for fraternity, at least, has been somewhat dented by Anne Phillips's compelling and disquieting discussion of that subject.[11] And while agreeing that some socialists, Marx among them, have put forward distinctive accounts of the freedom of "the all-round man," I do not want to rely on any suggestion that if socialism achieves liberty, it is a special, socialist kind of liberty; in my view, the kind of liberty capitalists and socialists ought to be keen on as a minimum is the same kind.[12]

If we have a right to freedom, it is at least a right not to be coerced by others without very good reason. But the impossibility of deriving private property rights from the right not to be coerced by others without good reason seems to me clear enough. Property, as Bentham observed, is born and dies with the law.[13] In the absence of a legal system, people would be able to secure a precarious possession of various things, but others would equally be able to dispossess them too. For A to *own* what he or she possesses—let alone to own what is not within his or her physical grasp—a necessary though not a sufficient condition is that there should be rules in force requiring B, C, D, . . . Z to keep their hands off whatever it is, unless they have A's leave to interfere with it. The more interesting question, however, is how far toward property rights a system of rights would reach if its basis was something like the right set out in Mill's *On Liberty* not to be coerced by others except in self-defense.[14]

This right would allow us to exercise our natural abilities, either singly or in cooperation with others, wherever this did not harm others. If I were to take and use some previously unpossessed object and put it to harmless use, then presumably I should have the right to remain undisturbed in my possession and use of it. Would this amount to ownership? The answer seems to me to be no. An essential element in property is the ability unilaterally to alter the position of third parties by your own acts. So, for example, if you make a will and pass on to your heirs the right to the royalties payable to you by your publisher, you change the legal relationship between your heirs and the publisher without having to ask either of them to consent to it. But, more importantly, for your will to be effective, something has to happen over and above your exercise of your natural capacities—other people have to go along with giving effect to your wishes after you, being dead, are unable to give effect to them yourself.[15] This aspect of ownership seems quite impossible to accommodate within an analysis that relies on our obligation to permit non-harm-threatening behavior. Quite a lot of what is normally protected by property rights can be so protected—one might build and occupy a house, allow a friend to move in, move out oneself and leave her in occupation, say—but most of the more interesting uses of property require analysis of the positive contribution of the law.[16]

If a concern for noncoercion is to be connected with private property, then it cannot be by saying simply that a Mill-like right not to be coerced except to prevent harm to others entails the existence of private property. What it does plausibly entail is such institutionalizable rights as the right to choose what employment to follow—except in such desperate straits as when your decision to paint abstracts rather than stand sentry duty might cost us all our lives. That is, you may do whatever harmless things you can do by using the gifts of nature rather than by employing the conventional powers granted by others and needing their assistance for their use.

It is this that suggests that arguments from noncoercion can put tight constraints on the sort of socialism that will be acceptable to us. That is, even if private property is a social privilege and not a natural right, it may well be that there are only a small number of property systems that will score at all well in minimizing the amount of direct, illicit coercion they involve. Slavery is obviously ruled out; systems involving forced labor are out; much of feudalism is out. Indeed, many writers who have defended private property as essential to freedom have recognized the point that all property rights imply some sort of coercive background in being conventional rights at all, but have thought it possible to minimize the day-to-day exercise of coercion—especially coercion by government—only under a system of private ownership. The socialist reply must be that it all depends, and that what it all depends on is not so much the formal property law of the society as political and judicial behavior. So, for instance, if all industrial and commercial capital were supplied by a state bank, or a series of state investment trusts, but was borrowed by workers' cooperatives that nobody could be formally penalized for joining or leaving, there would be no more coercion implicit here than under contemporary capitalism. The proneness of the system to illicit coercion or quasi coercion would depend a good deal on the constitutional arrangements for running the central bank; but on the face of it, we could organize it to deal with cooperators no more coercively than banks and insurance companies deal with firms in present-day capitalist economies.[17]

This analysis begs some questions. It relies heavily on a commonsense view of what coercion comes to and what sort of "harms" we are to count as entitling others to use coercion to prevent. All I can say is that I have not tried to argue that the private ownership of the means of production is intrinsically coercive in the sense of being a weapon that one man can employ to force somebody else to do his bidding. It plainly can sometimes be so used, but I am, for the present, content to agree that when the rich man says to the poor man, "I will employ you at such and such a wage," this really is an offer and not a threat and is not best understood as amounting to "part with your surplus value or I'll starve you to death." The sense in which coercion is inevitably present is that behind both the rich and poor man stands the state, saying, "If you touch his person or his possessions without his leave, you will suffer for it."[18]

The argument becomes more interesting when we turn to choice enlargement and self-government. I begin with the observation that noncoercion is only half the story about freedom; the other half is plainly the issue of choice enlargement. Indeed, in some views, choice enlargement is the whole story and coercion is important as one element in the deliberate restriction of our choices by others. To my mind, the invention of property rights is a freedom-creating act; it works not by diminishing coercion but by allowing for the creation of novelty. The ability to make elaborate contractual arrangements for the future, which a secure system of property rights permits, is the first step toward a world in which new possibilities may constantly arise. In allowing people to plan ahead, it gives them an incentive to innovate. Marx's praise of the bourgeoisie in the *Communist Manifesto* may have been misdirected—seeing as the innovators who got the Industrial Revolution going were landowners and agriculturalists rather than members of anything much like a bourgeoisie—but the spirit of his remarks was quite right. He and Henry Sumner Maine disagreed about practically everything else, but the one thing they shared was the belief that western European civilization had been uniquely progressive because the property system had encouraged innovation rather than stagnation.[19] It was not only the existence of an appropriate property system, of course, but also the crucial thing the property system had done was to disperse the ability to make new starts into innumerable private hands, a process that was aided by the willingness of the legal and political authorities to bless after the event bargains and arrangements that private individuals had made.

Socialism faces an obvious problem. The standard defense of the innovative Western world is that it links individual reward to individual effort—or luck—by allowing successful entrepreneurs to pocket the profits they make. The easiest and simplest way of so doing seems to be to allow people to own firms in the simple and outright way that the capitalist economy presupposes. Of course, this does not mean there is anything sacrosanct about tying together the rights that *we* now tie together. It is all a matter of what results from so doing. From the point of view of the workers in an enterprise, there is nothing particularly "natural" about allowing the owners of the capital funds to appoint the management and to walk off with any increase in the capital value of the firm. The only justification for letting them do so is that this is the only way to enlarge the workers' choices too. Thus, the real problem is that of creating some other system of rights that will be equally conducive to entrepreneurial initiative and thence to choice enlargement.

It is not at all easy to work one's way consecutively through the problems involved, but one might begin by suggesting that one important distinction is between socialist theories that suppose that human nature will change drastically under socialism and theories that do not. The higher stage of socialism to which Marx looked forward in the *Critique of the Gotha Programme* plainly supposes that our motivation will have changed quite dramatically. If people spontaneously contribute according to their abilities out of sheer creative exuberance, there will be no problems about incentives, though there may be some about coordination. But Marx's account has two drawbacks. The first is that it is, even in principle, very difficult to make clear sense of it; we seem to be told at every point only that whatever problems we envisage will somehow disappear at the point where individual and social production will immediately coincide. This, however, simply evades all the serious questions about how decisions will get taken and what sort of decisions they will be. The second stems from the first; in practice, Marx's blueprint has been quite catastrophic. Workers in primitive conditions have been exhorted to behave like the new socialist man and have been shot or imprisoned when they have failed to live up to those exhortations.[20]

This does not impugn the plausibility of what Marx treats as the lower stage of socialism. In that stage, it will be recalled, bourgeois conceptions of right and justice continue to operate, but with the abolition of the functionless capitalist, there will be no rewards going to anyone who either has not earned them by his or her productive contribution, or has claims of need or justice on the social fund—children and the nonworking elderly, for instance. Here there is a lot of room for questions about how we secure entrepreneurial initiative without at once reintroducing full-fledged capitalism. To my mind, the only plausible story is that we must allow would-be entrepreneurs to bid for the use but not, of course, the outright ownership of capital resources.

There is no reason why a socialist economy should not be even more competitive and fast moving than a capitalist economy. Under capitalism, slow-moving owners of capital resources can always decline to take any notice of the plans laid before them by entrepreneurs, and since they own the capital they control, there is no way of making them take any notice— no doubt, they will eventually be driven to take some notice by market forces, but if there are lots of slow movers about, market forces will not work very swiftly. Under socialism, the rules that make the holders of invest-

ment funds or the ultimate owners of production goods lease them to entrepreneurs could be made much fiercer; if all anyone ever had was a use right
over productive equipment, and to keep the use right he or she had to outbid
anyone who had a decently worked-out plan for using the equipment more
productively, you might get much fiercer competition than in most capitalist
economies. Whether the rewards that this system could offer to entrepreneurs would be enough is a difficult question to answer; to suppose that
entrepreneurs would remain in the woodwork unless they were allowed to
have outright ownership of the firms they put together is to believe that
dynastic considerations are a basic element in human nature. But it is always
possible that very high levels of consumption, the pleasures of power, and
the intrinsic rewards of success would not be enough to motivate them. My
own guess is that the symbolic rewards would be sufficient without capitalist private ownership sneaking in through the back door, but that is only a
guess.[21] The main point is that we could envisage a system—though it is
hard to imagine anything other than a system in which most enterprises
were either one-person (or few-persons) firms or worker-managed cooperatives doing it—that could replicate all the innovative and competitive features of a capitalist economy and would therefore score no less well along
the dimension of choice enlargement. Of course, as Peter Kellner points out,
this then leaves a large question to be answered—how much do we mind
about the inequalities that such a system would produce?[22] In my view of
the matter, we might not mind very much, since they would not be permanent and bequeathable inequalities and would not wash over into inequalities of esteem.[23]

The subject is one that raises all sorts of awkward empirical questions
that do not yield to philosophical or conceptual analysis. Three things seem
to me to explain the slow progress we have made in sorting out the empirical consequences of this sort of decentralized socialism. One is that
nineteenth-century socialists, whether Marx, Morris, Bellamy, the English
Fabians, or whoever, were uninterested in and unastute about the role of the
entrepreneur under capitalism and therefore were uninterested in and unastute about the performance of entrepreneurial functions under socialism.
The second is that numbers of sociologists—Tawney, Weber, and Schumpeter among them—were convinced that all economic activity would become a matter of professional, public-spirited administration; it has not, but
intellectual curiosity and imagination have not kept up with reality. The
third thing is that in any case, no generalizations about what makes for innovation and progress in economic matters seem to be exactly and excep-
tionlessly true across cultures. Hardship and security, closely knit and
loosely knit families, strong and weak religious affiliations, all seem capable
of making people more or less economically adventurous. Why the overseas
Chinese are, and the overseas Irish are not, remarkable for their mercantile
aptitude and entrepreneurial vigor remains deeply mysterious. For my purposes, it is enough that no empirical evidence forbids us to believe that a

system of ownership rights could be recognizably socialist, could score as high as any capitalist regime on the noncoercion test, and would neither frustrate nor be frustrated by whatever psychological traits are essential to entrepreneurial vigor.[24]

None of this is to say that choice enlargement is exhausted by replicating the choices offered under capitalism. There are choices that capitalism systematically thwarts, and there are many "revealed preferences" that reflect adaptation to the economic realities rather than genuine underlying tastes. The preference for more money rather than more leisure, which is consistently exhibited by the British working class, may well be an artifact of the tax system and the accounting system rather than the reflection of an ultimate preference or a real enthusiasm for what the extra income will enable them to buy. Since all the evidence suggests that the motives behind present choices are rather altruistic—looking after one's family, saving to buy houses and furnish them, clothing one's children and so on—it is possible that people would change their views about work if they could provide these benefits rather differently and implement a different preference structure through their own managerial decisions. (Would they, for instance, vote to pay people very much more for overtime, or would they vote to have more members of the firm?) Nor is it the case that we should expect every firm to end up behaving like every other firm; enthusiasts for working their backsides off could do so without forcing everyone else to do so in self-defense.

I said earlier that one component in freedom is self-government; and this I distinguished from self-mastery in the sense in which Isaiah Berlin objects to the notion. It is remarkable how reluctant socialists have been to stress the one dimension in which capitalism is plainly deficient, that of industrial self-government. Capitalism has never mounted a convincing defense of itself in this area. Consumers have often enough been said to be "sovereign" in the marketplace, and this has provided a sort of defense against the idea that the capitalists themselves have exercised anything you could call industrial tyranny or dictatorship.[25] If consumers are really sovereign, all the capitalists can do is transmit the consumers' demands to the workers; they do not exercise an independent power, and their authority has nothing of what you might call a "political" flavor about it. The intermediary role of the capitalist in the process of reflecting demand in supply raises no interesting moral questions. But this has always been a pretty unpersuasive story, not least because it simply begs the crucial question of why the ownership of the capital that a company employs in trading should entitle its owners to automatic and absolute authority over how the company is run. We do not think that the landowners who own the land on which London is situated should thereby obtain all the political authority that is actually located in borough and county councils.[26] There is, therefore, a case to be made before we have to agree that the owners of the capital employed in commerce and industry may exercise all the authority exercised in commercial and industrial undertakings.

A simple answer would be that the capitalist is entitled to as much authority as is needed for the performance of his entrepreneurial functions. But this reply, reasonable as it is, too swiftly closes the gap between the capitalist as rentier and the capitalist as entrepreneur. The capitalist as rentier does only one thing, and that is to advance the funds needed to enable production to proceed. He seems on the face of it entitled to no more authority than the investor in National Savings bonds can exercise over the way the government spends the money he lends it. The rentier has a right to protection against mismanagement and speculation; it is not obvious that he has more rights than that. If anyone has a right to authority, it must be the entrepreneur. Whatever the pattern of ownership, he cannot do his job at all unless he can get others to do what he wants, the way he wants it, and when he wants it. In that sense, he, like a political leader, needs authority to do his job; he has the same sort of claim to be given that authority, a claim based on the kind of job it is and the importance of its being done. Even so, it is worth noting that two distinct issues are at stake. Generals, prime ministers, and entrepreneurs all need to be able to say "go" with a confidence that he goeth. But this is a different issue from that of who it is who ought to bestow that authority upon them. What authority is needed and how it may legitimately be had are different questions.

Prime ministers need large but not absolute powers and should get them through the ballot box, not through a military coup. The socialist view is surely that entrepreneurs need large discretionary powers but should get them from the votes of the workers instead of from the say-so of the rentiers. How socialist self-government can work without succumbing either to inefficiency, on the one hand, or to erosion in the face of expertise and deference in the face of expertise, on the other, is a difficult empirical question. It is precisely the sort of question that socialist economists and sociologists ought to think about in a grimly realistic frame of mind. But the conceptual issue is simple enough. Capitalist management has been chronically non-democratic and nonparticipatory. The view that workers can sign away their industrial citizenship but cannot sign away their political citizenship has needlessly gone unchallenged. Yet any defense of socialism's greater potential for freedom ought to make much of it.[27] It is, of course, a case that is very much easier to make on behalf of a decentralized socialism based on worker cooperatives than on behalf of a command economy. To the socialist who thinks that there is something special about working life, the importance of self-government at the workplace will need no argument. It ought to go without saying that for any of these arguments to be morally compelling, the relationships between men and women with respect to the allocation of different kinds of work will also need to be opened up.

Turning, more briefly, to freedom in education, we can advance along similar lines, but add one or two points more specific to issues of an educational sort. A concern to minimize coercion suggests that educational activities can properly shelter under the principle that where people do something that harms nobody else, others have no right to interfere. Educational self-help seems on the face of it to be something that is absolutely immune from legitimate interference. No doubt some of our property rights will have to be employed, even in very small-scale educational work; if I teach half a dozen five-year-olds to read, I shall still need to use my front room and be able to buy pencils and paper.

This perhaps sounds like a defense of private education. And it seems to suggest that we can have what you might call market socialism in schooling. Objectors to this will argue that the condition of "harmlessness to others" will be continuously violated, either in the present or in prospect. If some people now use their resources for educational purposes, they either now deprive others of them or threaten to give some children such advantages in the future that their employment of them constitutes "harm to others." Do those who find that they do less well in this process, either now or in future, have a case for saying that they have been harmed and that they may restrict the activities of my supposed "self-help" educators? My own view is that they do; I agree that the successful have not limited the freedom of the unsuccessful to compete, but they have limited their freedom of choice and have lessened their "life chances." If what you want to do is occupy a certain job, the person who defeats you because they are better qualified certainly lessens your life chances.

The committed natural-rights theorists who have recently walked off with the label of "libertarians" would, of course, rest all their arguments on the proposition that so long as the losers were no less free than the winners to use their resources, nobody's rights would have been infringed and there is an end of it. I want to argue something different. We are concerned here with noncoercion, choice-enlargement, and self-government. It is therefore important to ask whether there is some way of settling the issue between the more and less successful in the competitive use of educational resources that will sort out the question whether we should prevent the talented—or merely likable—from getting ahead of the less talented or less likable. If the freedom of choice created by a competitive or self-help-allowing system is great enough to give the least assisted a greater range of options (both in education and in life chances thereafter) than they would otherwise have had, it is hard to resist a Rawls-like argument to the effect that they would, if rational, have voted for such a system and must now accept that it is a just system.[28] This is different from arguing, as Mill did in *On Liberty*, that we should allow educational and other forms of competition because the gains overall outweigh the losses of the losers.

Ideal utilitarians like Mill place such a value on the discovery of truth and the encouragement of intellectual liveliness among the elite that they make the argument turn on a direct, though not very easy, utilitarian argument in which gains are set against losses in a straightforward balancing act. My case is not a balancing act. The question we ask is whether those people whose choices are most frustrated or most narrowed as a result of the free operation of self-help nonetheless have their choices widened as far as possible. Competitors who lose do suffer harm—they do not do as well as they would have if all resources had been there and their abler competitors disabled—but they may (since this is another case in which everything turns on the way it is institutionalized) get a better deal in terms of choice enlargement by not disabling them.

The second place where we can borrow from what was said before is in thinking of the role of educational entrepreneurship under socialism. There has to be some equivalent of what works rather badly under the existing system, namely, the possibility of someone trying out his or her educational ideas by renting buildings and hiring staff and seeing whether parents are willing to pay for what is on offer. My arguments about self-help obviously suffer from the fact that they do not seem to match a reality in which the resources needed are much beyond using one's own front room and pencils and paper. Schools are hefty pieces of capital equipment for a flow of services. What we need to put our minds to is ways in which educators can outbid existing users of them in order to keep up innovation and quality alike. This is the rational kernel in the arguments about education vouchers, and the question is whether any more likable device might encourage innovation and high quality. As things stand, educational authorities seem to behave in a thoroughly proprietorial way—in effect saying what is no doubt true, that there are not enough resources to give every group with a bright idea a whole new school to try it out in and, what is a lot less true, that nothing can be done to approach that utopian condition.

All I want to say is that this is the sort of question that has to be settled constitutionally under socialism. This is not to say that we must wait for the millennium to introduce a greater variety of educational provision and to encourage parents and teachers to conspire together for the good of their charges. But under socialism, the principle of decentralization has to operate to the extent of not penalizing the "self-help" educators who can get by on their own resources, and then to match this at the more complicated and elaborate level by obliging the authorities who own an educational plant to make it available to users who can get the support of parents and teachers. The analogy with the competitive cooperatives of the rest of the economy is not perfect; there are all sorts of problems, identified back in the 1770s, about the extent to which the consumer's judgment is a reliable one, and so on. Nonetheless, that aside, the structure of the problem is not dissimilar.

But what about self-government? Again, the case of education raises peculiar problems because there are interesting questions about the nature of the "product" that do not arise anywhere else. The obvious answer is that a concern for self-government implies that the running of schools, universities, and other institutions has to be altered in the direction of self-management—which universities and they alone at present practice, however imperfectly, to an extent that makes the management of polytechnics and colleges, let alone schools, look appallingly autocratic—and that the educational program has to be deliberately slanted to encourage students to develop the self-reliance, public spirit, and range of knowledge that will enable them to make something of self-government everywhere else in adult life. Will this amount to "indoctrination"?

It surely should not; there is no question of telling children that self-government is wonderful and doing so with all the aids of Madison Avenue. Self-government is not wholly wonderful; as Oscar Wilde observed, it cuts into your evenings in the most terrible way, and it makes a good many demands on you in the daytime. But as John Stuart Mill observed at the end of *The Subjection of Women*, grown adults do not seriously want to go back home to their parents, no matter how comfortable their parents' home may be; independent countries do not contemplate renouncing their independence for the sake of prosperity; nobody really wants to go back to school, however much they may look back on "the happiest days of their lives." Very little in this essay has been about why freedom is worth having. I have mostly made a limited case about what freedom is and which elements of it should be likely to flourish under socialism if we took various institutional steps to help it flourish. I do not think that only knaves and madmen doubt the value of liberty, and I do think that it would be perfectly possible to teach children the skills of citizenship without begging all the questions about why those skills were worth having. I do, however, think that arguments about freedom are the most important of all political arguments and that freedom is a value that can look after itself in an argument. But this is precisely why policies to advance liberty in the workplace and in education are mutually dependent and why they must not smack of imposition. A libertarian socialist party need not be committed to making slow progress; but it has to be committed to making only such progress as is consistent with recognizing its supporters' intellectual liberty.

Notes

2: FREEDOM

1. This essay is substantially as read to the Moral Sciences Club at Cambridge in November 1963 and to the Jowett Society at Oxford in February 1964.
2. Most of this section is highly derivative; sources of particular importance are Gilbert Ryle, "Ordinary Language," *Philosophical Review* (1953), and Stanley Cavell, "Must We Mean What We Say?" *Inquiry* (1958).
3. Bernard Williams, review *Sense and Sensibilia*, by J. L. Austin, *Oxford Magazine*, December 1962.
4. This is unfair to Flew's later views, but perhaps not to the view expressed in *New Essays in Philosophical Theology*.

3: CULTURE AND ANXIETY

1. Charles Murray and Richard J. Herrnstein, *The Bell Curve: Intelligence and Class Structure in American Life* (New York: Free Press, 1994); Russell Jacoby and Naomi Glauberman, eds., *The Bell Curve Debate: History, Documents, Opinions* (New York: Times Books, 1995).
2. Michael Young, *The Rise of the Meritocracy* (Harmondsworth: Penguin, 1959).
3. Richard Hofstadter, *Anti-Intellectualism in American Life* (New York: Knopf, 1963), 345.
4. The German title of Sigmund Freud's *Civilization and Its Discontents* (New York: Norton, 1951) could more literally have been translated as "anxiety in culture," but the sense of culture was the anthropologist's rather than Arnold's.
5. Max Weber, *The Protestant Ethic and the Spirit of Capitalism* (New York: Scribner's, 1930), originally published 1904–5.
6. W. B. Carnochan, *The Battleground of the Curriculum: Liberal Education and American Experience* (Stanford, Calif.: Stanford University Press, 1993).
7. Christopher J. Lucas, *American Higher Education: A History* (New York: St. Martin's, 1994), 155ff.
8. J. S. Mill, *Considerations on Representative Government* (London: Dent, 1910), 261n.

4: THE LIBERAL COMMUNITY

1. I acknowledge with pleasure the criticism of the first version of this chapter that I received from Nancy Rosenblum, Martin Golding, and Ian Shapiro. I have paid them what I hope is the compliment of silently amending my text where they have shown it to be unclear, but I have not restructured my argument nor altered

contentious claims. Our readers and I will learn more if I offer my critics a good fat target than if I beat a premature retreat.

2. It thus follows Alan Ryan, "Communitarianism: The Good, the Bad, and the Muddly," *Dissent*, Summer 1989, 350–54; and Charles Taylor, "Cross-Purposes: The Liberal Communitarian Debate," in *Liberalism and the Moral Life*, ed. Nancy Rosenblum, 159–82 (Cambridge, Mass.: Harvard University Press, 1989). Supervising Dr. Mimi Bick's D.Phil. dissertation, "The Liberal-Communitarian Debate: A Defense of Holistic Individualism" (University of Oxford, 1987), taught me a great deal. For an excellent overview of the subject, see Will Kyrnlicka, *Community, Individuality and Culture* (Oxford: Clarendon Press, 1989).

3. Taylor's view that "the heirs of Mill" have forgotten the legacy of Humboldt is, in this view, quite wrong ("Cross-Purposes," 163). Rather, recent American liberals have forgotten the legacy of Mill.

4. But see L. A. Siedentop, "Two Liberal Traditions," in *The Idea of Freedom*, ed. Alan Ryan, 153–74 (Oxford: Oxford University Press, 1979), on the sociologically sophisticated character of French liberalism early in the nineteenth century too. The Oxford D.Phil. dissertation of my former student Avital Simchoni, "The Social and Political Thought of the English Idealists" (University of Oxford, 1980), is uniquely illuminating on the politics of the English Idealists.

5. John Stuart Mill, "Coleridge," in *The Collected Works of John Stuart Mill* [cited as *CW*], ed. John M. Robson (Toronto: University of Toronto Press, 1969), 10:117–63.

6. L. T. Hobhouse, *Liberalism* (London: Longman, Green, 1911); Stefan Collini, *Liberalism and Sociology* (Cambridge: Cambridge University Press, 1979).

7. Bernard Bosanquet, *The Philosophical Theory of the State* (London, Macmillan, 1958 [1899]), 59–62; T. H. Green, *The Principles of Political Obligation*, in *The Philosophical Works of Thomas Hill Green* [cited as *PW*], ed. R. L. Nettleship (London, Macmillan, 1894), 2:522–23.

8. F. H. Bradley, *Ethical Studies* (Oxford: Oxford University Press, 1976 [1874]), 39n.

9. John Stuart Mill, *An Examination of Sir William Hamilton's Philosophy*, *CW* 9: chaps. 12, 18; Bradley, *Ethical Studies*, 36–41.

10. Green, *PW* 1:297–98.

11. Green, *Principles of Political Obligation*, *PW* 2:512–21; conversely, Bosanquet shows a more conservative Idealist agreeing with some of *On Liberty*, disagreeing with much else, and always claiming that Mill's foundations are flawed (*Philosophical Theory of the State*, 61–65).

12. John Stuart Mill, *A System of Logic*, book 6, chap. 2, sec. 3, *CW* 8:840–41.

13. John Stuart Mill, "Utilitarianism," *CW* 10:215–16, 228, 238.

14. Mill, *Examination of Hamilton*, chap. 26, *CW* 9:452.

15. Though it bulks larger than that for Michael Sandel, *Liberalism and the Limits of Justice* (Cambridge: Cambridge University Press, 1982), 1–11.

16. As I argued in Alan Ryan, *The Philosophy of John Stuart Mill* (London, Macmillan, 1970), chap. 13.

17. Hobhouse, *Liberalism*, 54–55; T. H. Green, "Liberal Legislation and Freedom of Contract," *PW* 3:365–86.

18. Bertrand Russell, *The Principles of Social Reconstruction* (London: Allen and Unwin, 1916), 11–13.

19. Green, *Principles of Political Obligation*, *PW* 2:451–54.

20. Charles Taylor, *The Sources of the Self* (Cambridge, Mass.: Harvard University Press, 1989), part 1.

21. Mill, "Coleridge," *CW* 10:134–36.

22. Mill, *System of Logic*, *CW* 8:919–20.

23. John Stuart Mill, *Considerations on Representative Government*, *CW* 19:535–39.

24. John Stuart Mill, *On Liberty*, *CW* 18:276.

25. Émile Durkheim, *Professional Ethics and Civic Morals* (London: Routledge and Kegan Paul, 1957); Steven Lukes, *Emile Durkheim: His Life and Work* (London: Allen Lane, 1973), 264–76.

26. The detachability of commitment from method leads Richard Rorty to recommend that we just dispense with philosophical "foundations"; even he admits that we shall find it helpful to engage in the philosophical "articulation" of our commitments; see Richard Rorty, "The Priority of Democracy to Philosophy," in *Philosophical Papers* (Cambridge: Cambridge University Press, 1991), 1:178.

27. Bernard Williams, *Ethics and the Limits of Philosophy* (London, Fontana, 1985), chap. 10.

28. Taylor, *Sources of the Self*, 495ff.

29. Bruce Ackerman, *Social Justice in the Liberal State* (New Haven, Conn.: Yale University Press, 1980), chap. 2.

30. John Rawls, "A Theory of Justice, Political Not Metaphysical," *Philosophy and Public Affairs* 14 (1985): 215–35.

31. Bick relies on three paired distinctions: between "ontology and advocacy" as a general organizing distinction, between "atomists" and "holists" in ontology, and between "individualists" and "collectivists" in advocacy. I am uneasy about ontology, so I stick with the distinction between methodological-cum-conceptual issues on the one hand and prescriptive issues on the other. There is, I hope, nothing much at stake here.

32. Taylor, "Cross-Purposes," 169.

33. G.W.F. Hegel, *The Philosophy of History* (New York: Dover, 1956), 266–68.

34. Edward Bellamy, *Looking Backward* (New York: Modern Library, 1951), 90–91.

35. Alasdair MacIntyre, *Three Rival Versions of Moral Enquiry* (London, Duckworth, 1990), makes much of authority, and thus of those who exercise it, but less of the community of the faithful who sustain that authority.

36. Alasdair MacIntyre, *After Virtue* (London, Duckworth, 1981), 114–21.

37. Charles Taylor argues that social, political, and psychological theories have a "value slope" because they point out the ways in which people get what they want; he agrees, of course, that the critic may say they want the wrong things or get what they want at too high a price ("Neutrality in Political Science," in *The Philosophy of Social Explanation*, ed. Alan Ryan [Oxford: Oxford University Press, 1973], 75–77).

38. MacIntyre, *After Virtue*, 243–45.

39. Ackerman, *Social Justice in the Liberal State*, 3–9; Jürgen Habermas, *Toward a Rational Society* (Boston, Beacon Press, 1970), chap. 4; Richard Rorty, "Postmodernist Bourgeois Liberalism," in *Philosophical Papers* 1:197–202.

40. Richard Rorty, *Contingency, Irony, and Solidarity* (Cambridge: Cambridge University Press, 1988).

41. This would, in my view, allow an approach to abortion that was sensitive to

moral convictions—for example, by forbidding abortion based on sex selection, by providing plenty of room for those who conscientiously objected to performing abortions to keep well away from the whole business—while allowing ready access to abortion in cases of hardship. It would not be very hospitable to treating the issue as a clash between a mother's right to choose and a fetus's right to life; cf. Mary Ann Glendon, *Abortion and Divorce in Western Law* (Cambridge, Mass.: Harvard University Press, 1987).

42. The British Public Order Acts allow the police to prevent marches and demonstrations that pose a threat to the peace, and allow local authorities to impose restrictions, amounting to prohibition, on such demonstrations in a way that U.S. courts would find unconstitutional (Geoffrey Robertson, *Freedom, the Individual, and the Law* [Harmondsworth: Penguin, 1990], 66–76).

5: LIBERAL IMPERIALISM

1. I am grateful to the participants in the Charlottesville conference that resulted in the book from which this chapter is taken for many very instructive comments.

2. He represented his employment at the East India Company as a form of not too mindless drudgery that gave him enough spare time to write; seeing that, by the end of his career, he occupied a position of much the same importance as a permanent secretary for the colonies, this was unduly dismissive.

3. Biographically, one perhaps should take into account Mill's view that as an irrevocable contract whose terms were profoundly disadvantageous to women, marriage was a form of slavery; objections to Mormons having lots of quasi slaves on the part of people who thought it fine to have one each would have cut less ice with Mill than with most of his contemporaries.

4. Consider Mugabe's theft of the parliamentary and presidential elections in Zimbabwe; if it were possible to remove him "surgically"—as I do not for one moment imagine that it is—this would not be forcing Zimbabweans to be free in the sense at issue here, but analogous to the case of the hostage taker. It might, of course, be the case that if one asked the people of Zimbabwe whether they wished to be saved from Mugabe by outside invasion, they would answer that they did not; then they would be in the position of having been forced to be free. Analogies with Serbia and Iraq are there for the drawing.

5. Conor Cruise O'Brien, *The Long Affair: Thomas Jefferson and the French Revolution, 1785–1800* (Chicago: University of Chicago Press, 1996).

6. This is a fairly simple-minded thought in the following sense: the Europeans had such a police force in the form of NATO, and they did not use it. They could and should have used it; first to ensure that Croatia did not become an independent state before it had put in place measures to protect its Serb minority (whose memories of World War II do not incline them to trust a Croat government), second to ensure that neither Croatia nor Serbia set about ruining the lives of the Muslim inhabitants of Bosnia-Herzogovina, and third to ensure that Serbia did not behave abominably in Kosovo. European governments could not bring themselves to act; the squeamishness that made them *feel* the horrors of what was happening also made them reluctant to get their own people killed. World War I having started in the streets of Sarajevo, so to speak, their fears were not absurd, but under the cir-

cumstances, they were cowardly. So having a police force is no use without the willingness to use it.

7. I hasten to point out that I go much further than Mill does in "A Few Words on Non-Intervention." Mill's line was that it was up to the oppressed to throw off their oppression and that outsiders ought not to do it for them; the British had no obligation to help the Hungarians turf out the Austrian monarchy. *However*, if the Austrian government were to rely on Russia to act in its old role as the gendarme of Europe, the British could come in on the side of the Hungarians. This is an argument to be handled with kid gloves; Gertrude Himmelfarb used to like it because she thought it justified the Vietnam War, but one can imagine the Bertrand Russell fan club thinking with equal warrant that it justified Russian intervention on the side of the Vietcong—indigenous revolutionaries oppressed by a South Vietnamese government sustained by American power. Those of us who dislike talk of sovereignty do not much like treating nations as anything but a term of convenience; for us, the question is not *who* is involved but whether one can do something effective to establish a nonbrutal, and preferably a nonbrutal and minimally liberal, regime. The trouble with the brightest and the best is that they think it is easier to achieve than it is; hence the caution apparent in the paper.

6: STATE AND PRIVATE, RED AND WHITE

1. R. M. Hare, *Applications of Moral Philosophy* (London: Macmillan, 1972), 1–3.

2. Thomas Hobbes, *Leviathan* (Harmondsworth: Penguin, 1968), 188, 727–28.

3. Ibid., chap. 13.

4. G.W.F. Hegel, introduction to *The Philosophy of Right* (Oxford: Clarendon, 1941).

5. G.W.F. Hegel, *The Philosophy of History* (New York: Dover, 1954).

6. Walter Kaufmann seems to me to plead too hard for such an interpretation in *Nietzsche: Philosopher, Psychologist, Anti-Christ* (Princeton, N.J.: Princeton University Press, 1950).

7. Georges Sorel, "Apology for Violence," app. 2 in *Reflections on Violence* (New York: Collier, 1961).

8. Franz Fanon, *The Wretched of the Earth* (New York: Grove, 1965); Jean-Paul Sartre, *Critique de la raison dialectique* (Paris: Gallimard, 1960).

9. As was argued by Regis Debray, *Revolution within the Revolution* (Cambridge, Mass.: MIT Press, 1967).

10. Karl Marx, "The Civil War in France," in *Karl Marx: Selected Writings*, ed. David McLellan, 539–58 (Oxford: Oxford University Press, 1977).

11. John Harris, "'Non-Violent' Violence," chap. 2 in *Violence and Responsibility* (London: Routledge and Kegan Paul, 1980).

12. John Dunn, *Modern Revolutions*, 2nd ed. (Cambridge: Cambridge University Press, 1989), 204ff.

13. Hannah Arendt, *On Violence* (New York: Harcourt Brace, 1970), 56.

14. Ibid., 84–87.

15. Anthony Giddens, "Power in the Writings of Talcott Parsons," chap. 10 in *Studies in Social and Political Theory* (London: Hutchinson, 1977).

16. George Kateb stresses the extent to which political action in Arendt's sense of

the term is a violent business that often eventuates in harm to a good many people (*Hannah Arendt: Politics, Conscience, and Evil* [Totowa, N.J.: Rowman and Allanheld, 1983], 38–40). This is a proper emphasis; not the least of one's difficulties in understanding *On Violence* is that of squaring its account of politics with the enthusiasm for Machiavelli expressed in *The Human Condition*. This paragraph is only about *On Violence* and does not pretend to be an adequate account of Arendt's views more generally considered.

17. Ted Honderich, *Violence for Equality* (New York: Routledge, 1989). See also C.A.J. Coady, "The Morality of Terrorism," *Philosophy* 60 (January 1985): 47–69.

18. As argued some years ago in Frank Parkin, *Inequality and Political Order* (London: McGibbon and Kee, 1971).

19. Honderich, *Violence for Equality*, 187–210; Harris, *Violence and Responsibility*, chap. 2; Barrington Moore, Jr., *Social Origins of Dictatorship and Democracy* (Boston: Beacon, 1967), 103.

20. Harris, *Violence and Responsibility*, 21–23.

21. The force of this varies a good deal according to whether writers think that there is something especially evil about violent methods; Honderich and Coady plainly represent different views of this issue.

22. Arendt, *On Violence*, 45–48.

23. This is plainly the proper interpretation of Hobbes's account of political obligation; see Brian Barry, "Warrender and His Critics," in *Hobbes and Rousseau*, ed. M. Cranston and R. S. Peters, 36–38 (London: Macmillan, 1972).

24. Joseph de Maistre, *Works*, trans. and ed. J. Lively (New York: Macmillan, 1965), 192.

25. Arendt, *On Violence*, 80.

26. Though Honderich takes the simplicity of the IRA's aims much more for granted than I would (*Violence for Equality*, 198–99).

27. R. M. Hare, "The Lawful Government," in *Applications of Moral Philosophy*, 84ff.

28. H.L.A. Hart, "Prolegomenon to the Principles of Punishment," in *Punishment and Responsibility: Essay in the Philosophy of Law* (Oxford: Clarendon, 1968), 1–27.

29. In 1986, there were 61 sectarian killings in Ulster, and 91 in 1987, but in 1988 there were 332 murders in Washington, D.C., whose population is less than a third of the province's.

30. The best account of the Baader-Meinhof gang is Jillian Becker, *Hitler's Children* (Philadelphia: Lippincott, 1977), 227–40.

31. Carl Friedrich, ed., *Totalitarianism* (New York: Grosset and Dunlap, 1954); Hannah Arendt, *The Origins of Totalitarianism* (New York: Meridian, 1958).

32. St. Augustine, *The City of God* (Harmondsworth: Penguin, 1984), 139.

33. John Simpson and Jana Bennett, *The Disappeared* (New York: St. Martin's, 1985).

34. Hugo Young, *One of Us* (London: Macmillan, 1989).

35. Jeane Kirkpatrick, *Dictatorships and Double Standards: Rationalism and Reason in Politics* (New York: Simon and Schuster, 1982).

36. Bob Woodward, *Veil: The Secret Wars of the CIA, 1981–87* (New York: Simon and Schuster, 1988).

37. But see Paul Fussell, *Thank God for the Atomic Bomb, and Other Essays* (New York: Summit, 1988).

38. Bruce Catton, *The Terrible Swift Sword* (New York: Doubleday, 1963).

7: The Right to Kill in Cold Blood

1. The story is told in Michael St. John Packe, *The Life of John Stuart Mill* (1956), 463–72.

2. See a series of articles by Ken Armstrong and Steve Mills: "Flawed Trials Lead to Death Chamber: Bush Confident in System Rife with Problems," *Chicago Tribune*, June 11, 2000; "Gatekeeper Court Keeps Gates Shut; Justices Prove Reluctant to Nullify Cases," *Chicago Tribune*, June 12, 2000 (on Governor Bush); "Ryan Suspends Death Penalty; Illinois First State to Impose Moratorium on Executions," *Chicago Tribune*, Jan. 31, 2000 (on Governor Ryan); "Ryan: 'Until I Can Be Sure' Illinois Is First State to Suspend Death Penalty," *Chicago Tribune*, Feb. 1, 2000 (on Ryan).

3. See the *Harris Report*, July 11–17, 2000 (reporting 64 percent support today against a low of 38 percent in 1964 and a high in Harris polls of 75 percent in 1995).

4. See Gordon Hawkins and Franklin Zimring, *The Death Penalty and the American Agenda* (1986).

5. The antipedophile riots at the Portsdown housing complex in the summer of 2000 suggest the passions that can be unleashed when the public sees its children potentially at risk, but no sustained pressure for the reinstatement of capital punishment has resulted from such outbreaks.

6. And true to form, the British government at first proposed not to adopt the Sixth Protocol, because it wishes to be able to reinstate the death penalty—should there be reason to do so—without the need to denounce the entire convention.

7. Indeed, thus far the majority of retests have saved the life of the convicted criminal, but a minority of retests have confirmed their guilt; see Gregg Easterbrook, "The Myth of Fingerprints: DNA and the End of Innocence," *New Republic*, July 31, 2000.

8. A thought implicit in the ECHR's second article.

9. H.L.A. Hart, "Prolegomena to a Theory of Punishment," in *Punishment and Responsibility: Essays in the Philosophy of Law* (1968).

10. This, of course, is explicitly denied by the Supreme Court's judgment in *Woodson v. North Carolina*, 428 U.S. 280 (1976), in which it is argued that the Eighth Amendment requires that the amount of punishment must not be excessive, but not that it must be the minimum necessary. Just how much is to be inflicted is a matter for the legislature.

11. Immanuel Kanat, *Critique of Judgment*, trans. J. H. Bernard, 1968.

12. *Furman v. Georgia*, 408 U.S. 238 (1972).

13. Leviticus, chap. 20, contains an impressive catalogue of capital offenses.

8: Hobbes's Political Philosophy

1. On religion, see Patricia Springborg, "Hobbes on Religion," in *The Cambridge Companion to Hobbes*, edited by Tom Sorell, 346–80 (Cambridge: Cambridge University Press, 1996). I have written on this elsewhere: see Ryan, "Hobbes, Toleration, and the Inner Life," in *The Nature of Political Theory*, edited by David Miller and Larry Siedentop, 197–218 (Oxford: Clarendon Press, 1983), reprinted as chapter 10 of the present volume; and "Hobbes and Individualism," in *Perspectives on Thomas Hobbes*, edited by G.A.J. Rogers and Alan Ryan, 81–105 (Oxford: Clarendon Press, 1989), reprinted as chapter 9 of the present volume. Two much more extended and

very useful recent accounts, differently oriented but not wholly at odds with each other, are S. A. Lloyd, *Ideals as Interests in Hobbes's "Leviathan": The Power of Mind over Matter* (Cambridge: Cambridge University Press, 1992), and A. P. Martinich, *The Two Gods of Leviathan: Thomas Hobbes on Religion and Politics* (Cambridge: Cambridge University Press, 1992). David Johnston, *The Rhetoric of "Leviathan": Thomas Hobbes and the Politics of Cultural Transformation* (Princeton, N.J.: Princeton University Press, 1986), is an elegant argument for the view that Hobbes's purpose in his discussion of religion is to remove religious controversy from politics. My general perspective on Hobbes is not unlike that of Michael Oakeshott in *Hobbes on Civil Association* (Oxford: Blackwell, 1975).

2. John Aubrey, *Brief Lives*, ed. Oliver Lawson Dick (Harmondsworth: Penguin, 1972), 316; everyone comments on the fact that Hobbes's physical timidity was quite at odds with his intellectual boldness. Leslie Stephen, *Hobbes* (London: Macmillan, 1904), is still a very engaging account of its subject.

3. Thomas Hobbes, *Leviathan*, ed. Richard Tuck (Cambridge: Cambridge University Press, 1991), 76–77; citations to *Leviathan* are to this edition.

4. Thomas Hobbes, *De Mirabilibus Pecci: Being the Wonders of the Peak in Darby-Shire* (1636).

5. *The Collected English Works of Thomas Hobbes* [cited as *EW*], ed. William Molesworth (London, 1839–45), 8:viii.

6. Ibid., 8:xvi.

7. Ibid., 8:xvi–xvii, 221: "It was in name, a state democratical; but in fact a government of the principal man." For two very different views of the place of Thucydides in Hobbes's political thought, see Leo Strauss, *The Political Philosophy of Hobbes* (Chicago: University of Chicago Press, 1952), and John Watkins, *Hobbes's System of Ideas: A Study in the Political Significance of Philosophical Theories* (London: Hutchinson, 1965).

8. *EW* 8:vii.

9. Thomas Hobbes, *A Dialogue between a Philosopher and a Student of the Common Laws of England*, ed. Joseph Cropsey (Chicago: University of Chicago Press, 1971).

10. Hobbes, *Leviathan*, 149.

11. Ibid., 257.

12. See Steven Shapin and Simon Schaffer, *Leviathan and the Air-Pump: Hobbes, Boyle, and the Experimental Life* (Princeton, N.J.: Princeton University Press, 1989), for Hobbes's controversy with Robert Boyle; for Hobbes's (failed) relations with the Royal Society, see Noel Malcolm, "Hobbes and the Royal Society," in *Perspectives on Thomas Hobbes*, ed. G.A.J. Rogers and Alan Ryan, 43–66 (Oxford: Clarendon Press, 1989).

13. Hobbes, *Leviathan*, 38; for the problems of Hobbes's account of science, see Watkins, *Hobbes's System of Ideas*. The best recent account of these is in Tom Sorell, *Hobbes* (London: Routledge and Kegan Paul, 1986), and on the bearing of Hobbes's science on his politics, the same author's "The Science in Hobbes's Politics," in *Perspectives on Thomas Hobbes*, ed. G.A.J. Rogers and Alan Ryan, 67–80 (Oxford: Clarendon Press, 1989).

14. Karl Popper, *The Poverty of Historicism* (London: Routledge and Kegan Paul, 1957), 115–16.

15. This idea is particularly associated with Karl Popper, *The Logic of Scientific Discovery* (London: Hutchinson, 1957); it sets the context for the discussion in Watkins, *Hobbes's System of Ideas*.

16. See Popper, *Poverty of Historicism*, for an account of situational logic; also see Martin Hollis, *The Cunning of Reason* (Cambridge: Cambridge University Press, 1988).

17. I have long been in Martin Hollis's debt for this insight; see his "Theory in Miniature," *Mind* 82 (1973): 525–41.

18. The most sustained discussion from this standpoint comes in David Gauthier, *The Logic of Leviathan* (Oxford: Clarendon Press, 1969), and Jean Hampton, *Hobbes and the Social Contract Tradition* (Cambridge: Cambridge University Press, 1986).

19. *The Political Works of James Harrington*, ed. J.G.A. Pocock (Cambridge: Cambridge University Press, 1977), 161–63.

20. Ibid., 161.

21. Hobbes, *Leviathan*, 37.

22. Thomas Hobbes, *De Cive*, ed. Howard Warrender (Oxford: Clarendon Press, 1983), 36.

23. Ibid., 37.

24. Ibid., 36–37.

25. As he did in *De Cive* and *The Elements of Law Natural and Politic*, where he simply presumes the truth of the psychological basis of our problems in the state of nature.

26. Hobbes, *Leviathan*, 9; incidentally, Martinich's view that Hobbes's use of this analogy shows how seriously he took religion seems rather forced, especially since Martinich emphasizes the sharpness of the distinction that Hobbes drew between the behavior of human beings and the essentially unintelligible behavior of God.

27. Ibid., 89.

28. *The Politics of Aristotle*, trans. Ernest Barker (Oxford: Clarendon Press, 1948), 6 (i.e., 1.2.9).

29. Hobbes, *Leviathan*, 119; the account in *De Cive*, 87–88, is equally insistent on the role of pride or "eminence" in creating discord.

30. Aristotle, *Politics*, 7 (1.2.10).

31. Hobbes, *Leviathan*, 107–8.

32. Ibid., 126, 128.

33. Jean-Jacques Rousseau, *Social Contract and Discourses* (London: Everyman, 1993); Émile Durkheim, *Montesquieu and Rousseau: Pioneers of Sociology* (Ann Arbor: University of Michigan Press, 1961); François Tricaud, "Hobbes's Conception of the State of Nature from 1640 to 1651," in *Perspectives on Thomas Hobbes*, ed. G.A.J. Rogers and Alan Ryan, 107–23 (Oxford: Clarendon Press, 1989), explores ambiguities in Hobbes's account, and especially variations between his accounts in *Elements*, *De cive*, and *Leviathan*, that I do not touch on here.

34. Hobbes, *Leviathan*, 89–90; *De Cive*, 32–33, 45.

35. Hobbes, *Leviathan*, 89; Anthony Pagden, *The Fall of Natural Man* (Cambridge: Cambridge University Press, 1982), provides a riveting account of the role of American Indians in European accounts of "natural man."

36. Hobbes, *Leviathan*, 75–76; incidentally, this passage, founding religion on "some peculiar quality, or at least in some eminent degree thereof, not to be found in other Living creatures," shows how much closer Rousseau and Hobbes were than is commonly thought.

37. Hobbes, *Leviathan*, 70.

38. Ibid., 87.

39. Ibid., 170.

40. Cf. Hobbes's comparison of life to a race (EW 4:53) in which there is no other goal but to come first.

41. Cf. Hobbes, *Leviathan*, 221.

42. Ibid., 91.

43. Ibid., 111; *De cive*, 76; the question whether Hobbes made their status as divine commands central to the analysis of the laws of nature has been much debated. Martinich's claim in *Two Gods* is the most recent defense of the view that he does. My own view is that he may well have thought that God commanded obedience to them, but that he still thought that they could bring men to agreement by virtue of their status as "convenient articles of peace."

44. John Locke, *Two Treatises of Government* (Cambridge: Cambridge University Press, 1969), *Second Treatise*, sec. 4.

45. Hobbes, *Leviathan*, 90; *De Cive*, 42–43.

46. This is not to slight the interesting work of David Gauthier and Jean Hampton cited above; it is, however, to say that they discuss some issues that I do not think Hobbes's account in fact raises. That it is too late in the day to deny the label "Hobbesian" to such problems is very likely true, just as it is, as Hampton agrees, too late to relabel Hobbes's argument if it is, as she thinks, not a "contractual" argument in the strict sense at all; see Hampton, *Hobbes and the Social Contract Tradition*, 186–88, and David Gauthier, "Hobbes's Social Contract," in *Perspectives on Thomas Hobbes*, ed. G.A.J. Rogers and Alan Ryan, 125–52 (Oxford: Clarendon Press, 1989). Gauthier agrees that the state of nature is not a pure prisoner's dilemma, but he remains (I think) firmly wedded to a utility-maximizing psychology. The title of Gregory Kavka's *Hobbesian Moral and Political Theory* (Princeton, N.J.: Princeton University Press, 1986) is entirely apt, of course, because he focuses on issues of mutual deterrence that arise whether or not all parties are utility maximizers.

47. Hobbes, *Leviathan*, 93; *De Cive*, 63. One of the many insights made by Brian Barry is the special status of contractual agreement as an obligation-undertaking device ("Warrender and His Critics," *Philosophy* 43 [1968]: 117–37).

48. Hobbes, *Leviathan*, 117.

49. This is famously spelled out in Anatol Rapaport, *The Evolution of Cooperation* (New York: Basic Books, 1984), and discussed in passing in Gauthier, "Hobbes's Social Contract."

50. Hobbes, *Leviathan*, 120.

51. Ibid., 97–98; cf. 138–39.

52. Ibid., 138–39; it is to be noticed that Hobbes's account has a curious internal flaw. I do not follow Don Herzog (in *Happy Slaves*) in his cheerful view that Hobbes's contradictions were the small price Hobbes had to pay for the rhetorical effect he wanted to make, so I wish I could see some way out of them. We begin with a right to all things in the state of nature; thus we have a right to the obedience of others, but one that they have no obligation to recognize, because they cannot save their lives by recognizing it, and that, in any case, is at odds with their equal right to have the obedience of everyone else. Hobbes often suggests that the covenant is necessary only because a human sovereign needs the help of others to exercise his rights; God, whose kingdom is "gotten by violence," needs none. Then the interesting question is whether the victor in battle has a right to my obedience. It looks as though he has, because I cannot resist, and the victor has that right—that is, to my obedience—in the state of nature. On the other hand, Hobbes insists that I am under an obligation only once I have submitted; that is, I have agreed to obey. This introduces an asym-

metry between the right to command and the obligation to obey. The one view of obligation I think we may reject is John Plamenatz's in *Man and Society: A Critical Examination of Some Important Social and Political Theories from Machiavelli to Marx*, 2 vols. (London: Longmans, 1963), according to which "I am obliged" means "I had better." It is clear this does not make sense of obligations stemming from covenant.

53. Hobbes, *Leviathan*, 484; Hampton, in arguing for a noncontractual interpretation of Hobbes, insists that all agreements must be upon terms, and therefore cannot confer absolute power (*Hobbes and the Social Contract Tradition*); Locke, in *Second Treatise*, sec. 8, argues against the suggestion that we might contract into servitude on that basis.

54. Hobbes, *Leviathan*, 18, 121–29.

55. Ibid., 101; cf. note 52 above.

56. Ibid., 141; cf. note 53 above.

57. Ibid., 142.

58. Ibid., 231.

59. Ibid., 216.

60. Ibid., 127.

61. Ibid., 231.

62. Thomas Hobbes, *An Historical Discourse and Narration Concerning Heresy* (1680); Richard Tuck points out that Hobbes and Locke were, in fact, of one mind on toleration in the 1670s. Locke later hardened his position on toleration, not in the sense of becoming more or less tolerant, but in the sense of refusing to accept toleration as a concession from the monarch ("Hobbes and Locke on Toleration," in *Thomas Hobbes and Political Theory*, ed. Mary Dietz, 153–71 [Lawrence: University of Kansas Press, 1990]).

63. Hobbes, *Leviathan*, 479.

64. Ibid., 239; the portrait of Hobbes as the great proto-theorist of market society by C. B. Macpherson in *The Political Theory of Possessive Individualism: Hobbes to Locke* (London: Oxford University Press, 1962) is wonderfully imaginative but entirely implausible.

65. Hobbes, *Leviathan*, 149.

66. Ibid., 91; cf. 145.

67. Marginal note to *Leviathan*, 152.

68. Hobbes, *Leviathan*, 226; Hobbes was certain that the only role of Parliament was to give advice to the sovereign, and many times said that it was no accident that people called their king a sovereign but did not so call Parliament—not entirely fairly to the usage of "king-in-Parliament." Deborah Baumgold argues a delicate case for the implicit constitutionalism of Hobbes's theory (*Hobbes's Political Theory* [Cambridge: Cambridge University Press, 1988]).

69. Hobbes, *Leviathan*, 232.

70. Ibid., 214.

71. One interesting place where Hobbes's argument was indeed simply reinvented three hundred years later was the 1950s attempt to deal with the issue of unjust "punishment" by the definitional maneuver of pointing out that only a penalty inflicted on the guilty for a crime could *count* as "punishment." Here, Hobbes's chapter 28 surely is three hundred years ahead of its time, whatever one thinks of the quality of the argument itself.

72. Hobbes, *Leviathan*, "Review and Conclusion," 484–85.

9: HOBBES AND INDIVIDUALISM

1. Alan Ryan, "The Nature of Human Nature in Hobbes and Rousseau," in *The Limits of Human Nature*, ed. Jonathan Benthall, 3–19 (London, 1973), reprinted as chapter 11 in the present volume; Ryan, "Hobbes, Toleration, and the Inner Life," in *The Nature of Political Theory*, ed. David Miller and L. A. Siedentop, 197–218 (Oxford, 1981), reprinted as chapter 10 in the present volume. This present essay is a companion to Ryan, "A More Tolerant Hobbes?" in *Essays on Toleration*, ed. Susan Mendus, 37–59 (Cambridge, 1988).

2. C. B. Macpherson, "Hobbes's Bourgeois Man," in *Hobbes Studies*, ed. Keith Brown, 169–83 (Oxford, 1965); Macpherson, *The Political Theory of Possessive Individualism* (Oxford, 1962); Macpherson, introduction to Thomas Hobbes, *Leviathan* (Harmondsworth, 1968).

3. Leo Strauss, *The Political Philosophy of Hobbes* (Oxford, 1936); Sheldon Wolin, *Politics and Vision: Continuity and Vision in Western Political Thought* (Princeton, 1960).

4. Michael Oakeshott, *Hobbes on Civil Association* (Oxford, 1975).

5. On which see Maurice Goldsmith, *Hobbes's Science of Politics* (New York, 1968) and J.W.N. Watkins, *Hobbes's System of Ideas*, 2nd ed. (London, 1973), both of them at odds with Strauss, *Political Philosophy of Hobbes*.

6. Alexander Ross, *Leviathan Drawn Out with a Hook* (London, 1653), A5.

7. John Aubrey, *Brief Lives* (Harmondsworth, 1962), 314.

8. Edward Hyde, *A Brief Review of Mr Hobbes's Leviathan* (London, 1670), "Epistle Dedicatory."

9. Thomas Hobbes, *Leviathan*, ed. C. B. Macpherson (Harmondsworth, 1968), 171.

10. Ross complains of this (*Leviathan Drawn Out*, 24–25).

11. Hobbes, *Leviathan*, 112.

12. John Eachard, *Mr Hobbes's State of Nature Examined* (London, 1672), preface.

13. John Shafto, *The Great Law of Nature* (London, 1672), A3–4.

14. Watkins, *Hobbes's System of Ideas*, 17ff.

15. Karl Popper, *The Open Society and Its Enemies* (London, 1945), 1:124–27.

16. John Locke, *An Essay Concerning Human Understanding* (Oxford, 1975), 417–20.

17. Roger Woolhouse, *Locke's Philosophy of Science and Knowledge* (Oxford, 1971), 10ff.

18. Hobbes, *Leviathan*, 118.

19. Ibid., 115.

20. Ross, *Leviathan Drawn Out*, 12–13; Hobbes, *Leviathan*, 82.

21. Aubrey, *Brief Lives*, 309.

22. Hobbes, *Leviathan*, 142; cf. 134–36.

23. Ibid., 111–12.

24. Karl Popper, *Objective Knowledge* (Oxford, 1972), 153–61.

25. Popper, *Objective Knowledge*; Jean-Jacques Rousseau, "A Discourse on the Origins of Inequality," in *The Social Contract and Discourses* (London, 1973).

26. Ernest Gellner, *The Legitimation of Belief* (Cambridge, 1974), 27 ff.

27. Thomas Hobbes, *De Cive* (Oxford, 1983), 50.

28. Brian Barry, "Warrender and His Critics," in *Hobbes and Rousseau*, ed. Mau-

rice Cranston and Richard Peters, 37–65 (London, 1972); John Plamenatz, "Mr. Warrender's Hobbes," in Brown, *Hobbes Studies*, 76–78; Howard Warrender, *The Political Philosophy of Hobbes* (Oxford, 1964), 287ff.

29. Hobbes, *Leviathan*, 256.
30. Clarendon, *Short Review*, "Epistle Dedicatory."
31. Hobbes, *Leviathan*, p. 189
32. Hobbes, *Leviathan*, 189, 217.
33. Barry, "Warrender and His Critics," 36ff.
34. David Gauthier, *The Logic of Leviathan* (Oxford, 1969), 76ff.
35. Hobbes, *Leviathan*, 161.
36. Hobbes, *De Cive*, 168.
37. Hobbes, *Leviathan*, 217.
38. Ibid., 396.
39. Hobbes, *De Cive*, 199.
40. Ibid., 179.
41. Ibid., 186.
42. Hobbes, *Leviathan*, 398.
43. Ibid., 397.
44. Ross, *Leviathan Drawn Out*, 2.
45. Hobbes, *Leviathan*, 75–76; Strauss, *Political Philosophy of Hobbes*, 115ff.
46. Hobbes, *Leviathan*, 376.
47. F. C. Hood, *The Divine Politics of Thomas Hobbes* (Oxford, 1964).
48. Hobbes, *Leviathan*, 718–19.
49. Clarendon *Short Review*.
50. Hobbes, introduction to *Leviathan*, 11ff.
51. Strauss, *Political Philosophy of Hobbes*, 120ff.
52. Shafto, *Great Law of Nature*, A2.
53. Thomas Tenison, *The Creed of Mr Hobbs Examined* (London, 1670).
54. Hannah Arendt, *The Human Condition* (Chicago: University of Chicago Press, 1958).
55. Oakeshott, *Hobbes on Civil Association*.

10: HOBBES, TOLERATION, AND THE INNER LIFE

1. See particularly, John Plamenatz, *Man and Society: A Critical Examination of Some Important Social and Political Theories from Machiavelli to Marx* (London: Longmans, 1963), 1: chap. 4; his introduction to Hobbes, *Leviathan* (London, Collins, 1962), 3–55; and Plamenatz, "Mr Warrender's Hobbes," *Political Studies* 5 (1957): 295–308.
2. John Plamenatz, *The English Utilitarians* (Oxford: Blackwell, 1958), chaps. 4 and 6.
3. Plamenatz, *Man and Society*, 1:207.
4. Plamenatz, introduction to *Leviathan*, 55.
5. Sheldon Wolin, *Politics and Vision* (London: Allen and Unwin, 1961), 280.
6. Thomas Hobbes, *Leviathan* (London: Dent, 1914), 93.
7. Ibid., 88–89.
8. *The English Works of Thomas Hobbes* [cited as *EW*], ed. William Molesworth (London: John Bohn, 1841), 2:2.

9. Hobbes, *EW* 2:292–97.

10. M. M. Goldsmith, *Hobbes's Science of Politics* (New York: Columbia University Press, 1966), 214–20.

11. Hobbes, "Behemoth," *EW* 6:167–69.

12. Leslie Stephen, *Hobbes* (Ann Arbor: University of Michigan Press, 1961), 31, 34; his hostility is unabated in "Behemoth," *EW* 6:169–75.

13. Hobbes, *EW* 2:315.

14. Ibid.

15. Ibid., 316; but cf. *Leviathan*, 328.

16. Hobbes, *Leviathan*, 219.

17. Hobbes, *EW* 4:388; cf. *EW* 6:174.

18. Hobbes, *Leviathan*, 391.

19. Hobbes, *EW* 2:203.

20. Hobbes, *EW* 4:215; cf. *EW* 2:178–80; Stephen, *Hobbes*, 31.

21. D. D. Raphael, *Hobbes* (London: Allen and Unwin, 1977), 33.

22. Hobbes, *Leviathan*, 24.

23. Ibid., 34.

24. J. S. Mill, *Three Essays* (London: Oxford University Press, 1975), 22–23; Hobbes, *Leviathan*, 283–84.

25. Hobbes, *Leviathan*, 53.

26. Ibid.

27. Ibid., 194.

28. Ibid., 56.

29. Ibid., 83.

30. F. C. Hood, *The Divine Politics of Thomas Hobbes* (Oxford: Clarendon Press, 1964), 180–81.

31. Hobbes, *EW* 6:45.

32. Hobbes, *Leviathan*, 24.

33. J. S. Mill, "Utilitarianism," in *Collected Works* (Toronto: Toronto University Press, 1969), 10:229–32.

34. Hobbes, *EW* 2:1–3.

35. Maurice Cowling, *Mill and Liberalism* (Cambridge: Cambridge University Press, 1963); cf. Shirley Letwin, *The Pursuit of Certainty* (Cambridge: Cambridge University Press, 1965), chap. 21.

36. This is not wholly surprising: he thought *Brave New World* had been lifted from his own book *The Scientific Outlook*. R. W. Clark, *The Life of Bertrand Russell* (Harmondsworth: Penguin, 1978), 566.

37. Hobbes, *Leviathan*, 89.

38. Wolin, *Politics and Vision*, 281.

39. Keith Thomas, "The Social Origins of Hobbes's Political Thought," in *Hobbes Studies*, ed. Keith Brown, 185–236 (Oxford: Blackwell, 1965).

40. Hobbes, *Leviathan*, 131; cf. *EW* 2:157 and 178, where sumptuary laws are recommended.

41. Leo Strauss, *The Political Philosophy of Hobbes* (Oxford: Clarendon Press, 1936), 121.

42. Hobbes, *EW* 4:53.

43. Stephen, *Hobbes*, 23–24; Thomas, "Social Origins," 220–21.

44. Bertrand Russell, *Principles of Social Reconstruction* (London: Allen and Unwin, 1916), chap. 1; Mill, *Three Essays*, 73.

11: THE NATURE OF HUMAN NATURE IN HOBBES AND ROUSSEAU

1. Immanuel Kant, *Groundwork of the Metaphysics of Morals*, ed. H. J. Patton (London: Hutchinson, 1952); R. M. Hare, *The Language of Morals* (Oxford: Oxford University Press, 1953).
2. This phrase from his *Discourse on the Origins of Inequality* may have been intended to avoid too obvious a conflict with the creation story of Genesis.
3. Quentin Skinner, "The Ideological Context of Hobbes's Political Thought," *Historical Journal* 9 (1966): 286–317.
4. Leo Strauss, *The Political Philosophy of Hobbes* (Chicago: University of Chicago Press, 1952).
5. F. C. Hood, *The Divine Politics of Thomas Hobbes* (Oxford: Oxford University Press, 1964).
6. John Aubrey, *Brief Lives*, ed. Oliver Lawson Dick (Harmondsworth: Penguin, 1961).
7. See D. E. Broadbent, *Behaviour* (London: Methuen, 1968).
8. Noam Chomsky, "A Review of B. F. Skinner's *Verbal Behavior*," *Language* 35 (1959): 26–58.
9. See, for example, his account of the prisoner's dilemma in Rapaport, *Fights, Games, and Debates* (Ann Arbor: University of Michigan Press, 1960).
10. John Watkins, *Hobbes's System of Ideas: A Study in the Political Significance of Philosophical Theories* (London: Hutchinson, 1965).
11. Stuart Hampshire, *Morality and Pessimism* (Cambridge: Cambridge University Press, 1972).
12. Émile Durkheim, *Montesquieu and Rousseau: Forerunners of Sociology* (Ann Arbor: University of Michigan Press, 1960).
13. Marshall Berman, *The Politics of Authenticity: Radical Individualism and the Emergence of Modern Society* (London: Allen and Unwin, 1970).
14. Judith Shklar, *Men and Citizens: A Study of Rousseau's Social Theory* (Cambridge: Cambridge University Press, 1969).
15. See the long chapter on *Julie* in Berman, *Politics of Authenticity*.

12: LOCKE ON FREEDOM: SOME SECOND THOUGHTS

1. Knud Haakonssen, ed., *Traditions of Liberalism: Essays on John Locke, Adam Smith, and John Stuart Mill* (Sydney: Centre for Independent Studies, 1988). The present essay first appeared in this collection.
2. Quotations from Locke's *Treatises* are identified in the text by 1 (*First Treatise*) and 2 (*Second Treatise*) and the section number.
3. I say this in spite of Hobbes's insistence that a law of nature is a truth found out by reason whereby we are forbidden to do what is destructive of our own welfare; Hobbes's summary of natural law in the negative Golden Rule—"Do not unto others what you would not have them do unto you"—precisely is to reduce natural law to rules of mutual forbearance.
4. Shirley Robin Letwin, "John Locke: Liberalism and Natural Law," in *Traditions of Liberalism*, ed. Knud Haakonssen, 3–29 (Sydney: Centre for Independent Studies, 1988); see 7ff., 13ff.
5. I had not read Shirley Robin Letwin's essay when writing my own. She and I

are wholly in agreement that Locke's conception of individual rights does not rest on any kind of moral pluralism. The only pluralism in Locke is supplied by the thought that God has given us diverse talents and placed us in diverse situations, so that the practical implications of the injunction to employ God's bounty to the best of our abilities are different for different people. But she and I are at odds on the political implications of this. Locke's sense of the sanctity of the individual's private concerns seems to me to be quite as firm a basis for the rule of law as one could ask.

13: MILL'S ESSAY ON LIBERTY

1. J. S. Mill, *On Liberty*, ed. Gertrude Himmelfarb (London: Penguin, 1974). All citations to *Liberty* are to this edition.

14: SENSE AND SENSIBILITY IN MILL'S POLITICAL THOUGHT

1. See Alan Ryan, *The Philosophy of John Stuart Mill* (London: Macmillan, 1970) and my introduction to vol. 9 of John Stuart Mill, *Collected Works of John Stuart Mill* (hereafter cited as *CW*), 33 vols., edited by J. M. Robson (Toronto: University of Toronto Press, 1963–91); see also John Skorupski, *John Stuart Mill* (London: Routledge and Kegan Paul, 1989).

2. Not that this stopped us trying; see Alan Ryan, "The Family Mill," review of *James and John Stuart Mill: Father and Son in the Nineteenth Century*, by Bruce Mazlish, *New York Review of Books*, 29 May 1975, 4–8, and Gertrude Himmelfarb's deftly but even more comprehensively destructive review, "Clio and Oedipus," *Times Literary Supplement*, 23 May 1975, 565–66.

3. As Himmelfarb's *On Liberty and Liberalism* (New York: Knopf, 1974) seems to suppose it does.

4. There can, of course, be fruitful and sympathetic ways of linking Mill's feminism to his larger liberalism; Nadia Urbinati, "John Stuart Mill on Androgyny and the Ideal Marriage," *Political Theory* 19 (1991): 626–48, gives a very persuasive instance.

5. See, for instance, some notably intransigent assaults and rebuttals in James Tully, ed., *Meaning and Context: Quentin Skinner and His Critics* (Princeton, N.J.: Princeton University Press, 1988).

6. J. S. Mill, *CW* 1:5.

7. Ibid.

8. See Robert Cumming, "Mill's History of His Opinions," *Journal of the History of Ideas* 25 (1965): 235–56.

9. J. S. Mill, *CW* 1:5.

10. All of these are perfectly fascinating subjects, of course. They are treated with unusual judiciousness and good sense in Gail Tulloch, *Mill and Sexual Equality* (Brighton, UK: Harvester, 1989).

11. J. S. Mill, *CW* 12:28–30.

12. On Mill and Eyre, see Michael St. John Packe, *The Life of John Stuart Mill* (London: Secker and Warburg, 1954), 467–72; on Marx's essay "The Civil War in France," see J. S. Mill, *CW*, 17:1754n3.

13. Or who had fought his father to an honorable draw, as in Edmund Gosse's *Father and Son*.

14. J. S. Mill, *On Liberty*, CW 18:258–59, 262–63.

15. Alan Ryan, *The Philosophy of John Stuart Mill* (London: Macmillan, 1970); John Gray, *Mill on Liberty: A Defence* (London: Routledge and Kegan Paul, 1981); Fred Berger, *Happiness, Justice and Freedom* (Berkeley and Los Angeles: University of California Press, 1984).

16. See particularly the works by Gray and Berger cited in note 15.

17. J. S. Mill, CW 21:337.

18. Ibid., 1:145.

19. Ibid., 13:655–57.

20. Ibid., 10:329–30.

21. Ibid., 13:697–98.

22. Ibid., 1:609.

23. Ibid., 14:155, 181–82.

24. See Quentin Skinner, "Meaning and Interpretation," in Tully, *Meaning and Context*, 29–67.

25. T. S. Kuhn, *The Structure of Scientific Revolutions* (Chicago: Chicago University Press, 1962).

26. J. S. Mill, CW 18:261.

27. Robert Nozick, *Anarchy, State, and Utopia* (New York: Basic Books, 1974).

28. J. S. Mill, CW 18:255.

29. Ibid., 8:840–41.

30. Ibid., 1:211.

31. Howard Williams, *Kant's Political Philosophy* (Oxford: Blackwell, 1983), 118–21.

32. See Susan Mendus, "To Have and to Hold: Liberalism and the Marriage Contract," and Mary Stokes, "A Comment on Mendus," both in *Liberalism and Recent Legal and Social Philosophy*, ed. Richard Bellamy, 70–85 (Stuttgart: Steiner Verlag, 1989).

15: Mill in a Liberal Landscape

1. See the interesting collection of the first reviews of *On Liberty* assembled by Pyle (1994).

2. As Hamburger (1991) is the latest of a long line of critics to argue.

3. My discussion of utilitarianism (Ryan [1970], 227–29), made a similar though not identical point.

4. On Mill's career in the service of the East India Company, see the works by Zastoupil (1994) and Moir (1990).

5. For instance, I pay no attention to the difficulty of giving an account of the concept of harm, since I can add nothing to the discussion by Feinberg (1984), and I am content to endorse Waldron's (1987) insistence that Mill would have counted the mental discomfort caused when our prejudices are shaken not as harmful but as good for us.

6. For those in search of something sharper, Himmelfarb (1974) offers a notably unkind account of the conception, purposes, content, and effects of the book.

7. J. M. Robson's "Textual Introduction" to volume 10 of Mill's *Collected Works* gives a complete account of the writing of *Auguste Comte and Positivism*; Mill was deterred from tackling Comte in 1854 by his own antipathy to Harriet Martineau, whose recent translations and commentaries would have been the ostensible occasion for his *compte rendu*, and even more by Harriet Taylor's antipathy to Mrs. Martineau. See *CW* 10:cxxix–cxxxii.

8. "The grand, leading principle, towards which every argument unfolded in these pages directly converges, is the absolute and essential importance of human development in its richest diversity," Wilhelm von Humboldt, *Sphere and Duties of Government*; epigraph to J. S. Mill, *On Liberty*, *CW* 18:215.

9. "It is proper to state that I forgo any advantage which could be derived to my argument from the idea of abstract right, as a thing independent of utility. I regard utility as the ultimate appeal on all ethical questions; but it must be utility in the largest sense, grounded on the permanent interests of man as a progressive being. Those interests, I contend, authorize the subjection of individual spontaneity to external control, only in respect to those actions of each, which concern the interest of other people" (*CW* 18:224).

10. See, for instance, the analysis by Gray (1983).

11. See Gray (1983) for a book-length elaboration of that claim, and *Utilitarianism* (*CW* 10:250–51), for Mill's explanation of rights.

12. He acquired it as a result of the savagery of his reviews in the *Saturday Review*; it was bestowed on him by his friends, who admired his prose but winced for his victims' sensibilities.

13. Popper's 1974 work is, perhaps surprisingly, not the classic source of the doctrine that science progresses by the process of making hypotheses and testing them against the evidence; his 1959 study, first published in German in 1934, is that.

14. For the distinction between "negative" and "positive" liberty, see Berlin (1969).

15. See, for example, the work by Musgrave et al. (1970).

16. See also his letters to Theodore Gomperz and Arnold Ruge in which he suggests that the essay is less needed in Germany "than here" (*CW* 10:539, 598).

17. See Rawls (1971, 205–11) for a discussion of liberty of conscience.

18. See Rawls (1933a, 48–62); there is already a substantial critical literature.

19. Raz (1983) hints at such possibilities; the argument of Wollheim (1979, 253–69) provides yet another route.

20. This is partly a prudential argument against such measures, not an argument from high principle; and the moral principle in question is simple utilitarianism—the misery caused is not justified by the good achieved.

21. See Ryan (1995, chap. 3); and for a much longer and more detailed account, Rockefeller (1991, 76–124).

22. Cf. the study by Taylor (1989).

23. See, for instance, Berlin (1969), "Two Concepts of Liberty."

24. Ryan 1970, chaps. 12–13.

16: Utilitarianism and Bureaucracy: The Views of J. S. Mill

1. Quentin Skinner, "The Limits of Historical Explanations," *Philosophy* 41 (1966): 199–215, and "The History of Ideas," *History and Theory* 8 (1969): 3–53.

2. Jenifer Hart, "Nineteenth Century Social Reform: A Tory Interpretation of History," *Past & Present* 31 (1965): 45.

3. R. K. Webb, "Benthamites and Unitarians" (mimeo), 3. I am grateful to Professor Webb for permission to cite his paper here.

4. Cf. P. G. Winch, *The Idea of a Social Science* (London, 1958), chap. 2, and W. Dray, *Laws and Explanation in History* (Oxford, 1957), chap. 5.

5. A. Schutz, "The Phenomenology of the Social World," in *Philosophy of the Social Sciences*, ed. M. Natanson, 183ff. (New York, 1963).

6. T. S. Kuhn, *The Structure of Scientific Revolutions* (Chicago, 1962), and cf. S. S. Wolin, "Political Theory and Paradigms," in *Politics and Experience*, ed. P. King and B. C. Parekh, 125–52 (Cambridge, 1968).

7. O.O.G.M. MacDonagh, "The Nineteenth Century Revolution in Government: A Reappraisal," *Historical Journal* 1 (1958): 52–67.

8. A. V. Dicey, *Lectures on the Relation between Law and Public Opinion in England during the Nineteenth Century* (London, 1905).

9. Hart, "Nineteenth Century Social Reform," 41.

10. MacDonagh, "Revolution in Government," 65–66.

11. Kuhn, *Scientific Revolutions*, chaps. 4 and 5.

12. Webb, "Benthamites and Unitarians," 6–8.

13. Mill-Taylor Collection (manuscripts and letters), British Library of Political and Economic Science, file 1, nos. 27 and 28.

14. J. S. Mill, *Autobiography* (New York, 1956), 113 ff.

15. J. S. Mill, *A System of Logic*, 8th ed. (London, 1906), 3.

16. E. Stokes, *The English Utilitarians and India* (Oxford, 1959), chap. 1.

17. Parliamentary Papers 1854–55, vol. 20, *Report and Papers relating to the Reorganisation of the Civil Service*: *Papers*, 87–98 (Mill and Vaughan), and *Report*, 24–31 (Jowett).

18. E. Hughes, "Sir Charles Trevelyan and Civil Service Reform, 1853–5," pt. 1, *English Historical Review* 64 (1949): 62.

19. Stokes, *English Utilitarians and India*, 13–16, and chaps. 1–3 generally.

20. To House of Lords Select Committee, June 1852 (Parliamentary Papers 1852–53, 30:300–32).

21. Ibid., 30:301.

22. *Plus ça change*: The essays in the present volume originally appeared in scattered books and journals; they were put into an electronic form suitable for editing by a retyping service in India.

23. S. R. Letwin, *The Pursuit of Certainty* (Cambridge, 1965), chap. 12.

24. James Mill, *History of British India* (London, 1856), 6:13.

25. Stokes, *English Utilitarians and India*, 64.

26. J. S. Mill, *On Liberty* (Everyman Edition, n.d.), 73–74.

27. J. S. Mill, *System of Logic*, 3.

28. J. S. Mill, *On Liberty*, 73.

29. M. Seliger, *The Liberal Politics of John Locke* (London, 1968), 241ff., 262–63.

30. James Mill, *Essay on Government* (Cambridge, 1937), 3–4.

31. Parliamentary Papers 1857–58, vol. 43, *Memorandum ... of the Improvements in the Administration of India during the Last Thirty Years*.

32. James Mill, *Essay on Government*, 6–7, 13.

33. Parliamentary Papers 1852–53, 30:303.

34. Ibid.

35. Ibid.

36. Ibid., 331.

37. Ibid., 321.

38. Ibid., 322.

39. Ibid., 325.

40. Ibid., 305.

41. H. Parris, "The Nineteenth Century Revolution in Government: A Reappraisal Reappraised," *Historical Journal* 3 (1960): 19ff.

42. G. Himmelfarb, "The Haunted House of Jeremy Bentham," in *Victorian Minds*, 32–81 (London, 1968).

43. Stokes, *English Utilitarians and India*, 52–58.

44. Ibid., 47–48.

45. Parliamentary Papers 1857–58, vol. 43, *Memorandum*, 17.

46. Ibid., 35.

47. *Examiner*, May 1873.

48. Stokes, *English Utilitarians and India*, 49–50.

49. Parliamentary Papers 1852–53, 30:316 (Mill's evidence).

50. *Examiner*, May 1873.

51. The pamphlets were all published by William Penny, London, during 1858; they are anonymous, but Mill's own bibliography of his published writings lists them as his work. I should like to express my gratitude to Mr. Martin Moir of the India Office Records for his help in finding these pamphlets and various other East India Company tracts. The pamphlets are *A Constitutional View of the India Question*, *Practical Observations on the First Two of the Proposed Resolutions on the Government of India*, *A President in Council the Best Government for India*, and *The Moral of the India Debate*.

52. *Hansard*, 3rd ser., vol. 148, appendix, *Petition of the East India Company* (presented to Earl Grey in the Lords, Feb. 11, 1858), col. 1.

53. Parliamentary Papers 1852–53, 30:313.

54. *Hansard*, 3rd ser., vol. 148, *Petition*, col. 2.

55. Ibid., col. 3.

56. [J. S. Mill], *The Moral of the India Debate*, 3.

57. J. S. Mill, *Representative Government* (Everyman Edition, n.d.), 333–34.

58. Parliamentary Papers 1857–58, 43:43.

59. *Hansard*, 3rd ser., vol. 148, *Petition*.

60. J. S. Mill, *Representative Government*, 334–35.

61. Ibid., 232.

62. Parliamentary Papers 1854–55, vol. 20, *Papers*; the evidence of Stephen, Cornewall Lewis, and Booth, among others.

63. Ibid., 95.

64. M. St. J. Packe, *The Life of John Stuart Mill* (London, 1954), 349–57.

65. Ibid., 368.

66. Parliamentary Papers 1854–55, vol. 20, *Papers*, 92.

67. Ibid., 76.

68. Quoted in Hughes, "Trevelyan and Civil Service Reform," 56.

69. Parliamentary Papers 1854–55, vol. 20, *Papers*, 95.

70. Ibid., 96n.

71. Ibid., 94.

72. Ibid., 92.

73. Ibid., 98.

74. Ibid., 92.

75. Parliamentary Papers 1854–55, vol. 20, *Report*, 3.

76. Mill, *On Liberty*, 68–70, cf. Alan Ryan, *The Philosophy of John Stuart Mill* (London, 1970), chap. 13.

77. Mill, *On Liberty*, 140.

78. See, e.g., ibid., 159–63, so far as education is concerned.

79. Stokes, *English Utilitarians and India*, 64.

80. See, e.g., the quotation from Humboldt that stands at the beginning of *On Liberty*; the well-known essay "Coleridge" does more than justice to the latter's influence.

81. A. Briggs, *Victorian People* (London, 1954), 117–18.

82. Ibid., 68–72.

83. J. S. Mill, *Representative Government*, 260–67.

84. Ibid., 235–9.

85. Ibid., 237.

86. Parliamentary Papers 1854–55, vol. 20, *Report*, 3.

87. J. S. Mill, *Representative Government*, 333–35.

88. Ibid., 335.

89. Ibid., 244–46.

90. Ibid., 248–49.

91. G. O. Trevelyan, *The Life and Letters of Lord Macaulay* (London, 1906), 279.

92. I should like to record my thanks for the help and comments I received from Gillian Sutherland and Jenifer Hart.

17: MILL AND ROUSSEAU: UTILITY AND RIGHTS

1. G. C. Duncan and S. M. Lukes, "The New Democracy," *Political Studies* 11 (1963); 156–77; Carole Pateman, *Participation and Democratic Theory* (Cambridge, 1970), 1–35.

2. L. Davis, "The Cost of Realism: Contemporary Restatements of Democracy," *Western Political Quarterly* 17 (1964): 37–46.

3. J. A. Schumpeter, *Capitalism, Socialism, and Democracy* (London, 1943), 269.

4. Ibid., 282–83, 295.

5. S. M. Lipset, *Political Man* (London, 1960), chaps. 4 and 5.

6. Davis, "Cost of Realism," 39.

7. Pateman, *Participation and Democratic Theory*, chap. 2.

8. Ibid., 109; Robert Dahl, *After the Revolution?* (New Haven, Conn., 1970), 143–66.

9. Pateman, *Participation and Democratic Theory*, 22ff.

10. J.-J. Rousseau, *Social Contract and Discourses*, trans. G.D.H. Cole (London, 1973; rev. ed.), 218 (bk. 3, chap. 4).

11. Ibid., 217.

12. Ibid., 219 (bk. 3, chap. 5).

13. J. S. Mill, *Utilitarianism, Liberty, and Representative Government* (London, 1964), 229–30.

652 • Notes to Essay 17

14. Dahl, *After the Revolution?* 140ff.

15. Rousseau, *Social Contract*, 240 (bk. 3, chap. 15).

16. Ibid.

17. R. Dworkin, "Liberalism," in *Public and Private Morality*, ed. Stuart Hampshire, 133–34 (Cambridge, 1978).

18. R. P. Wolff, *In Defense of Anarchism* (New York, 1970), 27.

19. Rousseau, *Social Contract*, 169 (bk. 1, chap. 4).

20. R. M. Hare, "The Lawful Government," in *Philosophy, Politics, and Society*, ser. 3, ed. P. Laslett and W. G. Runciman (Oxford, 1967), 157–72.

21. It is also open to us to dilute the notion of consent as Locke does, and count as tacit consenters all those who derive benefits from the government; then, the nonconsenting will become a different group, posing different problems; see J. Locke, *Two Treatises of Government*, ed. P. Laslett (Cambridge, 1967; 2nd ed.), 365–67 (2nd treatise, secs. 119–22).

22. T. Hobbes, *Leviathan* (London, 1962), 97 (chap. 19).

23. Ibid.

24. Rousseau, *Social Contract*, 245 (bk. 4, chap. 18).

25. Ibid., 249–51 (bk. 5, chap. 2).

26. Wolff, *Anarchism*, 70.

27. Rousseau, *Social Contract*, 240 (bk. 4, chap. 15).

28. Ibid., 193 (bk. 2, chap. 6).

29. J. Lively, *Democracy* (Oxford, 1975), 17.

30. Rousseau, *Social Contract*, 250 (bk. 4, chap. 2).

31. Ibid.

32. R. M. Hare, "Political Obligation," in *Social Ends and Political Means*, ed. T. Honderich (London, 1976), 1–12.

33. James Mill, *An Essay on Government* (Indianapolis, 1955), 66–67.

34. Ibid., 60.

35. Ibid., 75–77.

36. Alan Ryan, "Utilitarianism and Bureaucracy," in *The Growth of Nineteenth Century Government*, ed. G. Sutherland, 33–62 (London, 1972), reprinted as chapter 16 of the present volume.

37. James Mill, Essay on Government, 73–74.

38. Rousseau, *Social Contract*, 242–43 (bk. 3, chap. 16).

39. Ibid., 244 (bk. 3, chap. 17).

40. Ibid.

41. Ibid.

42. Ibid., 227–30 (bk. 3, chap. 8).

43. Ibid., 253ff. (bk. 4, chap. 4).

44. Ibid., 183–84 (bk. 2, chap. 3).

45. Ibid., 245 (bk. 3, chap. 18).

46. Ibid.

47. Ibid., 247 (bk. 4, chap. 1).

48. J. L. Talmon, *The Origins of Totalitarian Democracy* (London, 1952).

49. J. S. Mill, *Utilitarianism*, 202.

50. Ibid., 205–6.

51. Ibid., 73.

52. Ryan, "Utilitarianism and Bureaucracy," 45.

53. This, of course, does not entail that each man has only one vote; Mill defends plural votes as well as the equality of the sexes (*Utilitarianism*, 290–91).

54. J. S. Mill, *Principles of Political Economy* (Toronto, 1965), 793.
55. Ibid., 763–64.
56. J. S. Mill, *Utilitarianism*, 247.
57. Ibid., 216–17.
58. Rousseau, *Social Contract*, 192–93 (bk. 2, chap. 6)
59. Ibid., 182 (bk. 2, chap. 1).
60. *Kant's Political Writings*, ed. H. Reiss, 79 (Cambridge, 1970).
61. J. Rawls, *A Theory of Justice* (Oxford, 1972).
62. J.-J. Rousseau, *The Government of Poland* (Indianapolis, 1972), 5ff.
63. J. S. Mill, *Utilitarianism*, 74, 132.
64. Ibid., 68–69.
65. C. L. Ten, *Mill on Liberty* (Oxford, 1980).

18: Bureaucracy, Democracy, Liberty: Some Unanswered
Questions in Mill's Politics

1. See, for instance, Jennifer Pitts (2005), chap. 5.
2. See, for example, Mill's letter to the *Morning Chronicle*, July 5, 1853 (CW 25:1193–94).
3. Mill to the *Penny Newsman*, Mar. 15, 1863 (CW 25:1201–4).

22: Alexis de Tocqueville

1. François Furet, *Penser la révolution française* (Paris, 1974).
2. André Jardin, *Tocqueville: A Biography* (New York: Farrar, Straus and Giroux, 1988), 37.
3. Ibid., 47.
4. But see Joel Schwartz, "The Penitentiary and Perfectibility in Tocqueville," *Western Political Quarterly* 38, no. 1 (1985): 7–26.
5. G. W. Pierson, *Tocqueville and Beaumont in America* (New York: Oxford University Press, 1938).
6. David Riesman, *The Lonely Crowd* (New York: Doubleday, 1952).
7. L. A. Siedentop, "Two Liberal Traditions," in *The Idea of Freedom*, ed. Alan Ryan, 153–74 (Oxford, 1979).
8. See Claude Lamberti, *Tocqueville and the Two Democracies* (New York, 1989).
9. J. L. Mesick, *The English Travellers in America, 1785–1835* (New Haven, 1922).
10. This is discussed at length by Phillips Bradley in his introduction to the 1945 Knopf edition of *Democracy in America* (1:viii–c in the 1991 printing).
11. Citations are to the Everyman's Library edition of the work: Alexis de Tocqueville, *Democracy in America* (New York: Knopf, 1994).

23: Staunchly Modern, Nonbourgeois Liberalism

1. This is an abbreviated treatment of issues I tackle at much greater length in *John Dewey and the High Tide of American Liberalism* (New York: Norton, 1995); toward the end, in particular, it gets pretty hasty, therefore. For "Postmodernist Bourgeois Liberalism," see Richard Rorty, *Philosophical Papers* (Cambridge: Cam-

bridge University Press, 1991), 1:197–202. I ought to say, what I hope is obvious enough, that Rorty and I are not at odds, but rather at nuances. I think there is more a "philosophical metanarrative" in Dewey than Rorty does, though it surely does not invoke "noumena"; and I demur at the thought that the institutions that liberalism requires are informatively described as "bourgeois," especially in light of Dewey's own attachment to something like guild socialism. But these are complaints from under the same umbrella.

2. Thus, in Dewey's *Democracy and Education* (New York: Macmillan, 1916), "modern" means after the Reformation and the scientific revolution of the seventeenth century, while in *Liberalism and Social Action* (New York: Putnam, 1935), "modern" means the twentieth century as opposed to the nineteenth century. There is no particular confusion here: liberalism of all kinds is a modern phenomenon, but "new liberalism" was a response within that liberal tradition to new problems as they emerged in the late nineteenth and early twentieth centuries.

3. Dewey to Scudder Klyce, Apr. 16, 1915, quoted in Steven Rockefeller, *John Dewey: Religious Faith and Democratic Humanism* (New York: Columbia University Press, 1991), 328.

4. In this, as much else, he admitted a debt to G.D.H. Cole's work and espoused a view very like that offered by Russell in *Roads to Freedom* and *Principles of Social Reconstruction*.

5. John Dewey, "The Ethics of Democracy," in *The Early Works of John Dewey, 1882–1898*, ed. J. A. Boydston et al., 5 vols. (Carbondale: Southern Illinois University Press, 1967–72), 1:227–49.

6. John Dewey, "Liberalism and Social Action," in *The Later Works of John Dewey, 1925–1953*, ed. J. A. Boydston et al., 17 vols. (Carbondale: Southern Illinois University Press, 1981–87), 11:46ff.

7. Rorty says just what I am tempted to say, namely, that Dewey and others such as Michael Oakeshott "take over Hegel's criticism of Kant's conception of moral agency while either naturalizing or junking the rest of Hegel" ("Post-Modernist Bourgeois Liberalism," *Philosophical Papers* 1:197–98). But the interesting issue that this buries is what of the rest is "naturalized" and what "junked."

8. See John Dewey, "The Psychological Standpoint" and "Psychology as Philosophic Method," in *Early Works* 1:122–43, 144–67 (the essays were first published in *Mind*, January and April 1886).

9. It is true, too, that Dewey could have turned the charge of residual Absolutism against Russell if he had thought to; Russell always hankered after what Bernard Williams has called "the absolute conception of the world," and it seems that Dewey really did not. On this, Hilary Putnam is illuminating (*Renewing Philosophy* [Cambridge, Mass.: Harvard University Press, 1992], chap. 5).

10. The book that makes this case most straightforwardly is Charles Taylor, *The Ethics of Authenticity* (Cambridge, Mass.: Harvard University Press, 1992), but it is also the burden of Taylor's *Sources of the Self* (Cambridge, Mass.: Harvard University Press, 1989). Habermas's interest in Dewey goes back to *Toward a Rational Society*, but a perhaps even more interesting link (though not, I think, one explored by Habermas) is their common obsession with communication.

11. This "must" is, of course, mere bullying in the absence of the argument, which this remark threatens but does not offer; there is certainly a sense in which Heidegger, say, was attuned to the modern world. I am tempted to say that the disastrousness of Heidegger's career is as good an argument as any for that "must," but

here, at any rate, cannot do more than refer the skeptical to Taylor's *Ethics of Authenticity* for the kind of case that we need to make.

12. The story is told in George Dykhuizen, *Life and Mind of John Dewey* (Carbondale: Southern Illinois University Press, 1973), 22–24; the essay is reprinted in *Early Works* 1:3–8.

13. John Dewey, "Christianity and Democracy," *Early Works* 4:9.

14. John Dewey, *Human Nature and Conduct: An Introduction to Social Psychology*, in *The Middle Works of John Dewey, 1899–1924*, ed. J. A. Boydston et al., 15 vols. (Carbondale: Southern Illinois University Press, 1977–83), 14:227.

15. John Dewey, "The Reflex Arc Concept in Psychology," *Early Works* 5:96–107.

16. John Dewey, *The School and Society, Middle Works* 1:3–109. It was an accidental best seller; the University of Chicago decided in 1899 to lay on a series of lectures and publications to publicize the university's work, and Dewey's lectures were part of that program. It was also an occasion to reflect on his Laboratory School's work since it had opened in 1896—the topic of the lectures as delivered, in fact. It very rapidly made its way as a statement of "progressive" views about elementary education, and was a commercial as well as an intellectual hit. There is some unhappy correspondence between Dewey and the publisher at the University of Chicago Press in the Dewey Papers; Dewey was not bashful about money, but the press plainly felt that he had been less than open about his plan to have the second printing done by Macmillan. It may also have been a decision provoked by his growing irritation with the university and its administration.

17. See, for instance, Avital Simhony, "The Social and Political Ideas of the English Idealists" (D.Phil. thesis, Oxford University, 1980).

18. John Dewey, "The University Elementary School: General Outline of Study," *Middle Works* 1:337.

19. A subject on which I shall not touch is Dewey and the city; critics have been more or less equally divided between complaining that he focuses exclusively on the city and thus neglects much else that he ought to attend to, and complaining that he hankers after an essentially rural way of life and thus spends his time trying to turn the school into an agency of rural patterns of socialization in spite of its urban setting. See Robert Westbrook, *Dewey and American Democracy* (Ithaca, N.Y.: Cornell University Press, 1991), 150–94, for a great deal on all this. I think it is a noncontroversy; Dewey got interested in education in the Chicago of Jane Addams, which was much more like the environment that inspired the British (and, of course, the American) settlement movement than it was like anything we have encountered in the late twentieth century.

20. John Dewey, "From Absolutism to Experimentalism," *Later Works* 5:156.

21. It is not an accident that this kind of claim should sound so much like G. H. Mead; it was Mead and James Hayden Tufts who got Dewey to come to Chicago, and with the latter, Dewey wrote the most successful text in ethics ever to be put before American students, while the former's work on the "I" and the "Me" so impressed Dewey that he later said he had stopped trying to do any original work in psychology and had simply taken over Mead's results. It is to the Meads, incidentally, that the relatively felicitous prose of "The School and Society" was due; they reconstituted a publishable text from Dewey's lecture notes.

22. Bernard Williams, *Ethics and the Limits of Philosophy* (London: Fontana/Collins, 1985).

23. John Dewey, "Art as Experience," *Later Works* 10; see, e.g., 143–44.

24. I say this slightly hesitantly, partly because it leaves out the role of ideals, which certainly mattered a lot to Dewey, and partly because it underplays the role of the individual's responsibility and answerability to others. If one were to ask what differentiates ethics from other sorts of decision-guiding thinking in Dewey, I think one would have to say that it is the role of "answering to others" for our decisions, and this may sit awkwardly with an emphasis on individual healthy functioning. Of course, in the ideal it does not, because in the ideal we find our own satisfaction in seeing our ideals realized in the community's achievements; but even though Dewey was happy to take up the offer of a "moral holiday" that this rather Hegelian thought allows us, he was much too down to earth to ignore the importance of conflicts of interest. The difficulty is that once they are placed in the foreground, the "healthy individual in the healthy community" ideal can easily look like a fudge or wishful thinking.

25. See Westbrook, *Dewey and American Democracy*, 179–83.

26. John Dewey, "What Are We Fighting For?" *Middle Works* 11:105.

27. John Dewey, "In Explanation of Our Lapse," *Middle Works* 10:292ff.

28. John Dewey, "The Future of Pacifism," *Middle Works* 10:266–68.

25: Deweyan Pragmatism and American Education

1. The title of Cornel West's quick tour of the pragmatist tradition is nicely chosen: not only the title but the content, too, of *The American Evasion of Philosophy* (Madison: University of Wisconsin Press, 1989) leaves it squarely up to the reader to decide whether Americans—Dewey foremost among them—have simply ducked the hard issues of philosophy or have cleverly escaped the snares traditional philosophy sets for the unwary.

2. John Dewey, "The School and Society," in *The Middle Works of John Dewey, 1899–1924* [cited as *MW*], ed. Jo Ann Boydston et al., 15 vols. (Carbondale: Southern Illinois University Press, 1977–83), 1:81. In this essay, I cite also *The Early Works of John Dewey, 1882–1898* [*EW*], ed. Jo Ann Boydston et al., 5 vols. (Carbondale: Southern Illinois University Press, 1967–72).

3. John Dewey, "My Pedagogic Creed," *EW* 5:84–95. I am not the first commentator to have had that sensation: "One is tempted to continue indefinitely quoting from this Creed," wrote William H. Kilpatrick ("Dewey's Influence on Education," in *The Philosophy of John Dewey*, ed. Paul Arthur Schilpp, 2nd ed. [New York: Open Court, 1971], 463).

4. Dewey, "My Pedagogic Creed," *EW* 5:95.

5. Lawrence A. Cremin, *The Transformation of the School* (1961; New York: Vintage, 1964), 100.

6. Dewey, "My Pedagogic Creed," *EW* 5:86.

7. Ibid.

8. John Dewey, *The School and Society*, *MW* 1:8.

9. Ibid., 1:9.

10. Ibid.

11. The latter was Christopher Lasch's criticism in *The New Radicalism in America* (New York: Knopf, 1965).

12. Dewey, *The School and Society*, *MW* 1:10.

13. Ibid., 1:39.

14. Ibid., 1:41–43.

15. Ibid., 1:81.

16. Ibid.

17. In fact, the Prussian government banned the establishment of kindergartens in 1851; this seems to have been the result not of an authoritarian government's suspicion of all forms of freedom, but of the Ministry of Education confusing the apolitical, mystical Friedrich Froebel with his nephew, Karl, a socialist (Harry G. Good and James D. Teller, *A History of Western Education* [New York: Macmillan, 1969], 287).

18. Bertrand Russell's two short books on education, *On Education*, and *Education and the Social Order*, do not go off on long metaphysical excursions, but there is something to be said for the thought that Russell's attachment to Froebel and Montessori teaching methods was part of a desire to protect children *from* society rather than a desire to integrate them into society.

19. See, e.g., John Dewey, "The Interpretation of the Savage Mind," *MW* 2:39–52.

20. Cremin, *Transformation of the School*, 141.

21. John Dewey, "Interest in Relation to Training of the Will," *EW* 5:111–50.

22. John Dewey, *How We Think*, *MW* 6:208.

23. Ibid., 6:215.

24. Ibid., 6:338.

25. Ibid., 6:339.

26. Ibid., 6:237.

27. I do not mean that this can never be done in the public school system. Debbie Mayers's success with the East Harlem school shows what can be done with an unusually talented principal and unusually devoted teachers; but nobody supposes that there is something here that can be set down as a recipe, whereas it is not too hard to see how a small school with a generous staff-student ratio would allow a Deweyan approach to flourish.

27: Locke and the Dictatorship of the Bourgeoisie

1. I should like to say how much I owe to the late G. A. Paul in this essay; it amounts to a good deal as to doctrine, and all but everything as to method.

2. See J. Locke, *Two Treatises of Government*, ed. P. Laslett (Cambridge, 1967), sec. 124, cf. sec. 134; all references, by section number, are to this to edition.

3. C. E. Vaughan, *Studies in the History of Political Philosophy Before and After Rousseau*, 2 vols. (1925; New York, 1960).

4. W. Kendall, *John Locke and the Doctrine of Majority-Rule* (Urbana, Ill., 1965).

5. J. W. Gough, *John Locke's Political Philosophy: Eight Studies* (Oxford, 1950).

6. R. H. Cox, *Locke on War and Peace* (Oxford, 1960).

7. C. B. Macpherson, *Political Theory of Possessive Individualism*, chap. 5; cf. "Locke on Capitalist Appropriation," *Western Political Quarterly* 4 (1951): 550–66, and "The Social Bearing of Locke's Political Theory," *Western Political Quarterly* 7 (1954): 1–22.

8. Macpherson, *Possessive Individualism*, 221.

9. Macpherson, *Possessive Individualism*, 198, 230–31, 247–50.

10. Ibid., 221, 227.
11. Ibid., 256.
12. Ibid., 251.
13. Ibid., 236–37.
14. See J. P. Day, review of *Political Theory of Possessive Individualism*, by C. B. Macpherson, *Philosophical Quarterly* (1964): 266–68.

28: Hegel on Work, Ownership, and Citizenship

1. Charles Reich, "The New Property," in *Property*, ed. C. B. Macpherson, 179–98 (Oxford, 1979).
2. G.W.F. Hegel, *Hegel's Philosophy of Right*, trans. T. M. Knox (Oxford, 1942). All quotations from *The Philosophy of Right* [*PhR*] are from this edition.
3. M. Djilas, *The New Class* (New York, 1957).
4. L. Trotsky, *The Revolution Betrayed* (New York, 1973), 248–50.
5. A. Giddens, *The Class Structure of the Advanced Societies* (London, 1973), chap. 13.
6. Ibid.; R. Dahrendorf, *Class and Class-Conflict in Industrial Society* (London, 1959).
7. J. Locke, *Two Treatises on Government* (Cambridge, 1960), bk. 2, chap. 5.
8. J.-J. Rousseau, *The Social Contract and Discourses* (London, 1973), 83.
9. H. Reiss, ed., *Kant's Political Writings* (Cambridge, 1970), 41–53.
10. James Mill, *Essay on Government* (Indianapolis, 1955), 52–54.
11. Ibid., 89–91.
12. D. Hume, "Idea of a Perfect Commonwealth," in *Essays*, 499–515 (Oxford, 1963).
13. Charles Taylor, *Hegel* (Cambridge, 1975), 456ff.
14. L. Easton and K. Guddat, *Writings of the Young Marx* (New York, 1967), 320.
15. A. Kojève, *Introduction to the Reading of Hegel*, trans. Allan Bloom (New York, 1969).
16. R. Dworkin, "Liberalism," in *Public and Private Morality*, ed. B. Williams and S. Hampshire (Cambridge, 1979).
17. Locke, *Two Treatises*, 305–6.
18. R. Nozick, *Anarchy, State, and Utopia* (Oxford, 1975), 174–82.
19. Locke, *Two Treatises*, 311 and note.
20. A. Honoré, "Ownership," in *Oxford Essays in Jurisprudence*, ed. A. G. Guest, 107–47 (Oxford, 1961).
21. H. Arendt, *The Human Condition* (Chicago, 1953), 136–37.
22. K. Marx, *Critique of Hegel's "Philosophy of Right"* (Cambridge, 1970), 106.

29: Utility and Ownership

1. R. Nozick, *Anarchy, State, and Utopia* (Oxford: Blackwell, 1974), 228.
2. A. M. Honore, "Ownership," in *Oxford Essays in Jurisprudence*, ed. A. G. Guest, 107ff. (Oxford: Clarendon Press, 1961).

3. G.W.F. Hegel, *The Philosophy of Right* (Oxford: Clarendon Press, 1941), 54, 57.

4. J. S. Mill, *The Principles of Political Economy*, vols. 2 and 3 in *The Collected Works of John Stuart Mill*, ed. J. M. Robson, (Toronto: University of Toronto Press, 1965), 2:201ff.

5. T. Hobbes, *Leviathan* (London: Dent, 1914), 113.

6. N. Machiavelli, *The Discourses* (Harmondsworth: Penguin, 1970), 42–43.

7. J. Bentham, *Theory of Legislation* (London: Trubner French, 1887), 93–198.

8. J.-J. Rousseau, *Social Contract and Discourses* (London: Dent, 1973), 117–53.

9. Hobbes, *Leviathan*, 110–11.

10. J. S. Mill, *A System of Logic*, vols. 7 and 8 in *Collected Works*, 8:841.

11. Bentham, *Theory of Legislation*, 112–13.

12. H.L.A. Hart, "Are There Any Natural Rights?" *Philosophical Review* 64 (1955): 175–91.

13. J. Locke, *Two Treatises of Government* (Cambridge: Cambridge University Press, 1967), 289 (II, ii, 6).

14. Ibid., 318 (II, v, 47).

15. Ibid., 188–89 (I, iv, 42–43).

16. Nozick, *Anarchy, State, and Utopia*, 175–76.

17. Hegel, *Philosophy of Right*, 259.

18. Mill, *Principles of Political Economy*, 2:208.

19. Ibid., 233.

20. A. Ryan, *The Philosophy of John Stuart Mill* (London: Macmillan, 1970), 213–30.

21. J. S. Mill, *Principles of Political Economy*, 2:233.

22. Bentham, *Theory of Legislation*, 119–22.

23. Nozick, *Anarchy, State, and Utopia*, 219.

24. James Mill, *An Essay on Government* (Indianapolis: Bobbs-Merrill, 1955), 48–49.

25. Bentham, *Theory of Legislation*, 109.

26. Ibid., 122.

27. Nozick, *Anarchy, State, and Utopia*, 213ff.

28. H. Reiss, ed., *Kant's Political Writings* (Cambridge: Cambridge University Press, 1970), 147–48.

29. A. A. Berle and G. C. Means, *The Modern Corporation and Private Property*, rev. ed. (New York: Harcourt, Brace & World, 1968), 293ff.

30. F. H. Lawson, *The Law of Property* (Oxford: Clarendon Press, 1958), 59ff.

31. Nozick, *Anarchy, State, and Utopia*, 75–76.

32. Reiss, *Kant's Political Writings*, 147.

33. J. S. Mill, *Utilitarianism, Liberty, Representative Government* (London: Dent, 1914), 157–59.

34. Nozick, *Anarchy, State, and Utopia*, 206.

35. Locke, *Two Treatises on Government*, 306 (II, v, 28).

36. Lawson, *Law of Property*, 98.

37. J. P. Day, "Locke on Property," *Philosophical Quarterly* 16 (1966): 207–21.

38. Hegel, *Philosophy of Right*, 40–41.

39. J. S. Mill, *Principles of Political Economy*, 2:214ff.

40. R. Tuck, *Natural Rights Theories* (Cambridge: Cambridge University Press, 1979), 78–79.

41. Hegel, *Philosophy of Right*, 52–54.

42. Bentham, *Theory of Legislation*, 202–3.

43. J. S. Mill, *Utilitarianism*, 157.

44. V. Haksar, *Liberty, Equality, and Perfectionism* (Oxford: Clarendon Press, 1979), 253–55.

45. J. S. Mill, *Utilitarianism*, 158.

46. J. S. Mill, *Principles of Political Economy*, 2:233.

47. J. S. Mill, *Utilitarianism*, 11.

48. J. S. Mill, *Principles of Political Economy*, 3:800ff.

49. Ibid., 2:222–14.

50. J. S. Mill, *Essays on Economics and Society*, vols. 4 and 5 in *Collected Works*, 5:463–98.

51. J. S. Mill, *Principles of Political Economy*, 3:758–96.

52. J. S. Mill, *Essays on Economics and Society*, 5:749–52.

53. J. Harris, "The Survival Lottery," *Philosophy* 50 (1975): 81–87.

54. P. Singer, "Utility and the Survival Lottery," *Philosophy* 52 (1977): 218–20.

55. Reiss, *Kant's Political Writings*, 136.

56. J. Glover, *Causing Death and Saving Lives* (Harmondsworth: Penguin, 1977).

30: MAXIMIZING, MORALIZING, AND DRAMATIZING

1. Goffman, *The Presentation of Self in Everyday Life* (New York, 1959), 254.

2. I. Jarvie, *Concepts and Society* (London, 1972), chap. 1.

3. G. C. Homans, *The Nature of Social Science* (New York, 1967).

4. S. F. Nadel, *The Theory of Social Structure* (London, 1957), 20ff.

5. Goffman, *Frame Analysis*, 573ff.

6. Cf. S. M. Lyman and M. B. Scott, *The Drama of Social Reality* (New York, 1975), and R. Harré and P. F. Secord, *The Explanation of Social Behaviour* (Oxford, 1972).

7. E. Goffman, *Encounters* (New York, 1961), chap. 3.

8. A. de Saint-Exupéry, *Sand, Sea and Stars* (Harmondsworth, 1966), 25.

9. A. Downs, *An Economic Theory of Democracy* (New York, 1957), 261ff.

10. Cf. A. Heath, "The Rational Model of Man," *European Journal of Sociology* 15 (1974): 200ff.

11. J.W.N. Watkins, "Imperfect Rationality," in *Explanation in the Behavioural Sciences*, ed. R. Borger and F. Cioffi, 172–79 (Cambridge, 1970).

12. R. D. Laing, *The Divided Self* (Harmondsworth, 1965), 18–38.

13. I. Jarvie and J. Agassi, "The Problem of the Rationality of Magic," in *Rationality*, ed. B. R. Wilson, 173 (Oxford, 1970).

14. Downs, *Economic Theory of Democracy*, 29n.

15. B. M. Barry, *Sociologists, Economists, and Democracy* (London, 1970), 45ff.

16. Ibid., 17–18.

17. T. B. Macaulay, "Mill on Government," in *Works* (Edinburgh, 1902 [reprint]), 7:354.

18. Goffman, *Frame Analysis*, chap. 5.

19. Ibid., 362–63.
20. M. Banton, *Roles* (London, 1965).
21. Lyman and Scott, *The Drama of Social Reality*, 168n1.
22. Ibid., 102.
23. J. D. Douglas, *The Social Meanings of Suicide* (Princeton, 1967), 315ff.
24. Lyman and Scott, *Drama of Social Reality*, 66–67.
25. Ibid., chap. 2.
26. D. Richards, *A Theory of Reasons for Action* (Oxford, 1971), 3–71.
27. It is impossible to do very much to take advantage of the discussion that the paper received. The main point to make is, perhaps, that not only Goffman's work but also Goffman himself resists both the attempt to erect a general theory on the basis of his observations and any further attempt to draw strenuous morals from them. It appears that the only general moral to which Goffman might be willing to subscribe is that social life is very much more intricate than the naked eye tends to notice, and that we employ a remarkable range of communicative skills, and rely on all sorts of hidden communicative conventions, to facilitate even the most everyday activities. There are gestures that the man standing on the curb employs to signal his intentions to car drivers; there are hosts of gestures that pedestrians in a busy street employ not to collide with one another, to keep each other in invisible lanes—invisible to the pedestrian, but detectable by careful plotting. The suggestion that some of us had thought we detected in *Encounters* and elsewhere, to the effect that social life is hard and emotionally wearing work, is not part of Goffman's case. There is a great deal of *busy* work, but not in any plausible sense hard work.

This suggests that the information-transmitting aspect of behavior is, indeed, the central aspect of the argument. In this case, the idea that "dramatic" explanations are parasitic on other sorts of explanation is reinforced, for what a drama turns out to be is a particular mode of telling a story. The story itself must, presumably, have a coherence of its own already that is, in principle at least, there to be elicited before the dramatization occurs. But we are still left with the question with which the paper ended—a question that, of course, is one that literary theorists have wrestled with for ages—namely, what makes a particular form of presentation uniquely or specially apt for transmitting a given sort of information, and why should expressing it in this way satisfy individuals' desire to learn, or remind themselves of, truths about themselves? Whether this is a question for sociological theorists, I do not know.

31: THE ROMANTIC THEORY OF OWNERSHIP

1. G.W.F. Hegel, *The Philosophy of Right*, trans. T. M. Knox (Oxford, Clarendon Press, 1942), sec. 207.
2. See Alan Ryan, "Two Concepts of Politics and Democracy: James and John Stuart Mill," in *Machiavelli and the Nature of Political Thought*, ed. Martin Fleisher, 76-113 (New York, Croom Helm, 1972).
3. Thomas Hobbes, *Leviathan* (London, Andrew Crooke, 1651), chap. 6; David Hume, *A Treatise of Human Nature* (Oxford: Clarendon Press, 1888), bk. 2.
4. J. P. Day, "Locke on Property," *Philosophical Quarterly* 16 (1966): 207–21.
5. Jeremy Bentham, *The Theory of Legislation*, ed. by C. K. Ogden (London: Routledge, 1931), 201ff.

6. A. M. Honoré, "Ownership," in *Oxford Essays in Jurisprudence*, ed. A. G. Guest, 107–47 (Oxford, Clarendon Press, 1961).

7. Bentham, *Theory of Legislation*, 109–23.

8. See Robert Nozick, *Anarchy, State, and Utopia* (Oxford: Blackwell, 1974), 219.

9. William Godwin, *Enquiry Concerning Political Justice*, ed. by K. Codell Carter (Oxford: Clarendon Press, 1971), 236.

10. K. Marx, *Economic-Philosophical Manuscripts*, in *Collected Works* (London: Lawrence and Wishart, 1975), 3:299–301.

11. Hegel, *Philosophy of Right*, addition 26 to sec. 44.

12. W. Hastie, *Kant's Philosophy of Law* (Edinburgh: Black, 1887), 81–84.

13. Ibid., 108–13, 237–38.

14. H. Reiss, ed., *Kant's Political Writings* (Cambridge: Cambridge University Press, 1970), 43–45.

15. Ibid., 45–46.

16. Marx, *Economic-Philosophical Manuscripts*, 3:332–33.

17. Hegel, *Philosophy of Right*, sec. 44.

18. Ibid.

19. Ibid., sec. 57 and addition.

20. Ibid., sec. 197 and addition.

21. Hannah Arendt, *The Human Condition* (Chicago: Chicago University Press, 1958), 139ff.

22. K. Marx, "A Contribution to the Critique of Hegel's Philosophy of Right," *Collected Works* (London: Lawrence and Wishart, 1975), 3:100–1.

23. Marx, *Economic-Philosophical Manuscripts*, 3:306ff.

24. Thomas Carlyle, *Past and Present* (New York: New York University Press, 1977), 193.

25. In essence, this is to say that such notions as that of "self-expression" are indefinitely contestable; see W. B. Gallie, "Essentially Contested Concepts," chap. 8 of *Philosophy and the Historical Understanding* (London: Chatto and Windus, 1964).

32: Justice, Exploitation, and the End of Morality

1. I am indebted for discussion to Onora O'Neill, Stephen Clark, and the other participants at the Royal Institute of Philosophy Conference in Belfast, also to Steven Lukes, Jenifer Hochschild, and Jim Griffin, and to the Balliol Cerberus Society and the Politics Department at Princeton University. From the vast literature on all aspects of Marx and Marxism I would single out as particularly helpful the studies by Buchanan (1982), Elster (1985), Roemer (1982, 1986), Lukes (1985), and Wood (1981).

33: Liberty and Socialism

1. Robert Nozick, *Anarchy, State, and Utopia* (Oxford: Blackwell, 1974), 158ff.

2. John Stuart Mill, *Principles of Political Economy* (Toronto: Toronto University Press, 1965), 765–69.

3. Peter Archer, "The Constitution," in *Fabian Essays in Socialist Thought*, ed. Ben Pimlott (London: Heinemann, 1984).

4. Bertrand Russell, *The Principles of Social Reconstruction* (London: Allen and Unwin, 1916), 100ff.

5. F. H. Lawson makes it clear that many of the powers of owners in developed legal systems are inventions; societies in which they did not exist are not just conceivable—such powers did not exist in an earlier England (*The Law of Property* [Oxford, Clarendon Press, 1958]).

6. Isaiah Berlin, "Two Concepts of Liberty," in *Four Essays on Liberty* (Oxford: Oxford University Press, 1969), 118ff.

7. Ibid., 131ff.

8. John Stuart Mill, *Utilitarianism, Liberty, and Representative Government* (London: Dent, 1912), 72.

9. Hannah Arendt, "What Was Freedom," in *Between Past and Future* (London: Faber, 1961), interestingly and perceptively discussed by Margaret Canovan, *The Political Thought of Hannah Arendt* (London: Methuen, 1977), 72–79.

10. See Alan Ryan, "Utility and Ownership," in *Utility and Rights*, ed. Raymond Frey, 175–95 (Oxford: Blackwell, 1984); reprinted as chapter 29 in the present volume.

11. Anne Phillips, "Fraternity," in *Fabian Essays in Socialist Thought*, ed. Ben Pimlott, 230–41 (London: Heinemann, 1984).

12. C. B. Macpherson defends a version of negative liberty ("counterextractive" liberty) that implies that capitalist property relations systematically deprive the worker of his freedom; but I think that this is to win one's case by a definitional maneuver ("Berlin's Divisions of Liberty," in *Democratic Theory*, 117ff. [Oxford: Clarendon Press, 1973]).

13. J. Bentham, *Theory of Legislation* (London: Trubner, French, 1883), 94.

14. J. S. Mill, *Utilitarianism*, 73.

15. A. M. Honoré, "Ownership," in *Oxford Essays in Jurisprudence*, ed. A. G. Guest, 107ff. (Oxford: Clarendon Press, 1961).

16. Bentham, *Theory of Legislation*, 94ff.

17. Alec Nove, *The Economics of Feasible Socialism* (London: Allen and Unwin, 1983).

18. G. A. Cohen, "Robert Nozick and Wilt Chamberlain: How Patterns Preserve Liberty," *Erkenntnis* 11 (1977): 5–23.

19. Karl Marx, "Manifesto of the Communist Party," in *The Revolutions of 1848* (Harmondsworth: Penguin, 1973), 70; J. W. Burrow, *Evolution and Society* (Cambridge: Cambridge University Press, 1966), 158ff.

20. Leszek Kolakowski, "The Myth of Human Self-Identity," in *The Socialist Idea*, ed. Leszek Kolakowski and Stuart Hampshire, 25ff. (London: Quartet, 1977).

21. Nozick supposes that "capitalist acts between consenting adults" would have to be forbidden if capitalism is not to reemerge (*Anarchy, State, and Utopia*, 162–63).

22. Peter Kellner, "Are Markets Compatible with Socialism," in *Fabian Essays in Socialist Thought*, ed. Ben Pimlott, 146–56 (London: Heinemann, 1984).

23. Michael Walzer, *Spheres of Justice* (Oxford: Robertson, 1983), 17–20.

24. George Gilder, *Wealth and Poverty* (New York: Basic Books, 1981), contains some strange ideas about the connections between sexuality and capitalism, but is properly obsessed by entrepreneurial energy.

25. J. K. Galbraith discusses this myth at some length in *The Anatomy of Power* (London: Hamish Hamilton, 1984).

26. Michael Walzer, *Radical Principles* (New York: Basic Books, 1980), 128–38.

27. Oddly, Raymond Plant's *The Market, Equality, and the State* (London: Fabian Society, 1984), hardly touches on this issue of liberty for the worse off.

28. John Rawls, *A Theory of Justice* (Oxford: Clarendon Press, 1971), 60ff.

Index